Lecture Notes in Artificial Intell

Edited by J. G. Carbonell and J. Siekmann

Subseries of Lecture Notes in Computer Science

Stefan Kramer   Bernhard Pfahringer (Eds.)

Inductive
Logic Programming

15th International Conference, ILP 2005
Bonn, Germany, August 10-13, 2005
Proceedings

 Springer

Series Editors

Jaime G. Carbonell, Carnegie Mellon University, Pittsburgh, PA, USA
Jörg Siekmann, University of Saarland, Saarbrücken, Germany

Volume Editors

Stefan Kramer
Technische Universität München, Institut für Informatik/I12
Boltzmannstr. 3, 85748 Garching/München, Germany
E-mail: kramer@in.tum.de

Bernhard Pfahringer
University of Waikato, Department of Computer Science
Hamilton, New Zealand
E-mail: bernhard@cs.waikato.ac.nz

Library of Congress Control Number: 2005930339

CR Subject Classification (1998): I.2.3, I.2.6, I.2, D.1.6, F.4.1

ISSN   0302-9743
ISBN-10   3-540-28177-0 Springer Berlin Heidelberg New York
ISBN-13   978-3-540-28177-1 Springer Berlin Heidelberg New York

Springer is a part of Springer Science+Business Media

springeronline.com

© Springer-Verlag Berlin Heidelberg 2005
Printed in Germany

Typesetting: Camera-ready by author, data conversion by Scientific Publishing Services, Chennai, India
Printed on acid-free paper   SPIN: 11536314   06/3142   5 4 3 2 1 0

Preface

"Change is inevitable."[1] Embracing this quote we have tried to carefully experiment with the format of this conference, the 15th International Conference on Inductive Logic Programming, hopefully making it even better than it already was. But it will be up to you, the inquisitive reader of this book, to judge our success. The major changes comprised broadening the scope of the conference to include more diverse forms of non-propositional learning, to once again have tutorials on exciting new areas, and, for the first time, to also have a discovery challenge as a platform for collaborative work.

This year the conference was co-located with ICML 2005, the 22nd International Conference on Machine Learning, and also in close proximity to IJCAI 2005, the 19th International Joint Conference on Artificial Intelligence. Co-location can be tricky, but we greatly benefited from the local support provided by Codrina Lauth, Michael May, and others. We were also able to invite all ILP and ICML participants to shared events including a poster session, an invited talk, and a tutorial about the exciting new area of "statistical relational learning". Two more invited talks were exclusively given to ILP participants and were presented as a kind of stock-taking—fittingly so for the 15th event in a series—but also tried to provide a recipe for future endeavours.

Abstracts of all invited events as well as full-length papers of 24 presentations comprise this volume. All the presentations of the "Work-in-Progress" track as well as all submissions to the "ILP Challenge" should be available both as a technical report and on the Web.

We gratefully acknowledge the continued support of Kluwer Academic Publishers for the "Best Student Paper" award on behalf of the *Machine Learning* journal; and Springer for continuing to publish the proceedings of these conferences. The German Gesellschaft für Informatik acted as a guarantor for the conference budget, relieving us from any imminent dangers of bankruptcy. Additional support was provided by the SIGILP of the PASCAL network of excellence. Finally, we are especially grateful for the efforts of Anne Einenkel, who ran the online services of the conference in a very smooth and effective way. *Danke schön.*

June 2005

Stefan Kramer
Bernhard Pfahringer

---

[1] —except from a vending machine. –Robert C. Gallagher

Organization

Program Committee Chairs

Stefan Kramer   TU München, Germany
Bernhard Pfahringer   University of Waikato, New Zealand

Organising Committee

Michael May   Fraunhofer AIS Bonn, Germany
Codrina Lauth   Fraunhofer AIS Bonn, Germany
Anne Einenkel   TU München, Germany

Challenge Chairs

Amanda Clare   University of Wales, United Kingdom
Andreas Karwath University of Freiburg, Germany
Wenjin Lu   University of Wales, United Kingdom

Invited Speakers

Stephen Muggleton Imperial College London, United Kingdom
Ashwin Srinivasan   IBM India Research Laboratory, India
Lise Getoor   University of Maryland, USA
Gerhard Widmer   Johannes Kepler University Linz, Austria

Program Committee

Hendrik Blockeel   Katholieke Universiteit Leuven, Belgium
Rui Camacho   Universidade do Porto, Portugal
James Cussens   University of York, United Kingdom
Luc Dehaspe   PharmaDM and Katholieke Universiteit Leuven, Belgium
Kurt Driessens   University of Waikato, New Zealand
Sašo Džeroski   Jožef Stefan Institute, Slovenia
Floriana Esposito   Università degli Studi di Bari, Italy
Peter Flach   University of Bristol, United Kingdom
Johannes Fürnkranz TU Darmstadt, Germany
Lise Getoor   University of Maryland, USA
Tamás Horváth   University of Bonn and Fraunhofer AIS, Germany

Katsumi Inoue	National Institute of Informatics, Japan
David Jensen	University of Massachusetts Amherst, USA
Andreas Karwath	University of Freiburg, Germany
Roni Khardon	Tufts University, USA
Jörg-Uwe Kietz	Zurich, Switzerland
Ross King	University of Wales, United Kingdom
Joost Kok	Leiden University, The Netherlands
Nada Lavrač	Jožef Stefan Institute, Slovenia
Francesca Lisi	Università degli Studi di Bari, Italy
John Lloyd	The Australian National University, Australia
Donato Malerba	Università degli Studi di Bari, Italy
Stan Matwin	University of Ottawa, Canada
Hiroshi Motoda	Osaka University, Japan
Stephen Muggleton	Imperial College London, United Kingdom
Ramon Otero	University of Corunna, Spain
David Page	University of Wisconsin, USA
Jan Ramon	Katholieke Universiteit Leuven, Belgium
Céline Rouveirol	Université de Paris XI, France
Michèle Sebag	Université Paris-Sud, France
Jude Shavlik	University of Wisconsin, USA
Takayoshi Shoudai	Kyushu University, Japan
Arno Siebes	Universiteit Utrecht, The Netherlands
Ashwin Srinivasan	IBM India Research Laboratory, India
Tomoyuki Uchida	Hiroshima City University, Japan
Lyle Ungar	University of Pennsylvania, USA
Christel Vrain	Université d'Orléans, France
Takashi Washio	Osaka University, Japan
Stefan Wrobel	Fraunhofer AIS and University of Bonn, Germany
Akihiro Yamamoto	Kyoto University, Japan
Mohammed Zaki	Rensselaer Polytechnic Institute, USA
Gerson Zaverucha	Universidade Federal do Rio de Janeiro, Brazil
Filip Železný	Czech Institute of Technology in Prague, Czech Republic
Jean-Daniel Zucker	University of Paris XIII, France

Sponsoring Institutions

Gesellschaft für Informatik (GI)
Bioinformatics Initiative Munich (BIM)
TU München
PASCAL European Network of Excellence
"Machine Learning" journal of Kluwer Academic Publishers

Additional Referees

Annalisa Appice
Margherita Berardi
Michelangelo Ceci
Nicola Di Mauro
Nicola Fanizzi
Stefano Ferilli

Daan Fierens
Mark Goadrich
Simon Rawles
Jan Struyf
Lisa Torrey
Antonio Varlaro

Table of Contents

Research Papers

Invited Papers

An Output-Polynomial Time Algorithm for Mining Frequent Closed Attribute Trees

Hiroki Arimura[1],[*] and Takeaki Uno[2]

[1] Hokkaido University, Kita 14-jo, Nishi 9-chome, Sapporo 060-0814, Japan
arim@i.kyushu-u.ac.jp
[2] National Institute of Informatics, Tokyo 101–8430, Japan
uno@nii.jp

Abstract. Frequent closed pattern discovery is one of the most important topics in the studies of the compact representation for data mining. In this paper, we consider the *frequent closed pattern discovery problem* for a class of structured data, called *attribute trees* (AT), which is a subclass of labeled ordered trees and can be also regarded as a fragment of description logic with functional roles only. We present an efficient algorithm for discovering all frequent closed patterns appearing in a given collection of attribute trees. By using a new enumeration method, called the *prefix-preserving closure extension*, which enable efficient depth-first search over all closed patterns without duplicates, we show that this algorithm works in polynomial time both in the total size of the input database and the number of output trees generated by the algorithm. To our knowledge, this is one of the *first result for output-sensitive algorithms* for frequent closed substructure disocvery from trees and graphs.

Keywords: frequent closed pattern mining, tree mining, attribute tree, description logic, semi-structured data, the least general generalization, closure operation, output-sensitive algorithm.

1 Introduction

Frequent closed pattern discovery [19] is the problem of finding all the frequent closed patterns in a given data set, where *closed patterns* are the maximal patterns among each equivalent class that consists of all frequent patterns with the same occurrence sets in a tree database. It is known that the number of frequent closed patterns is much smaller than that of frequent patterns on most realworld datasets, while the frequent closed patterns still contain the complete information of the frequency of all frequent patterns. Closed pattern discovery is useful to increase the performance and the comprehensivity in data mining.

On the other hand, rapid growth of semi-structured data [1] such as HTML and XML data enabled us to accumulate a massive amount of weakly structured data on the networks. There is a potential demand for efficient methods

---

[*] Present address: LIRIS, University Claude-Bernard Lyon 1, France.

S. Kramer and B. Pfahringer (Eds.): ILP 2005, LNAI 3625, pp. 1–19, 2005.

for extracting useful patterns from these semi-structured data, so called *semi-structured data mining*. For the last years, a number of researches on efficient algorithms for semi-structured data mining have been done for ordered trees [3,27], unordered trees [4,11,15,22] , and general graphs [14,26]. Presently, one of the major topics in semi-structured data mining is so-called *closed tree mining*, an extension of closed pattern mining framework to semi-structured data [11,23,26].

In this paper, we consider the frequent closed pattern discovery problem for a class of structured data, called *attribute trees* ($\mathcal{AT}$), which is a subclass of labeled ordered trees and can be also regarded as a fragment of description logic [9] with functional roles only. We present an efficient algorithm for discovering all frequent closed patterns appearing in a given collection of attribute trees.

Most of the present closed tree mining algorithms adopted an approach that combines fast enumeration of frequent patterns and explicit checking of its maximality [11,23,26]. Unfortunately, this approach does not yield any efficient algorithms with theoretical performance guarantee, in terms of output-sensitive algorithms or enumeration algorithm. To overcome this problem, we developed a new enumeration technique, called the *prefix-preserving closure expansion*, which is originally introduced to frequent closed itemset discovery by Uno *et al.* [24], with combining the notions of the rightmost expansion [3,18,27] and the least general generalization [20] for trees.

Based on these techniques, we present an efficient algorithm CLOATT (Closed Attribute Tree Miner) that enumerates all frequent closed attribute trees in a given collection of attribute trees without duplicates in polynomial time per closed tree in the total size n of the database using a small amount of memory space that only depends on n. The key of the algorithm is a tree-shaped search space generated by the prefix-preserving closure expansion, that enables us to make efficient enumeration using depth-first search of closed patterns, without storing any of the previously discovered patterns for maximality check.

To the best of our knowledge, this is one of the first results on output-polynomial time closed pattern miners for structured objects. Hence, this is a first step towards efficient closed pattern discovery for general structured objects including trees and graphs.

Related Works: Termier *et al.* [23] recently considered the frequent closed tree discovery problem for a class of trees with same constraint as attribute trees in $\mathcal{AT}$. Though they presented an efficient algorithm using an interesting idea of *hooking*, its output-sensitive complexity is not yet analyzed. Cumby and Roth [13] presented a framework for learning and inference with relation data using a fragment of description logic, called *feature description logic*, which is similar to the class $\mathcal{AT}$ of attribute trees considered in this paper. However, the focus is on the knowledge representation issues in complex structural data domains, and closed pattern discovery is not considered [13]. Wang and Liu [25] studied the frequent tree discovery problem for the class of sets of paths from a given collection of labeled trees, which is closely related to frequent discoverry problem for the class AT.

Organization of This Paper: The rest of this paper is organized as follows. In Section 2, we give basic notion and definitions on attribute trees and closed patterns. In Section 3, we give a characterization of closed trees in terms of least general generalization. In Section 4, we develop the ppc-expansion (prefix-preserving expansion) and then present an output-polynomial time algorithm for frequent closed attribute trees. In Section 4, we show an experimental result, and in Section 5, we conclude.

2 Preliminaries

In this section, we introduce basic definitions on the class of ranked trees and closed tree discovery.

For a set A, $|A|$ denotes the cardinality of A and $\varepsilon \in A^*$ denotes the *empty sequence* of length zero. We denote by A^* and $A^+ = A^* \backslash \{\varepsilon\}$, respectively, the sets of all finite sequences and all non-empty finite sequences over A. For sequences $\alpha, \beta \in A^*$, we denote by $\alpha\beta$ the concatenation of α, and β and by $|\alpha|$ the length of α. If $\alpha\gamma = \beta$ holds for some possibly empty sequence $\gamma \in A^*$ then we say that α is a *prefix* of β. Furthermore, if γ is not the empty sequence then the prefix α is said to be *proper*. For a binary relation $R \subseteq R^2$ over a set X, R^+ denotes the *transitive closure* relation of R.

2.1 Attribute Trees

In this subsection, we model semi-structured data by a special type of labeled rooted trees, called attribute trees.

Let $\mathcal{A} = \{a_0, a_1, a_2, \ldots\}$ be a countable set of *labels* associated with a total order $\leq$ over $\mathcal{A}$. Sometimes, we call the elements of $\mathcal{A}$ *attributes* or *value*, too. For simplicity, we use a single alphabet A, and think of the labels at internal nodes and leaves as the encodings of attributes and values, respectively, as in [10]. Throughout this paper, we assume without loss of generality that $\mathcal{A}$ is the set of all nonnegative integers $\mathcal{A} = \{0, 1, 2, \ldots\}$ and $\leq$ is the partial order over integers.

Definition 1. *Let $\mathcal{A}$ is an alphabet of labels. An* attribute tree on $\mathcal{A}$ *(tree, for short) is a rooted, node labeled, directed acyclic graph $T = (V, E, r, label)$, where*

1. *The set $V = \{v_1, \ldots, v_n\}$ $(n \geq 0)$ is a finite set of nodes.*
2. *The set $E \subseteq V \times V$ is a finite set of edges. If $(u, v) \in E$ then we say that either u is the parent of v or v is a child of u.*
3. *The node $r \in V$ is a distinguished node, called the root. Any node v except r has exactly one parent.*
4. *The function label : $V \to \mathcal{A}$ is a labeling function for assigning a label $label(v)$ to each node v of T.*
5. *For every label $a \in \mathcal{A}$, each node $v \in V$ has at most one child w labeled by a. Then, the unique node w is called the a-child of v.*

We assume that $V_T = \{1, \ldots, n\}$ and identify the isomorphic patterns. The *size* of T, denoted by $|T|$, is defined by the number $|V|$ of the nodes in T. Let $u, v \in V$. If $(u, v) \in (E)^+$ then we say that either u is an *ancestor* of v or v

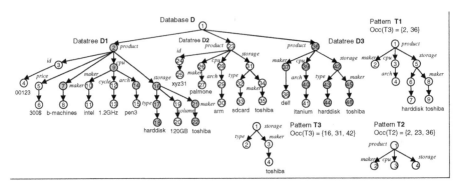

Fig. 1. An example of a tree database and patterns in attribute trees, where each circle indicates a node, each number in a circle indicates the node number, and each name in italic or bold face next to a circle indicates a node label. For instance, the pattern T_1 occurs in the database at positions 2 and 36.

is a *descendant* of u, where (E^+) is the transitive closure of E. A *path* in T is a sequence of nodes $\pi = (v_1, \ldots, v_d)$, $d \geq 0$, such that $(v_i, v_{i+1}) \in E$ for every $i = 1, \ldots, d-1$ and its *length* is the number of its nodes $|\pi| = d$. The *depth* of node v is the length of the unique path from the root to v. Other notions on trees such as height can be found in a standard textbook, e.g., [2]. We denote by $\mathcal{AT}$ the *class of all attribute trees* over $\mathcal{A}$. In what follows, for an attribute tree $T = (V, E, r, label)$, we refer to $V, E, \leq, r, label$ as V_T, E_T, r_T, and $label_T$, respectively if it is clear from context.

In Fig. 1, we show an example of attribute trees, where nodes are numbered in the preorder (as ordered trees), and each label is used to represents either an *attribute* (in italic face) or a *value* (in block face). These labels can be used to represent edge labels, too, since we deal with trees only.

2.2   Tree Matching Relation

The semantics of attribute trees is given by the *matching functions* as follows [3,8,16,17].

Definition 2. Let S and $T \in \mathcal{AT}$ be attribute trees over $\mathcal{A}$. Then, S *matches* T, denoted by $S \sqsubseteq T$, if there exists some function $\varphi : V_S \to V_T$ that satisfies the following conditions (i)–(iv) for any $v, v_1, v_2 \in V_S$.

(i) φ is a *one-to-one mapping*: $v_1 \neq v_2$ implies $\varphi(v_1) \neq \varphi(v_2)$.
(ii) φ *preserves the parent-child relation*: $(v_1, v_2) \in E_S$ iff $(\varphi(v_1), \varphi(v_2)) \in E_T$.
(iii) φ *preserves the node labels*: $label_S(v) = label_T(\varphi(v))$.

The function φ is called a *matching function* from S to T.[1] We denote by $\Phi(S, T)$ the set of all matching function from S to T.

---

[1] In Kilpelainen and Mannila [16], φ is called a path inclusion since it preserves the parent-child relationship. The fuction φ is called an *embedding*.

Example 1. In the example of Fig. 1, the tree T_2 with node set $V_{T_2} = \{1, 2, 3, 4\}$ occurs in the data tree $\mathcal{D}$ with matching functions $\varphi_1 = (2, 7, 9, 16)$, $\varphi_2 = (23, 26, 28, 31)$, and $\varphi_3 = (36, 37, 39, 42)$, where each φ is represented by tuple of its images $(\varphi(1), \varphi(2), \varphi(3), \varphi(4))$.

If $S \sqsubseteq T$ holds, then we also say that S *occurs* in T, S *is included* by T, or S *subsumes* T. If $S \sqsubseteq T$ and $T \not\sqsubseteq S$ then we define $S \sqsubset T$ and say that S is *properly included* in T or S *properly subsumes* T. For convention, we assume a special tree $\perp$ of size 0, called the *empty tree*, such that $\perp \sqsubseteq T$ for every $T \in \mathcal{AT}$.

Lemma 1. *The subsumption relation $\sqsubseteq$ is a partial order over $\mathcal{AT}$.*

The *matching problem* w.r.t. $\sqsubseteq$ is the problem to decide if a pattern tree P matches a data tree D, i.e., $P \sqsubseteq D$ holds.

Lemma 2. *The matching problem w.r.t. $\sqsubseteq$ is computable in $O(mn)$ time for attribute trees, where m and n are the sizes of a pattern tree and a data trees.*

2.3   Databases, Patterns, Denotations, and Closed Patterns

Let $\mathcal{D} = \{D_1, \ldots, D_m\}$ be a *tree database* (*database*, for short), where each $D_i \in \mathcal{AT}$ is an attribute tree, called a *data tree*, and the node sets $V_{D_1}, \ldots, V_{D_m}$ are mutually disjoint. In the later sections, we often identify $\mathcal{D}$ as a single database tree with a virtual master root v_0 labeled by a null label.[2] We define the domain and the size of $\mathcal{D}$ by $V_{\mathcal{D}} = \bigcup_i V_{D_i}$ and $||\mathcal{D}|| = |V_{\mathcal{D}}|$, respectively.

A *pattern* or *tree* in $\mathcal{D}$ is any attribute tree $T \in \mathcal{AT}$ that occurs in $\mathcal{D}$. A *position* in $\mathcal{D}$ is any node $v \in V_{\mathcal{D}}$. If there exists some matching function $\varphi \in \Phi(T, \mathcal{D})$ such that $p = \varphi(r_T)$, then we say that either T *occurs at* position p or p is an *occurrence* of T. For attribute trees, each occurrence $p = \varphi(r_T)$ of tree T determines the matching function φ in a unique way. The *occurrence set* of T in $\mathcal{D}$, denoted by $Occ_{\mathcal{D}}(T)$, is the set of all occurrences of T in $\mathcal{D}$, that is, $Occ_{\mathcal{D}}(T) = \{ \varphi(r_T) \mid \varphi \in \Phi(T, \mathcal{D}) \}$. Trees S and T are *equivalent* if $Occ_{\mathcal{D}}(S) = Occ_{\mathcal{D}}(T)$. The equivalent class for T on $\mathcal{D}$ is denoted by $EQ(T) = \{ T' \in \mathcal{AT} \mid Occ_{\mathcal{D}}(T') = Occ_{\mathcal{D}}(T) \}$. From now on, we fix a database $\mathcal{D}$, and we may omit the subscript $\mathcal{D}$ if no confusion arises in the future sections.

Let $0 \leq \sigma \leq ||\mathcal{D}||$ be a nonnegative integer, called a *minimum frequency threshold* or a *min-freq*. Then, a tree $T \in \mathcal{AT}$ is *frequent* in $\mathcal{D}$ if $|Occ_{\mathcal{D}}(T)| \geq \sigma$ holds. Both of $Occ_{\mathcal{D}}(T)$ and $|Occ_{\mathcal{D}}(T)|$ are computable in $O(|T| \cdot ||\mathcal{D}||)$ time.

Definition 3 (Closed trees). *A frequent tree T is* closed *in $\mathcal{D}$ if there exists no equivalent tree to T within $\mathcal{AT}$ that properly includes T, that is, there exists no such $T' \in \mathcal{AT}$ that (i) $T \sqsubset T'$ and (ii) $Occ_{\mathcal{D}}(T') = Occ_{\mathcal{D}}(T)$.*

Example 2. In the database of Fig. 1, patterns T_1 and T_2 have the occurrence sets $Occ_{\mathcal{D}}(T_1) = \{2, 36\}$ and $Occ_{\mathcal{D}}(T_2) = \{2, 23, 36\}$, respectively. We also see

---

[2] Note that the whole database tree $\mathcal{D}$ with the master root v_0 is not an attribute tree and represents a forest of data trees, since v_0 may have children with possibly same labels. However, it is justified whenever no pattern is allowed to occur at v_0.

that $T_2 \sqsubseteq T_1$ holds. Let $\sigma = 2$ be a minimum frequency threshold. $T_1, T_2,$ and T_3 are frequent patterns in $\mathcal{D}$ since. T_1 is closed in $\mathcal{D}$.

In other words, a closed tree T is a maximal element of $EQ(T)$. For threshold σ, $\mathcal{F}_\sigma$ and $\mathcal{C}_\sigma$ denotes the classes of all frequent trees and all frequent closed trees, respectively, in $\mathcal{D}$. We write $\mathcal{F}$ and $\mathcal{C}$ for the threshold $\sigma = 1$. Now, we state our data mining problem as follows.

CLOSED PATTERN MINING PROBLEM FOR ATTRIBUTE TREES
Given a database $\mathcal{D} = \{D_1, \ldots, D_m\}$ $(m \geq 0)$ of attribute trees and a minimum frequency threshold $0 \leq \sigma \leq ||\mathcal{D}||$, find all frequent closed trees $T \in \mathcal{AT}$ in $\mathcal{D}$ without duplicates.

Our goal in this paper is to design an output-polynomial time algorithm for the frequent closed pattern problem for the class $\mathcal{AT}$ using as small memory footprint as possible. An algorithm $\mathcal{M}$ solves an enumeration problem Π in *output-polynomial time* [5] if the running time of $\mathcal{M}$ is bounded by a polynomial time in m and n, where $m = |\mathcal{C}_\sigma|$ and $n = ||\mathcal{D}||$.

Since a transaction database with attributes $\mathcal{A}$ can be encoded by a forest of depth three over alphabet $\mathcal{A} \cup \{\ell_{\mathrm{db}}, \ell_{\mathrm{record}}\}$, the following lemmas for attribute trees follows from the corresponding lemmas for transaction databases.

Lemma 3. *There exist some database $\mathcal{D} \subseteq \mathcal{AT}$ and $\sigma \geq 0$ such that $|\mathcal{C}|$ is exponentially larger than the input size $||\mathcal{D}||$.*

Lemma 4 (Uno et al. [24]). *There exists some database $\mathcal{D} \subseteq \mathcal{AT}$ and $\sigma \geq 0$ such that $|\mathcal{F}_\sigma|$ is exponentially larger than $|\mathcal{C}_\sigma|$.*

From Lemma 3 and Lemma 4, we see that a naïve generate-and-test algorithm with enumeration of all frequent patterns cannot be output-sensitive.

2.4   Relationship to Other Models of Semi-structured Data

The class $\mathcal{AT}$ of attribute trees can be related in several ways to the existing models of structured and semi-structured data as follows.

- $\mathcal{AT}$ is a slight modification of *ranked trees* in the studies of tree automata and formal logic. In ranked trees, the domain of indices is restricted to non-negative integers rather than arbitrary countable set $\mathcal{A}$. Also the number of children of each node, called *rank* is determined by the symbol attached to the node.
- $\mathcal{AT}$ is a special case of *labeled ordered trees* [3,18,27] and *labeled unordered trees* [4,15], which are extensively studied in semi-structured data mining. Trees in $\mathcal{AT}$ have the constraint that the labels of the children of each node are mutually distinct.
- $\mathcal{AT}$ is corresponds to the class of complex objects with the tuple constructor only [6,10] where a *complex object* over an attribute alphabet A is either an empty object $O = \emptyset$ or a hierarchical tuple $O = \{a_1 : O_1, \ldots, a_n : O_n\}$ for attributes $a_1, \ldots, a_n \in A$ and complex objects $O_1, \ldots, O_n$.

- $\mathcal{AT}$ can be considered as a fragment of *description logic* [9] where only functional roles/attributes are allowed and equivalence constraints and complex logical constructs are not allowed. The relation $\sqsubseteq$ corresponds to the subsumption relation of such logic. Furthermore, roughly speaking, if we regard a tree database $\mathcal{D}$ as a model $I_\mathcal{D}$ and a tree pattern T as a formula ϕ_T in this version of description logic, then the occurrence set $Occ(T)$ of T corresponds to the extension of ϕ_T in $I_\mathcal{D}$, where a matching function is not necessarily one-to-one.

- $\mathcal{AT}$ corresponds to a simple subclass of *conjunctive queries* in deductive databases and first-order logic programs. The database has monadic predicates $Q_1(\cdot), \ldots, Q_m(\cdot)$ for labels and a binary predicate $R(\cdot, \cdot)$ for edges. A database has tree structure in the edge predicate, and a pattern is a definite clause of the form

$$P(X) \leftarrow Q_1(X_1), \ldots, Q_m(X_m), E_1(Y_1, Z1), \ldots, E_n(Y_n, Z_n)$$

with an underlying variable dependency structure of tree-shape, with some constraint on the appearance of monadic predicate corresponding to the definition of attribute trees.

A natural question is how useful the class of attribute trees is. Clearly, not all XML databases are attribute trees. For a non-attribute labeled tree T, there are two possible ways to derive an attribute tree version of T as follows. The first way is to simply remove all but first nodes with the same label in siblings. The second way is recursively merge the siblings with the same labels starting from the root node of T. In Section 5, we give an example of such an attribute tree derived from a real world dataset.

3   Characterization of Closed Attribute Trees

In this section, we give a characterization for closed attribute trees, which plays a central role in our output-polynomial time algorithm for frequent closed tree mining. This characterization used the notion of least general generalization for trees, and is a natural generalization of properties of closed itemsets to attribute trees.

In this and the next sections, we identify a tree in $\mathcal{AT}$ and its address set representation if no confusion arises.

3.1   A Representation for Attribute Trees

In this subsection, we introduce the address set representation of attribute trees, which is a combination of sequence representation for frequent itemsets [7] with tree domains for ranked trees.

For an attribute tree $T \in \mathcal{AT}$, each node v of T has the unique path π from the root to v. Then, the *address* of v, denoted by $dom(v)$, is the sequence $\alpha = (a_1, \ldots, a_m) \in \mathcal{A}^*$ of node labels spelled out by the path π. We also call any element of $\mathcal{A}^*$ an *address* on $\mathcal{A}$. The *address set* (or *domain*) of a tree $T \in \mathcal{AT}$ is defined by the set $dom(T) = \{\, dom(v) \in \mathcal{A}^* \mid v \in V_T \,\} \cup \{\varepsilon\}$, the set of all

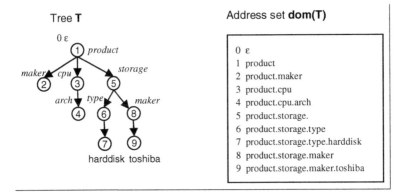

Fig. 2. A attribute tree T and its address set $dom(T)$

addresses for the nodes of T. For the empty tree $\bot$, we define $dom(\bot) = \{\varepsilon\}$.[3] Intuitively, an address and an address set over $\mathcal{A}^*$ correspond to a node and a tree in $\mathcal{A}$, respectively.

For an address $\alpha = (a_1, \ldots, a_{d-1}, a_d)$ of length $d \geq 1$, the *parent address* of α is the address $pa(\alpha) = a_1, \ldots, a_{d-1}$ of length $d - 1$. A set $A \subseteq \mathcal{A}^*$ is *prefix-closed* if $\alpha \in A$ implies $pa(\alpha) \in A$ for any address $\alpha \in \mathcal{A}^*$. The following lemmas are well known saying that the address set precisely encodes an attribute tree.

Lemma 5. *Let $A \subseteq \mathcal{A}^*$ be any set of addresses. Then, $dom(T) = A$ for some tree $T \in \mathcal{AT}$ iff A is prefix-closed.*

Lemma 6. *Trees T_1 and $T_2 \in \mathcal{AT}$ are isomorphic iff $dom(T_1) = dom(T_2)$ holds.*

The conversion between T and $dom(T)$ can be done in each direction in linear time of the input size.

Consider the set $\mathcal{A}^*$ of all addresses and the lexicographic order $<_{\text{lex}}$ over $\mathcal{A}^*$. It is often convenient to regard an address set $A = \{\alpha_1, \ldots, \alpha_n\}$ as an ordered sequence $(\alpha_{i_1}, \ldots, \alpha_{i_n})$, where $\alpha_{i_1} <_{\text{lex}} \cdots <_{\text{lex}} \alpha_{i_n}$ for some permulation $\{i_1, \ldots, i_n\} = \{1, \ldots, n\}$. With this sequence notation, we have the following definition. Let $\gamma \in \mathcal{A}^*$ be any address. The γ-*prefix* and the *strict* γ-*prefix* of A are the elements of A that are less than or equal to γ and strictly less than γ, that is, $A(\gamma) = \{\alpha \in A \mid \alpha \leq_{\text{lex}} \gamma\}$, and $A(\gamma - 1) = \{\alpha \in A \mid \alpha <_{\text{lex}} \gamma\}$, respectively.[4] The *head* and the *tail* of A is the the minimum and the maximal elements $hd(A) = \min(A)$ and $tl(A) = \max(A)$, respectively (They are equivalent to α_{i_1} and α_{i_n} in the sequence notation above).

For a tree A, an address $\alpha \in \mathcal{A}^*$ is *open* for an address set A if $pa(\alpha) \in A$ and $\alpha \notin A$ hold. We denote by $Open(A)$ the set of all open addresses for A.

---

[3] Here, we assume that every tree T contains an invisible *grand root* with the address ε. This treatment is just necessary to ensure a tree domain to be the prefix-closed.

[4] If $\mathcal{A}$ is finite then actually the address $\gamma - 1$ exists as the predecessor of address γ. It is not the case when $\mathcal{A}$ is countably infinite and γ ends with the smallest letter in $\mathcal{A}$. However, we can still use this notation safely if A is finite as in our case.

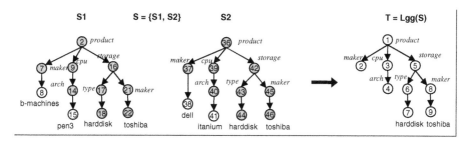

Fig. 3. The least general generalization $T = Lgg(S)$ of set of trees $\{S_1, S_2\}$. The tree T is the unique maximal tree that is more general than both of S_1 and S_2.

3.2   The Least General Generalization and Closure Operation

In this subsection, we introduce the least general generalization for attribute trees by extending the original definition for atomic formulas by Plotkin [20] and Reynolds [21]. Then, we give the closure operation for trees in $\mathcal{AT}$.

We define a binary relation $\preceq$ over $\mathcal{AT}$, called the *generalization relation*, as follows. For any trees $S, T \in \mathcal{AT}$, if there exists some $\varphi \in \Phi(S,T)$ such that $\varphi(r_S) = r_T$ then we define $S \preceq T$ and say that S is *more general than* T or T is *more specific than* S. If $S \preceq T$ but $T \not\preceq S$ then S is *properly more general than* T or T is *properly more specific than* S. Clearly, $S \preceq T$ implies $S \sqsubseteq T$, and thus, $\preceq$ is a partial order. However, the converse does not hold in general since φ have to map the root of S into the root of T in the case for $\preceq$.

Lemma 7. *For any* $S, T \in \mathcal{AT}$, $S \preceq T$ *iff* $dom(S) \subseteq dom(T)$.

The generalization relation satisfies the following anti-monotonicity.

Lemma 8. *Let* $S, T \in \mathcal{AT}$ *be any trees.*

1. *If* $S \preceq T$ *then* $Occ(S) \supseteq Occ(T)$.
2. *If* $S \preceq T$ *then* $|Occ(S)| \geq |Occ(T)|$.

Then, the least general generalization of a set of trees is defined as follows. Let $\mathcal{S} \subseteq \mathcal{AT}$ be a finite set of trees. A tree $T \in \mathcal{AT}$ is a *common generalization* for $\mathcal{S}$ if $T \preceq S$ for every $S \in \mathcal{S}$. A common generalization T of $\mathcal{S}$ is the *least general generalization* (*lgg*) of $\mathcal{S}$ if T is more specific than any common generalization for $\mathcal{S}$, i.e., $T' \preceq T$ for any common generalization T' for $\mathcal{S}$. We denote the lgg of $\mathcal{S}$ by $Lgg(\mathcal{S})$. The following theorem says that $Lgg(\mathcal{S})$ always exists and unique.

Lemma 9. *For any set* $\mathcal{S} \subseteq \mathcal{AT}$, $Lgg(\mathcal{S})$ *is the unique tree* $T_\cap$ *such that* $dom(T_\cap) = \bigcap_{S \in \mathcal{S}} dom(S)$.

Proof: Let $\mathcal{S} = \{S_1, \ldots, S_n\} \subseteq \mathcal{AT}$ be a finite set of trees, where $m \geq 0$. Then, we can show that $Lgg(\mathcal{S})$ is the unique tree $T_\cap \in \mathcal{AT}$ whose address set is given by the intersection of all address sets $A_1, \ldots, A_n$, that is, $A_\cap = \bigcap_i A_i$, where $A_i = ad(S_i)$ for every $i = 1, \ldots, m$. Now, we give the proof for the above claim. Let $T_\cap \in \mathcal{AT}$ be the tree defined in the above statement. If both sets A_1 and A_2 are prefix-closed then so is $A_1 \cap A_2$. Thus, the intersection $A_\cap$ is also prefix-closed. From Lemma 6 and Lemma 5, such a tree $T_\cap$ always exists and is unique. On the other hand, assume that we have a common p-generalization T' of $\mathcal{S}$. If $T' \preceq S_i$ then $A' = ad(T')$ is included in $A_i = ad(S_i)$ for every i. Thus, $A' \subseteq \bigcap_i ad(S_i) = A_\cap$ holds. From Lemma 7, this implies that $T' \preceq T$ for any common generalization T'. Hence, we know that T is the unique least general generalization of $\mathcal{S}$ w.r.t. $\preceq$. $\qquad\square$

Theorem 1. *The least general generalization $Lgg(\mathcal{S})$ for a finite set $\mathcal{S} \subseteq \mathcal{AT}$ of attribute trees is unique, of polynomial size, and polynomial time computable in the total size of $\mathcal{S}$.*

From the proof of the above theorem, we present an $O(mn)$ time algorithm for $Lgg(\mathcal{S})$ as in [20]. Cohen *et al.* [12] studied the least general generalization for a more general fragment of description logic, called CLASSIC.

Now, we give the closure operation for trees.

For a position $v \in V_\mathcal{D}$, the *subtree (or half-tree) rooted at position v* is the tree S whose domain is given by $dom(S) = \{\, \beta \in \mathcal{A}^* \,|\, \alpha\beta \in dom(\mathcal{D}) \,\}$ for the address α of v. For a set $P \subseteq V_\mathcal{D}$ of positions, the *tree set* of tree T for P, denoted by $Tree(T)$, is the set of all subtrees of $\mathcal{D}$ rooted at some positions in P.

Definition 4 (The closure operation). *Let $\mathcal{D}$ be a database. The* closure *of a tree $T \in \mathcal{AT}$ is the tree $Clo_\mathcal{D}(T) = Lgg(Tree_\mathcal{D}(Occ_\mathcal{D}(T)))$.*

Lemma 10. *$Clo(T)$ is computable in $O(mn)$ time in the size $m = |T|$ of T and the total size $n = ||\mathcal{D}||$ of $\mathcal{D}$.*

Theorem 2. *$Clo(T)$ is the unique maximal tree in the equivalence class $EQ(T)$*

Proof: Let $\mathcal{S}$ be the set of all half-trees in $\mathcal{D}$ rooted at the occurrences of T in the database. Then, the closure of T is $L = Lgg(\mathcal{S})$. Now, we show that if P is any member of $EQ(T)$ then the pattern P is also more general than the closure $Lgg(\mathcal{S})$. Let P be any member of $EQ(T)$. Then, P occurs at all occurrences of T in the database, i.e., $Occ(T) \subseteq Occ(P)$. By the definition of half-trees, this implies that P is more general than all half-trees in $\mathcal{S}$. From the definition, $Lgg(\mathcal{S})$ is the unique greatest tree that is more general than all half-trees in $\mathcal{S}$. Thus, it immediately follows that P is more general than $Lgg(\mathcal{S})$. Since this is valid for all $P \in EQ(T)$, we see that $Lgg(\mathcal{S})$ is the greatest member of $EQ(T)$ in terms of $\preceq$. $\qquad\square$

Theorem 3. *A tree $T \in \mathcal{AT}$ is a closed tree in $\mathcal{D}$ iff $Clo(T) = T$.*

From Theorem 3 and Lemma 10, we can test if T is closed or not in polynomial time in $|T|$ and $||\mathcal{D}||$. We listed below some properties of closed trees, which are useful in show in the above theorems and also for the discussion in the later sections.

Lemma 11. *For any trees $T, T_1, T_2 \in \mathcal{AT}$, the following properties hold:*

1. $T \preceq Clo(T)$.
2. *If $T_1 \preceq T_2$ then $Clo(T_1) \preceq Clo(T_2)$.*
3. *If $Occ(T_1) \subseteq Occ(T_2)$ then $Clo(T_1) \preceq Clo(T_2)$.*
4. $Clo(Clo(T)) = Clo(T)$.
5. $Clo(T)$ *is the unique smallest closed tree including T.*
6. *For closed trees $T_1, T_2 \in \mathcal{C}$, $T_1 \preceq T_2$ iff $Occ(T_1) \preceq Occ(T_2)$.*

4 Output-Polynomial Time Algorithm for Closed Trees

In this section, we present an efficient algorithm for enumerating all frequent closed trees in polynomial time per tree without duplicates in the total size of the input database.

4.1 Possible Approaches

In this subsection, we consider and briefly summarize the possible approaches for computing frequent closed trees and point out some problems in them.

The first approach is to use a frequent tree mining algorithm. In mining of labeled ordered trees, an efficient enumeration technique, called *rightmost expansion* in [3], is used for generating all frequent labeled ordered trees with depth-first search. In our representation for attribute trees with address set, the definition is given as follows.

Definition 5 (Rightmost expansion). *Let $k \geq 1$ and $S \in \mathcal{AT}$ be a tree of size $k - 1$. Then, a tree T of size k is said to be a* rightmost expansion *of S if $T = S \cup \{\beta\}$ for some open address $\beta \in Open(S)$ such that $\beta >_{\text{lex}} td(S)$.*

Using rightmost expansion, we can implement an algorithm that enumerates all frequent trees in $\mathcal{AT}$ without duplicate, which starts from the empty tree, and searches all frequent trees from smaller to larger by the rightmost expansion as Asai *et al.* showed for the computation of frequent ordered trees [3].

We can modify this algorithm to compute all frequent closed trees by first enumerating each tree, and then testing if it is closed. This algorithm requires at least time proportional to $||\mathcal{F}_\sigma|| > ||\mathcal{C}_\sigma||$. Thus, it cannot be an output-polynomial time algorithm at all.

The second approach is to use the closure operation to generate closed trees. T is an *expansion* for S if $T = S \cup \{\beta\}$ for some open address $\beta \in Open(S)$.

Definition 6 (Closure expansion). *Let $k \geq 1$ and $S \in \mathcal{AT}$ be a tree of size $k - 1$. Then, a tree T of size k is said to be a* closure expansion *of S if T is the closure of an expansion for S, that is, $T = Clo_\mathcal{D}(S \cup \{\beta\})$ for some $\beta \in Open(S)$.*

It is not hard to see that any closed tree T is a closure expansion of some closed tree S. Then, we can implement an algorithm for computing all frequent closed trees working with level by level using breadth-first search or level-wise search as Uno *et al.* showed for the computation of frequent closed itemsets [24].

This algorithm starts from the set of frequent closed trees of size one, and for every level $k = 1, 2, \ldots$ then iteratively computes from the set C_k of trees of size k the set C_{k+1} by using closure expansion. Since the same tree can be generated more than one parent tree by closure expansion, we have to check if each generated closed tree is not repeated, using the current set of closed trees in a breadth-first manner.

We can prove that the computation time of this approach can be output-polynomial in $||\mathcal{D}||$, using the results to be shown in the following sections.

Corollary 4. *There exists an output-polynomial time algorithm in $||\mathcal{D}||$ for the frequent closed pattern problem using the space proportional to the output size $||\mathcal{C}_\sigma||$.*

However, this algorithm with closure expansion alone requires at least the memory space proportional to the total size $||\mathcal{C}_\sigma||$ of outputs due to its breadth-first search scheme.

Overall, neither of the approaches with rightmost expansion alone and with closure expansion alone are not satisfactory yet. To overcome these problems, we combine both approaches in the following sections to achieve efficient enumeration with small amount of space proportional to $||\mathcal{D}||$ rather than $||\mathcal{F}_\sigma||$ and $||\mathcal{D}||$.

4.2   Tree-Shaped Search Space for Closed Trees

In this subsection, we introduce a tree-shaped search structure over $\mathcal{C}$, which is based on a search technique, called reverse search [5].

We first give a parent function over closed trees. Let $\mathcal{D}$ be a database. Then, the *root closed pattern* is the smallest tree $root_\mathcal{C} = Clo(\bot)$ equivalent to the empty pattern $\bot$ and always exists. Let $A \subseteq \mathcal{A}^*$ be an address set of a tree. Recall that we introduced the notations $A(\gamma)$ and $A(\gamma-1)$ for an address $\gamma \in \mathcal{A}^*$ in Section 3.1, where $A(\gamma)$ is the set of addresses in A less than or equal to γ and $A(\gamma-1)$ is the set of addresses strictly less than γ. We define the *core index* of A by

$$core\_i(A) = \min\{\, \gamma \in A \mid Occ(A) = Occ(A(\gamma)) \,\},$$

that is, the minimum address $\gamma \in A$ such that $Occ(A) = Occ(A(\gamma))$. For $root_\mathcal{C}$, we define $core\_i(root_\mathcal{C}) = -1$.

Definition 7 (The parent tree). *Let $T \in \mathcal{C} \backslash \{root_\mathcal{C}\}$ be any non-root closed tree. Then, the* parent *of T, denoted by $\mathcal{P}(T) \in \mathcal{AT}$, is defined by*

$$\mathcal{P}(T) = Clo(T(core\_i(T) - 1)).$$

Lemma 12. *For any non-root closed tree $T \in \mathcal{C} \backslash \{root_\mathcal{C}\}$, the parent tree $\mathcal{P}(T)$ always exists, is unique, and is also a member of $\mathcal{C}$.*

Proof: Since $T \in \mathcal{C} \backslash \{root_\mathcal{C}\}$, T is not equivalent to the empty tree $\bot$ in its occurrence set. Thus, its core index $\gamma = core\_i(T)$ must be greater than zero, and thus the prefix $T(\gamma-1)$ is defined. For any tree T, its closure $Clo(T)$ always exists. Hence, the result follows.   □

Lemma 13. *For any non-root closed tree $T \in \mathcal{C} \setminus \{root_\mathcal{C}\}$, the following properties hold:*

1. $|\mathcal{P}(T)| < |T|$ *holds.*
2. $\mathcal{P}(T) \prec T$ *holds.*

Proof: The proof follows from Lemma 11.   □

Let us consider a directed graph $\mathcal{T} = (\mathcal{C}, \mathcal{P}, root_\mathcal{C})$, called a *search graph* for $\mathcal{C}$, where each node is a closed tree T and there exists an edge (a reverse edge) from a tree T to tree S if $\mathcal{P}(T) = S$. From Lemma 12 and Lemma 13, we have the following lemma.

Lemma 14 (Existence of tree-shaped search space for $\mathcal{C}$). *The search graph $\mathcal{T} = (\mathcal{C}, \mathcal{P}, root_\mathcal{C})$ for $\mathcal{C}$ is a spanning tree over all closed trees in $\mathcal{C}$ with the unique root $root_\mathcal{C}$.*

Lemma 14 is also valid for frequent closed trees in $\mathcal{C}_\sigma$ with min-freq threshold σ since the parent edge satisfies the anti-monotonicity in frequency (Lemma 8).

4.3   Prefix-Preserving Closure Expansion

In this subsection, we give the prefix-preserving closure expansion. Let $S, T \in \mathcal{AT}$ be trees. $T \in \mathcal{AT}$ is said to be a *prefix-preserving closure expansion* (ppc-expansion) of S if

(i) $T = Clo(S \cup \{\beta\})$ for some $\beta \in Open(S)$, that is, T is obtained by first adding a new node to S, and then taking its closure.
(ii) the address β satisfies $\beta > core\_i(S)$.
(iii) $S(\beta - 1) = T(\beta - 1)$, that is, the strict β-prefix of S is preserved.

In the search, starting from the root tree $root_\mathcal{C}$, we search the search tree $\mathcal{T}$ by growing the present tree by taking its ppc-expansions. The next lemma says that the core index can be recursively computed.

Lemma 15. *Let S be a closed tree and $T = Clo(S \cup \{\beta\})$ be a ppc-expansion of S. Then, β is the core index of T.*

Proof: Since $Clo(T(\beta)) = T$ by assumption, we at least know that $core\_i(T) \leq \beta$. Assume to contradict that $core\_i(T) < \beta$ and that $Clo(T(\delta)) = T$ holds for some $\delta < \beta$ such that $\delta \notin S$. Then, we can show that $Clo(S \cup \{\delta\}) = T$ holds. However, this implies the contradiction that $S(\beta) \neq T(\beta)$ since $\delta \notin S$ but $\delta \in T$. Thus, we conclude that $core\_i(T) = \beta$.   □

Lemma 16. *Let S be a closed tree. Then, all ppc-expansions of S can be generated in polynomial time per ppc-expansions in $|S|$ and $\|\mathcal{D}\|$.*

We show that any non-root tree T can be generated from its parent $\mathcal{P}(T)$ by ppc-expansion. In the following proofs, we assume that $\mathcal{A}$ is finite for simplicity. However, these lemmas also hold for infinite $\mathcal{A}$.

Lemma 17. *Let T be a non-root closed tree, and $S = \mathcal{P}(T)$ be the parent tree of T. Then, T is a ppc-expansion of S.*

Proof: Let $\gamma = core\_i(T)$. We will show that $T = Clo(S \cup \{\gamma\})$. By assumption, $S = Clo(T(\gamma - 1))$. Thus, the core index of S is at least strictly smaller than γ and this satisfies condition (ii) of ppc-expansion. Since $T(\gamma) = T(\gamma - 1) \cup \{\gamma\}$. By Lemma 11, we have $T(\gamma) \preceq S \cup \{\gamma\} \preceq T$. Since $Clo(T(\gamma)) = T$ for the core index γ, it follows from Lemma 11 that condition (i) $Clo(S \cup \{\gamma\}) = T$ of ppc-expansion. Since $S = Clo(T(\gamma - 1))$, $S(\gamma - 1)$ already includes $T(\gamma - 1)$. The converse is also true T is a closure of $S \cup \{\gamma\}$. Thus, we have condition (iii) $S(\gamma - 1) = T(\gamma - 1)$ of ppc-expansion.   □

Lemma 18. *Let S be a closed tree, and T be a ppc-expansion of S. Then, S is the parent tree of T, i.e., $S = \mathcal{P}(T)$.*

Proof: By assumption, (i) $T = Clo(S \cup \{\beta\})$ for some $\beta > core\_i(S)$. Then, by condition (iii) of ppc-expansion $S(\beta - 1) = T(\beta - 1)$, we know that $\gamma = core\_i(T)$ is at least larger than β, and thus strictly larger than $core\_i(S)$. This implies that $\gamma - 1$ is larger than or equal to $core\_i(S)$. Since $\gamma - 1 \geq \beta - 1$, we have $S(\gamma - 1) \preceq T(\gamma - 1)$. On the other hand, since $\gamma - 1 \geq core\_i(S)$ as above, we have $Clo(S(\gamma - 1)) = S$. This implies that $Clo(T(\gamma - 1))$ is at least as general as S, and thus equivalent to S. This shows that $\mathcal{P}(T(core\_i(T) - 1)) = S$.   □

Combining Lemma 17 and Lemma 18, we show that the ppc-expansion correctly generates the children of a closed pattern in the search graph.

Theorem 5. *Let S and T be a closed tree such that $T \neq root_C$. Then, S is the parent tree of T iff T is a ppc-expansion of S.*

4.4   Algorithm

In Fig. 4, we show our algorithm CLOATT (Closed Attribute Tree Miner) for discovering all frequent closed trees in a given database. This algorithm uses ppc-expansion introduced in the previous section. Starting from the smallest closed tree $root_C$, the algorithm performs depth-first search for closed trees by finding the children of the present closed tree using ppc-expansion.

Theorem 6. *Let $\mathcal{D} \subseteq \mathcal{AT}$ be a database and $\sigma \geq 1$ be a minimum frequency threshold. Then, the algorithm CLOATT of Fig. 4 finds all frequent closed trees $T \in \mathcal{AT}$ appearing in $\mathcal{D}$ in $O(bm^2 n)$ amortized time per tree without duplicates using $O(n)$ memory space, where b is the maximal branching of each data trees in $\mathcal{D}$, $m = |T|$ is the size of the tree found, and $n = ||\mathcal{D}||$ is the total size of the database $||\mathcal{D}||$.*

Proof: From Lemma 14 and Theorem 5, the algorithm CLOATT correctly searches all closed trees on the spanning tree $\mathcal{T}$ for $\mathcal{F}$. Since this search space forms tree, each closed tree is generated exactly once. For each closed tree T, we can compute $Occ(T)$ in $O(mn)$ time. From Lemma 16, we can also compute all ppc-expansions of T in polynomial time, more exactly in $O(bm^2 n)$ time

---

1   **Algorithm** CLOATT
2   *input*: a database $\mathcal{D}$ and a min-frequency threshold $1 \leq \sigma \leq ||\mathcal{D}||$.
3   *output*: all frequent closed patterns in $\mathcal{D}$ with min-freq σ;
4       $T_0 := Clo(\bot)$.   // Most general closed pattern $root_C$
5       $\gamma_0 := core\_i(T_0)$.   // Core index of T_0
6       $PPC\text{-}Expand(T_0, \gamma_0, Occ(T_0), \mathcal{D}, \sigma)$.

7   **Proc.** $PPC\text{-}Expand(S, \gamma, Occ(S), \mathcal{D}, \sigma)$
8   If $|Occ(S)| < \sigma$ then return   // Not frequent
9   Else if $Clo(S) \neq S$ then return   // Not closed
10   Else   // Closed pattern
11   Output S.
12   For each address $\beta \in Open(S)$ such that $\beta >_{\text{lex}} \gamma$ do:
                // PPC-Expansion
13              $T := Clo(S \cup \{\beta\})$;
14   If $S(\gamma - 1) \neq T(\gamma - 1)$ then return.
15              $PPC\text{-}Expand(T, \beta, Occ(T), \mathcal{D}, \sigma)$.

16   Prefix$(\gamma) := \{\, \alpha \in \mathcal{A}^* \,|\, \alpha <_{\text{lex}} \gamma \,\}$.

Fig. 4. A frequent closed pattern miner using prefix-preserving closure (PPC) expansion. This algorithm runs in output-polynomial time also with a small amount of memory due to the pure depth-first search.

since there are at most bm ppc-extensions of T. From the recursive computation scheme of the algorithm, if all ppc-expansions of T are not closed then this branch of computation is terminated and the algorithm backtracks. Therefore, the amortized computation time per generated tree is again $O(bm^2n)$ time. Since the recursive call for the subprocedure $PPC\text{-}Expand$ can be implemented by using a stack of length at most $m = |T|$ where each entry contains a pair of an ancestor tree S of T and its occurrence set $Occ(S)$, the memory space used is $O(\ell) = O(mn)$, where ℓ is the sum of $|Occ(S)| = O(||\mathcal{D}||)$ for all ancestors of the current tree T. Furthermore, this can be reduced to $O(n)$ by recording only the differences of these occurrence lists. This completes the proof.   □

Corollary 7. *There exists an output-polynomial time algorithm for the frequent closed pattern problem using the space proportional to the total database size.*

5   Experiments

In this section, we present some experimental results on a qualitative assessment at the utility of closed attribute tree mining. In particular, we examine how much reduction is possible by closed pattern discovery on a real world dataset.

Table 1. The size of original and pruned datasets

Dataset	# documents	# nodes	Is AT?
dblp1830.xml	986	37,276	No
dblp1830at.xml	986	33,468	Yes

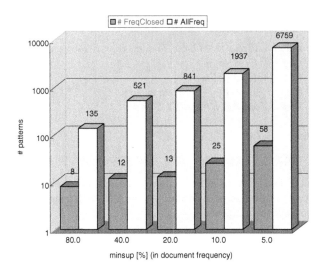

Fig. 5. The number of frequent closed trees and all frequent trees against the minimum frequency thresholds

We first build a pruned dataset consisting of attribute trees derived from a real world dataset as follows. The orignal dataset is a subset of an XML dataset dblp1830.xml consisting of 986 XML documents extracted from a bibliographic database DBLP (dblp.xml).[5] Since this dataset contains repeated occurrences of the same label, such as author and ee in siblings, we prune the dataset by removing all but first occurrences of the repeated attributes and its subtrees in siblings. The resulting dataset, called dblp1830at.xml, consists only of attribute trees. In Table 1, we show statistics of the original and pruned datasets. From the table, we can see that the dataset retains a large part of the structure in the original datasets.

Then, we compute the sets of all frequent closed trees and frequent trees in the pruned dataset dblp1830at.xml. To compute all frequent attribute trees, we used an implementation of a frequent unordered tree miner UNOT [4]. Since

---

[5] http://www.informatik.uni-trier.de/~ley/db/

we have not implemented the algorithm CLOATT in the previous section, we compute all closed patterns by explicitly checking if the condition of Definition 3 holds for each frequent trees computed by UNOT. In Figure 5, we show the number of the frequent closed trees and the number of all frequent trees when we vary the minimum frequency threshold from 80.0% to 5.0% in document frequency. From this figure, we can observe that the number of the frequent closed trees is order of magnitude smaller than the number of all frequent trees for most minimum frequency threshold values. Some of the discovered closed trees corresponded to a schema structure inherent to the DBLP database.

6   Conclusion

In this paper, we presented an output-polynomial time algorithm for mining all frequent closed patterns for the class of attribute trees.

This algorithm computes all frequent closed trees in polynomial time per closed tree without duplicates in the total size of the input database using a small amount of memory with depth-first search. For the purpose, we gave a characterization of closed trees in terms of the least generalization for attribute trees, and an efficient enumeration method, called pcc-expansion, for realizing direct enumeration of closed trees only using the depth-first search.

The class $\mathcal{AT}$ of attribute trees can be related in several ways to the existing models of structured and semi-structured data. In particular, $\mathcal{AT}$ has a close relationship to a fragment of description logic with functional roles only. Thus, it is an interesting future work to generalize the result of this paper to richer fragment of description logic. This may include the introduction of equivalence constraints and non-functional roles.

In this paper, we are working only with theoretical framework for efficient closed tree miners using ppc-extension. The implementation of the proposed algorithm CLOATT and the estimation of its efficiency on realworld datasets will be future works.

Acknowledgment

The authors would like to thank Ken Satoh, Shinichi Nakano, Ryutaro Ichise, Hideaki Takeda, Akihiro Yamamoto, Hiroshi Sakamoto, and Shinichi Shimozono for their valuable discussions and comments. The first author also would like to thank Fabien de Marchi and Salima Benbernou of UCBL1 and Makoto Haraguchi of Hokkaido University for their introduction to and discussions on description logic and to also thank Mohand-Said Hacid of UCBL1 and Yuzuru Tanaka of Hokkaido University for giving the opportunity for the research. The authors also thank anonymou referees for their valuable comments that greatly improve the quality of this paper. This research is partly supported by Grant-in-Aid for Scientific Researchon Priority Areas on "Informatics," Ministry of Education, Culture, Sports, Science and Technology of Japan, and Cooperative Fund by National Institute of Informatics, Japan.

References

1. S. Abiteboul, P. Buneman, D. Suciu, Data on the Web, Morgan Kaufmann, 2000.
2. Aho, A. V., Hopcroft, J. E., Ullman, J. D., *Data Structures and Algorithms*, Addison-Wesley, 1983.
3. T. Asai, K. Abe, S. Kawasoe, H. Arimura, H. Sakamoto, and S. Arikawa. Efficient substructure discovery from large semi-structured data. In *Proc. the 2nd SIAM Int'l Conf. on Data Mining (SDM2002)*, 158–174, 2002.
4. T. Asai, H. Arimura, T. Uno, S. Nakano, Discovering frequent substructures in large unordered trees, In *Proc. the 6th Int'l Conf. on Discovery Science (DS'03)*, LNAI 2843, Springer-Verlag, 47-61, 2003.
5. D. Avis, K. Fukuda, Reverse search for enumeration, Discrete Applied Mathematics, 65(1–3), 21–46, 1996.
6. Bancilhon, Khoshafian, A calculus for complex objects, In *PODS'86*, 53–59, 1986.
7. R. J. Bayardo Jr., *Efficiently Mining Long Patterns from Databases*, In Proc. SIGMOD98, 1998, pp. 85–93.
8. B. Bringmann, Matching in Frequent Tree Discovery, In *'Proc. IEEE ICDM 2004*, 335–338, 2004.
9. A. Borgida, R. J. Brachman, D. L. McGuinness, L. A. Resnick, CLASSIC: A Structural Data Model for Objects, In *Proc. SIGMOD'89*, ACM, 58–67, 1989.
10. P. Buneman, S. B. Davidson, G. G. Hillebrand, D. Suciu, A query language and optimization techniques for unstructured data, In *Proc. SIGMOD'96*, ACM, 505–516, 1996.
11. Y. Chi, Y. Yang, Y. Xia, and R. R. Muntz, Cmtreeminer: Mining both closed and maximal frequent subtrees, In *Proc. PAKDD'04*, 2004.
12. W. W. Cohen, A. Borgida, H. Hirsh, Computing Least Common Subsumers in Description Logics, In *Proc. AAAI'92*, 754-760, 1992.
13. C. M. Cumby and D. Roth, Learning with feature description logic, In *Proc. ILP 2002*, LNAI 2583, 23–47, 2003.
14. A. Inokuchi, T. Washio, H. Motoda, An Apriori-Based Algorithm for Mining Frequent Substructures from Graph Data, In *Proc. PKDD 2000*, 13–23, LNAI 1910, Springer-Verlag, 2000.
15. S. Nijssen, J. N. Kok, Effcient Discovery of Frequent Unordered Trees In *Proc. the First International Workshop on Mining Graphs, Trees and Sequences (MGTS'03)*, Sep. 2003.
16. P. Kilpelainen, H. Mannila, Ordered and Unordered Tree Inclusion, SIAM J. Computing, 24(2), 340–356, 1995.
17. Kosaraju, S. R., Efficient tree pattern matching, In *Proc. 30th FOCS*, 178–183, 1989.
18. S. Nakano, Efficient generation of plane trees, Information Processing Letters, 84, 167–172, Elsevier,2002.
19. N. Pasquier, Y. Bastide, R. Taouil, L. Lakhal, Discovering Frequent Closed Itemsets for Association Rules, In Proc. ICDT'99, 398–416, 1999.
20. G. D. Plotkin, A note on inductive generalization. *Machine Intelligence*, 5, 153–163, Edinburgh University Press.
21. J. C. Reynolds, Transformational systems and the algebraic structure of atomic formulas, Machine Intelligence 5, 135–151, Edinburgh University Press.
22. A. Termier, M.-C. Rousset, M. Sebag, Treefinder: a first step towards xml data mining, In *Proc. ICMD'02*, 2002.
23. A. Termier, M.-C. Rousset, M. Sebag, DRYADE: a new approach for discovering closed frequent trees in heterogeneous tree databases, In *Proc. ICMD'04*, 2004.

24. T. Uno, T. Asai, Y. Uchida, H. Arimura, An efficient algorithm for enumerating closed patterns in transaction databases, In *Proc. DS'04*, LNAI 3245, Springer-Verlag, 16-30, 2004.
25. K. Wang, H. Liu, Schema Discovery for Semistructured Data, In *Proc. KDD'97*, 271–274, 1997.
26. X. Yan, J. Han,   CloseGraph: Mining Closed Frequent Graph Patterns   In *Proc. SIGKDD'03*, ACM, 2003.
27. M. J. Zaki. Efficiently mining frequent trees in a forest, In *Proc. SIGKDD'02*, ACM, 2002.

Guiding Inference Through Relational Reinforcement Learning

Nima Asgharbeygi, Negin Nejati, Pat Langley, and Sachiyo Arai

Computational Learning Laboratory
Center for the Study of Language and Information
Stanford University, Stanford CA 94305, USA
{nimaa, negin}@stanford.edu
langley@csli.stanford.edu
arai@tu.chiba-u.ac.jp

Abstract. Reasoning plays a central role in intelligent systems that operate in complex situations that involve time constraints. In this paper, we present the Adaptive Logic Interpreter, a reasoning system that acquires a controlled inference strategy adapted to the scenario at hand, using a variation on relational reinforcement learning. Employing this inference mechanism in a reactive agent architecture lets the agent focus its reasoning on the most rewarding parts of its knowledge base and hence perform better under time and computational resource constraints. We present experiments that demonstrate the benefits of this approach to reasoning in reactive agents, then discuss related work and directions for future research.

1   Introduction

A fundamental goal of artificial intelligence is to develop systems that demonstrate intelligent behavior in complex environments. Such systems should be capable of assessing situations, reasoning about them, and making informed decisions even when confronted with constraints involving time and computational resources. For example, an embodied agent can benefit greatly by drawing inferences (internal beliefs) about its immediate situation (as perceived through sensors) using knowledge about the world (inference rules).

Because we are concerned with reactive agents, we focus here on data-driven bottom-up approaches to inference, rather than query-based top-down ones. Such agents need a belief state about the world in order to make a decision and take an action in any situation, so bottom-up inference over relational inference rules is the natural choice. However, it is clear that a reactive agent operating under time constraints cannot afford to exhaustively make all possible inferences. Rather, like humans, it must give priority to drawing more important conclusions and delay others. Such an informed agent may overlook important items on occasion, but it can still respond rapidly and its performance will degrade gracefully as complexity increases. This approach differs significantly from most

S. Kramer and B. Pfahringer (Eds.): ILP 2005, LNAI 3625, pp. 20–37, 2005.

AI research on efficient matching and inference, which has combined exhaustive methods with clever indexing schemes (Doyle [1], Forgy [2]).

In this paper, we assume that a knowledge-rich reactive agent cannot afford to make all possible inferences, and thus must focus its attention. We are interested in an "anytime" inference mechanism that achieves high utility by inferring the most useful inferences within a given time limit. Moreover, under no time constraint, it should generate the same belief state as the exhaustive inference mechanism. As an implication, we prefer not to modify the structure of inference rules (unlike previous work on speedup learning, such as Zelle and Mooney [3]), but rather to have an adaptive reasoning system that learns *over* the relational structure in order to use it more efficiently.

Our solution, called the Adaptive Logic Interpreter (ADLIN), consists of two components—a value-driven inference process that iteratively selects the implied instantiated inference rule with the highest expected utility, and a learning mechanism that estimates these utilities based on received rewards. The latter uses a variation of relational reinforcement learning over the logical structure of inference rules. It incorporates a generalization mechanism that models the values estimated for instances of each first-order inference rule using regression methods. This model is then used to estimate the initial expected utility for new instances of the corresponding inference rule.

We should mention that, since the problem involves relationally represented states and actions, it is naturally posed as relational reinforcement learning (Tadepalli *et al.* [4]). Nevertheless, our generalization mechanism differs from the methods employed in earlier works on this topic. For example, Dzeroski *et al.* [5] applied inductive logic programming methods to induce first-order regression trees as generalizers. However, our approach represents the generalization knowledge as a set of linear regression models over the first-order predicates. We claim that our approach to relational reinforcement learning uses the prior knowledge encoded in the relational structure of a given domain effectively, and that it is capable of generalizing across distinct objects of the same class and transferring to tasks of different sizes.

Furthermore, in contrast with traditional reinforcement learning over physical actions, our formulation deals with actions that are internal to the agent. More specifically, we interpret each inference step as a mental action taken at some internal state that updates the agent's belief state but not the physical world. We hypothesize that the resulting adaptive attention method will let reactive agents make informed inferences under time constraints, and thus respond appropriately in complex environments.

We begin by reviewing ICARUS, a reactive agent architecture that currently relies on exhaustive inference to characterize situations and decide on its actions. After this, we describe ADLIN's method for giving priority to high-utility beliefs and an associated mechanism for learning their values. Next, we formalize our hypotheses about the benefits of this method and report experimental studies that demonstrate them empirically. In closing, we discuss related research on controlled inference and suggest directions for future work.

2   Architectural Framework

Our vehicle for studying controlled inference has been ICARUS, a reactive architecture for physical agents that has been described at length in Choi *et al.* [6]. Here we summarize the framework briefly, emphasizing those aspects most relevant to our current topic. We believe our approach will be applicable to other knowledge-rich reactive agent architectures that include an inference component.

An ICARUS agent lives in an *environment* composed of a dynamic collection of objects whose attributes and mutual relations change over time. Like other agent architectures, ICARUS operates in cycles. On each iteration, descriptions of objects perceivable to the agent (*perceptions*) are deposited into a perceptual buffer from which the system bases its inferences and generates a belief state. The interpreter then finds which *skills* match against the resulting belief state, selects the best applicable skill instance, and executes it in the environment.

Skills are Prolog-like rules that let the agent respond to different situations in the environment. These are organized in a hierarchy, so that each skill calls on lower-level skills or executable actions. Each skill specifies initiation conditions that match against descriptions of perceived objects or inferred relations among those objects. Unlike many reactive frameworks, ICARUS bases its decisions not only on primitive perceptions but also on its inferred beliefs.

In this paper we are mainly concerned with ICARUS' inference mechanism which, on each cycle, generates the agent's belief state based on the perceptions and the domain knowledge. Knowledge about the domain is stored in a long-term conceptual memory as a set of *concept* definitions. Concepts are first-order logical inference rules, each stated in terms of relations that must hold among objects, relations that must not hold for them, and arithmetic tests. In addition, associated with each concept is a reward function that specifies its utility to the agent when an instance of the concept holds. Like skills, concepts are defined in terms of perceptual entities and lower-level concepts, thus producing a hierarchical structure.

Table 1 presents three concept definitions from the blocks world. The first concept determines if the perceived object `?b` is a block. The second concept defines a `left-of` relation between two blocks. It holds between two perceived objects `?b1` and `?b2` of type `block` (specified in `:percepts`) whenever `is-block` predicate holds for both of them and their x positions satisfy the condition specified in `:tests`, which simply states that the x position of `?b1` must be less than that of `?b2`. The reward associated with this concept is always zero. The relation defined by the next concept, `between`, can be interpreted similarly, but notice that its reward is a function of the attributes of the perceived objects, in this example the x positions of the blocks involved.

On each execution cycle, the architecture initiates its inference procedure by examining the lowest-level concepts at the bottom of the hierarchy and inferring matched instances. Inferring a concept instance means checking whether its conditions hold based on the current belief state and, if so, adding the instance to the belief state. ICARUS then proceeds up the hierarchy, checking concepts that include newly inferred elements in their definitions. The process recurses

Table 1. Three examples of ICARUS concept definitions from the blocks world.

```
(is-block (?b)                        (between (?b1 ?b2 ?b3)
 :percepts  ((block ?b xpos ?x))       :percepts  ((block ?b1 xpos ?x1)
 :reward    0.0)                                   (block ?b2 xpos ?x2)
                                                   (block ?b3 xpos ?x3))
(left-of (?b1 ?b2)                     :positives ((left-of ?b1 ?b2)
  :percepts ((block ?b1 xpos ?x1)                 (left-of ?b2 ?b3))
            (block ?b2 xpos ?x2))      :reward (* 10 (- 30 ?x3 ?x2 ?x1)))
 :positives ((is-block ?b1)
            (is-block ?b2))
 :tests     ((< ?x1 ?x2))
 :reward    0.0)
```

upwards, continuing until the entire hierarchy has been processed or, in the time-constrained case, until reaching the deadline.

We will refer to this inference method as *exhaustive*, because it considers concepts in a bottom-up, breadth-first manner with no control over the reasoning strategy. Clearly, this approach will not scale well to complex domains in which the knowledge base is large. Even worse, when the agent operates under time constraints, early termination can produce an inaccurate description of the environment, which in turn can produce undesirable behavior for the agent.

3   A Method for Controlled Inference

In order to overcome the drawbacks of exhaustive inference, a reasoning system requires some way to focus its cognitive attention on useful candidates. In this section, we introduce ADLIN, our adaptive logic interpreter. We begin by presenting a method for *value-driven* inference that gives priority to beliefs with higher expected utilities. After this, we describe a learning method that estimates these utilities from experienced rewards. Finally, we consider ADLIN's generalization mechanism for compactly modelling the knowledge learned over belief instances. The resulting system should fare better than an exhaustive version when the number of possible inferences exceeds the number that can be made in the time the agent has available.

3.1   Value-Driven Inference

Our approach to value-driven inference assumes that, for each candidate belief, the agent computes an expected utility, which it then uses to select the next instance to consider. The technique incorporates an agenda mechanism that inserts items into a list sorted by their priority levels, selects the topmost item to process, and iterates. This method is flexible enough to control inference, yet simple enough to incur little computational overhead.

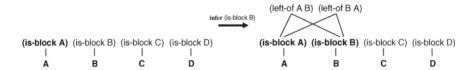

Fig. 1. A simple example of state and fringe update from the blocks world. The literals in bold belong to the belief state, whereas the others belong to the fringe.

More formally, we can specify a set of real values $V : \mathcal{U} \mapsto \mathcal{R}$ that is defined over $\mathcal{U}$, the set of all concept instances. These values differ from the rewards associated with concept definitions and may be specified in order to achieve a desired objective or reasoning strategy. As we will see later, ADLIN learns the values V to capture not only the immediate rewards, but also the future benefits of inferring different belief instances. Also notice that assigning scalar values to concept definitions would not be sufficient. The number of instantiated beliefs derived from one concept definition can be very large, in which case the inference system should be able to prioritize between them and infer only those with highest expected utility. This will let the system guide the inference process in a best-first manner, rather than a depth-first or breadth-first one.

Before describing the inference process, we should introduce a few more technical terms. We define the mental state, s_t, as the set of instances inferred to be true after t inference steps within the current execution cycle. Each inference step consists of selecting an instance that has not yet been inferred and checking whether it holds. This involves examining whether its child instances are believed and whether all its variable constraints and arithmetic tests are satisfied. At the beginning of each reasoning cycle, s_0 is empty. The *fringe* F_{s_t} at any state s_t is the set of all *inferrable* concept instances, that is, those instances not yet inferred within the current execution cycle whose children are already included in the state s_t.

A *valid action* a_u is an inference step that infers the instance $u \in F_{s_{t-1}}$ at the current step t. Finally, a *value-driven inference mechanism* is one that performs a valid action $a(V, F_{s_{t-1}})$ at each step t. In other words, every inference step depends entirely on the value assignment V and the contents of the current fringe. In this paper, we use a special *greedy* case of this mechanism class that always selects the highest value instance in the fringe. More precisely, we define $a_{greedy}(V, F_{s_{t-1}})$ as the action to infer the instance $\arg\max_{u \in F_{s_{t-1}}} V(u)$. This choice will prove reasonable when we consider the objective of the inference process shortly.

An example from the blocks world should illustrate the approach more clearly. Suppose the knowledge base consists of the three concept definitions introduced in Table 1 and there are four blocks in the environment. Figure 1 shows how executing an action updates the belief state and the fringe. Once the system selects inferring (is-block B) as the action, it checks whether this concept instance holds. Because B is a block, ADLIN adds this instance to its belief state and, because (is-block A) is already in the state, (left-of B A) and (left-of A B) become inferrable, so it adds them both to the fringe.

3.2   Value-Learning Mechanism

As mentioned earlier, the nature and computation of expected utilities are contingent upon the objective of the value-driven inference mechanism. Here we define the objective in terms of reward, r_u, produced by an inference action a_u, which we define as

$$r_u = \begin{cases} R_u(x_u), & \text{if } u \text{ is inferred to true;} \\ 0, & \text{otherwise,} \end{cases} \tag{1}$$

where R_u is the reward function associated with concept u and x_u denotes the attribute vector for perceived objects on which u depends. As we have noted, this reward function quantifies the desirability to the agent of instances for the given concept. When an instance does not match, it contributes zero reward. Therefore, r_u provides a reasonable measure for the immediate success of the corresponding inference action.

We assume the agent aims to maximize the cumulative absolute reward over each execution cycle, that is $W_T = \sum_{u \in s_t} |r_u|$, subject to the constraint that the t inference steps in this cycle take no more than T units of time. This objective is equivalent to minimizing $W_\infty - W_T$, which represents the error in calculated utility of the time-constrained system with respect to the utility calculated under no time constraints. In the terminology of value-driven inference, this objective translates to finding V values such that the inference strategy (approximately) maximizes W_T under a given time constraint T.

These values should capture not only the immediate expected reward for each inference action, but also its benefit for later inference steps. To this end, we adapt an approximate reinforcement learning method based on the account of states and actions presented earlier. We will let $Q(s_t, a)$ indicate the expected value of taking inference action a at state s_t. Recall that, unlike most work on reinforcement learning, our states and actions are completely internal to the agent. Furthermore, as equation (1) suggests, the source of reward is distributed over the entire knowledge base. This lets the learning element consider only the relevant parts of reward at each step.

Because the state space $\mathcal{S}$ of all possible states s_t can be intractably large, the classical tabular representations of $Q(s_t, a)$ for Q learning or $V(s_t)$ for value learning are impractical. Inspired by the MAXQ framework [7], we introduce a value decomposition that expresses the Q function in terms of V values:

$$Q(s_t, a) = \sum_{u \in s_t} V(u) + V(u_a) , \tag{2}$$

where u_a denotes the concept instance inferred by action a. While making the problem tractable, this approximation establishes a relationship between the reinforcement learning method and value-driven inference. In fact, equation (2) lets us rewrite the standard stochastic Q function update rule for V values:

$$V(u) := \overline{\alpha}V(u) + \alpha[r_u + \max_{u' \in F_{s_t}^u} V(u')] , \tag{3}$$

where $F_{s_t}^u \subseteq F_{s_t}$ is the set of instances in the current fringe for which u is a child. Furthermore, we define α as

$$\alpha = \frac{1}{1 + visits(u)} , \tag{4}$$

in which $visits(u)$ indicates the number of updates performed on $V(u)$, and $\overline{\alpha}$ is given by

$$\overline{\alpha} = \begin{cases} 1, & \text{if } u \in s_t; \\ 1 - \alpha, & \text{if } u \notin s_t . \end{cases} \tag{5}$$

We derive the update rule provided in equation (3) from the standard stochastic Q function update rule [8]:

$$Q(s,a) := (1 - \alpha)Q(s,a) + \alpha[R(s,a) + \gamma \max_{a'} Q(s',a')].$$

We can safely assume $\gamma = 1$, since we are dealing with a finite-horizon problem. Substituting the value decomposition in (2) and the definition of reward in (1) into this update rule gives

$$\sum_{u \in s_{t-1}} V(u) + V(u_a) := (1 - \alpha)(\sum_{u \in s_{t-1}} V(u) + V(u_a))$$

$$+ \alpha[r_{u_a} + \max_{\text{valid } a'} (\sum_{u \in s_t} V(u) + V(u_{a'}))]$$

$$:= (1 - \alpha) \sum_{u \in s_{t-1}} V(u) + (1 - \alpha)V(u_a)$$

$$+ \alpha[r_{u_a} + \sum_{u \in s_t} V(u) + \max_{u_{a'} \in F_{s_t}} V(u_{a'})] \tag{6}$$

Observe that

$$\sum_{u \in s_t} V(u) = \sum_{u \in s_{t-1}} V(u) + V(u_a) \cdot \mathbf{1}(u_a \in s_t) , \tag{7}$$

in which

$$\mathbf{1}(u_a \in s_t) = \begin{cases} 1, \text{if } u_a \in s_t; \\ 0, \text{if } u_a \notin s_t \end{cases} \tag{8}$$

As a result, the update rule simplifies to

$$V(u_a) := \overline{\alpha}V(u_a) + \alpha[r_{u_a} + \max_{u_{a'} \in F_{s_t}} V(u_{a'})] , \tag{9}$$

with $\overline{\alpha}$ being defined by (5). Notice that the only difference between the update rules in (9) and (3) lies in the argument of max. In fact, we have restricted the

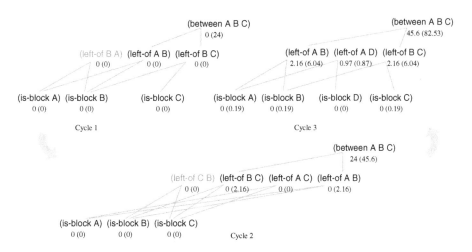

Fig. 2. An example of value propagation for three successive cycles in the blocks world. Updated values are shown in parentheses whereas others have been used to guide inference. The literals in grey have been inferred to be false.

argument in (3) to the set of instances that depend directly on u. This reflects the intuition that the values of instances which depend on u are more indicative of the desirability of inferring u than the values of other instances in the fringe.

Figure 2 shows how the values are learned and propagated in our example from the blocks world. Each diagram illustrates part of the agent's belief state at the end of the corresponding inference cycle. For an easier visualization of the procedure, the instances are ordered from left to right according to the order in which ADLIN infers them, the leftmost being the first. Having no previous experience in this domain, the system initializes the values to zero. As Table 1 shows, only the highest level concept, `between`, has nonzero reward and therefor the values remain zero until an instance of `between` is inferred as true. Once the system infers (`between A B C`), it updates this belief's value in proportion to its reward. Equation 3 propagates this value to the immediate children, (`left-of B C`) and (`left-of A B`), in the next cycle and consequently to the grandchildren—(`is-block A`), (`is-block B`), and (`is-block C`)—two cycles later. Note that the value updates occur after the instances are inferred and, as a result, the updated values participate in guiding the inference one cycle later.

3.3   Generalization Mechanism

The learning method described so far attempts to guide inference toward the most rewarding parts of the instance space $\mathcal{U}$ and maximize cumulative reward by propagating the rewards down the concept hierarchy. However, the value learned for a single instance lives only as long as the instance remains in $\mathcal{U}$. Thus, the agent would also benefit from a *generalization* mechanism that summarizes the learned knowledge about concept instances and stores it as compact models for future use. ADLIN uses such models to initialize the expected value V for new candidate beliefs in the instance space. Without a generalization model, the inference system would need to relearn the value functions for every new instance, which is certainly undesirable.

Our generalization mechanism learns a linear model $h_c(x) = \theta^T x$ for every concept definition c. More precisely, it applies linear regression methods to incrementally update the linear model h_c associated with each concept definition c, using the training examples $S_c = \{(V(u), x(u)) \mid u \in \mathcal{U}_c \cap s_t\}$ at the end of each execution cycle. Here, $x(u)$ indicates the vector of numeric attributes for the perceptions that appear in concept instance u and $\mathcal{U}_c \subseteq \mathcal{U}$ denotes the set of all instances derived from concept definition c. Later, when a new concept instance is created, its corresponding linear model is evaluated to initialize the expected value V for the candidate belief. Given this prior knowledge, the inference mechanism can perform more efficiently, as we will demonstrate shortly. Despite their simplicity, these linear models appear to help significantly in improving ADLIN's overall performance.[1]

Figure 2 illustrates how generalization affects the priorities of inferring various instances. Once the value for (left-of A B) becomes 2.16, the generalization module takes advantage of the relational structure of the state space to update a linear model for the concept definition left-of. ADLIN uses the numeric attributes of blocks A and B, namely their x positions, and the value 2.16 to update the model, which it revises further based on other instances. However, when entirely new instances of the left-of concept become inferrable, the system uses this model to initialize their values. For example when (left-of A D) becomes inferrable after adding (is-block D), it uses the learned model and the x positions of A and D to generate the initial value 0.97. In this example, the resulting value is higher than the value of (is-block C) and therefor the system prefers to infer (left-of A D) first.

Table 2 summarizes the ADLIN inference system, including its method for value-driven inference, its mechanism for reinforcement learning, and its technique for generalizing over instances of relational concepts.

4   Experimental Evaluation

Our primary goal for designing a value-driven inference mechanism, as stated earlier, is to make time-limited reasoning more effective by focusing cognitive attention on relevant parts of the instance space. To collect evidence that our approach has the desired effects, we carried out experiments within ICARUS that compared ADLIN's value-driven inference with exhaustive reasoning and also ADLIN without its generalization mechanism, all under time constraint and var-

---

[1] Another application of the generalization models, especially in highly dynamic environments, lies in updating the V values when the sensory attributes of the instance change. The update frequency should be increased with the frequency and variance of the change in sensory values.

Table 2. An outline of ADLIN inference process for one execution cycle.

---

1. INITIALIZATION
    i. At the beginning of each cycle, start with an empty state $s_0 = \emptyset$ and let $t = 0$.
    ii. If a new perceived object is added in this cycle, update $\mathcal{U}$ by adding the new instances and initialize their V values by evaluating their h_c functions.
    iii. If a perceived object is deleted, update $\mathcal{U}$ by removing all instances that depend on it. Initialize the fringe F_{s_0} with all primitive concept instances.

2. VALUE-DRIVEN INFERENCE AND VALUE-LEARNING
    Repeat the following steps run until time runs out:
    i. Set $t \leftarrow t + 1$ and infer the instance $u = \arg\max_{u' \in F_{s_{t-1}}} V(u')$.
    ii. Let $s_t = s_{t-1}$ and $F_{s_t} = F_{s_{t-1}}$.
    iii. If u is true, add it to s_t, compute its reward r_u, and update the fringe F_{s_t} .
    iv. Perform the V-value update for u:

    $$V(u) := \overline{\alpha} V(u) + \alpha[r_u + \max_{u' \in F_{s_t}^u} V(u')] ,$$

    where $\alpha = 1/[1 + visits(u)]$ and $\overline{\alpha}$ is given by (5).

3. GENERALIZATION
    For each concept definition c:
    i. Consider the function $h_c(x) = \theta^T x$.
    ii. For every sample point in $S_c = \{(V(u), x(u)) \mid u \in \mathcal{U}_c \cap s_t\}$, perform the update:

    $$\theta \leftarrow \theta + \alpha(V(u) - h_c(x(u))) \cdot x(u) .$$

---

ious circumstances. We present experimental evidence in two different domains, which we describe in detail below.

Naturally, we chose *reward accuracy* as the performance measure for our comparisons. Reward accuracy refers to the ratio between the cumulative reward obtained by the inference system under time constraints on a particular execution cycle to the total reward that would be accumulated on the same cycle by making all possible inference under no time constraints. This gives a measure on how successful our inference system is in guiding inference toward the most rewarding parts of the current instance space. Using the notation introduced in the previous section, we can express accuracy on some specific cycle as $A = W_T/W_\infty$. Recall that W_T denotes the cumulative absolute reward obtained in one cycle under time limit T. Similarly, we can state the reward error as $E = (W_\infty - W_T)/W_\infty$.

4.1 Blocks-World Domain

Our first experiments used a simple blocks-world environment because it gave us systematic control over factors of interest. The only objects in the environment are blocks placed in line, each with a name and a position specified as its distance from a reference point, which we call the origin. We used the three relational

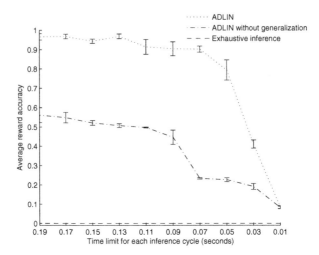

Fig. 3. Comparison between reward accuracies of three inference systems in the blocks-world environment over decreasing amounts of available time for each inference cycle.

concepts defined in Table 1. Clearly, when a large number of blocks are present, the number of feasible **between** relation instances will be enormous. We assume that the agent is located at the origin and prefers to interact with blocks sitting close to it. Therefore, we assigned a reward function to the highest level concept as a linear function that favors relations whose corresponding blocks are closer to the origin. The other two concept definitions had no assigned reward function.

We expected ADLIN to outperform exhaustive inference in terms of reward accuracy. However, we also anticipated that the degree of dominance would depend on factors such as the time limit for each inference cycle, domain complexity, and the rate of environmental change. First we considered the effect of time constraints on the behavior of three different inference systems: ADLIN, ADLIN without generalization, and exhaustive inference.[2] We expected that, as the available time for inference decreases, all three inference mechanisms would become less accurate, but we hypothesized that ADLIN's performance would degrade more gracefully.

We let each system learn for 200 cycles under a fixed time limit of 0.04 seconds in an initial world state with six blocks. We then tested the system under various time limits ranging from 0.19 to 0.01 seconds, in a dynamic environment in which a new block was added every 25 cycles, for a total of 100 cycles. At the end we measured the average inferred reward during the last 10 cycles and averaged the results over 20 independent runs. Figure 3 summarizes the results for the three inference systems considered. The accuracy of the exhaustive inference

---

[2] One might also consider an inference system that uses a greedy policy based on the immediate rewards of individual belief instances. In our example domains, however, there is no reward function assigned to low level concepts and hence such an inference mechanism should perform no better than exhaustive inference.

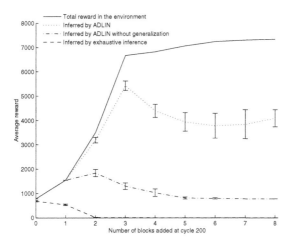

Fig. 4. Performance comparison between three inference systems over increasingly complex blocks-world environments.

method is almost zero for this range of time limits. Clearly, ADLIN provides a superior reward accuracy for most values of the time constraint. Its performance degrades only for extremely tight time limits (0.03 to 0.01 seconds), which is mainly caused by the computational overhead of its generalization mechanism.

Next we studied the effects of domain complexity, which refers to the size of the instance space. We let each system operate in a situation similar to the previous experiment, but we increased the complexity by abruptly adding objects, ranging from one to eight blocks, at cycle 200 and then ran the system for 100 more cycles. As before, we measured the average inferred reward over the final 10 cycles for 20 independent runs. Figure 4 depicts the results as a function of the number of blocks added. As expected, exhaustive inference performs very poorly. ADLIN without generalization gives better performance, but it cannot handle the excess complexity in the environment and, eventually, when the environment becomes too complex, it only obtains as much reward as it could in the initial world state.

In contrast, when equipped with generalization, ADLIN demonstrates substantially better performance, as shown by the dotted line in Figure 4. This result signifies that the generalization mechanism plays an important role in dealing with new inference instances. Notice, however, that ADLIN's performance degrades considerably when more than three blocks are added. This is because the first three new blocks are close to the origin and hence contribute a significant increase to the total reward, whereas the other new blocks are far from the origin and hence much less important. Nonetheless, these blocks distract ADLIN to some extent and cause the degradation in its performance.

The last factor we considered was the rate of change in the environment. We set up a similar experiment to the one above but, after the 200-cycle learning period, instead of introducing an abrupt change, we inserted the new blocks

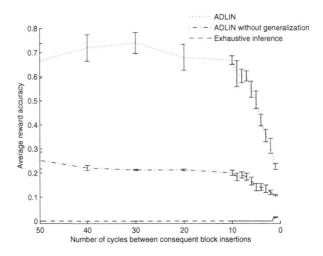

Fig. 5. Accuracy of different inference systems over increasing rates of environmental change in the blocks-world domain.

one at a time with a specific number of cycles between consequent insertions. Thus, we systematically varied the rate of change in the world and measured the average performance of each inference system over its last 10 cycles. As Figure 5 illustrates, ADLIN is the most robust of the three systems across a wide range of rates. However, for very rapidly changing environments, even ADLIN's performance degrades significantly, as seen when we added one block per cycle. In the closing section, we propose some responses to this issue.

4.2   In-City Driving Domain

As a more realistic, and hence more interesting, domain for evaluating ADLIN we chose an in-city driving environment. This is an appropriate domain both because of its complexity and its inherent time constraints in collision-like situations. In this simulated environment [6], all objects take a rectangular form on a Euclidean plane. The simulator supports static objects such as road segments, intersections, lane lines, and buildings, as well as dynamic ones like vehicles. One of the vehicles is controlled by an ICARUS agent and all others follow realistic physical laws but with predetermined behavior.

The vehicle controlled by the agent can perceive objects that are in its field of view, defined by the radius of a circle centered at its current position. The objects are described by numeric attributes like distance, angle, relative velocity, and angular velocity. The ICARUS agent also perceives its own properties, including distance and angle with respect to lane lines, as well as its speed and the angle of its steering wheel. The agent must drive the vehicle safely by staying on the right side of the road, making necessary turns, and avoiding collisions. These constraints produce a complex environment which requires reasoning about many objects with different priorities.

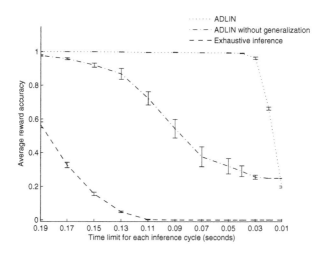

Fig. 6. Comparison between reward accuracies of three inference systems in the in-city driving environment over decreasing amounts of available time for each inference cycle.

In our first experiment in the driving domain, we again considered time constraint as the independent variable, while holding complexity and rate of change fixed. Figure 6 summarizes the results for the three inference systems in our study, namely ADLIN, ADLIN without generalization, and exhaustive inference.

In this experiment, we had the agent drive around a block in the simulated city at a constant speed of 15 miles per hour. We let each system learn under a fixed time limit of 0.5 seconds while making a complete turn around the block. Then we measured the average reward inferred by the system when turning around the same block at the same speed, but under different time constraints ranging from 0.19 to 0.01 seconds. Figure 6 presents the resulting accuracies averaged over 20 independent runs for each system. ADLIN demonstrates a higher tolerance of time constraints, especially for time limits between 0.13 to 0.03 seconds. However, we observed a similar sudden degradation of performance for extremely tight time constraints as seen earlier in the blocks-world study.

In the driving domain, the rate of change and complexity of the environment are mainly determined by the agent's speed of driving. Therefore, we cannot vary these factors separately while keeping the other fixed. In response, our next experiment evaluated each inference system in the driving domain for different driving speeds. As the agent drives faster both complexity and the rate of change in the environment increase. The complexity increases since the overlap of the visible areas across the cycles decreases and therefore more of the perceived objects are new. Figure 7 shows the average reward achieved by different inference systems for different driving speeds, compared to the total reward that is available in the environment.

We let each system learn under a time constraint of 0.4 seconds while the agent was driving on a straight street at a speed of 5 miles per hour. Then we tested the system under a 0.08-second time limit while driving at different

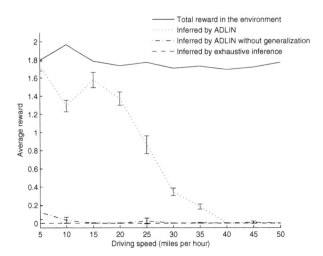

Fig. 7. Average inferred rewards achieved by different inference systems in the driving domain for different driving speeds.

constant speeds that ranged from 10 to 50 miles per hour. We computed inferred rewards over the entire test period, again averaged over 20 independent runs. The curves of Figure 7 show the superior performance of ADLIN for speeds under 35 miles per hour, although its reward accuracy decreases at higher speeds. Clearly, even ADLIN has difficulty in dealing with highly dynamic environments, here represented as driving speeds over 40 miles per hour. Again, we will return to this issue in Section 6.

5   Related Research on Inference and Learning

The challenge of reasoning under resource constraints is nearly as old as the field of artificial intelligence, but the problem has typically been neglected in classical theories of normative behavior. The common approach to mitigating the problem in practical intelligent systems has been to employ heuristic, and usually domain-dependent, control strategies to guide reasoning. For example, the meta-level reasoning system developed by Genesereth and Ginsberg [9] lets the designer write Prolog-like control clauses that specify how inference rules should be prioritized.

However, research on the topic of *bounded rationality* has attempted to deal with the problem in a domain-independent way. Early work by Simon [10] examined humans' reliance on satisficing strategies when confronted with complex decision-making tasks. More recently, Horvitz [11] has discussed limitations of traditional normative approaches in dealing with real-world complexity and proposed adapting such methods to reason about the reasoning process itself. Similarly, Russell and Wefald [12,13] sought to develop a theoretical framework for meta-reasoning that was based on probability and decision theory. Our approach shares the idea of considering computations as mental actions with Russell and Wefald analysis.

Other work has focused on learning control rules to reduce search or speed up processing (see for example Minton [14]), some of which has dealt with monotonic inference. Zelle and Mooney [3] combined explanation-based learning techniques with inductive logic programming ideas to learn such control conditions over inference rules. In a different approach, Cohen and Singer [15] used bootstrapping to learn similar rules. These approaches assumed a query-based, top-down inference mechanism and sought to modify the logic program itself in order to achieve performance gains. In our work, however, we consider a data-driven, bottom-up inference process that is more appropriate for reactive agents, for the reasons discussed earlier. In addition, our approach operates on top of a fixed logic program and modifies the way it is utilized by the logic interpreter.

Our approach has more in common with research on relational reinforcement learning, at least in its broad sense defined by Tadepalli *et al.* [4], and hierarchical reinforcement learning [7]. However, as mentioned earlier, our variation on relational reinforcement learning differs from the initial work by Dzeroski *et al.* [5] in its use of linear regression models distributed over first-order concepts to support generalization. Moreover, in contrast to most work on these topics, our states and actions are cognitive rather than physical and they are completely internal to the agent.

Our work also shares some of its basic ideas with the recent work by Guestrin *et al.* [16], including relational representation of states and actions, distributed reward over the relational structure of first-order predicates, additive approximation of value function, and class-based generalization. Nevertheless, there are significant differences in problem setting and approach. Guestrin *et al.* considered a planning problem modeled by a relational Markov decision process with fixed relations in the world, discrete attributes, and given transition probabilities. They also took a linear programming approach to solving their problem. In contrast, we have addressed an inference problem modeled as a reinforcement learning problem over a relational state structure with dynamic relations and continuous attributes. Our approach holds the promise of rapid learning and the ability to scale to large state spaces, which makes it closer in spirit to work on explanation-based reinforcement learning (e.g., Dietterich and Flann [17]).

6   Concluding Remarks

In this paper, we introduced the Adaptive Logic Interpreter (ADLIN), which uses a value-driven inference mechanism combined with reinforcement learning to deal with the challenge of data-driven inference under time constraint. Our experiments in dynamic domains showed that ADLIN performs well in guiding the reasoning process toward high-utility parts of the knowledge base and outperforms exhaustive inference system. This difference was especially large under short time limits and high rates of environmental change.

However, when the time constraint is extremely strict or the environment is changing too rapidly, ADLIN does not provide a satisfying performance gain. This is partly due to the computational overhead involved in the system and partly because, in the current system, every instance in the agent's belief state is inferred on the current execution cycle, regardless of whether it was true or false on the previous cycle. Although this simplification did not appear to be a crucial restriction in our experimental studies, it should certainly be addressed in future extensions.

One basic approach to dealing with this issue is to incorporate the simple idea behind truth maintenance systems and Rete matchers [2]. These systems maintain the truth value of each inference instance unless the evidence supporting that instance changes, in which case its truth value is updated. It should be straightforward to extend ADLIN to consider only instances with changed evidence as candidates for inference, from which it then selects high value instances to actually infer. This should let the system concentrate on the belief instances that need to be reinferred. Nevertheless, a more refined approach would consider the intensity of change in the environment and its corresponding effect on each belief instance. More precisely, we propose the idea of *probabilistically persistent belief*, in which the agent persists in maintaining a belief instance and only updates it with some probability that depends on its intrinsic variance given the amount of change in evidence for that instance. Such a probabilistic measure can be applied either to reduce the number of candidate inferences or to modulate their expected values to incorporate the effect of their change of evidence into the value-driven inference process.

Clearly, our design of ADLIN assumes that the domain's reward structure is additively decomposable over the concepts (first-order predicates). However, this does not impose any fundamental restriction on generality of our approach, for two reasons. First, interactions among different concepts in the reward function can be expressed by their relational structure. For example, imagine a predator/prey scenario in which proximity of a predator lowers the reward of proximity of a mate for a prey animal. This effect can be captured by defining a higher level concept that describes the relational situation (proximity of mate given the proximity of a predator) and assigning it a low reward function. Second, the behavior produced by a non-decomposable reward structure can often be well-approximated by a decomposable one. In the above example, suppose the reward function assigned to "predator proximity" (or to the concepts built on top of it) is higher than the reward associated with "mate proximity." Then ADLIN would pay more attention to the former and, should it hold, to reasoning on top of it, effectively being less concerned about the latter.

Finally, from the point of view of agent architectures, a complete attention mechanism must consider not only the concept instances that the agent believes, but also the skills by which it interacts with its environment. Therefore, in the longer term, a promising direction is to extend our attention mechanism to cover skill inference and selection. Such an extension would require considering both the temporal effects and the top-down nature of skill execution. Despite the need for further improvements, ADLIN has already revealed its potential for the effective control of inference, which in turn has taken us closer to a practical attention mechanism for reactive agents.

References

1. Doyle, J.: A truth maintenance system. Artificial Intelligence **12** (1979) 231–272
2. Forgy, C.L.: Rete: A fast algorithm for the many pattern/many object pattern match problem. Artificial Intelligence **19** (1982) 17–37
3. Zelle, J.M., Mooney, R.J.: Combining FOIL and EBG to speed-up logic programs. In: Proceedings of the Thirteenth International Joint Conference on Artificial Intelligence, Chambery, France, Morgan Kaufmann (1993) 1106–1111
4. Tadepalli, P., Givan, R., Driessens, K.: Relational reinforcement learning: An overview. In: Proceedings of the ICML-2004 workshop on Relational Reinforcement Learning, Banff, Canada (2004)
5. Dzeroski, S., Raedt, L.D., Driessens, K.: Relational reinforcement learning. Machine Learning **43** (2001) 7–52
6. Choi, D., Kaufman, M., Langley, P., Nejati, N., Shapiro, D.: An architecture for persistent reactive behavior. In: Proceedings of the Third International Joint Conference on Autonomous Agents and Multi Agent Systems, New York, ACM Press (2004) 988–995
7. Dietterich, T.G.: Hierarchical reinforcement learning with the MAXQ value function decomposition. Journal of Artificial Intelligence Research **13** (2000) 227–303
8. Mitchell, T.M.: Machine Learning. McGraw Hill, New York (1997)
9. Genesereth, M.R., Ginsberg, M.L.: Logic programming. Communications of the ACM **28** (1985) 933–941
10. Simon, H.A.: Administrative behavior. 2nd edn. Free Press, New York (1965)
11. Horvitz, E.: Reasoning about beliefs and actions under computational resource constraints. Journal on Uncertainty in Artificial Intelligence **3** (1989) 301–324
12. Russell, S., Wefald, E.: Principles of metareasoning. In: Proceedings of the First International Conference on Principles of Knowledge Representation and Reasoning, San Mateo, CA, Morgan Kaufmann (1989)
13. Russell, S., Wefald, E.H.: Do the Right Thing: Studies in Limited Rationality. MIT Press, Cambridge, MA (1991)
14. Minton, S.: Quantitative results concerning the utility of explanation-based learning. In: Proceedings of the Seventh National Conference on Artificial Intelligence, Saint Paul, MN, AAAI Press (1988) 564–569
15. Cohen, W.W., Singer, Y.: A simple, fast, and effective rule learner. In: Proceedings of the Forteenth National Conference on Artificial Intelligence. (1999) 335–342
16. Guestrin, C., Koller, D., Gearhart, C., Kanodia, N.: Generalizing plans to new environments in relational MDPs. In: Proceedings of International Joint Conference on Artificial Intelligence, Acapulco, Mexico (2003)
17. Dietterich, T.G., Flann, N.S.: Explanation-based learning and reinforcement learning: A unified view. Machine Learning **28** (1997) 169–210

Converting Semantic Meta-knowledge into Inductive Bias*

John Cabral, Robert C. Kahlert, Cynthia Matuszek, Michael Witbrock,
and Brett Summers

Cycorp, Inc., 3721 Executive Center Drive, Suite 100,
Austin, TX 78739
{jcabral, rck, cynthia, witbrock, bsummers}@cyc.com

Abstract. The Cyc KB has a rich pre-existing ontology for representing common sense knowledge. To clarify and enforce its terms' semantics and to improve inferential efficiency, the Cyc ontology contains substantial meta-level knowledge that provides definitional information about its terms, such as a type hierarchy. This paper introduces a method for converting that meta-knowledge into biases for ILP systems. The process has three stages. First, a "focal position" for the target predicate is selected, based on the induction goal. Second, the system determines type compatibility or conflicts among predicate argument positions, and creates a compact, efficient representation that allows for syntactic processing. Finally, mode declarations are generated, taking advantage of information generated during the first and second phases.

1 Introduction

Because of the general complexity of machine learning, the discipline has devoted significant attention to the use of inductive bias in improving algorithmic efficiency. Inductive logic programming (ILP) is in an interesting position on this topic because its declarative representations can be extended to include the representation of the ILP system itself, including the biases its algorithms employ. Tausend [1], [2], Nedellec et al. [3] have investigated the utility of declaratively representing biases as part of the background knowledge for ILP systems. They have noted that such representations allow for an explicit and modular representation of bias, such that biases used by different systems can be meaningfully compared and the settings of an individual system can be easily manipulated. McCreath [4], McCreath and Sharma [5], and DiMauro, et. al. [6] have begun the next phase of this work by developing algorithms for inducing type and mode biases from data. The implementation of these algorithms in pre-processors promises to reduce the burden on the human users of ILP systems. An alternative source for inductive biases is the language of the data, when that language is part of a larger ontology. Using the knowledge contained in the Cyc knowledge base (KB) – a very large, non-domain-specific ontology of formalized knowledge – provides a novel approach to automating the generation of inductive biases.

---

* Distribution Statement A: Approved for public release; distribution is unlimited.

S. Kramer and B. Pfahringer (Eds.): ILP 2005, LNAI 3625, pp. 38–50, 2005.

2   An Overview of the Cyc Project

The Cyc project is an ambitious, decades-long effort to generate a store of common-sense knowledge that enables reasoning in a broad array of domains.   Human knowledge engineers have so far constructed most of the knowledge base (KB). However, one of the underlying premises of the Cyc project is that certain kinds of machine learning require the existence of a pre-existing body of knowledge into which new knowledge can be integrated (Lenat and Guha [7]). So, the long-term goal of the project is to invest human effort in the creation of a necessary foundation for effective, future machine learning. The goal of the research described in this paper is to begin the work of converting the existing knowledge into a basis for more effective automated learning. Since the representational language of Cyc is an extension of first-order predicate logic, inductive logic programming is the natural fit for the type of machine learning that would eventually drive the growth of the knowledge base.

The Cyc KB is represented using the language CycL, a LISP-like language that includes features like quantification over predicates and complete sentences, modal operators, and an extensive meta-language. All expressions are wrapped within parentheses and the leftmost entity within the parentheses being the predicate or function. Constants of the language are tagged with a prefixed '#$' and variables are composed of all capital letters and a prefixed '?'. All aspects of the language are represented within CycL. So, logical connectives follow the same syntactic rules. The following Prolog clause (a translation of "For any birth event E in which some M plays the role of female parent and some C is the child born during E, then M is C's biological mother"):

```
biologicalMother(C,M)  :-
birthEvent(E),  femaleParentActor(E,M),  birthChild(E,C)
```

would be represented in CycL as:

```
(#$implies
(#$and
(#$isa ?BIRTH #$BirthEvent)
(#$femaleParentActor ?BIRTH ?MOTHER)
(#$birthChild ?BIRTH ?CHILD))
(#$biologicalMother ?CHILD ?MOTHER)).¹
```

The above example illustrates a significant feature of the Cyc ontology. First, classes are denoted with constant names, not predicates. This choice is based on certain requirements of ontological engineering. First, it allows for multiple instance-to-class relations to be introduced into the vocabulary. Thus, we can specialize the predicate to specific types of collection to more precise relations such as occupations, ethnicities, and nationalities. Introducing these more specific relations increases the precision of the language and, as a consequence, allows for greater inferential

---

[1] When variables are unbound, the system assumes universal quantifiers with scope over the entire sentence.

efficiency because problems can be more narrowly defined. Second, because there is a significant inferential cost to reasoning with unbound predicates and it is quite common quantify over classes, introducing classes as named entities allows rules to be written at the right level of generality without incurring a significant computational cost.

The Cyc KB is structured using a hierarchical arrangement of microtheories. Microtheories represent contexts in which sentences are true. Microtheories inherit content from other microtheories to which they are linked. So, if MT_1 is more general than MT_2 than everything that is true in MT_1 is also true in MT_2. This relationship among microtheories is transitive and reflexive, but not symmetric. Sentences that hold universally are those which are expressed in the "highest," most general microtheories, while sentences that are true in very limited contexts (i.e., the content of a person's testimony or a work of fiction) are represented in microtheories that are much "lower" in the hierarchy. The great advantage of microtheories is that contradictory assertions can be represented within the KB without introducing formal contradictions because those assertions can be represented in microtheories that are not linked to one another.

As of March 2005, the Cyc KB contains over 296,000 reified terms, including over 55,000 classes, 198,000 individuals, and 22,000 relations (predicates and functions). These terms are linked by 3.3 million assertions. The Cyc KB operates in conjunction with an inference engine, with deductive and abductive capabilities. The inference engine is composed of more than 800 special-purpose reasoning modules, each of which handles a very specific type of query. These modules range in complexity from the very simple (special index-lookup code for a specific predicate) to the extremely complex (modules for temporal reasoning). The modules are interlinked via a blackboard system, which allows very general modules to handles cases for which more specific support does not exist; the final fall back is a general theorem prover. This architecture allows for the addition of new modules as needed.

An important aspect in the design of the system comes from the design of the ontology. Specifically, because of the explosive growth of search spaces during deductive inferences with transformation, the ontology needs to be designed such that it can make inference more efficient. The choice not to represent classes with unary predicates is one illustration of this. Another significant illustration of this point is the inclusion of definitional assertions on the elements of the ontology and the enforcement of the semantics represented by those assertions at different stages within the system. The definitional assertions for predicates are used to constrain the values that the predicate's arguments can take (I will refer to these assertions content as "semantic meta-knowledge"). During the knowledge entry process, this enables the system to exclude assertions as "semantically ill-formed" and, thus, ensure the integrity of the content of the KB. Thus, if #$biologicalMother can hold only between an animal and a female animal and female animal and integer are disjoint classes (i.e., they do not and cannot have any common instances), then an attempt to enter into the KB that someone's mother is the number 12 would be rejected.

By preserving the integrity of the knowledge entered into the KB, these semantic restrictions maintain the correctness of the answers derived through deductive inference and spare inference the cost of checking for the satisfaction of constraints.

Another application of this knowledge is with abductive inference. Cyc implements abduction through hypothesizing entities or relations such that the hypothesized facts satisfy the antecedents of deductive implication rules. The inference engine uses this knowledge about the meaning and proper usage of predicates to reject hypotheses that could never be true. Thus, it will not hypothesize that an office building was destroyed because it was a meteor that burned up upon entering the atmosphere, because no office building is a meteorite.

As a first step toward using the knowledge in the Cyc ontology and KB to enhance machine learning, we will be investigating the use of semantic meta-knowledge to provide inductive biases to ILP systems. The next two sections of this paper discuss the declarative representation of bias used by ALEPH, and McCreath and Sharma's [5] algorithm for learning modes and types from data. The remainder of the paper will provide more detail on one form of semantic meta-knowledge for predicates, discuss how to convert them into inductive biases, and discuss additional approaches for handling more complex cases.

3   The Declarative Representation of Bias in ALEPH

ALEPH is an implementation of the inverse entailment algorithm underlying the Progol system (Muggleton [8]). We are interested in this formalism because it combines mode and type information and, so, offers a scheme that could be used among different ILP systems. The system represents mode and type biases using the predicate mode/2.[2] The general form of these clauses is:

mode(RecallNumber,pred(ModeType₁,…,ModeTypeₙ)).

RecallNumber is either the maximum number of successful calls to the predicate that appears in the second argument position, or an asterisk, meaning the predicate has unbounded indeterminacy. The number of instances of ModeType$_i$ equals the arity of the predicate pred. If these mode types are simple, the expressions that will replace ModeType$_i$ begin with a symbol designating the mode of the variables that will fill that argument position, followed by a name for the type constraint on that argument. In ALEPH, input variables are designated with a '+', output variables are designated with a '-', and constant arguments are designated with a '#'.[3] For example, if the predicate addition/3 has all of its arguments constrained to integers and an expression of the form addition(X,Y,Z) means that Z is the sum of X and Y, then the following is an appropriate mode declaration for the predicate:

mode(*,addition(+integer, +integer,-integer)).

This clause states that addition/3 has unbounded indeterminacy, that all of its arguments take instances of the same type, and that the first two arguments are input

---

[2] This following description of ALEPH is based on the documentation available at: http://web.comlab.ox.ac.uk/oucl/research/areas/machlearn/Aleph/aleph.html

[3] This paper will not discuss the creation of constants, but that is an important piece of future research.

variables while the third argument is an output variable. It is important to note that the names given to the types are not used for type reasoning by ALEPH. So, no special significance attaches to the names used in the mode/2 statements.

The mode settings contained in mode/2 clauses are used by ALEPH to constrain the set of hypotheses, by shaping the construction of the bottom clause from which the algorithm generalizes. The modes constrain the hypotheses' variables in the following ways:

- An input variable of a given type in a body literal must appear as an input variable of the same type in the head literal or as an output variable of the same type in an earlier body literal of that clause.
- An output variable of a given type in the head literal must appear as an output variable of the same type in some body literal of that clause.
- Any predicate's arguments declared to be a constant of a given type, must take a ground instance of that type as a value in that argument.

The user need not program the mode and type information. ALEPH includes an implementation of McCreath and Sharma's (1995) algorithm for inferring mode and type constraints from the background knowledge and examples.

4   McCreath and Sharma's Algorithm: Bias Induction from Data

4.1   The Algorithm

McCreath and Sharma's [5] algorithm aims to induce meta-knowledge from only the data given to the system. For determining mode biases, the algorithm initially assumes that all possible combinations of modes for a predicates' arguments are valid. It then works through the available data to find counter-examples. When a counter-example is found, the contradicted modes are eliminated. Counter-examples are based on the assumption that modes represent functional dependencies. So, a counter-example would involve the values for a set of input arguments being matched to different values for an associated output argument. For example, this algorithm would originally assign the binary predicate p/2 the set of possible modes: p(+,+), p(+,-), p(-,+) and p(-,-). If p(a,b) and p(a,c) were positive examples, then the mode setting p(+,-) would be eliminated from the set because the examples contradict the claim that the value of the second argument is a function of the first argument.

For determining types, McCreath and Sharma's algorithm begins with the assumption that every argument of every predicate in the language of the learning problem is constrained to a different type. As the algorithm processes the data, if the same value appears in two different argument positions, then the algorithm redistributes the type constraints and assigns the same type to the argument positions that shared that value. For example, if we have two binary predicates p/2 and r/2, then the algorithm would initially assign every argument a different type constraint: p(type1,type2) and r(type3,type4). If p(a,a) and r(a,b) appeared within the examples, then the types would be modified to show that the same type can appear in both of `p/2`'s arguments and in the first argument of `r/2`. So, the revised types would be `p(type1,type1)` and `r(type1,type4)`.

4.2 Weaknesses of the Algorithm

With any form of learning, there is the possibility of error; but there are two types of error to which McCreath and Sharma's original algorithm and a modified version implemented within ALEPH are susceptible.   Both relate to type constraints. Excluding available type constraints reduces efficiency, while including too many type constrains puts too much of a restriction on the search space and, so, causes the system to miss legitimate hypotheses.

McCreath and Sharma's basic algorithm is susceptible to including too few type restrictions.   For instance, consider the following representation of a section of a family tree.

```
father(abe,bob).
mother(abe,carol).
father(bob,david).
father(carol,fred).
```

In this example, Bob and Carol both appear in the first argument positions of `father/2` clauses.   This causes the types on the second argument positions of `mother/2` and `father/2` to be merged, even though they should be constrained to disjoint types: female and male animals, respectively. So, in this situation, there would be only one type for all of the argument positions.

ALEPH includes an alternative implementation of the algorithm that allows for the merging of types between argument positions based on the degree of overlap in the values for two different positions, where the degree of overlap is the proportion of values of one position that are also values for the second position.   This approach faces the problem of not recognizing that argument positions can be merged.   For instance, in the above example, because there is only one value that appears in both the second argument of mother and the first argument of father, a sufficiently high overlap threshold between those arguments would prevent them from being linked. Thus hypotheses that link mothers to their fathers could be missed.

5   Semantic Meta-knowledge in Cyc

5.1 Basic Meta-knowledge for Predicates

A first step in the addition of a new predicate to the Cyc ontology is the creation of definitional assertions that express the predicate's meaning by setting constraints on its applicability. For example, the predicate `#$hasHeadquartersInRegion` relates an organization to the geographical region where that organization's headquarters are located. If `#$BMWInc` denotes the Bayerische Motoren Werke corporation and `#$CityOfMunich` denotes the city of Munich, Germany one could assert:

```
(#$hasHeadquartersInRegion #$BMWInc #$CityOfMunich)
```

To enforce the semantics of this predicate, a number of other assertions that constrain `#$hasHeadquartersInRegion` would be used. For example, `#$arg1Isa` and `#$arg2Isa` are, respectively, used to state that the first and second argument positions of a particular predicate must be instances of particular collections.[4] In order to express that the first argument of `#$hasHeadquartersInRegion` must be an organization and second argument must be a geographical area, the following assertions would be made:

```
(#$arg1Isa #$hasHeadquartersInRegion #$Organization)

(#$arg2Isa #$hasHeadquartersInRegion
#$GeographicalRegion)
```

The effect of these two statements is that if a knowledge engineer tries to enter a new assertion using the predicate `#$hasHeadquartersInRegion` and the value of one of its arguments can be proved to not be an instance of the required type, then the semantic validation process would reject the assertion.

Many predicates in the Cyc ontology take collections as values. The predicate `#$argIsa` can be used to state that a value must be a collection. Additional assertions can further specify the collection. First, the predicate `#$argGen1` can be used to state that the value must be a sub-collection of some collection. Alternatively, instead of `#$Collection`, `#$argIsa` could refer to a second-order collection – a collection whose instances are collections. `#$PersonTypeByPositionInOrg` is a second-order collection whose instances are types of occupation that refer to organizations (e.g., `#$PrimeMinister`, `#$ChiefExecutiveOffice`). The predicate `#$personHasPositionInOrg` relates a person to a type of occupation and an organization. The following definitional assertions hold of its second argument:

```
(#$arg2Isa #$positionOfPersonInOrg
          #$PersonTypeByPositionInOrg)

(#$arg2Gen1 #$positionOfPersonInOrg    #$Person)
```

So, although an instance of the collection `#$PrimeMinister` (e.g., Tony Blair) could fill the first argument of a `#$positionOfPersonInOrg` assertion, the appearance of the same value in the second argument position would not be semantically well-formed because the collection of individuals is disjoint with the collection of occupation types, `#$PersonTypeByPositionInOrg`.

5.2 Representing the Determination

The first step is the process is the representation of the problem, or determination. Specifically, there is the representation of the target predicate (i.e. the predicate for

---

[4] The Web Ontology Language, OWL, based on its inheritance of certain portions of the Resource Description Framework, includes similar vocabulary for defining the properties of predicates. The Cyc ontology includes a larger vocabulary with that function, but the particular process described here can be applied to OWL ontologies as well.

the head of learned clauses) and the set of predicates for the background knowledge (i.e., the predicates that could appear in the bodies of learned clauses). The Cyc ontology uses the function #$ILPDeterminationFn for denoting determinations. It is a binary function whose first argument position is the target predicate and whose second argument is the list of background predicates. In order for the target predicate to be considered a possible body predicate, it would need to be included in the list of predicates as well.

For example, the following expression represents a determination that targets the predicate #$hasHeadquartersInRegion with the possible body predicates: #$residesInRegion, #$seniorExecutives, #$importantCompany, and #$positionOfPersonInOrg:

```
(#$ILPDeterminationFn
        #$hasHeadquartersInRegion
        (#$TheList #$residesInRegion
        #$seniorExecutives #$importantCompany
        #$positionOfPersonInOrg))
```

For simplicity's sake, during the remainder of this section the term #$Determination01 will be used as a name for the determination denoted by the above expression.

5.3 Deriving Types

Given a specific determination, Cyc uses its semantic meta-knowledge and its type hierarchy to determine a more compact representation of the relevant type constraints. This more compact representation allows us to communicate information to ILP engines like ALEPH that do not do type reasoning when using inductive biases. The goal is to try to capture all and only the appropriate linkages among arguments, while minimizing the size of the representation. Because of the size of the Cyc ontology and the different representational tasks of different predicates, they have type constraints at different levels of generality. The basic strategy implemented here is to look for subsumption relations among argument constraints and then to use only the most specific types that are used as constraints.

The first step in the process is to generate the set of collections that constrain the argument positions for the predicates in the determination. The set of these collections for #$Determintion01 is:

```
{#$Animal, #$PersonTypeByPositionInOrg #$Person,
#$Organization, #$CommercialOrganization,
#$GeographicalRegion}
```

The next step is to reduce the set by eliminating any collections that have at least one sub-collection that is also element of the set. #$Person is a sub-collection of #$Animal and #$CommercialOrganization is a sub-collection of #$Organization. So, #$Organization and #$Animal would be eliminated to produce the new set:

```
{#$Person, #$PersonTypeByPositionInOrg
#$CommercialOrganization, #$GeographicalRegion}
```

For the remainder of this paper, any reference to a "relativized type" should be taken to refer to an element of this reduced set. Given the original semantic meta-knowledge about the predicates, knowledge of the subsumption and disjointness of collections, a set of rules are invoked that conclude to the predicate #$argIsaWRTSpec. ("argument is an instance of type with regard to determination"). This predicate is used to represent more focused type constraints for a predicate within the context of a given determination. For example, relative to the determination above, Cyc would infer

```
(#$argIsaWRTSpec
#$hasHeadquartersInRegion 1 #$CommercialOrganization
#$Determination01)
```

This statement states that, relative to #$Determination01, the first argument of the predicate #$hasHeadquartersInRegion should be treated as if it were constrained to #$CommercialOrganization. In cases where the reduced set contains several collections that are subsumed by the predicate's original argument-constraining collection, they are all represented with #$argIsaWRTSpec assertions for that predicate's argument.

5.4 Deriving Modes

For certain predicates, modes are readily definable based on the content of the underlying relation. For example, in the case of a predicate that relates a list to one of its members, a mode that requires the list value to be provided (i.e., an input) and the member value to be derived (i.e., an output) is more efficient than the inverse would be since the member value is a member of an unlimited number of possible lists. For the vast majority of predicates in the Cyc ontology, a similar judgment is not as readily available. The issue is magnified by the fact that the choice of mode settings can greatly influence the behavior of the ILP system.

As Cyc is an engineering project, the choice of how to proceed with establishing those connections occurs in the context of improving Cyc's ability to answer questions. Specific applications of Cyc will likely focus on a central set of queries that share a common set of predicates, most of those predicates will be used to describe a small set of types of entities. Assuming that induction will be geared to improving inference with regard to a particular topic, the current strategy for generating modes is to focus on one argument of the target predicate. We expect that this focal argument will be bound during a query. In practice, this binding would be the entity that is the topic of the question. So, if we wanted to know information about commercial organizations, we would ask the following sort of query:

```
(#$hasHeadquartersInRegion #$BMWInc ?PLACE)
```

Given that the focal type for these queries is #$Organization and that the first argument of #$hasHeadquartersInRegion is the only one constrained to

#$Organization, we would include the following assertion to specify that the organization argument is focal for this determination:

```
(#$focalArgumentOfDeterminationTarget
#$Determination01 1)
```

Once a focal argument has been designated, the following rules are used to determine the modes for the determination's predicates:

- The focal argument of the target predicate has an input mode.
- If the target predicate has an input argument of relativized type T, and a predicate (either target or background) also has an argument of relativized type T, then that second argument has an input mode.
- If the target predicate has an input argument of relativized type T_1, a predicate (either target or body) has an argument of relativized type T_1, and T_1 and T_2 are disjoint collections, then that second argument has an output mode. [5]

This algorithm utilizes the user-provided information of the focal argument for the target predicate in conjunction with semantic knowledge regarding all of the predicates in the determination to derive modes for each argument.

In CycL, the process concludes with the derivation of assertions represent the combination of the relativized type for a predicate's arguments and that argument's mode. The predicates #$argIsaInputModeForDetermination and #$argIsaOutputModeForDetermination are used for this task. In the case of #$Determination01, we have assumed a focal argument that is constrained to organizations. Since organizations are disjoint with geographical regions, the system would draw the following conclusions for the predicate #$importantCompany, which relates a commercial organization to a geographical region in which it plays a significant economic role:

```
(#$argIsaInputModeForDetermination
        #$importantCompany
        #$CommercialOrganization 1
        #$Determination01)

(#$argIsaOutputModeForDetermination
        #$importantCompany
        #$GeographicalRegion 2
        #$Determination01)
```

The first argument is an input mode because it shares the same relativized type as the focal argument, #$CommercialOrganization. The second argument is an output mode because its relativized type, #$GeographicalRegion, is disjoint with the focal argument's relativized type.

---

[5] This is a rough reconstruction of the general pattern found in the data sets found in the archive at: http://web.comlab.ox.ac.uk/oucl/research/areas/machlearn/applications.html. The development of more sophisticated algorithms is a topic for future research.

5.5 More Complex Cases

The method described above is most efficient in cases where the set of type constraints all involve disjointness and subsumption relationships. First, the subsumption allows us to minimize the number of collections that need to be considered. So, we can send out a more compact representation to the ILP engine. Further, when two collections are disjoint, then there should be no relationship between two arguments that are constrained by those collections. However, for any pair of collections that are chosen from the ontology, a significant chance exists that they are neither disjoint nor does one subsume the other. As of March 2005, the probability that two randomly selected collections from the Cyc KB are orthogonal is 0.35. While such 'orthogonal collections' are a minority in the set of collections used for semantic constraints on predicates, they do occur. For example, the second argument of #$father is constrained to #$MaleAnimal, while the first argument of #$rulerInDynasty is constrained to #$Monarch-HeadOfState. Neither of these collections subsumes the other and they share instances. Depending on the focal argument of the determination, the rules described might not return modes for such cases. There are four solutions that present themselves for handling cases where this situation is violated.

First, one could introduce a framework that allows for type conversions of individuals within the rules that govern the use of modes. Such conversions would be made in the case of individuals that are instances of multiple collections. A second strategy is the introduction of more general collections that subsume the orthogonal collections to link the different argument. Third, a more specific collection could be introduced that represents the intersection of the various orthogonal collections. Finally, temporally created specialized predicates could be introduced when communicating the background knowledge to ALEPH. The new predicates would be specialized in the sense that their argument constraints be the intersection of the orthogonal collections. This would establish subsumption relations and make them compatible with the simple algorithm described above.

First, the "Casting" strategy is intended for cases where predicates are constrained by orthogonal collections and they have values that are instances of those orthogonal classes (e.g. a father who is a ruler in a dynasty). The strategy focuses on type constraints of predicates, but also takes into account the fact that some entities will be instances of more than one collection. So, if an argument is constrained to a particular type that is orthogonal to another predicates' constraining type and the value of that argument is also an instance of the orthogonal collection, then that value should be used with the other predicate. The principle cost of this strategy is a dramatic increase in the number of predicates in relation to the number of individuals that are instances of multiple collections. In addition, since type conversion has to be bi-directional, there is the potential of catching ALEPH in a conceptual loop, as it oscillates back and forth between two facets of a term.

Second, the "Type Generalization" strategy walks up the type hierarchy to find the least general collection that subsumes the orthogonal collections. From a strictly semantic perspective, the use of the more general types violates the meaning of the predicate. This violation translates into a decrease in the utility of type knowledge. Since fewer distinctions are being made, there is a weaker partitioning of the search space. In the degenerate case, all type knowledge is lost if the least general collection remains general enough to subsume all the argument constraints of all the predicates in the determination.

Third, the "Type Specialization" strategy introduces more specific types that allow the system to maintain the semantic integrity of the predicates and the benefits that follow from the splitting up of the search space. However, this strategy requires the generation of significantly more types and a proportionately larger group of mode statements that properly connect them to the predicates.

Fourth, the "Predicate Specialization" strategy introduces more specific predicates. It requires creating more specialized predicates whose argument positions have significantly tighter constraints and then distributing the original data to the new predicates based on the types of their values. Here, the problem of having multiple linkages to the same argument positions is eliminated because the examples will be partitioned based on the new predicates' tighter semantics. However, there are two problems with the approach. First, the strategy increases the likelihood of the system returning over-fitted rules. If the invented predicate has a very small extent, the likelihood increases that it will satisfy some of the positive examples even though the more general predicate from which it was derived would not. Alternatively, if the system's evaluation function has a relatively high threshold for acceptability (e.g., its minimum number of positive examples covered), the split might be such that hypotheses with the new predicate falls beneath that threshold while a rule formed with the original predicate would be above it.

6   Conclusions and Future Research

The next and most important stage in this work is the empirical investigation of the utility of this strategy for ILP systems. Existing data sets need to be ontologized such that a system like ALEPH can be tested with ontologically derived settings versus hand-generated settings and the settings provided by other mode learning algorithms.

In addition, our presentation has focused on only a subset of the types of semantic meta-knowledge that are available within the Cyc. Cyc contains a large amount of unexploited meta-knowledge, such as that expressed by #$interArgReln and #$interArgIsa. The former predicate is used to say that a particular binary relation must hold between the values of some predicate. The latter predicate dictates that when an instance of one collection appears in one argument of a predicate, then an instance of a specified collection must appear in some other argument (e.g., a human child can only have a human as a parent).

The content of the Cyc KB itself can also serve as a resource for generating inductive biases. It contains a large body of rules expressed as either implications or as ground assertions that can be expanded to implications via templates. These rules could be used to divert the search away from known rules or hypotheses that are entailed by existing rules. Preliminary work has been done to convert rules into formats that use ALEPH's pruning mechanism toward this end.

Finally, we have introduced only a simple methodology for generating mode settings based on type constraints. More sophisticated strategies for deriving modes from the focal type and the relationships among the type constraints of the determination should become available with further research. Given that the rules for generating modes are declaratively represented, representing the modes themselves and rules for interpreting them could lead to further rule-learning improvements.

References

1. Tausend, B.: Biases and their Effects in Inductive Logic Programming. In: F. Bergadano and L. De Raedt (eds.): Proceedings of the 7th European Conference on Machine Learning. Lecture Notes in Artificial Intelligence, Vol. 784. Springer-Verlag, Berlin Heidelberg New York (1994) 431–434.
2. Tausend, B.: Representing Biases for Inductive Logic Programming. In: F. Bergadano and L. De Raedt, (eds.): Proceedings of the 7th European Conference on Machine Learning. Lecture Notes in Artificial Intelligence, Vol. 784. Springer-Verlag, Berlin Heidelberg New York (1994) 427–430.
3. Nedellec, C., Rouveirol, C., Ade,H., Bergadano, F., Tausend, B.: Declarative Bias in ILP. In: L. De Raedt (ed.): Advances in Inductive Logic Programming. IOS Press, Amsterdam (1996) 82-103.
4. McCreath, E.: Induction in First Order Logic from Noisy Training Examples and Fixed Example Set Sizes. PhD Thesis, University Of New South Wales (1999).
5. McCreath, E. and Sharma, A.: Extraction of Meta-Knowledge to Restrict the Hypothesis Space for ILP Systems. Yao, X. (ed): Eighth Australian Joint Conference on Artificial Intelligence. World Scientific Publishing, Singapore (1995) 75-82.
6. Di Mauro, N., Esposito, F., Ferilli, S. and Basile, T.M.A.: An Algorithm for Incremental Mode Induction. In Orchard, B., Yang, C., Moonis, A. (eds.): Innovations in Applied Artificial Intelligence: 17th International Conference on Industrial and Engineering Applications of Artificial Intelligence and Expert Systems, IEA/AIE 2004. Lecture Notes in Computer Science, Vol. 3029. Springer-Verlag, Berlin Heidelberg New York (2004) 512-522.
7. Lenat, D. and Guha, R.: Building Large Knowledge Based Systems: Representations and Inference in the Cyc Project. Addison-Wesley, Reading (1989).
8. Muggleton, S.H.: Inverse Entailment and Progol. *New Generation Computing* **13** (1995): 245-286.

Learning Teleoreactive Logic Programs from Problem Solving

Dongkyu Choi and Pat Langley

Computational Learning Laboratory
Center for the Study of Language and Information
Stanford University, Stanford, CA 94305 USA
dongkyuc@stanford.edu, langley@csli.stanford.edu

Abstract. In this paper, we focus on the problem of learning reactive skills for use by physical agents. We propose a new representation for such procedures, teleoreactive logic programs, along with an interpreter that utilizes them to achieve goals. After this, we describe a learning method that acquires these structures in a cumulative manner through problem solving. We report experiments in three domains that involve multiple levels of skilled behavior. We also review related work and discuss directions for future research.

1 Introduction

Humans typically acquire complex procedures in a cumulative manner, first mastering simple tasks and then utilizing them to learn higher-level abilities. At each stage, the learner must have reasonably automatized procedures before he can incorporate them into more sophisticated structures. The end result is a set of hierarchically organized skills that can be executed automatically, but at intermediate stages the person must rely at least partly on problem solving, which may require search to find solutions.

In this paper, we examine the task of learning such complex skills from a sequence of training problems. We are concerned with acquiring the structure and organization of skills, rather than tuning their parameters, which we view as a secondary learning issue. We assume the learner begins with primitive skills for the domain, including knowledge of their effects, and that training problems are presented in order of increasing complexity, much as in human instruction.

We focus here on procedures that involve action in the world, but ones that are more complex than those usually studied in research on reinforcement learning (Sutton & Barton, 1998) and behavioral cloning (Sammut, 1996). We assume that the agent encodes its knowledge in a formalism – teleoreactive logic programs – designed specifically for such tasks, and our learning methods take advantage of this notation to constrain the acquisition process. As we will see, these are similar in spirit to early techniques for learning macro-operators and search-control rules, but they also differ in important ways.

In the next section, we specify the formalism used to encode initial and learned knowledge, along with performance mechanisms that interpret them to

S. Kramer and B. Pfahringer (Eds.): ILP 2005, LNAI 3625, pp. 51–68, 2005.

Table 1. Examples of concepts from an in-city driving domain.

```
(parked (?self ?lane)
 :percepts ((self ?self speed ?speed))
 :positives ((in-rightmost-lane ?self ?lane)
             (stopped ?self)))
(in-lane (?self ?lane)
 :percepts ((self ?self segment ?sg)
             (lane-line ?lane segment ?sg dist ?dist))
 :tests    ((> ?dist -10)
             (<= ?dist 0)))
```

produce behavior. After this, we present an approach to problem solving on novel tasks and a learning mechanism that transforms the results of this process into executable logic programs. Next, we report experimental studies of the method in three domains, including an in-city driving task that we use to illustrate our ideas. In closing, we review related work on learning and consider directions for additional research.

2   Teleoreactive Logic Programs

As noted, our approach revolves around a representational formalism, called teleoreactive logic programs, that are designed to support the execution and acquisition of complex procedures. We refer to these structures as "logic programs" because their syntax is similar to the Horn clauses used in Prolog and related languages. We have borrowed the term "teleoreactive" from Nilsson (1994), who used it to refer to systems that are goal driven but that also react to their current environment. His examples incorporated symbolic control rules but were not cast as logic programs, as we assume here.

A teleoreactive logic program consists of two knowledge bases. One specifies a set of concepts that recognize classes of situations in the environment and describe them at higher levels of abstraction. These monotonic inference rules have the same semantics as traditional Horn clauses and a similar syntax. Each clause includes a single head, stated as a predicate with zero or more arguments, along with a body that includes one or more positive literals, negative literals, or arithmetic tests. The same head can appear in more than one clause, expressing different ways to satisfy the named concept.

We distinguish between primitive clauses, which refer only to percepts that the agent can perceive in the environment, and complex conceptual clauses, which refer to other concepts in their body. Specific percepts play the same role as ground literals in traditional logic programs, but, because they can change rapidly, we do not consider them part of the program. Table 1 presents some concepts from an in-city driving domain. The concept *parked* is defined in terms of the concepts *in-rightmost-lane* and *stopped*, whereas *in-lane* is defined in terms of the percepts *self* and *lane-line*, along with arithmetic tests on their attributes.

Table 2. Examples of skills from an in-city driving domain. The complex skill (first) has typed variables, a start condition, and a set of ordered subskills. The primitive (second) skill has a set of actions (marked by an asterisk) and effects instead of subskills.

```
(driving-in-segment (?self ?sg ?lane)
 :percepts ((lane-line ?lane) (segment ?sg) (self ?self))
 :start    ((steering-wheel-straight ?self))
 :skills   ((in-lane ?self ?lane)
            (centered-in-lane ?self ?sg ?lane)
            (aligned-with-lane-in-segment ?self ?sg ?lane)
            (steering-wheel-straight ?self))
(steering-wheel-straight (?self)
 :percepts ((self ?self))
 :start    ((steering-wheel-not-straight ?self))
 :actions  ((*straighten))
 :effects  ((steering-wheel-straight ?self)))
```

A second knowledge base contains a set of skills that the agent can execute in the world. Each skill clause includes a single head (a predicate with zero or more arguments) and a body that specifies a single start condition and one or more components. Primitive clauses refer to executable actions that affect the environment. They also specify the effects of their execution, stated as literals that hold after their completion, and may state requirements that must hold during their execution. Primitive skill clauses are similar in structure and spirit to STRIPS operators, although they may be executed in a durative manner.

In contrast, complex skill clauses specify how to decompose activity into subskills. Because a skill may refer to itself, either directly or through a subskill, the formalism supports recursive definitions. For this reason, nonprimitive skills do not specify effects, which can differ for different levels of recursion, nor do they state requirements. However, the head of each complex skill corresponds to some concept that the skill aims to achieve, with its head using the same predicate and taking the same number of arguments as the concept. This connection between skills and concepts figures centrally in the learning methods we describe later. Table 2 presents some skills for the driving domain, including a complex skill, *driving-in-segment*, and a component primitive skill, *steering-wheel-straight*.

Note that every skill S can be expanded into one or more sequence of primitive skills. For each skill S in a teleoreactive logic program, if S has concept C as its head, then every expansion of S into such a sequence must, if executed successfully, produce a state in which C holds. This second constraint does not guarantee that, once initiated, the sequence will achieve C, since other events may intervene or it may encounter states in which one of the primitive skills may not apply. However, if the sequence of primitive skills can be run to completion, then it will achieve the goal literal C. The approach to learning that we report later is designed to acquire programs with this characteristic, although we do not yet have a formal proof to that effect.

3   Inference and Execution Mechanisms

The performance mechanisms of a teleoreactive logic program reflect the fact that it operates in a physical setting that changes over time. As we have described elsewhere (Choi et al., 2004), the basic architecture proceeds in discrete cycles, in each case invoking an inference process that elaborates on the agent's perceived state and an execution process that generates behavior in the environment.

The inference module operates in a bottom-up, data-driven manner that starts from descriptions of perceived objects, such as (segment G1113 street 1 dist −5.0 latdist 15.0 dir WE), and deduces all beliefs that they imply in combination with the conceptual clauses, such as (in-lane ME G1213). This inference process augments the agent's perceptions with higher-level descriptions of the environment that may be useful for its decision making. Although this mechanism reasons over structures similar to Horn clauses, its operation is closer in spirit to the bottom-up elaboration process in Soar (Laird et al., 1986) than to the query-driven reasoning in Prolog.

In contrast, the execution module proceeds in a top-down manner, starting from high-level intentions, such as (delivered-package ME package5), and finding applicable paths through the skill hierarchy that terminate in primitive skills with executable actions, such as (∗steer −0.5). A *skill path* is a chain of skill instances that starts from the agent's top-level intention and descends the skill hierarchy, unifying the arguments of each subskill consistently with those of its parent. A path is *applicable* if the concept instance that corresponds to the intention is not satisfied, if the requirements of the terminal (primitive) skill instance are satisfied, and if, for each skill instance in the path not executed on the previous cycle, the start conditions are satisfied. This last constraint is necessary because skills may take many cycles to achieve their desired effects, making it important to distinguish between their initiation and their continuation.

Both conceptual inference and skill execution play essential roles in complex domains like in-city driving. On each cycle, the agent perceives nearby objects and infers instances of conceptual relations that they satisfy. For each intention, the system then uses these beliefs to check the conditions on skill instances and to determine which paths are applicable, which in turn constrains which actions it executes. The environment changes, either in response to these actions or on its own, and the agent begins another inference-execution cycle. This looping continues until the concepts associated with each of the agent's top-level intentions are satisfied, when it halts.

The interpreter incorporates two preferences that provide a balance between reactivity and persistence. First, given a choice between two or more subskills, it selects the first one for which the corresponding concept instance is not satisfied. This bias supports reactive control, since the agent reconsiders previously completed subskills and, if unexpected events have undone their effects, reexecutes them to correct the situation. Second, given a choice between two or more applicable skill paths, it selects the one that overlaps most with the path executed on the previous cycle. This bias encourages the agent to keep executing a high-level skill it has started until it achieves the associated goal or becomes inapplicable.

4   Problem Solving and Learning Mechanisms

Although one can construct teleoreactive logic programs manually, this process is time consuming and prone to error. In response, we have developed a problem solver that chains primitive skills to solve novel tasks and an associated learning method that composes the solutions into executable programs, which we describe in this section. Both mechanisms are interleaved with the execution process, with the problem solver being invoked whenever the agent encounters a situation for which it finds no applicable skill paths. As in Laird et al.'s Soar, problem solving and learning are driven by impasses, although the details are quite different.

4.1   Means-Ends Problem Solving

As noted, our system resorts to problem solving when there are no applicable skill paths that would take it toward the current goal. We utilize a variant of means-ends analysis (Newell et al., 1960) which chains backward from the goal, pushing the result of each reasoning step onto a goal stack that stores information about the agent's efforts toward achieving the goal. As the pseudocode in Table 3 indicates, two distinct forms of chaining play a role in problem solving.

Backward chaining off a skill involves retrieving a skill clause with effects or a head that indicates its execution would achieve the current goal. If such a clause exists in skill memory, the system associates an instance of this clause with the goal.[1] If the clause's start condition is met, the system executes the clause instance in the environment until it achieves the goal, which is then popped from the stack. If the condition is not satisfied, the system makes it the current goal by pushing it onto the stack.

If the problem solver cannot find any skill clause that would achieve the current goal, it resorts to concept chaining. Here it uses the definition of the goal concept to decompose the problem into subgoals. Some subgoals may already be satisfied in the current situation, which the system stores as such with the current goal. If more than one subgoal is unsatisfied, the problem solver selects one at random and makes it the current goal by pushing it onto the goal stack.

The system continues along these lines, pushing new goals onto the stack until it finds one it can achieve with an applicable skill clause. In such cases, it executes the skill and pops the goal from the stack. If the parent goal involved skill chaining, then this leads to execution of its associated skill and achievement of the parent, which is in turn popped. If the parent goal involved concept chaining, one of the other unsatisfied subconcepts is pushed onto the goal stack or, if none remain, then the parent is popped. This process continues until the system achieves the top-level goal.

Of course, the problem-solving procedure must make decisions about which skills to select during skill chaining and the order in which it should tackle

---

[1] When there are multiple relevant clauses, the problem solver selects the one with the fewest conditions unsatisfied in the current situation. Because skills always have a single start condition, this means expanding the concept into its primitive components. If the candidates tie on this criterion, then it selects the clause that requires fewer expected steps, and if ties occur on this dimension, it selects one at random.

Table 3. Pseudocode for means-ends problem solving and associated learning through goal-driven composition of component skills.

```
Solve(G)
  Push the goal literal G onto the empty goal stack GS.
  On each cycle,
     If the top goal G of the goal stack GS is satisfied,
     Then pop GS and let New be Learn(G).
        If G's parent P involved skill chaining,
        Then store New as P's first subskill.
        Else if G's parent P involved concept chaining,
           Then store New as P's next subskill.
     Else if the goal stack GS does not exceed the depth limit,
        Let S be the skill instances whose heads unify with G.
        If any applicable skill paths start from an instance in S,
        Then select one of these paths and execute it.
        Else let M be the set of primitive skill instances that
              have not already failed in which G is an effect.
           If the set M is nonempty,
           Then select a skill instance Q from M.
              Store Q with goal G as its last subskill.
              Push the start condition C of Q onto goal stack GS.
              Mark goal G as involving skill chaining.
           Else if G is a complex concept with the unsatisfied
                 subconcepts H and with satisfied subconcepts F,
              Then if there is a subconcept I in H that has not yet failed,
                 Then push I onto the goal stack GS.
                    Store F with G as its initially true subconcepts.
                    Mark goal G as involving concept chaining.
                 Else pop G from the goal stack GS.
                    Store information about failure with G's parent.
              Else pop G from the goal stack GS.
                 Store information about failure with G's parent.

Learn(G)
  If the goal G involves skill chaining,
  Then let S₁ and S₂ be G's first and second subskills.
     If subskill S₁ is empty,
     Then return the literal for clause S₂.
     Else create a new skill clause N with head G,
          with S₁ and S₂ as ordered subskills, and
          with the same start condition as subskill S₁.
        Return the literal for skill clause N.
  Else if the goal G involves concept chaining,
     Then let C_{k+1}, ..., C_n be G's initially satisfied subconcepts.
        Let C₁, ..., C_k be G's stored subskills.
        Create a new skill clause N with head G,
        with C_{k+1}, ..., C_n as ordered subskills, and
        with the conjunction of C₁, ..., C_k as start condition.
        Return the literal for skill clause N.
```

subconcepts during concept chaining. The system may well make the incorrect choice at any point, which leads it to pop the current goal and backtrack when the goal goal reaches its maximum depth or when it has no alternatives it has not already tried. As a result, it carries out depth-first search through the problem space, which can require considerable time on some tasks.

Figure 1 shows an example of the problem solver's behavior in our in-city driving domain. When the system is given the objective *driving-in-segment*, it looks for any executable skill with this goal as its head. When this fails, it looks for a skill that has the objective as one of its effects. Since it has no such skills,

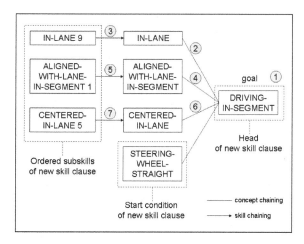

Fig. 1. A trace of successful problem solving in the in-city driving domain. Circled numbers correspond to the steps explained in the text.

it chains off the concept definition, which involves four subconcepts. The first three are not satisfied, from which the system chooses *in-lane* as its subgoal. It finds skill clauses with this head and selects (in-lane 9), which is applicable and which it executes to achieve the subgoal.

Later, the problem solver does the same for the subconcepts *aligned-with-lane-in-segment* and *centered-in-lane*, selecting the skills (aligned-with-lane-in-segment 1) and (centered-in-lane 5), which the system executes in turn to achieve them. At this point, it notes that the original goal is satisfied. This example describes a trace of successful problem solving, but we have omitted missteps that require backtracking and search for the sake of clarity.

4.2   Learning Through Goal-Driven Composition

Fortunately, learning can transform the results of search into a teleoreactive logic program that can be executed efficiently. Whenever the agent achieves a goal during problem solving, it stores a new skill clause, unless its solution involves immediate execution of an existing clause or unless the new clause would be equivalent to an existing one. The learning mechanism, which we call *goal-driven composition*, operates somewhat differently for each form of chaining.

When the agent reaches an objective through skill chaining, say by achieving a goal G by first applying skill S_1 to satisfy the start condition for S_2 and executing the skill S_2, the learning mechanism constructs a new clause[2] with head G and ordered subskills S_1 and S_2. The start condition for the new clause is the same as that for S_1, since when S_1 is applicable, the successful completion of this skill will ensure the start condition for S_2, which in turn will achieve G.

---

[2] If the skill S_2 can be executed without invoking another skill to meet its start condition, the method creates a new clause G with S_2 as its only subskill.

This differs from traditional methods for constructing macro-operators, which analytically combine the preconditions of the first operator and those preconditions of later operators it does not achieve. However, S_1 was either selected because it achieves S_2's start condition or it was learned during its achievement, both of which mean that S_1's start condition is sufficient for the composed skill.

In contrast, successful concept chaining leads to the creation of slightly different skill clauses. Suppose the agent achieves a goal concept G by satisfying the subconcepts $G_1, \ldots, G_k$, in that order, while subconcepts $G_{k+1}, \ldots, G_n$ were true at the outset. In this case, the system constructs a new skill clause with head G and the ordered subskills $G_1, \ldots, G_k$.[3] In this case, the start condition for the new clause is the conjunction of subgoals that were already satisfied beforehand. This prevents execution of the learned clause when some of $G_{k+1}, \ldots, G_n$ are not satisfied, in which case the sequence $G_1, \ldots, G_k$ may not achieve the goal G.

Goal-driven composition operates in a bottom-up fashion, with new skills being formed whenever a goal on the stack is achieved. The method is fully incremental, in that it learns from single training cases, and it is interleaved with problem solving and execution. Unlike most techniques for learning macro-operators, it can acquire both disjunctive and recursive skills. Moreover, learning is cumulative in that skill clauses learned from one problem are available for use on later tasks. However, the system invokes a learned clause only when it is applicable in the current situation, so the problem solver never chains off its start condition. Mooney (1989) relied on a similar strategy to avoid the utility problem (Minton, 1990), in which learned knowledge leads to slower behavior.

Our approach to learning takes advantage of three insights that make it effective. First, although means-ends analysis is seldom used in the AI planning community, it has the distinct advantage that, when successful, it produces an AND tree that decomposes the original problem into subproblems. This determines the structure of the learned clauses. Second, the problem-solving trace indicates the goal literal being pursued in each subproblem, which provides the head for the learned clause. Because the same goal may be achieved in different ways, this leads naturally to both disjunctive and recursive structures. Finally, the skill clauses in a teleoreactive logic program are interpreted not in isolation but as parts of chains through the skill hierarchy. This lets the learning method store very abstract conditions with new clauses without a danger of overgeneralization. Taken together, these features make goal-driven composition a simple yet powerful approach to learning logic programs for reactive control.

5   Experimental Studies of Learning

Preliminary studies in a number of domains suggested that the learning mechanism described above constructs appropriate teleoreactive logic programs. Given the same or isomorphic problems, the agent retrieves and executes the learned programs in a reactive manner, without resorting to means-ends problem solv-

---

[3] Each of these subskills was either already known and used to achieve the associated subgoal or it was learned from the successful solution of one of the subproblems.

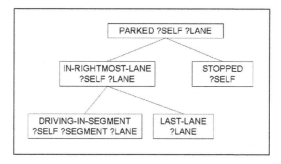

Fig. 2. Portion of the concept hierarchy given to the system that it uses to decompose the goal instance (parked ME LANE1). Skills that achieve these concepts are learned through problem solving.

ing. These informal results encouraged us to test the system in a more dynamic domain that involved in-city driving, which we present below. We also carried out more systematic experiments with two domains that are less dynamic but that involve recursive structure, which should let the learned programs scale to more complex problems.

5.1   In-City Driving

In-city driving is a demanding task that involves the reactive use of complex skills. To study this problem, we have implemented a simulated environment that makes simplifications but retains the dynamic nature and complexity of the real world. Objects in the environment are represented as rectangles of various sizes on a Euclidean plane. These include static objects like road segments, intersections, lane lines, and buildings, but they also include moving vehicles.

One vehicle is controlled by the agent, whereas others follow standard driving customs but make random decisions about whether to drive through intersections or turn. The agent can invoke actions for accelerating, decelerating, and turning its steering wheel left or right. These inputs affect the associated control variables of the vehicle according to realistic physical laws. The agent can perceive objects around it up to 60 feet away, including other vehicles and buildings, each of which is described in agent-centered polar coordinates that give its distance, angle, relative velocity, and angular velocity. The agent also perceives its own properties, including its current speed and its steering wheel angle.

For this domain, we provided the system with 19 concepts and eight primitive skills to achieve a goal that we stated as an instance of some defined concept. The particular task we report in this paper involves achieving the goal (parked ME LANE1), which has subconcept instances (in-rightmost-lane ME LANE1) and (stopped ME). The first subconcept can be decomposed further into (driving-in-segment ME SEGMENT1 LANE1) and (last-lane LANE1), as shown in Figure 2. As the concepts clarify, this task can be done by first changing to the rightmost lane (by achieving *driving-in-segment* and *in-rightmost-lane*, in that order), if the vehicle is not already in that lane, and then slowing to a stop.

Table 4. Skill clauses learned from a run in the in-city driving domain.

```
driving-in-segment (?ME ?G1101 ?G1152)
 :percepts ((lane-line ?G1152) (segment ?G1101) (self ?ME))
 :start    ((steering-wheel-straight ?ME))
 :skills   ((in-lane ?ME ?G1152)
            (centered-in-lane ?ME ?G1101 ?G1152)
            (aligned-with-lane-in-segment ?ME ?G1101 ?G1152)
            (steering-wheel-straight ?ME))
in-rightmost-lane (?ME ?G1152)
 :percepts ((self ?ME) (lane-line ?G1152))
 :start    ((last-lane ?G1152))
 :skills   ((driving-in-segment ?ME ?G1101 ?G1152))
parked (?ME ?G1152)
 :percepts ((lane-line ?G1152) (self ?ME))
 :start    ( )
 :skills   ((in-rightmost-lane ?ME ?G1152)
            (stopped ?ME))
```

Table 4 shows the teleoreactive logic program acquired from one learning run. All the skill clauses are constructed from concept chaining. During problem solving, the objective (driving-in-segment ME G1101 G1152) of the first skill clause is achieved by *in-lane, centered-in-lane, aligned-with-lane-in-segment*, and *steering-wheel-straight*, in that order. When execution of the first subskill was started, the concept (steering-wheel-straight ME) was true, so it is included in the start condition. Since the goal (in-rightmost-lane ME G1152) was at the next level of the stack, the system creates the second skill clause, *in-rightmost-lane*, immediately after the first clause and used the first learned clause *driving-in-segment* as its only subskill. Again, because the concept instance (last-lane G1152) held when the chaining that led to this skill clause began, it is included in the start condition. In turn, it uses the skill *in-rightmost-lane* as the first subskill of the skill clause *parked* followed by the primitive clause *stopped*. Note that these learned clauses are organized hierarchically, but they all expand into primitive skills with executable actions. When combined with the original skills, the learned program shows the desired behavior. Moreover, they generalize correctly to situations with different numbers of lanes and other starting lanes.

These results are encouraging, but we also desired to answer two questions that required a more formal experiment. First, we wanted to know whether the learning method produces teleoreactive logic programs that are more effective for the task than the primitive skills combined with means-ends problem solving. To this end, we ran the system on the task of achieving (parked ME LANE1) both with learning turned on and with it turned off. Second, we wanted to determine whether cumulative learning on subtasks of increasing complexity produced more rapid improvement than learning on the goal task. For the former, we first let the system master the component task of achieving (driving-in-segment ME

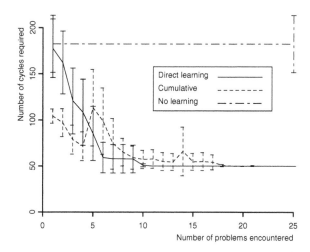

Fig. 3. Execution cycles required to achieve the goal (parked ME) in the driving domain as a function of the number of trials with no learning, non-cumulative learning, and cumulative learning. Each learning curve shows the mean over 25 runs and 95 percent confidence intervals.

SEGMENT1 LANE1) and then (in-rightmost-lane ME LANE1) before finally letting it learn how to achieve the top-level goal, (parked ME LANE1).

In each of these three conditions, we ran the system 25 times on the driving task. We measured the number of decision-making cycles the system took to solve the task on each trial, which differ due to the randomness of selection in the chaining process. Based on these data, we computed the mean and 95% confidence interval as a function of the trial number, which we plot in Figure 3. With learning disabled, performance on this task does not improve and the agent continues to take 180 cycles to solve the problem. With learning activated, the number of cycles dramatically decreases over the first few trials and converges to about 50 cycles after ten trials, which is the fewest cycles needed for this particular task. This suggests that learning is effective for the problems that arise in the in-city driving domain.

We also compared the basic learning condition to the cumulative learning case, in which we presented the system with subgoals in order of increasing difficulty. The system begins taking fewer cycles than the non-cumulative case, mainly because we gave it a relatively simple goal first. Around the fifth trial, it completes learning on the first simple problem and moves on to the second one. Since this task is new to the system, it needs more cycles for problem solving, which produced the peak on the graph. However, this peak is still lower than the level at which non-cumulative learning began, since the learned skills from the first task reduced effort. After learning to achieve the second subgoal, the most difficult task became noticeably easier than without prior learning, and the graph shows no detectable peak. Even though cumulative learning requires more trials to complete the learning process, on average it needs fewer cycles per trial.

Table 5. Recursive skills learned from a Blocks World problem in which C is on B and B is on A in the initial state and the goal is to make A clear. Some start conditions have been expanded for the sake of clarity.

```
unstackable (?C ?B)                    hand-empty ( )
:percepts  ((block ?B)(block ?C))      :percepts  ((block ?D)(table ?T1))
:start     ((on ?C ?B)(hand-empty))    :start     ((putdownable ?D ?T1))
:skills    ((clear ?C)(hand-empty))    :skills    ((putdown ?D ?T1))

clear (?B)                             holding (?D)
:percepts  ((block ?C)(block ?B))      :percepts  ((block ?D)(block ?C))
:start     ((on ?C ?B)(hand-empty))    :start     ((unstackable ?D ?C))
:skills    ((unstackable ?C ?B)        :skills    ((unstack ?D ?C))
            (unstack ?C ?B))

clear (?C)
:percepts  ((block ?D)(block ?C))
:start     ((unstackable ?D ?C))
:skills    ((unstack ?D ?C))
```

Although in-city driving is a challenging physical domain, its structure does not take full advantage of our method's capabilities. We predict that, combined with a cumulative training regime, it will be especially effective in domains with recursive structure, since its ability to learn recursive logic programs will let it train on simple problems and generalize to more complex ones. To test this prediction, we also carried out experiments with two other domains, the Blocks World and FreeCell solitaire, that are known to have recursive structure,

5.2   Blocks World

The Blocks World consists of a table with cubical blocks and a gripper. For this domain, we provided the system with nine concepts and four primitive skills, along with one concept for each of four distinct goals. These are sufficient, in principle, to solve all the problems in the domain, but means-ends analysis would require extensive search when there are more than a few blocks. Instead, we want a teleoreactive logic program that can solve problems with arbitrary numbers of blocks without significant search. For this study, we developed a simulated environment that let the agent perceive the positions of objects and manipulate blocks by grasping, lifting, carrying, and ungrasping them. Table 5 presents the recursive skills learned from one training problem that required clearing the lowest object in a stack of four blocks.

To determine whether the control programs our method constructs are useful on more complex tasks, we carried out a transfer experiment that involved two conditions. In one condition, we presented the system with 20 training problems with three blocks, another 20 problems with four blocks, and a third set of

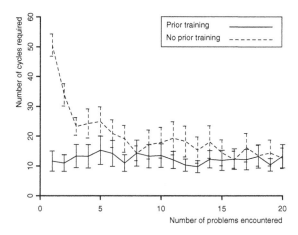

Fig. 4. Execution cycles required to solve a 20-block problem in the Blocks World as a function of the number of training tasks with and without prior training on simpler problems. Each learning curve shows the mean over 500 different training orders and 95 percent confidence intervals.

the same size with five blocks. Each problem involved one of four conjunctive goals that referred to configurations of one, two, or three blocks. After this, we presented the system with 20 new problems that referred to analogous goals but that each involved 20 blocks. In the second condition, we asked the system to solve the same 20 tasks, but without the benefit of working on the simpler problems. Learning was active in both conditions, but the former had the benefit of prior training when it encountered the transfer set.

Figure 4 shows the number of execution cycles required for both conditions, averaged over 500 runs using transfer problems with different randomized orders. For each problem, we let the system run a maximum of 50 cycles before starting over and attempt the task at most ten times before giving up. In both conditions, the system managed to solve 99 percent of the problems, but there was considerable difference in the effort required. When the system worked on simpler problems first, it constructed a recursive logic program that, in nearly all cases, handled the 20 block tasks without resorting to means-ends analysis. This condition shows no improvement because the system had learned all there was to learn in the simpler setting. However, this does not mean they would not challenge traditional learning methods that cannot acquire recursive structures.

In contrast, without the benefit of this prior experience, the system had to invoke its problem solver, leading to much longer runs on the initial tasks. Even in this case, the learning mechanism rapidly acquired a teleoreactive logic program, with the system reaching apparent asymptotic performance after only five problems. However, its performance under this condition did not quite reach the same level as under the transfer condition, suggesting that training on simpler problems provides an overall advantage. We repeated this study with tasks that involved 30 blocks and obtained almost identical results.

5.3   FreeCell Solitaire

FreeCell is a solitaire game that involves stacks of cards on eight columns, all faced up and visible to the player. There are four free cells, which serve as temporary holding spots for a single card at a time, and four foundation cells that correspond to four different suits. The goal is to move all the cards on the eight columns to the foundation cells in ascending order and grouped by suit. At any given time, only the cards on the top of the stack on each column and the ones in free cells are available for movement, and they can shift to a free cell, to the proper foundation column, or to an empty column. We again provided a simulated environment that let the agent make legal moves, as well as perceive card locations and the status of cells.

For this domain, we provided the system with 24 concepts and 12 primitive skills that are sufficient to handle any initial configurations capable of solution. But again, means-ends analysis may require an inordinate amount of effort to handle problems with more than a few cards or convenient configurations. We hoped our learning mechanism would acquire a teleoreactive logic program that could solve arbitrary FreeCell tasks in the simulated environment with little or no need to invoke the problem-solving module. To this end, we carried out a transfer experiment similar to that we reported for the Blocks World.

In the transfer condition, we trained the system on 20 randomly generated FreeCell tasks that involved eight cards, another 20 problems with 12 cards, and a third set of the same size with 16 cards. We then asked the system to tackle a set of 20 harder tasks that involved configurations of 20 cards. In the control condition, we presented the system with the similar 20 card problems but we did not let it work on the simpler ones first. Figure 5 displays the number of execution cycles needed for each condition, averaged over 300 random sequences of the harder problems. As for the Blocks World, the system in the transfer condition shows no improvement beyond what it gained from working on the simpler tasks. However, in the control condition, the system requires much more effort at the outset and it continues to require substantially more effort than the version that trained on easier problems.

In this domain, the system cannot solve all of the more complex problems. The recursive program learned from simpler problems, in the transfer condition, handles around 72 percent of the 20 card FreeCell tasks. Prior experience leads to the creation of useful structures, but the training problems do not produce any skills for moving from one column to another, which are needed for some 20 card tasks. However, without the benefit of this earlier training, the system can initially solve only 39 percent of these problems, and its solution probability remains below that for the other condition through the learning curve.[4] When we used harder problems for the transfer set, this effect was far more pronounced. This result provides even stronger evidence that our method benefits from a cumulative approach to learning.

---

[4] With learning turned off, the system could solve none of the 20 card problems.

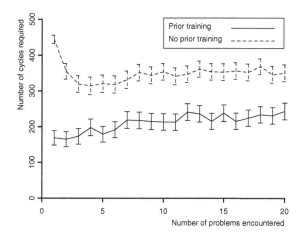

Fig. 5. Execution cycles required to solve a 20 card FreeCell problem as a function of the number of training tasks with and without prior training on simpler problems. Each learning curve shows the mean over 300 different training orders and 95 percent confidence intervals.

6   Related Research

The basic framework we have reported in this paper incorporates ideas from a number of traditions. Our representation and organization of knowledge draws directly from the paradigm of logic programming, whereas its utilization in a recognize-act cycle has more in common with production system architectures. The reliance on heuristic search to resolve goal-driven impasses, coupled with the caching of generalized solutions, comes closest to the performance and learning methods used in problem-solving architectures like Soar (Laird, Rosenbloom, & Newell, 1986) and PRODIGY (Minton, 1990). Finally, we have already noted our debt to Nilsson (1994) for the notion of a teleoreactive system.

However, our approach differs from earlier methods for learning from problem solving in the nature of the acquired knowledge. In contrast to Soar and PRODIGY, which create flat control rules, our framework constructs hierarchical logic programs that incorporate nonterminal symbols. Methods for learning macro-operators (e.g., Iba, 1988; Mooney, 1989) have a similar flavor, in that they explicitly specify the order in which to apply operators, but they do not typically support recursive references, nor do they produce reactive skills that can be used in dynamic domains like driving.

Equally important, our learning method differs substantially from earlier techniques used for improving efficiency of problem solvers. These have used either analytical methods that rely on goal regression to collect conditions on control rules or macro-operators, a relational approach to induction like inductive logic programming, or some combined method (e.g., Estlin & Mooney, 1997). Instead, our method transforms traces of successful means-ends search directly into teleoreactive logic programs, determining their preconditions by a simple method that involves neither analysis or induction, as normally defined.

The cumulative nature of our approach further distinguishes it from earlier efforts. There has been remarkably little work on cumulative learning in problem-solving domains. Ruby and Kibler's (1991) SteppingStone learns to solve more difficult problems based on solutions generalized from simpler ones, which it obtains through a mixture of problem reduction and forward-chaining search. A closer relative is Reddy and Tadepalli's (1997) X-Learn, which acquires goal-decomposition rules from a sequence of training exercises. Their system does not include an execution engine, but it generates recursive hierarchical plans in a cumulative manner using a mixture of analytical and relational learning.

Benson's (1995) TRAIL acquires teleoreactive control programs for use in physical environments. However, it utilizes inductive logic programming to determine the conditions on its rules, which focus on individual actions rather than hierarchical structures. Fern et al. (2004) report another approach to learning reactive controllers that trains itself on increasingly complex problems, but that also acquires flat rules for action selection. Stone and Veloso (2000) describe a system that learns a hierarchical controller for playing robotic soccer, but it acquires quite different types of structure at each level of description. Other work on cumulative learning deals with tasks other than problem solving and reactive control. Sammut and Banerji's (1986) Marvin learns logical concept definitions that are stated in terms of other concepts, whereas Stracuzzi and Utgoff's (2002) STL algorithm incorporates a similar idea but handles many concepts in parallel.

We should also mention another research paradigm that deals with speeding up the execution of logic programs. For instance, Zelle and Mooney (1993) report one such system that combines ideas from explanation-based learning and inductive logic programming to infer the conditions under which clauses should be considered. Work in this area starts and ends with logic programs, whereas our system transforms a weak problem-solving method into an efficient program for reactive control. In summary, although our learning technique incorporates ideas from earlier frameworks, it remains distinct on a number of dimensions.

7   Concluding Remarks

In the preceding pages, we proposed a new representation of knowledge – teleoreactive logic programs – and described how they can be executed over time to control physical agents. In addition, we explained how a means-ends problem solver can utilize them to solve novel tasks and, more important, transform the traces of problem solutions into new clauses that can be executed efficiently. The responsible learning method, goal-driven composition, bears little resemblance to previous techniques, and it acquires recursive, executable skills. We reported experiments that demonstrated the method's ability to learn both reactive driving skills and logic programs for two recursive domains, along with its capacity to benefit from training on tasks of increasing difficulty.

Despite the promise of this new approach to representing, utilizing, and learning knowledge for physical agents, our work remains in its early stages. Future research should demonstrate the acquisition of more complex skills in the driving domain. This will require adding the ability to chain backward off the start conditions of learned clauses, which the problem solver currently avoids. In addition, our method fares well on the domains reported here, but we have observed slight overgeneralization on the Tower of Hanoi, where it acquires a recursive strategy that does not distinguish between the goal and other peg. The learned program has a 50 percent chance of making the wrong choice, which becomes apparent when it runs to completion without reaching the goal. We can avoid this problem by adding some lookahead ability, as in work on hierarchical task networks (e.g., Erol et al., 1994), which have very similar structure. This will require additional effort, but still far less than solving the problem with means-ends analysis.

We should note that, although our approach learns recursive logic programs that generalize to different numbers of objects, its treatment of goals is less flexible. For example, it can acquire a general program for clearing a block that does not depend on the number of others involved, but it cannot learn a program for constructing a tower with arbitrarily specified components. Extending the method's ability to learn about recursive goal structures is an important direction for future research. We should also finds ways to decrease the method's reliance on initial concepts, which it uses to index and organize learned clauses. One approach involves defining a new concept for the start condition of each created clause, which would then be available to support future learning.

In conclusion, our work on learning teleoreactive logic programs is still in its early stages, but it appears to provide a novel and quite promising path to the acquisition of effective control systems that differs significantly from earlier research in this area. We hope to present reports on our progress in future conferences on approaches to learning relational knowledge.

Acknowledgements

This research was funded in part by Grant HR0011-04-1-0008 from DARPA IPTO and by Grant IIS-0335353 from the National Science Foundation. Discussions with Kirstin Cummings, Glenn Iba, Seth Rogers, and Stephanie Sage contributed to the ideas we have presented in this paper.

References

Benson, S. (1995). Induction learning of reactive action models. *Proceedings of the Twelfth International Conference on Machine Learning* (pp. 47–54). San Francisco: Morgan Kaufmann.

Choi, D., Kaufman, M., Langley, P., Nejati, N., & Shapiro, D. (2004). An architecture for persistent reactive behavior. *Proceedings of the Third International Joint Conference on Autonomous Agents and Multi Agent Systems* (pp. 988–995). New York: ACM Press.

Erol, K., Hendler, J., & Nau, D. S. (1994). HTN planning: Complexity and expressivity. *Proceedings of the Twelfth National Conference on Artificial Intelligence* (pp. 1123–1128). Seattle: MIT Press.

Estlin, T. A., & Mooney, R. J. (1997). Learning to improve both efficiency and quality of planning. *Proceedings of the Fifteenth International Joint Conference on Artificial Intelligence* (pp. 1227–1232). Nagoya, Japan.

Fern, A., Yoon, S. W., & Givan, R. (2004). Learning domain-specific control knowledge from random walks. *Proceedings of the Fourteenth International Conference on Automated Planning and Scheduling* (pp. 191–199). Whistler, BC: AAAI Press.

Iba, G. A. (1989). A heuristic approach to the discovery of macro-operators. *Machine Learning*, *3*, 285–317.

Laird, J. E., Rosenbloom, P. S., & Newell, A. (1986). Chunking in Soar: The anatomy of a general learning mechanism. *Machine Learning*, *1*, 11–46.

Minton, S. N. (1990). Quantitative results concerning the utility of explanation-based learning. *Artificial Intelligence*, *42*, 363–391.

Mooney, R. J. (1989). The effect of rule use on the utility of explanation-based learning. *Proceedings of the Eleventh International Joint Conference on Artificial Intelligence* (pp. 725–730). Detroit: Morgan Kaufmann.

Newell, A., Shaw, J. C., & Simon, H. A. (1960). Report on a general problem-solving program for a computer. *Information Processing: Proceedings of the International Conference on Information Processing* (pp. 256–264). UNESCO House, Paris.

Nilsson, N. (1994). Teleoreactive programs for agent control. *Journal of Artificial Intelligence Research*, *1*, 139–158.

Reddy, C., & Tadepalli, P. (1997). Learning goal-decomposition rules using exercises. *Proceedings of the Fourteenth International Conference on Machine Learning* (pp. 278–286). San Francisco: Morgan Kaufmann.

Ruby, D., & Kibler, D. (1991). SteppingStone: An empirical and analytical evaluation. *Proceedings of the Tenth National Conference on Artificial Intelligence* (pp. 527–532). Menlo Park, CA: AAAI Press.

Sammut, C. (1996). Automatic construction of reactive control systems using symbolic machine learning. *Knowledge Engineering Review*, *11*, 27–42.

Sammut, C., & Banerji, R. B. (1986). Learning concepts by asking questions. In R. S. Michalski, J. G. Carbonell, & T. M. Mitchell (Eds.), *Machine learning: An artificial intelligence approach* (Vol. 2). Los Altos, CA: Morgan Kaufmann.

Shavlik, J. W. (1989). Acquiring recursive concepts with explanation-based learning. *Proceedings of the Eleventh International Joint Conference on Artificial Intelligence* (pp. 688–693). Detroit, MI: Morgan Kaufmann.

Stone, P., & Veloso, M. M. (2000). Layered learning. *Proceedings of the Eleventh European Conference on Machine Learning* (pp. 369–381). Barcelona. Springer-Verlag.

Sutton, R. S. & Barto, A. G. (1998). *Reinforcement learning*. Cambridge, MA: MIT Press.

Utgoff, P., & Stracuzzi, D. (2002). Many-layered learning. *Proceedings of the Second International Conference on Development and Learning* (pp. 141–146).

Zelle, J. M., & Mooney, R. J. (1993). Combining FOIL and EBG to speed up logic programs. *Proceedings of the Thirteenth International Joint Conference on Artificial Intelligence* (pp. 1106–1111). Chambery, France: Morgan Kaufmann.

A Framework for Set-Oriented Computation in Inductive Logic Programming and Its Application in Generalizing Inverse Entailment*

Héctor Corrada Bravo[1], David Page[1,2], Raghu Ramakrishnan[1],
Jude Shavlik[1,2], and Vitor Santos Costa[2,3]

[1] Department of Computer Sciences,
[2] Department of Biostatistics and Medical Informatics,
University of Wisconsin-Madison, USA
[3] COPPE/Sistemas UFRJ, Brasil
{hcorrada, raghu, shavlik}@cs.wisc.edu
{page, vitor}@biostat.wisc.edu

Abstract. We propose a new approach to Inductive Logic Programming that systematically exploits caching and offers a number of advantages over current systems. It avoids redundant computation, is more amenable to the use of set-oriented generation and evaluation of hypotheses, and allows relational DBMS technology to be more easily applied to ILP systems. Further, our approach opens up new avenues such as probabilistically scoring rules during search and the generation of probabilistic rules. As a first example of the benefits of our ILP framework, we propose a scheme for defining the hypothesis search space through Inverse Entailment using multiple example seeds.

1 Introduction

The goal of Inductive Logic Programming (ILP) [1] is to autonomously learn first-order logic programs that model relational data. However, the current approach to ILP has limitations in its scalability and computational efficiency. Recent efforts extend ideas from relational database query optimization to this setting [2,3,4,5,6]. Along the same line, we present a new formulation of ILP that systematically exploits caching to achieve greater efficiency and flexibility, and present theoretical results that characterize it.

The fundamental building blocks for our approach are a new data structure and an extension operation for hypotheses that expose and exploit opportunities for caching the results of previous computation. This provides an immediate benefit by avoiding the redundant computation pervasive in the standard ILP search and score paradigm. Further, the extension operation is formulated as a set-oriented computational strategy defined in terms of (extended) relational

---

* Work was supported by Air Force Grant F30602-01-2-0571, DARPA ISTO Grant HR0011-04-0007 and a Ford Fellowship from the National Academy of Sciences.

S. Kramer and B. Pfahringer (Eds.): ILP 2005, LNAI 3625, pp. 69–86, 2005.
© Springer-Verlag Berlin Heidelberg 2005

database operations, facilitating the use of relational query-processing techniques in ILP systems.

Extensional representations of hypotheses are treated as first-class objects. Consequently, statistics derived from these objects are easily maintained, and can be used to define alternatives to guide the search process in ILP. For example, probabilistic methods for search [7,3,4,8,9] can directly use statistics derived from our new data structure for representing hypotheses.

Additionally, statistics derived from an extensional representation of hypotheses offer new avenues for learning a class of rules richer class than Horn clauses. For example, rules containing statements about aggregates [10], and rules containing probabilistic statements, such as statements about missing values [11], can be generated. While these extensions are beyond the scope of this paper, we investigate a scheme for restricting the hypothesis search space using Inverse Entailment based on a set of multiple seed examples. Our algorithm for Generalized Inverse Entailment offers flexibility and robustness in hypothesis space restriction, including alternative seed-coverage measures (which we study in this paper) and cost-based measures that can be readily obtained from our hypothesis representation.

Our main contributions are as follows:

(1) New data representation and extension-join operation (Section 3), with a discussion of potential benefits (Section 3.2).
(2) New set-oriented hypothesis generation framework, with proof of soundness and completeness with respect to inverse entailment under subsumption for the single-seed case (Section 4).
(3) Generalization of inverse entailment to the multiple-seeds case; extension of our hypothesis generation framework to this case; and a proof of soundness and completeness with respect to a generalized coverage measure (Section 5).

2 Mode-Restricted Languages

The ILP task consists of learning a logic program that models a dataset of ground facts, given as two disjoint sets of positive examples and negative examples. We are also given "background knowledge" in the form of additional facts or predicates defined as Horn clauses. The learned program is a set of Horn clauses that, when added to the background knowledge, entails as many of the positive example facts as possible while entailing as few of the negative example facts as possible. Each clause, or hypothesis, in the learned program is built from the predicates given in the background knowledge, and we assume they are functor-free Horn clauses. In this section we define the space of hypotheses we seek to represent.

We borrow the concept of user-specified "modes" that constrain the space of allowable hypotheses from the Aleph [12] and Progol [13] ILP systems.

Definition 1. *A mode is defined by* $(p/n, B, F)$ *where:* p *is an* n-*ary background predicate,* B *is the list of arguments of* p *specified to be* bound, F *is the list of arguments of* p *specified to be* free.

Further restrictions are that B and F are disjoint sets, every argument in the predicate is specified as either *bound* or *free*, and at least one *bound* argument is specified. (We do not include the case where modes specify arguments to be constants, but our results apply to this case as well.)

Definition 2. *A moded literal* $p^*(A, \ldots, N)$ *is the adornment of a literal as specified by the binding pattern in a mode.*

As an example, let q be a background predicate. If $q(A, B)$ is a literal, and mode $(q/2, [1], [2])$ is defined, then $q^{bf}(A, B)$ is an allowed moded literal. The first argument of q is specified as bound, that is, an input argument in the usual ILP nomenclature, while the second is specified as free, that is, an output argument. In the rest of this paper, we treat arguments in literals as implicit when their details are not required, and use p^* to denote moded literals.

For convenience, we define the following operations on moded literals: let p^* be the moded literal specified by mode $(p/n, B, F)$, then: $\text{bound}(p^*) = B$, $\text{free}(p^*) = F$, $\text{vars}(p^*) = B \cup F$, and $\text{pred}(p^*) = p$.

Given a set of modes, we denote the set of allowable moded literals as $\mathcal{M}$. From now on, we assume every literal in a hypothesis is a moded literal and leave the adornment implicit when not needed. With this set of allowable moded literals the mode-restricted set of hypotheses can be defined recursively as follows:

Definition 3. *Given a set of allowable moded literals* $\mathcal{M}$, *and a target predicate* h, *the set* $H(\mathcal{M}, h)$ *of hypotheses allowable in the mode-restricted language is recursively defined as:* $H(\mathcal{M}, h) = \{(h \leftarrow \text{true.})\} \cup \{(h \leftarrow r_1, \ldots, r_n, p.) : (h \leftarrow r_1, \ldots, r_n.) \in H(\mathcal{M}, h), p \in \mathcal{M}, \text{ and } \text{bound}(p) \subseteq \text{Vars}(h \leftarrow r_1, \ldots, r_n.)\}$

The set of variables $\text{Vars}(h \leftarrow r_1, \ldots, r_n.)$ of a hypothesis is the union of the variable sets of its literals. That is, $\text{Vars}(h \leftarrow r_1, \ldots r_n.) = \text{vars}(h) \bigcup_{i=1}^{n} \text{vars}(r_i)$. The given positive facts we want to model are instances of the target predicate h. For example, let r and q be background predicates and let there be modes that specify the adornments r^{bf} and q^{fb}. Then, $\hat{h} = (h(A) \leftarrow r^{bf}(A, B), q^{fb}(C, B).) \in H(\mathcal{M}, h)$, while $\hat{h} = (h(A) \leftarrow r^{bf}(A, B), q^{fb}(B, C).) \notin H(\mathcal{M}, h)$.

The set $H(\mathcal{M}, h)$ in Definition 3 is the set of hypothesis we want to capture using our representation.

3   The WILD Representation

We seek to represent hypotheses in $H(\mathcal{M}, h)$ in such a way that, intuitively, the result of operating on a hypothesis is reused when operating on an extension of the hypothesis. For instance, when measuring the coverage of a hypothesis, the substitution found in proving that a hypothesis covers an example contains bindings which could potentially make an extension of the hypothesis cover the same example. Our representation should reuse those bindings when measuring the coverage of the extended hypothesis.

Another objective is that useful statistics regarding a hypothesis should be easy to derive and maintain from the representation of hypotheses. Continuing with the example, we want the coverage of a hypothesis for a given example to be easily recoverable from our data structure. However, we are interested in maintaining statistics that are useful for measures other than coverage. We now define a data representation and extension operation for hypotheses that meet these goals.

Definition 4. *Hypothesis* $\hat{h} \in H(\mathcal{M}, h)$ *is represented by the pair* $\langle \hat{h}, t \rangle$, *where* t *is a database table.* t *has schema* $t[id, fid, A, \ldots, N]$, *where* id *is a unique (across all existing tables) row identifier;* fid *is the unique identifier of the 'parent' row; and* $A, \ldots, N$ *are variable names appearing in* $\hat{h}$.

Each row of t is a binding that makes $\hat{h}$ cover a fact e in a set of seeds E. The schema of t serves to share common subsets of bindings between hypotheses by its use of the *id* and *fid* fields. Given a set of seeds, an initial table is built where *fid* is *null* and each seed is represented by one row.

As an example, consider hypothesis $\hat{h}_1 = (h(X, Y) \leftarrow q^{bf}(X, Z).)$, along with seed table t_0 shown in Fig. 1(a), built for the seed set $\{h(a, b), h(a', b)\}$. Let the facts $q(a, c)$ and $q(a', c')$ be in the table for background predicate q. $\hat{h}_1$ is represented as the intensional/extensional pair $\langle h(X, Y) \leftarrow q^{bf}(X, Z)., t_1 \rangle$, where t_1 is shown in Fig. 1(b).

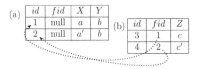

Fig. 1. (a) Initial table t_0. (b) Table for pair $\langle \hat{h}_1 = (h(X, Y) \leftarrow q^{bf}(X, Z).), t_1 \rangle$.

Continuing this example, let the facts $r(b, d)$ and $r(b, e)$ be in the base table for background predicate r. We represent the hypothesis $\hat{h}_2 = (h(X, Y) \leftarrow q^{bf}(X, Z), r^{bf}(Y, W).)$ as pair $\langle \hat{h}_2, t_2 \rangle$, where t_2 is shown in Fig. 2(a) along with its references to t_1 for illustration.

We could avoid indirection and store all variable bindings for a corresponding seed in each row. However, significant savings are obtained by not storing shared bindings redundantly. For example, given pair $\langle \hat{h}_1, t_1 \rangle$ above, all hypotheses that are extensions of $\hat{h}_1$, including $\hat{h}_2$, share bindings for variables appearing in table t_1. Using chained tables allows these bindings to be stored once, and extensions then refer to these bindings through indirection. Otherwise, each new table would store a copy of table t_1 along with any new bindings. The use of unique row ids allows tables to be unambiguously reconstructed from the chained tables when necessary. For the running example, the reconstructed table for t_2 is shown in Fig. 2(b).

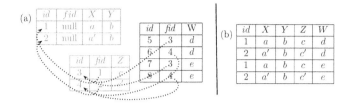

Fig. 2. (a) Table t_2 in pair $\langle \hat{h}_2, t_2 \rangle$ with its references to t_0 and t_1. (b) Reconstructed version of t_2.

3.1   Extension-Join

Using this representation, we formulate hypothesis extension as a stylized join operation on database tables [14]. This operation takes as input two intensional/extensional pairs as described above. The first $\langle \hat{h}_n = (h \leftarrow r_1, \ldots, r_n), t_n \rangle$ is a hypothesis pair as in definition 4. The second, $\langle p, \mathrm{pred}(p) \rangle$, consists of a moded literal p and its corresponding base table $\mathrm{pred}(p)$. The result of the operation is a new hypothesis pair $\langle \hat{h}_{i+1} = (h \leftarrow r_1, \ldots, r_n, p), t_{i+1} \rangle$. Each substitution in t_i is extended according to the moded literal and those that make the new hypothesis h_{i+1} cover the corresponding seed $e \in E$ are retained in the new table t_{i+1}. We denote this operation as $\langle \hat{h}_{i+1}, t_{i+1} \rangle = \langle \hat{h}_i, t_i \rangle \bowtie \langle p, \mathrm{pred}(p) \rangle$.

The extension-join operation combines a number of steps, the most significant of which is an equi-join of the input tables. The remaining steps are for bookkeeping, and set up the equi-join to capture the proper variable bindings of the extension. Extension-join is defined by Algorithm 1.

Algorithm 1: The Extension-Join operation
Input: Hypothesis pair $\langle h_i, t_i \rangle$ and extension $\langle p, \mathrm{pred}(p) \rangle$
Output: Extended hypothesis pair $\langle h_{i+1}, t_{i+1} \rangle$
X-JOIN($\langle h_i, t_i \rangle, \langle p, \mathrm{pred}(p) \rangle$)
(1)   compute projection of t_i
(2)   build join constraints and result projection list
(3)   execute join and result projection
(4)   **if** result is not empty make new table t_{i+1}
(5)   let $h_i = (h \leftarrow r_1, \ldots, r_n.)$, and set $h_{i+1} = (h \leftarrow r_1, \ldots, r_n, p.)$
(6)   output $\langle h_{i+1}, t_{i+1} \rangle$

We present the details of these steps using the running example. To create pair $\langle \hat{h}_2, t_2 \rangle$ we calculate $\langle \hat{h}_1, t_1 \rangle \bowtie \langle r^{bf}(Y, W), \mathrm{pred}(r) \rangle$, where t_1 is shown in Fig. 1(b) and the table $\mathrm{pred}(r)$ contains the facts $r(b, d)$ and $r(b, e)$.

1. Compute projection of t_i. We project the input hypothesis table to only those columns containing the bound arguments of the extension, following *fid* fields to gather necessary variable bindings. We also keep the id and fid columns required for chaining rows in the result t_{i+1} to rows in t_i. In our example, t_1 is projected to table t_1' shown in Fig. 3(a). For extension $r^{bf}(Y, W)$ only column Y is needed since Y is the only *bound* argument of $r^{bf}(Y, W)$.

(a)

id	fid	Y
3	1	b
4	2	b

(b)

$t.id$	$t.fid$	$\mathrm{pred}(r).2$
3	1	d
4	2	d
3	1	e
4	2	e

Fig. 3. (a) Table t_1', the projection of t_1 to bound arguments of extension. (b) Result of equi-join of t_1' and $\mathrm{pred}(r)$ after projection to identifier and free argument columns.

In principle, several extensions to a given hypothesis require the same bound variables from the input hypothesis table. The result of extension-joining each of these extensions and the input hypothesis can be computed simultaneously using a single projection of the input hypothesis table. This first step in the extension-join operation permits set-oriented optimizations of this kind.

2. Build join constraints and result projection list . This step finds common bindings between the input hypothesis and its extension using the input moded literal. These bindings are expressed as constraints on an equi-join operation, the result of which is then projected to only those columns required for chaining and those containing new variables.

For a given pair of operands, a list c of join constraints of the form $t_i.j = p.k$ is constructed, where j is a variable column in t_i and k is a column of base table p. For our current example, $c = \{t_1'.Y = \mathrm{pred}(r).1\}$ since the first column of $\mathrm{pred}(r)$ is specified as a *bound* argument and variable Y is assigned to that column in $r^{bf}(Y, W)$. A list of column names l is constructed as $\{t_i.id, t_i, fid, p.x_1, \ldots, p.x_m\}$ where $p.x_1, \ldots, p.x_m$ are the columns of base table p that do not appear in the join constraints in list c. In the example $l = \{t_1'.id, t_1'.fid, \mathrm{pred}(r).2\}$ since column 2 of $\mathrm{pred}(r)$ is not involved in any constraint in list c.

3. Execute join and projection . The result of the previous step is used to execute an equi-join on the two input tables. This operation is defined by the relational algebra [14] expression $\pi_l(t_i \bowtie_c p)$ where $\bowtie_c$ is an equi-join under the constraints given in list c, and π_l is a projection to the columns listed in l. This has the effect of extending substitutions in input table t_i with bindings from the input base predicate. For our running example, the result of $\pi_{\{t_1'.id, t_1'.fid, \mathrm{pred}(r).2\}}(t_1' \bowtie_{t_1'.Y = \mathrm{pred}(r).1} \mathrm{pred}(r))$ is shown in Fig. 3(b).

4. If result is not empty, build new table t_{i+1} . This step transforms the result of the previous step so it conforms to the hypothesis schema. It also chains the rows in t_{i+1} to rows of t_i by making the proper entries in the *fid* column of the new table. Column names for the new table are derived from the moded literal and a unique id is generated for each row in the result. The final result for our example, t_2, was shown in Fig. 2.

By Definition 4 and the extension-join in Algorithm 1, all hypothesis tables contain a unique identifier for each row, and refer to the unique identifier of a parent row. Since the seed table t_0 contains exactly one row for each seed example e in seed set E, a row identifier e_{id} can be uniquely associated with each seed example. Thus, any row in subsequent tables can be associated with a seed example $e \in E$ using the row identifier e_{id} in seed table t_0, by following fid links. We define a selection operation, denoted $\sigma_e(t)$, and a projection operation, denoted $E(t)$, that use these row identifiers:

Definition 5. *Let* $\hat{h} = (h \leftarrow r_1, \ldots, r_n)$ *and*

$$\langle \hat{h}, t \rangle = \langle (h \leftarrow .), t_0 \rangle \bowtie \langle r_1, \mathrm{pred}(r_1) \rangle \bowtie \cdots \bowtie \langle r_n, \mathrm{pred}(r_n) \rangle$$

such that seed table t_0 *is built from a seed example set* E, *and* t_x *is the reconstruction of* t *through* fid *fields as described above. Then:*

1. *$E(t) \stackrel{def}{=} \pi_{id}(t_x)$ is the projection of t to its example identifiers, where π is the relational algebra projection operator.*
2. *$\sigma_e(t) \stackrel{def}{=} \sigma_{id=e_{id}}(t_x)$ is the selection of t to rows involving seed e, where e_{id} is the row identifier for seed $e \in E$ in the initial table t_0, and σ is the relational algebra selection operator.*

A useful property of the extension-join operation is that selection on examples for a hypothesis table can be pushed to a selection on the original table of seeds t_0. We formalize this with the following lemma:

Lemma 1. *Let* $\hat{h}_m = (h \leftarrow r_1, \ldots, r_m.) \in H(\mathcal{M}, h)$,

$$\langle \hat{h}_m, t_m \rangle = \langle (h \leftarrow \mathrm{true.}), t_0 \rangle \bowtie \langle r_1, \mathrm{pred}(r_1) \rangle \bowtie \cdots \bowtie \langle r_m, \mathrm{pred}(r_m) \rangle,$$

such that seed table t_0 *is built from a seed example set* E, *and let* $\langle \hat{h}_n, t_n \rangle = \langle \hat{h}_m, t_m \rangle \bowtie \langle r_n, \mathrm{pred}(r_n) \rangle$.

For every $e \in E$, *if* $\langle \hat{h}_n, t_e \rangle \stackrel{def}{=} \langle \hat{h}_m, \sigma_e(t_m) \rangle \bowtie \langle r_n, \mathrm{pred}(r_n) \rangle$, *then* $t_e = \sigma_e(t_n)$, *where* σ_e *is the selection operation of Definition 5.*

Proof. Let e_{id} be the unique row identifier for example e in seed table t_0.

$(\sigma_e(t_n) \subseteq t_e)$. Let $t_e \subset \sigma_e(t_n)$, then there is a tuple $s \in \sigma_e(t_n)$ such that $s \notin t_e$. Let s be the result of joining tuples $s' \in t_m$ and $s'' \in \mathrm{pred}(r_n)$ according to the definition of extension-join. Since $s \in \sigma_e(t_n)$, the $s.id = e_{id}$, by definition of extension-join, $s'.id = s.id. = e_{id}$. However, since $s \notin t_e$, the definition of extension-join implies $s' \notin \sigma_e(t_m)$. This is a contradiction since we established $s'.id = e_{id}$.

$(t_e \subseteq \sigma_e(t))$. Conversely, let $\sigma_e(t_n) \subset t_e$, then there is a tuple $s \in t_e$ such that $s \notin \sigma_e(t_n)$. Let s be the result of joining tuples $s' \in \sigma_e(t_m)$ and $s'' \in \mathrm{pred}(r_n)$ according to the definition of extension-join. Since $s' \in \sigma_e(t_m)$, $s' \in t_m$

which implies by definition of extension-join that $s \in t_n$. Furthermore, since $s' \in \sigma_e(t_m)$, we have $s'.id = e_{id}$, and the definition of extension-join implies $s.id = e_{id}$. We have shown that $s \in t_n$ and $s.id = e_{id}$, but $s \notin \sigma_e(t_n)$. This is a contradiction. $\square$

It is worth noting that existing work addresses issues we present here. For example, data structures used in algorithms for testing θ-subsumption [15,16,17] store multiple substitutions compactly to avoid backtracking when finding satisfying substitutions. However, the compact representation used can make maintaining statistics of the type we discuss below difficult. On the other hand, the data structure for storing multiple substitutions used in the LogAn-H system [18] uses the reconstructed tables we discuss above which store information redundantly.

Techniques that store only coverage lists or some computed answers meet some, but not all, of our goals. For example, storing coverage lists [19] or a technique such as tuple-id propagation [20] allows for compact storage and fast retrieval of statistics used to determine coverage measures of a hypothesis in a classification setting. However other types statistics, those not involving coverage as used in some probabilistic models, for example, are not easily derivable. We present a formulation that seeks to balance the two goals of caching and availability of general statistics.

3.2   Benefits of the WILD Representation

We identify two general areas in which our representation offers advantages:

1. Within the current search and score paradigm in ILP, this framework allows for efficiency, scalability and flexibility.
2. This framework easily adapts to settings where learning theories in languages other than Horn clauses is desired.

We discuss these benefits below.

Caching Benefits. Each table contains those bindings required to determine the coverage properties of a hypothesis $\hat{h}$ with respect to the seed table t_0. Once these bindings are cached by pair $\langle \hat{h}, t \rangle$, they can be reused to determine coverage properties of extensions to $\hat{h}$. This is exploited in the context of search-space restriction in the next section.

Set-oriented Hypothesis Extension. The extension-join operation can be carried out efficiently in a relational database system since it is defined in terms of relational operations. Thus, ILP could potentially be carried out on disk-resident data.

There are also set-oriented optimizations that can be performed at the tuple level during extension-join. For instance, earlier we described an optimization where extension-join on a particular hypothesis and a set of its extensions (for example, modes that share a base table) is executed in a set-oriented fashion. This optimization is in the spirit of the query packs presented by Blockeel et al. [5]

Alternative Search Methods. The cached table for a hypothesis pair can be used to maintain statistics that help in defining the hypothesis search-space, and in exploring that space. In this paper we present an application in which statistics from extensional tables are used to restrict the space of allowable hypotheses.

As another example, stochastic search methods can use prior distributions over the space to guide search towards probably useful parts of the space [7,8]. A hypothesis space generated and, thus, defined using our representation can use an informative prior derived from coverage statistics derivable from cached tables.

Similarly, estimates of a given property of hypotheses can also be used to guide search. For example, estimates of the coverage of a hypothesis may be used to specify which parts of the hypothesis space to explore [4,9]. Under our representation, these estimates are derived from a cached table resulting from the extension-join of background predicates to some representative set of seeds. Another method might use our representation to estimate how efficiently a hypotheses can be evaluated. For example, Struyf and Blockeel [3] estimate a prior on the selectivity of literals to decide an efficient literal reordering for a given hypothesis. Statistics derived from our representation can provide good estimates of the selectivity of a literal.

Language Extensions. This framework permits learning rules in languages other than sets of Horn clauses. For example, we can use statistics in the cached table for a hypothesis to train a statistical model that infers missing values in other instances of similar datasets. This is the formulation for CLP(BN) [11], a language easily incorporated into our hypothesis framework.

Alternatively, we can use statistics in the cached table to make distributional statements regarding variables in a hypothesis. For example, we can estimate the distribution of a column in our target predicate and determine its correlation to subsets of other columns in the background knowledge using statistics derived from cached tables. This allows for statements of the type *rich people tend to live in big houses* to be made in the learned program.

Extensions to the Datalog language have been proposed that add the ability to group constants and calculate aggregates on these groups [21]. By having cached tables available, these groups can be defined and aggregates calculated on the fly during the learning process. This may allow for statements about aggregates like those described by Vens et al. [10]. Another Datalog extension is the use of negated literals in clauses. This is allowed through the requirement that programs be stratified with respect to negation. Since we assume a set-oriented, bottom-up evaluation strategy in our system, we can expect to learn stratified programs with negated literals.

The remainder of this paper presents an initial example of the benefits of the WILD representation and the avenues it opens when defining the ILP task. We look at how the space of allowable hypotheses can be defined using background knowledge about multiple facts in the target predicate.

4   An Initial Application

The Aleph and Progol systems restrict the set of hypotheses in the search space through *Inverse Entailment* [13]. A specific seed example is chosen to generate a set of literals, known as the bottom clause, by finding facts in the background knowledge that are relevant to the chosen seed example. The space of hypotheses is restricted to include only generalizations of this bottom clause, consequently, all hypotheses generated will cover the seed example. This process seeks to restrict search to useful hypotheses. However, a seed defines a space of hypotheses that are useful only in respect to that seed.

In the presence of noise in data, restricting the search space based on a single seed is potentially wasteful. For instance, suppose that a few positive examples are mislabelled, and are in fact negative examples. Using any of these examples as seeds will restrict the search space to hypotheses that probably cover many negative examples. Hypothesis evaluation based on coverage will then try to find a, possibly non-existent, very specific clause that differentiates between negative examples. While search parameters can be used to alleviate this, a minimum positive example coverage constraint for example, a principled method that avoids this phenomenon while defining the search space is best.

If a 'usefulness' restriction is imposed on the search space defined in terms of multiple seeds, then the effect of an unfavorable choice of seed might be mitigated by true representative seeds in the set. Furthermore, it would be useful to provide a degree of freedom in how the space restriction is defined in terms of the multiple seeds. We show how a hypothesis generation strategy using the WILD representation meets these goals by generalizing Inverse Entailment to multiple seeds.

First, we describe Inverse Entailment in more detail and then show how the WILD representation is used to define a hypothesis space. Specifically, how it is used to define a space using Inverse Entailment in the single-seed case. Finally, we define a generalization of Inverse Entailment and show it defines a class of 'usefulness' restrictions that can be imposed on the hypothesis space.

4.1   Inverse Entailment

Inverse Entailment constructs a set of literals that defines the allowable hypotheses in the search space. In practice, this construction is done using a partitioning approach: the first partition contains the constants appearing in the seed example; at each step of the iteration, instances of the constants in the current partition are found in each background predicate as specified in any of the binding patterns defined by the given modes; each ground literal containing instances is added to the bottom clause and new constants appearing in these literals are added to the next partition if the corresponding argument is specified as *free* in some mode. This is repeated until no new constants are added to the next partition or a user-defined bound on the number of iterations performed is met. To finalize, the ground literals in the bottom clause are 'variabilized' according to the given set of modes. Here and below we leave out a bound on hypothesis length for clarity, but this can be easily implemented.

Allowable hypotheses in the search space are valid ordered subsets of the literals in the bottom clause. Literals can only be used to extend a hypothesis if it appears in the bottom clause and variables appearing in its *bound* arguments must appear in the hypothesis to be extended. The subset of $H(\mathcal{M}, h)$ built from a given bottom clause can now be defined.

Definition 6. *Given a set of allowable moded literals* $\mathcal{M}$, *target predicate* h, *seed example* e, *depth bound* k *and background knowledge* $\mathcal{B}$, *let* $\perp_e$ *be the bottom clause built from seed example* e. *Define the set of hypotheses* $H_A(e)$ *generated from* $\perp_e$ *as* $H_A(\mathcal{M}, h, e, k, \mathcal{B}) = \{(h \leftarrow \text{true}.)\} \cup \{h \leftarrow r_1, \dots, r_n, p. : (h \leftarrow r_1, \dots, r_n.) \in H_A(\mathcal{M}, h, e, k, \mathcal{B}), p \in \perp_e,$ *and* $\text{bound}(p) \subseteq \text{Vars}(h \leftarrow r_1, \dots, r_n.).\}$

Remark 1. We stated previously that all hypotheses in set $H_A(\mathcal{M}, h, e, k, \mathcal{B})$ will cover the seed example e. Muggleton proved in [13] that Inverse Entailment is complete under θ-subsumption, thus if the depth bound is relaxed, that is, if $k = \infty$, for a given $\hat{h} \in H(\mathcal{M}, h)$, $\hat{h} \wedge \mathcal{B} \vdash e$ if, and only if, $\hat{h} \in H_A(\mathcal{M}, h, e, \infty, \mathcal{B})$.

4.2   WILD Hypothesis Generation

This process of Inverse Entailment can be generalized to a set-oriented formulation. Instead of a single seed example being used to restrict the search space, a set of examples is used along with a filter function that determines which candidate hypotheses can be included in the search space. This generalized version of Inverse Entailment, like the original Aleph/Progol version, benefits from bottom-up computation. Using the representation and the extension-join operation of Section 3, we propose the following algorithm for generating hypotheses:

Algorithm 2: WILD Hypothesis Generator
Input: Set of allowable moded literals $\mathcal{M}$, target predicate h, seed fact set E, depth bound k, background knowledge $\mathcal{B}$, filter-function ϕ
Output: Set of hypotheses
GENERATEH$(\mathcal{M}, h, E, k, \mathcal{B}, \phi)$
(1)   openset $= \{\langle (h \leftarrow \text{true}.), t_0 \rangle\}$, ($t_0$ built from seed set E)
(2)   output $\langle (h \leftarrow \text{true}.), t_0 \rangle$
(3)   **while** openset is not empty
(4)   choose and remove $\langle \hat{h}_i, t_i \rangle$ from openset
(5)   **foreach** moded predicate p that is a valid extension to $\hat{h}_i$
(6)   compute $\langle \hat{h}_{i+1}, t_{i+1} \rangle = \langle \hat{h}_i, t_i \rangle \bowtie \langle p, \text{pred}(p) \rangle$
(7)   **if** $\phi(t_{i+1})$ is true
(8)   output $\langle \hat{h}_{i+1}, t_{i+1} \rangle$ as an allowable hypothesis
(9)   **if** depth of $\hat{h}_{i+1} \leq k$
(10)   add $\langle \hat{h}_{i+1}, t_{i+1} \rangle$ to openset

Valid extensions here are as in set $H(\mathcal{M}, h)$, that is: $\text{bound}(p) \subseteq \text{Vars}(h_i)$ so that arguments marked *bound* are assigned a variable already appearing in the hypothesis to be extended. In step 9, the depth of h_{i+1} as defined by Muggleton in [13] is easily obtained from t_{i+1}. First, we define $\hat{h}_0 = (h \leftarrow \text{true})$ to have depth 0. If the depth of $\hat{h}_i$ is j, and table t_{i+1} has columns for variables not appearing in t_i, then the depth $\hat{h}_{i+1}$ is $j + 1$.

Using the WILD hypothesis generator we formulate a strategy to enumerate the set of hypotheses generated by Inverse Entailment in the single-seed case. First, we make the seed set $E = \{e\}$ a singleton set. We then set the filter function ϕ to take a table as input, and return true if the table is not empty. We'll denote this emptiness-testing function as ϕ_{empty}. We prove in the following proposition that with these parameters, we can generate a complete and sound set of hypotheses that cover the given single seed e.

Proposition 1. Soundness and Completeness of WILD Generation for a Single Seed. *Let $H_B(e) = \text{GENERATEH}(\mathcal{M}, h, \{e\}, \infty, \mathcal{B}, \phi_{\text{empty}})$. Hypothesis $\hat{h} \in H(\mathcal{M}, h)$ covers e if, and only if, there exists table t such that $\langle \hat{h}, t \rangle \in H_B(e)$.*

Proof. (Only if). Proceeds by induction on n, the number of literals in $\hat{h}$. If $n = 1$ we have that $\hat{h}$ must be of the form $(h \leftarrow \text{true.})$. $\hat{h}$ covers e by a unique substitution θ that maps variables in h to constants in e such that $h[\theta] = e$. That is, the result of applying substitution θ to literal h is e. By construction, in Step 2 of Algorithm 2, we have $\langle \hat{h}, t_0 \rangle \in H_B(e)$.

Let the 'only if' direction of the Proposition be true for all $n \leq m - 1$; thus we assume that for each $\hat{h}_{m-1} = (h \leftarrow r_1, \ldots, r_{m-1}.) \in H$ that covers e, there exists a table t_{m-1} such that $\langle \hat{h}_{m-1}, t_{m-1} \rangle \in H_B(e)$. We show that for each extension $\hat{h}_m$ to $\hat{h}_{m-1}$ such that $\hat{h}_m = (h \leftarrow r_1, \ldots, r_{m-1}, r_m.)$ covers e, there is a pair $\langle \hat{h}_m, t_m \rangle \in H_B(e)$.

Since $\hat{h}_m$ covers e we must have that $\hat{h}_{m-1}$ also covers e, and thus by the inductive hypothesis, there is table t_{m-1} such that $\langle \hat{h}_{m-1}, t_{m-1} \rangle \in H_B(e)$. Also, since $\hat{h}_m$ covers e, there exists a substitution θ such that $h[\theta] = e$ and for each i, $1 \leq i \leq m$ there is a tuple $s \in \text{pred}(r_i)$ such that $r_i[\theta] = s_i$, specifically there is a tuple $s_m \in \text{pred}(r_m)$ such that $r_m[\theta] = s_m$. Let

$$\langle \hat{h}_m, t_m \rangle = \langle \hat{h}_{m-1}, t_{m-1} \rangle \bowtie \langle r_m, \text{pred}(r_m) \rangle,$$

then due to tuple $s_m \in \text{pred}(r_m)$ and the definition of extension-join, there is at least one tuple in t_m, that is, $\phi_{\text{empty}}(t_m) = \text{true}$. This implies $\langle \hat{h}_m, t_m \rangle \in H_B(e)$ as desired.

(If). Now we prove that if there is a pair $\langle \hat{h}, t \rangle \in H_B(e)$, then $\hat{h}$ covers e. Proceed by induction on n, the number of literals in $\hat{h}$. If $n = 1$ then we have $\langle \hat{h} = (h \leftarrow \text{true.}), t_0 \rangle \in H_B(e)$, and by construction we have that t_0 is built from the constants appearing in e. We build a substitution θ from t_0 such that $h[\theta] = e$ which makes $\hat{h}$ cover e.

Let the 'if' direction of the claim be true for all $n \leq m - 1$, and assume that if $\langle \hat{h}_{m-1} = (h \leftarrow r_1, \ldots, r_{m-1}.), t_{m-1} \rangle \in H_B(e)$ then $\hat{h}_{m-1}$ covers e. We show that for each extension $\langle \hat{h}_m, t_m \rangle = \langle \hat{h}_{m-1}, t_{m-1} \rangle \bowtie \langle r_m, \text{pred}(r_m) \rangle \in H_B(e)$, $\hat{h}_m = (h \leftarrow r_1, \ldots, r_{m-1}, r_m.)$ covers e.

Since $\langle \hat{h}_m, t_m \rangle \in H_B(e)$, we have that $\langle \hat{h}_{m-1}, t_{m-1} \rangle \in H_B(e)$. By the inductive hypothesis, there is a substitution θ' such that $h[\theta'] = e$ and there is a tuple $s_i \in \mathrm{pred}(r_i)$ for all i, $1 \leq i \leq m - 1$, such that $r_i[\theta'] = s_i$. Since $\langle \hat{h}_m, t_m \rangle \in H_B(e)$ we know that $\phi_{\mathrm{empty}}(t_m) = \mathrm{true}$, thus there is at least one tuple $s_m \in t_m$. We build a substitution σ with a domain consisting of variables not appearing in θ', which corresponds to arguments of r_m in $\mathrm{free}(r_m)$. We bind the variables in σ to the constants appearing in the corresponding arguments in tuple s_m. Since $\mathrm{bound}(r_m)$ is a subset of the domain of θ', we can build the substitution $\theta = \theta'\sigma$. The result is that $h[\theta] = e$, and there is a tuple $s_i \in \mathrm{pred}(r_i)$ for all i, $1 \leq i \leq m - 1$ such that $r_i[\theta] = s_i$. Finally due to the definition of equi-join, there is a tuple $s_m \in \mathrm{pred}(r_m)$ such that $r_m[\theta] = s_m$. This implies $\hat{h}_m$ covers e as desired.   □

The following corollary follows from Proposition 1 and Remark 1.

Corollary 1. *WILD Generates the Inverse Entailment Space for a Single Seed.* Let $H_B(e) = \mathrm{GENERATEH}(\mathcal{M}, h, \{e\}, \infty, \mathcal{B}, \phi_{\mathrm{empty}})$, and $H_A(e)$ be as in Definition 6, then for every $\hat{h} \in H(\mathcal{M}, h)$, $\hat{h} \in H_A(e)$ if, and only if there exits table t such that $\langle \hat{h}, t \rangle \in H_B(e)$.

Proof. Follows trivially from Proposition 1 and Remark 1. as both sets contain exactly the subset of $H(\mathcal{M}, h)$ that cover single seed e.   □

5   Generalized Inverse Entailment

We now present a scheme for generalizing Inverse Entailment using multiple seeds. It uses the parameters in the WILD generation algorithm to restrict the set of allowable hypotheses. Specifically, the filter function is used to only allow generation of hypotheses that meet some coverage criteria. Inverse Entailment is generalized in the sense that while the criterion used for restriction in Inverse Entailment is that hypotheses cover a single seed, we use a class of measures of the coverage of a hypotheses over the set of seed examples. This class of measures is implemented as the filter function ϕ of the WILD generation algorithm.

Given a set of seed examples we denote the subset of seeds covered by a hypothesis $\hat{h} \in H(\mathcal{M}, h)$ as $E(\hat{h})$.

Definition 7. Let $\hat{h} \in H(\mathcal{M}, h)$, then: $E(\hat{h}) = \{e \in E \mid \hat{h} \in H_A(e)\}$, where $H_A(e)$ is the set of hypotheses generated by Inverse Entailment from the single seed example e as in Definition 6.

Intuitively, $e \in E(\hat{h})$ if $\hat{h}$ is a hypothesis generated from the bottom clause built from seed e. This is equivalent to stating, due to Remark 1, that $e \in E(\hat{h})$ if $\hat{h}$ covers e.

We define two filter functions we propose and evaluate in this paper. Given a subset $E' \subseteq E$, define:

1. *Intersection:* $\phi_{\mathrm{int}}(E') = $ true if $E' = E$. We will claim in Proposition 2 that the hypotheses generated by the WILD hypothesis generator using this filter are those hypotheses that would be generated by *every* bottom clause built, in turn, by a seed in E. That is, the resulting space is the intersection of the spaces defined by the set of Aleph bottom clauses.
2. *Support:* $\phi_{\mathrm{sup}}(E') = $ true if, for a given threshold η, $|E'|/|E| \geq \eta$. We borrow this concept from frequent itemset and relational pattern mining algorithms, [22,23] and use it to generalize the coverage assumptions of Inverse Entailment. This introduces an extra parameter that can be used to determine the amount of filtering to apply. We will claim in Proposition 2 that the hypotheses generated using this filter are those that cover at least $\eta|E|$ seed examples. Notice that if $\eta = 1$, this is equivalent to ϕ_{int} above.

Notice that these functions are monotonic on the size of seed subset E' and that they return true for the entire set E. We formalize this in the following definition and use these properties when proving our main result in Proposition 2.

Definition 8. *Proper Filter Function.* *Let E be a set of seed examples and $E' \subseteq E$. A filter function ϕ is **proper** when (1) if $\phi(E') = $ true then for any superset $E'' \supseteq E'$: $E'' = $ true; and (2) $\phi(E) = $ true.*

Below, we take $\phi(t)$ where t is a table in an intensional/extensional pair, to mean $\phi(E(t))$ where $E(t)$ is the projection of t to its example identifiers as in Definition 5.

We can now present our main result regarding generalized Inverse Entailment which states that the WILD generator will produce only, and all, hypotheses in $H(\mathcal{M}, h)$ that meet the criteria imposed by the filter function. That is, it generates those hypotheses we deem as useful with respect to the set of seed examples.

Proposition 2. *Soundness and Completeness of WILD Generation for Multiple Seeds.* *Let $H_W(E) \overset{def}{=} $ GENERATEH$(\mathcal{M}, h, E, \infty, \mathcal{B}, \phi)$ be the set of hypotheses generated by the WILD generator for seed set E such that ϕ is a proper filter as specified in Definition 8. For all $\hat{h} \in H(\mathcal{M}, h)$, $\phi(E(\hat{h})) = $ true if, and only if, there exists a table t such that $\langle \hat{h}, t \rangle \in H_W(E)$.*

We use two Lemmas to prove this result. Once these are stated and proven we present the proof of Proposition 2. Throughout we denote as $H_B(e) \overset{def}{=} $ GENERATEH$(\mathcal{M}, h, \{e\}, \infty, \mathcal{B}, \phi_{\mathrm{empty}})$ the set of hypotheses described in Proposition 1, that is, the set of hypotheses generated by the WILD hypothesis generator for single seed e, using the emptiness-testing function ϕ_{empty}. Also, we denote as $H_A(e)$ the set from Definition 6, that is, the set of hypotheses generated by Inverse Entailment using single seed e. Recall from Corollary 1 that sets $H_A(e)$ and $H_B(e)$ are equal.

First, we use the selection result in Lemma 1 to reason about pairs $\langle \hat{h}, t \rangle$, built from multiple seeds, in terms of the single-seed space $H_B(e)$. We state in the next Lemma the conditions in which the projection of t to its seed row identifiers contains the identifier for a particular example e. We show this occurs if, and only if, the pair $\langle \hat{h}, \sigma_e(t) \rangle$ is in the single-seed space $H_B(e)$, or equivalently, due to Proposition 1, when $\hat{h}$ covers e. Here $\sigma_e(t)$ is the selection of rows in t involving seed e as defined in Definition 5

Lemma 2. *Let* $\hat{h}_n = (h \leftarrow r_1, \ldots, r_n.) \in H(\mathcal{M}, h)$, *and*

$$\langle \hat{h}_n, t_n \rangle = \langle (h \leftarrow .), t_0 \rangle \bowtie \langle r_1, \mathrm{pred}(r_1) \rangle \bowtie \cdots \bowtie \langle r_n, \mathrm{pred}(r_n) \rangle,$$

such that seed table t_0 *is built from a seed example set* E *as described in Section 3. Let* e_{id} *be the unique row identifier associated with seed example* $e \in E$ *in table* t_0. *For every* $e \in E$, $e_{id} \in E(t)$ *if, and only if,* $\langle \hat{h}, \sigma_e(t) \rangle \in H_B(e)$.

Proof. (If). If $\langle \hat{h}, \sigma_e(t) \rangle \in H_B(e)$, by definition of ϕ_{empty}, $\sigma_e(t_n) \neq \emptyset$. This implies $e_{id} \in E(t)$.

(Only if). We proceed by induction on n, the number of literals in the body of $\hat{h}$. If $n = 1$, then by construction $\langle \hat{h}, \sigma_e(t) \rangle \in H_B(e)$.

Let the 'only if' direction of the Lemma be true for all $n \leq m - 1$; we assume that for every

$$\langle \hat{h}_{m-1}, t_{m-1} \rangle = \langle (h \leftarrow .), t_0 \rangle \bowtie \langle r_1, \mathrm{pred}(r_1) \rangle \bowtie \cdots \bowtie \langle r_{m-1}, \mathrm{pred}(r_{m-1}) \rangle,$$

such that seed table t_0 is built from a seed example set E as described in Section 3, and $e \in E$, $e_{id} \in E(t_{m-1})$ implies $\langle \hat{h}_{m-1}, \sigma_e(t_{m-1}) \rangle \in H_B(e)$.

Let $\langle \hat{h}_m, t_m \rangle = \langle \hat{h}_{m-1}, t_{m-1} \rangle \bowtie \langle r_m, \mathrm{pred}(r_m) \rangle$, and $e_{id} \in E(t_m)$, we now show $\langle \hat{h}, \sigma_e(t_m) \rangle \in H_B(e)$. Since $e_{id} \in E(t_m)$ the selection $\sigma_e(t_m) \neq \emptyset$. By the definition of extension-join and σ_e, this implies that $\sigma_e(t_{m-1}) \neq \emptyset$, and thus $e_{id} \in E(t_{m-1})$. By the inductive hypothesis pair $\langle \hat{h}_{m-1}, \sigma_e(t_{m-1}) \rangle \in H_B(e)$. Therefore, since $\langle \hat{h}_{m-1}, \sigma_e(t_{m-1}) \rangle \in H_B(e)$, and $\sigma_e(t_m) \neq \emptyset$, $\langle \hat{h}_m, \sigma_e(t_m) \rangle \in H_B(e)$ as desired. □

The result of $E(t)$ is a set of row identifiers for examples in seed set E. Given this set of identifiers a subset of examples in seed set E can be uniquely specified. The next Lemma shows that under some conditions, for a hypothesis pair $\langle \hat{h}, t \rangle$ the set of example identifiers in t can be mapped to the set of examples covered by $\hat{h}$. We denote this relationship as $E(t) = E(\hat{h})$. This mapping will lead directly to the desired result for Proposition 2, except for the issues presented by the filter function ϕ. Addressing those effects will be the bulk of the proof of Proposition 2.

Lemma 3. *Let* $\hat{h} = (h \leftarrow r_1, \ldots, r_n.) \in H(\mathcal{M}, h)$, *and*

$$\langle \hat{h}, t \rangle = \langle (h \leftarrow .), t_0 \rangle \bowtie \langle r_1, \mathrm{pred}(r_1) \rangle \bowtie \cdots \bowtie \langle r_n, \mathrm{pred}(r_n) \rangle,$$

such that seed table t_0 *is built from a seed example set* E *as described in Section 3. Let* e_{id} *be the unique row identifier associated with seed example* $e \in E$ *in table* t_0. *Then for every* $e \in E$, $e_{id} \in E(t)$, *if and only if,* $e \in E(\hat{h})$, *where* $E(t)$ *is the projection of table* t *as in Definition 5 and* $E(\hat{h})$ *is the set of examples covered by hypothesis* $\hat{h}$ *as in Definition 7. That is,* $E(t) = E(\hat{h})$.

Proof. (*If*). By Definition 7, $e \in E(\hat{h})$ if $\hat{h} \in H_A(e)$. By Proposition 1, if $\hat{h} \in H_A(e)$ then there exists table t_e such that $\langle \hat{h}, t_e \rangle \in H_B(e)$. This implies by Lemma 1 that $e_{id} \in E(t)$ the projection of t to its seed example identifiers.

(*Only if*). By Lemma 1, $e_{id} \in E(t)$ implies $\langle \hat{h}, \sigma_e(t) \rangle \in H_B(e)$. By Proposition 1, $\langle \hat{h}, t_e \rangle \in H_B(e)$ implies $\hat{h} \in H_A(e)$. Then by definition, $e \in E(\hat{h})$, that is, $\hat{h}$ covers single seed e.   □

We now prove Proposition 2 proceeding by induction on the number of literals in the hypothesis. We note that if a hypothesis $\hat{h}_n \in H(\mathcal{M}, h)$ is an extension of hypothesis $\hat{h}_{n-1} \in H(\mathcal{M}, h)$, the set of examples covered by $\hat{h}_n$ is a subset of the examples covered by $\hat{h}_{n-1}$. We use the monotonicity of the *proper* filter function ϕ to reason about the result of applying ϕ to the set of examples covered by $\hat{h}_n$. Finally, Lemmas 2 and 3 provide a mapping from the set of examples covered by a hypothesis to the examples present in a table resulting from a chain of multiple extension-joins starting from the seed table.

Proof. (*If*). Let $\hat{h} = (h \leftarrow r_1, \ldots, r_n.) \in H(\mathcal{M}, h)$. If $\langle \hat{h}, t \rangle \in H_W(E)$, then

$$\langle \hat{h}, t \rangle = \langle (h \leftarrow .), t_0 \rangle \bowtie \langle r_1, \text{pred}(r_1) \rangle \bowtie \cdots \bowtie \langle r_n, \text{pred}(r_n) \rangle,$$

such that seed table t_0 is built from a seed example set E as described in Section 3 and $\phi(t) \stackrel{\text{def}}{=} \phi(E(t)) = \text{true}$. We have by Lemma 3 that $E(\hat{h}) = E(t)$, and thus, $\phi(E(\hat{h})) = \text{true}$ since $\phi(E(t)) = \text{true}$.

(*Only if*). We proceed by induction on n, the number of literals in the body of $\hat{h}$. If $n = 1$, then $\hat{h} = (h \leftarrow \text{true}.)$. By construction there is a t_0 such that $\langle \hat{h}_n, t_0 \rangle \in H_W(E)$.

Let the 'only if' direction of the Proposition be true for all $n \leq m - 1$; we assume that for every $\hat{h}_{m-1} = (h \leftarrow r_1, \ldots, r_{m-1}.) \in H(\mathcal{M}, h)$, $\phi(E(\hat{h}_{m-1})) = \text{true}$ implies that there is a table t_{m-1} such that $\langle \hat{h}_{m-1}, t_{m-1} \rangle \in H_W(E)$. Let $\hat{h}_m = (h \leftarrow r_1, \ldots, r_{m-1}, r_m.) \in H(\mathcal{M}, h)$ and $\phi(E(\hat{h}_m)) = \text{true}$. We show there is a table t_m such that $\langle \hat{h}_m, t_m \rangle \in H_W(E)$.

By the monotonicity of ϕ, $\phi(E(\hat{h}_{m-1})) = \text{true}$ since $E(\hat{h}_m) \subseteq E(\hat{h}_{m-1})$ and $\phi(E(\hat{h}_m)) = \text{true}$. Then, by the inductive hypothesis, there exists $\langle \hat{h}_{m-1}, t_{m-1} \rangle \in H_W(E)$ where

$$\langle \hat{h}_{m-1}, t_{m-1} \rangle = \langle (h \leftarrow .), t_0 \rangle \bowtie \langle r_1, \text{pred}(r_1) \rangle \bowtie \cdots \bowtie \langle r_{m-1}, \text{pred}(r_{m-1}) \rangle,$$

such that table t_0 is built from a seed example set E as described in Section 3 and $\phi(t_{m-1}) \stackrel{\text{def}}{=} \phi(E(t_{m-1})) = \text{true}$. Let $\langle \hat{h}_m, t_m \rangle = \langle \hat{h}_{m-1}, t_{m-1} \rangle \bowtie \langle r_m, \text{pred}(r_m) \rangle$. By Lemma 3, we have $E(t_m) = E(\hat{h}_m)$ which implies $\phi(t_m) \stackrel{\text{def}}{=} \phi(E(t_m)) = \text{true}$. This implies $\langle \hat{h}_m, t_m \rangle \in H_W(E)$ as desired.   □

In the case of the strict intersection filter function, this Proposition states that only hypotheses that cover every seed are generated. On the other hand, in the case of the support filter function, only hypotheses that cover the required number of seeds are generated.

In future work we will experimentally evaluate the effect of alternative settings of the parameters exposed for hypothesis space restriction by this framework. In particular, we want to observe their effect on the accuracy of learned hypothesis found under spaces restricted by Generalized Inverse Entailment. For example, determining what effect different support thresholds have on accuracy is important. Determining how robust this approach is to sampling effects as compared to Inverse Entailment would test the conjecture that the effect caused by a bad choice of a single seed is in fact mitigated by this proposed framework. Characterizing the types of datasets that benefit from this approach would be enlightening.

6   Conclusion

We presented a framework for ILP that exploits caching and avoids redundant computation. This framework is built upon a data structure and hypothesis extension operation that makes opportunities for caching explicit. We presented this structure and defined the extension operation in terms of relational database operations, suggesting a way to incorporate ILP in a relational database environment.

We also discussed how current methods that seek to improve efficiency and alternative search definition can directly benefit from the framework presented here. In addition, new variants of search restriction and strategy are direct results of this framework. We discussed one such variant, which generalizes Inverse Entailment to multiple seeds, and presented theoretical results that offer a foundation for this generalization.

Finally, this framework enables us to learn theories in languages other than sets of Horn clauses, including theories that make probabilistic statements, statements about aggregates, and that contain negation.

Each of the directions mentioned above holds the potential for significant improvement in some aspect of ILP, and we believe that the work in this paper is a first step that opens many promising avenues for future research.

References

1. Dzeroski, S., Lavrac, N., eds.: Relational Data Mining. Springer-Verlag New York, Inc. (2001)
2. Blockeel, H., Sebag, M.: Scalability and efficiency in multi-relational data mining. SIGKDD Explor. Newsl. **5** (2003) 17–30
3. Struyf, J., Blockeel, H.: Query optimization in inductive logic programming by reordering literals. In: ILP. (2003) 329–346
4. Bockhorst, J., Ong, I.M.: FOIL-D: Efficiently scaling FOIL for multi-relational data mining of large datasets. In: ILP. (2004) 63–79
5. Blockeel, H., Dehaspe, L., Demoen, B., Janssens, G., Ramon, J., Vandecasteele, H.: Improving the efficiency of inductive logic programming through the use of query packs. J. Artif. Intell. Res. (JAIR) **16** (2002) 135–166

6. Costa, V.S., Srinivasan, A., Camacho, R., Blockeel, H., Demoen, B., Janssens, G., Struyf, J., Vandecasteele, H., Laer, W.V.: Query transformations for improving the efficiency of ILP systems. Journal of Machine Learning Research **4** (2003) 465–491
7. Cussens, J.: Using prior probabilities and density estimation for relational classification. In: ILP. (1998) 106–115
8. Zelezný, F., Srinivasan, A., Page, D.: A Monte Carlo study of randomised restarted search in ILP. In: ILP. (2004) 341–358
9. DiMaio, F., Shavlik, J.W.: Learning an approximation to inductive logic programming clause evaluation. In: ILP. (2004) 80–97
10. Vens, C., Assche, A.V., Blockeel, H., Dzeroski, S.: First order random forests with complex aggregates. In: ILP. (2004) 323–340
11. Costa, V.S., Page, D., Qazi, M., Cussens, J.: CLP(BN): Constraint logic programming for probabilistic knowledge. In: International Conference on Uncertainty in Artificial Intelligence. (2003)
12. Srivasanan, A.: The Aleph manual. Source code available at http://web.comlab.ox.ac.uk/oucl/research/areas/machlearn/Aleph/aleph.html (2004)
13. Muggleton, S.: Inverse entailment and Progol. New Generation Comput. **13** (1998) 245–286
14. Ramakrishnan, R., Gehrke, J.: Database Management Systems. Third edn. McGraw-Hill (2003)
15. Ferilli, S., Mauro, N.D., Basile, T.M.A., Esposito, F.: Theta-subsumption and resolution: A new algorithm. In Zhong, N., Ras, Z.W., Tsumoto, S., Suzuki, E., eds.: ISMIS. Volume 2871 of Lecture Notes in Computer Science., Springer (2003) 384–391
16. Mauro, N.D., Basile, T.M.A., Ferilli, S., Esposito, F., Fanizzi, N.: An exhaustive matching procedure for the improvement of learning efficiency. [24] 112–129
17. Maloberti, J., Sebag, M.: Fast theta-subsumption with constraint satisfaction algorithms. Machine Learning **55** (2004) 137–174
18. Arias, M., Khardon, R.: Bottom-up ilp using large refinement steps. In Camacho, R., King, R.D., Srinivasan, A., eds.: ILP. Volume 3194 of Lecture Notes in Computer Science., Springer (2004) 26–43
19. Fonseca, N., Rocha, R., Camacho, R., Silva, F.M.A.: Efficient data structures for inductive logic programming. [24] 130–145
20. Yin, X., Han, J., Yang, J., Yu, P.S.: Crossmine: Efficient classification across multiple database relations. In: ICDE, IEEE Computer Society (2004) 399–411
21. Ramakrishnan, R., Srivastava, S., Sudarshan, S.: Efficient bottom-up evaluation of logic programs. In Dewilde, P., Vandewalle, J., eds.: Computer Systems and Software Engineering: State-Of-The-Art. Kluwer Academic Publishers (1992)
22. Agrawal, R., Mannila, H., Srikant, R., Toivonen, H., Verkamo, A.I.: Fast discovery of association rules. In: Advances in Knowledge Discovery and Data Mining. AAAI/MIT Press (1996) 307–328
23. Dehaspe, L., Toivonen, H.: Discovery of frequent datalog patterns. Data Min. Knowl. Discov. **3** (1999) 7–36
24. Horváth, T., ed.: Inductive Logic Programming: 13th International Conference, ILP 2003, Szeged, Hungary, September 29-October 1, 2003, Proceedings. In Horváth, T., ed.: ILP. Volume 2835 of Lecture Notes in Computer Science., Springer (2003)

Distance Based Generalisation*

V. Estruch, C. Ferri, J. Hernández-Orallo, and M.J. Ramírez-Quintana

DSIC, Univ. Politècnica de València , Camí de Vera s/n, 46020 València, Spain
{vestruch, cferri, jorallo, mramirez}@dsic.upv.es

Abstract. Many distance-based methods in machine learning are able
to identify similar cases or prototypes from which decisions can be made.
The explanation given is usually based on expressions such as "because
case a is similar to case b". However, a more general or meaningful pattern, such as "because case a has properties x and y (as b has)" is usually
more difficult to find. Even in this case, the connection of this pattern
with the original distance-based method is generally unclear, or even inconsistent. In this paper, we study the connection between the concept of
distance (or similarity) and the concept of generalisation. More precisely,
we define several conditions which, in our view, a sensible distance-based
generalisation must have. From that, we are able to tell whether a generalisation operator for a pattern representation language is consistent
with the metric space defined by the underlying distance. We show that
there are pattern languages and generalisation operators which comply
with these properties for typical data types: nominal, numerical, sets and
lists. We also show the relationship between the well-known concepts of
lgg and distances between terms, and the definition of generalisation presented in this paper.

Keywords: Distance-based methods, generalisation operators, lgg, metric space.

1   Introduction

The concept of distance is key in many areas such as case-based reasoning [1],
machine learning [6], diagnosis, information retrieval [2], etc. Distance, as the
mathematical concept of dissimilarity, allows many learning techniques to be
applied to quite different kinds of data and situations, provided we are able to
define a distance for the instances or cases at hand. Distance-based methods,
then, are easily adaptable to any kind of applications. However, the problem of
converting the similarity traits into a numerical value (the distance) is that the
information on the matches or coincidences is lost. Consequently, many distance-
based methods cannot give an explanation of their answers. For instance, a
distance-based method [5] such as k-nearest neighbours can output that the film

---

* This work has been partially supported by the EU (FEDER) and the Spanish
  MEC, under grant TIN 2004-7943-C04-02, the Acción Integrada Hispano-Austriaca
  HU2003-0003, and the Generalitat Valenciana (MEDIM, GV04B/477).

S. Kramer and B. Pfahringer (Eds.): ILP 2005, LNAI 3625, pp. 87–102, 2005.

X is likely to be appropriate for a customer because the k-nearest neighbours of X were appropriate for the customer, but are not able to give a general *pattern* of why it is the case, such as the film X is likely to be appropriate for the customer because X is an action movie where the good guys win, and the customer liked all the films with these traits s/he hired before.

The connection of distance and pattern, or more precisely, the connection of distance and generalisation is not new. Many learning techniques (e.g. clustering or classification) generate a prototype (or centroid) and the generalisation area is based on a certain distance ball from the prototype. However, a good distance-based generalisation can have no meaningful pattern which is able to express the generalisation or, in other words, a generalisation can have no good representation. For instance, the generalisation "all the films with more than 4 traits in common with film X" is a well-defined general region according to a distance based on the number of common traits, but it lacks a meaningful pattern. Vice versa, a meaningful pattern can lead to very bad or unintuitive generalisations. For instance, the pattern "all the documents that contain the string *inductive logic programming*" is a meaningful pattern but is not a good generalisation if edit distances are taken into account, since two very similar documents can just differ on this string or two very different documents can just match on this sequence.

Consequently, if we are using a distance-based method to determine similar objects or to establish centroids or prototypes, we need a representation pattern that is consistent with the metric space defined by the underlying distance. In order to do this, we have to identify a series of conditions that a pattern representation language and a generalisation operator must fulfil.

Let us illustrate this idea with a more detailed example. Consider an intruder-detection problem where we want to detect whether a user might be an intruder. For each user, we record the machines (1, 2, 3) where they have made a 'ping' (p), have connected (c) or have failed to connect (f). For each user we record a 'sequence' of actions. For instance, "$p_1 f_2 c_2$" means a user that first *pinged* to machine 1, then failed to connect to machine 2 and finally connected to machine 2. With this data we apply case-based reasoning to determine for a new user whether s/he is an intruder or not. More specifically, we compute edit distances between the sequences of actions and then use a k-nearest neighbour (k-nn) to determine the class of each new case. Figure 1 shows the case of determining whether "$p_1 f_1 f_2 f_3$" is an intruder when we use 7-nn and the seven nearest examples (with distances 2, 4, 4, 3, 3 for the positives and 3, 5 for the negatives). Since among the 7-nearest neighbours there are five positive cases and two negative cases, the sequence "$p_1 f_1 f_2 f_3$" is labelled as a possible 'intruder'.

A different thing is when we want to extract a pattern to explain the 7-nn classification. The pattern can be determined taking into account the five positive examples and trying to ascertain what they have in common. A possible pattern for the 5 positive cases could be $\{*f_1 f_1 *, *f_3 f_3 *\}$, meaning that any instance containing two consecutive f_1 or two consecutive f_3 is an intruder. Apparently,

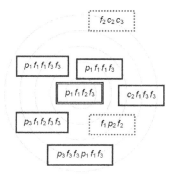

Fig. 1. 7-nn with 5 positive (solid line) and 2 negative (dotted line) cases for classifying the new case "$p_1 f_1 f_2 f_3$"

this is a good pattern, since it covers all the five positive examples, and none of the two negative examples. Additionally, it is not too specific and it is not too general, and it is meaningful. Despite this idealistic picture, the pattern conceals a surprise: it does not cover the centre point "$p_1 f_1 f_2 f_3$"! Even worse, the point "$p_1 f_1 f_2 f_3$" has a distance 2 to "$p_1 f_1 f_1 f_3$" and has distance 3 to "$p_3 f_1 f_2 f_3 f_3$", where these two latter examples have distance 5. That is, two examples are in the pattern, but a middle point is not in it. These two observations show that any meaningful pattern in a general situation may be inconsistent w.r.t. the underlying distance. The pattern is then useless to explain or represent the behaviour of the distance-based technique.

Consequently, if we use a pattern representation language for explaining some distance-based generalisation we have to check first whether the language and the generalisation operator meet some properties.

In this paper, we study the connection between the concept of distance (or similarity) and the concept of generalisation, and the pattern representation languages that are able to express sensible generalisations. This is the first step in order to make the idea of obtaining meaningful explanations of the answers given by a distance-based learning method applicable to the broadest kind of distance-based techniques as possible. In the following section, we analyse which generalisations are considered unintuitive in a metric space, and we define two properties a generalisation operator must satisfy. In Section 3 we show sensible pattern languages and binary generalisation operators for the typical data types: nominal, numerical, sets and lists. Next, we analyse the relationship between our generalisation concept and the lgg operator defined by Plotkin. We show that, using the metric defined in [9] which is based on the lgg concept, this operator satisfies the conditions of a good generalisation operator to be used as a pattern constructor for first-order logic language. This puts some (but not all) some generalisation operators (such as lgg) and some (but not all) metric spaces used in ILP as special cases of metric-based generalisations. This suggests the applicability of other distance-based methods in ILP as well as the applicability of ILP methods (top-down/ bottom-up) to other areas outside ILP.

Finally, in the conclusions, we discuss on the application of this integrated view to distance-based methods such as k-nearest neighbours, clustering, distance-based decision trees and other case-based reasoning techniques. We also propose some ideas for the future work.

2   Generalisation in Metric Spaces

In this section, we propose a notion of generalisation for metric spaces. From now, we will work with metric spaces[1].

Definition 1. *Given* $\Delta : X \times X \rightarrow 2^X, \Delta$ *is a k-generalisation* $(k \geq 1)$ *if* $\forall a, b \in X$ *these two conditions hold:*
1 (No Isolation)

$$\forall x \in \Delta(a, b) \text{ and } \forall \epsilon > 0, \text{ if } \{x\} \subsetneq B(x, \epsilon) \text{ then } B(x, \epsilon) \cap \Delta(a, b) \neq \{x\}$$

where $B(x, \epsilon) = \{x' \in X : d(x, x') < \epsilon\}$.
2 (Scope)

$$\forall x \in X, \text{ if } d(a, x) + d(x, b) \leq k \cdot d(a, b) \text{ then } x \in \Delta(a, b)$$

Note that Condition 2 implies that $a, b \in \Delta(a, b)$. We employ the term k-generalisation instead of generalisation, because in this way we have a more flexible definition. The value of k establishes the level of generality, i.e. for greater values of k more instances are allowed inside the generalisation. The underlying idea to the parameter k consists of introducing a least generalisation notion in a similar way ILP and the *lgg* operator do. Note that a k-generalisation is also a $(k-1)$-generalisation and so on.

Both conditions are important when considering generalisations. The first one (No isolation) restricts the definition in the following way; if there is an example that belongs to the generalisation, for any ball centered in this example if there are other examples in this ball, at least one must belong to the generalisation. This condition rejects the generalisations that have isolated points. The following example shows how this condition is useful to reject some unintuitive generalisations.

Example 1. Let us consider a metric space formed by three elements a, b and c where $d(a, b) = 1$, $d(b, c) = 2$, $d(a, c) = 2$. If we define a generalisation $\Delta(a, c) = \{a, c\}$, we can see that it trivially verifies Condition 2 $(d(a, b) + d(b, c) > d(a, c))$. However this generalisation does not satisfy condition 1 (consider a ball of radius 2 centered in a, then $B(a, 2) = \{a, b\}$ but $b \notin \Delta(a, c)$).

---

[1] A metric space (X, d) is a set of points with an associated distance function (also called a metric) $d : X \times X \rightarrow \Re$ which satisfies the following conditions: $\forall x, y \in \Re$, $d(x, y) \geq 0$, $d(x, y) = 0$ if and only if $x = y$ (identity of indiscernibles), $d(x, y) = d(y, x)$ (symmetry), $d(x, z) \leq d(x, y) + d(y, z)$ (triangle inequality).

The second condition (Scope) rejects the generalisations that are much too specific in the sense that do not consider all the points between two generalised points. The following example illustrates this:

Example 2. Let us consider the metric space $\Re$ where the metric is defined as the absolute difference. If we define $\Delta(4,5)$ formed by $[3.8, 4.2] \cup [4.8, 5.2]$ we can see that this is not a valid 1-generalisation since it is much too restricted. $\Delta(4,5)$ satisfies Condition 1, but not Condition 2 because $d(4.5, 5) + d(4.5, 4) = d(4, 5)$, and 4.5 is not inside the generalisation.

3   Suitable Generalisation for Several Data Types

In this section we study some generalisation operators for several well-known data types: nominal, numerical, sets and lists. First, we define a distance function d over each data type T such that the pair (T, d) is a metric space. Then, we define a binary operator which generalises a pair of elements of T and we show that this function verifies the conditions defined in Section 2. Obviously, the scope condition establishes the dependency between a generalisation and the underlying distance function. In fact, in some cases, it is possible to define a function over a data type which is a generalisation operator if we use a certain metric, but it does not verify the definition using a different metric. We illustrate this point by means of an example over lists.

3.1   Nominal Data Types

A nominal or discrete data type T is a finite collection of values $\{a_1, \ldots, a_n\}$ such that $a_i \neq a_j$ for all $i \neq j$. For instance, $\{red, yellow, blue\}$ is a nominal data type. Let d be the discrete metric defined as $d(a, b) = 0$ if $a = b$ and $d(a, b) = 1$ if $a \neq b$, where $a, b \in T$. Then, (T, d) is a metric space. The next proposition shows that the set of two discrete values is an admissible generalisation for this data type.

Proposition 1. *Given* $T = \{a_1, \ldots, a_n\}$ *a discrete data type and d the discrete distance, then the operator Δ defined as $\Delta(a_i, a_j) = \{a_i, a_j\}$ is a 1-generalisation.*

Proof. We first prove the no isolation condition. Any ball centered in a_i (equivalently in a_j) which verifies the premise of this condition contains, at least, a_j (equivalently a_i), by the definition of d. But a_j (equivalently a_i) also belongs to $\Delta(a_i, a_j)$ (by definition of $\Delta(a_i, a_j)$). Therefore, $a_j \in B(a_i, \epsilon) \cap \Delta(a_i, a_j)$, which verifies condition 1.

Also, $\Delta(a_i, a_j)$ trivially satisfies condition 2 since there does not exist any $x \in T$ (different from a_i and a_j) which verifies $d(a_i, x) + d(x, a_j) = d(a_i, a_j)$ because of the definition of the distance.

The generalisation derived from this operator resembles the "explanation" computed by decision tree learning algorithms such as $ID3$ or $C4.5$ [8] for nominal splits.

3.2   Numerical Data Types

The next data type we consider is the real number set $\Re$. The usual distance function over $\Re$ is defined as $d(a, b) = | a - b |$. In this case, the pair $(\Re, d)$ is also a metric space.

There are many ways of generalising a pair of real numbers, but not all of them are sensible generalisations in the sense of Definition 1. The following proposition shows that given a pair of real numbers a and b, $a \leq b$, the interval $[a, b]$ is a good generalisation.

Proposition 2. *Let $\Re$ be the real number set with the usual metric and let $a, b \in \Re$ such that $a \leq b$. Then $\Delta(a, b) = [a, b]$ is a 1-generalisation.*

Proof. Any ball centered in any of the interval limits contains real numbers which belong to the interval. Obviously, this is the worst case and the rest of values in $]a, b[$ also verifiy condition 1. Hence, $\Delta(a, b)$ verifies condition 1. On the other hand, any $x \in \Re$ that verifies $d(a, x) + d(x, b) = d(a, b)$ (premise of condition 2) also belongs to the interval $[a, b]$, which proves that condition 2 is satisfied.

Other possible generalisations also based on the interval concept are, for instance, $\Delta'(a, b) = [a - | a - b |, b]$ or $\Delta''(a, b) = [a - \delta, b + \delta]$, $\delta \geq 0$. In this last case, if $\delta = (k - 1) | a - b | / 2$, then it is a k-generalisation. Note that if c is the upper bound of this interval, then $d(a, c) + d(c, b) \leq k \cdot d(a, b)$. However, a generalisation based on two disjoint balls centred in a and b respectively, is not a proper one since there will always exist a point placed between a and b which will not be covered by any of the two balls.

3.3   The Set Data Type

Let $\Sigma = \{a_1, a_2, \ldots\}$ be a set of items (not necessarily finite). Let us consider the set of all finite sets over Σ, denoted by S_Σ, and define the function $d : S_\Sigma \times S_\Sigma \rightarrow \Re$ as the cardinality of the symmetric set difference between two sets belonging to S_Σ. Then, the pair (S_Σ, d) is a metric space. Now, given $A, B \in S_\Sigma$ we define $\Delta(A, B)$ as,

$$\Delta(A, B) = \{C \in S_\Sigma : A \cap B \subseteq C\}$$

Note that, as follows from the definition of $\Delta(A, B)$, if A and B are two disjoint sets, then $\Delta(A, B) = S_\Sigma$.

Proposition 3. *The above operator Δ defined over sets is a 1-generalisation.*

Proof. According to the introduced metric, the minimum permitted distance between two different sets is equal to 1. Hence, it is sufficient to prove that condition 1 holds for balls that contain sets which are at the minimum distance. In this case, for any V in $\Delta(A, B)$, it is possible to build a set W which keeps at distance 1 and belongs to $\Delta(A, B)$, by only inserting a new item into V. Then, the first condition of the generalisation definition holds.

Let us glance at the second one. We prove it by contradiction. Suppose that there exists a set C which verifies $d(A, C) + d(C, B) = d(A, B)$, but $C \notin \Delta(A, B)$. Then, the following relations hold:

$$d(A, C) + d(C, B) = d(A, B)$$
$$\Downarrow \text{ (by the definition of } d)$$
$$(\mid A \mid + \mid C \mid - 2 \mid A \cap C \mid) + (\mid B \mid + \mid C \mid - 2 \mid B \cap C \mid) =$$
$$\mid A \mid + \mid B \mid - 2 \mid A \cap B \mid$$
$$\Updownarrow \text{ (by simplification)}$$
$$\mid C \mid = \mid A \cap C \mid + \mid B \cap C \mid - \mid A \cap B \mid \quad (1)$$

On the other hand, if C verifies $d(A, C) + d(C, B) = d(A, B)$ it is possible to transform A into B going through C. Then, C contains at least some elements that also belong to A and some elements that also belong to B. Hence,

$$\mid C \mid \geq \mid A \cap C \mid + \mid B \cap C \mid - \mid A \cap B \cap C \mid$$

where $\mid A \cap B \cap C \mid$ is the number of elements in C belonging to both A and B. By replacing this expression in (1), we obtain

$$\mid A \cap C \mid + \mid B \cap C \mid - \mid A \cap B \mid \geq \mid A \cap C \mid + \mid B \cap C \mid - \mid A \cap B \cap C \mid$$
$$\Updownarrow \text{ (by simplification)}$$
$$\mid A \cap B \mid \leq \mid A \cap B \cap C \mid \quad (2)$$

By hypothesis, $C \not\subseteq \Delta(A, B)$. Then $A \cap B$ is not included in C and $\mid A \cap B \cap C \mid = 0$. But then, $\mid A \cap B \mid = 0$ by (2) which implies that $\Delta(A, B) = S_\Sigma$. Therefore, $C \subseteq \Delta(A, B)$, which contradicts the hypothesis.

To conclude this subsection, we sketch an example of a bad-generalisation for sets. Just consider $\Delta(A, B) = \{C \in S_\Sigma : A \cup B \subseteq C\}$. Setting $A = \{a, x\}$ and $B = \{b, x\}$, then the set $D = \{x\}$ verifies $d(A, B) = d(A, D) + d(D, B)$ but it does not belong to $\Delta(A, B)$.

3.4   The List Data Type

The last data type we deal with is the list or sequence data type, i.e. words constructed from symbols of a finite alphabet $\Sigma = \{a_1, \ldots, a_n\}$. Before defining a generalisation operator for this data type, we introduce some preliminary concepts.

Definition 2. *The alignment of two words $s, t \in \Sigma^*$ is the process of juxtaposing them such that there exist matched symbols.*

For instance, if $s = abc$ and $t = bca$, there are two alignments of s and t.

$$(i) \quad a\ b\ c \quad (ii)\ a\ b\ c$$
$$b\ c\ a \qquad\quad b\ c\ a$$

Definition 3. *Given two words s and t, the edit distance d between s and t is defined as the minimum number of deletions or insertions required to transform s into t.*

For instance, in the above example, $d(s,t) = 2$. The edit distance is obtained when the number of symbols matched in an alignment is maximal. If it is the case, we say that the alignment is maximal. Note that, in general, it is possible to have more than one maximal alignment. For instance, if $s = cbc$ and $t = abcbd$ then we have two maximal alignments giving $d(s,t) = 4$:

$$(i) \quad c\ b\ c \quad (ii)\ c\ b\ c$$
$$\quad a\ b\ c\ b\ d \qquad a\ b\ c\ b\ d$$

By $M_{s,t}$ we denote the number of matched symbols in the maximal alignments of s and t.

   If there is an alignment of s and t, then it is possible to find a more general expression which includes s and t as special cases. We call this expression *pattern* of s and t. More formally,

Definition 4. *Given $s,t \in \Sigma^*$, a pattern p of s and t is an expression constructed from an alignment of s and t by keeping the matched symbols and replacing the sequences of un-matched symbols by $*$.*

For instance, following with the above example, there are two patterns, $*bc*$ and $*cb*$.

Definition 5. *A pattern p covers a word w, if w can be obtained from p by replacing any ocurrence of $*$ by a (possibly empty) sequence of alphabet symbols. In this case, we say that w is an instance of p.*

Note that, it follows from this definition that a pattern represents the set of its instances.

Definition 6. *Given the metric space (Σ^*, d), where d is the edit distance, and $x, y \in \Sigma^*$, we define the operator $\Delta(x, y)$ as the set of words covered by the patterns obtained when the edit distance between x and y is calculated.*

For instance, in our example, $\Delta(cbc, abcbd) = \{bc, abc, cbca, \ldots, cb, cba, acb, \ldots\}$ and can be represented by the set of patterns $\{*bc*, *cb*\}$. In order to show that this operator is a k-generalisation, the first question to rise is whether it is necessary that $\Delta(x, y)$ contains instances of the patterns of x and y obtained from all maximal alignments or if it is sufficient only to consider one of them. We clarify this point with our example (see the left hand side of Figure 2). Given s and t, the word $w = cbd$ verifies $d(s, w) + d(w, t) = d(s, t)$ and, however, it is not an instance of the pattern $*bc*$. But $*cb*$ is also a pattern for s and t and w is an instance of it. Hence, we need to take the patterns obtained from all the maximal alignments into account.

As we have said at the begining of this section, it is possible to define an operator which is not a generalisation w.r.t. a distance function, but indeed verifies the

Fig. 2. (Left picture) All the maximal patterns must be considered in the generalisation.**(Right picture)** Edit distance with substitution does not work.

definition w.r.t. another distance metric. We show this fact with an example using the edit distance with substitution (right hand side of Figure 2). Let $w_1 = cbc$ and $w_2 = aaaab$ be two words. In this case, there is only one maximal alignment giving the pattern $*b*$, but $w_3 = aaa$ verifies $d(w_1, w_3) + d(w_3, w_2) = d(w_1, w_2)$ and, however, it is not an instance of this pattern.

Proposition 4. *Let (Σ^*, d) be a metric space, and let $x, y \in \Sigma^*$. Then, the operator $\Delta(x, y)$ in Definition 6 is a 1-generalisation.*

Proof. The proof is quite similar to that of proposition 3. The minimum distance between two words is 1. Then, if we extract any word, namely u, from $\Delta(x, y)$, we can find a different expression, namely v, which is at a distance 1 from u and belongs to $\Delta(x, y)$. For this purpose, it is enough to add or delete one symbol from u which does not match with the explicit symbols in v. This proves that condition 1 holds.

Now, we prove condition 2 by contradiction. Suppose that there exists a word z such that $d(x, z) + d(z, y) = d(x, y)$ and $z \notin \Delta(x, y)$. By the definition of the edit distance, given two words s and t, $d(s, t) = |s| + |t| - 2 \cdot M_{s,t}$, where $|w|$ denotes the length of s. Hence

$$d(x, z) + d(z, y) = d(x, y) \Leftrightarrow$$

$$|x| + |z| - 2 \cdot M_{x,z} + |z| + |y| - 2 \cdot M_{z,y} = |x| + |y| - 2 \cdot M_{x,y} \Leftrightarrow$$

$$|z| = M_{x,z} + M_{z,y} - M_{x,y} \quad (3)$$

On the other hand, we know that

$$|z| \geq M_{x,z} + M_{z,y} - Agree_{<x,z>,<y,z>}$$

where $Agree_{<x,z>,<y,z>}$ is the number of coincidental symbols in the alignment of x with z, and y with z. By replacing this expression in (3), we obtain

$$M_{x,y} < Agree_{<x,z>,<y,z>}$$

But if $z \notin \Delta(x, y)$ then $Agree_{<x,z>,<y,z>} < M_{x,y}$ which is a contradiction. Thus, we conclude that condition 2 holds.

With this we show that there are metric spaces which can be associated generalisation patterns such that the team works in an appropiate way. We have shown this for nominal, numeric, set and lists. The next case, and most usual in ILP, is the term and the atom data type.

4   The Lgg Operator in Metric Spaces of Atoms

One of the most popular generalisation operators in ILP is the least general generalisation, *lgg*, introduced by Plotkin in [7]. In this section we study the relationship between this operator and Definition 1, in the framework of a first-order logic language. We will show that using a metric defined over this language and based on the lgg, the Δ function and the lgg are connected so that we could use the lgg as a pattern constructor over the first-order language. In order to do this, we first establish a distance over the set of atoms and then we provide a Δ definition which is also based on the lgg operator.

In what follows L denotes a first order language defined over the signature $\langle \mathcal{F}, \Pi, \mathcal{X} \rangle$ where $\mathcal{F}$ (respectively Π) is a family indexed on N (non negative integers) being $\mathcal{F}_n (\Pi_n)$ a set of n−adic function (predicate) symbols and $\mathcal{X}$ is a (infinite) denumerable set of variable symbols. In case of no ambiguity, both predicate and function symbols will be referred as symbols, and variable symbols as variables. Also $H_{\mathcal{X}}$ and $B_{\mathcal{X}}$ denote the non-ground Herbrand Universe and the non-ground Herbrand base respectively as is introduced in [3].

4.1   A Distance Based on Lgg

In [9] is presented a distance between non-ground atoms such that the set of atoms in L along with this distance is a metric space. Basically, the mentioned distance between two atoms is expressed as a pair of integer values (F, V) reflecting the differences of them w.r.t. their *lgg*. The distance defintion is based on an auxiliary function $size(a) = (F, V)$ which reflects the structure of the atom a. Roughly speaking, F is a function which counts the number of ocurrences of predicate and function symbols occurring in a, and the function V returns the sum of the squared frequency of appearance of each variable in a. More formally,

Definition 7. *Given a_1 and a_2 be two atoms, then*

$$d(a_1, a_2) = [size(a_1) - size(lgg(a_1, a_2))] + [size(a_2) - size(lgg(a_1, a_2))]$$

Example 3. Consider the atoms $a_1 = p(a, b)$ and $a_2 = p(b, b)$. The distance $d(a_1, a_2)$ is calculated as follows. First, we compute the *lgg* of both atoms, that is, $lgg(a_1, a_2) = p(X, b)$ and then, we measure each atom structure by means of the function *size*: $size(a_1) = size(a_2) = (3, 0)$ and $size(lgg(a_1, a_2)) = (2, 1^2)$. Finally, the distance between a_1 and a_2 is

$$d(a_1, a_2) = [(3, 0) - (2, 1)] + [(3, 0) - (2, 1)] = (1, -1) + (1, -1) = (2, -2)$$

Note that with this definition of distance the proximity relation (how near two atoms are) is not as intuitive as in a conventional metric space where its associated distance returns only a positive real number (and not a pair of values). For this reason, the authors introduce a total order relation over the pair of values which allows to specify a proximity notion. Given two ordered pairs $A = (F_1, V_1)$ and $B = (F_2, V_2)$, $A < B$ iff $F_1 < F_2$ or $F_1 = F_2$ and $V_1 < V_2$ (lexicographic order). Let us illustrate how this order relation can be used to determine the proximity among atoms.

Example 4. Let $a_1 = p(a, b)$, $a_2 = p(a, a)$ and $a_3 = p(b, b)$ be three atoms. Since $d(a_1, a_3) = (2, -2)$ and $d(a_2, a_3) = (4, -8)$ we can conclude according to the order relation that a_3 is closer to a_1 than to a_2.

4.2   Defining Δ

Now we are ready to define a generalisation Δ over the metric space of atoms.

Definition 8. *Given two atoms from B_χ a_1 and a_2, the Δ function is defined as follows:*

$$\Delta(a_1, a_2) = \{a \in B_\chi : \exists \sigma, a = lgg(a_1, a_2)\sigma\}$$

where σ is a substitution and $e\sigma$ denotes the instance of an expression e by σ.

Note that with this defintion, $lgg(a_1, a_2)$ is an atom that also belongs to $\Delta(a_1, a_2)$. Additionally, it is the most general atom in $\Delta(a_1, a_2)$. For these reasons we use the lgg as the canonical representant of the set Δ, or in other words, $lgg(a_1, a_2)$ would be used as the pattern representing $\Delta(a_1, a_2)$.

In the following 4 pages, we will prove that this Δ function verifies the conditions of the Definition 1.

In order to prove the *Scope* condition a formal problem arises. Note that this one is formulated thinking of standard metric functions, which return a positive real value. In principle, the concept of ball, $B(x, \epsilon)$, would not make sense in the current metric space. But we can address this proof thanks to the following observation. This condition restricted to discrete spaces is equivalent to consider that given any a_3 belonging to $\Delta(a_1, a_2)$ then, at least, one of the nearest atoms to a_3 must belong to $\Delta(a_1, a_2)$. This alternative definition can already be managed for the current metric space using the established order relation over the set of pairs (F, V).

Before tackling the proof, some preliminary definitions and propositions are introduced. We consider the usual representation of a term as a labelled tree. Then, a position p in a term t is represented by a sequence of natural numbers. $p \cdot q$ denotes the concatenation of positions p and q.

Definition 9. *Let a be an atom, and let t_1 and t_2 be two (sub)-terms in a at positions $p = p_1 \cdot p_2 \cdot \ldots \cdot p_n$ and $q = q_1 \cdot q_2 \cdot \ldots \cdot q_m$, respectively. We will say that p is deeper than q if $n > m$. Additionally, by saying that a (sub)-term t is placed at $p \cdot *$ in a, we mean that the exact position of t has the sequence p as a prefix.*

Example 5. Given the atom $a = p(b, f(g(c)))$, the position of b in a is 1 and the position of $g(c)$ in a is $2 \cdot 1$. Thus, $g(c)$ is placed at a deeper position in a than b is. We can also say that c is placed at $2 \cdot *$ since its position is $2 \cdot 1 \cdot 1$.

Definition 10. *Let a be an atom, the skeleton of a (denoted by $sk(a)$) is just the term obtained from a by replacing any variable by a dot.*

Example 6. Given the atom $a = p(a, f(X), g(h(X)))$ then, $sk(a) = p(a, f(\cdot), g(h(\cdot)))$.

Note that the dot symbol simply informs about an unknown subterm at that position, just like an anonymous variable. Thus, the skeleton would be interpreted as an atom with all its variables different from each other.

Definition 11. *Let sk_1 and sk_2 two skeletons, we will say that sk_1 and sk_2 overlap, if there exists a subset of symbols in sk_1 such that each symbol of this set occurs at same position in sk_2. The common skeleton between sk_1 and sk_2 will de denoted by $sk_1 \cap sk_2$.*

Example 7. Given $sk_1 = p(a, \cdot, g(b))$ and $sk_2 = p(b, \cdot, g(b))$ then, sk_1 and sk_2 overlap and $sk_1 \cap sk_2 = p(\cdot, \cdot, g(b))$.

Definition 12. *Let a_1 and a_2 two atoms. Then, we will say that the $sk(a_2)$ is a sub-skeleton of $sk(a_1)$ (denoted by $sk(a_2) \subset sk(a_1)$), if for each symbol in $sk(a_2)$, the same symbol occurs at the same position in $sk(a_1)$.*

Example 8. Given the atoms $a_1 = p(a, f(X), g(h(X)))$ and $a_2 = p(a, X, g(Y))$ then, $sk(a_2) = p(a, \cdot, g(\cdot))$ is a sub-skeleton of $sk(a_1) = p(a, f(\cdot), g(h(\cdot)))$.

Definition 13. *Let sk_1 and sk_2 be two skeletons, we will say that both are equal $(sk_1 = sk_2)$ if $sk_1 \subset sk_2$ and $sk_2 \subset sk_1$.*

Given three atoms a_1, a_2 and a_3 such that $d(a_1, a_2) = d(a_1, a_3) + d(a_3, a_2)$, the following proposition establishes that a_3 overlaps a_1 and a_2 at the same positions as a_1 and a_2 overlap, and a_3 overlaps at the rest of positions either with a_1 or a_2.

Proposition 5. *Let a_1, a_2 and a_3 be three atoms. If the equation $d(a_1, a_2) = d(a_1, a_3) + d(a_3, a_2)$ is verified, then the $sk(lgg(a_1, a_2)) \subset sk(a_3)$ and those (sub)-terms in a_3 which are not covered by the $sk(lgg(a_1, a_2))$ will be the same as those (sub)-terms placed at the same position in a_1 or in a_2.*

Proof. Let $d(a_1, a_2) = (F_1, V_1)$, $d(a_2, a_3) = (F_2, V_2)$ and $d(a_1, a_3) = (F_3, V_3)$ be the distances among a_1, a_2 and a_3 (for convenience the function $F(\cdot)$ will be applied over skeletons as well). Then, using the distance definition, F_1 can be written as $F_1 = F(a_1) + F(a_2) - 2F(lgg(a_1, a_2))$, and the same thing for the rest of F_i values.

Now, by the well-known equality between tuples, we have that $F_1 = F_2 + F_3$ and operating in both sides of the equation we obtain,

$$F(a_3) - F(lgg(a_1, a_3)) - F(lgg(a_2, a_3)) = -F(lgg(a_1, a_2))$$

Note that the atom $lgg(a_i, a_j)$ contains less or equal number of symbols than a_i and a_j. So, if the skeletons of $lgg(a_1, a_3)$ (for simplicity, denoted by $sk_{1,3}$) and $lgg(a_2, a_3)$ (denoted by $sk_{2,3}$) did not have some parts in common then, the left hand side of the identity above could not be negative. Thus, both skeletons must overlap. This overlapping will be expressed by $sk_{1,3} \cap sk_{2,3}$. Clearly, the symbols in a_3 belonging to $sk_{1,3} \cap sk_{2,3}$ are counted twice. Note that $sk_{1,3} \cap sk_{2,3}$ is equal to $sk(lgg(lgg(a_1, a_3), lgg(a_2, a_3)))$ and that it is a sub-skeleton of $lgg(a_1, a_2)$. Hence, we can write the equation above as,

$$F(a_3) - F(sk_{1,3}^*) - F(sk_{2,3}^*) - 2F(sk_{1,3} \cap sk_{2,3}) =$$

$$= -F(lgg(a_1, a_2))$$

where $sk_{1,3}^*$ (equivalently $sk_{2,3}^*$) stands for that part of the skeleton of $lgg(a_1, a_3)$ (equivalently $lgg(a_2, a_3)$) which does not take part of $sk_{1,3} \cap sk_{2,3}$. Setting $A = F(a_3) - F(sk_{1,3}^*) - F(sk_{2,3}^*) - F(sk_{1,3} \cap sk_{2,3})$, then $A \geq 0$ since sk^* expressions and $sk_{1,3} \cap sk_{2,3}$ do not overlap and $F(sk_{1,3} \cap sk_{2,3}) \leq F(lgg(a_1, a_2))$. The only way $A - F(sk_{1,3} \cap sk_{2,3}) = -F(lgg(a_1, a_2))$ holds, is that $sk(a_3)$ can be perfectly ensambled from the skeletons of $sk_{1,3}^*$, $sk_{2,3}^*$ and $sk_{1,3} \cap sk_{2,3}$ (this fact implies that $A = 0$) and finally, that $F(sk_{1,3} \cap sk_{2,3}) = F(lgg(a_1, a_2))$, from which it can be deduced that $sk_{1,3} \cap sk_{2,3} = sk(lgg(a_1, a_2))$ and that those subterms in a_3 not covered by the $sk(lgg(a_1, a_2))$ coincide with those subterms placed at the same position in a_1 or a_2. Summing up, a_3 is built from the (sub)-terms in a_1 or in a_2.

Before presenting the next proposition, a preliminary concept must be introduced.

Definition 14. *Let a_1, a_2 and a_3 be three atoms such that $d(a_1, a_2) = d(a_1, a_3) + d(a_3, a_2)$. Then, we will say that a variable occurring in $lgg(a_1, a_2)$ at position p is reflected in $lgg(a_1, a_3)$ or in $lgg(a_2, a_3)$, if there exists a variable (modulo renaming) at position $p \cdot *$ in $lgg(a_1, a_3)$ or in $lgg(a_2, a_3)$.*

Example 9. In Figure 3, the variable X in $lgg(a_1, a_2)$ is reflected in $lgg(a_2, a_3)$, whereas the variable Y in $lgg(a_1, a_2)$ is reflected in $lgg(a_1, a_3)$. Note that the reflection is not a one-to-one association. A variable in $lgg(a_1, a_2)$ could be reflected in $lgg(a_1, a_3)$ or $lgg(a_2, a_3)$ several times. For example imagine that a variable X occurs in $lgg(a_1, a_2)$ at position $2 \cdot 1$, and two variables Y and Z are placed at position $2 \cdot 1 \cdot 1$ and $2 \cdot 1 \cdot 2$ respectively in $lgg(a_1, a_3)$, then X is reflected twice in $lgg(a_1, a_3)$.

The next proposition shows the relationship between the variables in the lgg's of three atoms a_1, a_2 and a_3 which satisfy $d(a_1, a_2) = d(a_1, a_3) + d(a_3, a_2)$.

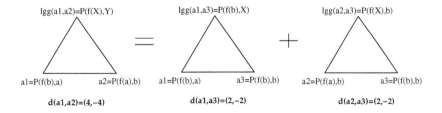

Fig. 3. An illustrative example

Proposition 6. *Let a_1, a_2 and a_3 be three atoms such that $d(a_1, a_2) = d(a_1, a_3) + d(a_3, a_2)$. Then, each variable appearing in $lgg(a_1, a_2)$ will be reflected either in $lgg(a_1, a_3)$ or in $lgg(a_2, a_3)$ only once. If a variable in $lgg(a_1, a_2)$ has multiple occurrences and one of these occurrences is reflected in $lgg(a_1, a_3)$ (equivalently $lgg(a_2, a_3)$) then, the rest of occurrences of the same variable will be also reflected in $lgg(a_1, a_3)$ (equivalently $lgg(a_2, a_3)$). Hence, $lgg(a_1, a_3)$ (equivalently $lgg(a_2, a_3)$) is a more specific atom than $lgg(a_1, a_2)$.*

Proof. The first part of the proposition is a derived consequence from Proposition 5. Recall that if $sk(lgg(a_1, a_2)) \subset sk(a_3)$ then, for each variable in position $p \cdot *$ in $lgg(a_1, a_3)$ or in $lgg(a_2, a_3)$ there exists a variable (modulo renaming) which occur in $lgg(a_1, a_2)$ at position $p \cdot *$. Additionally, those terms in a_3 which are not covered by the $sk(lgg(a_1, a_2))$ coincide with those terms placed at the same position either in a_1 or in a_2. Thus, all the variables in $lgg(a_1, a_2)$ will be reflected either in $lgg(a_1, a_3)$ or in $lgg(a_2, a_3)$ only once. An immediate effect of this part of the proposition is that the number of variables in $lgg(a_1, a_2)$ is equal to the number of variables in $lgg(a_1, a_3)$ plus the number of variables in $lgg(a_1, a_2)$.

Now let us prove the second part of the proposition (we use the function $V(a, X)$ employed in [9] which values the occurrences of variable X in the atom a.). Imagine that a variable X occurs n times in $lgg(a_1, a_2)$ then, $V(lgg(a_1, a_2), X) = n^2$. Now, let us suppose that n_1 occurrences of X are reflected in $lgg(a_1, a_3)$ and the rest of them, n_2, in $lgg(a_2, a_3)$ then, we would have $V(lgg(a_1, a_3), X) + V(lgg(a_2, a_3), X) = n_1^2 + n_2^2$. As $n = n_1 + n_2$ trivially we have $n^2 < n_1^2 + n_2^2$. So the only possibility for $V(lgg(a_1, a_2), X) = V(lgg(a_1, a_3), X) + V(lgg(a_2, a_3), X)$ to be hold is that the occurrences of any variable, namely Y, in $lgg(a_1, a_3)$ or in $lgg(a_2, a_3)$ increase. But it cannot happen because a_3 is built from (sub)-terms in a_1 and in a_2. Therefore, all the occurrences of one variable X in $lgg(a_1, a_2)$ are reflected either in $lgg(a_1, a_3)$ or in $lgg(a_2, a_3)$. This fact implies that the $lgg(a_1, a_3)$ and the $lgg(a_2, a_3)$ are more specific atoms than $lgg(a_1, a_2)$.

Now, we are ready to proof the feasibility of Δ for the current metric space.

Theorem 1. *The Δ function defined in Definition 8 is a 1-generalisation.*

Proof. — *(No Isolation).* Given an atom a, its nearest atoms are obtained by changing one of its constant (sub)-term by a variable. Calling a' to this new atom, it is trivial to see that the $lgg(a, a') = a'$ and, as we know, the number of symbols in a' is one less than the number of symbols in a whereas the number of variable occurrences in a' is one more than in a. Thus, the distance between a and a' is

$$d(a, a') = [size(a) - size(a')] + [size(a') - size(a')]$$
$$= (1, -1) + (0, 0) = (1, -1)$$

Therefore, given an atom a all its nearest atoms are $(1, -1)$ away. As the symbols are counted, the distance is not affected by the relative position of those different sub-terms between two atoms. Hence, it does not matter if the substituted (sub)-term constant symbol in a is placed at a higher or at a deeper position, the distance between a and a' will be the same. Thus, given two atoms a_1 and a_2, their generalisation $\Delta(a_1, a_2)$ and a new atom a_3 belonging to $\Delta(a_1, a_2)$, from the Definition 8 we know that there exists a substitution σ such that $a_3 = lgg(a_1, a_2)\sigma$. If we change any of the constant symbols appearing in σ by a variable (denoting this new substitution by σ'), we will obtain a new atom $a'_3 = lgg(a_1, a_2)\sigma'$ such that $d(a_3, a'_3) = (1, -1)$. Obviously, a'_3 belongs to $\Delta(a_1, a_2)$ and a'_3 is one of the nearest possible atoms to a_3.

– (*Scope*). The aim of this proof will consist of showing that if this identity $d(a_1, a_2) = d(a_1, a_3) + d(a_3, a_2)$ is preserved, where a_i are atoms, then a_3 is an instance of the $lgg(a_1, a_2)$ and consequently, a_3 belongs to $\Delta(a_1, a_2)$. By Proposition 6 it is followed that there exists a substitution σ_1 such that $lgg(a_1, a_3) = lgg(a_1, a_2)\sigma_1$. Then, by lgg definition, we know that there also exists a substitution σ_2 such that $a_3 = lgg(a_1, a_3)\sigma_2$. Hence, $a_3 = lgg(a_1, a_2)\sigma_1\sigma_2$ and a_3 belongs to $\Delta(a_1, a_2)$.

After the previous results on a generalisation operator (lgg), a pattern language (first-order logic) and a metric ([9]), it may see a little bit arduous to get positive results for another combination of generalisation, pattern language and metric. Nonetheless, this is important, because when we prove the properties we are more confident that the contribution can work better for extracting meaningful patterns from generalisation methods.

5   Conclusions

In this paper we have analysed the connection of three different, but highly related, notions: distance, pattern and generalisation. Although these notions are extremely related, there have not been many theoretical works that have studied the relationships among these three topics at the same time. This work intends to be a first step for this purpose. We have introduced a generalisation definition to identify the representation patterns which can behave as proper generalisations in the context of an underlying metric space. We have shown that given a metric, not every general pattern is a good generalisation. On the other hand, we have shown that we can have suitable generalisation patterns for the most usual metrics defined for well-known data types. One of the combinations we have analysed is lgg as a generalisation operator, first-order logic atoms as patterns and data language, and the [9] metric. We have shown that this metric could be used for many distance-based methods (as the authors claimed) and that the classification can be accompanied by a proper and well-behaving pattern for this metric: in this case the lgg. Other ILP generalisation operators and metrics could be studied as well, but maybe this combination is "natural" in many ways, since lgg is at the core of first-order logic.

As an immediate future work, we are studying the extension of the notion to generalisation operators applied to pairs of a set and an element, thus allowing the generalisation to be applied incrementally, and the extension of the definition to the Cartesian product of different types. All this could constitute an integrated framework that can be applied to many distance-based methods. For instance, in k-nearest neighbours, we could use an incremental generalisation operator to generate patterns which would be consistent with the clustering or classification performed by the k-nearest neighbour based on the underlying distance, starting from the closest elements to the farthest. Other case-based reasoning techniques based on distances can benefit from this as well. In a similar way, we could be able to give explanations to other methods that use distances. For instance, in a previous work, we have defined a distance-based decision tree, where the splits are determined by metric conditions, as the centre-splitting technique does. The generalisation operators introduced in section 3 can be used to give a comprehensible representation to the partitions, and hence to the overall decision tree, even if the problem contains non-standard data types such as lists or sets. In some way, this is a general approach to obtaining comprehensible patterns when distances are computed from structured data types. For instance, in [4], they compute kernels, and hence distances, for structured data types.

Finally, we would also like to study the "nested composability" of the generalisation conditions, i.e., lists of lists, or sets of lists of trees, that could deal with deeply complex structures. Other topics of research would be to analyse the associativity of the incremental generalisation operator (which we consider a minor issue for the applications considered), or the definition of a restricted generalisation if we use negative cases into account.

Acknowledgements. We gratefully acknowledge the referees for their many useful and helpful comments.

References

1. D. W. Aha, D. Kibler, and M. K. Albert. Instance-based learning algorithms. *Machine Learning*, 6(1):37–66, January 1991.
2. Ricardo A. Baeza-Yates and Berthier A. Ribeiro-Neto. *Modern Information Retrieval*. ACM Press / Addison-Wesley, 1999.
3. M. Falaschi, G. Levi, M. Martelli, and C. Palamidessi. Declarative Modeling of the Operational Behavior of Logic Languages. *Theoretical Computer Science*, 69(3):289–318, 1989.
4. T. Gartner, J. W. Lloyd, and P. A. Flach. Kernels and distances for structured data. *Machine Learning*, 57, 2004.
5. A. K. Jain, M. N. Murty, and P. J. Flynn. Data clustering: a review. *ACM Comp. Surveys*, 31(3):264–323, 1999.
6. T. M. Mitchell. *Machine Learning*. McGraw-Hill, 1997.
7. G. Plotkin. A note on inductive generalization. *Machine Intelligence*, 5:153–163, 1970.
8. J. R. Quinlan. *C4.5: Programs for Machine Learning*. Morgan Kaufmann, San Mateo, CA, 1993.
9. J. Ramon, M. Bruynooghe, and W. Van Laer. Distance measures between atoms. In *CompulogNet Area Meeting on Computational Logic and Machine Learing*, pages 35–41. University of Manchester, UK, 1998.

Automatic Induction of Abduction and Abstraction Theories from Observations

Stefano Ferilli, Teresa M.A. Basile, Nicola Di Mauro, and Floriana Esposito

Department of Computer Science, University of Bari, Italy
{ferilli, basile, ndm, esposito}@di.uniba.it

Abstract. Traditional Machine Learning approaches are based on single inference mechanisms. A step forward concerned the integration of multiple inference strategies within a first-order logic learning framework, taking advantage of the benefits that each approach can bring. Specifically, abduction is exploited to complete the incoming information in order to handle cases of missing knowledge, and abstraction is exploited to eliminate superfluous details that can affect the performance of a learning system. However, these methods require some background information to exploit the specific inference strategy, that must be provided by a domain expert.

This work proposes algorithms to automatically discover such an information in order to make the learning task completely autonomous. The proposed methods have been tested on the system INTHELEX, and their effectiveness has been proven by experiments in a real-world domain.

1 Introduction

In real-life domains, learning systems often have to deal with various kinds of imperfections in data: presence of random errors in both training examples and background knowledge (*noise*); too sparse training examples from which it is difficult to reliably detect correlations (*incompleteness*); inappropriateness of the description language which does not contain/facilitate an exact representation of the target concept (*inexact data*). Another kind of imperfection, more difficult to be dealt with, is represented by missing values in the training examples. As a solution, various noise-handling mechanisms have been exploited.

In dealing with such situations, most traditional Machine Learning approaches that exploit simple or constrained knowledge representations for the sake of efficiency, and are based on single (often simple or simplified) inference mechanisms, have reached their limits [16]. In order to investigate how to broaden the applicability of machine learning schemes, it is necessary to make different inference strategies work together, taking advantage of the benefits that each approach can bring. Many studies presented in the literature aimed at enforcing the integration of multiple inference strategies within a logic programming framework for first-order logic learning.

S. Kramer and B. Pfahringer (Eds.): ILP 2005, LNAI 3625, pp. 103–120, 2005.

The general schema of the inductive concept-learning paradigm ($BK \cup T \models O$) involves four variables, namely: the language $\mathcal{L}$, for which in this work the *single representation trick* [1] will be assumed, the background knowledge BK and the theory T that contains concept definitions explaining the occurrence of some observations O. Observations O stand for the extensional representation of concepts, and the aim is building an intensional description T, expressed in the language $\mathcal{L}$, that explains such concepts, supposed that BK is insufficient to give such an explanation. Most approaches focus on inductive mechanisms to fine-tune T in order to achieve the learning goal.

Two problems of the traditional approach to concept-learning can be singled out: the partial relevance of the available evidence O and the insolvability of a learning problem when the language $\mathcal{L}$ is not enough powerful to express a proper predicate definition in T. Abduction and abstraction can be exploited, respectively, to overcome such limitations: the former could bridge the gap between the observations and the definitions in the theory. The latter could shift to a higher language bias when the current one does not allow to capture the target predicate definition. From an operational viewpoint, abduction should somehow complete the observations with unknown facts that are likely to take place in the given situation and that can help in solving the learning problem at hand; it can be carried out by an abductive proof procedure, that shares the falsity-preserving nature with the inductive refinement operators [14]. As regards abstraction, it should deal with cases when learning can be more effective if it can take place at multiple (different) levels of complexity, which can be compared to the language bias shift considered in [2]; a useful perspective for the integration of this inference operator in an inductive learning framework was given in [23].

According to such a perspective, the incremental ILP system INTHELEX was extended in previous works to exploit abduction and abstraction to support the learning process [5]. However, it assumes that the information needed to apply the additional inference strategies is provided by the user. The objective of this work is investigating solutions for the automatic inference of such information from the same observations that are input to the inductive process, assuming that they are sufficiently significant. Abstraction should simplify the description language by grouping or eliminating correspondences that hold often or seldom, respectively, among the given observations. Abduction should consider as integrity constraints combinations of properties and relations that do not hold in the available observations. In the former case, the method focuses on the discovery of sets of common features in the observations; in the latter, sets of mutually exclusive features have to be singled out.

2   The General Framework

2.1   Handling Incomplete Information: Abduction

The problem of abduction, defined as *inference to the best explanation* according to a given domain theory, can be formalized as follows [4]: **Given** a theory T^1,

---

[1] Here, the theory T is assumed to include also the background knowledge.

some observations O and some constraints I, **Find** an explanation H such that: $T \cup H$ is consistent and satisfies I, $T \cup H \models O$. Candidate explanations H should be described in terms of domain-specific predicates, referred to as *abducibles*, that are not (completely) defined in T, but contribute to the definition of other predicates. They carry all the incompleteness of theory T: if it was possible to complete these predicates then the theory would be correctly described. The integrity constraints I should provide indirect information about them [10].

Since abduction is able to capture *default reasoning* (a form of reasoning which deals with incomplete information [10]), it can be exploited to face the problem of relevance and incompleteness. Indeed, when partial relevance is assumed, it could be the case that not only the set of all observations is partially known, but also any single observation may turn out to be incomplete. The usual *Abductive Logic Programming* framework [14, 6] can be adapted to concept learning theory revision problem as follows:

Definition 1. *An* abductive logic theory *is a triple $AT = (T, \mathcal{A}, \mathcal{I})$ where T is a (hierarchical) normal logic program; $\mathcal{A}$ is the set of abducible predicates; $\mathcal{I}$ is a set of integrity constraints represented as program clauses.*

In the original ALP framework, the theories are full normal logic programs interpreted according to the Stable Model semantics [11]. We restrict to *hierarchical* theories in order to exploit the Least Herbrand Models semantics, where if $T \models P_1$, ..., $T \models P_n$ then it also holds that $T \models P_1 \wedge \cdots \wedge P_n$, which is fundamental in an incremental setting, where examples are provided over time, to check correctness of the refined hypotheses with respect to older examples by testing them separately. This cannot be done when stable models semantics is adopted (cf. [6] for an example). Additionally, Least Herbrand Models semantics allows to cope with negation by means of the Negation as Failure rule, without transforming the theory and goals into their *positive version*, as required by the original framework. The integrity constraints $\mathcal{I}$ can be represented in principle as any first order formulæ. Some restrictions are to be applied: in the integrated framework described in [3], they are represented as range-restricted Horn clauses.

An abductive proof procedure can find explanations that make hypotheses (abductive assumptions) on the state of the world, possibly involving new abducible concepts, and is generally goal-driven by the observations that it tries to explain. The abductive proof procedure proposed in [12] works just like a standard SLD derivation [15], only when a literal cannot be proved the procedure does not fail immediately but first checks if it can be (or has already been) abductively hypothesized. In such a case, a consistency-check subroutine must ensure that no integrity constraints $\mathcal{I}$ is violated, by inductively or abductively deriving the falsity of at least one literal in each of them. Thus, the two procedures may call each other both when a new abductive assumption requires further consistency checks against the constraints and vice-versa.

2.2   Shifting Representation Language: Abstraction

Abstraction is defined as a mapping between representations that are related to the same reference set but contain less detail (typically, only the information that is relevant to the achievement of the goal is maintained). It is useful in inductive learning when the current language bias proves not to be expressive enough for representing concept descriptions that can explain the examples.

Definition 2. *Given two clausal theories T (ground theory) and T' (abstract theory) built upon different languages $\mathcal{L}$ and $\mathcal{L}'$ (and derivation rules), an ab-straction is a triple (T, T', f), where f is a computable total mapping between clauses in $\mathcal{L}$ and those in $\mathcal{L}'$.*

An Abstraction Theory (an operational representation of f) is used to perform such a *shift of language bias* [22, 2] to a higher level representation:

Definition 3. *An abstraction theory from $\mathcal{L}$ to $\mathcal{L}'$ is a consistent set of clauses $c : -d_1, \ldots, d_m$ where c is a literal built on predicates in $\mathcal{L}'$, and d_j, $j = 1, \ldots, m$ are literals built on predicates of $\mathcal{L}$.*

i.e., it is a collection of intermediate concepts represented as a disjunction of al-ternative definitions. *Inverse resolution* operators [17] (inter-construction, intra-construction and absorption) can be a valuable mechanism to build and exploit abstraction theories, as introduced in [9]. This work is interested in the case of Datalog programs, as in [19], where clauses are *flattened*, hence function-free.

Definition 4 (absorption). *Let C and D be two Datalog clauses. If $\exists \theta$ unifier such that $S = body(D)\theta \subset body(C)$, then applying the absorption operator yields the new clause C' such that $head(C') = head(C)$ and $body(C') = (body(C) \setminus S) \cup \{head(D)\theta\}$.*

i.e., if all conditions in D are verified in the body of C, the corresponding literals are eliminated and replaced by $head(D)$.

According to the framework proposed in [23], abstraction takes place by means of a set of operators, that generally includes operators for grouping indis-tinguishable objects into equivalence classes; grouping ground objects to form a compound object (that replaces them in the abstract world); ignoring terms (that disappear in the abstract world); merging values that are considered indis-tinguishable; reducing the arity of a function or relation (even up to elimination of *all* arguments). Modifications are performed by mappings.

2.3   Learning Background Knowledge for Multi-inference Strategies

As already pointed out, the exploitation of the two strategies reported above and their integration in an inductive concept learning framework is based on the assumption that the knowledge needed to use them is provided by an expert of the application domain. Here we propose an approach to automatically learn such knowledge to be exploited by the abduction/abstraction operators. It is worth recalling that the feasibility of reaching the target solution requires that the number of values for the domains to be identified and the amount of available knowledge about observations to be strictly proportional. Indeed, the more the values, the more the possible interrelations that can take place between them. If the available observations are not sufficiently significant, i.e. too many existing interrelations are not recognizable in them, then knowledge about the actual biases in the given domain would be too loose for the algorithm to properly infer significant and correct information.

3 Learning Abduction Theories

The exploitation of the abductive proof procedure presented in Section 2.1 requires the specification of an abductive theory for the specific application domain. Usually, it is provided by a domain expert; in the following we propose a methodology for automatically inferring it starting from the available observations, in order to make the learning system completely autonomous.

3.1 Abducibles

In setting up an abductive logic programming task, the logic program is typically to be learnt, while abducibles and integrity constraints have to be provided by the domain expert. Thus, a first problem is deciding on which properties and/or relations abduction can be carried out, i.e. listing the abducibles. Indeed, abductive reasoning needs to know them in order to assess on which concepts abductions (i.e., guesses about unknown facts) can be made. We assume that all predicates that make up the description language, and have no definition in the theory (in order to fulfil the requirements for abducibles [4]), are considered as abducibles since by hypothesis some of their instances could be missing in the available dataset. Indeed, in the absence of further information, any fact that can help in solving the problem at hand is useful, and the automatic system should be allowed to hypothesize it, in order to provide the abductive reasoner with all the freedom it needs for hypothesizing information.

3.2 Integrity Constraints

The other issue, far more complex, concerns the definition of the integrity constraints. It is, at the same time, a fundamental and difficult task, whose quality can determine the very feasibility of the learning process. Hence, the motivation for automatically inferring such constraints, this way overcoming possible problems related to omissions and/or wrong formalization of the human expert.

Learning denials (the form in which integrity constraints are coded in an abductive theory) cannot be simply cast as a supervised learning task, since it aims at inducing rules whose head is empty. Rather, it can be seen as a specific case of unsupervised learning aimed at finding regularities (specifically, conditions that are never verified) in a first-order logic database. Thus, the data mining approaches are better suited to carry out this task. Some systems are present in the literature that can learn denials. One of them is Claudien [18], that actually implements a more general algorithm for finding regularities that occur in a set of unlabelled observations represented as facts. It requires a template of the clauses to be induced, and can limit the corresponding search space using heuristics and resource bounds. By properly setting its parameters, it can be applied for learning classification rules, association rules, (non necessarily definite) clauses and also denials. Such a system inspired a number of successive works, among which the development of the systems Primus and its successor Tertius [8]. They are based on the generation of possible (H, B) couples, where H and B are sets of literals in the given description language to be interpreted, possibly negated, as candidate head and body, respectively, of a clause to be generated. The frequency with which each candidate rule is (or is not) verified in the dataset is computed, and statistical approaches are exploited to decide if such frequencies are significant, in which case a corresponding rule is generated. Background knowledge (i.e., derived predicates such as *ancestor* in a family environment) can be used, but increasing the number of literals in H and B causes high computational costs, thus sampling and non-redundant operators are exploited. Another widely known learning system that can induce integrity constraints is Aleph [21], that works in a similar way as Claudien. All of these systems can actually learn denials, but this is just a specific setting or a side-effect of a wider range of possibilities that the implemented algorithms provide. Thus, the aim of this paper is devising simpler procedures, purposely devoted to the generation of integrity constraints for an abductive theory, that being limited to this specific task can carry out it in a more focused and effective way.

The starting point in doing this is the fact that integrity constraints represent situations that cannot occur in the described world. Thus, the available observations cannot actively help in defining them. Rather, the aim is identifying combinations of descriptors and of the related arguments that cannot hold. In doing so, one possible strategy is generating a number of such combinations, according to a given strategy, and then exploiting the available observations passively to check if the generated combination occur in at least one case or not. In the former case, it cannot be a constraint, according to the assumption that observations are correct and report only true information. In the latter case, this can be taken as a suggestion, but not of course as a guarantee (since its absence could be due to just the fact that by chance that situation did not ever occur in the specific observations at hand), that the combination does not occur because it in fact makes no sense in the considered world[2]. This, of course, raises the problem of having a set of observations that is significant not only numerically, but also in the sense that they depict a significant amount of different cases. Nevertheless, such a significance should be assumed, because otherwise the learning task itself, to be carried out on such observations, would hardly make sense.

Now, the point is how to proceed in generating the literals (and variables) combinations to be tested. Indeed, it is clear that generating and testing all possible combinations becomes soon impossible even for relatively small datasets. Bounding the cardinality of the combinations to be generated to a given l, al-

---

[2] In any case, this makes useless counting the frequencies as in Tertius, since every combination that is verified is not a constraint, no matter how many times it happens.

though useful, is not sufficient to avoid the combinatorial explosion. Thus, it is necessary to identify specific classes of constraints that can be considered meaningful in general (i.e., without reference to specific datasets or environments) and thus are worth checking. A first important class is that of object properties, represented by unary predicates. Indeed, it is undoubtedly interesting to know which combinations of attributes are (im-)possible for a given object, in order for the abductive proof procedure to avoid them (e.g., it generally holds that a line is either tall or wide, but cannot be both at the same time). In this case, the problem can be significantly simplified since the presence of just one variable in the predicates allows to focus on just the predicates combinations, excluding the generation of duplicate literals and the presence of unrelated variables. The procedure is detailed in Algorithm 1.. *NotConstraints* and *Constraints* are two (initially empty) lists, containing the currently identified non-constraints and constraints, respectively. The presence of each potential constraint in the observations is checked: in case of success, it is added to the list of constraints, provided that the *not_trivial* function succeeds. A constraint is considered trivial if it is a superset of some other (shorter) constraint that is already present in the Constraints list, so the *not_trivial* function avoids generating (and learning) redundant constraints, just like in related work. In the first step, all possible n-tuples (with $2 \leq n \leq N$ for a fixed N) of unary predicates, all applied to the same variable, are generated and checked for occurrence in the available observations. The generation proceeds from lower to higher values of n. First, all pairs of unary predicates are generated and checked for occurrence: those that are not satisfied by the observations are considered constraints and added to the *Constraints* list; conversely, those that happen at least once are added to the *NotConstraints* list. Then, all non-constraints of cardinality 2 are extracted from *NotConstraints* and extended with one more unary predicate, checked for occurrence and added to *NotConstraints* or *Constraints* accordingly. Then, all newly found non-constraints of cardinality 3 are extended and checked, and so on until the fixed N is reached.

However, although very useful, constraints on properties are not sufficient. It is often important, for the purpose of learning a significant abduction theory, to consider also constraints built on n-ary predicates. Without loss of generality, in this work we restrict to binary predicates, and propose a set of typical relationships among the arguments that appear in pairs of such predicates that are deemed as significant to be exploited as constraints. Specifically, given two *predicate variables* P and Q (not necessarily distinct) ranging on binary predicates of the representation language $\mathcal{L}$, and three variables X, Y, Z, the *rules schemas* [13] (denials) that we propose to check are $\leftarrow P(X,X)$. (*reflexivity*), $\leftarrow P(X,Y), Q(Y,X)$. (*symmetry*), $\leftarrow P(X,Y), Q(Y,Z)$. (*transitivity*), $\leftarrow P(X,Y), Q(Z,Y)$. (*convergence*), and $\leftarrow P(X,Y), Q(X,Z)$. (*divergence*).

In the next step, all binary predicates are considered, and checked for occurrence of the reflexive, symmetric, transitive, converging and diverging relationships. Again, when a relationship has no counterpart in the available observations, it is added to the *Constraints*, otherwise it is added to the *NotConstraints*.

Algorithm 1. Induction of Integrity Constraints made up of unary predicates

Create_Constraints(N; $\mathcal{E}$; $UnaryPreds$; $NotConstraints$; $Constraints$);
$\{$ N: Maximal cardinality of constraints to generate; $\mathcal{E}$: Set of observations;
$UnaryPreds$: Set of Unary Predicates; $NotConstraints$: Set of non-Constraints;
$Constraints$: Set of Integrity Constraints $\}$
$NotConstraints := \emptyset$; $Constraints := \emptyset$
for all $a, b \in UnaryPreds, a \neq b$ **do**
  if $\mathcal{E} \vdash \{a(X), b(X)\}$ **then**
    $NotConstraints := NotConstraints \cup \{\{a(X), b(X)\}\}$
  else
    $Constraints := Constraints \cup \{\{a(X), b(X)\}\}$
for $n := 3..N$ **do**
  for all $NC \in NotConstraints, |NC| = n - 1$ **do**
    for all $a(X) \in UnaryPreds$ **do**
      if $not\_trivial(Constraints, \{a(X)\} \cup NC)$ **then**
        if $\mathcal{E} \vdash \{\{a(X)\} \cup NC\}$ **then**
          $NotConstraints := NotConstraints \cup \{\{a(X)\} \cup NC\}$
        else
          $Constraints := Constraints \cup \{\{a(X)\} \cup NC\}$

Lastly, all possible combinations of non-constraints on binary predicates relationships and on unary predicates (applied to any of the variables appearing in the former), whose cardinality does not exceed the fixed N, are checked for occurrence and added to the *Constraints*, if it is the case, according to Algorithm 2.. It starts the process taking as input the list of *non-constraints*, both unary and binary, built so far. $UnaryNotConstrs$ and $BinaryNotConstrs$ are the sets of non-constraints found in the previous steps. Since all constraints on unary predicates have at least cardinality 2, a preliminary step in which all possible combinations of constraints on binary predicates with a single unary predicate must be separately checked. Note that, in this step, no candidate constraint can be trivial, since its binary component is not a constraint by itelf and its unary component is just a singleton. Conversely, in the loop that combinates unary and binary constraints, the only way a constraint can be trivial is being a superset of a constraint obtained in the previous loop, since none of its components is a constraint by itself.

Example 1.   Consider the description language made up of the predicates:
{ block/1, line/1, low/1, medium/1, high/1, narrow/1, wide/1, part_of/2, on_top/2, to_right/2 }. Let the available observations be:
{ part_of(a,b), part_of(a,c), part_of(a,d), part_of(a,e), part_of(a,f), line(b), medium(b), narrow(b), block(c), high(c), wide(c), line(d), low(d), wide(d), block(e), medium(e), wide(e), block(f), medium(f), wide(f), on_top(d,b), on_top(d,e), on_top(d,f), on_top(b,c), on_top(e,c), on_top(f,c),to_right(b,e), to_right(f,b) } (representing the block world in Figure 1) and N be fixed to 4.

- Step 1:
  - Pairs of unary predicates: ***Constraints*** = { $\{block(X), line(X)\}$, $\{block(X), low(X)\}$, $\{block(X), narrow(X)\}$, $\{line(X), high(X)\}$,

---

Algorithm 2. Integrity Constraints made up of unary/binary predicates

---

Create_constraints_with_binary_and_unary_literals(N;   *Unary*;   *Constrs*;
UnaryNotConstrs; *BinaryNotConstrs***)**;
{N: Maximal cardinality of constraints to generate; $\mathcal{E}$: Set of observations; *Unary*:
Set of Unary Predicates; *Constrs*: Set of Integrity Constraints made up of unary or
binary predicates; *UnaryNotConstrs*: Set of non-constraints made up of unary predicates; *BinaryNotConstrs*: Set of non-constraints made up of binary predicates.}
for all $NC \in BinaryNotConstrs, X \in vars(NC), p \in Unary$ **do**
  if $|NC| < N \wedge \mathcal{E} \not\vdash NC \cup \{p(X)\}$ **then** $Constrs := Constrs \cup \{\{p(X)\} \cup NC\}$
for all $BNC \in BinaryNotConstrs$ **do**
  V := vars(BNC); $TentativeConstr$:= BNC;
  for all $S \subseteq V$ **do**
    apply a $UNC \in BinaryNotConstrs$ to each $X \in S$, add it to $TentativeConstr$
    if $|TentativeConstr| \leq N \wedge not\_trivial(Constrs, TentativeConstr) \wedge$
    $\mathcal{E} \not\vdash TentativeConstr$ **then**
      $Constrs := Constrs \cup \{TentativeConstr\}$

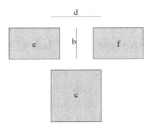

Fig. 1. Sample block world

$\{low(X), medium(X)\}, \{low(X), high(X)\}, \{low(X), narrow(X)\},$
$\{medium(X), high(X)\}, \{high(X), narrow(X)\}, \{narrow(X), wide(X)\}$ }
NotConstraints = { $\{block(X), medium(X)\}, \{block(X), high(X)\},$
$\{block(X), wide(X)\}, \{line(X), low(X)\}, \{line(X), medium(X)\},$
$\{line(X), narrow(X)\}, \{line(X), wide(X)\}, \{low(X), wide(X)\},$
$\{medium(X), narrow(X)\}, \{medium(X), wide(X)\}, \{high(X), wide(X)\}$ }

- Triplets of unary predicates (extending couples of *NotConstraints*):
  Constraints=$\{\{line(X), medium(X), wide(X)\}, \{line(X), high(X), wide(X)\}\}$
  NotConstraints = { $\{block(X), medium(X), wide(X)\},$
  $\{block(X), high(X), wide(X)\}, \{line(X), low(X), wide(X)\},$
  $\{line(X), medium(X), narrow(X)\}$ }
  All other possible extensions of binary non-constraints are trivial.
- 4-tuples of unary predicates: all 4-tuples obtained extending ternary non-
  constraints are trivial, thus in this step both Constraints and NotConstraints
  are empty. As a side effect, there are no non-constraints of cardinality 4 to be
  extended, and hence no constraints of cardinality larger than 4 can be found.
– Step 2:
  - Reflexivity: ***NotConstraints*** = $\emptyset$
    Constraints = { $\{part\_of(X, X)\}, \{on\_top(X, X)\}, \{to\_right(X, X)\}$ }

- Symmetry: **NotConstraints** $= \emptyset$
  Constraints$=\{\{part\_of(X,Y), part\_of(Y,X)\}, \{on\_top(X,Y), on\_top(Y,X)\},$
  $\{to\_right(X,Y), to\_right(Y,X)\}, \{part\_of(X,Y), on\_top(Y,X)\},$
  $\{part\_of(X,Y), to\_right(Y,X)\}, \{on\_top(X,Y), to\_right(Y,X)\}$ $\}$
- Transitivity: **NotConstraints** $= \{$ $\{on\_top(X,Y), on\_top(Y,Z)\},$
  $\{to\_right(X,Y), to\_right(Y,Z)\}, \{part\_of(X,Y), on\_top(Y,Z)\},$
  $\{part\_of(X,Y), to\_right(Y,Z)\}, \{to\_right(X,Y), on\_top(Y,Z)\}$ $\}$
  Constraints$=\{\{part\_of(X,Y), part\_of(Y,Z)\}, \{on\_top(X,Y), part\_of(Y,Z)\},$
  $\{to\_right(X,Y), part\_of(Y,Z)\}, \{on\_top(X,Y), to\_right(Y,X)\}\}$
- Convergence: **NotConstraints** $= \{$ $\{on\_top(X,Y), on\_top(Z,Y)\},$
  $\{on\_top(X,Y), part\_of(Z,Y)\}, \{to\_right(X,Y), part\_of(Z,Y)\},$
  $\{on\_top(X,Y), to\_right(Z,Y)\}$ $\}$
  Constraints $= \{$ $\{part\_of(X,Y), part\_of(Z,Y)\},$
  $\{to\_right(X,Y), to\_right(Z,Y)\}$ $\}$
- Divergence: **NotConstraints** $= \{$ $\{part\_of(X,Y), part\_of(X,Z)\},$
  $\{on\_top(X,Y), on\_top(X,Z)\}, \{on\_top(X,Y), to\_right(X,Z)\}$ $\}$
  Constraints $= \{$ $\{to\_right(X,Y), to\_right(X,Z)\},$
  $\{on\_top(X,Y), part\_of(X,Z)\}, \{to\_right(X,Y), part\_of(X,Z)\}$ $\}$;
- Step 3 (omitted due to lack of space)

3.3   Descriptors Type Domains and Abducibles

At the end of the procedure reported in Algorithm 1., the set of constraints of cardinality 2 can be input to the type induction procedure presented in [7] in order to infer type domains. Then, all pairs of unary predicates belonging to the same domain can be eliminated from the set $Constraints$, thus reducing the complexity of the abductive proof procedure, and a new kind of constraint will be introduced to represent types, such that no two values from the same type domain will be allowed applied to the same object. For example, if the descriptor type domain for the color property is $\{blue, red, yellow, black, green\}$, and the object X is part of an observation, it will be impossible to abduce two different color descriptors from the above set applied to X.

4   Learning Abstraction Theories

As pointed out in Section 2.2, abstraction aims at discarding or hiding the information that is irrelevant to achieve the goal. To be able to perform abstraction during the learning task, the system must be provided with an abstraction theory for the specific application domain, that (according to Definitions 2 and 3) contains the operators encoding the abstraction mapping f between languages $\mathcal{L}$ and $\mathcal{L}'$ represented as a set of clauses, i.e. domain rules.

Usually, such domain rules are hand-coded by the domain expert; this section proposes a methodology aimed at automatically learning them. The main idea underlying the proposed strategy consists in searching for correspondences that often or seldom hold among the available set of observations. These correspondences are then exploited to simplify the description language in two different

---

Algorithm 3. Identification of shifting/neglecting rules

Require: $\mathcal{E}^+$: set of positive observations; $\mathcal{E}^-$: set of negative observations; e: seed;
  Provide: AT: set of domain rules that make up an abstraction theory;
  if $\exists$ unary predicates in e **then**
    $S := \emptyset$, $UnaryPreds :=$ set of unary predicates in e
    $C := \{c_1, c_2, \ldots, c_n\}$ set of constants in the description of e
    for all $c_i \in C$ **do**
      $S_i := \{l_i \in UnaryPreds$ s.t. c_i is argument of $l_i\}$
      if $\mid S_i \mid \neq 0$ and $\mid S_i \mid \neq 1$ **then** $S := S \bigcup S_i$
    for i=1..n **do**
      for all $S_j \in S$ **do**
        find all the subsets s_{jm} of S_j s.t.
          $(0 - \alpha \leq Score(s_{jm}) \leq 0 + \alpha)$ OR $(Max - \alpha \leq Score(s_{jm}) \leq Max + \alpha)$
        create the rule: $rule_{s_{jm}}(c_i) \leftarrow s_{jm}$
        replace in $\mathcal{E}^+$, in $\mathcal{E}^-$ and in e, s_{jm} with $rule_{s_{jm}}(c_i)$
  while F ($:=$ set of all leaf predicates of e) $\neq \emptyset$ **do**
    for all $l_i \in F$ **do**
      if l_i has only one parent (let $g_i(a_i, \ldots, a_n)$ be the l_i's parent) **then**
        create the rule: $rule_{l_i}(a_i, ...a_n) \leftarrow g_i, l_i$; H := true
        replace in $\mathcal{E}^+$, in $\mathcal{E}^-$ and in e, g_i, l_i with $rule_{l_i}(a_i, ...a_n))$
    for all $rule_i \leftarrow l_{i_1}, \ldots, l_{i_n}$ generated **do**
      if $\{l_{i_1}, \ldots, l_{i_n}\}$ occurs in some rule $rule_j$ **then**
        replace $l_{i_1}, \ldots, l_{i_n}$ in $rule_j$ by $rule_i$
        eliminate $rule_i$ form the set of rules generated
  Evaluate the set of generated rules

---

ways: by generating *shifting rules* that replace significant, characteristic or discriminant groups of literals by one single literal representing their conjunction, or by generating *neglecting rules* that eliminate groups of literals that are not significant[3]. Both kinds of rules will be applied in order to perform the shift of language bias according to the absorption operator presented in Definition 4.

Algorithm 3. sketches the overall procedure conceived to discover common paths in the application domain that potentially could make up the Abstraction Theory. It firstly generates domain rules involving unary predicates only, that represent the characteristics of an object in the description, and then the rules involving predicates whose arity is greater than 1, that represent the relationships between two or more objects contained in the descriptions. Crucial point of the algorithm is the choice of the observation (referred to in the following as the *seed*) that will act as the representative of the concept that one would abstract. It is currently selected as the first encountered observation.

Once the seed is identified, for each constant c_i in its description, the algorithm finds the set of all the unary predicates having that constant as an argument, and computes all its possible subsets (except the empty set, that does

---

[3] The loss in detail is evident in the latter, while in the former derives from the impossibility to handle independently subsets of the grouped literals.

not give information about the object, or the singleton subsets, that express just single properties of the objects). Each subset identified in this way is a potential candidate to become the body of a rule, in the Abstraction Theory, made up of unary predicates. The selection among these subsets is done considering those that are the best representative for the class of the concept to be abstracted according to the seed e. Specifically, each subset is assigned a *score* based on the number of times that it occurs in the descriptions of positive and negative examples in the whole training set. Such a value represents the *coverage rate* of the subset with respect to the observations and indicates the quality of the subset. The selection aims at choosing those subsets that are neither too specific, because they are present in few observations, nor too general, because they are encountered in almost all the observations. Each selected subset s_j, interpreted as a conjunction of literals, becomes the body of a rule in the Abstraction Theory, formulated in the following way:

$$abstract\_predicate(c_i) \leftarrow s_j \quad \text{iff} \quad score(s_j) \geq P \quad \text{(shifting rule)}$$
$$\leftarrow s_j \quad \text{iff} \quad score(s_j) \leq P \quad \text{(neglecting rule)}$$

where P is a threshold that depends on the application domain at hand[4]. In the former case s_j is present in almost all the observations, hence it is considered significant as a whole for the learning process and thus it is taken as the body of a shifting rule, to be replaced by a single abstract predicate. In the latter case s_j is assumed to indicate a detail in the description that is not very significant for the learning process and thus it is eliminated (replaced by an empty head). In both cases, the abstraction operators will replace each occurrence in the description of the observations of the rule's body with the corresponding head, this way reducing the description length of observations and hence making the learning process more efficient.

The algorithm continues with the identification of rules made up of predicates whose arity is greater than 1 representing the relationships between two or more objects. Thus, once the abstraction rules, that are identified in the previous step, are replaced in all the observations, they don't contain any unary predicates. At this point, an iteration that groups together the n-ary predicates is performed until one of the following conditions succeeds: 1) the description of the seed e does not contain *leaf predicates* (predicates that share arguments with at least another predicate); 2) the step n generates exactly the same rules already built in the step $n - 1$. The search of the leaf predicates is particularly complex due to the large number of relationships that could hold between the objects in the descriptions. The identification of such predicates is done by representing the observation with a tree in which each level is determined by the propagation of the variables: the root is the head of the observation and its direct descendants are all the predicates that share with it at least one argument. This procedure is iterated until all the predicates in the description have been inserted in the tree (a considered predicate does not participate anymore to the tree construction).

---

[4] In order to make P independent on the specific domain, the score can be normalized as a percentage of the maximum score actually computed in the given dataset.

After the tree is constructed, we select the set of leaf nodes (predicates) that have only one parent, let it be $L = l_1, l_2, \ldots, l_n$. Successively, for each element $l \in L$ its parent, let be it the literal $g(a_1, \ldots, a_m)$, is extracted from the tree and the following rule is generated:

$$rule(a_1, \ldots, a_m) \leftarrow g(a_1, \ldots, a_m), l$$

Finally, for each rule $rule_i \leftarrow l_{i_1}, \ldots, l_{i_n}$ if the body of $rule_i$, i.e. $l_{i_1}, \ldots, l_{i_n}$, appears in some rule $rule_j$ then $l_{i_1}, \ldots, l_{i_n}$ is replaced in $rule_j$ by $rule_i$ and $rule_i$ is eliminated by the set of rules that are being generated. At the end of this step again the evaluation phase of the potential rules to make up the Abstraction Theory is performed according to the procedure above mentioned.

As to the *score* function, we need a statistical model able to take into account the significance of the subset for (i.e., its frequency in) the descriptions. Specifically, a significant subset should be able to characterize a concept, or to discriminate it from the others, better than other subsets. Conversely, a subset that is not characterizing or discriminant could be assumed as non-significant. An indication for such a setting could come from the distribution of the subset in the whole set of observations: in this perspective, an high significance value is associated to subsets that appear frequently in instances of one concept but rarely in instances of others (and hence help to distinguish a concept from the others), while a low significance value is associated to subsets that appear uniformly throughout different concepts (and hence are superfluous for the learning process). A statistical model that reflects such considerations is represented by the *Term Frequency - Inverse Document Frequency* (TF-IDF) [20]. Here, it must be adapted to a work context facing with positive and negative observations. In the following a brief description of the adapted method is provided.

Each subset s_i is associated with a vector $V_i = (V_{i1}, V_{i2}, \ldots, V_{iN})$ where N is the number of available observations and V_{ij} is the weight of the i-th subset in the j-th observation, computed as:

$$V_{ij} = FREQ_{ij} * (\lg \tfrac{N}{IFREQ_i} + 1)$$

The term $(\lg \tfrac{N}{IFREQ_i} + 1)$ represents the inverse of the frequency of subset s_i in the whole set of observations. Notice that the result of this computation will be positive if the j-th observation is positive, negative otherwise, thus the resulting vector will be of the form $V_i = (+, -, +, +, -, +, \ldots)$. This will allow to distinguish the significance of the subset according to its presence in the positive and negative observations. Now, having for each subset s_i the vector of its weights in the various observations, its score can be computed as follows:

$$score(s_i) = |\sum_{j=1,\ldots,N} V_{ij}|$$

It is worth noting that this score will be around zero if the subset equally occurs in both positive and negative observations, in which case it is considered insignificant and could be exploited as a neglecting rule in the abstraction phase. Conversely, an high absolute value indicates a strong correlation of the subset with the positive or the negative observations. Specifically, highly positive (resp., negative) scores indicate that the subset is very frequent in the positive (resp., negative) observations. In both cases, it is considered significant and hence it could be exploited to build shifting rules for the abstraction phase.

Example 2. Let $h(1) : -p(1,2), p(1,4), p(1,5), c(2,3), f(5,6), d(4), s(6)$ the seed chosen in the observations (in this case it represents the set of observations too).

- **Step 1**:
  - *Grouping unary predicates:* $S = \emptyset$ (no groups of unary predicates, referred to the same constant, with cardinality strictly greater than 1 can be recognized);
- **Step 2**:
  - *Recognize Leaf Nodes:* $F = \{c(2,3),\ d(4),\ s(6)\}$, indeed $c(2,3)$ has only one parent $p(1,2)$; $d(4)$ has only one parent $p(1,4)$; $s(6)$ has only one parent $f(5,6)$.
  - *Create the rules -* $rule_{l_i}(a_i, ...a_n) \leftarrow g_i, l_i$:
    $c(2,3)$ with parent $p(1,2) \rightarrow rule1(X,Y) : -p(X,Y), c(Y,Z)$.
    $d(4)$ with parent $p(1,4) \rightarrow rule2(X,Y) : -p(X,Y), d(Y)$.
    $s(6)$ with parent $f(5,6) \rightarrow rule3(X,Y) : -f(X,Y), s(Y)$.
  - *Replace the rule in the set of the observations:*
    $h(1) : -p(1,2), p(1,4), p(1,5), c(2,3), f(5,6), d(4), s(6). \rightarrow$
    $h(1) : -rule1(1,2), rule2(1,4), p(1,5), rule3(5,6)$.
- **Step 3**:
  - *Recognize Leaf Nodes:*
    $F = \{rule3(5,6)\}$, indeed $rule3(5,6)$ has only one parent $p(1,5)$.
  - *Create the rules -* $rule_{l_i}(a_i, ...a_n) \leftarrow g_i, l_i$:
    $rule3(5,6)$ with parent $p(1,5) \rightarrow rule4(X,Y) : -p(X,Y), rule3(Y,Z)$.
  - *Replace the rule in the set of the observations:*
    $h(1) : -rule1(1,2), rule2(1,4), p(1,5), rule3(5,6). \rightarrow$
    $h(1) : -rule1(1,2), rule2(1,4), rule4(5,6)$.
- **Step 4**: END - No more Leaf Nodes can be recognized

The procedure continues with the evaluation of the generated rules, that are:

$rule1(X,Y) : -p(X,Y), c(Y,Z)$.　　　　　　$rule2(X,Y) : -p(X,Y), d(Y)$.
$rule3(X,Y) : -f(X,Y), s(Y)$.　　　　　　　$rule4(X,Y) : -p(X,Y), rule3(Y,Z)$.

Now, supposing that $P = 95\%$ and that the scores of the rules are:
$Score1 = 95\%$; $Score2 = 99\%$; $Score3 = 75\%$; $Score4 = 86\%$,
$rule1$ and $rule2$ will be shifting rules, while $rule3$ and $rule4$ will be neglecting rules:

$rule1(X,Y) : -p(X,Y), c(Y,Z)$.　　　　　　$rule2(X,Y) : -p(X,Y), d(Y)$.
$: -f(X,Y), s(Y)$.　　　　　　　　　　　　$: -p(X,Y), rule3(Y,Z)$.

5   Experiments

The proposed methods were implemented in SICStus Prolog, and tested on the learning system INTHELEX with various experiments, whose results are reported in the following. 33 repetitions of each learning task were carried out, in each of which the dataset was randomly split into a training set (including 70% of the observations), exploited also to induce the rules for the abstraction operators) and a test set (made up of the remaining 30%).

Table 1. System performance with the exploitation of the discovered abductive theories

		Without abduction	With abduction Without type domains	With abduction With type domains
Lgg	Min - Max	3 - 13	2 - 8	0 - 2
	Med - StDev	7.72 - 2.08	5.48 - 1.5	1 - 0.66
Claus.	Min - Max	2 - 6	2 - 5	1 - 3
	Med - StDev	4.09 - 1.12	3.18 - 0.95	1.72 - 0.72
Accur.	Min - Max	89% - 100%	94% - 100%	91% - 100%
	Med - StDev	96.24% - 2.27	99.32% - 1.61	98.75% - 3.02
Runtime	Min - Max	3.20 - 13.36	4.98 - 170.36	3.06 - 84.40
	Med	5.16	40.05	24.29

5.1   Exploitation of the Learned Abductive Theories

The first experiment aimed at checking whether the *abducibles* and the *integrity constraints* automatically learned according to the proposed algorithms are effective to allow the abductive procedure implemented in INTHELEX to handle cases of missing information in the observations. The experiments concern the induction of layout-based classification rules for scientific papers belonging to ICML series. The available dataset was corrupted by eliminating the 8% of the descriptors for each observation contained in the tuning set. The learning system was applied on this dataset firstly without exploiting the abductive procedure. Successively, the learning process was repeated, allowing the system to exploit its abductive capability and the abduction theory automatically learned. We focused our attention on binary constraints made up of unary and binary predicates. One more experiment was run to test the usefulness of replacing groups of simple integrity constraints belonging to the same type by means of type constraints automatically inferred.

Table 1 reports the system performance in the various cases as regards the amount of performed refinements, lgg's and added clauses, predictive accuracy and runtime (sec). As we can note, the system performance improved with the exploitation of abduction with respect to all parameters except runtime. Actually, runtime increases because of the additional reasoning carried out by the abductive procedure; however, as expected, exploiting the type domains significantly reduces runtime because of the fewer constraints to be taken into account. According to a paired t-test, all differences are statistically significant except the predictive accuracy between the second and third rows. Thus, exploiting the automatically learned abduction theory allows the system to significantly improve its performance in the presence of missing data. The number of theory refinements and learned clauses decreases both using abduction and, even more, when type domains are exploited, indicating that the system was able to correctly complete the corrupted observations without applying the refinement procedure. Noticeably, except for accuracy, also the standard deviation constantly decreases, revealing more stability in the system behavior.

Table 2. System performance exploiting the discovered abstraction theories

	ICML		SVLN		IEEET	
	With Abs	No Abs	With Abs	No Abs	With Abs	No Abs
Lgg	5.81	5.54	7.36	8.12	8.03	8.30
Cl	1.21	1.27	2.75	2.69	2.03	2.27
Accuracy	96.93%	96.75%	86.54%	87.36%	90.69%	90.57%
Runtime	2.00	3.16	11.34	19.46	7.64	27.55

Table 3. Abstraction on ICML logic type components

	Author		Page Number		Title	
	With Abs	No Abs	With Abs	No Abs	With Abs	No Abs
Lgg	8.9	8.96	8.15	8.12	8.81	9.09
Cl	2.33	2.06	2.39	2.45	2.42	2.54
Accuracy	97.18%	97.12%	97.81%	97.54%	98.12%	97.87%
Runtime	14.44	29.07	34.06	76.22	27.70	51.67

5.2 Exploitation of the Abstraction Theories

The second experiment aimed at checking the effectiveness of the abstraction theories learned according to the proposed algorithms. Such rules were provided to INTHELEX, that was allowed to exploit the abstraction operators. The learning tasks involved the induction of classification rules for three classes of scientific papers (96 documents of which 28 for ICML, 32 for SVLN, 36 for IEEET), and of rules for identifying the logical components *Author* [36+, 332-], *Page Number* [27+, 341-] and *Title* [28+, 340-] in the ICML papers (in square brackets the number of positive and negative instances for each label are reported). To build neglecting rules, the threshold for considering low significance (i.e. the score near to zero) was empirically set to $P = 5\%$. To build shifting rules that have high significance (i.e. very frequent in positive observations and rarely present in negative observations and *vice versa*) the threshold was empirically set to $P = 95\%$ for the classification task and to $P = 75\%$ for the understanding task.

The average results on the 33 folds, along with the number of refinements and of clauses learned, the predictive accuracy of the learned theories and the runtime (sec), are reported in Tables 2 and 3. According to a paired t-test, there is no statistical difference between the results with and without abstraction, except for runtime. Having the same performance (predictive accuracy) and behavior (no. of clauses and refinements) both with and without abstraction means that the proposed technique was actually able to eliminate superfluous details only, leaving all the information that was necessary for the learning task, which was a fundamental requirement for abstraction. Conversely, runtime was dramatically reduced when using abstraction thanks to the shorter descriptions obtained by eliminating the details, which was exactly the objective of using abstraction.

An example of neglecting rule identified with the proposed strategy is:

```
:- type_graphic(A), pos_lower(A).
```

by which we understand that a graphics being placed in lower position is not discriminant between positive and negative examples. As expected, exploiting the abstraction operators the system learns shorter clauses. For instance, the theory learned for *author* contains two clauses made up of 18 and 15 literals (against the 19 and 37 without using abstraction):

```
logic_type_author(A) :- height_medium_small(A), pos_upper_type_text(A),
    part_of(B, A), part_of(B, C), height_very_small_type_text(C),
    pos_upper_type_text(C), part_of(B, D), width_very_large(D),
    height_smallest(D), type_hor_line(D), pos_center_pos_upper(D),
    alignment_left_col(D, E), on_top(F, E), part_of(B, E), part_of(B, F),
    part_of(B, G), type_text_width_medium_large(G), pos_left_type_text(G).
logic_type_author(A) :- part_of(B, A), part_of(B, C),
    pos_upper_type_text(A), pos_center_pos_upper(A),
    pos_upper_type_text(C), pos_left_type_text(C),
    height_very_very_small_type_text(C), on_top(C, D),
    part_of(B, D), on_top(E, A), width_very_large(E), height_smallest(E),
    pos_center_pos_upper(E), on_top(F, E), alignment_center_col(F, E).
```

where the presence of several abstract predicates confirms that the automatically generated abstraction theory was able to identify discriminative intermediate concepts. An example of shifting rule learned (and exploited above) is:

```
pos_upper_type_text(A) :- type_text(A), pos_upper(A).
```

6   Conclusion and Future Works

This paper presented a technique for automatically inferring meta-information needed to apply abduction and abstraction operators in and inductive learning framework, exploiting the same observations that are input to the inductive algorithm. Application of the proposed technique in a real learning system proved their viability for learning from incomplete observations without loosing predictive accuracy and for significantly improving learning time in complex real-world domains. Future work will concern a deeper investigations of which properties can be considered significant to infer integrity constraints for abduction, development of strategies to improve the generation of abductive theories, and design of techniques that can provide information for further abductive operators.

References

[1] P.R. Cohen and E.A. Feigenbaum, editors. *The Handbook of Artificial Intelligence*, volume 3. Morgan Kaufmann, 1981.
[2] L. De Raedt. *Interactive Theory Revision - An Inductive Logic Programming Approach*. Academic Press, 1992.
[3] Y. Dimopoulos, S. Džeroski, and A. Kakas. Integrating explanatory and descriptive learning in ILP. In *Proceedings of IJCAI97*, pages 900–906, 1997.
[4] Y. Dimopoulos and A. Kakas. Abduction and learning. In L. De Raedt, editor, *Advances in Inductive Logic Programming*, pages 144–171. IOS Press, 1996.

[5] F. Esposito, S. Ferilli, N. Fanizzi, T.M.A. Basile, and N. Di Mauro. Incremental multistrategy learning for document processing. *Applied Artificial Intelligence: An Internationa Journal*, 17(8/9):859–883, 2003.

[6] F. Esposito, E. Lamma, D. Malerba, P. Mello, M. Milano, F. Riguzzi, and G. Semeraro. Learning abductive logic programs. In *Proceedings of the ECAI96 Workshop on Abductive and Inductive Reasoning*, 1996.

[7] S. Ferilli, F. Esposito, T.M.A. Basile, and N. Di Mauro. Automatic induction of first-order logic descriptors type domains from observations. In Rui Camacho, Ross D. King, and Ashwin Srinivasan, editors, *ILP*, volume 3194 of *LNCS*, pages 116–131. Springer, 2004.

[8] P.A. Flach and N. Lachiche. Confirmation-guided discovery of first-order rules with **Tertius**. *Machine Learning*, 42(1/2):61–95, 2001.

[9] A. Giordana, D. Roverso, and L. Saitta. Abstracting concepts with inverse resolution. In *Proceedings of the 8th International Workshop on Machine Learning*, pages 142–146, Evanston, IL, 1991. Morgan Kaufmann.

[10] A.C. Kakas, R. Kowalski, and F. Toni. Abductive logic programming. *Journal of Logic and Computation*, 2(6), 1993. 718–770.

[11] A.C. Kakas and P. Mancarella. Generalized stable models: a semantics for abduction. In *Proceedings of ECAI90*, pages 385–391. Pitman Publishing, 1990.

[12] A.C. Kakas and P. Mancarella. On the relation of truth maintenance and abduction. In *Proceedings of the 1st Pacific Rim International Conference on Artificial Intelligence*, Nagoya, Japan, 1990.

[13] J-U. Kietz and S. Wrobel. Controlling the complexity of learning in logic through syntactic and task-oriented models. In S. Muggleton, editor, *ILP91*, pages 107–126, 1991.

[14] E. Lamma, P. Mello, M. Milano, F. Riguzzi, F. Esposito, S. Ferilli, and G. Semeraro. Cooperation of abduction and induction in logic programming. In A. Kakas and P. Flach, editors, *Abductive and Inductive Reasoning: Essays on their Relation and Integration*. Kluwer, 2000.

[15] J. W. Lloyd. *Foundations of Logic Programming*. Springer-Verlag, Berlin, second edition, 1987.

[16] R.S. Michalski. Inferential theory of learning. developing foundations for multistrategy learning. In R.S. Michalski and G. Tecuci, editors, *Machine Learning. A Multistrategy Approach*, volume IV, pages 3–61. Morgan Kaufmann, 1994.

[17] S.H. Muggleton and L. De Raedt. Inductive logic programming. *Journal of Logic Programming: Theory and Methods*, 19:629–679, 1994.

[18] L. De Raedt and L. Dehaspe. Clausal discovery. *Machine Learning*, 26(2):99–146, 1997.

[19] C. Rouveirol and J. Puget. Beyond inversion of resolution. In *Proceedings of ICML97*, pages 122–130, Austin, TX, 1990. Morgan Kaufmann.

[20] G. Salton and C. Buckley. Term-weighting approaches in automatic text retrieval. *Information Processing and Management*, 24(5):513–523, 1988.

[21] A. Srinivasan. The aleph manual version 4, 2003. http://web.comlab.ox.ac.uk/oucl/research/areas/machlearn/Aleph/.

[22] P.E. Utgoff. Shift of bias for inductive concept learning. In R.S. Michalski, J.G. Carbonell, and T.M. Mitchell, editors, *Machine Learning: an artificial intelligence approach*, volume II, pages 107–148. Morgan Kaufmann, Los Altos, CA, 1986.

[23] J.-D. Zucker. Semantic abstraction for concept representation and learning. In R. S. Michalski and L. Saitta, editors, *Proceedings of the 4th International Workshop on Multistrategy Learning*, pages 157–164, 1998.

Logical Bayesian Networks and Their Relation to Other Probabilistic Logical Models

Daan Fierens, Hendrik Blockeel, Maurice Bruynooghe, and Jan Ramon

Department of Computer Science, Katholieke Universiteit Leuven, Celestijnenlaan
200A, 3001 Leuven, Belgium
{daanf, hendrik, maurice, janr}@cs.kuleuven.ac.be

Abstract. Logical Bayesian Networks (LBNs) have recently been introduced as another language for knowledge based model construction of Bayesian networks, besides existing languages such as Probabilistic Relational Models (PRMs) and Bayesian Logic Programs (BLPs). The original description of LBNs introduces them as a variant of BLPs and discusses the differences with BLPs but still leaves room for a deeper discussion of the relationship between LBNs and BLPs. Also the relationship to PRMs was not treated in much detail.

In this paper, we first give a more compact and clear definition of LBNs. Next, we describe in more detail how PRMs and BLPs relate to LBNs. Like this we not only see what the advantages and disadvantages of LBNs are with respect to PRMs and BLPs, we also gain more insight into the relationships between PRMs and BLPs.

Keywords: Probabilistic-logical models, Bayesian networks, knowledge representation, Bayesian Logic Programs, Probabilistic Relational Models.

1   Introduction

Probabilistic logical models are models combining aspects of probability theory with aspects of Logic Programming, first-order logic, or relational languages. In recent years a variety of such models has been introduced in the literature (see the overview by Kersting and De Raedt [26]). An important class of such models are those based on the principle of *Knowledge Based Model Construction* (KBMC) [2]. The idea of KBMC is that a general probabilistic logical knowledge base can be used to generate a specific propositional probabilistic model (when given a specific problem). We focus on the case where the propositional model is a Bayesian network [32]. The most developed and best known models of this kind are Probabilistic Relational Models by Getoor et al. [14] and Bayesian Logic Programs by Kersting and De Raedt [23, 24].

We recently introduced Logical Bayesian Networks (LBNs) as yet another model for knowledge based model construction of Bayesian networks [12]. In the original description, we introduced LBNs as a variant of BLPs. In designing LBNs, focus was specifically on introducing all necessary language components

S. Kramer and B. Pfahringer (Eds.): ILP 2005, LNAI 3625, pp. 121–135, 2005.

to make knowledge representation with LBNs as simple as possible. First, LBNs cleanly separate deterministic, logical knowledge and probabilistic knowledge. Second, LBNs have different language components to determine different parts of a Bayesian network (the nodes in the graph, the directed edges and the conditional probability distributions).

In this paper, we first give a new, more compact and clear but essentially equivalent definition of LBNs. Next, we compare LBNs with PRMs, which was done only very briefly in [12]. Then we compare LBNs to BLPs. We approach this comparison differently than in [12] by explicitly using LBNs as a reference point and go more into detail. Such a comparison not only teaches us more about LBNs, but also about the mutual relations between PRMs and BLPs.

For several probabilistic logical models techniques for learning from data have been developed. At recent ILP conferences a substantial number of papers (and invited lectures) have been presented on this topic (e.g. [24, 22, 37, 11]). Our paper complements this work in that we do not discuss learning directly, but focus on the knowledge representation used by the different learning systems.

We proceed as follows. In Section 2 we review LBNs, give a new, more compact definition of LBNs and discuss the methodology behind their design. In Section 3 we compare LBNs with Probabilistic Relational Models and Bayesian Logic Programs. In Section 4 we conclude. We assume familiarity with the basic concepts of Bayesian networks [32] and Logic Programming [29].

2   Logical Bayesian Networks

We review Logical Bayesian Networks (LBNs) [12] by means of an example. Then we formally define the syntax and declarative semantics of LBNs. Finally, we discuss the methodology behind the design of LBNs.

2.1   Logical Bayesian Networks by Example

Consider the following running example (based on the 'university'-example by Getoor et al. [14]).

> *There are students and courses. We know which students take which courses. Each student has an IQ and a final ranking and each course has a difficulty level. A student taking a certain course, gets a grade for that course. The grade of a student for a course depends on the IQ of the student and the difficulty of the course. The final ranking of a student depends on his grades for all the courses he's taking.*

LBNs explicitly distinguish deterministic, logical knowledge and probabilistic knowledge. To do so, LBNs use two disjoint sets of predicates: the set of *logical predicates* and the set of *probabilistic predicates* (an idea introduced by Ngo and Haddawy [33]). Logical predicates are used to specify logical background knowledge describing the domain of discourse for the world considered (this is supposed to be deterministic information). Probabilistic predicates in LBNs (like predicates in Bayesian Logic Programs [23]) have an associated range and are used to represent random variables. Precisely, a random variable is represented as a ground atom built from a probabilistic predicate and has a range equal to the range of that predicate. Note that it is debatable whether 'predicates' is the right name since these 'predicates' behave more like (typed) functors than like ordinary predicates (similarly logical atoms behave more like terms than like ordinary atoms). The main reason for calling them predicates is because like this we stay in line with the terminology of Bayesian Logic Programs (since we introduced LBNs as a variant of Bayesian Logic Programs we believe this to be important).

LBNs have four components. The first one is a set of clauses called the *random variable declarations*. The second one is a set of clauses called the *conditional dependency clauses*. The third one is a set of *logical Conditional Probability Distributions (logical CPDs)*, quantifying the conditional dependencies determined by the conditional dependency clauses. The fourth one is a set of normal logic clauses for the logical predicates used to specify deterministic background information.

We now illustrate some of these notions on our running example. The logical predicates are *student*/1, *course*/1 and *takes*/2, the probabilistic predicates are *iq*/1, *diff*/1, *ranking*/1 and *grade*/2 (having as associated range for example respectively {low,high}, {low,middle,high}, {A,B,C} and {A,B,C}). The random variable declarations are:

```
random(iq(S)) <- student(S).
random(ranking(S)) <- student(S).
random(diff(C)) <- course(C).
random(grade(S,C)) <- takes(S,C).
```

Here *random*/1 is a special-purpose logical predicate. The first clause, for instance, should be read as: "*iq(S)* is a random variable if *S* is a student". The conditional dependency clauses are:

```
ranking(S) | grade(S,C) <- takes(S,C).
grade(S,C) | iq(S), diff(C).
```

The first clause should be read as: "the ranking of *S* depends on the grade of *S* for *C* if *S* takes *C*" and the second "the grade of *S* for *C* depends on the iq of *S* and the difficulty of *C*". We do not mention anything about the logical CPDs here, leaving this issue for the next section.

The semantics of a LBN is that it defines a mapping from specific problems (or worlds) to Bayesian networks. We use a normal logic program [29] to describe the specific problem. For our running example this could look as follows (the meaning is obvious):

```
student(john).      student(pete).
course(ai).         course(db).
takes(john,ai).     takes(john,db).     takes(pete,ai).
```

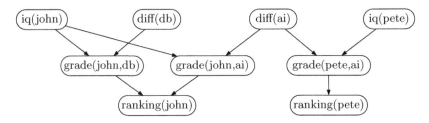

Fig. 1. The structure of the Bayesian network induced for our running example

The structure of the Bayesian network induced by the above LBN given this logic program is shown in Figure 1.

2.2 Syntax of Logical Bayesian Networks

We now define the syntax of LBNs. In the next section we define the semantics.

Remember that LBNs use two disjoint sets of predicates: the logical predicates and the probabilistic predicates having an associated range (we use these sets implicitly in our definitions). We call an atom built from a probabilistic predicate a *probabilistic atom* (it has the same range as the predicate). Similarly we talk about *logical atoms* and *logical literals*. Remember that a random variable is represented as a ground probabilistic atom.

Definition 1 (random variable declaration). *A random variable declaration is a range-restricted clause of the form*

$$random(pAtom) \leftarrow lit_1, \ldots, lit_n.$$

where $n \geq 0$, pAtom is a probabilistic atom and lit_1, ..., lit_n are logical literals.

A clause is *range-restricted* iff all free variables that occur in the head also occur in a positive literal in the body.

Definition 2 (conditional dependency clause). *A conditional dependency clause is a clause of the form*

$$pAtom \mid pAtom_1, \ldots, pAtom_n \leftarrow lit_1, \ldots, lit_m.$$

where $n, m \geq 0$, pAtom, $pAtom_1$, ..., $pAtom_n$ are probabilistic atoms and lit_1, ..., lit_m are logical literals.

As will become clear in the next section, these clauses need not be range-restricted. If $m = 0$, we write the clause as $pAtom \mid pAtom_1, ..., pAtom_n$.

Definition 3 (logical CPD). *A logical CPD for a probabilistic predicate p is a function mapping a set of ground probabilistic atoms to a conditional probability distribution on the range of p.*

When referring to the logical CPD for a ground probabilistic atom, we mean the logical CPD for the predicate that atom is built from.

Logical CPDs in LBNs play the same role as *combining rules* in Bayesian Logic Programs [23]. This means that a logical CPD not only quantifies a dependency indicated by a single conditional dependency clause but also combines the influences of multiple conditional dependency clauses with the same head.

In [12] we argued that one way to specify a logical CPD is as a *logical decision tree* [5, 43]. Working this out in detail is beyond the scope of this paper.

Definition 4 (Logical Bayesian Network). *A* Logical Bayesian Network *is a tuple* $(\mathcal{V}, \mathcal{D}, \mathcal{B}, \mathcal{L})$ *with* $\mathcal{V}$ *a set of random variable declarations,* $\mathcal{D}$ *a set of conditional dependency clauses,* $\mathcal{B}$ *a set of normal logic clauses for the logical predicates and* $\mathcal{L}$ *a set of logical CPDs, one for each probabilistic predicate.*

The above definitions differ slightly from the original definitions in [12]. First, we use a slightly different notation for the random variable declarations (using *random*/1). Second, we explicitly introduced in our definitions the normal clauses $\mathcal{B}$ describing deterministic background knowledge (in [12] this was left implicit). Third, we tried to make the definition of logical CPD easier.

2.3   Declarative Semantics of Logical Bayesian Networks

The semantics of a LBN is that it defines a mapping from specific problems or worlds (described by a normal logic program P_l defining the logical predicates) to Bayesian networks. In other words, a LBN induces a ground Bayesian network. We use the *well-founded semantics* [41]: every normal logic program P_l has a unique well-founded model $WFM(P_l)$ (for a program without negation, this semantics is equivalent to the least Herbrand semantics).

Definition 5 (Induced Bayesian Network). *The* Bayesian Network induced by a LBN $(\mathcal{V}, \mathcal{D}, \mathcal{B}, \mathcal{L})$ *given a normal logic program* P_l *is the Bayesian network determined by the directed graph containing*

- *a node (random variable)* V *iff* V *is a ground probabilistic atom and random* (V) *is true in* $WFM(P_l \cup \mathcal{B} \cup \mathcal{V})$,
- *an edge from a node* V_{parent} *in the graph to a node* V_{child} *in the graph iff there is a ground instance* $V_{child} \mid body \leftarrow context.$ *of a clause in* $\mathcal{D}$ *such that* $V_{parent} \in body$ *and context is true in* $WFM(P_l \cup \mathcal{B})$,

and where the CPD for a node V *is obtained by applying the logical CPD for* V *in* $\mathcal{L}$ *to the set of ground probabilistic atoms that are parents of* V *in the graph.*

Obviously the Bayesian network induced by a LBN given a logic program P_l is only well-defined (i.e. specifies a unique probability measure) under certain conditions[1].

---

[1] These conditions are similar to the conditions for a Bayesian Logic Program to be well-defined, see [23].

Proposition 1. *The Bayesian network induced by a LBN given P_l is well-defined iff the directed graph induced is non-empty and acyclic, each node in the graph has a finite number of ancestors and the CPD associated to each node is conditioned only on the parents of that node.*

2.4   Discussion

The language of LBNs was designed from the point of view of knowledge representation. We explicitly tried to unravel the different types of knowledge that one might want to represent and tried to reflect these different types of knowledge in the different components of LBNs. This can be seen on two levels.

First, as LBNs define a mapping from specific worlds to Bayesian networks and a Bayesian network is determined by its nodes, directed edges and CPDs, LBNs have a first component to determine the nodes, a another one to project a set of directed edges on these nodes and yet another one to determine the CPDs.

Second and more general, LBNs explicitly distinguish deterministic and probabilistic knowledge (under the form of two sets of predicates). In Section 3.2 we go into detail about the problems that arise when this distinction is not made.

LBNs have a number of advantages as compared to models offering a language as 'uniform' as possible (i.e. with as few language components as possible, as was for instance the original motivation behind Bayesian Logic Programs [27, 21]). First, LBNs are very easy to understand. Second, as argued in [12] knowledge representation with LBNs is very easy. Third, LBNs can be used to gain insight into other probabilistic logical models by investigating how the language components of these models map to the components of LBNs. We illustrate this last point in the next section.

3   Comparing Logical Bayesian Networks to Other Probabilistic Logical Models

We now compare LBNs to Probabilistic Relational Models (Section 3.1) and Bayesian Logic Programs (Section 3.2). We also briefly review other related models (Section 3.3).

3.1   Probabilistic Relational Models

Introduction. Probabilistic Relational Models (PRMs) [13, 15, 14, 16] are based on the entity-relationship model and consist of three components. The relational schema describes the set of classes and their attributes. The dependency structure defines the set of parents that an attribute conditionally depends on. Associated to the dependency structure is a quantitative component: a set of aggregate functions and CPDs. The semantics of a PRM is that it induces a Bayesian network on the so-called relational skeleton. The latter specifies all the objects for all the classes and the values of the (primary and foreign) key-attributes for all objects but leaves the values of all other attributes ('descriptive' attributes) unspecified. The Bayesian network then specifies a probability distribution on these unspecified values. Algorithms for learning the dependency structure and the CPDs have been developed [13, 15, 14, 16].

The graphical representation of the dependency structure for our running example is shown in Figure 2 (it is similar to the example in [14]).

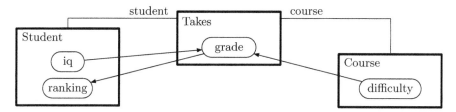

Fig. 2. The dependency structure of the PRM for our running example. Rectangles represent classes, ovals represent descriptive attributes, lines represent relationships through foreign keys and arrows represent conditional dependencies.

Discussion. LBNs can be seen as the counterpart of PRMs in a Logic Programming based language. First, the distinction logical vs. probabilistic predicates in LBNs corresponds to the distinction key-attributes vs. descriptive attributes in PRMs (as key-attributes in PRMs are supposed to be deterministic and are used to specify the objects in the domain of discourse and their relations)[2]. Second, there is a one-to-one correspondence as to functionality between the components of PRMs and those of LBNs. In LBNs we use the random variable declarations to determine the nodes in the Bayesian network, where PRMs use the relational schema. In LBNs we use the conditional dependency clauses to determine the directed edges, where PRMs use dependency structure. In LBNs we use logical CPDs to determine the CPDs in the Bayesian network, where PRMs use a combination of aggregate functions with ordinary CPDs.

Due to this correspondence between the components of LBNs and PRMs, it is trivial to translate any PRM to an equivalent LBN. As a consequence, LBNs can help to clarify the relationships between PRMs and probabilistic logical models based on concepts of Logic Programming [23, 10, 38, 33, 42, 34, 35].

The main advantage of LBNs over PRMs is that LBNs are more flexible and more expressive. This is the result from the transition from the entity-relationship language of PRMs to the full Logic Programming language of LBNs.

LBNs are more flexible than PRMs. First, in LBNs the knowledge that determines the random variables and the dependencies (i.e. the knowledge specified by the logical predicates) can be anything. In PRMs this knowledge can only be knowledge about class-membership and relations (i.e. knowledge contained in the relational skeleton). For example, suppose that we want to specify that only undergraduate students get a final ranking. In LBNs we simply write

---

[2] Extensions of PRMs exist where key-attributes do not have to be deterministic: PRMs with 'structural uncertainty' [15, 14, 16].

`random(ranking(S)) <- undergrad(S)`. In PRMs we can only specify this if we adapt the relational schema of our running example by explicitly making a new (sub)class for undergraduate students [14]. As the conditions we want to specify get more complex, this process of adapting the relational schema of the PRM becomes more and more cumbersome. In LBNs, this can be handled in a much more uniform way. Second, in the same way it is easier to specify deterministic background knowledge in LBNs than in PRMs (in LBNs we can simply use the normal clauses in $\mathcal{B}$).

LBNs are also more expressive than PRMs. PRMs do not have functor symbols. Functor symbols are needed to elegantly represent temporal processes such as Hidden Markov Models, or more generally, to represent recursive concepts. For a further discussion we refer to the remarks on recursion and PRMs in [38]. Also, PRMs have no concept of negation. One application of negation is dealing with exceptions, e.g. expressing that a student has a grade for a course if he was taking that course *unless* he was absent on the exam. This cannot be expressed directly in PRMs. We further discuss negation in Section 3.2.

3.2 Bayesian Logic Programs

Introduction. Bayesian Logic Programs (BLPs) combine Bayesian networks with definite Logic Programming. BLPs were defined in [23, 24, 22, 25]. Recently, a modified definition has been given in [10, 28]. We now discuss the original (and probably best known) definition. We come to the new definition later on in this section.

The core of a BLP is a set of Bayesian clauses. An example of such a clause is:

`grade(S,C) | iq(S), diff(C), takes(S,C).`

All predicates in BLPs are 'Bayesian' predicates having an associated range (like probabilistic predicates in LBNs). Ground atoms represent random variables. The semantics of a BLP is that it induces a Bayesian network. The random variables are the ground atoms in the least Herbrand model LH of the set of Bayesian clauses (treating these clauses as pure logical clauses). The ground instances of the Bayesian clauses encode directed edges: there is an edge from $V_{parent} \in LH$ to $V_{child} \in LH$ iff V_{parent} is in the body of a ground instance with V_{child} in the head. As a quantitative component BLPs use CPDs and combining rules. Algorithms for learning the Bayesian clauses and the CPDs have been developed [24, 22, 25].

To model our running example with a BLP, we need the following Bayesian clauses (*student*/1, *course*/1, *takes*/2, *iq*/1, *ranking*/1, *diff*/1 and *grade*/2 are all Bayesian predicates):

```
iq(S) | student(S).
ranking(S) | student(S).
diff(C) | course(C).
grade(S,C) | takes(S,C).
grade(S,C) | iq(S), diff(C), takes(S,C).
```

```
ranking(S) | grade(S,C), takes(S,C).
student(john).      student(pete).
course(ai).         course(db).
takes(john,ai).     takes(john,db).     takes(pete,ai).
```

The first four clauses are essentially needed to specify the random variables, the fifth and the sixth clause to specify the dependencies[3] and the Bayesian ground facts to specify the domain of discourse.

Discussion. The most important difference between BLPs as defined above and LBNs is that BLPs do not have standard logical predicates. In the philosophy of BLPs logical predicates are a special kind of Bayesian predicates with range {true,false}. This leads to a number of problems from a knowledge representation point of view:

1. *Compared to the Bayesian network induced by a LBN or PRM, the network induced by a BLP typically contains more nodes and, as a consequence, has CPDs that cannot be filled in meaningfully.* The reason is that for instance `student(john).` in the above BLP is not a logical fact stating that *john* is a student, but a Bayesian fact stating that *student(john)* is a random variable (with an associated CPD which we do not show here). The Bayesian network induced by the above BLP is shown in Figure 3a (only partially because of space restrictions). As a reference, Figure 3b shows the corresponding part of the Bayesian network induced by a LBN (this is a fragment of Figure 1). Note that network induced by the LBN does not contain e.g. *student(john)* as a random variable.

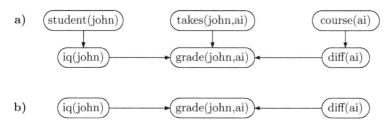

Fig. 3. Part of the structure of the Bayesian network induced for the running example a) by a BLP, b) by a LBN. The former typically contains more nodes than the latter.

In the network of Figure 3b (for LBNs), the node *iq(john)* needs a CPD that is unconditioned, for example the following table:

	$p(iq(john))$
low: 0.4	high: 0.6

---

[3] In the clause `grade(S,C) | iq(S), diff(C), takes(S,C).`, the atom `takes(S,C)` is needed to ensure that *grade(S, C)* is a random variable *only* if *S* takes *C*.

In the network of Figure 3a (for BLPs), the node $iq(john)$ needs a CPD that is conditioned on $student(john)$, for example the following table:

$student(john)$	$p(iq(john)\|student(john))$	
true	low: 0.4	high: 0.6
false	?	

The problem here is that no meaningful probability distribution can be filled in for the case where $student(john)$ is false (the question mark). The reason is that in our example we wanted to model that something has an iq only if it is a student. So if $student(john)$ is false, the random variable $iq(john)$ is meaningless and should not even exist. The same problem appears when trying to specify a CPD for the dependence of $diff(ai)$ conditioned on $course(ai)$ and also for $grade(john, ai)$ conditioned on $takes(john, ai)$. To summarize, the Bayesian networks induced by BLPs contain CPDs that cannot be filled in meaningfully while for LBNs (or PRMs) this problem does not exist.

One might think that the approach taken by BLPs is 'more general' than the approach taken by LBNs in that BLPs allow knowledge about the $student/1$ predicate to be non-deterministic and LBNs do not. This is wrong, however. LBNs leave the user the freedom to decide for each application which predicates should be logical and which probabilistic. As such the user could for instance decide to make $student/1$ a probabilistic predicate if needed, accepting the above problems with meaningless entries in CPDs (essentially, the same approach is taken by PRMs with structural uncertainty [15, 14, 16]). Our point, however, is that if $student/1$ is deterministic we can make it a logical predicate in LBNs, avoiding the above problems. In BLPs, this is not possible since it has been decided by design that all predicates are probabilistic. In other words, in BLPs we cannot express the fact that certain knowledge is deterministic, while in LBNs we can.

As a more practical side-remark, note that larger CPDs typically result in slower inference [7]. As such, inference in networks induced by BLPs is expected to be slower than for LBNs or PRMs.

2. *Since BLPs do not have logical atoms, no negated atoms are allowed.* One of the possible applications of negation is default reasoning (dealing with exceptions [6]). For instance, suppose we want to express that a student has a grade for a course if he was taking that course *unless* he was absent on the exam (being absent is considered as an exception). In LBNs, we would simply write:

```
random(grade(S,C)) <- takes(S,C), not(absent(S,C)).
```

In BLPs, however, we cannot express this since no negated atoms are allowed. Note that the above form of negation, which cannot be captured by BLPs, is *non-monotonic negation* [1]. *Classical negation*, in contrast, can be simulated by BLPs inside the CPDs [23]. For instance, to model that someone is male if and only if he is not female, we can write a Bayesian clause `male(X) | female(X)` with the following CPD:

$female(X)$	$p(male(X)\|female(X))$
true	true: 0.0 false: 1.0
false	true: 1.0 false: 0.0

3. In addition to the previous remarks (but less important because somewhat subjective), *it is more difficult to read and write clauses in a BLP than clauses in a LBN.* This is because clauses in a BLP have a double meaning:
   - They should be seen as a definite logic program to find the random variables in the Bayesian network (through the least Herbrand model). In this reading, each atom in each clause should be seen as a standard logical atom.
   - At the same time they should be seen as statements about conditional dependencies between random variables. In this reading, each atom should be seen as a random variable (or set of random variables).

   This is not the case in LBNs. First, each clause is either a random variable declaration or a conditional dependency clause. Second, each atom in each clause is either a standard logical atom or a random variable. Moreover, both distinctions are clearly visible in the syntax of LBNs.

BLPs Redefined. The above problems are all caused by the fact that BLPs as defined originally [23, 24, 22, 25] do not have standard logical predicates. BLPs have recently been redefined [10, 28] and now indeed distinguish logical predicates and Bayesian predicates. In the new definition only ground Bayesian atoms (in the least Herbrand model of the BLP) become random variables in the induced Bayesian network. Ground logical atoms are kept out of the network. This is also the way BLPs are implemented [28].

Note, that at the time LBNs were first published [12], all literature about BLPs [23, 24, 22, 25] still used the original definition, i.e. the one without this distinction. Also, the 'new' literature about BLPs [10, 28] does not give any reasons why this redefinition is needed (in fact, it does not even mention that it is different from the original definition). In our discussion above we tried to show these reasons by explicitly pointing out the problems with the original definition. As such this paper can contribute to the understanding of BLPs.

This redefinition obviously brings BLPs closer to LBNs. The main remaining difference is that LBNs use one set of clauses to specify the random variables in the Bayesian network and a separate set of clauses to specify the directed edges, whereas BLPs use the same set of clauses for both purposes. While this might make LBNs slightly easier to read than BLPs (especially for people acquainted with PRMs), it is not an essential difference.

3.3   Other Probabilistic Logical Models

A variety of probabilistic logical models has been described in the literature (see the overview by Kersting and De Raedt [26]). On a high level, these models can be divided into two classes.

Models of the first class combine Bayesian networks with logic and mainly follow the knowledge based model construction approach. We already discussed LBNs, Probabilistic Relational Models and Bayesian Logic Programs. Some others models of this class are Relational Bayesian Networks [19], Probabilistic Logic Programs (also known as Context-Sensitive Probabilistic Knowledge Bases) [33], MIA (the 'meta-interpreter approach', which is the origin of some ideas incorporated in LBNs) [4], CLP($\mathcal{BN}$) [38], Hierarchical Bayesian Networks [17] and Markov Logic Networks [11, 36] (the latter are based on Markov networks). Learning algorithms exist for Probabilistic Relational Models [13, 15, 14, 16], Bayesian Logic Programs [24, 22, 25], CLP($\mathcal{BN}$) [38], Hierarchical Bayesian Networks [17] and Markov Logic Networks [36].

Models of the second class integrate probabilities into Logic Programming, staying as close as possible to pure Logic Programming. The most important of these models are Probabilistic Horn Abduction [34], Independent Choice Logic [35], PRISM [39, 40], Stochastic Logic Programs [8, 9, 30, 31] and Logic Programs with Annotated Disjunctions [42]. Learning algorithms exist for the last three models [20, 40, 9, 31, 37].

4   Conclusions

We reviewed Logical Bayesian Networks introduced in [12]. We have given more compact and clear but essentially equivalent definitions of syntax and semantics of LBNs than in [12]. We carried out a more detailed comparison of LBNs with Probabilistic Relational Models and Bayesian Logic Programs, hereby clarifying and motivating the difference between the original definition of Bayesian Logic Programs [23, 24, 22, 25] and their recent redefinition [10, 28].

A lot of future work remains. As for knowledge representation, comparing LBNs to other probabilistic logical models is promising given the wide variety of such models. As for learning, we are currently working on learning logical CPDs in LBNs under the form of first order logical probability trees (Tilde [5, 43]). In a next step, algorithms for learning the conditional dependency clauses of LBNs can be developed.

The methodology behind the design of LBNs can also be followed for other graphical models than Bayesian networks. Languages for knowledge based model construction of dependency networks [18], Markov networks [36] or neural networks [3] can all be defined having the same components as LBNs: a component for determining the nodes in the graph, one for the edges and one for the quantitative local models (CPDs for dependency networks, potential functions for Markov networks, activation functions for neural networks).

Acknowledgements

Daan Fierens is supported by the Institute for the Promotion of Innovation through Science and Technology in Flanders (IWT Vlaanderen). Hendrik

Blockeel and Jan Ramon are post-doctoral fellows of the Fund for Scientific Research (FWO) of Flanders. The authors would like to thank Kristian Kersting and the reviewers for useful comments.

References

[1] J. Alferes, L. Pereira, and T. Przymusinski. 'Classical' negation in Nonmonotonic Reasoning and Logic Programming. *Journal of Automated Reasoning*, 20:107–142, 1998.

[2] F. Bacchus. Using first-order probability logic for the construction of Bayesian networks. In *Proceedings of the Sixth Conference on Uncertainty in Artificial Intelligence (UAI-1993)*, pages 219–226, 1993.

[3] C. M. Bishop. *Neural Networks for Pattern Recognition*. University Press, Oxford, 1999.

[4] H. Blockeel. Prolog for Bayesian networks: a Meta-Interpreter Approach. In *Proceedings of the 2nd International Workshop on Multi-Relational Data Mining (MRDM-2003)*, pages 1–13, 2003.

[5] H. Blockeel and L. De Raedt. Top-down induction of first order logical decision trees. *Artificial Intelligence*, 101(1-2):285–297, June 1998.

[6] R. Brachman and H. Levesque. *Knowledge Representation and Reasoning*. Morgan Kaufmann Publishers, 2004.

[7] G. F. Cooper. The computational complexity of probabilistic inference using bayesian belief networks. *Artificial Intelligence*, 42(2-3):393–405, 1990.

[8] J. Cussens. Stochastic logic programs: Sampling, inference and applications. In *Proceedings of the Sixteenth Annual Conference on Uncertainty in Artificial Intelligence (UAI-2000)*, pages 115–122, San Francisco, CA, 2000. Morgan Kaufmann.

[9] J. Cussens. Parameter estimation in stochastic logic programs. *Machine Learning*, 44(3):245–271, 2001.

[10] L. De Raedt and K. Kersting. Probabilistic Inductive Logic Programming. In *Proceedings of the 15th International Conference on Algorithmic Learning Theory (ALT-2004)*, pages 19–36, October 2004. Invited paper.

[11] P. Domingos. Learning, logic, and probability: A unified view. In *Proceedings of 14th International Conference on Inductive Logic Pogramming (ILP-2004)*, Porto, Portugal, page 359, 2004. Invited paper.

[12] D. Fierens, H. Blockeel, M. Bruynooghe, and J. Ramon. Logical bayesian networks. In *Proceedings of the 3rd Workshop on Multi-Relational Data Mining (MRDM-2004), Seattle, WA, USA*, pages 19–30, 2004.

[13] N. Friedman, L. Getoor, D. Koller, and A. Pfeffer. Learning probabilistic relational models. In *Proceedings of the 16th International Joint Conference on Artificial Intelligence (IJCAI-1999)*, pages 1300–1309, 1999.

[14] L. Getoor, N. Friedman, D. Koller, and A. Pfeffer. Learning Probabilistic Relational Models. In S. Džeroski and N. Lavrač, editors, *Relational Data Mining*, pages 307–334. Springer-Verlag, 2001.

[15] L. Getoor, N. Friedman, D. Koller, and B. Taskar. Learning probabilistic models of relational structure. In *Proc. 18th International Conf. on Machine Learning (ICML-2001)*, pages 170–177. Morgan Kaufmann, San Francisco, CA, 2001.

[16] L. Getoor, N. Friedman, D. Koller, and B. Taskar. Learning probabilistic models of link structure. *Journal of Machine Learning Research*, 3:679–707, 2002.

[17] E. Gyftodimos and P. Flach. Hierarchical Bayesian Networks: an Approach to Classification and Learning for Structured Data. In *Proceedings of the ECML/PKDD - 2003 Workshop on Probablistic Graphical Models for Classification*, pages 25–36, 2003.

[18] D. Heckerman, D. Chickering, C. Meek, R. Rounthwaite, and C. Kadie. Dependency Networks for Inference, Collaborative Filtering, and Data Visualization. *Journal of Machine Learning Research*, 1:49–75, 2000.

[19] M. Jaeger. Relational Bayesian networks. In *Proceedings of the Thirteenth Annual Conference on Uncertainty in Artificial Intelligence (UAI-1997)*, pages 266–273. Morgan Kaufmann Publishers, 1997.

[20] Y. Kameya and T. Sato. Efficient EM learning with tabulation for parameterized logic programs. In *Proceedings of the 1st International Conference on Computational Logic (CL-2000)*, volume 1861 of *Lecture Notes in Artificial Intelligence*, pages 269–294, 2000.

[21] K. Kersting and L. De Raedt. Bayesian logic programs. In *Proceedings of the tenth international conference on Inductive Logic Programming, work in progress track*, 2000.

[22] K. Kersting and L. De Raedt. Adaptive Bayesian Logic Programs. In *Proceedings of the 11th International Conference on Inductive Logic Programming (ILP-2001)*, pages 104–117, 2001.

[23] K. Kersting and L. De Raedt. Bayesian logic programs. Technical Report 151, Institute for Computer Science, University of Freiburg, Germany, April 2001.

[24] K. Kersting and L. De Raedt. Towards combining inductive logic programming and Bayesian networks. In *Proceedings of the 11th International Conference on Inductive Logic Programming (ILP-2001)*, pages 118–131, 2001.

[25] K. Kersting and L. De Raedt. Basic principles of learning bayesian logic programs. Technical Report 174, Institute for Computer Science, University of Freiburg, Germany, June 2002.

[26] K. Kersting and L. De Raedt. Probabilistic logic learning. In S. Dzeroski and L. De Raedt, editors, *SIGKDD Explorations, special issue on Multi-Relational Data Mining*, volume 5(1), pages 31–48, 2003.

[27] K. Kersting, L. De Raedt, and S. Kramer. Interpreting bayesian logic programs. In *Proceedings of the AAAI-2000 Workshop on Learning Statistical Models from Relational Data*, 2000.

[28] K. Kersting and U. Dick. Balios - The Engine for Bayesian Logic Programs. In *Proceedings of the 8th European Conference on Principles and Practice of Knowledege Discovery in Databases (PKDD-2004)*, pages 549–551, September 2004. Demonstration paper.

[29] J. Lloyd. *Foundations of Logic Programming*. Springer-Verlag, 2nd edition, 1987.

[30] S. Muggleton. Stochastic logic programs. In L. de Raedt, editor, *Advances in Inductive Logic Programming*, pages 254–264. IOS Press, 1996.

[31] S. Muggleton. Learning stochastic logic programs. In L. Getoor and D. Jensen, editors, *Proceedings of the AAAI2000 workshop on learning statistical models for relational data*, 2000.

[32] R. Neapolitan. *Learning Bayesian Networks*. Prentice Hall, New Jersey, 2003.

[33] L. Ngo and P. Haddawy. Answering queries from context-sensitive probabilistic knowledge bases. *Theoretical Computer Science*, 171(1–2):147–177, 1997.

[34] D. Poole. Probabilistic Horn abduction and Bayesian networks. *Artificial Intelligence*, 64:81–129, 1993.

[35] D. Poole. The Independent Choice Logic for modelling multiple agents under uncertainty. *Artificial Intelligence*, 94(1–2):5–56, 1997.

[36] M. Richardson and P. Domingos. Markov Logic Networks. Technical report, Department of Computer Science, University of Washington, 2004.

[37] F. Riguzzi. Learning logic programs with annotated disjunctions. In *Proceedings of 14th International Conference on Inductive Logic Pogramming (ILP-2004), Porto, Portugal*, 2004.

[38] V. Santos Costa, D. Page, M. Qazi, and J. Cussens. CLP(BN): Constraint logic programming for probabilistic knowledge. In *Proceedings of 19th Conference on Uncertainty in Artificial Intelligence (UAI-2003)*, 2003.

[39] T. Sato and Y. Kameya. PRISM: A symbolic-statistical modeling language. In *Proceedings of the 15th International Joint Conference on Artificial Intelligence (IJCAI-1997)*, pages 1330–1335, 1997.

[40] T. Sato and Y. Kameya. Parameter learning of logic programs for symbolic-statistical modeling. *Journal of Artificial Intelligence Research*, 15:391–454, 2001.

[41] A. Van Gelder, K. Ross, and J. Schlipf. The well-founded semantics for general logic programs. *Journal of the ACM*, 38(3), 1991.

[42] J. Vennekens, S. Verbaeten, and M. Bruynooghe. Logic programs with annotated disjunctions. In *Proceedings of the 20th International Conference on Logic Programming (ICLP-2004)*, 2004.

[43] C. Vens, A. Van Assche, H. Blockeel, and S. Džeroski. First order random forests with complex aggregates. In R. Camacho, R. King, and A. Srinivasan, editors, *Proceedings of the 14th International Conference on Inductive Logic Programming*, pages 323–340. Springer, 2004.

Strategies to Parallelize ILP Systems

Nuno A. Fonseca[1], Fernando Silva[1], and Rui Camacho[2]

[1] DCC-FC & LIACC, Universidade do Porto,
R. do Campo Alegre 823, 4150-180 Porto, Portugal
{nf, fds}@ncc.up.pt
[2] Faculdade de Engenharia & LIACC, Universidade do Porto,
Rua Dr. Roberto Frias, s/n 4200-465 Porto, Portugal
rcamacho@fe.up.pt

Abstract. It is well known by Inductive Logic Programming (ILP) prac-
tioners that ILP systems usually take a long time to find valuable models
(theories). The problem is specially critical for large datasets, preventing
ILP systems to scale up to larger applications. One approach to reduce
the execution time has been the parallelization of ILP systems. In this
paper we overview the state-of-the-art on parallel ILP implementations
and present work on the evaluation of some major parallelization strategies for ILP. Conclusions about the applicability of each strategy are
presented.

Keywords: Parallelism, Scaling-up.

1 Introduction

There are two major motivations for using ILP. First, ILP provides an excellent
framework for learning in multi-relational domains. Second, the theories learned
by general purpose ILP systems are in a high-level formalism often understand-
able and meaningful for the domain experts. We believe that these two reasons
mostly explain the success of ILP systems in several well known industrial and
scientific relevant problems [1,2,3,4]. The success usually comes at a price, and
in the case of ILP systems the price is long execution times. For complex applications, ILP systems can take several hours, even days, to return a theory.

Research on reducing the execution time of ILP systems has deserved plenty
attention in the last years. The proposed approaches are very diverse, ranging from new algorithms (see e.g., [5,6,7]), reducing the number of hypotheses generated (see e.g., [8,9,10]), to efficiently testing candidate hypotheses (see
e.g., [11,12]), just to mention a few. A quite different line of research to reduce the execution time of ILP systems is through parallelization. This has
been pointed out as a promising approach to improve efficiency by several researchers [13,14,15].

In this paper we survey the current state-of-the-art research on parallel ILP.
The many implementations described in the literature are succinctly presented
together with reported results. A comparison of the algorithms based only on

S. Kramer and B. Pfahringer (Eds.): ILP 2005, LNAI 3625, pp. 136–153, 2005.

their reported results is hard since they were observed on different systems, datasets, and platforms. We thus implemented three parallel algorithms, that accomplish the main parallelization strategies that we have identified, and studied their performance using three well known applications and the same test environment (i.e., the same underlying ILP system and the same parallel architecture). The three parallel implementations were evaluated on a distributed memory architecture.

The remainder of this paper is organized as follows. Section 2 provides some background on parallelism and describes a generic ILP algorithm. Section 3 describes the main strategies to parallelize ILP systems and in Section 4 a survey of the parallel ILP implementation is made. In Section 5 is made an evaluation of three parallel algorithms. In Section 6 we present the conclusions.

2   Background

In this section we start by providing a small introduction to parallelism and then describe a generic sequential covering algorithm.

2.1   Parallelism

By expressing parallelism in an algorithm one aims to improve its performance. However, designing efficient parallel algorithms is still a difficult task as there are many factors that can influence efficient parallel execution, for example balancing the work among the available processors and controlling communication costs in a distributed parallel architecture.

In order to clarify the discussion about parallel algorithms in ILP, we shall first briefly define common terms. A *task* is typically a program (or set of instructions) that is executed by a processor. *Parallel tasks* are tasks whose computations are independent of each other, so that all such tasks can be performed simultaneously with correct results. The maximum number of tasks that can be executed simultaneously at any time in a parallel algorithm, determines the *degree of parallelism* of the application program. The granularity of a task measures the ratio between the time a task takes to be executed and the corresponding overhead time required to schedule that task. The higher the ratio (*coarse-grain parallelism*) the better to scale up parallel execution.

A sequential algorithm is usually evaluated in terms of its execution time (sometimes expressed as a function of the size of its input data). The execution time of a parallel algorithm depends on the number of processors used, interprocess communication speed, and size of the input data.

One would expect that increasing the number of processors results in a proportional decrease of the execution time of a program, but this is rarely observed due to overheads associated with parallelism. There are three major sources of overheads: interprocess communication, idling, and extra computation.

A number of performance metrics have been devised to be used in the study of parallel algorithms performance [16]. The *serial runtime* (T_S) of a program is the time elapsed between the beginning and the end of its execution on a sequential computer. The *parallel runtime* (T_P) is the elapsed time from the beginning of the parallel computation until it ends. Speedup (S) is the most often used measure when studying the performance of parallel algorithms. It captures the relative benefit of solving a problem in parallel and is defined as the ratio between the time taken to solve a problem on a single processor and the time required to solve the same problem on a parallel computer with p identical processors.

$$S = \frac{T_S}{T_P}$$

Theoretically, the speedup can never exceed the number of processors p. In practice, a speedup greater than p, called *super-linear speedup*, is sometimes observed. This happens when the work performed by a sequential algorithm is greater than its parallel version or due to hardware features that slowdown the sequential algorithm (for instance, as a result of using slower memory, i.e., disk).

2.2   Generic ILP Algorithm

A plethora of rule learning algorithms [17], ILP algorithms included, use a variant of the generic *covering algorithm* (also called *separate-and-conquer*). An example of a generic covering algorithm is presented in Figure 1. This algorithm learns one rule at a time using some generalization procedure that performs a search through an ordered space of legal rules. After finding a rule, all covered positive examples are separated (removed) from the training set and the next rule is learned from the remaining examples. Rules are learned until no positive examples are left or some other stopping criteria is met.

---

covering(E^+,E^-,B)
Input: set of positive (E^+) and negative (E^-) examples, and background knowledge (B)
Output: A set of rules (*RulesLearned*)
 1. *Rules_Learned* = ∅
 2. **while** $E^+ \neq \emptyset$ **do**
 3. $R = learn\_rule(E^+, E^-, B)$
 4.   *Rules_Learned* = *Rules_Learned* ∪ $\{R\}$
 5. $B = B \cup \{R\}$
 6. $E^+ = E^+ \setminus \{Examples\ Covered\ by\ R\}$
 7. **end while**
 8. **return** *Rules_Learned*

Fig. 1. A generic covering algorithm. `learn_rule()` should return a (the best) rule that explains a subset of the positive examples(E^+).

Most ILP systems use some variant of the generic covering algorithm. The main difference between the existing ILP systems and algorithms that use a variant of this covering algorithm (e.g., [18,19,20]) concerns the `learn_rule()` procedure (step 3). Given a set of examples and prior knowledge, the procedure returns a consistent rule (clause) that explains some or all positive examples. This procedure is the most time consuming and will be described next in more detail.

---

learn_rule(E^+,E^-,B)
Input: set of positive (E^+) and negative (E^-) examples, and background knowledge (B)
Output: The "best" rule
  1. $Good = \varnothing$
  2. $S = START\_RULE$
  3. $Pick = pickRule(S)$
  4. $NewRule = genNewRule(Pick)$
  5. $Val = evalOnExamples(NewRule)$
  6. if $is\_good(NewRule,Val)$ then $Good = NewRule$endif
  7. $S = S \setminus \{Pick\}$
  8. if $stop\_criterium\_satisfied$ then return $bestOf(Good)$ endif
  9. goto 3

Fig. 2. An example of a generic `learn_rule()` procedure

The `learn_rule()` procedure, as described in Figure 2, searches the (potentially infinite) hypothesis space for a rule that optimizes some quality criteria. At each node of the search one rule is generated and evaluated. The evaluation of a rule usually requires the computation of its coverage, i.e., computing how many examples the rule explains. The time taken to compute the coverage of a rule depends, primarily, on the number of examples. Thus, scalability problems may arise when dealing with a large number of examples or/and when the computational cost of evaluating a rule is high.

3   Strategies for Parallelizing ILP Systems

Parallel algorithms aim to divide the work among the available processors so that a solution is achieved as fast as possible. The main difficulty faced by implementors is how to efficiently divide the work. Ideally, one would want to divide the computation and data evenly, and, at the same time, minimize the communication among processors, striving for a coarse-grained parallelism.

We classify the strategies to parallelize ILP systems described in the literature into four main approaches: parallel exploration of independent hypotheses [21]; parallel exploration of the search space [22,21,23,24]; parallel coverage test [21,25,26]; parallel execution of an ILP system over a partition of the data [27,22,25]. Surely, one could consider other views, however, we consider that these cover the main approaches to parallelize an ILP system. A parallel algorithm may not fit solely in a single strategy, but may combine several. Each strategy is next described in detail.

3.1   Parallel Exploration of Independent Hypotheses

Parallel exploration of independent hypotheses is performed as follows. Let n be the number of classes of the target predicate. Learning each class value is an independent task and can be done in parallel. This procedure requires that each processor owns a replica of the whole data.

Parallel exploration of independent hypotheses has a major drawback: it is not a general approach. It is adequate only for applications where the target predicate is composed by several independent predicates. Learning a definition of the target predicate can be seen as learning several sub-concepts, corresponding each subconcept to a class value. Since the induction of sub-concepts is inherently independent, it can be easily performed in parallel, For instance, consider the task of learning a predicate that classifies emails into categories such as `priority(+Email,-Priority)`, where $Priority \in \{low, medium, high\}$. The task of learning can thus be divided into 3 subtasks, one learning task for `priority(+Email,low)`, other for `priority(+Email,medium)`, and `priority(+Email, high)`.

The degree of parallelism of this strategy corresponds to the number of sub-concepts. The granularity is very high, since the learning of each subconcept corresponds to calling an ILP system to learn n sub-concepts independently.

3.2   Parallel Exploration of the Search Space

The search for a hypothesis involves traversing the generalization lattice in some way (e.g., top-down, bottom-up, bidirectional). The search space can be divided and explored in parallel by each processor to find a hypothesis.

The degree of parallelism and granularity of this strategy depends on the approach adopted to divide the search space.

3.3   Data Parallelism

Data parallelism consists in partitioning the data in subsets, assigning each subset of data to a processor. Each processor applies an algorithm (or part of an algorithm, e.g., coverage test) or the whole sequential ILP algorithm, on its local data. Generally, data partitioning is usually performed in the beginning of the execution. This happens because it is expensive to reassign the examples during execution, i.e., perform load-rebalancing.

A problem arises when a sequential ILP algorithm is applied to a subset of the training data: the hypotheses may be locally consistent and complete, but they may not be globally consistent. A solution to this problem may involve sharing the locally good hypotheses among all processors to obtain a global view.

Another problem, that results from partitioning the set of positive examples, is the impossibility of learning recursive rules. The only solution to this problem is the replication of the set of positive examples through all processors while dividing the set of negative examples.

The degree of parallelism of this strategy depends on the size of the data. The granularity depends on the algorithm applied to the dataset and size of the data.

3.4   Parallel Coverage Tests

The time to compute a hypothesis coverage depends on the cardinality of E^+ and E^-. Each example can be independently tested to determine if it is entailed by a rule h and the background knowledge B. The parallel coverage test strategy consists in performing the coverage test in parallel, i.e., for each example $e \in E$ the coverage test $(B \wedge h \vdash e)$ is performed in parallel.

The degree of parallelism depends on the number of examples evaluated in parallel by each processor. The granularity in this strategy is, relatively, low. However, the granularity can be enlarged either by increasing the number of examples of each processor or/and by evaluating several rules in parallel instead of a single one.

4   Parallel ILP Systems

We next survey the parallel ILP implementations, focusing on the strategy used and results reported.

The first parallel ILP system we are aware of is Claudien [27]. The algorithm followed a strategy based on parallel exploration of the search space where each processor keeps a pool of clauses to specialize, and shares part of them to idle processors (processors with an empty pool). In the end, the p set of clauses found are combined and returned as the solution. One should note that Claudien follows a non-monotonic setting of ILP instead of the usual normal ILP setting. The parallel system was evaluated on a shared-memory computer with two datasets and exhibited a linear speedup up to 16 processors.

Matsui et al. [22] evaluated and compared data parallelism (background knowledge and the set of examples) and, what they called, parallel exploration of the search space. The later approach consisted in evaluating, in parallel, the refinements of a clause, therefore, corresponding to a strategy based on parallel coverage tests. The two strategies were implemented in the FOIL [19] system and were evaluated on a distributed memory computer using the *trains* dataset [28]. The results of the search space parallel approach showed very low speedups. The reason pointed out by the authors for the poor results was that the size of the divided tasks may not be all the same, hence reducing the efficiency. The other two approaches based on data parallelism (background knowledge and the set of examples) showed a linear speedup up to 4 processors. The speedup decreased above 4 processors as a result of an increase in communication due to the exchange of the training set.

Ohwada and Mizoguchi [21] implemented an algorithm (based on Inverse Entailment) using a logic programming parallel language that explored three types of parallelism: parallel coverage tests; parallel exploration of independent hypotheses; and parallel exploration of the search space (each processor followed a branch of the search space). The parallel system was applied to three variants of an email classification dataset and the experiments performed evaluated each strategy. The results on a shared-memory parallel computer showed a non linear speedup in all strategies. The strategy that appears to show better results, on average, was the parallel coverage tests.

Ohwada et. al [23] implemented an algorithm that explores the search space in parallel. The job allocation (set of nodes to be explored) was dynamic and was implemented using contract-net [29] communication. The parallel system was evaluated on two datasets and showed an almost linear speedup on a ten-processor parallel machine.

Wang and Skillicorn [25] parallelized the Progol [30] system by partitioning the data and applying a sequential algorithm to each partition. The data partitioning consisted in dividing the positive examples among all processors and by replicating the negative examples. Each processor applies the sequential algorithm on its local data to find a locally good clause. Such clause is then shared among all processors to evaluate its quality on the whole training set. If a processor considers that a clause is globally good then it exchanges this information with all processors, so that all processors may add the clause to the local theory and remove the examples explained by the clause. It is important to point out that this algorithm is not complete in relation to the sequential algorithm, i.e., the theory found by the parallel algorithm may be different to the one found with the sequential algorithm. The evaluation of the algorithm focused on speedup and did not allow the assessment of the impact on accuracy. They reported double and linear speedups in their experiments with three datasets. The experiments were performed on shared-memory machines (with 4 and 6 processors).

Graham et al. [26] implemented a parallel ILP system, using the PVM [31] message passing library. They employ data partition and parallel coverage tests of parts of the search space on each processor. They reported an almost linear speedup up to 16 processors on a shared memory machine.

Konstantopoulos [32] implemented a data parallel version of the Aleph [20] system using MPICH [33] MPI [34] library. His algorithm performs the coverage tests evaluation in parallel. This approach, although very similar to the one of Graham et al., it only evaluates in parallel a single clause at a time while Graham et al. evaluates a set of clauses. The smaller granularity of the parallel tasks, in Konstantopoulos' approach, is, probably, the main reason for the poor results presented.

Wielemaker [24] implemented a parallel version of Aleph for shared memory machines. The strategy adopted was parallel exploration of the search space. The algorithm exploits parallelism by executing concurrently several randomized local searches [6] and was implemented on top of the Aleph system. The implementation was evaluated on the Carcinogenesis [4] dataset. The Aleph system was configured to perform 16 random restarts, and made 10 moves per restart, on each processor. The reported speedups (e.g., 7 on 16 processors) can be considered low when compared to other shared memory implementations. In spite of the results, this is an interesting proposal that could accomplish better results if the granularity of the tasks is enlarged. This can be easily accomplished by increasing the number of moves or the number of restarts done by each thread.

PolyFarm [35] is a parallel ILP system for the discovery of association rules targeted to distributed memory architectures. The system follows a master-worker scheme. The master generates the rules and reports the results. The workers perform the coverage tests of the set of rules received from the master on the local data. The counts are aggregated by a special type of worker (Merger) that reports the final counts to the master. No empirical evaluation of the system was presented in [35].

Table 1. Summary of the parallel ILP implementations and reported results

Strategy	Arch.	Speedup/#procs.	Work
Parallel exploration of the search space	Shared Memory	linear/16	[27]
		3/6	[21]
		7/16	[24]
		8/10	[23]
Parallel exploration of independent hypotheses	Shared Memory	2/6	[21]
Parallel coverage tests	Distributed Memory	1/15	[22]
		no	[32]
	Shared Memory	4/6	[21]
		5/8	[26]
Data Parallelism	Distributed Memory	4/15 (linear upto 5)	[22]
		not reported	[35]
	Shared Memory	linear and super-linear/6	[25]
		5/8	[26]

Table 1 summarizes the survey by presenting for each parallelization strategy the implementations made, targeted computer architecture, and reported results. The first observation concerns the fact that the majority of the parallel implementations were made for shared memory architectures, where the cost of data transmission is very low when compared to distributed memory architectures. In spite of the high cost of the communication, parallel ILP systems targeted for distributed memory computers may still achieve good speedups (see e.g., [22]). The results reported are generally good on all strategies except the parallel coverage test. The results reported with this strategy differ considerably if the target architecture is shared memory or distributed memory. The poor results of the latter can be explained by the higher communication cost not being compensated by the granularity of the tasks.

Even though most implementations just described were for shared memory machines, we share the view of the recent work reported [32,26], that is, to target distributed memory architectures when parallelizing ILP systems, therefore favoring coarse grain approaches.

5   An Evaluation of Parallelization Strategies

In the previous section we summarized current state-of-the-art research on parallel ILP algorithms. It is hard to compare the results of the referred implementations since they were observed on different systems, platforms, and datasets. We implemented on a distributed memory architecture three parallel algorithms based on the most general strategies, namely parallel exploration of the search space, parallel coverage tests, and data parallelism. No algorithm was implemented based on parallel exploration of independent hypotheses because, as discussed before, this strategy is not applicable to all applications. By implementing these strategies on the same platform, using the same techniques to distribute work among the processing units, and the same applications, we were able to make a fair comparison.

5.1   Parallel Algorithms

We started with a sequential implementation of the April [36] ILP system. The main loop of April's algorithm is similar to the covering algorithm presented in Section 2.2. For simplicity of presentation, all algorithms follow a master-worker scheme. In the beginning of the execution the worker enters a loop and waits for requests from the master. The master shares one processing unit with one of the workers.

The parallel algorithms were implemented using the Prolog language. For the communication layer we used LAM [37] MPI. LAM is a high-quality open-source implementation of the Message Passing Interface (MPI) specification, that can be used for applications running in heterogeneous clusters or in grids. Since the development was made in Prolog and LAM does not provide a native YAP Prolog interface, we had to develop a Prolog module for YAP, using the C language, to act as an interface between Prolog and LAM/MPI libraries.

The implemented algorithms are next described. For each algorithm, we refer the reader to Figure 3 for a schema of the messages exchanged between the master and the workers.

Parallel Coverage Tests (*pct*). A clause is dispatched for a processor to be evaluated on the local subset of examples. The master algorithm is similar to the covering algorithm of Section 2.2 with two main changes: first, the examples are divided evenly among the processors in the beginning of the execution (this could be done in the first line of the **covering** algorithm) and are then loaded by each worker; secondly, line 5 of the **learn_rule** is changed to

$broadcast(evalOnExamples(NewRule))$ $Val = collectAndCombine()$

where **broadcast()** is a procedure that sends a command to all processors to be executed, each processor executes the command and returns the result to the master. This corresponds to each slave evaluating a rule against its local set of examples and then returning the coverage value. The master collects and combines the coverage information using the **collectAndCombine()** procedure. This algorithm is basically the algorithm implemented by Konstantopoulos [32]. However, there are two main differences at the implementation level: i) we used asynchronous message passing communication for all operations involving the sending of a message, while Konstantopoulos only used synchronous message passing operations; ii) our implementation was done with LAM as opposed to the MPICH platform used by Konstantopoulos.

Data Parallel Learn Rule (*dplr*). This algorithm is based on the Wang et al. [25] algorithm mentioned in the previous section but it is next described in more detail.

$Rules\_Learned = \varnothing$
$< (E_1^+, E^-), \dots, (E_p^+, E^-) >= partition\ \ E^+\ \ into\ p\ subsets$
broadcast$(load\_files)$
while $\cup_{k=1}^{p} E_k^+ \neq \varnothing$ **do**
  $RulesBag=$**collect**$($**broadcast**$(learn\_rule()))$
  while $RulesBag \neq \varnothing$ **do**
    $Results=$**collect**$($**broadcast**$(eval(RulesBag)))$
    $R=pickBest(RulesBag)$
    $RulesBag=RulesBag \setminus \{R\}$
    $Rules\_Learned=Rules\_Learned \cup \{R\}$
    collect$($**broadcast**$(addRule2Theory(R)))$
  end while
end while
return $Rules\_Learned$

The algorithm consists of 1) dividing the set of positive examples among all processors and replicating the negative examples; 2) learning p rules in parallel (line 3 of the covering algorithm) starting at different points of the search space (using different seeds), where p is the number of processors available; 3) exchanging rules found among all processors to obtain their coverage values on the whole training set; 4) selecting a rule and mark examples covered on all subsets.

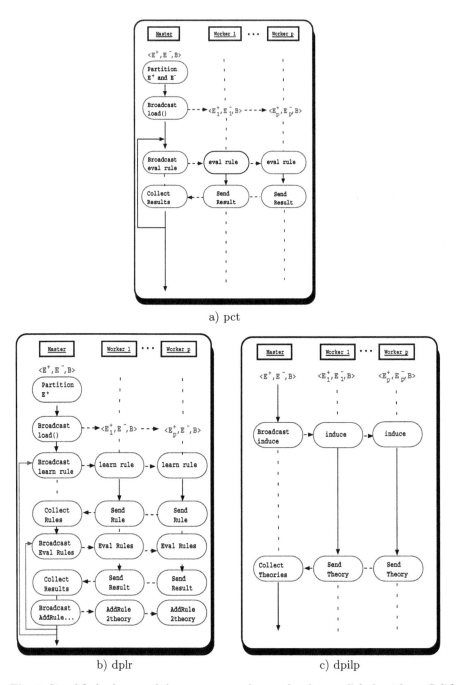

Fig. 3. Simplified schemes of the messages exchanges by the parallel algorithms. Solid lines represent the execution flow, horizontal dashed lines message passing between the processes, and vertical dashed lines idleness. The algorithms are ordered by the granularity of their parallel tasks, from the finest-grained to the most coarse-grained.

The `AddRule2theory(R)` performs steps 5 and 6 of the covering algorithm of Section 2.2, i.e., adds the rule to the background knowledge, marks the examples locally covered, and returns the number of examples locally covered.

Note that the first algorithm described in this section returns the same solution as the sequential algorithm, whereas this algorithm *may* not return the same solution due mainly to the order by which the rules are found and added to the theory.

Data Parallel ILP (*dpilp*). This algorithm starts by dividing the set of examples (positive and negatives) among all processors. It then induces p theories in parallel, using the covering algorithm on each subset, and then combines the p theories found using the whole training set. The combination of the theories (i.e., rules that compose the theories) can be made using several strategies (e.g., [38]). In order to make the comparison with the sequential algorithm more clear, we chose a simple strategy, very similar to the one used by the sequential algorithm. The rules are ordered using a metric (coverage in our implementation). The best rule is added to the theory and the remaining rules are reevaluated and reordered. The process is repeated while there are good rules to add to the theory. Like the previous algorithm, the solution returned by this algorithm may not be the same as the sequential version. It is obvious that this algorithm has the largest granularity of the three algorithms.

5.2 Materials

We used 3 ILP applications in the experiments. Table 2 characterizes the datasets used, in terms of number of examples (positive and negative) as well as background knowledge size (i.e., number of relations used in the learning task). *AET* is the average time required to test if an example is explained by a rule. This value is presented in microseconds and was estimated by dividing the sequential execution time by the number of examples evaluated during execution. This estimative of the cost of evaluating an example is a useful indicator when one considers the use of a parallelization strategy based on parallel coverage tests.

Table 2. Datasets Characterization

Dataset	$|E^+|$	$|E^-|$	$|B|$	AET (μs)
Carcinogenesis [4]	162	136	38	305
Mesh [2]	2272	223	29	46
Mutagenesis [1]	114	57	21	20846

The experiments were performed on a Beowulf Cluster composed by 8 nodes. Each node is a dual processor computer with 2GB of memory, and running the Linux Fedora OS. We used the YAP Prolog system version 4.5. The ILP system was configured to perform breadth-first search to find a rule. The search was guided using a heuristic that relies on the number of positive and negative examples.

We used 3-fold cross validation. The evaluation was focused on training time speedup and accuracy. We measured the accuracy because two of the implemented parallel algorithms may produce theories different from the ones obtained with the sequential version. The accuracy variation is the ratio between the predictive accuracy observed when using P processors and the predictive accuracy observed when using a single processor.

Table 3. Settings

Dataset	i-depth	Nodes	Noise	Minacc	CL
Carc	4	20000	5%	-	10
Mesh	4	10000	10%	85%	8
Mut	2	500	25%	70%	4

We tuned the settings so that the sequential runs would not take more than one hour to complete (except for the **Mut** dataset). Table 3 shows the main settings used for each dataset. The parameter *nodes* specifies an upper bound on the number of rules generated during a search for a rule. The *i*-depth [39] corresponds to the maximum depth of a literal with respect to the head literal of the rule. *MinAcc* specifies the minimum accuracy that a rule must have in order to be considered good. The parameter *CL* defines the maximum length that a rule may have. Finally, the *noise* parameter defines the percentage of negative examples that a rule may cover in order to be accepted.

5.3   Results

Table 4 presents the execution time (in seconds) and speedups observed, on each dataset and algorithm, for 1, 2, 4, 6, 8 and 16 processors. Some runs were not performed for one of two reasons: i) no speedup would be achieved; ii) the subset of data associated to each processor becomes too small (for the *dplr* or *dpilp* algorithms).

The effects on execution time of the parallel coverage tests approach (*pct*) show quite different behaviors. In the **Carc** and **Mesh** datasets the parallel version is slower than the sequential one, while in the **Mut** dataset a considerable speedup is observed. Since the **Mut** dataset has less examples than the other two, we can only deduct that the higher cost of evaluating an example (see Table 2) is the main reason for the speedups. However, when the subset becomes too small, as is the case for 16 processors, we stop obtaining gains.

The poor results with the **Carc** and **Mesh** suggest that the distribution of the work, and consequent parallel evaluation of the examples, is not compensated by the cost of message passing. Clearly, this fine-grain approach to parallelize ILP system seems only suited for datasets with a complex background knowledge, where the cost of evaluating an example is high, or for very large datasets (as the

Table 4. Execution time (T) and speedup (S)

Dataset		1	2	4	8
Carc	T	416	554	999	-
	S		**0.75**	**0.42**	-
Mesh	T	717	948	912	901
	S		**0.76**	**0.79**	**0.80**
Mut	T	8,022	4,565	2,502	-
	S		**1.75**	**3.20**	-

a) *pct*

Dataset		1	2	4	8	16
Carc	T	416	311	180	530	-
	S		**1.34**	**2.31**	**0.79**	-
Mesh	T	717	1,904	1,347	608	592
	S		**0.38**	**0.53**	**1.18**	**1.21**
Mut	T	8,022	6,339	3756	-	-
	S		**1.26**	**2.13**	-	-

b) *dplr*

Dataset		1	2	4	8	16
Carc	T	416	347	129	81	-
	S		**1.20**	**3.23**	**5.17**	-
Mesh	T	717	260	207	165	164
	S		**2.75**	**3.46**	**4.35**	**4.37**
Mut	T	5,865	6,339	3,756		
	S		**1.26**	**2.13**	-	-

c) *dpilp*

number of examples is concerned) where the parallel evaluation of the examples
on a subset outweighs the parallel overhead. A way of increasing the granularity
of the parallel task is to evaluate in parallel a set of rules, as proposed in [35],
instead of evaluating a single rule.

The impact of the *dplr* algorithm on the execution time is variable. In the
Carc dataset a speedup is observed up to four processors and is nonexistent for
eight processors. Interestingly, in the **Mesh** dataset, although we do not get a
speedup for two and four processors, we observe a decrease in the execution time
as the number of processors increases. A small speedup is observed with 8 and
16 processors.

One should note that the order by which the rules are found and added to
the theory is a crucial factor to the execution time since it conditions the amount
of the hypotheses space traversed. Recall that each worker gets a subset of E^+
but all E^-. If one of the workers does not find a globally "good" rule using its
local subset, it will have to do a more extensive search. This may happen when
a rule has an accuracy bellow the threshold, in the subset of the data where is
being generated (thus not being considered good), and is above the threshold if
the whole dataset is considered We observed that the final set of rules found by
the *dplr* algorithm is far bigger than the set found by the sequential algorithm
and that the rules are also lengthier. This suggests that the algorithm is unable
to find a small number of simple rules.

The *dplr* is a master-worker implementation of the algorithm described by
Wang et al. [25]. The results reported here are quite different from the ones previously reported. In [25] super-linear speedups (up to 6 processors) were reported
while the speedups we found are not even linear or, in some cases, inexistent.
The reason for this is two-fold. First, Wang et al. run the experiments in a shared

Table 5. Variation on predictive accuracy

Dataset	Alg.	2	4	8	16
Carc	dplr	+5%	+14%	-1%	-
(56%)	dpilp	+4%	-5%	+10%	-
Mesh	dplr	-25%	-25%	-	-
(72%)	dpilp	+17%	+21%	+23%	+25%
Mut	dplr	-2%	-13%	-	-
(86%)	dpilp	-1%	-12%	-	-

memory machine while we run on a distributed memory machine (a cluster, in fact). Second, in the experiments performed by Wang et al. no good rules were lost while learning because they did not define parameters, such as minimum accuracy or minimum coverage. These parameters are used when considering if a rule is good or not. However, when dealing with real world applications, these parameters are often used to make the learning process more tractable and to discard rules with very low coverage that may represent "overfitting".

Since the *dplr* is not complete, when compared to the sequential algorithm, the predictive accuracy of the theory found may vary. In Table 5 we can see that predictive accuracy is affected negatively by the use of this algorithm. The reason for this is also related to loosing "good" rules while looking for a rule in the subsets. The theories found by the algorithm are composed by much more specific and lengthier rules than the ones found by the sequential version.

The results obtained with the *dpilp* algorithm are clearly the best ones. This algorithm not only provides a consistent speedup but can also improve the theory predictive accuracy. *dpilp* differs from *dplr* in the amount of negative examples. In *dpilp* a worker gets a percentage of the total negatives whereas in *dplr* each worker gets a percentage of the positives but all of the negatives. *dpilp* also needs much less communication among the processors. This confirms the theory that greater task granularity results in bigger speedups.

6   Final Remarks

This paper has two main contributions: first, it surveys the state-of-the-art on parallel ILP implementations; secondly, the performance impact of three parallel algorithms on a distributed memory computer is studied using real world applications.

The parallel ILP algorithms described in the literature were grouped into four main approaches: parallel exploration of independent hypotheses; parallel exploration of the search space; parallel coverage test; parallel execution of an ILP system over a partition of the data. Parallel exploration of independent hypotheses is not a general approach since it is only adequate for applications where the target concept is composed by several independent subconcepts. However, when this approach is applicable it can be combined with other approaches to learn the subconcepts.

Three algorithms were implemented based on the three more generic strategies: parallel exploration of the search space; parallel coverage test; parallel execution of an ILP system over a partition of the data. The results show that a good approach to parallelize ILP systems in a shared-memory computer is one of the simplest to implement: divide the set of examples into p subsets; run the ILP system in parallel on each subset; combine the theories found. This approach not only reduces the execution time but can also improve predictive accuracy.

We have also noticed a significant difference between shared and distributed memory machines. In shared memory machines the communication overhead is significantly reduced and strategies, like *dlpr*, may give super-linear speedups. However, in distributed memory machines, where the communication costs are higher, fine-grained strategies are severely penalized.

A natural extension of this work is to perform a larger experimental evaluation over a greater number of datasets. This could provide us more insights about the applicability of each strategy. It would also be interesting to extend the evaluation of the strategies to shared memory architectures.

Acknowledgments. We are thankful to the anonymous referees for their valuable comments. The work presented in this paper has been partially supported by project APRIL (Project POSI/SRI/40749/2001) and funds granted to *LIACC* through the *Programa de Financiamento Plurianual, Fundação para a Ciência e Tecnologia* and *Programa POSI*. Nuno Fonseca is funded by the FCT grant SFRH/BD/7045/2001.

References

1. A. Srinivasan, S. Muggleton, R.D. King, and M.J.E. Sternberg. Mutagenesis: Ilp experiments in a non-determinate biological domain. In S. Wrobel, editor, *Proceedings of the 4th International Workshop on Inductive Logic Programming*, volume 237 of *GMD-Studien*, pages 217–232, 1994.

2. B. Dolsak, I. Bratko, and A. Jezernik. *Machine Learning, Data Mining and Knowledge Discovery: Methods and Applications*, chapter Application of machine learning in finite element computation. John Wiley and Sons, 1997.

3. Muggleton S., King R.D., and Sternberg M.J.E. Predicting protein secondary structure using inductive logic programming. *Protein Engineering*, (5):647–657, 1992.

4. A. Srinivasan, R. D. King, S. Muggleton, and M. J. E. Sternberg. Carcinogenesis predictions using ILP. In S. Džeroski and N. Lavrač, editors, *Proceedings of the 7th International Workshop on Inductive Logic Programming*, volume 1297, pages 273–287. Springer-Verlag, 1997.

5. Lappoon R. Tang, Raymond J. Mooney, and Prem Melville. Scaling up ilp to large examples: Results on link discovery for counter-terrorism. In *Proceedings of the KDD-2003 Workshop on Multi-Relational Data Mining (MRDM-2003)*, pages 107–121, 2003.

6. F. Železný, A. Srinivasan, and D. Page. Lattice-search runtime distributions may be heavy-tailed. In S. Matwin and C. Sammut, editors, *Proceedings of the 12th International Conference on Inductive Logic Programming*, volume 2583 of *LNAI*, pages 333–345. Springer-Verlag, 2003.

7. A. Srinivasan. A study of two probabilistic methods for searching large spaces with ilp. Technical Report PRG-TR-16-00, Oxford University Computing Laboratory, 2000.
8. Rui Camacho. Improving the efficiency of ilp systems using an incremental language level search. In *Annual Machine Learning Conference of Belgium and the Netherlands*, 2002.
9. A. Srinivasan, R.D. King, and M.E. Bain. An empirical study of the use of relevance information in inductive logic programming. *JMLR*, 2003.
10. Nuno Fonseca, Vitor Santos Costa, Rui Camacho, and Fernando Silva. On avoiding redundancy in Inductive Logic Programming. In Rui Camacho, Ross D. King, and Ashwin Srinivasan, editors, *Proceedings of the 14th International Conference on Inductive Logic Programming*, volume 3194 of *Lecture Notes in Artificial Intelligence*, pages 132–146, Porto, Portugal, September 2004. Springer-Verlag.
11. H. Blockeel, L. Dehaspe, B. Demoen, G. Janssens, J. Ramon, and H. Vandecasteele. Improving the efficiency of Inductive Logic Programming through the use of query packs. *Journal of Artificial Intelligence Research*, 16:135–166, 2002.
12. V.S. Costa, A. Srinivasan, R. Camacho, H. Blockeel, and W. Van Laer. Query transformations for improving the efficiency of ilp systems. *JMLR*, 2002.
13. Luc De Raedt. A perspective on inductive logic programming. In *The logic programming paradigm - a 25 year perspective*, pages 335,346. Springer-Verlag, 1999.
14. David Page. ILP: Just do it. In J. Cussens and A. Frisch, editors, *Proceedings of the 10th International Conference on Inductive Logic Programming*, volume 1866 of *LNAI*, pages 3–18. Springer-Verlag, 2000.
15. David Page and Ashwin Srinivasan. Ilp: a short look back and a longer look forward. *J. Mach. Learn. Res.*, 4:415–430, 2003.
16. Ananth Grama, Anshul Gupta, George Karypis, and Vipin Kumar. *Introduction to Parallel Computing*. Addison-Wesley, 2nd edition, 2003.
17. Johannes Fürnkranz. Separate-and-conquer rule learning. *Artificial Intelligence Review*, 13(1):3–54, February 1999.
18. S. Muggleton. Inverse entailment and Progol. *New Generation Computing, Special issue on Inductive Logic Programming*, 13(3-4):245–286, 1995.
19. J. R. Quinlan and R. M. Cameron-Jones. FOIL: A midterm report. In P. Brazdil, editor, *Proceedings of the 6th European Conference on Machine Learning*, volume 667, pages 3–20. Springer-Verlag, 1993.
20. Ashwin Srinivasan. Aleph manual, 2003.
21. Hayato Ohwada and Fumio Mizoguchi. Parallel execution for speeding up inductive logic programming systems. In *LNAI*, number 1721, pages 277–286. Springer-Verlag, 1999.
22. T. Matsui, N. Inuzuka, H. Seki, and H. Itoh. Comparison of three parallel implementations of an induction algorithm. In *8th Int. Parallel Computing Workshop*, pages 181–188, Singapore, 1998.
23. Hayato Ohwada, Hiroyuki Nishiyama, and Fumio Mizoguchi. Concurrent execution of optimal hypothesis search for inverse entailment. In J. Cussens and A. Frisch, editors, *Proceedings of the 10th International Conference on Inductive Logic Programming*, volume 1866 of *LNAI*, pages 165–173. Springer-Verlag, 2000.
24. Jan Wielemaker. Native preemptive threads in swi-prolog. In *ICLP*, pages 331–345, 2003.
25. Y. Wang and D. Skillicorn. Parallel inductive logic for data mining. In *Workshop on Distributed and Parallel Knowledge Discovery, KDD2000*, Boston, 2000. ACM Press.

26. James Graham, C. David Page, and Ahmed Kamal. Accelerating the drug design process through parallel inductive logic programming data mining. In *Proceeding of the Computational Systems Bioinformatics (CSB'03)*. IEEE, 2003.
27. L. Dehaspe and L. De Raedt. Parallel inductive logic programming. In *Proceedings of the MLnet Familiarization Workshop on Statistics, Machine Learning and Knowledge Discovery in Databases*, 1995.
28. R.S. Michalski. Pattern recognition as rule-guided inductive inference. In *Proceedings of IEEE Transactions on Pattern Analysis and Machine Intelligence*, pages 349–361, 1980.
29. R.G. Smith. "The contract net protocol: High-level communication and control in a distributed problem solver". *IEEE Trans. Computers*, 29(12):1104–1113, Dec 1980.
30. Stephen Muggleton and John Firth. Relational rule induction with cprogol4.4: A tutorial introduction. In Saso Dzeroski and Nada Lavrac, editors, *Relational Data Mining*, pages 160–188. Springer-Verlag, September 2001.
31. Pvm:parallel virtual machine. http://www.csm.ornl.gov/pvm/.
32. Stasinos K. Konstantopoulos. A data-parallel version of aleph. In *Proceedings of the Workshop on Parallel and Distributed Computing for Machine Learning, co-located with ECML/PKDD'2003*, Dubrovnik, Croatia, September 2003.
33. W. Gropp, E. Lusk, N. Doss, and A. Skjellum. A high-performance, portable implementation of the MPI message passing interface standard. *Parallel Computing*, 22(6):789–828, September 1996.
34. Message Passing Interface Forum. MPI: A message-passing interface standard. Technical Report UT-CS-94-230, 1994.
35. Amanda Clare and Ross D. King. Data mining the yeast genome in a lazy functional language. In *PADL*, pages 19–36, 2003.
36. Nuno Fonseca, Fernando Silva, Rui Camacho, and Vitor S. Costa. Induction with April - A preliminary report. Technical Report DCC-2003-02, DCC-FC & LIACC, Universidade do Porto, 2003.
37. Jeffrey M. Squyres and Andrew Lumsdaine. A Component Architecture for LAM/MPI. In *Proceedings, 10th European PVM/MPI Users' Group Meeting*, number 2840 in LNCS, Venice, Italy, September / October 2003. Springer-Verlag.
38. Ronaldo Cristiano Prati and Peter Flach. Roccer: an algorithm for rule learning based on roc analysis. In *Nineteenth International Joint Conference on Artificial Intelligence (IJCAI'2005)*, 2005.
39. S. Muggleton and C. Feng. Efficient induction in logic programs. In S. Muggleton, editor, *Inductive Logic Programming*, pages 281–298. Academic Press, 1992.

Inducing Causal Laws by Regular Inference

Katsumi Inoue[1], Hideyuki Bando[2], and Hidetomo Nabeshima[3]

[1] National Institute of Informatics,
2-1-2 Hitotsubashi, Chiyoda-ku, Tokyo 101-8430, Japan
ki@nii.ac.jp
[2] Mitsubishi Electric Control Software Corporation,
8-1-1 Tsukaguchi-Honmachi, Amagasaki, Hyogo 660-0001, Japan
bando@mcr.ita.melco.co.jp
[3] Department of Computer and Media Engineering, Yamanashi University,
4-3-11 Takeda, Kofu, Yamanashi 400-8511, Japan
nabesima@iw.media.yamanashi.ac.jp

Abstract. Recent work on representing action and change has introduced high-level action languages which describe the effects of actions as causal laws in a declarative way. In this paper, we propose an algorithm to induce the effects of actions from an incomplete domain description and observations after executing action sequences, all of which are represented in the action language $\mathcal{A}$. Our induction algorithm generates effect propositions in $\mathcal{A}$ based on regular inference, i.e., an algorithm to learn finite automata. As opposed to previous work on learning automata from scratch, we are concerned with explanatory induction which accounts for observations from background knowledge together with induced hypotheses. Compared with previous approaches in ILP, an observation input to our induction algorithm is not restricted to a narrative but can be any fact observed after executing a sequence of actions. As a result, induction of causal laws can be formally characterized within action languages.

1 Introduction

In a dynamic domain, an agent needs the ability to react against environment changes to generate a robust plan for a long-term goal. In planning, one should prepare knowledge about actions, i.e., the precondition and the effects of each action in the form of *causal laws*. In the real world, however, it is difficult or impossible to describe the complete causal laws for a domain. Then, it is easier to get observations after executing several actions. Such observations include fluents which hold in a narrative as well as information obtained by contacting with environments through some actions. Hence, we have the problem of *inducing causal laws*: given an incomplete description of a domain and observations after executing action sequences, find missing causal laws which enable to make the action sequences actually perform planning.

Induction of causal laws has recently become important for agents to reason about actions in dynamic worlds. Moreover, emergent applications such as robotics, bioinformatics and environmental problems involve temporal aspects

S. Kramer and B. Pfahringer (Eds.): ILP 2005, LNAI 3625, pp. 154–171, 2005.
© Springer-Verlag Berlin Heidelberg 2005

and state changes. However, although there have been many tools to discover association rules, their applications would merely discover fluents that change together, which mostly fail to find causal relationships. Hence, induction of causal laws requires taking temporal aspects into account. In ILP, some previous attempts contribute to this problem [12,11,10,9,15,16]. Unfortunately, they are not sufficiently powerful to induce causal laws in a general setting. In particular, previous methods often assume the existence of (complete) narratives.

On the other hand, recent work on representing action and change has introduced high-level *action languages* [6] to describe the effects of actions in a systematic and theoretically sound way. Gelfond and Lifschitz [5] firstly used this approach by introducing the action language $\mathcal{A}$, which is a simple action language allowing only deterministic actions without state constraints. The language $\mathcal{A}$ enables us to encode causal laws[1] in a domain, and is adequate to capture commonsense reasoning with the *law of inertia*, whose implementation can be realized in *extended logic programs* with two kinds of negation [5]. The formal semantics of $\mathcal{A}$ is mathematically of interest since each model represents a *state transition system*, which is a directed graph whose vertices represent the states of the world, and whose edges correspond to the execution of actions. Various extensions of $\mathcal{A}$ have been proposed in the literature, e.g., [2,7,17], yet all languages have the semantics similar to that of $\mathcal{A}$ in principle [6]. Recent work on *causal theories* [8] has also strong relationships with action languages [7]. In [14], it is shown that the expressive power of $\mathcal{A}$ is exactly the same as that of *finite automata* (FAs) in the sense that each language can precisely simulate the other. The equivalence result between $\mathcal{A}$ and FAs enables us to characterize the set of all possible solutions of a planning problem by a *regular expression*.

Although the language $\mathcal{A}$ is very simple, it has two unique features that cannot be seen in other extended action languages: (1) $\mathcal{A}$ can be used as both action *description language* and action *query language* [2], and (2) $\mathcal{A}$ can be used not only for *temporal projection*, i.e., reasoning from the initial state to the goal state, but for *temporal explanation*, i.e., reasoning about the past. These features enable us to use the language $\mathcal{A}$ for inducing causal laws from an incomplete domain description and observations. In this paper, we propose an algorithm to induce causal laws from incomplete domain description and observations after executing action sequences, in which all knowledge are represented in $\mathcal{A}$. By equivalence between $\mathcal{A}$ and FAs, we adopt an algorithm for *regular inference*, i.e., an algorithm to learn FAs [1,3], and call it in finding a missing part of a state transition system. As a regular inference algorithm, we use one by Dupont *et al.* [3] which infers the canonical FAs accepting all strings in the given sample. Our induction algorithm takes action sequences deriving some goal fluents as the positive sample and action sequences deriving states that contradict goals as the negative sample. Then, we infer automata which agree with the state transition by those input action sequences, and then generate causal laws

---

[1] When $\mathcal{A}$ was proposed in [5], the notion of *causality* has not been fully identified yet. Now a "causal law" is reserved for a different kind of law in action theories [8], but we adopt this term since it is in common use to denote cause and effect.

from the induced automata. However, as opposed to previous work on learning automata from scratch, we are concerned with explanatory induction which accounts for observations from background knowledge together with induced hypotheses. Moreover, compared with previous approaches in ILP, an observation input to our induction algorithm is not restricted to a narrative with complete information of intermediate states, but can be any fact observed after executing a sequence of actions.

The rest of this paper is organized as follows. Section 2 reviews the language $\mathcal{A}$ and shows equivalence between $\mathcal{A}$ and FAs, and Section 3 reviews regular inference. Section 4 presents an algorithm to induce causal laws in $\mathcal{A}$, and proves the correctness of the algorithm, then applies it to infer the models of a causal theory. Section 5 discusses related work, and Section 6 concludes the paper.

2   Action Language $\mathcal{A}$

The action language $\mathcal{A}$ consists of two sets of symbols, *action names* and *fluent names*, and two sets of propositions, *value propositions* and *effect propositions*. In this paper, we assume that the numbers of symbols and propositions in a domain description are finite.

A *fluent* is an attribute that may depend on states. For a fluent name f, $\neg f$ is a *negative fluent*, and f is a *positive fluent*. When we say a *fluent f*, it means either a positive fluent or a negative fluent. For a set of fluents $F = \{f_1, \ldots, f_n\}$, $|F|^\pm$ denotes the set of positive and negative fluents constructed with the fluent names appearing in F, that is, $|F|^\pm = \{f_1, \ldots, f_n\} \cup \{\neg f_1, \ldots, \neg f_n\}$.

A *value proposition* is an expression of the form:

$$f \textbf{ after } a_1; \cdots; a_m \quad (m \geq 0) \tag{1}$$

where f is a fluent, $a_1, \ldots, a_m$ are action names, and $a_1; \cdots; a_m$ denotes the sequence of actions starting from a_1 until a_m. The expression of the form (1) is also called a value proposition *with respect to f*. Each value proposition represents an *observation* that f holds after executing an action sequence $a_1; \cdots; a_m$ at the initial state. If $m = 0$, we write (1) simply as

$$\textbf{initially } f. \tag{2}$$

An *effect proposition* is an expression of the form:

$$a \textbf{ causes } f \textbf{ if } p_1, \ldots, p_m \quad (m \geq 0) \tag{3}$$

where a is an action name, and f and p_i $(i = 1, \ldots, m)$ are fluents. Each effect proposition represents a *causal law* specifying the *precondition* $p_1 \wedge \cdots \wedge p_m$ and the *effect* f for each action a. If $m = 0$, we will write (3) simply as

$$a \textbf{ causes } f.$$

For an effect proposition $P = (a \textbf{ causes } f \textbf{ if } p_1, \ldots, p_m)$, the fluents in the precondition and the effect of P are denoted as $cond(P) = \{p_1, \ldots, p_m\}$ and $effect(P) = f$, respectively.

A *domain description* is a set of value and effect propositions. For a domain description D, $action(D)$ is the set of all action names appearing in D, and $fluent(D)$ is the set of all fluent names included in D. Also, the set of value propositions in D is denoted as $V(D)$, and the set of effect propositions in D is denoted as $E(D)$. Note that $D = V(D) \cup E(D)$ and $V(D) \cap E(D) = \emptyset$.

A *state* q is defined as:[2]

$$q = S \cup \{\neg f \mid f \in fluent(D) \setminus S\}, \quad \text{where } S \subseteq fluent(D). \tag{4}$$

The set of states constructed from a domain description D is written as $state(D)$. A *transition function* Φ is a mapping $state(D) \times action(D) \rightarrow state(D)$. A *structure* I is a pair (Φ, q_0), where Φ is a transition function and q_0 is the *initial state*. For any structure $I = (\Phi, q_0)$ and any action sequence $a_1; \cdots; a_m$, we define

$$I^{a_1;\cdots;a_m} = \Phi(\Phi(\cdots \Phi(\Phi(q_0, a_1), a_2), \ldots, a_{m-1}), a_m).$$

A value proposition of the form (1) is *true* in a structure I if $f \in I^{a_1;\cdots;a_m}$; otherwise, it is *false*.

A structure I is a *model* of a domain description D if (i) every value proposition in D is true in I, and (ii) for any action name a and any state q, the transition function Φ satisfies that

$$\Phi(q, a) = (q \setminus |\mathcal{F}|^{\pm}) \cup \mathcal{F}, \tag{5}$$
$$\text{where } \mathcal{F} = \{effect(P) \mid P \in E(D), \ cond(P) \subseteq q\}.$$

The equation (5) represents that any fluent which is not influenced by execution of an action keeps its truth value at the state resulting by the execution of the action. This condition represents the *law of inertia*, which is how the semantics of $\mathcal{A}$ solves the *frame problem*. Since there exists at most one transition function Φ satisfying (5), different models of the same domain description differ only by their initial states. A domain description is *consistent* if it has a model, and is *categorical* if it has exactly one model. A value proposition (1) is *entailed* by a domain description D if it is true in every model of D, and is denoted as:

$$D \models (f \textbf{ after } a_1; \cdots; a_m).$$

Example 2.1. Here is the *Yale Shooting* domain represented in $\mathcal{A}$ [5].

> **initially** $\neg loaded$.
> **initially** $alive$.
> $load$ **causes** $loaded$.
> $shoot$ **causes** $\neg loaded$.
> $shoot$ **causes** $\neg alive$ **if** $loaded$.

Let D be this domain description. Then, $action(D) = \{load, shoot\}$ and $fluent(D) = \{loaded, alive\}$. The initial state is $q_0 = \{\neg loaded, alive\}$. Moreover, it holds that

$$D \models (\neg alive \textbf{ after } load; shoot).$$

---

[2] In [5], a state is defined as a set of fluent names, where the absence of f denotes the negative fluent $\neg f$. This definition is essentially equivalent to ours.

A *(finite) automaton* (FA) is a quintuple $(Q, \Sigma, \delta, q_0, G)$, where Q is a finite set of *states*, Σ is a *alphabet*, $q_0 \in Q$ is the *initial state*, $G \subseteq Q$ is the set of *final states*, and $\delta : \Gamma \rightarrow Q$ such that $\Gamma \subseteq Q \times \Sigma$ is the *transition function*. If a FA has the transition function $\delta : Q \times \Sigma \rightarrow Q$, i.e., $\Gamma = Q \times \Sigma$, it is a *(completely) deterministic* FA (DFA); otherwise, it is *incomplete*. Now, suppose a domain description D in $\mathcal{A}$. For each model $M = (\Phi, q_0)$ of D and a given $G \subseteq state(D)$, we can associate the DFA $(state(D), action(D), \Phi, q_0, G)$. Then, it is shown in [14] that the class of domain descriptions represented in $\mathcal{A}$ and the class of FAs are equivalent. The equivalence result is proved by defining the following algorithms:

- **Init**(D): computes the initial states of DFAs from a domain description D (Fig. 1).
- **Trans**(D): computes every transition function Φ of every DFA from a domain description D (Fig. 2).
- **RevTrans**(M): computes (the effect propositions of) the domain description D from a FA M (Fig. 4).
- **Compress**(D): removes redundant effect propositions from a domain description D (Fig. 5).

The algorithm **Init** computes initial states efficiently using the concept of *sub-states* by representing multiple states together after executing some action. A *substate* q is an incomplete description of a state:

$$q = S_1 \cup \{\neg f \mid f \in S_2\}, \quad \text{where } S_1, S_2 \subseteq fluent(D) \text{ and } S_1 \cap S_2 = \emptyset.$$

For example, if $fluent(D) = \{loaded, alive\}$, the substate $\{loaded\}$ expresses two states: $\{loaded, alive\}$ and $\{loaded, \neg alive\}$. The empty substate $\emptyset$ expresses all states. For any fluent name f, the *absolute value* of f is defined as $|f| = f$, $|\neg f| = f$. Similarly, for a substate q, we define $|q| = \{|f| \mid f \in q\}$. The *relevant fluents* of an action a is defined as

$$rel(a) = \{\, |f| \mid P \in E(D),\, f \in cond(P) \cup \{effect(P)\} \,\}.$$

For any set Q of substates and a fluent f, the function $div(Q, f)$ *divides* every substate $q \in Q$ into the two substates, $q \cup \{f\}$ and $q \cup \{\neg f\}$, as:

$$div(Q, f) = \begin{cases} \bigcup_{q \in Q} \{\, q \cup \{f\},\ q \cup \{\neg f\} \,\} & \text{if } |f| \notin |q| \text{ for any } q \in Q \\ Q & \text{otherwise.} \end{cases}$$

Similarly, for a set of fluents, we define:

$$div(Q, \{f_1, \ldots, f_n\}) = div(\cdots div(div(Q, f_1), f_2), \ldots, f_n).$$

Proposition 2.1. [14] *Let D be a consistent domain description in $\mathcal{A}$, and $\mathcal{I}$ the set of models of D. Suppose that the set $\mathcal{M}$ of DFAs is translated from D, i.e., $\mathcal{M} = \textbf{Trans}(D, \textbf{Init}(D))$. Then, there is a one-to-one correspondence between $\mathcal{I}$ and $\mathcal{M}$. Moreover, there is a model (Φ, q_0) in $\mathcal{I}$ iff there is a DFA in $\mathcal{M}$ whose initial state is q_0 and transition function is Φ.*

Init(D) Input: a consistent domain description D in $\mathcal{A}$
              Output: the set $\mathcal{Q}_0$ of initial states of D.
begin
  $Q^0 := \{\emptyset\}$;
  for $j := 1$ **to** $|V(D)|$ **do**
    j-th value proposition: $(f \ \textbf{after} \ a_1; \cdots; a_m) \in V(D)$;
    $T_0^j := div(Q^{j-1}, f)$;
    for $i := 1$ **to** m **do**
      $T_0^j := div(T_0^j, rel(a_i))$; $T_{i-1}^j := div(T_{i-1}^j, rel(a_i))$;
      $T_i^j := \{\textbf{NextState}(a_i, q, D) \mid q \in T_{i-1}^j\}$;
    $Q^j := \{q_0 \in T_0^j \mid f \in q_m, \ q_m \in T_m^j, \ \textbf{NextState}^*(a_1; \cdots; a_m, q_0, D) = q_m\}$;
  $\mathcal{Q}_0 := div(Q^k, fluent(D))$
end.

NextState(a, q, D) Input: an action a, a state q, a domain description D in $\mathcal{A}$.
                      Output: the state q_1 after executing a at q.
begin
  $q' := \{effect(P) \mid P \in E(D) \text{ and } cond(P) \subseteq q\}$;
  $q_1 := q' \cup \{f \in q \mid |f| \notin |q'|\}$
end.

NextState$^*(a_1; \cdots; a_m, q, D)$ extends **NextState** to an action sequence $a_1; \cdots; a_m$.

Fig. 1. Algorithm to compute the set of initial states

Trans$(D, \mathcal{Q}_0)$ Input: a domain description D in $\mathcal{A}$, a set $\mathcal{Q}_0$ of initial states.
                    Output: the set $\mathcal{M}$ of DFAs corresponding to D and $\mathcal{Q}_0$.
begin
  $Q := div(\{\emptyset\}, fluent(D))$;
  for all $q \in Q$ and all $a \in action(D)$ **do**
    $\delta(a, q) := \textbf{NextState}(a, q, D)$;
  $\mathcal{M} := \{(Q, action(D), \delta, q_0, Q) \mid q_0 \in \mathcal{Q}_0\}$
end.

Fig. 2. Algorithm to compute the transition function

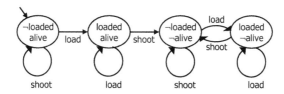

Fig. 3. DFA for the Yale Shooting domain

Example 2.2. Fig. 3 shows the result of translation of the domain description D in Example 2.1. Since this domain is categorical, it is translated into a single DFA. Note that we do not distinguish the final states G here. If we set G as the two states containing $\neg alive$, then the unique minimal solution for *planning* to realize $\neg alive$ is represented by the regular expression *load; shoot*, which is the minimal string accepted by the FA.

The reverse translation algorithm translates a (possibly incomplete) FA into a domain description in $\mathcal{A}$. To deal with each state of a FA in the same way as $\mathcal{A}$, any state of a FA must be represented as a set of fluents in the form (4). Here, when a FA has n states, $\lceil \log_2 |n| \rceil$ fluents have to be prepared. To remove redundant effect propositions from a domain description, the **Compress** algorithm can be used not only in the translation of FAs to $\mathcal{A}$ but in any situation for simplifying domain descriptions in $\mathcal{A}$.

RevTrans(M) Input: a FA $M = (Q, \Sigma, \delta, q_0, G)$.
                     Output: a domain description D.
begin
  $D := \{(\textbf{initially } f) \mid f \in q_0\};$
  $D := D \cup \{(a \textbf{ causes } f \textbf{ if } p_1, \ldots, p_n) \mid a \in \Sigma,\ q = \{p_1, \ldots, p_n\} \in Q,\ f \in \delta(a, q)\}$
end.

Fig. 4. Algorithm to generate a domain description in $\mathcal{A}$

Compress(D) Input: a domain description D.
                     Output: a simplified domain description.
begin
  while (it is possible to remove redundant effect propositions from D) **do**
  1) $E = (a \textbf{ causes } f \textbf{ if } p_1, \ldots, p_n) \in D \quad (n \geq 1);$
    if $f \in \{p_1, \ldots, p_n\}$ **then** $D := D \setminus \{E\};$
  2) $E = (a \textbf{ causes } f \textbf{ if } p_1, \ldots, p_n) \in D \quad (n \geq 0);$
    $F = (a \textbf{ causes } f \textbf{ if } q_1, \ldots, q_m) \in D \quad (m \geq n);$
    if $\{p_1, \ldots, p_n\} \subseteq \{q_1, \ldots, q_m\}$ **then** $D := D \setminus \{F\};$
  3) $E = (a \textbf{ causes } f \textbf{ if } p_1, \ldots, p_n) \in D \quad (n \geq 0);$
    $F = (a \textbf{ causes } f \textbf{ if } q_1, \ldots, q_n) \in D;$
    if $\neg p_i = q_j$ and $\{p_1, \ldots, p_{i-1}, p_{i+1}, \ldots, p_n\} = \{q_1, \ldots, q_{j-1}, q_{j+1}, \ldots, q_n\}$
      then $D := (D \setminus \{E, F\}) \cup \{(a \textbf{ causes } f \textbf{ if } p_1, \ldots, p_{i-1}, p_{i+1}, \ldots, p_n)\};$
  4) $E = (a \textbf{ causes } f \textbf{ if } p_1, \ldots, p_n) \in D \quad (n \geq m \geq 1);$
    if $\neg f = p_i \quad (1 \leq i \leq n)$ and
      there is no $(a \textbf{ causes } \neg f \textbf{ if } q_1, \ldots, q_m)$ such that
        $f \in \{q_1, \ldots, q_m\}$ and $(\{q_1, \ldots, q_m\} \setminus \{f\}) \subset (\{p_1, \ldots, p_n\} \setminus \{\neg f\})$
      then $D := (D \setminus \{E\}) \cup \{(a \textbf{ causes } f \textbf{ if } p_1, \ldots, p_{i-1}, p_{i+1}, \ldots, p_n)\}$
end.

Fig. 5. Algorithm to simplify domain descriptions

Proposition 2.2. [14] *Let M be any FA, and $D = \mathbf{RevTrans}(M)$. Then, D is categorical, and its unique model has the same initial state and the same transition function as M.*

Proposition 2.3. [14] *Let D be a domain description in $\mathcal{A}$. Then, $\mathbf{Compress}$ (D) and D have the same set of models.*

3 Regular Inference

By *regular inference* [1,3], we mean induction of FAs which accept the *positive sample* of strings but do not accept the *negative sample* of strings. An *acceptance* of a string $a_1; \cdots; a_m$ by a FA $M = (Q, \Sigma, \delta, q_0, G)$ defines a sequence of $m + 1$ states $(q_0, \ldots, q_m)$ such that $q_m \in G$ and $q_{i+1} = \delta(q_i, a_{i+1})$ for $i = 1, \ldots, m-1$. In this case, the m transitions are said to be *exercised* by this acceptance, and q_m is called an *acceptance state*. A set R of strings over Σ is said to be *structurally complete* with respect to M if there exists an acceptance of the strings in R by M such that (1) every transition of M is exercised and (2) every final state of M is used as an acceptance state.

Given a positive sample $R = \{\omega_1, \ldots, \omega_n\}$, where ω_i $(i = 1, \ldots, n)$ is a string over Σ, the *prefix tree acceptor* (PTA) of R [1], $PTA(R) = (Q, \Sigma, \delta, q_0, G)$, is an automaton accepting R such that

$$
\begin{aligned}
&Q = \{(a_1; \cdots; a_i) \mid (a_1; \cdots; a_m) \in R,\ 1 \le i \le m\} \cup \{\varepsilon\}, \\
&\delta(v, a) = (v; a) \quad \text{for } v \in Q,\ a \in \Sigma,\ (v; a) \in Q, \\
&q_0 = \varepsilon, \\
&G = R,
\end{aligned}
$$

where ε is the empty string. For example, when $R = \{(a; b; c), (c; d)\}$, the state set of $PTA(R)$ is $Q = \{\varepsilon, a, (a; b), (a; b; c), c, (c; d)\}$, and the transition function δ satisfies $\delta(a, b) = (a; b)$ but $\delta(a, c)$ is not defined because $(a; c) \notin Q$.

For any FA $M = (Q, \Sigma, \delta, q_0, G)$ and a partition π, the *quotient automaton* $M/\pi = (Q', \Sigma, \delta', q_0', G')$ is defined as:

$$
\begin{aligned}
&Q' = Q/\pi = \{[q] \mid q \in Q\}, \\
&\delta'([q], a) = [r] \quad \text{for } \delta(q, a) = r, \\
&q_0' = [q_0], \\
&G' = \{q \in Q' \mid q \cap G \ne \emptyset\},
\end{aligned}
$$

where $[s]$ denotes the unique element of π containing $s \in Q$.

Let $\pi_1 = \{B_1, \ldots, B_n\}$ and π_2 be two partitions of the state set Q of a FA M. If $\pi_2 = \{B_j \cup B_k\} \cup (\pi_1 \setminus \{B_j, B_k\})$ holds for some $1 \le j, k \le n$ $(j \ne k)$, we define that $\pi_1 \preceq \pi_2$. Let $\ll$ be the transitive closure of the relation $\preceq$. Then, it holds that $\pi_1 \ll \pi_2$ implies $L(M/\pi_1) \subseteq L(M/\pi_2)$, where $L(M)$ represents the language accepted by an automaton M. The set of automata partially ordered by the relation $\preceq$ constitutes a Boolean lattice, which is denoted as $Lat(M)$, of which the bottom and top elements are M and the universal automaton that accepts every string, respectively. Let L be a regular language, $M(L)$ the canonical (i.e., minimal) FA accepting L, and R a positive sample of L. It is known that, if R is structurally complete with respect to $M(L)$, then $M(L)$ belongs to $Lat(PTA(R))$ [3]. Hence, given the positive sample R and the negative sample N, the algorithm **LearnFA**(R, N) induces the FAs $\mathcal{P}$ by (1) generating $PTA(R)$, (2) constructing $Lat(PTA(R))$, and (3) selecting $\mathcal{P}$ which do not accept N from $Lat(PTA(R))$.

4   Induction of Causal Laws

4.1   Problem Definition

We consider the problem of inducing causal laws in the action language $\mathcal{A}$, which is formally defined as follows. We are given a domain description D in $\mathcal{A}$ as input. Recall that D consists of the two subsets $E(D)$ and $V(D)$, which are the effect propositions and the value propositions in D, respectively. Here, we regard $E(D)$ as *background knowledge* B, and regard $V(D)$ as an *observation* O in the induction problem. Note that $D = B \cup O$ and $B \cap O = \emptyset$, where $B = E(D)$ and $O = V(D)$. Then, suppose that the given description D is *inconsistent*, that is, there is no model of D that makes O true. The purpose of induction is to compute a set γ of effect propositions in $\mathcal{A}$, called a *hypothesis*, such that $D \cup \gamma$ is consistent. If such a hypothesis γ is found, then for every model $I = (\varPhi, q_0)$ of $D \cup \gamma$, every value proposition in O is true in I, and the transition function $\varPhi$ agrees with the state transition determined by the effect propositions in $B \cup \gamma$.

In the above problem setting, it should not be surprising that $D \cup \gamma$ is consistent although D is inconsistent. When $D = B \cup O$ is inconsistent, there are two possible cases. First, if B is inconsistent, there is no transition function which agree with every effect proposition in B, so that addition of any set γ of new effect propositions cannot make $B \cup \gamma$ consistent. In this case, we cannot get any hypothesis for the induction problem. Second, if B is consistent but $B \cup O$ is inconsistent, the inconsistency of $B \cup O$ is due to the fact that O cannot be verified within D because some effect propositions are missing. In this case, there is a possibility to make O entailed from the augmented consistent description $D \cup \gamma$. In this sense, the inconsistency of $B \cup O$ here is caused by the *incompleteness* of B. By this reason, we often say that a domain description D (or background knowledge B) is *incomplete*, instead of saying that D is *inconsistent*.

In the following, we assume that every fluent change is observable. This means that, for any fluent g, if (1) g is true at the initial state, (2) the truth value of g changes after executing some action sequence $a_1; \cdots; a_m$ $(m \geq 1)$, and (3) the change is caused as the effect of some action a_i $(1 \leq i \leq m)$ by a missing effect proposition $P \notin B$, then the input observation O is assumed to contain the following value propositions with respect to g and $\neg g$:

$$\textbf{(initially } g) \quad \text{and} \quad (\neg g \textbf{ after } a_1; \cdots; a_m).$$

When a fluent g satisfies the above three condition, we call the fluent $\neg g$ a *goal fluent*. This assumption implies that, to induce an effect proposition $P \notin B$, there must be a value proposition with respect to the goal fluent $effect(P)$ in O.

4.2 Induction Algorithm

Now, we propose the induction algorithm **InduceCL**(B, O), which takes background knowledge B and an observation O as input, and outputs a set of hypotheses $\mathcal{H}$. An outline of **InduceCL** consists of the following three steps:

1. Induce a set of FAs $\mathcal{P}$ by calling **LearnFA** with the positive and negative samples constructed from O;
2. Construct an automaton T by subdividing each FA in $\mathcal{P}$ such that the transition function of T agrees with the effect propositions in B and that every value proposition in O is true in T;
3. Compute a set of effect propositions γ from the transition function of each automaton T by calling **RevTrans**.

In Algorithm **InduceCL**, the given observation O is first divided into three sets, the *initial value propositions* $valI$, the *positive observations* $valR$, and the *negative observations* $valN$. That is,

$$O = valI \cup valR \cup valN \quad \text{where } valI \cap valR \cap valN = \emptyset,$$

$valI$ is the set of value propositions with respect to any fluent of the form (2), $valR$ ($valN$) is the set of value propositions with respect to goal fluents (negations of goal fluents) of the form (1) such that $m \geq 1$. Then, the positive sample R is set to the action sequences appearing in $valR$, and the negative sample N is set to the action sequences appearing in $valN$.

Next, **LearnFA**(R, N) constructs a set $\mathcal{P}$ of FAs which accepts R and do not accept N. Here, each state of an automaton $\pi \in \mathcal{P}$ is defined as a set of prefixes of a string in R. Then, **InduceCL** converts each prefix set s into a fluent set s' according to the following rules. For each goal fluent $\neg g$,

$$\begin{array}{ll}
g \in s' & \text{if } \varepsilon \in s, \\
\neg g \in s' & \text{if } w \in s \text{ and } w \in R(\neg g), \\
g \in s' & \text{if } w \in s \text{ and } w \in N(\neg g), \\
g \in s' \text{ or } \neg g \in s' & \text{otherwise,}
\end{array} \tag{6}$$

where $R(\neg g) \subseteq R$ ($N(\neg g) \subseteq N$) is the set of action sequences appearing in the value propositions with respect to $\neg g$ (g). By (6), each state s is replaced with s' at Fig. 6 (i). Note that the resulting state set S in π is not defined as a set but as a multiset because different states can be converted to states named with the same set of fluents. The first case in (6) is the rule for the initial state, the second is for the final states accepting the positive sample R, and the third is for the states accepting the negative sample N. By definition of the positive sample R, R never contains ε, and hence the first and second cases cannot occur at the same time. The fourth rule in (6) is for the case that the truth value of g cannot be determined in a state s. This case happens when the truth value of g in an intermediate state is not explicitly given in the input observation O. Hence, we are dealing with the case that narratives are not completely specified as input.

InduceCL(B, O) Input: background knowledge B, observation O.
                                          Output: the set $\mathcal{H}$ of hypotheses.
begin
　Divide O into $valI$, $valR$, and $valN$;
　$\mathcal{P} :=$ **LearnFA**(R, N) ;
　for all $\pi \in \mathcal{P}$ **do**
　　Convert every state in π into a fluent by (6) ;   /* (i) */
　$\mathcal{H} := \emptyset$; $\Sigma := action(B \cup O)$;
　$initF := \{f \mid (\textbf{initially } f) \in valI\}$;
　$Q_0 := div(\{initF\}, fluent(B \cup O))$;   /* (ii) */
　$Q := div(\emptyset, fluent(B \cup O))$;   /* (iii) */
　for all $\pi := (S, \Sigma, \delta, s_0, G) \in \mathcal{P}$ **do**
　　begin
　　　for all $q_0 \in Q_0$ **do**
　　　　for all $\omega_i \in R$ **do**
　　　　　$\omega_i = a_1; \cdots; a_m$ where $m = |\omega_i|$;
　　　　　for $j := 1$ **to** m **do**
　　　　　　begin
　　　　　　　$s_j := \delta(s_{j-1}, a_j)$;
　　　　　　　$q_j := trans(q_{j-1}, a_j, s_j)$;   /* (iv) */
　　　　　　　if $trans(q_{j-1}, a_j, s_j)$ is undefined, or $\Phi(q_{j-1}, a_j) = q$
　　　　　　　　has already been defined and $q \neq q_j$ **then goto** L1 ;
　　　　　　　$\Phi(q_{j-1}, a_j) := q_j$
　　　　　　end ;   /* (v) */
　　　　for all $(q, a) \in Q \times \Sigma$ **do**
　　　　　if $\Phi(q, a)$ is not defined **then** $\Phi(q, a) := trans(q, a, \emptyset)$;   /* (vi) */
　　　　$T := (Q, \Sigma, \Phi)$;
　　　　$\gamma :=$ **Compress**(**RevTrans**$(T)) \setminus B$;
　　　　$\mathcal{H} := \mathcal{H} \cup \{\gamma\}$
　L1:
　　end ;
　return $\mathcal{H}$
end.

Fig. 6. Algorithm to induce causal laws

The rules (6) replaces the FAs $\mathcal{P}$ with the FAs whose initial and final states contain g and $\neg g$, respectively. Then, for each $\pi = (S, \Sigma, \delta, s_0, G) \in \mathcal{P}$, **InduceCL** executes several operations and finally outputs an automaton $T = (Q, \Sigma, \Phi)$. This T has the property that $\delta(s_{j-1}, a_j) = s_j$ implies $\Phi(q_{j-1}, a_j) = q_j$ such that $s_{j-1} \subseteq q_{j-1}$ and $s_j \subseteq q_j$. This makes every value proposition in O true in this automaton. Here, each target automaton T generated in **InduceCL** is defined as a triple (Q, Σ, Φ), where Q is a finite set of states of the form (4) in $\mathcal{A}$, the alphabet is $\Sigma = action(B \cup O)$, and Φ is a mapping $Q \times \Sigma \to Q$. Because the initial state and the final states are not used to produce effect propositions in the algorithm **RevTrans**, they need not explicitly appear in each automaton.

At the point (i), each state in $\pi \in \mathcal{P}$ contains either g or $\neg g$ for each goal fluent $\neg g$, and does not fully represent a state in a domain description of $\mathcal{A}$.

To get states in $\mathcal{A}$, the dividing operations (ii) and (iii) in Fig. 6 are applied. At (ii), the state set Q_0 is defined as the set of all possible initial states in $\mathcal{A}$. Then, the initial state of the resulting model of $\mathcal{A}$ must be in Q_0. From each state $q_0 \in Q_0$, the transition function Φ of the target automaton T is computed using the function $trans$, and then Φ is transitively determined at Fig. 6 (iv). Here, $trans(q, a, s)$ returns a state q' after executing an action a at a state q such that q' includes a substate s:

$$trans(q, a, s) = (q \setminus (|\mathcal{E}|^{\pm} \cup |s|^{\pm})) \cup \mathcal{E} \cup s$$
$$\text{where } \mathcal{E} = \{effect(P) \mid P \in E(D), \ cond(P) \subseteq q\}.$$

Note that if $\mathcal{E} \cup s$ is inconsistent, that is, contains both the positive and negative fluents $f, \neg f$ for some fluent name f, then $trans(q, a, s)$ is undefined. In such a case, we cannot get a corresponding hypothesis for this FA π (hence go to L1). If Φ is well-defined at Fig. 6 (v), then state transition is completed by computing $trans(q, a, \emptyset)$ for every missing pair of a state q and an action a at Fig. 6 (vi).

Finally, each automaton T is converted to a set γ of new effect propositions in $\mathcal{A}$ by computing **Compress(RevTrans(T))** $\setminus B$. This computation is done for every FA $\pi \in \mathcal{P}$, and the hypotheses $\mathcal{H}$ are output by **InduceCL**.

4.3   Examples

Example 4.1. Suppose the following domain description D:

$$load \text{ causes } loaded, \tag{7}$$
$$shoot \text{ causes } \neg loaded, \tag{8}$$
$$\textbf{initially } alive, \tag{9}$$
$$\neg alive \text{ after } load; shoot. \tag{10}$$

Here, $D = B \cup O$, where background knowledge is $B = \{(7), (8)\}$ and the observation is $O = \{(9), (10)\}$. We first observe that D is inconsistent. To see this, $alive$ must be in the initial state q_0 by (9) in O, and $\neg alive$ must be true after executing $load; shoot$ by (10) in O. However, both actions $load$ and $shoot$ have effects only on the fluent $(\neg)loaded$ by (7) and (8) in B, and thus never influence the truth value of $alive$. Hence, the sequence $load; shoot$ keeps $alive$ by law of inertia, which contradicts (10).

Now, $\neg alive$ is the goal fluent. Algorithm **InduceCL** first divides O into $valI$, $valR$ and $valN$. In this case, $valI = \{(9)\}$. The value propositions which changed the truth value of $alive$ into $\neg alive$ is $valR = \{(10)\}$, and its action sequence is set to the positive sample $R = \{load; shoot\}$. Because there is no value proposition with respect to $alive$ in the form of (1) in O, $valN = N = \emptyset$.

Next, **LearnFA**(R, N) infers the set of FAs in Fig. 7. Then, by the rules (6), they are converted into the FAs $\mathcal{P}$ in Fig. 8. Here, π_{31} and π_{32} in Fig. 8 are two automata converted from π_3 in Fig. 7. Note that the intermediate state $\{load\}$ is converted into either $\{alive\}$ or $\{\neg alive\}$ here, which indicates that we cannot determine at which point the fluent $alive$ has changed its truth value.

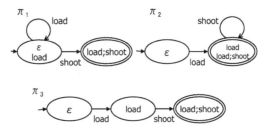

Fig. 7. FAs $\mathcal{P}$ obtained by **LearnFA**(R, N)

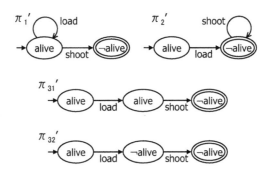

Fig. 8. FAs $\mathcal{P}$ after applying the rules (6)

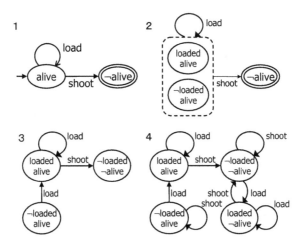

Fig. 9. Learning process for FA π_1'

The rest of learning process is shown in Fig. 9. For π_1, **InduceCL** first divides the initial state by div (Fig. 6 (ii) and Fig. 9-2). Then, those states after executing the action $load$ at $\{loaded, alive\}$ and $\{\neg loaded, alive\}$ are constructed by $trans$ (Fig. 6 (iv) and Fig. 9-3). After all other states are added, the transition function Φ is completed (Fig. 6 (vi) and Fig. 9-4).

Finally, from the resulting automaton T from π_1, the domain description in $\mathcal{A}$ is obtained by computing **Compress**(**RevTrans**(T)) as:

$$load \textbf{ causes } loaded,$$
$$shoot \textbf{ causes } \neg loaded,$$
$$shoot \textbf{ causes } \neg alive \textbf{ if } loaded.$$

Here, the first and second rules are already in B, and hence the new causal rules are obtained from π_1 as

$$\gamma_1 = \{(shoot \textbf{ causes } \neg alive \textbf{ if } loaded)\}.$$

Similarly, from π_2 and π_{32}, we obtain the common hypothesis

$$\gamma_2 = \{(load \textbf{ causes } \neg alive)\},$$

and from π_{31}, we obtain $\gamma_3 = \gamma_1 = \{(shoot \textbf{ causes } \neg alive \textbf{ if } loaded)\}$. Therefore, we get the final result $\mathcal{H} = \{\gamma_1, \gamma_2\}$. As expected, both $B \cup \gamma_1 \cup O$ and $B \cup \gamma_2 \cup O$ are consistent. Note here that there is no reason to reject the hypothesis γ_2.

Example 4.2. Suppose that the following new observation O' is additionally given to background knowledge B and the old observation O in Example 4.1:

$$alive \textbf{ after } load,$$
$$alive \textbf{ after } shoot.$$

Then, $valR$ and R are the same as those in Example 4.1, but now $valN$ and N become $valN = O'$ and $N = \{load, shoot\}$, respectively. In this case, **LearnFA** (R, N) produces π_{31} in Fig. 8 as the unique FA in $\mathcal{P}$. Hence, we have the unique hypothesis: $\{(shoot \textbf{ causes } \neg alive \textbf{ if } loaded)\}$. This result shows that, the more observations we have, the more accurate hypotheses we get by **InduceCL**.

4.4   Correctness

The soundness of **InduceCL** is given as follows.

Theorem 4.1. *Let B be consistent background knowledge, and O an observation. Suppose $\mathcal{H}$ is the output of **InduceCL**(B, O). Then, $B \cup \gamma \cup O$ is consistent for any $\gamma \in \mathcal{H}$.*

Proof. Suppose that a hypothesis γ is obtained from an automaton T which is constructed in **InduceCL**(B, O). We prove the following two statements.

1. The transition function determined by the effect propositions $B \cup \gamma$ coincides with the transition function Φ in T.

2. Each value proposition in O is true in any structure $I = (\Phi, q_0)$, where q_0 is a state in the set Q_0 constructed in **InduceCL**.

If these two claims are proved, then any structure I satisfying the above condition is a model of $B \cup \gamma \cup O$ by definition.

For the first claim, Φ is obtained by the function $trans/3$ in **InduceCL**, which is equivalent to the function $trans/2$ in the definition of models in $\mathcal{A}$ except that the latter is constrained by the extra third argument s. The condition s puts the result to the state containing s, but never changes the transition for the effect propositions from $E(B)$ because in that case $s = \emptyset$ is given. Hence, state transition determined by $B \cup \gamma$ is the same as that by Φ.

For the second claim, we will prove that, given a structure $I = (\Phi, q_0)$, it holds for any value proposition $(f \textbf{ after } a_1; \cdots; a_m) \in O$ that

$$f \in \Phi(\Phi(\cdots \Phi(q_0, a_1), \ldots, a_{m-1}), a_m). \tag{11}$$

By definition of **InduceCL**, O is divided into $valI$, $valR$ and $valN$, from which the positive sample R and the negative sample N are extracted. Because the initial state q_0 in I contains all fluents appearing in the value proposition in $valI$, every value proposition in $valI$ is immediately true in I.

Now suppose that the automaton T is constructed from a FA π in **Learn** (R, N), which is converted into a FA $(S, \Sigma, \delta, s_0, G)$ such that the state set S is defined by (6) and $f \in G \subseteq S$. Then, for any value proposition in $valR$ and $valN$, we have

$$f = \delta(\delta(\cdots \delta(s_0, a_1), \ldots, a_{m-1}), a_m). \tag{12}$$

Next, **InduceCL** generates the set Q_0 of all initial states that make every value proposition in $valI$ true. Then, the transition function Φ satisfies that, $\delta(s_{j-1}, a) = s_j$ $(s_{j-1}, s_j \in S)$ implies $\Phi(q_{j-1}, a) = q_j$ $(q_{j-1}, q_j \in Q)$ such that $s_j \subseteq q_j$ and $s_{j-1} \subseteq q_{j-1}$. Hence, $s_i \subseteq q_i$ holds for all i. Therefore, the equation (12) implies (11). This means that every value proposition in $valR$ and $valN$ is true in I.   □

The completeness of **InduceCL** is partially guaranteed in the sense that the algorithm can generate the *subsumption-minimal* hypotheses. For two effect propositions E and F, we say that E *subsumes* F if $effect(E) = effect(F)$ and $cond(E) \subseteq cond(F)$. For two sets of effect propositions α and β, we define that $\alpha \sqsubseteq \beta$ iff for any $F \in \beta$ there is $E \in \alpha$ such that E subsumes F.

Theorem 4.2. *Let B be consistent background knowledge, O an observation, and λ a set of effect propositions. If $B \cup O$ is inconsistent and $B \cup \lambda \cup O$ is consistent, then there is a hypothesis $\gamma \in \textbf{InduceCL}(B, O)$ such that $\gamma \sqsubseteq \lambda$.*

Proof. The completeness proof can be constructively shown according to the steps in **InduceCL** as follows.

1. The FAs $\mathcal{P} = \textbf{LearnFA}(R, N)$ cover all possible transition systems with respect to change of the goal fluent g.

2. The state set Q_0 covers all possible initial states by definition of *div*.
3. The transition function Φ achieves the indispensable transition by definition of *trans/3*.

Hence, **InduceCL** computes the automata with the requisite transition from all possible initial states by taking every possible change of g into account. The minimal requisites in this case corresponds to the subsumption minimality.   □

4.5   Model Inference

Algorithm **InduceCL** can be combined with the algorithm to translate domain descriptions in $\mathcal{A}$ into DFAs [14] (Section 2) for reasoning about action. Here, we consider the problem to predict the initial states of an incomplete domain description. Since any model in $\mathcal{A}$ is defined as a pair (Φ, q_0) of the transition function Φ and the initial state q_0, this problem is also called *model inference*.

Model inference of a domain description in $\mathcal{A}$ can be computed as follows. Suppose a domain description $D = B \cup O$, where B is a set of effect propositions and O is a set of value propositions. If D is consistent, then **Init**(D) gives the set of all initial states of D by Proposition 2.1. Otherwise, compute $\mathcal{H} = $ **InduceCL**(B, O). Then, $\mathcal{I}_\gamma = $ **Init**$(D \cup \gamma)$ gives the initial states of $D \cup \gamma$ for any $\gamma \in \mathcal{H}$. Note here that the **Init** algorithm can estimate the initial states of a (possibly non-categorical) domain description as long as it is consistent, but **Init** cannot be used for an incomplete domain description.

Example 4.3. Consider the domain description D in Example 4.1. Recall that D is not consistent. By augmenting B with either γ_1 or γ_2, the initial states of $D \cup \gamma_i$ $(i = 1, 2)$ are obtained as **Init**$(D \cup \gamma_i) = \{\{alive, \neg loaded\}, \{alive, loaded\}\}$. Hence, the domain $D \cup \gamma_i$ is not categorical. In fact, there is no information about *loaded* in the initial state.

Model inference is important for reasoning about action and change in incomplete domain descriptions. In particular, it is necessary to completely specify the initial and goal states for *planning*. Similarly, computation of the transition function is important to fill the gap between background knowledge and observations. Our induction algorithm constructs such a missing hypothesis and thus makes the given incomplete domain description complete.

5   Related Work

Moyle and Muggleton [12] first studied induction of logic programs in the *event calculus*, and Moyle [11] extends it to incorporate abduction as well as induction in *theory completion* [13]. These methods require the complete initial state as input and need to compute a complete set of narrative facts in advance, and thus cannot account for observations handled in this paper.

Lorenzo and Otero [10] propose an algorithm to learn causal relations in the *situation calculus* under a framework of *descriptive induction*. Lorenzo [9] extends it and discusses learning action theories with *ramification*, which has indirect effects on fluents through constraints. These methods also need complete narratives as input. On the other hand, we need neither a complete narrative nor a complete initial state. Otero [15,16] also considers the case of incomplete narratives. Given that the fluent g is true at a situation s_i but is false at a situation s_{i+k} and is unknown at s_j for every $j = i+1, \ldots, i+k-1$, his setting assumes that the truth value of g has changed only once. Our algorithm, on the other hand, can induce any case in which the fluent value has changed more than once in intermediate situations. Another difference appears in the output hypotheses. While causal laws are represented using new situation constants that represent missing situations in Otero's framework, we do not introduce any such new constants but consider every possible state transition in our framework.

All the above mentioned previous work in ILP do not use action languages. Then, representation needs either *frame axioms* or *inertia rules* in logic programs. The former causes the frame problem and the latter requires induction in nonmonotonic logic programs, both of which ought to be avoided [15]. Otero [16] tackles this problem by introducing the *causality predicate* for the goal fluent, thereby enables us to use a monotonic ILP method. In contrast, the language $\mathcal{A}$ we use in this work has the semantics that solves the frame problem inherently — any state change is represented as a set difference of fluents changed as effects of actions by keeping the status of other fluents unchanged. Moreover, the use of $\mathcal{A}$ enables us to represent observations concisely within the action language.

6   Concluding Remarks

This paper has considered a problem to induce causal laws in the action language $\mathcal{A}$. The proposed induction algorithm calls regular inference, and can be applied to a general form of observations in $\mathcal{A}$, which needs no restriction on the form of action sequences and observed fluents, as opposed to previous approaches.

It has been argued that regular inference is computationally hard in general because we need to search the Boolean lattice of a PTA. For this problem, an application of a genetic algorithm is proposed to partition the state set in an optimal way [4]. However, here we should claim that regular inference is only used as local calls in our induction algorithm so that only part of structures is induced by regular inference. This claim is important because the main difference from the previous approaches to learning automata from scratch also appears at this point. We utilize much information from *background knowledge*, and fill the gap between background knowledge and observations. Hence, our induction algorithm perfectly fits in the spirit of ILP. In this paper, we have established a theory of induction of causal laws based on the semantics of an action language, i.e., the state transition system. The next target will be to develop more efficient algorithms. Then, replacing regular inference of **LearnFA** with other popular ILP algorithms is of course promising in optimization of **InduceCL**.

Still, there are a lot of ways to improve the induction algorithm not by implementation techniques but in a semantic level. For example, information or heuristic that the last action has actually caused the change of the truth value of the goal fluent and information on how many times the truth value has changed in an action sequence should be used as great hints to prune the search space. It is also important to empirically verify the theoretical results in this paper on experiments with real data. Another important future work includes induction of causal laws involving concurrency and non-determinism as well as constraints within action languages that are more expressive than $\mathcal{A}$.

References

1. Angluin, D., Inference of reversible languages, *J. ACM*, 29(3):741–765, 1982.
2. Baral, C., Gelfond, M., and Provetti, A., Representing actions: laws, observations and hypotheses, *J. Logic Programming*, 31:201–243, 1997.
3. Dupont, P., Miclet, L., and Vidal, E., What is the search space of the regular inference?, in: *Proc. 2nd International Colloquium on Grammatical Intelligence*, LNAI 862, Springer, pp.26–37, 1994.
4. Dupont, P., Regular grammatical inference from positive and negative samples by genetic search: the GIG method, in: *Proc. 2nd International Colloquium on Grammatical Inference*, LNAI 862, Springer, pp.236–245, 1994.
5. Gelfond, M. and Lifschitz, V., Representing action and change by logic programs, *J. Logic Programming*, 17(2–4):301–321, 1993.
6. Gelfond, M. and Lifschitz, V., Action languages, *Electronic Transactions of AI*, 3:195–210, 1998.
7. Giunchiglia, E. and Lifschitz, V., An action language based on causal explanation: preliminary report, in: *Proc. AAAI-98*, AAAI Press, pp.623–630, 1998.
8. Giunchiglia, E., Lee, J., Lifschitz, V., McCain, N., and Turner, T., Nonmonotonic causal theories, *Artificial Intelligence*, 153:49–104, 2004.
9. Lorenzo, D., Learning non-monotonic causal theories, in: *Proc. 9th International Workshop on Non-monotonic Reasoning*, pp.349–355, 2002.
10. Lorenzo, D. and Otero, R.P., Learning to reason about actions, in: *Proc. 14th European Conference on Artificial Intelligence*, IOS press, Amsterdam, 2000.
11. Moyle, S., Using theory completion to learn a robot navigation control programs, in: *Proc. 12th International Conference on Inductive Logic Programming*, LNAI 2583, Springer, pp.182–197, 2003.
12. Moyle, S. and Muggleton, S., Learning programs in the event calculus, in: *Proc. 7th International Conference on Inductive Logic Programming*, LNAI 1297, Springer, pp.205–212, 1997.
13. Muggleton, S. and Bryant, C., Theory completion and inverse entailment, in: *Proc. 10th International Conference on Inductive Logic Programming*, LNAI 1866, Springer, pp.130–146, 2000.
14. Nabeshima, H. and Inoue, K., Automata theory for action language $\mathcal{A}$, *Trans. Information Processing Society of Japan*, 38(3):462–471, 1997 (in Japanese).
15. Otero, R.P., Induction of the effects of actions by monotonic methods, in: *Proc. 13th International Conference on Inductive Logic Programming*, LNAI 2835, Springer, pp.299–310, 2003.
16. Otero, R.P., Embracing causality in inducing the effects of actions, in: *Selection of papers from the 10th Conference of the Spanish Association for Artificial Intelligence*, LNAI 3040, Springer, pp.291–301, 2004.
17. Watanabe, H. and Muggleton, S., First-order stochastic action language, *Electronic Transactions in Artificial Intelligence*, 7, 2003.

Online Closure-Based Learning
of Relational Theories

Frédéric Koriche

LIRMM, UMR 5506, Université Montpellier II CNRS,
161, rue Ada 34392 Montpellier Cedex 5, France
koriche@lirmm.fr

Abstract. Online learning algorithms such as Winnow have received much attention in Machine Learning. Their performance degrades only logarithmically with the input dimension, making them useful in large spaces such as relational theories. However, online first-order learners are intrinsically limited by a computational barrier: even in the finite, function-free case, the number of possible features grows exponentially with the number of first-order atoms generated from the vocabulary. To circumvent this issue, we exploit the paradigm of closure-based learning which allows the learner to focus on the features that lie in the closure space generated from the examples which have lead to a mistake. Based on this idea, we develop an online algorithm for learning theories formed by disjunctions of existentially quantified conjunctions of atoms. In this setting, we show that the number of mistakes depends only logarithmically on the number of features. Furthermore, the computational cost is essentially bounded by the size of the closure lattice.

1 Introduction

A recurrent theme in machine learning is the development of efficient *online* learning algorithms, capable of producing better and better predictions in an incremental way [4]. Such algorithms are "anytime learners" that can be interrupted at each instant to provide a prediction whose correctness is related to the number of mistakes that have been made so far. The underlying model takes place in a sequence of trials. At any stage, the learner is first presented a new example, next it is asked to predict its associated class, and then it is told whether its prediction was correct or not. In case of mistake, an update procedure is activated and the current hypothesis is refined accordingly.

In a landmark paper [16], Littlestone introduced an elegant algorithm for learning k out of n variable disjunctions which he called Winnow. It resembles the perceptron algorithm in its simplicity, but employs multiplicative, rather than additive, weight updates on input variables. Consequently, the number of mistakes grows essentially as $k \log n$ instead of kn. The fact that the dependence on n is reduced to logarithmic, rather than linear, makes this algorithm potentially applicable even if the number of variables is enormous. For example, the SNoW algorithm, a variant of Winnow, has been shown to be effective in natural language settings with ten of thousands of features [10].

S. Kramer and B. Pfahringer (Eds.): ILP 2005, LNAI 3625, pp. 172–189, 2005.

This remarkable property has lead researchers to examine the possibility of applying multiplicative update algorithms to large concept classes where the number of patterns is exponential in the input dimension. In this setting, the key question is: just how can we preserve attribute-efficiency in order to learn, in a reasonable amount of time and space, a function of k relevant features in presence of a possibly exponential number $N - k$ of irrelevant features ?

Computational learning theory has supplied mixed results. On the one hand, it has been shown that several geometrical classes are indeed attribute-efficient learnable, using appropriate data structures [11, 17]. The basic idea is to exploit commonalities among features, partitioning them into a polynomial number of equivalence classes that are used for prediction. The number of mistakes still depends only logarithmically on the number of patterns and the computational cost remains essentially polynomial on the input dimension. On the other hand, for logical theories such as monotone DNF formulas, Khardon et al. [14] have recently shown that, unless $P = \#P$, there is no polynomial time algorithm capable of simulating Winnow over exponentially many conjunctive features.

Such a computational barrier does *not* necessarily imply that a brutal force implementation of Winnow is the sole option to obtain complete correctness. In fact, even if the resulting partition is not always guaranteed to be polynomial, the idea of "compiling" a large space can be more efficient than systematically exploring the set of N features. Furthermore, Blum [3] observed that, in many situations the problem at hand exhibits a three-stage hierarchy: a small number of relevant features in the target function, a larger number of features that appear in each example, and an enormous number of possible features. In such circumstances, the combined strategies of "focusing" on a limited fragment of the space and "compiling" this fragment into a compact data structure seem to provide a useful approach to circumvent the counting problem.

Following this research avenue, we investigate the paradigm of *closure-based* learning which allows a learner to focus on the closure space generated by the closure of the examples which have lead to a mistake. Based on a well-known property of closure operators, the data structure maintained by the learner is a complete lattice of features. During each trial, the learner first receives an unlabeled example, next predicts its class according to its lattice, and then receives the correct label. In case of mistake, the lattice is refined by taking the closure of the data structure with the current observation.

This paradigm is applied to the problem of learning relational theories formed by disjunctions of existentially quantified conjunctions of atoms. This class of formulas have the same expressive power as select-project-join-union database queries, which are the queries that occur most often in practice [1]. Furthermore, relational theories provide a substrate for many ILP systems that operate in a concept learning framework [18]. Namely, any existentially quantified conjunction of atoms can be regarded as a decision rule predicting the target concept. If any of the conjunctions in some theory "fires" for a given example, then the example is classified as positive. If none of them fires, the example is classified as negative.

In the relational setting, each candidate "feature" is an existentially quantified conjunction of atoms. Consequently, the number of possible features is exponential in the number of first-order atoms. The central aim of closure-based learning is to alleviate this combinatorial barrier by allowing the learner to limit exploration in the space of first-order conjunctions. Based on this paradigm, we develop an online algorithm that extends Winnow to relational theories. We show that the number of mistakes still depends only logarithmically on the number of possible features. Furthermore, the computational cost is polynomial in the size of the closure lattice. In the worst case, this structure can be exponential in the number of its maximal elements. Yet, experiments in formal concept analysis reveal that this case rarely occurs in practice; on average, the size of closure lattices increases polynomially with the number of atoms [5, 9]. These encouraging results corroborate the practical applicability of our approach.

Outline. Section 2 introduces the necessary background about online relational learning. Section 3 presents an algebraic setting for closure-based induction. Section 4 is devoted to the development and the analysis of the closure-based Winnow algorithm. Notably, a mistake bound and a computational bound for this algorithm are reported in this section. Finally, section 5 compares the present approach with other results in online relational learning, and concludes with some perspectives of further research.

2   Preliminaries

In this section, we begin to introduce a logical setting for relational theories and next, we present the "standard" Winnow algorithm applied to relational theories. We conclude this section by bringing to the fore the main computational bottleneck of online relational learning.

2.1   Relational Logic

The linguistic component of this study is an existential positive fragment of first-order logic defined from a finite and pre-fixed vocabulary. Function symbols including constants, are not allowed. The vocabulary consists in a finite set of *predicate symbols* $\{p_1, \cdots, p_p\}$ and a finite set of *variables* $\{x_1, \cdots, x_k\}$. Each predicate symbol has a finite arity, which is the number of its arguments. We consider that the maximum arity over all predicate symbols is bounded by a constant a. Such an assumption is commonly advocated in the relational learning literature [12, 22]. An *atom* $p(x_1, \cdots, x_t)$ is a t-ary predicate symbol followed by a bracketed t-tuple of variables. The set of all distinct atoms generated from the vocabulary is denoted **A**. Using the above notations, we remark that the cardinality of **A** is upper bounded by pk^a, which is polynomial in the number of predicate symbols and the number of variables.

A *relational conjunction* (henceforth called *feature*) is a closed formula in prenex normal form, containing only existential quantifiers, and whose matrix is a conjunction of atoms. A *relational theory* (or *theory*) is a disjunction of relational conjunctions. For convenience, we shall sometimes represent theories as sets of features and features as sets of atoms. The size of a feature F, denoted $|F|$, is the number of all atoms occurring in it. Note that the restriction on the number of variables does not limit the size of features to be constant. Indeed, long conjunctions of size $O(pk^a)$ can be constructed since variables can appear in more than one atom. The space of all features constructed from the vocabulary is denoted $\mathbf{F}$. The cardinality of this space is denoted N. Notably, we observe that N is upper bounded by 2^{pk^a}.

Example 1. Our running example is a variant of the so-called Bongard problem (see e.g. [13]). In this problem, the learner is presented some scenes involving objects and geometrical relationships among them. The underlying task is to distinguish positive scenes from negative ones. We consider here the vocabulary composed by the unary predicate symbols circle, square and triangle, the binary predicate symbols left, in and larger, and the variables x_1 and x_2. The theory T below involves three relational conjunctions.

$$\exists x_1 \exists x_2 (\mathsf{circle}(x_1) \wedge \mathsf{square}(x_2) \wedge \mathsf{in}(x_1, x_2)),$$
$$\exists x_1 \exists x_2 (\mathsf{circle}(x_1) \wedge \mathsf{square}(x_2) \wedge \mathsf{larger}(x_2, x_1)),$$
$$\exists x_1 \exists x_2 (\mathsf{circle}(x_1) \wedge \mathsf{circle}(x_2) \wedge \mathsf{in}(x_1, x_2))$$

Examples are interpretations that involve objects and relationships among them. A *domain* is a finite set of objects. A *ground atom* over a domain D is an expression $\mathsf{p}(o_1, \cdots, o_t)$, where p is a t-ary predicate symbol and $o_1, \ldots, o_t$ are objects in the domain D. An *interpretation* is a pair $I = (D^I, P^I)$ where D^I is a domain and P^I is a set of ground atoms over D^I. An interpretation I is a *model* of a relational conjunction F if there is a substitution θ mapping variables in the feature F to objects in D^I and such that $A\theta \in P^I$ for each atom A in F. By extension, an interpretation I is a *model* of a relational theory T if there is a relational conjunction F in T such that I is a model of F.

Example 2. Consider the following interpretation I involving three objects. We can observe that I is a model of the theory T examined in example 1. Indeed, we notice that I is a model of the first two conjunctions described in T.

$$I = (\{1, 2, 3\}, \{\mathsf{circle}(1), \mathsf{circle}(2), \mathsf{square}(3), \mathsf{in}(1, 3), \mathsf{larger}(1, 3)\})$$

Given an interpretation I, the *feature space* of I, denoted $\mathbf{F}(I)$, is the set of all features F in $\mathbf{F}$ such that I is a model of F. An element F of $\mathbf{F}(I)$ is called a *maximal feature* if there is no proper superset F' of F in $\mathbf{F}(I)$. The set of all maximal features of I is called the *basis* of I and denoted $B(I)$. The following property states that the problem of checking whether I is a model of some feature F can be reduced to a covering test of F in the basis of I.

Proposition 1. *Let I be an interpretation and F a relational conjunction. Then I is a model of F if and only if there is a feature F' in $B(I)$ such that $F \subseteq F'$.*

Proof. First, suppose that I is a model of F. Then F is an element of $\mathbf{F}(I)$ and hence, F is covered by at least one maximal feature in $B(I)$. Now, suppose that I is a model of a maximal feature F' in $B(I)$ such that $F \subseteq F'$. Then, there is a substitution θ mapping variables in F' to objects in D^I and such that $F'\theta \subseteq P^I$. It follows that $F\theta \subseteq P^I$ and hence, I is a model of F.   □

Interestingly, we remark that the cardinality of the basis of I is bounded by d^k, which is the number of possible substitutions over D^I. The basis of I can be found time quadratic in d^k. Namely, for each substitution θ over D^I, we first generate the saturated feature F formed by all atoms A in the language such that $A\theta \in I$. Next, we check whether a proper superset of F is present in the current basis of I. If this is not the case, we add F to the basis and we eliminate from it all proper subsets of F.

Example 3. The basis of the interpretation I specified in example 2 is given by the four following features.

$$\exists x_1 \exists x_2 (\mathsf{circle}(x_1) \wedge \mathsf{circle}(x_2))$$
$$\exists x_1 \exists x_2 (\mathsf{square}(x_1) \wedge \mathsf{square}(x_2))$$
$$\exists x_1 \exists x_2 (\mathsf{circle}(x_1) \wedge \mathsf{square}(x_2) \wedge \mathsf{in}(x_1, x_2) \wedge \mathsf{larger}(x_1, x_2))$$
$$\exists x_1 \exists x_2 (\mathsf{circle}(x_2) \wedge \mathsf{square}(x_1) \wedge \mathsf{in}(x_2, x_1) \wedge \mathsf{larger}(x_2, x_1))$$

2.2 Online Relational Learning

The online learning model can be regarded as a game between two players, the learner and the environment. A target relational theory T^* containing r features, is fixed by the environment and hidden from the learner. During each trial, the learner first receives an interpretation from the environment, next it makes a prediction based on its current hypothesis and then the learner receives the correct response. In the setting of online relational learning, the quantities that the learner would like to minimize are the number of mistakes it makes and the computational resources it spends along the process. Notice that learner is merely *passive* and cannot ask membership queries or statistical queries.

Before presenting the algorithm, we need additional definitions. Given a feature F, the *classifier* of F is a map that assigns to each interpretation I a boolean value given by: $F(I) = 1$ if I is a model of F, and $F(I) = 0$ otherwise. Similarly, given a theory T, the classifier of T is a map that assigns to each interpretation I the value $T(I) = 1$ if I is a model of T, and the value $T(I) = 0$ otherwise. A *linear threshold function of* $\mathbf{F}$ is a function Φ that associates to each feature F in $\mathbf{F}$ a weight in $\mathbb{R}^+$. Intuitively, $\Phi(F)$ captures the degree of relevance of the feature F in the learning process. The classifier of Φ is a map that assigns to each interpretation I a boolean value defined as follows:

$$\Phi(I) = \begin{cases} 1 \text{ if } \left(\sum_{F \in \mathbf{F}} \Phi(F) \cdot F(I)\right) \geq N, \text{ and} \\ 0 \text{ otherwise} \end{cases}$$

Initialization

₀ Set $\Phi(F) \leftarrow 2$ for each relational conjunction $F \in \mathbf{F}$

Trials

₁ Receive an interpretation I

₂ If $\left(\sum_{F \in \mathbf{F}} \Phi(F) \cdot F(I)\right) \geq N$ then

> predict $\Phi(I) \leftarrow 1$

else

> predict $\Phi(I) \leftarrow 0$

₃ Receive $T^*(I)$. If $T^*(I) \neq \Phi(I)$ then for each F such that $F(I) = 1$ do

> *Demotion:* if $\Phi(I) = 1$ then set $\Phi(F) \leftarrow \frac{1}{2}\Phi(F)$
>
> *Promotion:* if $\Phi(I) = 0$ then set $\Phi(F) \leftarrow 2\Phi(F)$

Fig. 1. Standard Relational Winnow

We have now all notions in hand to present the standard Winnow algorithm. The key idea is to maintain a linear threshold function that approximates the target theory. The algorithm is presented in figure 1. Initially, $\Phi(F) = 2$ for each feature in $\mathbf{F}$. On each received interpretation I, if $\Phi(I)$ predicts the correct class of I then no change is made. If $\Phi(I) = 1$ and I is a negative example, then a *demotion* occurs: the weights of each feature involved in the prediction are divided by 2. Dually, if $\Phi(I) = 0$ and I is a positive example, then a *promotion* occurs: the weights of each feature that predicted correctly are multiplied by 2. By an adaptation of Littlestone's analysis, the number of mistakes made by the learner depends on N only logarithmically and on r polynomially.

Although "feature-efficient", the standard Winnow algorithm is confronted with an important computational barrier. Namely, an explicit representation of a linear threshold function of $\mathbf{F}$ takes $\Omega(2^{pk^a})$ size. The complexity issue is exacerbated still further by the fact that for any received interpretation I, a covering test must be done for each candidate feature F in the space $\mathbf{F}$. This test can be performed by enumeration in $O(|F|d^k)$ time, where d is the number of objects in the domain D^I. A similar result is obtained if the test is performed by computing the basis of I. Based on these considerations, the prediction step takes $O(d^k 2^{pk^a})$ time. Consequently, even for constant values of a and k, a brutal force implementation of relational Winnow is clearly infeasible.

Example 4. Let us consider the vocabulary presented in example 1. Given 2 variables, 3 unary predicate symbols and 3 binary predicate symbols, the number of atoms is 18. If 64 bits are needed to encode each weight, then an explicit representation of a linear relational threshold function would require 2^{24} bits. For 3 and 4 variables, we would need 2^{44} bits and 2^{66} bits. The last requirement is well beyond the capacity of computational machinery into the foreseeable future.

3   Closure-Based Induction

As observed in the previous section, the main computational bottleneck of online relational learning lies in the cardinality of the feature space. To alleviate this barrier, we advocate the paradigm of closure-based induction that allows the learner to "focus" on a limited portion of its feature space and to "compile" this portion into a semantically equivalent data structure. In this section, we introduce a formal setting for closure-based induction. We begin to examine the notion of relational closure space, next we define a projection operator over closure spaces, and then we concentrate on linear functions of closure spaces.

3.1   Relational Closure Spaces

Let T be a relational theory. Then we say that T is *closed* if for any nonempty subset S of T, the feature $\bigcap S$ is an element of T. Furthermore, we say that T is a *closure space* if T is closed and contains the maximal feature $\mathbf{A}$. Interestingly, we remark that any relational closure space is a Moore family of subsets of $\mathbf{A}$. Consequently, by an application of a well-known theorem about Moore families of subsets (see e.g. [2, 8]), any relational closure space forms a complete lattice under set-inclusion.

Given a relational theory T, the *feature space* of T, denoted $\mathbf{F}(T)$, is the set of all features F in $\mathbf{F}$ such that F is included in some element F' of T. We can see that if T is a closure space, then its feature space covers all elements in $\mathbf{F}$. Now, given a feature F in $\mathbf{F}(T)$, the *closure of F with respect to T*, denoted $C_T(F)$, is the feature formed by the intersection of all supersets of F in T:

$$C_T(F) = \bigcap\{F' \in T : F \subseteq F'\}$$

The *closure of T*, denoted $C(T)$ is given by the set $\{C_T(F) : F \in \mathbf{F}(T)\}$. The following property states that the "closure" of a relational theory is necessarily "closed" under intersection.

Proposition 2. *Let T be a relational theory. Then T is closed iff $T = C(T)$.*

Proof. Let $T' = C(T)$ and $T'' = \{\bigcap S : S \subseteq T\}$. We must show that $T' = T''$. Let F be an element of T'. By construction of T', there exists a feature F' in $\mathbf{F}$ such that $F = C_T(F')$. Let S be the set of all supersets of F' in T. Since $C_T(F') = \bigcap S$, it follows that $F = \bigcap S$. Therefore, $F \in T''$. Now, let F be an element of T'' and V be the set of all supersets of F in T. By construction of T'', there exists a subset S of T such that $F = \bigcap S$. Since $S \subseteq V$ and $S \neq \varnothing$ it follows that $\bigcap V \subseteq \bigcap S$. Hence, $C_T(F) \subseteq F$. Furthermore, for every element F' in V, we have $F \subseteq F'$. It follows that $F \subseteq \bigcap V$. Thus $F \subseteq C_T(F)$. By combining the two results, we obtain $F = C_T(F)$, and hence $F \in T'$. □

Given two closed relational theories T and T', the *intersection product* of T and T', denoted $T \circ T'$, is defined by the set $\{F \cap F' : F \in T \text{ and } F' \in T'\}$. The intersection product provides a natural operator for constructing composite closed theories from basic building blocks. The following proposition states that the intersection product of two closed theories is necessarily a closed theory.

Proposition 3. *Let T and T' be two closed theories. Then $T \circ T'$ is closed.*

Proof. Let T'' denote $T \circ T'$. By proposition 2, T'' is closed if and only if for every nonempty subset S of T'', the feature $\bigcap S$ is an element of T''. Since the relational vocabulary is finite, we consider without loss of generality that $S = \{F_1'', \cdots, F_n''\}$. By construction, $F_i'' = F_i \cap F_i'$ for some F_i in T and F_i' in T'. It follows that $\bigcap S = (\bigcap_{i=1}^n F_i) \cap (\bigcap_{i=1}^n F_i')$. Since T and T' are closed, then the feature $\bigcap_{i=1}^n F_i$ is an element of T and the feature $\bigcap_{i=1}^n F_i'$ is an element of T'. Therefore $\bigcap S$ is an element of T''. □

The *congruence relation* of a theory T, denoted $\sim_T$, is the binary relation on $\mathbf{F}(T)$ defined by following condition: $F \sim_T F'$ if and only if $C_T(F) = C_T(F')$. Based on the axioms of equality, $\sim_T$ is an equivalence relation on $\mathbf{F}(T)$. The *congruence class* of a feature F with respect to T, denoted $[F]_T$, is the set of all features F' in $\mathbf{F}(T)$ such that $F \sim_T F'$. In the following, the cardinality of $[F]_T$ is denoted $\|F\|_T$. The following property states that congruence relations can be refined using the product operation.

Proposition 4. *Let T and T' be two closed theories. Then $\sim_{T \circ T'} = \sim_T \cap \sim_{T'}$.*

Proof. Let T'' be $T \circ T'$ and F be a feature in $\mathbf{F}(T'')$. We must prove that $C_{T''}(F) = C_T(F) \cap C_{T'}(F)$. Let S'' be the set of all supersets of F in T''. By construction, there exists a subset S of T and a subset S' of T' such that $\bigcap S'' = \bigcap S \cap \bigcap S'$. Let us show that $C_T(F) = \bigcap S$. Let V be the set of all supersets of F in T. Obviously, $S \subseteq V$. Let G be an element of V. We know that $F \subseteq G$. Furthermore, $F \subseteq F'$ for at least one element F' in S'. Therefore, $F \subseteq G \cap F'$ and hence, G must be an element of S. It follows that $V \subseteq S$. Therefore, $S = V$ and hence, $C_T(F) = \bigcap S$. Based on an analogue strategy, we can show that $C_{T'}(F) = \bigcap S'$. Since $C_{T''}(F) = \bigcap S''$, the result follows. □

We conclude this part by an important topological property of the closure operation. The following result states that the closure of a theory generates a complete partitioning of its feature space; the number of equivalence classes is determined by the size of the closure of the theory.

Proposition 5. *Let T be a relational theory. Then the congruence relation of T induces a complete partitioning of $\mathbf{F}(T)$ into $|C(T)|$ congruence classes.*

Proof. We know that the relation $\sim_T$ is an equivalence relation on the space $\mathbf{F}(T)$. Therefore, $\sim_T$ induce a complete partitioning of $\mathbf{F}(T)$. Now, let $T' = C(T)$ and $T'' = \{[F]_T : F \in \mathbf{F}\}$. We must show that $|T'| = |T''|$. Let f be the function that maps to each feature F in T' the congruence class $f(F) = [F]_T$ in T''. Let F and F' be two distinct elements of T'. Since $C_T(F) \neq C_T(F')$ it follows that $f(F) \neq f(F')$. Thus, f is injective and hence, $|T'| \leq |T''|$. Dually, let g be a function that associates to each class $[F]_T$ of T'' the feature $g([F]_T)$ in T' such that $g([F]_T) = C_T(F)$. Let $[F]_T$ and $[F']_T$ be two distinct congruence classes of T''. Since $C_T(F) \neq C_T(F')$, it follows that $g([F]_T) \neq g([F']_T)$. Thus g is injective and hence, $|T''| \leq |T'|$. □

3.2   The Projection Operation

The key idea of closure-based induction is to enable the learner to focus on limited regions of its feature space and to compile these regions into compact structures. This idea is captured by a projection operator that takes as input a closure space maintained by the learner and an interpretation sent by the environment, and that returns as output a closed theory which partitions the feature space of the interpretation into a set of congruence classes.

Let T be a closure space and I be an interpretation. Then, the *projection* of T onto I, denoted $P(T, I)$, is given by the intersection product of T and the closure of $B(I)$. In formal terms: $P(T, I) = T \circ C(B(I))$. The *update* of T by I, denoted $U(T, I)$, is given by the set $T \cup P(T, I)$. The next property states that the theories generated from projection and update are closed.

Proposition 6. *Let T be a closure space and I be an interpretation. Then $P(T, I)$ is closed and $U(T, I)$ is a closure space.*

Proof. By application of proposition 3, we know that $P(T, I)$ is closed. Let us examine $U(T, I)$. By definition:

$$U(T, I) = T \cup \left(T \circ C(B(I))\right)$$

We remark that $T = T \circ \{\mathbf{A}\}$. By reporting this observation in the equation:

$$U(T, I) = (T \circ \{\mathbf{A}\}) \cup \left(T \circ C(B(I))\right)$$

By factorizing, we obtain:

$$U(T, I) = T \circ \left(C(B(I)) \cup \{\mathbf{A}\}\right)$$

Since $\bigcap S = \bigcap(S \cup \{\mathbf{A}\})$ for any nonempty subset S of features, it follows that:

$$U(T, I) = T \circ \left(C(B(I) \cup \{\mathbf{A}\})\right)$$

The two terms in the right hand side of the equation are closed theories containing the element $\mathbf{A}$. Hence, by proposition 3, $U(T, I)$ is a closure space.   □

The salient characteristic of the projection operator is to compile the feature space $\mathbf{F}(I)$ of an interpretation I into a structure that exploits the commonalities between features. This is formalized in the next property.

Proposition 7. *Let T be a closure space and I be an interpretation. Then the congruence relation of $P(T, I)$ induces a complete partitioning of $\mathbf{F}(I)$ into $|P(T, I)|$ congruence classes.*

Proof. By proposition 6, $P(T, I)$ is closed. Thus, by proposition 5, it follows that the congruence relation of $P(T, I)$ induces a complete partitioning of the feature space of $P(T, I)$ into $|P(T, I)|$ congruence classes. So, we simply need to show that $\mathbf{F}(P(T, I)) = \mathbf{F}(I)$. Let F be an element of $\mathbf{F}(P(T, I))$. By construction, $F \subseteq F'$ for some element in F' in $P(T, I)$, and $F' \subseteq F''$ for some element F'' in $C(B(I))$. Thus, F is covered by some maximal element in the basis of I and hence, by proposition 1, $F \in \mathbf{F}(I)$. Conversely, let F be an element of $\mathbf{F}(I)$. Then, by proposition 1, $F \subseteq F'$ for some element F' in $B(I)$. Since $F' \cap \mathbf{A} = F'$, it follows that $F' \in P(T, I)$. Hence, $F \in \mathbf{F}(P(T, I))$.   □

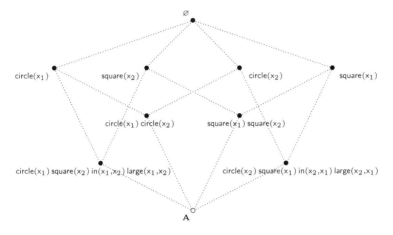

Fig. 2. Update of T by I

Example 5. Let $T = \{\mathbf{A}\}$ and consider the interpretation I given in example 2. The update of T by I is represented by the lattice in figure 2. The projection of T by I is formed by the set of all "•" nodes. Based on the above result, $P(T, I)$ induces a complete partitioning of $\mathbf{F}(I)$ into 9 congruence classes. By comparison, $\mathbf{F}(I)$ contains 33 features.

3.3   Linear Functions of Closed Theories

We have now all elements in hand to define online relational predictors in the setting of closure-based induction. Let T be a closure space. A *linear threshold function of* T is a map H that associates to each feature F in T a weight in $\mathbb{R}^+$. Intuitively, T can be regarded as a complied representation of $\mathbf{F}$ that is iteratively constructed during the mistakes made by the learner. The function H simply labels each closed feature F in T according to its degree of relevance. The *classifier* of H is a map that assigns to each interpretation I the boolean value $H(I)$ defined according to the following condition:

$$H(I) = \begin{cases} 1 \text{ if } \left(\sum_{F \in P(T,I)} H(C_T(F)) \cdot \|F\|_{P(T,I)} \right) \geq N, \text{ and} \\ 0 \text{ otherwise} \end{cases}$$

The prediction obtained from the classifier H can be explained as follows. Initially, the learner has at its disposal a closure space T and a linear threshold function H of T. Given an observation I, the learner first computes the projection of T onto I. Then, for each feature F in the projected set, the learner evaluates the degree of relevance of the congruence class of F. In doing so, the learner considers that each element in the class has the same weight, which is given by the feature $C_T(F)$ in T. Thus, the learner only needs to multiply this weight by the number of features in the congruence class. This strategy is applied for all congruence classes and the overall sum is compared with the threshold N.

We conclude this section by establishing a one-to-one correspondence between the two forms of linear functions investigated in this study. Let Φ be a linear threshold function of $\mathbf{F}$ and H be a linear threshold function of some given closure space T. Then, we say that H is a *closure-based representation* of Φ if $\Phi(F) = H(C_T(F))$ for every feature F in the space $\mathbf{F}$.

Proposition 8. *Let T be a closure space. Let Φ and H be linear threshold functions of $\mathbf{F}$ and T, respectively. If H is a closure-based representation of Φ, then for each interpretation I, $\Phi(I) = H(I)$.*

Proof. Suppose that H is a closure-based representation of Φ. Let F be an element of $P(T, I)$. By proposition 4, we know that $[F]_{P(T,I)} \subseteq [F]_T$. Since $\Phi(F) = H(C_T(F))$, then for each feature F' in the congruence class $[F]_{P(T,I)}$ we have $\Phi(F') = H(C_T(F')) = H(C_T(F))$. By adding up all weights:

$$\sum \{\Phi(F') : F' \in [F]_{P(T,I)}\} = H(C_T(F)) \cdot \|F\|_{P(T,I)}$$

Furthermore, by proposition 7, we know that the congruence relation of $P(T, I)$ induces a complete partitioning of $\mathbf{F}(I)$. It follows that:

$$\sum_{F \in \mathbf{F}(I)} \Phi(F) = \sum_{F \in P(T,I)} H(C_T(F)) \cdot \|F\|_{P(T,I)}$$

Using the definition of Φ, we therefore obtain:

$$\sum_{F \in \mathbf{F}} \Phi(F) \cdot F(I) = \sum_{F \in P(T,I)} H(C_T(F)) \cdot \|F\|_{P(T,I)}$$

Finally, since the classifiers Φ and H are defined on the same threshold N, we must have $\Phi(I) = H(I)$. $\square$

Example 6. Consider the following scenario. The learner starts from the theory $T = \{\mathbf{A}\}$ and the linear function H such that $H(\mathbf{A}) = 2$. After receiving the interpretation I given in example 2, the projection of T onto I forms the theory represented in figure 2. We remark that: $\sum_{F \in P(T,I)} H(C_T(F)) \cdot \|F\|_{P(T,I)} = 66$. Since $N = 2^{18}$, the example I is classified as negative. Suppose that I is, in fact, a positive example of the target concept. In this case, we consider that the new closure space T is obtained from the update of the initial theory $\{A\}$ by I. Furthermore, we consider that the new linear function H is obtained from the original function by multiplying by 2 the weight of each feature F in $P(T, I)$. Now suppose that the learner receives a new interpretation J given by:

$$J = (\{1, 2\}, \{\mathsf{triangle}(1), \mathsf{triangle}(2), \mathsf{larger}(1, 2), \mathsf{left}(1, 2)\})$$

The projection of T onto J is represented by the set of all "•" nodes in figure 3. We remark that: $\sum_{F \in P(T,J)} H(C_T(F)) \cdot \|F\|_{P(T,J)} = 62$. Again, the example is classified as negative. Suppose that J is, in fact, positive. Then, the new closure space T is obtained from the update of the original theory by J. This theory is represented by the complete lattice in figure 3. We notably remark that T partitions the feature space $\mathbf{F}$ into 15 congruences classes. By comparison, $\mathbf{F}$ contains $262, 144$ features.

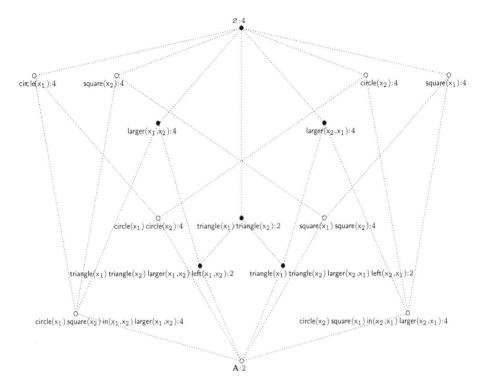

Fig. 3. Update of T by J

4 Online Closure-Based Learning

After an excursion into the algebraic aspects of our framework, we now focus on closure-based relational learning. In this section, we begin to present an online learning algorithm for relational committees, next we provide a mistake bound for this algorithm, and then we examine its computational cost.

The algorithm is specified in figure 4. The learner starts with the closure space $\{\mathbf{A}\}$, where $H(\{\mathbf{A}\})$ is set to 2. The order of the events in any trial is organized as follows. First, the learner receives an interpretation I from its environment. Next it predicts a class label for I by projecting its closure space T onto I and by computing the value $H(I)$ of its corresponding classifier. In doing so, the learner exploits the topological structure of its closure space T in order to determine the overall weight of the feature space $\mathbf{F}(I)$. Finally, the learner receives the correct label. If the algorithm has made a mistake, then it updates its linear threshold function H and its theory T. The learner starts by expanding the domain of H to $P(T, I)$. The weights of the features are increased or decreased, according to the type of mistake that has been made. Then, the learner updates its closure space T by I, and waits for a new example.

Initialization

₀ Set $T \leftarrow \{\mathbf{A}\}$ and $H(\mathbf{A}) \leftarrow 2$

Trials

₁ Receive an interpretation I

₂ If $\left(\sum_{F \in P(T,I)} H(C_T(F)) \cdot \|F\|_{P(T,I)}\right) \geq N$, then

$\qquad$ predict $H(I) \leftarrow 1$

$\quad$ else

$\qquad$ predict $H(I) \leftarrow 0$

₃ Receive $T^*(I)$. If $T^*(I) \neq H(I)$ then

$\qquad$ *Demotion:*   if $H(I) = 1$ then $\forall F \in P(T,I)$, set $H(F) \leftarrow \frac{1}{2} H(C_T(F))$

$\qquad$ *Promotion:* if $H(I) = 0$ then $\forall F \in P(T,I)$, set $H(F) \leftarrow 2 H(C_T(F))$

$\qquad$ Set $T \leftarrow T \cup P(T,I)$

Fig. 4. Closure-Based Relational Winnow

4.1   Mistake Bound

We have now all elements in hand to provide the first main result of this study. In the next theorem, we consider that the target expression T^* is a relational theory containing r relational conjunctions. The goal for the learner is to identify these r relevant features in a feature space $\mathbf{F}$ containing an exponential number $N - r$ of irrelevant features. Based on a natural correspondence between the standard algorithm and the closure-based algorithm, we can state that the number of mistakes depends only logarithmically on N and linearly on r.

Theorem 1. *For the class of relational theories containing r existentially quantified conjunctions of atoms defined over p predicate symbols and k variables, online closure-based Winnow has a mistake bound of:*

$$2(rpk^a + 1)$$

Proof. Let Φ and H be the linear threshold functions maintained by the standard algorithm (fig. 2) and the closure-based algorithm (fig. 4). We show that, if both algorithms have received the same sequence $\mathbf{I}$ of examples, then for any new received example J, we have $\Phi(J) = H(J)$. Based on proposition 8, a sufficient condition for this is to prove that H is a closure-based representation of Φ. This is demonstrated by induction on the size of the sequence $\mathbf{I}$.

First, suppose that the sequence $\mathbf{I}$ is empty. We remark that for each feature F in $\mathbf{F}$, $\Phi(F) = H(\mathbf{A}) = 2$. Since $C_{\{\mathbf{A}\}}(F) = \mathbf{A}$, it follows that $\Phi(F) = H(C_T(F))$. Hence, H is a closure-based representation of Φ.

Now, suppose that $\mathbf{I}$ is not empty. We focus on the last trial in the sequence. Let I be the example observed during this trial. Let E_{bef} and E_{aft}

denote the expression E at the beginning of the trial and at the end of the trial. Finally, let F be a feature in $\mathbf{F}$. By induction hypothesis, we assume that $\Phi_{\text{bef}}(F) = H_{\text{bef}}(C_{T_{\text{bef}}}(F))$ at the beginning of the trial. We must show that $\Phi_{\text{aft}}(F) = H_{\text{aft}}(C_{T_{\text{aft}}}(F))$. If this condition holds, then H is still a closure-based representation of Φ at the end of the last trial of the sequence. Consequently, $\Phi(J) = H(J)$ during any new trial involving J. Suppose that no mistake occurred. In this case, $\Phi_{\text{aft}} = \Phi_{\text{bef}}$. Similarly, $H_{\text{aft}} = H_{\text{bef}}$ and $T_{\text{aft}} = T_{\text{bef}}$. Hence, we have $\Phi_{\text{aft}}(F) = H_{\text{aft}}(C_{T_{\text{aft}}}(F))$. Suppose that a mistake occurred. Then both classifiers are either "demoted" or "promoted". We only examine the demotion case, since an analogue strategy applies to the promotion case.

We know that $T_{\text{aft}} = T_{\text{bef}} \cup P(T_{\text{bef}}, I)$. First, consider that $F \notin \mathbf{F}(I)$. In this case, $\Phi_{\text{aft}}(F) = \Phi_{\text{bef}}(F)$. Furthermore, F must be an element of some congruence class in T_{bef}. Therefore, $C_{T_{\text{aft}}}(F) = C_{T_{\text{bef}}}(F)$. Since $H_{\text{aft}}(C_{T_{\text{bef}}}(F)) = H_{\text{bef}}(C_{T_{\text{bef}}}(F))$, we have $H_{\text{aft}}(C_{T_{\text{aft}}}(F)) = H_{\text{bef}}(C_{T_{\text{bef}}}(F))$. Hence, $\Phi_{\text{aft}}(F) = H_{\text{aft}}(C_{T_{\text{aft}}}(F))$. Now, consider that $F \in \mathbf{F}(I)$. In this case, we must have $\Phi_{\text{aft}}(F) = \frac{1}{2}\Phi_{\text{bef}}(F)$. Furthermore, F is an element of some congruence class in $P(T_{\text{bef}}, I)$. It follows that, $C_{T_{\text{aft}}}(F) = C_{P(T_{\text{bef}}, I)}(F)$. Since $H_{\text{aft}}(C_{P(T_{\text{bef}}, I)}(F)) = \frac{1}{2} H_{\text{bef}}(C_{T_{\text{bef}}}(F))$, we have $H_{\text{aft}}(C_{T_{\text{aft}}}(F)) = \frac{1}{2} H_{\text{bef}}(C_{T_{\text{bef}}}(F))$. Therefore, $\Phi_{\text{aft}}(F) = H_{\text{aft}}(C_{T_{\text{aft}}}(F))$.

We thus have shown that closure-based Winnow is a simulation of standard Winnow. Consequently, if the later algorithm has a mistake-bound of m, then the former algorithm must have a mistake bound of m. By an adaptation of Littlestone's analysis (see also [21]), standard Winnow has a mistake bound of $2(r \log_2 N + 1)$. Since N is upper bounded by 2^{pk^a}, the result follows.   □

4.2   Computational Complexity

Obviously, the main source of complexity in closure-based Winnow resides in the prediction phase. This phase can be divided into two steps. Namely, given a closure space T and an interpretation I, the learner computes first the projection of T onto I. Then, for each closed feature F in the projection, the learner evaluates the weight of F and the cardinality of the congruence class of F. The following property suggests a simple incremental procedure to build projections.

Proposition 9. *Let T be a closure space and I be an interpretation. Suppose that the basis of I is given by the set $\{F_1, \cdots, F_n\}$ and let $(P_0, \cdots, P_n)$ be the sequence of sets of features recursively defined as follows:*

(1) $P_0 = \varnothing$,
(2) $P_n = P_{n-1} \cup \{F \cap F_i : F \in T \cup P_{i-1}\}$.

Then P_n is the projection of T onto I.

Proof. Let B_n denote the set $\{F_1, \cdots, F_n\}$. The proof is done by induction on n. First, suppose that $n = 1$. In this case, we know that $C(B_1) = B_1 = \{F_1\}$. Since $P_1 = \{F \cap F_1 : F \in T\}$, it follows that $T \circ C(B_1) = P_1$, as desired.

Now, consider that $n > 1$ and, by induction hypothesis, assume that P_{n-1} is given by $T \circ C(B_{n-1}(I))$. We first prove that

$$C(B_n) = C(B_{n-1}) \cup (C(B_{n-1}) \circ \{F_n\}) \cup \{F_n\}$$

We know that $C(B_n)$ is closed under intersection. Let C_n denote the set of all intersections of nonempty subsets of B_n containing F_n. By construction, C_n is given by $\{F_n\} \cup \{\bigcap S \cap F_n : \varnothing \subset S \subseteq B_{n-1}\}$. Since $C(B_{n-1})$ is the set $\{\bigcap S : \varnothing \subset S \subseteq B_{n-1}\}$, it follows that: $C_n = \{F_n\} \cup \{F_n \cap F : F \in C(B_{n-1})\}$. Finally, since the second term corresponds to $C(B_{n-1}) \circ \{F_n\}$, the result follows. Now, we examine the main property. By construction, we have:

$$T \circ C(B_n) = (T \circ C(B_{n-1})) \cup (T \circ \{F_n\}) \cup (T \circ C(B_{n-1}) \circ \{F_n\})$$

By induction hypothesis, we know that $T \circ C(B_n) = P_{n-1}$. By reporting this result, $T \circ C(B_n)$ is $P_{n-1} \cup (T \circ \{F_n\}) \cup (P_{n-1} \circ \{F_n\})$. By factorizing, it follows that $T \circ C(B_n) = P_{n-1} \cup ((T \cup P_{n-1}) \circ \{F_n\})$. Since the second term is the set $\{F \cap F_n : F \in T \cup P_{i-1}\}$, the result follows. $\qquad \square$

The following property suggests a simple method to evaluate the cardinality of any congruence class of a closed set.

Proposition 10. *Let T be a closed theory and $\{F_1, \cdots, F_n\}$ be a linear ordering of T where $F_i \subset F_j$ implies $i \leq j$ for any pair of indexes i and j. Then the cardinality of each congruence class in T is recursively determined as follows:*

(1) $\|F_1\| = 2^{|F_1|}$,
(2) $\|F_n\| = 2^{|F_n|} - \sum\{\|F_i\| : 1 \leq i < n \text{ and } F_i \subseteq F_n\}$.

Proof. Let T_n and $\mathbf{F}_n$ denote the sets of every subset of F_n in T and $\mathbf{F}(T)$, respectively. By proposition 5, we know that the congruence relation of T induces a complete partitioning of $\mathbf{F}(T)$. Since each element in $\mathbf{F}_n$ must be covered by some congruence class in T_n, it follows that the congruence relation of T_n induces a complete partitioning of $\mathbf{F}_n$. We thus have,

$$\mathbf{F}_n = \bigcup\{[F_i] : 1 \leq i \leq n \text{ and } F_i \subseteq F_n\}$$

We now examine the main property. First, consider that $n = 1$. In this case, $|\mathbf{F}_1| = \|F_1\|$. Since $|\mathbf{F}_1| = 2^{|F_1|}$, the result follows. Now, consider that $n > 1$. From the previous equation, we have:

$$[F_n] = \mathbf{F}_n - \bigcup\{[F_i] : 1 \leq i < n \text{ and } F_i \subseteq F_n\}$$

Since $|\mathbf{F}_n| = 2^{|F_n|}$ and congruence classes are mutually disjoint, we obtain:

$$\|F_n\| = 2^{|F_n|} - \sum\{\|F_i\| : 1 \leq i < n \text{ and } F_i \subseteq F_n\}$$

Based on these considerations, we are now in position to present the second key result of this paper. The next theorem states that the computational cost is polynomial in the size of the closure lattice.

Theorem 2. *Let s be the size of the closure space maintained by the learner at the beginning of some trial. Let d and b denote the number of objects and the size of the closure of the basis of the received interpretation. Then, the time complexity of the trial is in $O(b^2 s^2 + d^{2k})$.*

Proof. Let T be the closure space maintained by the learner and I be the received interpretation at the beginning of the trial (line 1). We assume that elements in T are sorted. We first examine the complexity of the prediction step (line 2). As observed earlier, the construction of the basis takes $O(d^{2k})$ time. Based on the method suggested by proposition 9, the projection of T onto I takes $O(bs)$ time. Furthermore, the resulting theory is sorted and contains at most bs features. For each feature F in $P(T, I)$, the weight $H(C_T(F))$ can be evaluated in $O(s)$ time. Furthermore, using the method suggested in proposition 10, the value $\|F\|_{P(T,I)}$ can be obtained in $O(bs)$ time. Since there are at most bs features in $P(T, I)$, the counting task takes $O(bs(s + bs))$ time, which is in $O(b^2 s^2)$. We now turn to the complexity of the update step (line 3). Updating the linear function H requires $O(bs)$ time since the weights were already computed in the prediction step. The update of T by I requires $O(bs \log_2(s))$ time.   □

If we consider constant values of the maximum arity a and the number of variables k, then the computational cost is essentially dependent on the size of the closure space T. This space T is isomorphic to a concept lattice [8] formed by the context (G, M, I) where the set of "objects" G is given by the set $B(T)$ of all maximal elements of T with respect to set-inclusion, the set of "attributes" M is given by $\mathbf{A}$ and the "incidence relation" I is given by the membership relation between $\mathbf{A}$ and $B(T)$. Following [15], this lattice can be exponential in the number of its maximal elements. Yet, as stressed in introduction to this paper, experiments in formal concept analysis suggest that such an exponential bound is rarely observed in practice. On average, the size of a closure lattice tends to be quadratic in the number of the attributes (or atoms) [5, 9].

5   Conclusions

Online relational learning is intrinsically characterized by a dilemma between effectiveness and computational complexity. On the one hand, the mistake bound of multiplicative weight algorithms is only logarithmic in the input dimension, making them useful to handle large spaces such as relational theories. On the other hand, standard online relational learners are fundamentally limited by the counting problem that requires a systematic exploration of these spaces. The key contribution of this study is to provide a model of closure-based learning that allows a learner to focus on limited regions of its hypothesis space and to compile these regions into a closure lattice. This paradigm was applied to the development of an online algorithm for learning relational theory. The number of mistakes depends only logarithmically on the number of features and the computational cost is polynomially bounded by the size of the closure lattice.

Related Work. In the past few years, there have been an increased an significant interest in the development of online learning algorithms for relational domains. In a seminal work, Golding and Roth [10] developed a relational architecture, the SNoW system, that learns linear threshold functions with quantified propositions. This architecture has been applied to several structured domains, including visual recognition [19] and information extraction [20]. The basic idea underlying the notion of quantified proposition is to limit the scope of each quantifier to a single predicate. In other words, only atoms are quantified and thus, any formula can be treated essentially as a logical combination of boolean variables [7]. Based on this representation, the number of mistakes still depends only logarithmically on the number of quantified atoms. Soon afterwards, Valiant [21, 22] extended this approach by addressing the class of quantified projections, an intermediate class between quantified disjunctions and quantified DNF formulas. Based on a combination of Winnow algorithms, the method preserves attribute-efficiency by exhibiting a logarithmic dependence on the number of quantified atoms.

The main interest of these approaches is to extend the expressiveness of pure propositional systems while maintaining a polynomial cost during the learning phase. By comparison, our paradigm is orthogonal to these approaches. Namely, the use of multi-class, first-order decision rules provides a far more expressive language. In particular, existentially quantified conjunctions of atoms are able to capture both relations among objects and dependencies between relations. Yet, despite the use of closure-based operations, the dependence of the computational cost on the input dimension is not guaranteed to be polynomial.

Finally, the recent work by Chawla et. al. [6] is also concerned with generalizing Winnow algorithms to large spaces. But their approach is essentially propositional and uses a randomized approximation technique that does not always guarantee complete correctness of the learning system.

Perspectives. Several directions of future research are possible. First and topmost, the practical issue of online closure-based learning needs to be explored. In particular, the development of a competence map for our algorithm is the subject of ongoing research. A second interesting research avenue is to develop pruning techniques for closure spaces. A potential strategy is to merge congruence classes that have the same weight vectors. An other approach is to use lower and upper bounds on the possible weights in order to limit the number of distributions. Third and finally, the framework described suggests a broader variety of relational classes that might be handled using the paradigm of closure-based learning. In particular, the extension of this approach to first-order Horn theories looks promising.

References

[1] S. Abiteboul, R. Hull, and V. Vianu. *Foundations of Databases.* Addison-Wesley, 1995.

[2] G. Birkhoff. *Lattice Theory.* American Mathematical Society, Third Edition, 1967.

[3] A. Blum. Learning boolean functions in an infinite attribute space. *Machine Learning*, 9(4):373–386, 1992.

[4] A. Blum. On-line algorithms in machine learning. In *Online Algorithms*, volume 1442 of *Lecture Notes in Computer Science*, pages 306–325, 1998.

[5] C. Carpineto, G. Romano, and P. d'Amado. Inferring dependencies from relations: a conceptual clustering approach. *Computational Intelligence*, 15(4):415–441, 1999.

[6] D. Chawla, L. Li, and S. Scott. Efficiently approximating weighted sums with exponentially many terms. In *Proceedings of the 14th Annual Conference on Computational Learning Theory*, pages 82–98, 2001.

[7] C. M. Cumby and D. Roth. Relational representations that facilitate learning. In *Principles of Knowledge Representation and Reasoning: Proceedings of the 7th International Conference*, pages 425–434, 2000.

[8] B. Ganter and R. Wille. *Formal Concept Analysis: Mathematical Foundations*. Springer-Verlag, 1997.

[9] R. Godin, R. Missaoui, and H. Alaoui. Incremental concept formation algorithms based on Galois lattices. *Computational Intelligence*, 11:246–267, 1995.

[10] A. R. Golding and D. Roth. A Winnow-based approach to context-sensitive spelling correction. *Machine Learning*, 34:107–130, 1999.

[11] S. A. Goldman, S. Kwek, and S. D. Scott. Agnostic learning of geometric patterns. *Journal of Computer and System Sciences*, 62(1):123–151, 2001.

[12] D. Haussler. Learning conjunctive concepts in structural domains. *Machine Learning*, 4:7–40, 1989.

[13] R. Khardon. Learning horn expressions with LogAn-H. In *Proceedings of the 17th International Conference on Machine Learning*, pages 471–478, 2000.

[14] R. Khardon, D. Roth, and R. A. Servedio. Efficiency versus convergence of boolean kernels for on-line learning algorithms. In *Advances in Neural Information Processing Systems*, volume 14, pages 423–430, 2001.

[15] S. Kuznetsov. On computing the size of a lattice and related decision problems. *Order*, 18(4):313–321, 2001.

[16] N. Littlestone. Learning quickly when irrelevant attributes abound: A new linear-threshold algorithm. *Machine Learning*, 2(4):285–318, 1988.

[17] W. Maass and M. K. Warmuth. Efficient learning with virtual threshold gates. *Information and Computation*, 141(1):66–83, 1998.

[18] T. M. Mitchell. Generalization as search. *Artificial Intelligence*, 18(2):203–226, 1982.

[19] D. Roth, M.-H. Yang, and N. Ahuja. Learning to recognize three-dimensional objects. *Neural Computation*, 14(5):1071–1103, 2002.

[20] D. Roth and W. Yih. Relational learning via propositional algorithms: An information extraction case study. In *Proceedings of the 17th International Joint Conference on Artificial Intelligence*, pages 1257–1263, 2001.

[21] L. G. Valiant. Projection learning. *Machine Learning*, 37(2):115–130, 1999.

[22] L. G. Valiant. Robust logics. *Artificial Intelligence*, 117(2):231–253, 2000.

Learning Closed Sets of Labeled Graphs for Chemical Applications

Sergei O. Kuznetsov and Mikhail V. Samokhin

All-Russia Institute for Scientific and Technical Information (VINITI),
Moscow, Russia

Abstract. Similarity of graphs with labeled vertices and edges is naturally defined in terms of maximal common subgraphs. To avoid computation overload, a parameterized technique for approximation of graphs and their similarity is used. A lattice-based method of binarizing labeled graphs that respects the similarity operation on graph sets is proposed. This method allows one to compute graph similarity by means of algorithms for computing closed sets. Results of several computer experiments in predicting biological activity of chemical compounds that employ the proposed technique testify in favour of graph approximations as compared to complete graph representations: gaining in efficiency one (almost) does not lose in accuracy.

1 Introduction

In last years the problem of learning from data given by labeled graphs attracted much attention in Machine Learning and Data Mining communities [1,2,3,4,5,6,7,8,9]. In our paper we address this issue using an approach based on generation of closed sets of labeled graphs and their approximations. On the one hand, this approach is related to computation of most specific (or least general) generalizations of positive (or negative) examples, which proved to be successful in real-life applications, including predictive toxicology [10]. On the other hand, generation of (frequent) closed itemsets turned out to be useful for computing the set of all well-supported association rules [11]. This explains recent attention to computing closed graphs in data mining [8]. As reported in [8], CloseGraph algorithm computes frequent graphs much faster than its forerunner gSpan [7], and WARMR [1], an ILP program.

An important application for learning with labeled graphs is the analysis of properties of chemical substances. Fragmentary Code of Substructure Superposition (FCSS) [12,10] has been designed and permanently refined for this purpose and proved to be a very efficient tool. For example, it was successfully applied (as estimated by ROC diagrams) in the open PTC competition [13,10,14]. As reported in [14], FCSS produced the largest number of useful attributes in comparison with other representations used in PTC. The drawbacks of FCSS are related to the loss of information about connection between molecular parts and the lack of flexibility w.r.t. different problems. To compensate for this, a similarity operation ⊓ on sets of labeled graphs, representing molecules, was proposed

S. Kramer and B. Pfahringer (Eds.): ILP 2005, LNAI 3625, pp. 190–208, 2005.

in [15,16,3]. This operation, defining similarity of sets of labeled (hyper)graphs, has the property of a semilattice: it is idempotent ($X \sqcap X = X$), commutative ($X \sqcap Y = Y \sqcap X$), and associative ($X \sqcap (Y \sqcap Z) = (X \sqcap Y) \sqcap Z$). This allows one to compute similarity of graph sets by means of algorithms for computing closed sets (see review [17]) well-known in Formal Concept Analysis [18].

The main problem with practical implementation of this operation is that of computational complexity: to compute similarity of two graphs one needs to make several tests of subgraph isomorphism (which is in general NP-complete), and make tests for graph isomorphism.

A theoretical means for approximate computation in semilattices, called projections, was proposed in [19] and the first computer implementation was described in [20]. In this paper we study projections for semilattices on graph sets and their use in learning models. Here we consider a realization of similarity operation on graph sets and their projections realized by means of certain order-theoretic and lattice-theoretic techniques. We consider several applied problems in the analysis of biological activity of chemical compounds. To predict target attribute values (biological activities) we employ and compare several learning models: induction of decision trees, Naive Bayes classifier (see, e.g., [21]) and JSM-method or concept-based learning [22,3,19]. In this paper the issues of program realization and efficiency are not considered in details, since our programs are Java prototypes. We concentrate mostly on combinations of learning models with representation languages, and evaluations of their predictive accuracy. Results obtained for learning with graph projections for various values of projection parameter are compared with those obtained with FCCS representation.

The paper is organized as follows. In the second section we describe the general theoretical framework for computing similarity (meet) of graph sets together with a means for its approximate computations. In the third section we discuss the learning models used in this work. In the fourth section we describe computer experiments in the analysis of molecular graphs (of chemical compounds from the PTC dataset [13], halogen-substituted aliphatic hydrocarbons, alcohols, etc.) where the above representations and learning models are used. In the fifth section the results are discussed and some conclusions are made.

2   Closed Sets of Labeled Graphs and Their Projections

In [15,16,3] a semilattice on sets of graphs with labeled vertices and edges was proposed. This lattice is based on a natural domination relation between graphs with labeled vertices and edges. Consider an ordered set P of connected graphs[1] with vertex and edge labels from the set $\mathcal{L}$ with partial order $\preceq$. Each labeled graph Γ from P is a quadruple of the form $((V, l), (E, b))$, where V is a set of vertices, E is a set of edges, $l: V \to \mathcal{L}$ is a function assigning labels to vertices, and $b: E \to \mathcal{L}$ is a function assigning labels to edges.

---

[1] Omitting the condition of connectedness, one obtains a (computationally harder) model that accounts for multiple occurrences of subgraphs.

For two graphs $\Gamma_1 := ((V_1, l_1), (E_1, b_1))$ and $\Gamma_2 := ((V_2, l_2), (E_2, b_2))$ from P we say that Γ_1 **dominates** Γ_2 or $\Gamma_2 \le \Gamma_1$ (or Γ_2 is a **subgraph** of Γ_1) if there exists an injection $\varphi: V_2 \to V_1$ such that it

- respects edges: $(v, w) \in E_2 \Rightarrow (\varphi(v), \varphi(w)) \in E_1$,
- fits under labels: $l_2(v) \preceq l_1(\varphi(v))$, if $(v, w) \in E_2$ then $b_2(v, w) \preceq b_1(\varphi(v), \varphi(w))$.

Obviously, $(P, \le)$ is a partially ordered set.

Example 1. Let $\mathcal{L} = \{C, NH_2, CH_3, OH, x\}$ then we have the following relations:

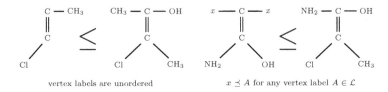

vertex labels are unordered $x \preceq A$ for any vertex label $A \in \mathcal{L}$

Now a *similarity operation* $\sqcap$ on graph sets can be defined as follows: For two graphs X and Y from P

$$\{X\} \sqcap \{Y\} := \{Z \mid Z \le X, Y, \forall Z_* \le X, Y \; Z_* \not\ge Z\},$$

i.e., $\{X\} \sqcap \{Y\}$ is the set of all maximal common subgraphs of graphs X and Y. Similarity of non-singleton sets of graphs $\{X_1, \ldots, X_k\}$ and $\{Y_1, \ldots, Y_m\}$ is defined as

$$\{X_1, \ldots, X_k\} \sqcap \{Y_1, \ldots, Y_m\} := \text{MAX}_{\le}(\cup_{i,j}(\{X_i\} \sqcap \{Y_j\})),$$

where $\text{MAX}_{\le}(X)$ returns maximal (w.r.t. $\le$) elements of X. Here is an example of applying $\sqcap$:

The similarity operation $\sqcap$ on graph sets is commutative: $X \sqcap Y = Y \sqcap X$ and associative: $(X \sqcap Y) \sqcap Z = X \sqcap (Y \sqcap Z)$.

A set X of labeled graphs from P for which $\sqcap$ is idempotent, i.e., $X \sqcap X = X$ holds, is called a *pattern*. For patterns we have $\text{MAX}_{\le}(X) = X$. For example, for each graph $g \in P$ the set $\{g\}$ is a pattern. On the contrary, for $\Gamma_1, \Gamma_2 \in P$ such that $\Gamma_1 \le \Gamma_2$ the set $\{\Gamma_1, \Gamma_2\}$ is not a pattern. Denote by D the set of all patterns, then $(D, \sqcap)$ is a semilattice with infimum (meet) operator $\sqcap$. The natural subsumption order on patterns is given by

$$c \sqsubseteq d : \Longleftrightarrow c \sqcap d = c.$$

Let E be a set of example names, and let $\delta : E \to D$ be a mapping, taking each example name to $\{g\}$ for some labeled graph $g \in P$ (thus, g is "graph description" of example e). The triple $(E, (D, \sqcap), \delta)$ is a particular case of a *pattern structure* [19]. Another example of an operation $\sqcap$ may be the following semilattice on closed intervals from [16]: for $a, b, c, d \in R$, $[a, b] \sqcap [c, d] = [\max \{a, c\},$ $\min \{b, d\}]$ if $[a, b]$ and $[c, d]$ overlap, otherwise $[a, b] \sqcap [c, d] = \emptyset$. This semilattice, where numbers are values of activation energy (computed for molecules by a standard procedure, e.g. see [23]) was used in predicting toxicity of alcohols and halogen-substituted hydrocarbons (see Section 4). The resulting similarity semilattice in this application is that on pairs, where the first element is a graph set and the second element is a numerical interval.

Derivation operators are defined as

$$A^\diamond := \sqcap_{e \in A} \, \delta(e) \qquad \text{for } A \subseteq E$$

and

$$d^\diamond := \{e \in E \mid d \sqsubseteq \delta(e)\} \qquad \text{for } d \in D.$$

For $a, b \in D$ the *pattern implication* $a \to b$ holds if $a^\diamond \sqsubseteq b^\diamond$. Implications are exact association rules (with confidence $= 1$). Operator $(\cdot)^{\diamond\diamond}$ is an algebraical closure operator [24,18] on patterns, since it is

idempotent: $d^{\diamond\diamond\diamond\diamond} = d^{\diamond\diamond}$,
extensive: $d \sqsubseteq d^{\diamond\diamond}$,
monotone: $d^{\diamond\diamond} \sqsubseteq (d \cup c)^{\diamond\diamond}$.

For a set X the set $X^{\diamond\diamond}$ is called *closure* of X. A set of labeled graphs X is called *closed* if $X^{\diamond\diamond} = X$. This definition is related to the notion of a closed graph [8], which is important for computing association rules between graphs. Closed graphs are defined in [8] in terms of "counting inference" as follows.

Given a labeled graph dataset D, support of a graph g or *support(g)* is a set (or number) of graphs in D, in which g is a subgraph. A graph g is called *closed* if no supergraph f of g (i.e., a graph such that g is isomorphic to its subgraph) has the same support.

Note that the definitions distinguish between a closed graph g and the closed set $\{g\}$ consisting of one graph g. Closed sets of graphs form a *meet semilatice* w.r.t. infimum or meet operator. A finite meet semilattice is completed to a lattice by introducing a unit (maximal) element. Closed graphs do not have this property, since in general, there can be nonunique supremums and infimums of two closed graphs.

Proposition. Let a dataset described by a pattern structure $(E, (D, \sqcap), \delta)$ be given. Then the following two properties hold:
1. For a closed graph g there is a closed set of graphs G such that $g \in G$.
2. For a closed set of graphs G and an arbitrary $g \in G$, graph g is closed.

Proof. 1. Consider the closed set of graphs $G = \{g\}^{\diamond\diamond}$. Since G consists of all maximal common subgraphs of graphs that have g as a subgraph, G contains as an element either g or a supergraph f of g. In the first case, property 1 holds. In the second case, we have that each graph in G that has g as a subgraph also has f as a subgraph, so f has the same support as g, which contradicts with the fact that g is closed. Thus, $G = \{g\}^{\diamond\diamond}$ is a closed set of graphs satisfying property 1.

2. Consider a closed set of graphs G and $g \in G$. If g is not a closed graph, then there is a supergraph f of it with the same support as g has and hence, with the same support as G has. Since G is the set of all maximal common subgraphs of the graphs describing examples from the set $G^{\diamond}$ (i.e., its support), $f \in G$ should hold. This contradicts the fact that $g \in G$, since a closed set of graphs cannot contain as elements a graph and a supergraph of it (otherwise, its closure does not coincide with itself).   □

Therefore, one can use algorithms for computing closed sets of graphs, e.g., the algorithm in [3], to compute closed graphs. With this algorithm one can also compute all *frequent* closed sets of graphs, i.e., closed sets of graphs with support above a fixed *minsup* threshold (by introducing a minor variation of the condition that terminates computation branches).

Computing $\sqcap$ may require considerable computation resources: even testing $\sqsubseteq$ is NP-complete. To approximate graph sets we consider projection (kernel) operators [19], i.e. mappings of the form $\psi \colon D \to D$ that are

monotone: if $x \sqsubseteq y$, then $\psi(x) \sqsubseteq \psi(y)$,
contractive: $\psi(x) \sqsubseteq x$, and
idempotent: $\psi(\psi(x)) = \psi(x)$.

Any projection of the semilattice $(D, \sqcap)$ is $\sqcap$-preserving, i.e., for any $X, Y \in D$

$$\psi(X \sqcap Y) = \psi(X) \sqcap \psi(Y),$$

which helps us to relate learning results in projections to those with initial representation (see Section 3).

As for practical complexity of computing $\sqsubseteq$ we can say the following. Using a Pentium PIII-1 GHz, 512 MB RAM, testing subgraph isomorphism for an average graph with 30-40 vertices and 30-40 edges took up to 5 seconds, but usually, less than a second.

In our computer experiments we used several types of projections of sets of labeled graphs that are natural in chemical applications:

- k-*chain* projection: a set of graphs X is taken to the set of all chains with k vertices that are subgraphs of at least one graph of the set X;
- k-*vertex* projection: a set of graphs X is taken to the set of all subgraphs with k vertices that are subgraphs of at least one graph of the set X;
- k-*cycles* projection: a set of graphs X is taken to the set of all subgraphs consisting of k adjacent cycles of a minimal cyclic basis of at least one graph of the set X.

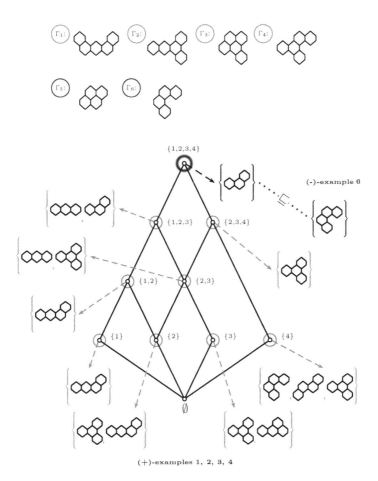

Fig. 1.

3 Learning Models

In this work we used several learning models realized within QuDA data miners' discovery environment [25][^2]: concept-based learning (JSM-method) [22,3,26] and several machine learning algorithms from the Weka workbench [27]: C4.5 algorithm for induction of decision trees, Naive Bayes classifier, and JRip (induction of ripple-down rules).

JSM-hypotheses were defined in [22] for standard object-attribute representation in a special logical language. These hypotheses were redefined as *JSM-* or *concept-based hypotheses* in [16,3,26,19] in terms of Formal Concept Analysis (FCA). For graph sets hypotheses can be defined as follows. Suppose we have a set of positive examples E_+ and a set of negative examples E_- w.r.t. a target attribute.

[^2]: Free download: http://www.intellektik.informatik.tu-darmstadt.de/~peter/

A graph set $h \in D$ is a *positive hypothesis* iff

$$h^{\circ} \cap E_- = \emptyset \text{ and } \exists A \subseteq E_+ : A^{\circ} = h.$$

Informally, a positive hypothesis is a similarity of positive examples, which does not cover any negative example. A *negative hypothesis* is defined analogously, by interchanging $+$ and $-$.

The meet-preserving property of projections implies that a hypothesis H_p in data under projection ψ corresponds to a hypothesis H in the initial representation for which the image under projection is equal to H_p, i.e., $\psi(H) = H_p$.

Hypotheses are used for classification of undetermined examples along the lines of [22] in the following way. If e is an undetermined example (example with the unknown target value), then a hypothesis h with $h \sqsubseteq \delta(e)$ is *for the positive classification* of g if h is a positive hypothesis and h is *for the negative classification* of e if h is a negative hypothesis.

An undetermined example e is *classified positively* if there is a hypothesis for its positive classification and no hypothesis for its negative classification. Example e is *classified negatively* in the opposite case. If there are hypotheses for both positive and negative classification, then some other methods (e.g., based on standard statistical techniques) may be applied. Obviously, for classification purposes it suffices to use only hypotheses minimal w.r.t. subsumption $\sqsubseteq$.

The definition of classification suggests that hypotheses can be considered as disjunctions of *lgg*s of positive and of negative examples. Notwithstanding its simplicity, the model of learning and classification with concept-based hypotheses proved to be efficient in numerous computer experiments, including PTC competition [13,10]. This learning/classification model, together with FCSS representation, produced Pareto-optimal classifications in each of the four sex/species groups (from {mice, rats} × {male, female}): in three groups the results were on the ROC curve and in the fourth group (male rats, MR) the result was slightly below the curve with no other strictly better classification result.

An algorithm for computing hypotheses on closed graph sets was described in [3]. Here we realize it by simulating $\sqcap$ operation with usual set-theoretic intersection $\cap$ in the following way. For each example e described by a labeled graph $\delta(e)$ first a set of all subgraphs of $\delta(e)$ is computed up to the projection level $k = N$. Each such subgraph is declared to be a binary attribute and example e is represented by the set $S(e)$ of binary attributes that correspond to subgraphs of $\delta(e)$. For two examples e_1 and e_2 intersection $S(e_1) \cap S(e_2)$ is equivalent to finding similarity $\psi(\delta(e_1)) \sqcap \psi(\delta(e_2))$.

Example 2. In Figure 1 consider JSM-hypotheses for the dataset with positive examples described by graphs $\Gamma_1,...,\Gamma_4$ and negative examples described by graphs Γ_5 and Γ_6. Here $\Gamma_1 \sqcap \Gamma_2 \sqcap \Gamma_3$ and $\Gamma_2 \sqcap \Gamma_3 \sqcap \Gamma_4$ are minimal positive hypotheses, whereas $\Gamma_1 \sqcap \Gamma_2 \sqcap \Gamma_3 \sqcap \Gamma_4$ is not a positive hypothesis.

Then standard Weka procedures for C4.5, Naive Bayes and JRip are run in QuDA environment. Computing concept-based hypotheses in QuDA is realized by means of algorithms for computing lattices of closed sets (or concept lattices), see review [17].

After that we perform *reduction of attributes* [18]: each column of the example/attribute binary table that is equal to the (component-wise) product (conjunction) of some other columns, is removed.

Reduction is realized by an efficient algorithm based on results from FCA [18]. Lattice-theoretical properties guarantee [18] that thus reduced set of columns gives rise to the isomorphic lattice of closed sets of attributes and thus, to the same set of concept-based hypotheses as defined above.

Since in practice reduction often results in diminishing sets of attributes in several times (see experimental results in Section 4), in our experiments we wanted to find out how reduction affects performance of other learning methods, such as C4.5, Naive Bayes and JRip. Upon reduction, every learning method was executed for data tables again. Results for reduced and nonreduced tables were compared.

The general **PBRL** (project-binarize-reduce-learn) procedure looks as follows:

1. For each example e and for k compute i-projections of $\delta(e)$ for $1 \leq i \leq k$. The subgraphs from this projections are declared to be binary attributes;
2. Compose example/attribute binary table;
3. For each learning method LM run LM, classify examples from test sets, compute cross validation;
4. Reduce the binary (example/attribute) table;
5. For reduced table and for each learning method LM run LM, classify examples from test sets, compute cross-validation.

General procedure for computing with FCSS looks similar with first two lines replaced by the following ones:

1*. For each example e compute FCSS code (set of FCSS descriptors) of its molecular graph;
2*. Compose example/attribute binary table, where each attribute stays for an FCSS descriptor;

Another approach that uses learning with graph sets was realized by means of Subdue and SubdueCL [28,9] systems. Subdue finds subgraphs that appear repetitively in graph databases. SubdueCL can learn from positive and negative examples. It generates graphs common to *many* positive examples that are common to a *small* amount of negative examples (the corresponding values are captured exactly within the *error* estimate). As reported in [9], SubdueCL slightly outperformed ILP systems FOIL [29] and Progol [30] on the PTC dataset.

SubdueCL pursues the covering strategy: having found a subgraph with the best error estimate, SubdueCL excludes positive examples covered by this subgraph (i.e., example descriptions that contain it as a subgraph) and iterates on the remaining set of positive examples. Thus, skipping certain generalizations of positive examples, Subdue performs efficiently, however may lose in learning accuracy. The latter is much more important in such domains as Predictive Toxicology, where SubdueCL [31], as estimated by ROC diagrams, was outperformed by the concept-based learning model [10] (classifications of SubdueCL were optimal only in one group (male rats) and were strictly worse than concept-based hypotheses [10] for male and female mice.

4   Experiments with Projections of Labeled Graphs

In this section we analyse results of applying the introduced data representation and learning models to the analysis of several chemical datasets [3]. For each dataset we computed graph projections (mostly, k-vertex projections, except for the 25PAH dataset (Section 4.5), where we computed k-cycles projections). Every subgraph of each graph in the projection (up to isomorphism) was declared to be a binary attribute, so each graph dataset was turned into a binary object-attribute table, which was then reduced. We also computed FCSS codes for each dataset. After that for each dataset we ran several learning methods realized within QuDA environment (JSM or concept-based hypotheses, induction of decision trees by C4.5, Naive Bayes, JRip). We computed 10-fold cross-validation and in several cases (PTC, halogen substituted hydrocarbons, alcohols, polycyclic aromatic hydrocarbons), where a known test set was available, we performed classifications for the test set. We compared cross-validation and results on the test set for each chemical dataset. Results of the analysis are presented in similar tables. For PTC datasets we plotted results of our experiments on the ROC curves of the PTC workshop [13].

4.1   Experiments with PTC Dataset

Participants of the workshop on Predictive Toxicology Challenge (PTC) [13] discussed results of competition of machine learning programs that generated hypothetical causes of toxicity from positive and negative examples.

The training dataset consisted of descriptions of 409 molecular graphs of chemical compounds with indication of whether a compound is toxic or not for a particular sex/species group out of four possible groups: {mice, rats} × {male, female}. For each group there were about 120 to 150 positive examples and 190 to 230 negative examples of toxicity. The test dataset consisted of 185 substances for which forecasts of toxicity should be made.

The average size of the initial graphs was 25 vertices and 26 edges in the training set, and 45 vertices and 46 edges in the test set. We generated graph k-vertex projections for k from 1 to 8, thus producing 8 binary object-attribute tables. For $k = 9$ we computed projections in 30 hours, but had to stop generation of the binary object-attribute matrix (which involves testing graph isomorphism) after 70 hours, having obtained 561921 attributes. With the growth of k, the number of attributes in the resulting tables becomes large, but reduction of attributes diminishes the size of tables in several times. Compared to computing projections of initial graphs (which comprises the major part of computation) and hypothesis generation, the reduction is relatively fast, see Table 1.

---

[3] These datasets can be downloaded from http://ilp05-viniti.narod.ru

Table 1. PTC dataset: number of attributes in representation tables before and after attribute reduction

projection size	1	2	3	4	5	6	7	8
# attributes in full table	22	95	329	1066	3275	9814	28025	76358
# attributes in reduced table	22	72	153	373	812	1548	2637	3981
reducing time (in sec.)	1	1	2	5	16	57	219	883

To estimate different classification strategies in combination with k-projections ($1 \leq k \leq 13$) the 10-fold cross-validation procedure was used for the given training dataset. Table 2 shows the best results w.r.t. predictive accuracy and total number of predictions. The best strategy for MR group w.r.t. predictive accuracy is the one based on JSM-hypotheses. This strategy attains predictive accuracy of 58% with k-projection representation. For FR group the best result (predictive accuracy of 66%) was obtained by JRip rules in combination with k-projections. The use of FCSS representation leads to the following results. For MR group the best strategies w.r.t. predictive accuracy are JSM-hypotheses and C4.5 algorithm, the both strategies attain predictive accuracy of 52%. For FR group JSM-hypotheses with FCSS codes also is the best strategy w.r.t. predictive accuracy. It attains predictive accuracy of 56%.

If we consider both precision and number of predictions then the best result for k-projections representation for MR group is obtained by Naive Bayes (it attains predictive accuracy of 56% and 64% of total number of predictions). For FR group JRip results in 66% of predictive accuracy with 40% of total number of predictions. Naive Bayes also turns out to be the best strategy in combination with FCSS representation for both groups (predictive accuracy of 51% and 49% of total number of predictions for MR group; corresponding values for FR group are 50% and 25%). The results of 10-fold cross-validation suggest that the performance of learning methods stabilizes with the growth of k.

Table 2. The results of 10-fold cross-validation procedure for PTC dataset obtained with JSM-hypotheses (**J**), C4.5 (**C**), Naive Bayes classifier (**N**), and JRip rules (**R**) with FCSS-encoding (**F**) and $3, \ldots, 14-$ projections (**PR**); **A** – predictive accuracy, **TP** – total number of predictions

	MR (male rats)								FR (female rats)							
	J-F	C-F	N-F	R-F	J-PR	C-PR	N-PR	R-PR	J-F	C-F	N-F	R-F	J-PR	C-PR	N-PR	R-PR
A	0.523	0.527	0.511	0.475	0.586	0.556	0.552	0.556	0.560	0.462	0.500	0.385	0.464	0.571	0.468	0.662
TP	0.164	0.397	0.493	0.199	0.266	0.643	0.552	0.448	0.123	0.263	0.246	0.044	0.109	0.403	0.429	0.395

4.2 Classification in Projections Estimated by ROC Curves

The results are shown in Figure 2, where the following abbreviations are used:

– J-PR1, J-PR2, ..., J-PR8 – the results obtained using 1- to 8-projection representations, respectively, in combination with JSM-hypotheses; similarly, for other methods (C4.5, Naive Bayes, JRip), the results marked as C45-PRi, NB-PRi and R-PRi (where $1 \leq i \leq 8$);

– WAI1, GONZ, KWAI, LEU3 are other Pareto-optimal models submitted to the Predictive Toxicology Challenge for this animal group.

Note that the Figure 2 shows both the "old" ROC-curve (composed by LEU3, KWAI, GONZ, and WAI1 models) and the "new" one (composed by LEU3, J-PR5, C45-PR3, NB-PR3, and R-PR7 models).

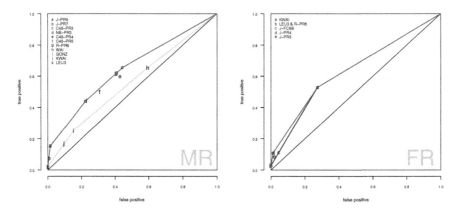

Fig. 2. Projected pattern structures "On the ROC" for groups MR (male rats) and FR (female rats)

For the MR group (male rats; see Figure 2) the following results were obtained. The use of k-projections (with $k \leq 3$) together with JSM-hypotheses does not lead to any good classifications. However, the C4.5 algorithm and Naive Bayes classifier appears on the "new" ROC-curve. The use of 4-projections in combination with JSM-hypotheses and C4.5 results in better classifications: the corresponding points are above the "old" ROC-curve. The 5-projections representation in combination with JSM-hypotheses happens to be one of the five "new" best strategies: it results in making 8 true positive predictions with only 2 false positive ones. As in the case with JSM-hypotheses the use of decision tree induction strategy leads to the classification that is also better than those on the "old" ROC-curve. The use of 6-projections with JSM-hypotheses, however, does not result in better classification: the number of true positives decreases to 6; the number of false positives remains the same. At the same time new classifications of the C4.5 are among the best ones. The corresponding point lies on the "new" ROC-curve. The use of 7-projections and JSM-hypotheses, with 4 true positives and 1 false positives again appears on the "new" ROC-curve. The classification based on the 8-projections representation and JSM-hypotheses increases the number of true positives to 6 but also increases the number of false positives to 2; this strategy is thus strictly worse than using 5-projections (assuming positive cost of making a true positive classification).

For the FR group (female rats; see Figure 2) the points corresponding to the results for 4-, 5-, 6-, and 8-projections in combination with JSM-hypotheses, also lie above the "old" PTC ROC-curve, where concept-based hypotheses were computed for FCSS representation. However, other methods do not lead to any good classifications. None of them in combination with k-projections appears above the "old" ROC-curve. There was only one exception: ripple-down rules (JRip) using 6-projections representation show the same result as LEU3.

Computer experiments with PTC data in comparison of FCSS, k-projections and reduced/nonreduced tables showed that the use of reduced tables, as compared with nonreduced ones, does not make any difference for concept-based hypotheses, makes a very slight difference (no more than 5%) for induction of decision trees and small difference (about 10-15%) for other methods such as Naive Bayes and JRip. As for comparison of projections of different type, first there is an obvious improvement with the growth of the projection parameter k. Starting from a certain value of k there is no further improvement.

4.3 Toxicity of Alcohols

In [32] the results of studies on the relationships between structures of miscellaneous alcohols (from [33]) and their acute toxicity for rats and mice using JSM-(concept-based) hypotheses with FCSS representation are described.

The training set contains descriptions of 89 molecular graphs of chemical compounds with indication of acute toxicity degree (high, moderate, and low). Separate computations were made for two target values: high and moderate. In the first case moderate and low toxic substances were considered as negative examples. In the second case only low toxic substances were considered as negatives. The test set consisted of 22 substances. The average size of a molecular graph was 24 vertices and 23 edges.

Tables 3 and 4 report on the results obtained with FCSS and k-projections ($4 \leq k \leq 13$) in combination with various learning models.

Table 3. Toxicity of alcohols: results obtained with JSM-hypotheses, FCSS-encoding (**F**) and $4-,\ldots,13-$projections

	F	4	5	6	7	8	9	10	11	12	13
# correct predictions	8	9	10	10	14	14	13	12	11	11	11
# incorrect predictions	2	0	3	1	1	2	3	3	3	3	3
# unclassified substances	12	13	9	11	7	6	6	7	8	8	8

Table 4. Predicting toxic potential of alcohols: the best results obtained with JSM-hypotheses (**J**), C4.5 (**C**), Naive Bayes classifier (**N**), and JRip rules (**R**) in combination with FCSS-encoding (**F**) and $3,\ldots,14-$ projections (**PR**)

	J-F	C-F	N-F	R-F	J-PR	C-PR	N-PR	R-PR
# correct predictions	8	19	16	19	14	19	12	17
# incorrect predictions	2	3	6	3	1	3	10	5

For k-projections with $1 \leq k \leq 3$ there was no classification with JSM-hypotheses whatsoever. For $k = 4$ with JSM-hypotheses a result is better than that for FCSS was obtained. For $k = 5$ and $k = 6$ results are not comparable with those for $k = 4$: the number of correct classifications is 10, but the numbers of incorrect predictions are equal to 3 and 1, respectively. The result obtained with JSM-hypotheses for 7-projections is among the best results for $1 \leq k \leq 13$: 14 correct predictions with only 1 mistake. Starting with $k = 8$ the growth of k results in the decrease of predictive accuracy for JSM-hypotheses. The predictive accuracy of other methods also decreases with the growth of k. For example, the use of C4.5 algorithm and 8-projections leads to the classification with 19 correct predictions and 3 incorrect predictions, but the use of 11-projections representation in combination with the same learning model results in 18 correct predictions with 4 mistakes.

In general, we observe that the use of reduced vs. nonreduced tables does not affect results obtained with the JSM-hypotheses and slightly affects results of other methods. The best classifications were obtained for average projection values ($4 \leq k \leq 8$). Experimental complexity of computing projections for this dataset, is given in Table 5

Table 5. Alcohol dataset: time of computing projections

size of projection	4	5	6	7	8	9	10	11	12	13
time elapsed, sec.	12	21	44	109	317	937	3163	12402	45822	156297

4.4 Predicting Carcinogenic Potential in Halogen-Substituted Aliphatic Hydrocarbons

The training set [34] contained descriptions of 57 molecular graphs with values of carcinogenic potential. The unique target property here was "to be carcinogenic". The test set consisted of 13 molecular graphs. The results for different k-projections and FCSS in combination with different learning models are shown in Table 6.

Table 6. Predicting carcinogenic potential in hydrocarbons: the results obtained with JSM-hypotheses and FCSS-encoding (**F**) and $3, \ldots, 14-$ projections

	F	3	4	5	6	7	8	9	10	11	12	13	14
# correct predictions	2	6	6	6	7	7	7	7	7	7	7	7	7
# incorrect predictions	0	0	0	0	0	0	0	1	1	1	1	1	1
# unclassified substances	11	7	7	7	6	6	6	5	5	5	5	5	5

The average size of the initial graphs was 8 vertices and 7 edges in the training set and 13 vertices and 12 edges in the test set. As the projection size increases the classification accuracy first grows and then (for $k \geq 9$) starts to decrease (Table 6).

For another dataset with 25 molecular graphs in the training set, 17 graphs in the test set, and the same sizes of molecules as above a numerical value (characteristic of a specific activation energy of a molecule) [35] was supplied for each substance. This value was treated by means of the semilattice on intervals as described in Section 2. The resulting similarity semilattice is that on pairs of the form (graph set, numerical interval). The computation results are shown in Table 7.

Table 7. Predicting indirect carcinogenic potential in hydrocarbons with JSM-hypotheses, FCSS-encoding (**F**), and $3, \ldots, 14-$ projections

	F	3	4	5	6	7	8	9	10	11	12	13	14
# correct predictions	6	8	9	11	11	11	11	11	11	11	11	11	11
# incorrect predictions	5	2	2	1	1	1	1	1	1	1	1	1	1
# unclassified substances	6	7	6	5	5	5	5	5	5	5	5	5	5

Again, we computed k-projections of the initial molecular graphs for $1 \leq k \leq 13$. The stratified 10-fold cross-validation procedure was used to estimate different classification strategies in combination with k-projections ($1 \leq k \leq 13$). Table 8 shows the best results w.r.t. predictive accuracy and total number of predictions. On the one hand the best strategies w.r.t. predictive accuracy are C4.5 algorithm, the one based on JSM-hypotheses, and JRip rules. C4.5 attains predictive accuracy of 83% with FCSS representation, JSM and JRip attained predictive accuracy of 78% with k-projections. On the other hand, if we consider both precision and number of predictions, then the best result is obtained with JRip rules (78% of predictive accuracy and 93% of total number of predictions with k-projections). 66% of total number of predictions was attained with the use of C4.5 and FCSS representation. Table 8 also shows the results of 10-fold cross-validation for reduced tables. The use of reduced tables, as compared with nonreduced ones, does not make any difference for concept-based hypotheses, makes a very slight difference (no more than 5%) for C4.5 and small difference (about 10-15%) for other methods such as Naive Bayes and JRip.

Table 8. The results of 10-fold cross-validation for hydrocarbons dataset obtained with JSM-hypotheses (**J**), C4.5 (**C**), Naive Bayes classifier (**N**), and JRip rules (**R**) in combination with FCSS-encoding (**F**) and $3, \ldots, 14-$ projections (**PR**); **A** – predictive accuracy, **TP** – total number of predictions

	nonreduced table								reduced table							
	J-F	C-F	N-F	R-F	J-PR	C-PR	N-PR	R-PR	J-F	C-F	N-F	R-F	J-PR	C-PR	N-PR	R-PR
A	0.800	0.833	0.722	0.765	0.778	0.750	0.765	0.778	0.800	0.833	0.722	0.765	0.778	0.812	0.750	0.765
TP	0.533	0.667	0.867	0.867	0.467	0.800	0.867	0.933	0.533	0.667	0.867	0.867	0.467	0.867	0.800	0.867

The predictions made by different strategies were compared with known experimental results from [34] the following evaluations were obtained. As in the previous experiment with the k-projections and JSM-hypotheses where $1 \leq k \leq$

2 no classification was made at all. The strategies based on 3-, 4-projections and JSM-hypotheses result in better classifications than those with FCSS-encoding. The same result was attained by the strategy based on induction of decision trees (C4.5 algorithm). It results in 12 correct predictions and 5 incorrect predictions. For $k \geq 5$ in combination with JSM-hypotheses the best result was obtained w.r.t. predictive accuracy. Other methods with k-projections ($k \geq 5$) made approximately the same number of correct predictions as the strategy based on JSM-hypotheses. However, the number of incorrect predictions is also a little bit larger. Starting from a certain value of k the results stabilize and no further improvement is made. For example, with JSM-hypotheses and Naive Bayes, k is equal to 5, while for C4.5, $k = 11$. Table 9 shows the best results obtained with different methods.

Table 9. Predicting of indirect carcinogenic potential in hydrocarbons: the best results obtained with JSM-hypotheses (**J**), C4.5 (**C**), Naive Bayes classifier (**N**), and JRip rules (**R**) in combination with FCSS-encoding (**F**) and $3, \ldots, 14-$ projections (**PR**)

	J-F	C-F	N-F	R-F	J-PR	C-PR	N-PR	R-PR
# correct predictions	6	12	8	8	11	15	13	12
# incorrect predictions	5	5	9	9	1	2	4	5

Thus, as for other datasets the best results were obtained for average projection values and were almost similar for reduced/nonreduced tables.

4.5   Analysis of Carcinogenicity of Polycyclic Aromatic Hydrocarbons

In the following experiment we considered data from [36]. The training dataset contains the descriptions of 25 molecular graphs of polycyclic aromatic hydrocarbons with indication of carcinogenic degree. As in Section 4.3 two separate computations were made for 2 target properties. To compare different classification methods in combination with k-cycles projections representation, we computed leave-one-out cross-validation. The best results w.r.t. predictive accuracy for the first target property are shown in Table 10. Learning with JSM-hypotheses attains the best results in most of the cases. However, other methods (e.g., C4.5) make more total predictions, see Table 10. Computer experiments with 25PAH data in comparison of FCSS, k-projections and reduced/nonreduced tables showed that the use of reduced tables, as compared with nonreduced ones, does not make any difference for any method.

To test the strength of methods we considered the test dataset from [37,38] and applied the hypotheses computed for k-cycles projections representation (with $1 \leq k \leq 7$) to classification of substances from the test set. There were 19 substances in the test dataset and Table 11 shows the best results obtained by different methods. From Table 11 we can conclude that among all methods w.r.t. predictive accuracy and completeness, the strategy based on JSM-hypotheses is

Table 10. The values of Leave-One-Out on 25PAH for the first target property, different methods, FCSS-encoding (**F**), and $3-,\ldots,7-$cycles projections

	J-F	C-F	N-F	R-F	J-PR	C-PR	N-PR	R-PR
predictive accuracy	0.818	0.688	1.000	0.846	0.909	0.818	1.000	0.846
total number of predictions	0.643	0.786	0.500	0.786	0.714	0.643	0.500	0.786

Table 11. Predicting indirect carcinogenic potential in PAH: different learning methods, FCSS-encoding (**F**) and $3-,\ldots,7-$ cycles projections

	J-F	C-F	N-F	R-F	J-PR	C-PR	N-PR	R-PR
# correct predictions	6	5	13	1	7	7	11	7
# incorrect predictions	5	14	6	18	6	12	8	12

the best one for the second target property in combination with k-cycles projections representation (for all values $1 \le k \le 7$). For the first target property the best result was obtained by Naive Bayes, next comes the JSM-method. At the same time we consider the combination of two target properties to predict the carcinogenic degree of a substance from the test dataset. Thus the comparison between different methods was drawn w.r.t. both target properties. From Table 11 we can conclude that best results w.r.t. predictive accuracy were obtained with JSM-hypotheses for both FCSS codes and k-cycles projections.

As for practical complexity, cyclic projections were generated in less than 0.5 second for all values of k, parameter of projection, since each graph in this dataset contains no more than 7 cycles in the minimal cyclic base.

5   Conclusions

Definitions of graph similarity operations and its approximations (projections), based on order- and lattice-theoretic ideas, were considered and studied experimentally on several chemical datasets with several learning models. In many cases the proposed graph representation results in better predictive accuracy as compared to that with standard FCSS language for the analysis of biological activity of chemicals. We experimentally studied a technique for lowering dimensionality of datasets, called reduction of attributes. For JSM or concept-based learning the reduction of attributes is strictly information lossless. The reduction proved to be useful for decision tree induction, Naive Bayes classifiers, and JRip: while lowering the number of attributes in several times, it results in almost no loss of accuracy in case of decision tree induction and results in minor loss of accuracy in case of Naive Bayes and JRip classifiers. On the other hand, we studied the performance of learning methods with respect to precision of graph approximation controlled by projection level. With the increase of representation accuracy (k, parameter of projection), the performance of learning methods first improves, then stabilizes and in some cases becomes worse after a certain threshold, seemingly due to overfitting effects. This picture, standard for the role of dimensionality in machine learning, suggests the use of molecular graph approximations instead of complete graphs: keeping dimensionality in a certain range, we can even gain in predictive accuracy. Further work on improving the representation model with labeled graphs will be related to accounting for 3D information, e.g. various types of isomerisms.

Acknowledgments. This work was supported by the Russian Foundation for Basic Research, project no. 05-01-00914a and by the Presidium of Russian Academy of Sciences, 2005 project "Problem solver for causal dependencies." The first author was partially supported by the Alexander-von-Humboldt Foundation.

References

1. King, R., Srinivasan, A., Dehaspe, L.: WARMR: A Data Mining tool for chemical data. J. of Computer-Aided Molecular Design **15** (2001) 173–181
2. Kramer, S.: Structural Regression Trees. In: Proc. 13th National Conference on Artificial Intelligence, AAAI-96, Cambridge/Menlo Park, AAAI Press/MIT Press (1996) 812–819
3. Kuznetsov, S.: Learning of Simple Conceptual Graphs from Positive and Negative Examples. In Zytkow, J., Rauch, J., eds.: Proc. Principles of Data Mining and Knowledge Discovery, Third European Conference, PKDD'99. Volume 1704 of Lecture Notes in Artificial Intelligence., Springer (1999) 384–392
4. Borgelt, C., Berthold, M.: Mining Molecular Fragments: Finding Relevant Substructures of Molecules. In Zhong, N., Yu, P., eds.: Proc. 2nd IEEE International Conference on Data Mining, ICDM'02, Piscataway, NJ, USA, IEEE Press (2002) 51–58
5. Inokuchi, A., Washio, T., Motoda, H.: Complete Mining of Frequent Patterns from Graphs: Mining Graph Data. Machine Learning **50** (2003) 321–354
6. Washio, T., Motoda, H.: State of the art of graph-based data mining. SIGKDD Explorations Newsletter **5** (2003) 59–68
7. Yan, X., Han, J.: gSpan: Graph-Based Substructure Pattern Mining. In: Proc. IEEE Int. Conf. on Data Mining, ICDM'02, IEEE Computer Society (2002) 721–724
8. Yan, X., Han, J.: CloseGraph: mining closed frequent graph patterns. In Getoor, L., Senator, T., Domingos, P., Faloutsos, C., eds.: Proc. of the 9th ACM SIGKDD Int. Conf. on Knowledge Discovery and Data Mining, KDD'03, ACM Press (2003) 286–295
9. Gonzalez, J., Holder, L., Cook, D.: Experimental Comparison of Graph-Based Relational Concept Learning with Inductive Logic Programming System. In Matwin, S., Sammut, C., eds.: Proc. Inductive Logic Programming, ILP'2002. Volume 2583 of Lecture Notes in Artificial Intelligence., Springer (2003) 84–100
10. Blinova, V., Dobrynin, D., Finn, V., Kuznetsov, S., Pankratova, E.: Toxicology analysis by means of the JSM-method. Bioinformatics **19** (2003) 1201–1207
11. Pasquier, N., Bastide, Y., Taouil, R., Lakhal, L.: Efficient Mining of Association Rules Using Closed Itemset Lattices. J. Inf. Systems **24** (1999) 25–46
12. Avidon, V., Pomerantsev, A.: Structure-Activity Relationship Oriented Languages for Chemical Structure Representation. J. Chem. Inf. Comput. Sci. **22** (1982) 207–214

13. Helma, C., King, R., Kramer, S., Srinvasan, A., eds.: Proc. of the Workshop on Predictive Toxicology Challegnge at the 5th Conference on Data Mining and Knowledge Discovery, PKDD'01, http://www.predictive-toxicology.org/ptc/ (2001, September 7)
14. Pfahringer, B.: (The Futility of) Trying to Predict Carcinogenicity of Chemical Compounds. In Helma, C., King, R., Kramer, S., Srinvasan, A., eds.: Proc. of the Workshop on Predictive Toxicology Challegnge at the 5th Conference on Data Mining and Knowledge Discovery, PKDD'01, http://www.predictive-toxicology.org/ptc/ (2001, September 7)
15. Kuznetsov, S.: Similarity operation on hypergraphs as a basis of plausible inference. In: Proc. 1st Soviet Conference on Artificial Intelligence. (1988) 442–448
16. Kuznetsov, S.: JSM-method as a machine learning method. Itogi Nauki i Tekhniki, ser. Informatika **15** (1991) 17–50 in Russian.
17. Kuznetsov, S., Obiedkov, S.: Comparing performance of algorithms for generating concept lattices. J. Exp. Theor. Artif. Intell. **14** (2002) 189–216
18. Ganter, B., Wille, R.: Formal Concept Analysis: Mathematical Foundations. Springer, Berlin, Heidelberg (1999)
19. Ganter, B., Kuznetsov, S.: Pattern Structures and Their Projections. In Stumme, G., Delugach, H., eds.: Proc. 9th Int. Conf. on Conceptual Structures, ICCS'01. Volume 2120 of Lecture Notes in Artificial Intelligence., Springer (2001) 129–142
20. Ganter, B., Grigoriev, P., Kuznetsov, S., Samokhin, M.: Concept-Based Data Mining with Scaled Labeled Graphs. In Delugach, H., Pfeiffer, H., Wolff, K., eds.: Proc. 12th Int. Conf. on Conceptual Structures, ICCS'04. Volume 3127 of Lecture Notes in Artificial Intelligence., Springer (2004) 94–108
21. Mitchell, T.: Machine Learning. The McGraw-Hill Companies (1997)
22. Finn, V.: Plausible Reasoning in Systems of JSM Type. Itogi Nauki i Tekhniki, Seriya Informatika **15** (1991) 54–101 in Russian.
23. Yan, L.S.: Study of carcinogenic mechanism of polycyclic aromatic hydrocarbons-extended bay region theory and its quantitative model. Carcinogenesis **6** (1985) 1–6
24. Birkhoff, G.: Lattice Theory. Amer. Math. Soc., Providence (1979)
25. Grigoriev, P.A., Yevtushenko, S.A.: Elements of an Agile Discovery Environment. In Grieser, G., Tanaka, Y., Yamamoto, A., eds.: Proc. 6th International Conference on Discovery Science, ICDS'03. Volume 2843 of Lecture Notes in Artificial Intelligence., Springer (2003) 309–316
26. Ganter, B., Kuznetsov, S.: Formalizing Hypotheses with Concepts. In Ganter, B., Mineau, G., eds.: Proc. 8th Int. Conf. on Conceptual Structures, ICCS'00. Volume 1867 of Lecture Notes in Artificial Intelligence., Springer (2000) 342–356
27. Witten, I., E.Frank: Data Mining: Practical Machine Learning Tools with Java Implementations. Morgan kaufmann, San Francisco (2000)
28. Cook, D., Holder, L.: Graph-Based Data Mining. IEEE Intelligent Systems **15** (2000) 32–41
29. Cameron-Jones, R., Quinlan, J.: Efficient Top-down Induction of Logic Programs. SIGART Bulletin **5** (1994) 33–42
30. Muggleton, S.: Inverse Entailment and Progol. New Generation Computing **13** (1995) 245–286
31. Gonzalez, J., Holder, L., Cook, D.: Application of Graph-Based Concept Learning to the Predictive Toxicology Domain. In Helma, C., King, R., Kramer, S., Srinvasan, A., eds.: Proc. Workshop on Predictive Toxicology Challegnge at the 5th Conference on Data Mining and Knowledge Discovery, PKDD'01, http://www.predictive-toxicology.org/ptc/ (2001, September 6)

32. Blinova, V.G., Dobrynin, D.A., Zholdakova, Z.I., Kharchevnikova, N.V.: Studies on the structure-activity relationships of alcohols by means of the JSM-method. Nauch. Tekh. Inf., ser. 2 (2001) 13–18 in Russian.
33. Guilian, W., Naibin, B.: Structure-activity relationships for rat and mouse LD50 of miscellaneous alcohols. Chemosphere **35** (1998) 1475–1483
34. Woo, Y.T., Lai, D., McLain, J., et al.: Use of mechanism-based structure-activity relationships analysis in carcinogenic ranking for drinking water desinfection by-products. Environ. Health Perspect. (2002) 75–87
35. Kharchevnikova, N.V., Blinova, V.G., Dobrynin, D.A., Maksin, M.V., Zholdakova, Z.I.: Application of JSM-method and quantum-chemical computations for predicting of carcinogenic potential and chronic toxicity in halogen-substituted aliphatic hydrocarbons. Nauch. Tekh. Inf., ser. 2 (2004) 21–28 in Russian.
36. Jerina, D., Lehr, R.: The bay-region theory: quantum mechanical approach to aromatic hydrocarbon-induced carcinogenecity. In: Microsomes and Drug Oxidation. Pergamon Press, Oxford (1977) 709–720
37. Dipple, A.: Polynuclear Aromatic Carcinogens. Number 172 in ACS Monograph. In: Chemical Carcinogens. Amer. Chem. Soc., Washington, DC (1976) 245–314
38. Lowe, J., Silverman, B.: Mo theory of ease of formation of carbocations derived from nonalternant polycyclic aromatic hydrocarbons. J. Amer. Chem. Soc. **106** (1984) 5955–5958

ILP Meets Knowledge Engineering: A Case Study

Francesca A. Lisi and Floriana Esposito

Dipartimento di Informatica, University of Bari, Italy
{lisi, esposito}@di.uniba.it

Abstract. The use of background knowledge is one of the distinguishing features of ILP with respect to other approaches to machine learning. Yet the representation formalisms traditionally chosen for the background knowledge in ILP seem to ignore the latest developments in Knowledge Engineering such as standard languages for ontologies. In this paper we present a case study that shows how current ILP systems can be made compliant with these standards in order to fulfill the expressive requirements of emerging application areas like the Semantic Web.

1 Introduction

ILP has been historically concerned with concept learning from examples and *background knowledge* within the representation framework of Horn clausal logic and with the aim of prediction. Though the use of background knowledge has been widely recognized as one of the strongest points of ILP when compared to other forms of inductive learning [22,24,16] and has been empirically studied in several application domains [17,29,27], the background knowledge in ILP systems is often not organized around a well-formed conceptual model. This practice seems to ignore latest developments in Knowledge Engineering (KE).

During the last decade increasing attention has been paid on *ontologies* and their role in Knowledge Engineering and (Intelligent) Information Systems [5,28]. In the philosophical sense, we may refer to an ontology as a particular system of categories accounting for a certain vision of the world. As such, this system does not depend on a particular language: Aristotle's ontology is always the same, independently of the language used to describe it. On the other hand, in its most prevalent use in Artificial Intelligence, an ontology refers to an engineering artifact (more precisely, produced according to the principles of *Ontological Engineering* [8]), constituted by a specific vocabulary used to describe a certain reality, plus a set of explicit assumptions regarding the intended meaning of the vocabulary words. This set of assumptions has usually the form of a first-order logical theory, where vocabulary words appear as unary or binary predicate names, respectively called concepts and relations. In the simplest case, an ontology describes a hierarchy of concepts related by subsumption relationships; in more sophisticated cases, suitable axioms are added in order to express other relationships between concepts and to constrain their intended interpretation.

S. Kramer and B. Pfahringer (Eds.): ILP 2005, LNAI 3625, pp. 209–226, 2005.

The two readings of ontology described above are indeed related each other, but in order to solve the terminological impasse the word conceptualization is used to refer to the philosophical reading as appear in the following definition, based on [9]: *An ontology is a formal explicit specification of a shared conceptualization for a domain of interest.* Among the other things, this definition emphasizes the fact that an ontology has to be specified in a language that comes with a formal semantics. Only by using such a formal approach ontologies provide the machine interpretable meaning of concepts and relations that is expected when using an ontology-based approach. Among the formalisms proposed by Ontological Engineering, the most currently used are *Description Logics* (DLs) [1]. DLs are fragments of first-order logic that are incomparable with Horn clausal logic as regards the expressive power [3].

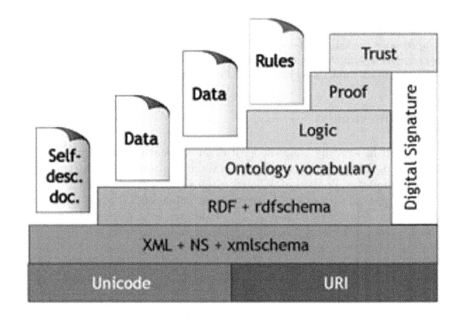

Fig. 1. Architecture of the Semantic Web

Ontology Engineering, notably its DL-based approach, is playing a relevant role in the definition of the *Semantic Web*. The Semantic Web is the vision of the World Wide Web enriched by machine-processable information which supports the user in his tasks [2]. The architecture of the Semantic Web is shown in Figure 1. It consists of several layers, each of which is equipped with an ad-hoc mark-up language. In particular, the design of the mark-up language for the *ontological layer*, OWL [12], has been based on the very expressive DL $\mathcal{SHIQ}$ [13].

In a very recent position paper, Page and Srinivasan have pointed out that the use of special-purpose reasoners in ILP is among the pressing issues that have arisen from the most challenging ILP applications of today [21]. In this paper we present a case study that shows how current ILP systems can meet the KE requirements and take benefit from the services offered by current KE tools in anticipation of an ILP application to the Semantic Web. In particular, we choose $\mathcal{AL}$-QuIn [19,18] as the ILP system and Protégé-2000 [20] as the KE tool. $\mathcal{AL}$-QuIn learns in $\mathcal{AL}$-log within the setting of characteristic induction from interpretations. $\mathcal{AL}$-log [6] is a hybrid language that integrates the DL $\mathcal{ALC}$ [25] and Datalog [4] by using $\mathcal{ALC}$ concept assertions essentially as *type constraints* on variables. Therefore $\mathcal{AL}$-QuIn can learn from relations and ontologies. Protégé-2000 is the most popular KE tool that supports OWL editing and reasoning. It has an extensible architecture, thus allowing for customization.

The paper is structured as follows. Section 2 describes $\mathcal{AL}$-QuIn. Section 3 describes Protégé-2000. Section 4 presents a data pre-processing module - implemented as an extension of Protégé-2000 - that allows $\mathcal{AL}$-QuIn to deal with OWL ontologies. Section 5 draws conclusions and outlines directions of future work. Appendix A and B briefly introduce $\mathcal{AL}$-log and OWL respectively.

2   The ILP System $\mathcal{AL}$-QuIn

The ILP system $\mathcal{AL}$-QuIn ($\mathcal{AL}$-log QUery INduction) [19,18] solves a variant of the frequent pattern discovery problem which takes concept hierarchies into account during the discovery process, thus yielding descriptions of a data set $\mathbf{r}$ at multiple granularity levels. More formally, given

- a data set $\mathbf{r}$ including a taxonomy $\mathcal{T}$ where a reference concept C_{ref} and task-relevant concepts are designated,
- a set $\{\mathcal{L}^l\}_{1 \leq l \leq maxG}$ of languages
- a set $\{minsup^l\}_{1 \leq l \leq maxG}$ of support thresholds

the problem of *frequent pattern discovery at l levels of description granularity*, $1 \leq l \leq maxG$, is to find the set $\mathcal{F}$ of all the patterns $P \in \mathcal{L}^l$ frequent in $\mathbf{r}$, namely P's with support s such that (i) $s \geq minsup^l$ and (ii) all ancestors of P w.r.t. $\mathcal{T}$ are frequent.

In $\mathcal{AL}$-QuIn the data set $\mathbf{r}$ is represented as an $\mathcal{AL}$-log knowledge base $\mathcal{B}$.

Example 1. As a running example, we consider an $\mathcal{AL}$-log knowledge base $\mathcal{B}_{\text{CIA}}$ that adds $\mathcal{ALC}$ ontologies to Datalog facts[1] extracted from the on-line 1996 CIA World Fact Book[2]. These ontologies contain concepts such as Country, EthnicGroup and Religion.

The language $\mathcal{L} = \{\mathcal{L}^l\}_{1 \leq l \leq maxG}$ of **patterns** allows for the generation of unary conjunctive queries, called $\mathcal{O}$-queries. Given a reference concept C_{ref}, an $\mathcal{O}$-*query* Q to an $\mathcal{AL}$-log knowledge base $\mathcal{B}$ is a (linked and connected) constrained Datalog clause of the form

---

[1] http://www.dbis.informatik.uni-goettingen.de/Mondial/mondial-rel-facts.flp
[2] http://www.odci.gov/cia/publications/factbook/

$$Q = q(X) \leftarrow \alpha_1, \ldots, \alpha_m \& X : C_{ref}, \gamma_2, \ldots, \gamma_n$$

where X is the *distinguished variable* and the remaining variables occurring in the body of Q are the *existential variables*. An $\mathcal{O}$-query $q(X) \leftarrow \& X : C_{ref}$ is called *trivial*. The language $\mathcal{L}$ of patterns for a given frequent pattern discovery problem is implicitly defined by a declarative bias specification. The *support* of an $\mathcal{O}$-query $Q \in \mathcal{L}^l$ w.r.t an $\mathcal{AL}$-log knowledge base $\mathcal{B}$ is defined as

$$supp(Q, \mathcal{B}) = | \ answerset(Q, \mathcal{B}) \ | \ / \ | \ answerset(Q_t, \mathcal{B}) \ |$$

where Q_t is the trivial $\mathcal{O}$-query for $\mathcal{L}$.

Example 2. Following Example 1, suppose that we are interested in finding hypotheses that characterize Middle East countries w.r.t. the religions believed and the languages spoken. An ad-hoc language $\mathcal{L}$ of patterns has been defined. Here `MiddleEastCountry` is the reference concept, and `Religion` and `Language` are task-relevant concepts. Examples of $\mathcal{O}$-queries belonging to $\mathcal{L}$ are:

Q_t= q(X) ← & X:MiddleEastCountry
Q= q(X) ← believes(X,Y), believes(X,Z)
         & X:MiddleEastCountry, Y:MonotheisticReligion

In particular, Q_t is the trivial $\mathcal{O}$-query for $\mathcal{L}$.

2.1   The Knowledge Base $\mathcal{B}$

In $\mathcal{AL}$-QuIn the knowledge base $\mathcal{B}$ is structured as illustrated in Figure 2.

The **background knowledge** is the portion $\mathcal{K}$ of $\mathcal{B}$ which encompasses the whole structural subsystem Σ and the intensional part of Π.

Example 3. The background knowledge $\mathcal{K}_{\mathrm{CIA}}$ of $\mathcal{B}_{\mathrm{CIA}}$ contains axioms such as

```
AsianCountry ⊑ Country.
MiddleEastEthnicGroup ⊑ EthnicGroup.
MiddleEastCountry ≡ AsianCountry ⊓ ∃Hosts.MiddleEastEthnicGroup.
MonotheisticReligion ⊑ Religion.
ChristianReligion ⊑ MonotheisticReligion.
MuslimReligion ⊑ MonotheisticReligion.
```

and membership assertions such as

```
'ARM':AsianCountry.
'IR':AsianCountry.
'Arab':MiddleEastEthnicGroup.
'Armenian':MiddleEastEthnicGroup.
<'ARM','Armenian'>:Hosts.
<'IR','Arab'>:Hosts.
'Armenian Orthodox':ChristianReligion.
'Shia':MuslimReligion.
'Sunni':MuslimReligion.
```

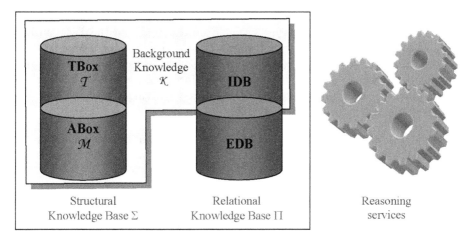

$\mathcal{AL}$-log Knowledge Base $\mathcal{B}$

Fig. 2. The hybrid knowledge base of $\mathcal{AL}$-QuIn

that define taxonomies for the concepts `Country`, `EthnicGroup` and `Religion` respectively. Note that Middle East countries (concept `MiddleEastCountry`) have been defined as Asian countries that host at least one Middle Eastern ethnic group. In particular, Armenia (`'ARM'`) and Iran (`'IR'`) are classified as Middle East countries. Also $\mathcal{K}_{\texttt{CIA}}$ includes constrained DATALOG clauses such as:

```
believes(CountryID, ReligionName)←
        religion(CountryID,ReligionName,Percent)
```

that defines a view on the relation `religion`.

Observations are in the form of $(q(a_i), \mathcal{A}_i)$ where a_i is an individual of C_{ref} and $\mathcal{A}_i$ are portions of $\mathcal{B} \setminus \mathcal{K}$, therefore portions of the extensional part of Π.

Example 4. By assuming `MiddleEastCountry` as reference concept, the observation $\mathcal{A}_{\texttt{IR}}$ contains DATALOG facts such as

```
language('IR','Persian',58).
religion('IR','Shia',89).
religion('IR','Sunni',10).
```

concerning the individual `'IR'` whereas the observation $\mathcal{A}_{\texttt{ARM}}$ consists of facts like

```
language('ARM','Armenian',96).
religion('ARM','Armenian Orthodox',94).
```

related to the individual `'ARM'`.

In $\mathcal{AL}$-QuIn the coverage problem reduces to a query answering problem. Indeed, an *answer* to an $\mathcal{O}$-query Q is a ground substitution θ for the distinguished variable of Q. An answer θ to an $\mathcal{O}$-query Q is a *correct (resp. computed) answer* w.r.t. an $\mathcal{AL}$-log knowledge base $\mathcal{B}$ if there exists at least one correct (resp. computed) answer to $body(Q)\theta$ w.r.t. $\mathcal{B}$. Therefore proving that an $\mathcal{O}$-query Q covers an observation $(q(a_i), \mathcal{A}_i)$ w.r.t. $\mathcal{K}$ equals to proving that $\theta_i = \{X/a_i\}$ is a correct answer to Q w.r.t. $\mathcal{B}_i = \mathcal{K} \cup \mathcal{A}_i$.

Example 5. Following Example 2 and Example 4, we want to check whether the $\mathcal{O}$-query Q covers the observation $(\mathtt{q('IR')}, \mathcal{A}_{\mathrm{IR}})$ w.r.t. $\mathcal{K}_{\mathrm{CIA}}$. This is equivalent to answering the query

$$Q^{(0)} = \leftarrow \mathtt{q('IR')}$$

w.r.t. $\mathcal{K}_{\mathrm{CIA}} \cup \mathcal{A}_{\mathrm{IR}} \cup Q$.

2.2   Saturation of the Observations w.r.t. the Background Knowledge

The internal representation language in $\mathcal{AL}$-QuIn is a kind of $\mathrm{DATALOG}^{OI}$ [18]. We would like to remind the reader that $\mathrm{DATALOG}^{OI}$ [26] is a subset of $\mathrm{DATALOG}^{\neq}$. In it the equational theory consists of the axioms of Clark's Equality Theory augmented with one rewriting rule that adds *inequality atoms* $s \neq t$ to any $P \in \mathcal{L}$ for each pair (s, t) of distinct terms occurring in P. Note that $\mathcal{ALC}$ constraints are rendered as *membership atoms*, e.g. $\mathtt{X:MiddleEastCountry}$ becomes $\mathtt{c\_MiddleEastCountry(X)}$. Thus, when implementing the coverage test in $\mathcal{AL}$-QuIn, the goal has been to reduce constrained SLD-resolution in $\mathcal{AL}$-log to SLD-resolution on $\mathrm{DATALOG}^{OI}$.

A crucial issue in this mapping is to deal with the satisfiability tests of $\mathcal{ALC}$ constraints w.r.t. Σ which are required by constrained SLD-resolution because they are performed by applying the tableau calculus for $\mathcal{ALC}$. The reasoning on the constraint part of $\mathcal{O}$-queries has been replaced by preliminary **saturation** steps of the observations w.r.t. the background knowledge $\mathcal{K}$. Saturation is a reformulation operator that enables ILP systems to take background knowledge into account during the generalization process [23]. It was originally proposed for the setting of learning from implications in Horn clausal logic where observations are represented as definite clauses. But it can be extended to the setting of learning from interpretations in $\mathcal{AL}$-log as follows: The observations are completed with concept assertions that can be derived from Σ.

Retrieving all the individuals of a concept C is known in DLs as the **retrieval** problem [1]. In $\mathcal{AL}$-QuIn, the retrieval for the *reference concept* is made only once at the beginning of the whole discovery process because it makes explicit knowledge of interest to all the levels of granularity. Conversely, retrieval for the *task-relevant concepts* follows the layering of $\mathcal{T}$: individuals of concepts belonging to the l-th layer $\mathcal{T}^l$ of $\mathcal{T}$ are retrieved before searching the space $\mathcal{L}^l$. This makes SLD-refutations of queries in $\mathcal{L}^l$ work only on extensional structural knowledge at the level l of description granularity (*levelwise saturation*).

Example 6. The concept assertions

```
'ARM':MiddleEastCountry.
'IR':MiddleEastCountry.
```

for the reference concept `MiddleEastCountry` are made explicit before the discovery process starts. Conversely the concept assertions

```
'Armenian Orthodox':MonotheisticReligion.
'Shia':MonotheisticReligion.
'Sunni':MonotheisticReligion.
```

for the task-relevant concept `MonotheisticReligion` (belonging to $\mathcal{T}^2$) are derived at the beginning of the search in $\mathcal{L}^2$.

The concept assertions returned by the retrieval tasks are then translated to DATALOG^{OI} and added to the facts derived from the intensional relational knowledge at the loading of each observation. The coverage test therefore concerns DATALOG^{OI} rewritings of both $\mathcal{O}$-queries and saturated observations.

Example 7. The DATALOG^{OI} rewriting

```
q(X) ← c_MiddleEastCountry(X), believes(X,Y), c_MonotheisticReligion(Y),
        believes(X,Z), Y≠Z
```

of Q covers the DATALOG^{OI} rewriting of the saturated observation $\hat{\mathcal{A}}_{\text{IR}}$:

```
c_MiddleEastCountry('IR')
believes('IR','Shia')
believes('IR','Sunni')
c_MonotheisticReligion('Shia')
c_MonotheisticReligion('Sunni')
...
```

Note that the translation from $\mathcal{ALC}$ to DATALOG^{OI} is possible because in $\mathcal{AL}$-QUIN *all* the concepts are named. This means that an equivalence axiom is required for each complex concept in the knowledge base. Equivalence axioms help keeping concept names (used within constrained DATALOG clauses) independent from concept definitions.

3   The KE Tool Protégé-2000

Protégé-2000[3] [7] is the latest version of the Protégé line of tools, created by the Stanford Medical Informatics (SMI) group at Stanford University, USA. It has a community of thousands of users. Although the development of Protégé has historically been mainly driven by biomedical applications, the system is domain-independent and has been successfully used for many other application areas as well.

---

[3] The   current   distribution   is   3.0   (February   2005),   freely   available   at http://protege.stanford.edu/ under the Mozilla open-source license.

3.1   The Architecture

Protégé-2000 is a Java-based standalone application to be installed and run in a local computer. The core of this application is the ontology editor. Like most other modeling tools, the architecture of Protégé-2000 is cleanly separated into a model part and a view part. Protégé-2000's model is the internal representation mechanism for ontologies and knowledge bases. Protégé-2000's view components provide a Graphical User Interface (GUI) to display and manipulate the underlying model.

Protégé-2000's **model** is based on a simple yet flexible metamodel [20], which is comparable to object-oriented and frame-based systems. It basically can represent ontologies consisting of classes, properties (*slots*), property characteristics (*facets* and *constraints*), and instances. Protégé-2000 provides an open Java API to query and manipulate models. An important strength of Protégé-2000 is that the Protégé-2000 metamodel itself is a Protégé-2000 ontology, with classes that represent classes, properties, and so on. For example, the default class in the Protege base system is called :STANDARD-CLASS, and has properties such as :NAME and :DIRECT-SUPERCLASSES. This structure of the metamodel enables easy extension and adaption to other representations.

Using the views of Protégé-2000's **GUI**, ontology designers basically create classes, assign properties to the classes, and then restrict the properties facets at certain classes. Using the resulting ontologies, Protégé-2000 is able to automatically generate user interfaces that support the creation of individuals (instances). For each class in the ontology, the system creates one form with editing components (*widgets*) for each property of the class. For example, for properties that can take single string values, the system would by default provide a text field widget. The generated forms can be further customized with Protégé-2000's form editor, where users can select alternative user interface widgets for their project. The user interface consists of panels (*tabs*) for editing classes, properties, forms and instances.

Protégé-2000 has an **extensible architecture**, i.e. an architecture that allows special-purpose extensions (aka *plug-ins*) to be easily integrated. These extensions usually perform functions not provided by the Protégé-2000 standard distribution (other types of visualization, new import and export formats, etc.), implement applications that use Protégé-2000 ontologies, or allow configuring the ontology editor. Most of these plug-ins are available in the Protégé-2000 Plug-in Library, where contributions from many different research groups can be found. Three kinds of plug-ins can be developed for Protégé-2000:

- *Tab plug-ins.* These are the most common types in Protégé-2000, and provide functions that are not covered by the standard distribution of the ontology editor. To perform their task, tab plug-ins extend the ontology editor with an additional tab so that users can access its functions from it.
- *Slot widget plug-ins.* These are used to display and edit slot values without the default display and edit facilities. There are also slot widgets for displaying images, video and audio, and for managing dates, for measurement units, for swapping values between slots, etc.

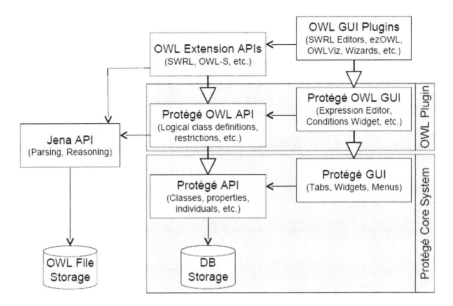

Fig. 3. Architecture of the OWL Plugin for Protégé-2000

- *Backend plug-ins.* These enable users to export and import ontologies in different formats. E.g., there is a backend for storing and retrieving ontologies from databases so that not only ontologies can be stored as CLIPS files (the default storage format used by Protégé-2000) but they can also be stored in any database JDBC compatible.

3.2 The OWL Plugin

As illustrated in Figure 3, the OWL Plugin [15] extends the Protégé-2000 model and its API with classes to represent the OWL specification. In particular it supports RDF(S), OWL Lite, OWL DL (except for anonymous global class axioms, which need to be given a name by the user) and significant parts of OWL Full (including metaclasses). The **OWL API** basically encapsulates the internal mapping and thus shields the user from error-prone low-level access. Furthermore the OWL Plugin provides a comprehensive mapping between its extended API and the standard OWL parsing library Jena[4]. The presence of a secondary representation of an OWL ontology in terms of Jena objects means that the user is able to invoke arbitrary Jena-based services such as interfaces to classifiers, query languages, or visualization tools permanently.

Based on the above mentioned metamodel and API extensions, the OWL Plugin provides several custom-tailored **GUI components** for OWL. When started, the system displays the five tabs shown in Figure 4. Most ontology designers will focus on the *OWL classes* and *Properties* tabs. The *Forms* and *Individuals* tabs are mostly geared for the acquisition of Semantic Web contents,

---
[4] http://jena.sourceforge.net

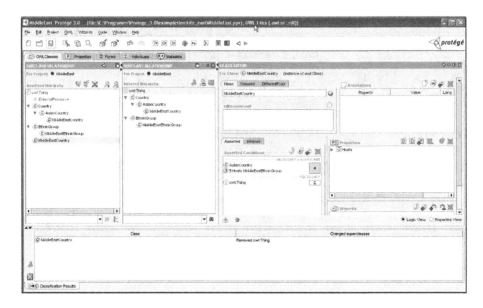

Fig. 4. Interface of the OWL Plugin for Protégé-2000

while the *Metadata* tab allows users to specify global ontology settings such as imports and namespaces. With reference to the OWL ontology displayed in Figure 4, conditions widget in the *OWL classes* tab shows the definition of the concept `MiddleEastCountry` in the form of an equivalence axiom. It has been composed with the *Expression Editor*. The stored OWL file for this ontology is reported in Figure 5.

The OWL Plugin provides **direct access to DL reasoners** such as RACER [10]. The current user interface supports two types of DL reasoning:

Consistency checking (i.e., the test whether a class could have instances) can be invoked either for all classes with a single mouse click, or for selected classes only. Inconsistent classes are marked with a red bordered icon.

Classification (i.e., inferring a new subsumption tree from the asserted definitions) can be invoked either for the whole ontology, or for selected subtrees only. When the classify button is pressed, the system determines the OWL species, because some reasoners are unable to handle OWL Full ontologies. This is done using the validation service from the Jena library. If the ontology is in OWL Full, the system attempts to convert the ontology temporarily into OWL DL. Once the ontology has been converted into OWL DL, a full consistency check is performed, because inconsistent classes cannot be classified correctly. Finally, the classification results are stored until the next invocation of the classifier, and can be browsed separately (see, e.g., the panel *Inferred Hierarchy* in Figure 4). Note that OWL files store only the subsumptions that have been asserted by the user. However, experience has shown that, in order to edit and correct their ontologies, users need to

Fig. 5. An example of OWL file generated by the OWL Plugin for Protégé-2000

distinguish between what they have *asserted* and what the classifier has *inferred*. The OWL Plugin addresses this need by displaying both hierarchies and making available extensive information on the inferences made during classification.

The OWL Plugin can be further extended, e.g. to support OWL-based languages like the Semantic Web Rule Language (SWRL) [11] or to implement DL reasoners directly on top of the OWL API or Jena.

4   From OWL to Datalog: A Data Pre-processing Module for $\mathcal{AL}$-QuIn

A module has been developed to support the saturation of observations w.r.t. a OWL background knowledge Σ in $\mathcal{AL}$-QuIn. To achieve this goal according to the requirements specified in Section 2.2, it supplies the following functionalities:

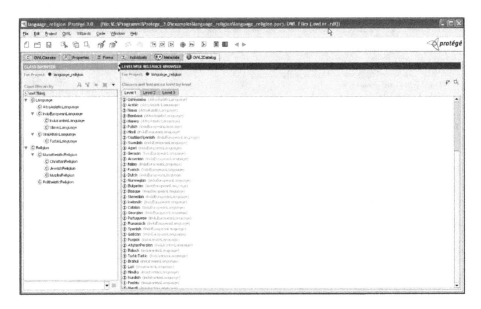

Fig. 6. Interface of the OWL2DATALOG Plugin for Protégé-2000

- levelwise retrieval w.r.t. Σ
- transformation of concept assertions of Σ to DATALOG facts

The latter relies on the former, meaning that the results of the levelwise retrieval are exported to DATALOG.

The module, called OWL2DATALOG, is implemented as an extension of Protégé-2000, more precisely on top of the OWL Plugin described in Section 3.2. Indeed, as shown in Figure 6, it adds a new *tab* to the standard interface of the OWL Plugin for Protégé-2000. The tab consists of two panels: a *Class Browser* and a *LevelWise Instance Browser*. The former shows the OWL classes of Σ and their hierarchical arrangement. The latter shows the instances and their membership, both the asserted one and the inferred one, to the classes of Σ in a levelwise manner. E.g., the individual **Arabic** has been asserted as instance of the concept **AfroAsiaticLanguage** (put in rounded brackets just after the instance name in the *LevelWise Instance Browser* panel). As an effect of the levelwise retrieval it appears among the instances of concepts belonging to the level $l = 1$ in the subsumption hierarchy. A button *Export Assertions to DATALOG* is available on the *LevelWise Instance Browser* panel for the export of the extensional part of Σ to DATALOG.

In Table 1 we have reported the results of a performance evaluation of the OWL2DATALOG Plugin on the OWL ontology, shown in Figure 6, concerning languages spoken and religions believed all over the world. For each of the three hierarchical levels of the ontology, Table 1 specifies the number of concepts, the number of asserted instances, the number of instances that have been inferred

Table 1. Performance of OWL2DATALOG on the OWL ontology shown in Figure 6

l	# concepts	# asserted instances	# inferred instances	retrieval (secs)	export (secs)
1	2	9	121	1.12	1.47
2	5	47	74	0.36	0.93
3	6	74	0	0.00	0.05

by retrieval, retrieval time and export time. Note that fast execution times of OWL2DATALOG are due to the underlying OWL reasoner.

5   Conclusions and Future Work

In this paper we have made $\mathcal{AL}$-QUIN, an existing ILP system, compliant with the latest developments in Knowledge Engineering. The solution proposed follows engineering principles because it promotes:

- the reuse of existing systems ($\mathcal{AL}$-QUIN and Protégé-2000)
- the adherence to standards (either normative - see OWL for KE - or *de facto* - see Prolog for ILP)

Furthermore the resulting artifact overcomes the capabilities of the two systems when considered stand-alone. In particular, $\mathcal{AL}$-QUIN was originally conceived to deal with $\mathcal{ALC}$ ontologies. Since OWL is equivalent to $\mathcal{SHIQ}$ and $\mathcal{ALC}$ is a fragment of $\mathcal{SHIQ}$, the Protégé-2000 plugin OWL2DATALOG allows $\mathcal{AL}$-QUIN to deal with more expressive ontological background knowlege.

The OWL2DATALOG Plugin supplies a saturation service to $\mathcal{AL}$-QUIN. In [18] saturation has been mentioned as a way of speeding-up the evaluation of candidate hypotheses in ILP systems. In this paper it is intended as a way of compiling DL-based background knowledge down to the usual DATALOG-like formalisms of ILP systems. A related work to ours is the pre-processing method proposed by Kietz [14] to enable legacy ILP systems to learn in the hybrid language CARIN-$\mathcal{ALN}$.

The OWL2DATALOG Plugin is just a preliminary 'real' step towards the application of $\mathcal{AL}$-QUIN to Semantic Web Mining. For the future we plan to make $\mathcal{AL}$-QUIN tighter-coupled with Protégé-2000 by developing a middleware component. Also we intend to implement a plugin for translating hypotheses generated by $\mathcal{AL}$-QUIN from $\mathcal{AL}$-log to SWRL.

Acknowledgement. We are grateful to Michèle Sebag and Peter Flach for the useful discussions on some issues faced in this paper. Also we acknowledge the financial support of the COFIN-PRIN 2003 project "Tecniche di Intelligenza Artificiale per il Reperimento di Informazione di Qualità sul Web" funded by the *Ministero dell'Istruzione, dell'Università, e della Ricerca Scientifica*.

Table 2. Syntax and semantics of $\mathcal{ALC}$

bottom (resp. top) concept	$\bot$ (resp. $\top$)	$\emptyset$ (resp. $\Delta^{\mathcal{I}}$)
atomic concept	A	$A^{\mathcal{I}} \subseteq \Delta^{\mathcal{I}}$
role	R	$R^{\mathcal{I}} \subseteq \Delta^{\mathcal{I}} \times \Delta^{\mathcal{I}}$
individual	a	$a^{\mathcal{I}} \in \Delta^{\mathcal{I}}$
concept negation	$\neg C$	$\Delta^{\mathcal{I}} \setminus C^{\mathcal{I}}$
concept conjunction	$C \sqcap D$	$C^{\mathcal{I}} \cap D^{\mathcal{I}}$
concept disjunction	$C \sqcup D$	$C^{\mathcal{I}} \cup D^{\mathcal{I}}$
value restriction	$\forall R.C$	$\{x \in \Delta^{\mathcal{I}} \mid \forall y \; (x,y) \in R^{\mathcal{I}} \rightarrow y \in C^{\mathcal{I}}\}$
existential restriction	$\exists R.C$	$\{x \in \Delta^{\mathcal{I}} \mid \exists y \; (x,y) \in R^{\mathcal{I}} \wedge y \in C^{\mathcal{I}}\}$
equivalence axiom	$C \equiv D$	$C^{\mathcal{I}} = D^{\mathcal{I}}$
subsumption axiom	$C \sqsubseteq D$	$C^{\mathcal{I}} \subseteq D^{\mathcal{I}}$
concept assertion	$a : C$	$a^{\mathcal{I}} \in C^{\mathcal{I}}$
role assertion	$\langle a,b \rangle : R$	$(a^{\mathcal{I}}, b^{\mathcal{I}}) \in R^{\mathcal{I}}$

A The KR&R System $\mathcal{AL}$-Log

The system $\mathcal{AL}$-log [6] integrates two KR&R systems: Structural and relational.

The **structural subsystem** Σ is based on $\mathcal{ALC}$ [25] and allows for the specification of knowledge in terms of classes (*concepts*), binary relations between classes (*roles*), and instances (*individuals*). Complex concepts can be defined from atomic concepts and roles by means of constructors (see Table 2). Also Σ can state both is-a relations between concepts (*axioms*) and instance-of relations between individuals (resp. couples of individuals) and concepts (resp. roles) (*assertions*). An *interpretation* $\mathcal{I} = (\Delta^{\mathcal{I}}, \cdot^{\mathcal{I}})$ for Σ consists of a domain $\Delta^{\mathcal{I}}$ and a mapping function $\cdot^{\mathcal{I}}$. In particular, individuals are mapped to elements of $\Delta^{\mathcal{I}}$ such that $a^{\mathcal{I}} \neq b^{\mathcal{I}}$ if $a \neq b$ (*unique names* assumption). If $\mathcal{O} \subseteq \Delta^{\mathcal{I}}$ and $\forall a \in \mathcal{O} : a^{\mathcal{I}} = a$, $\mathcal{I}$ is called $\mathcal{O}$-*interpretation*. The main reasoning task for Σ is the *consistency check*. This test is performed with a *tableau calculus* that starts with the tableau branch $S = \Sigma$ and adds assertions to S by means of *propagation rules* until either a contradiction is generated or an interpretation satisfying S can be easily obtained from it.

The **relational subsystem** Π extends DATALOG [4] by using the so-called *constrained* DATALOG *clause*, i.e. clauses of the form

$$\alpha_0 \leftarrow \alpha_1, \ldots, \alpha_m \& \gamma_1, \ldots, \gamma_n$$

where $m \geq 0$, $n \geq 0$, α_i are DATALOG atoms and γ_j are *constraints* of the form $s : C$ where s is either a constant or a variable already appearing in the clause, and C is an $\mathcal{ALC}$ concept. A constrained DATALOG clause of the form $\leftarrow \beta_1, \ldots, \beta_m \& \gamma_1, \ldots, \gamma_n$ is called *constrained* DATALOG *query*. For an $\mathcal{AL}$-*log knowledge base* $\mathcal{B} = \langle \Sigma, \Pi \rangle$ to be acceptable, it must satisfy the following conditions: (i) The set of predicate symbols appearing in Π is disjoint from the set of concept and role symbols appearing in Σ; (ii) The alphabet of constants used in Π coincides with $\mathcal{O}$; (iii) For each clause in Π, each variable occurring in the constraint part occurs also in the DATALOG part. The interaction between Σ and Π allows the notion of *substitution* to be straightforwardly extended from DATALOG to $\mathcal{AL}$-log. It is also at the basis of a model-theoretic semantics for $\mathcal{AL}$-log. An *interpretation* $\mathcal{J}$ for $\mathcal{B}$ is the union of an $\mathcal{O}$-interpretation $\mathcal{I}_{\mathcal{O}}$ for Σ and an Herbrand interpretation $\mathcal{I}_{\mathcal{H}}$ for Π_D (i.e. the set of DATALOG clauses obtained from the clauses of Π by deleting their constraints). The notion of *logical consequence* paves the way to the definition of *correct answer* and *answer set* similarly to DATALOG. Reasoning for an $\mathcal{AL}$-log knowledge base $\mathcal{B}$ is based on *constrained SLD-resolution*, i.e. an extension of SLD-resolution with the tableau calculus to deal with constraints. *Constrained SLD-refutation* is a complete and sound method for answering queries, being the definition of *computed answer* and *success set* analogous to DATALOG. A big difference from DATALOG is that the derivation of a constrained empty clause does not represent a refutation but actually infers that the query is true in those models of $\mathcal{B}$ that satisfy its constraints. Therefore in order to answer a query it is necessary to collect enough derivations ending with a constrained empty clause such that every model of $\mathcal{B}$ satisfies the constraints associated with the final query of at least one derivation.

B   The Semantic Mark-Up Language OWL

The Web Ontology Language OWL [12] is a semantic mark-up language for publishing and sharing ontologies on the World Wide Web. An OWL ontology is an RDF graph, which is in turn a set of RDF triples. As with any RDF graph, an OWL ontology graph can be written in many different syntactic forms. However, the meaning of an OWL ontology is solely determined by the RDF graph. Thus, it is allowable to use other syntactic RDF/XML forms, as long as these result in the same underlying set of RDF triples.

OWL provides three increasingly expressive sublanguages designed for use by specific communities of implementers and users.

- *OWL Lite* supports those users primarily needing a classification hierarchy and simple constraints. E.g., while it supports cardinality constraints, it only permits cardinality values of 0 or 1. It should be simpler to provide tool support for OWL Lite than its more expressive relatives, and OWL Lite provides a quick migration path for thesauri and other taxonomies. OWL Lite also has a lower formal complexity than OWL DL.
- *OWL DL* supports those users who want the maximum expressiveness while retaining computational completeness and decidability. OWL DL includes all OWL language constructs, but they can be used only under certain restrictions (e.g., while a class may be a subclass of many classes, a class cannot be an instance of another class). OWL DL is so named due to its correspondence with the very expressive DL $\mathcal{SHIQ}$ [13] which thus provides a logical foundation to OWL.
- *OWL Full* is meant for users who want maximum expressiveness and the syntactic freedom of RDF with no computational guarantees. For example,

in OWL Full a class can be treated simultaneously as a collection of individuals and as an individual in its own right. OWL Full allows an ontology to augment the meaning of the pre-defined (RDF or OWL) vocabulary. It is unlikely that any reasoning software will be able to support complete reasoning for every feature of OWL Full.

Each of these sublanguages is an extension of its simpler predecessor, both in what can be legally expressed and in what can be validly concluded.

The mapping from $\mathcal{ALC}$ to OWL is reported in Table 3.

Table 3. Mapping from $\mathcal{ALC}$ to OWL

$\neg C$	```<owl:Class>```
	``` <owl:complementOf><owl:Class rdf:ID="C" /></owl:complementOf>```
	```</owl:Class>```

$C \sqcap D$	```<owl:Class>```
	``` <owl:intersectionOf rdf:parseType="Collection">```
	``` <owl:Class rdf:ID="C" /><owl:Class rdf:ID="D" />```
	``` </owl:intersectionOf>```
	```</owl:Class>```

$C \sqcup D$	```<owl:Class>```
	``` <owl:unionOf rdf:parseType="Collection">```
	``` <owl:Class rdf:ID="C" /><owl:Class rdf:ID="D" />```
	``` </owl:unionOf>```
	```</owl:Class>```

$\exists R.C$	```<owl:Restriction>```
	``` <owl:onProperty rdf:resource="#R" />```
	``` <owl:someValuesFrom rdf:resource="#C" />```
	```</owl:Restriction>```

$\forall R.C$	```<owl:Restriction>```
	``` <owl:onProperty rdf:resource="#R" />```
	``` <owl:allValuesFrom rdf:resource="#C" />```
	```</owl:Restriction>```

$C \equiv D$	```<owl:Class rdf:ID="C">```
	``` <owl:sameAs rdf:resource="#D" />```
	```</owl:Class>```

$C \sqsubseteq D$	```<owl:Class rdf:ID="C">```
	``` <rdfs:subClassOf rdf:resource="#D" />```
	```</owl:Class>```

$a : C$	```<C rdf:ID="a" />```
$\langle a,b \rangle : R$	```<C rdf:ID="a"><R rdf:resource="#b" />```

References

1. F. Baader, D. Calvanese, D. McGuinness, D. Nardi, and P.F. Patel-Schneider, editors. *The Description Logic Handbook: Theory, Implementation and Applications.* Cambridge University Press, 2003.

2. T. Berners-Lee, J. Hendler, and O. Lassila. The Semantic Web. *Scientific American*, May, 2001.
3. A. Borgida. On the relative expressiveness of description logics and predicate logics. *Artificial Intelligence*, 82(1–2):353–367, 1996.
4. S. Ceri, G. Gottlob, and L. Tanca. *Logic Programming and Databases.* Springer, 1990.
5. B. Chandrasekaran, J.R. Josephson, and V.R. Benjamins. What are ontologies, and why do we need them? *IEEE Intelligent Systems*, 14(1):20–26, 1999.
6. F.M. Donini, M. Lenzerini, D. Nardi, and A. Schaerf. $\mathcal{AL}$-log: Integrating Datalog and Description Logics. *J. of Intelligent Information Systems*, 10(3):227–252, 1998.
7. J.H. Gennari, M.A. Musen, R.W. Fergerson, W.E. Grosso, M. Crubézy, H. Eriksson, N. Fridman Noy, and S. W. Tu. The evolution of Protégé: An environment for knowledge-based systems development. *International Journal of Human-Computer Studies*, 58(1):89–123, 2003.
8. A. Gómez-Pérez, M. Fernández-López, and O. Corcho. *Ontological Engineering.* Springer, 2004.
9. T. Gruber. A translation approach to portable ontology specifications. *Knowledge Acquisition*, 5:199–220, 1993.
10. V. Haarslev and R. Möller. Description of the RACER System and its Applications. In C.A. Goble, D.L. McGuinness, R. Möller, and P.F. Patel-Schneider, editors, *Working Notes of the 2001 Int. Description Logics Workshop*, volume 49 of *CEUR Workshop Proceedings*, 2001.
11. I. Horrocks and P.F. Patel-Schneider. A Proposal for an OWL Rules Language. In *Proc. of the 13th Int. World Wide Web Conference*, pages 723–731. ACM, 2004.
12. I. Horrocks, P.F. Patel-Schneider, and F. van Harmelen. From $\mathcal{SHIQ}$ and RDF to OWL: The making of a web ontology language. *Journal of Web Semantics*, 1(1):7–26, 2003.
13. I. Horrocks, U. Sattler, and S. Tobies. Practical reasoning for very expressive description logics. *Logic Journal of the IGPL*, 8(3):239–263, 2000.
14. J.-U. Kietz. Learnability of description logic programs. In S. Matwin and C. Sammut, editors, *Inductive Logic Programming*, volume 2583 of *Lecture Notes in Artificial Intelligence*, pages 117–132. Springer, 2003.
15. H. Knublauch, M.A. Musen, and A.L. Rector. Editing Description Logic Ontologies with the Protégé OWL Plugin. In V. Haarslev and R. Möller, editors, *Proc. of the 2004 Int. Workshop on Description Logics*, volume 104 of *CEUR Workshop Proceedings*, 2004.
16. N. Lavrač and S. Džeroski. Background knowledge and declarative bias in inductive concept learning. In Klaus P. Jantke, editor, *Analogical and Inductive Inference*, volume 642 of *Lecture Notes in Computer Science*, pages 51–71. Springer, 1992.
17. N. Lavrač, S. Džeroski, V. Pirnat, and V. Krizman. The utility of background knowledge in learning medical diagnostic rules. *Applied Artificial Intelligence*, 7(3):273–293, 1993.
18. F.A. Lisi and F. Esposito. Efficient Evaluation of Candidate Hypotheses in $\mathcal{AL}$-log. In R. Camacho, R. King, and A. Srinivasan, editors, *Inductive Logic Programming*, volume 3194 of *Lecture Notes in Artificial Intelligence*, pages 216–233. Springer, 2004.
19. F.A. Lisi and D. Malerba. Ideal Refinement of Descriptions in $\mathcal{AL}$-log. In T. Horvath and A. Yamamoto, editors, *Inductive Logic Programming*, volume 2835 of *Lecture Notes in Artificial Intelligence*, pages 215–232. Springer, 2003.

20. N. Fridman Noy, R.W. Fergerson, and M.A. Musen. The Knowledge Model of Protégé-2000: Combining Interoperability and Flexibility. In R. Dieng and O. Corby, editors, *Knowledge Acquisition, Modeling and Management*, volume 1937 of *Lecture Notes in Computer Science*, pages 17–32. Springer, 2000.
21. D. Page and A. Srinivasan. ILP: A short look back and a longer look forward. *Journal of Machine Learning Research*, 4:415–430, 2003.
22. M.J. Pazzani and D.F. Kibler. The utility of knowledge in inductive learning. *Machine Learning*, 9:57–94, 1992.
23. C. Rouveirol. Flattening and saturation: Two representation changes for generalization. *Machine Learning*, 14(1):219–232, 1994.
24. C. Rouveirol and L. De Raedt. The use of background knowledge for generalization in ILP. In C. Rouveirol, editor, *Proceedings of the ECAI-92 Workshop on Logical Approaches to Machine Learning*, 1992.
25. M. Schmidt-Schauss and G. Smolka. Attributive concept descriptions with complements. *Artificial Intelligence*, 48(1):1–26, 1991.
26. G. Semeraro, F. Esposito, D. Malerba, N. Fanizzi, and S. Ferilli. A logic framework for the incremental inductive synthesis of Datalog theories. In N.E. Fuchs, editor, *Proc. of 7th Int. Workshop on Logic Program Synthesis and Transformation*, volume 1463 of *LNCS*, pages 300–321. Springer, 1998.
27. A. Srinivasan, R.D. King, and M. Bain. An empirical study of the use of relevance information in inductive logic programming. *Journal of Machine Learning Research*, 4:369–383, 2003.
28. S. Staab and R. Studer, editors. *Handbook on Ontologies*. International Handbooks on Information Systems. Springer, 2004.
29. M. Turcotte, S. Muggleton, and M.J.E. Sternberg. The effect of relational background knowledge on learning of protein three-dimensional fold signatures. *Machine Learning*, 43(1/2):81–95, 2001.

Spatial Clustering of Structured Objects

Donato Malerba, Annalisa Appice, Antonio Varlaro, and Antonietta Lanza

Dipartimento di Informatica, Università degli Studi di Bari,
via Orabona, 4 - 70126 Bari - Italy
{malerba, appice, varlaro, lanza}@di.uniba.it

Abstract. Clustering is a fundamental task in Spatial Data Mining where data consists of observations for a site (e.g. areal units) descriptive of one or more (spatial) primary units, possibly of different type, collected within the same site boundary. The goal is to group structured objects, i.e. data collected at different sites, such that data inside each cluster models the continuity of socio-economic or geographic environment, while separate clusters model variation over the space. Continuity is evaluated according to the spatial organization arising in data, namely discrete spatial structure, expressing the (spatial) relations between separate sites implicitly defined by their geometrical representation and positioning. Data collected within sites that are (transitively) connected in the discrete spatial structure are clustered together according to the similarity on multi-relational descriptions representing their internal structure. CORSO is a novel spatial data mining method that resorts to a multi-relational approach to learn relational spatial data and exploits the concept of neighborhood to capture relational constraints embedded in the discrete spatial structure. Relational data are expressed in a first-order formalism and similarity among structured objects is computed as degree of matching with respect to a common generalization. The application to real-world spatial data is reported.

1 Introduction

Within both social and environmental sciences much of data is collected in a spatial framework, where data consists of measurements or observations of one or more attributes taken at specific sites which are spatially-referenced. This means that geometrical representation and relative positioning of sites are recorded to express the spatial organization arising in social and environmental data. A simple form of spatially referenced data is point data where observations are taken at fixed point sites of space and represented as triple $\{(x_i, y_i), z_i\}$, such that (x_i, y_i) references the location of a point i with respect to some coordinate system, while z_i is the vector of measured attributes observed at site i. However, operations and activities of private and public institutions generally deal with space in terms of areas (irregular partitions or regular grid) and not points.

Areal data can be represented as point data by identifying each area with its centroid [24], but this is restrictive when observations for an area are descriptive of one or more (spatial) primary units, possibly of different type, collected

S. Kramer and B. Pfahringer (Eds.): ILP 2005, LNAI 3625, pp. 227–245, 2005.
© Springer-Verlag Berlin Heidelberg 2005

within the same area boundary. In this case, data includes both attributes that relate to primary units or areas and attributes that refer to relations between primary units (e.g., contact frequencies between households) and between areal units (e.g., migration rates). Moreover, spatial-referencing poses a further degree of complexity due to the fact that the geometrical representation (point, line or polygon) and the relative positioning of primary units or areal units implicitly define spatial features (properties and relations) of different nature, that is, geometrical (e.g. area, distance), directional (e.g. north, south) and topological (e.g. crosses, on top) features. This relational information may be responsible for the spatial variation among areal units and it is extremely useful in descriptive modeling of different distributions holding for spatial subsets of data. An extra consequence is that observations across space cannot be considered independent due to the spatial continuity of events occurring in the space. Continuity of events over neighbor areas is a consequence of social patterns and environmental constraints that deal with space in terms of regions and allow to identify a mosaic of nearly homogeneous areas in which each patch of the mosaic is demarcated from its neighbors in terms of attributes levels. For instance, the spatial continuity of an environmental phenomenon such as air pollution may depend on the geographical arrangements of pollution sources. As a model for this spatial continuity, the regional concept encourages the analyst to exploit spatial correlation following from the first Law of Geography [22], according to which everything is related to everything else, but near things are more related than distant things. This means that primary units forming areal units of analysis will tend to be essentially identical members of same populations in nearby locations. In this spatial framework, relations among areal units of analysis are expressed in form of relational constraints that represent a discrete spatial structure arising in spatial data, while relations among primary units within an area model the spatial structure of each single areal unit of analysis.

Grouping connected areas to form clusters of homogeneous regions, i.e., spatial clustering, is a fundamental task of Spatial Data Mining. In this paper, we propose to represent the discrete spatial structure as a graph, where nodes are associated with relational descriptions of areal units to be clustered, while links express relational constraints which typically reflect spatial relations such as adjacency. In this way, discontinuity in the graph represents some obstacles in the space. Exploiting this graph-based representation, we present a clustering method, named CORSO (Clustering Of Related Structured Objects), that resorts to a multi-relational approach [2] to model homogeneity over relational structure embedded in spatial data and exploits the concept of graph neighborhood to capture relational constraints embedded in the graph edges. Units associated with (transitively) graph connected nodes are clustered together according to the similarity of their relational descriptions.

The paper is organized as follows. In the next section we discuss some related works. The method is presented in Section 3. Two applications of spatial clustering for topographic map interpretation and geo-referenced census data analysis are reported in Section 4, while conclusions are drawn in Section 5.

2   Background and Motivation

The problem of clustering spatial data has been investigated by some researchers, but while a lot of research has been conducted on detecting spatial clusters from point data, only few works deal with areal data. For instance, Ng and Han [18] have proposed to extend the k-medoid partitioning algorithm [12] to group point data in a set of k clusters. However, the k-medoid partitioning appears well suited only when spatial clusters are of convex shape and similar size, and the number k is reasonably a-priori estimated. Moreover, the method suffers from severe limitations when clustering large spatial dataset [5] due to the complexity of computing distance between medoid points representing each pair of clusters. These efficiency drawbacks are partially alleviated when adopting both proximity and density information to achieve high quality spatial clusters in a sub-quadratic time without requiring the user to a-priori specify the number of clusters [7]. Similarly, DBSCAN [6] exploits density information to efficiently detect clusters of arbitrary shape from point spatial data with noise. The key idea of density-based clustering is that for each point of a cluster, a neighborhood of a given radius has to contain a minimum number (cardinality) of data points. Neighborhood is determined according to the Euclidean distance. However, when observations concern areal units, Euclidean distance may not be appropriate to neighborhood determination. To this purpose, Sander et al. [21] have proposed GDBSCAN that generalizes DBSCAN in order to cluster not only point data but also spatially extended objects (lines or areas) taking into account both spatial and non spatial attributes when defining cardinality. Indeed, GDBSCAN extends the notion of neighborhood to any binary predicate that is symmetric and reflexive (e.g. distance, meet) and imposes a discrete spatial structure on data that guides the clustering detection. This discrete spatial structure can be equivalently modeled as links of a graph, namely neighborhood or proximity graph [23], whose nodes represent the units to be clustered. The graph-based representation of data, that is extensively used in pattern recognition [9], perfectly fits the spatial need of representing the relational constraints among spatial units to be clustered. In this perspective, it is clear that hybrid methods [17] which combine data clustering with graph-partitioning technique have some interesting applications properly in spatial clustering [8].

However even when clustering takes into account relational constraints forming discrete spatial structure, all methods reported above suffer from severe limitations due to the single-table representation [2]. Data to be clustered is represented in a single table (or relation) of a relational database, such that each row (or tuple) corresponds to a single unit of the sample population and the columns correspond to both spatial and a-spatial properties of these units. This representation is clearly inadequate when describing observations concerning several (spatial) primary units, eventually of different types, which are naturally modeled as many data tables as the number of object types and interactions. Some methods for mining clusters on (multi-)relational data have been investigated by resorting to the field of relational data mining. For instance, RDBC [13] forms clusters bottom-up in an agglomerative fashion that uses the distance metric introduced in [11] and handles relational representations with lists and other functional terms as well. In contrast, C0.5 [1] adopts logical decision trees for clustering purposes by choosing split literals that maximize the distance between two resulting subsets (clusters) of examples. However, differently from RDBC, distance in literal choice is in this case estimated according to a user-provided propositional distance.

Although these relational clustering methods present several interesting aspects, detecting spatial clusters is a more complex task. Indeed, relational clustering methods generally work in the learning from interpretation setting [20] that allows to mine examples and background knowledge stored as Prolog programs exploiting expressiveness of first-order representation during clustering detection. The interpretation corresponding to each example e given the background knowledge BK is here intended as the minimal Herbrand model of $e \land BK$ and the implicit assumption is that separate interpretations are independent. This leads to ignore relational constraints eventually relating separate interpretations (e.g. geographic contiguity of areal units). This problem also occurs in graph-based relational learning methods [10] where graphs appear as a flexible representation for relational domains. However, these methods generally continue to work in learning from interpretation settings and thus ignore relations among graphs representing separate examples. In contrast, we propose to combine a graph-based partitioning algorithm with a relational clustering method to mine both relational constraints imposing the discrete spatial structure and relational data representing structured objects (spatial unit) to be clustered.

3   The Method

In a quite general formulation, the problem of clustering structured objects (e.g., complex areal units), which are related by links representing persistent relations between objects (e.g., spatial correlation), can be defined as follows: *Given*: (i) a set of structured objects O, (ii) a background knowledge BK and (iii) a binary relation R expressing links among objects in O; *Find* a set of homogeneous clusters $\mathbf{C} \subseteq \wp(O)$ that is feasible with R.

Each structured object $o_i \in O$ can be described by means of a conjunctive ground formula (conjunction of ground selectors) in a first-order formalism, while background knowledge BK is expressed with first-order clauses that support some qualitative reasoning on O. In both cases, each basic component (i.e., *selector*) is a relational statement in the form $f(t_1, \ldots, t_n) = v$, where f is a function symbol or *descriptor*, t_i are terms (constant or variables) and v is a value taken from the categorical or numerical range of f.

Structured objects are then related by R that is a binary relation $R \subseteq O \times O$ imposing a discrete structure on O. In spatial domains, this relation may be either purely spatial, such as topological relations (e.g. adjacency of regions), distance relations (e.g. two regions are within a given distance), and directional relations (e.g. a region is on south of an other region), or hybrid, which mixes both spatial and non spatial properties (e.g. two regions are connected by a road). The relation R can be described by the graph $G = (N_O, A_R)$ where N_O is the set of nodes n_i representing each structured object o_i and A_R is the set of arcs $a_{i,j}$ describing links between each pair of nodes $\langle n_i, n_j \rangle$ according to the discrete structure imposed by R. This means that there is an arc from n_i to n_j only if $o_i R o_j$. Let $N_R(n_i)$ be the R-*neighborhood* of a node n_i such that $N_R(n_i) = \{n_j |$ there is an arc linking n_i to n_j in $G\}$, a node n_j is R-*reachable* from n_i if $n_j \in N_R(n_i)$, or $\exists n_h \in N_R(n_i)$ such that n_j is R-reachable from n_h.

According to this graph-based formalization, a clustering $\mathbf{C} \subseteq \wp(O)$ is feasible with the discrete structure imposed by R when each cluster $C \in \mathbf{C}$ is a subgraph G_C of the graph $G(N_O, A_R)$ such that for each pair of nodes $\langle n_i, n_j \rangle$ of G_C, n_i is R-reachable from n_j, or vice-versa. Moreover, the cluster C is homogeneous when it groups structured objects of O sharing a similar relational description according to some similarity criterion.

CORSO integrates a neighborhood-based graph partitioning to obtain clusters which are feasible with R discrete structure and resorts to a multi-relational approach to evaluate similarity among structured objects and form homogeneous clusters. This faces with the spatial issue of modeling spatial continuity of a phenomenon over the space. The top-level description of the method is presented in Algorithm 1. CORSO embeds a saturation step (function *saturate*) to make explicit information that is implicit in data according to the given BK. The key idea

---

Algorithm 1. Top-level description of CORSO algorithm

1: **function** CORSO($O, BK, R, h - threshold$) → $CList$;
2: $CList \leftarrow \oslash$; $O_{BK} \leftarrow$ saturate(O,BK); $C \leftarrow$ newCluster( );
3: **for** each $seed \in O_{BK}$ **do**
4:     **if** $seed$ is UNCLASSIFIED **then**
5:         $N_{seed} \leftarrow$ neighborhood($seed,O_{BK},R$);
6:         **for** each $o \in N_{seed}$ **do**
7:             **if** o is assigned to a cluster different from C **then**
8:                 $N_{seed} = N_{seed}/o$;
9:             **end if**
10:         **end for**
11:         $T_{seed} \leftarrow$ neighborhoodModel(N_{seed});
12:         **if** homogeneity(N_{seed}, T_{seed}) $\geq h - threshold$ **then**
13:             C.add($seed$); $seedList \leftarrow \oslash$;
14:             **for** each $o \in N_{seed}$ **do**
15:                 C.add(o); $seedList$.add(o);
16:             **end for**
17:             $\langle C, T_C \rangle \leftarrow$ expandCluster($C,seedList,O_{BK},R,T_{seed},h - threshold$);
18:             $CLabel$=clusterLabel(T_C); $CList$.add($\langle C, CLabel \rangle$); $C \leftarrow$ newCluster( );
19:         **else**
20:             $seed \leftarrow NOISE$;
21:         **end if**
22:     **end if**
23: **end for**
24: **return** CList;

---

is to exploit the R-neighborhood construction and build clusters feasible with R-discrete structure by merging partially overlapping homogeneous neighborhood units. Cluster construction starts with an empty cluster ($C \leftarrow newCluster()$) and chooses an arbitrary node $seed$ from G. The R-neighborhood N_{seed} of the node $seed$ is then built according to G discrete structure (function $neighborhood$) and the first-order theory T_{seed} is associated to it. T_{seed} is built as a generalization of the objects falling in N_{seed} (function $neighborhoodModel$). When the neighborhood is estimated to be an homogeneous set (function $homogeneity$), cluster C is grown with the structured objects enclosed in N_{seed} whcih are not yet assigned to any cluster. The cluster C is then iteratively expanded by merging the R-neighborhoods of each node of C (neighborhood expansion) when these neighborhoods result in homogeneous sets with respect to current cluster model T_C (see Algorithm 2.). T_C is obtained as the set of first-order theories generalizing the neighborhoods merged in C. It is noteworthy that when a new R-neighborhood is built to be merged in C, all the objects which are already classified into a cluster different from C are removed from the neighborhood. When the current cluster cannot be further expanded it is labeled with $CLabel$ and an unclassified seed node for a new cluster is chosen from G until all objects are classified. $CLabel$ is obtained by T_C (function $labelCluster$) to compactly describe C.

Algorithm 2. Expand current cluster by merging homogeneous neighborhood

---

    function expandCluster($C, seedList, O_{BK}, R, T_C, h - threshold$) $\rightarrow \langle C, T_C \rangle$;
2: **while** ($seedList$ is not empty) **do**
        $seed \leftarrow seedList.\text{first}()$; $N_{seed} \leftarrow \text{neighborhood}(seed, O_{BK}, R)$;
4:    **for** each $o \in N_{seed}$ **do**
            if o is assigned to a cluster different from C **then**
6:            $N_{seed} = N_{seed}/o$;
        end if
8:    **end for**
        $T_{seed} \leftarrow \text{neighborhoodModel}(N_{seed})$;
10:   **if** homogeneity($N_{seed}, \{T_C, T_{seed}\}$)$\geq h - threshold$ **then**
          for each $o \in N_{seed}$ **do**
12:       $C.\text{add}(o)$; $seedList.\text{add}(o)$;
          end for
14:    $seedList.\text{remove}(seed)$; $T_C \leftarrow T_C \cup T_{seed}$;
        end if
16: **end while**
    return $\langle C, T_C \rangle$;

    This is different from spatial clustering performed by GDBSCAN, although both methods share the neighborhood-based cluster construction. Indeed, GDB-SCAN retrieves all objects density-reachable from an arbitrary core object by building successive neighborhoods and checks density within a neighborhood by ignoring the cluster. This yields a density-connected set, where density is efficiently estimated independently from the neighborhoods already merged in forming the current cluster. However, this approach may lead to merge connected neighborhoods sharing some objects but modeling different phenomena. Moreover, GDBSCAN computes density within each neighborhood according to a weighted cardinality function (e.g. aggregation of non spatial values) that assumes single table data representation. CORSO overcomes these limitations by computing density within a neighborhood in terms of degree of similarity among all relationally structured objects falling in the neighborhood with respect to the model of the entire cluster currently built. In particular, following the suggestion given in [16], we evaluate homogeneity within a neighborhood N_{seed} to be added to the cluster C as the average degree of matching between objects of N_{seed} and the cluster model $\{T_C, T_{seed}\}$. Details on cluster model determination, neighborhood homogeneity estimation and cluster labeling are reported below.

3.1   Cluster Model Generation

Let C be the cluster currently built by merging w neighborhood sets $N_1, \ldots, N_w$, we assume that the cluster model T_C is a set of first-order theories $\{T_1, \ldots, T_w\}$ for the concept C where T_i is a model for the neighborhood set N_i. More precisely, T_i is a set of first-order clauses: $T_i : \{cluster(X) = c \leftarrow H_{i1}, \ldots, cluster(X) = c \leftarrow H_{iz}\}$, where each H_{ij} is a conjunctive formula describing a sub-structure shared by one or more objects in N_i and $\forall o_i \in N_i, BK \cup T_i \models o_i$. Such model can be learned by resorting to the ILP system ATRE [14] that adopts a separate-and-conquer search strategy to learn a model of structured objects from a set of training examples and eventually counter-examples. In this context, ATRE learns a model for each neighborhood set without considering any counter-examples. The search of a model starts with the most general clause, that is, $cluster(X) = c \leftarrow$, and proceeds top-down by adding selectors (literals) to the body according to some preference criteria (e.g. number of objects covered or number of literals).

Selectors involving both numerical and categorical descriptors are handled in the same way, that is, they have to comply with the property of linkedness and are sorted according to preference criteria. The only difference is that selectors involving numerical descriptors are generalized by computing the closed interval that best covers positive examples and eventually discriminates from contour-examples, while selectors involving categorical descriptors with same function value are generalized by simply turning all ground arguments into corresponding variables without changing the corresponding function value.

3.2   Neighborhood Homogeneity Estimation

The homogeneity of a neighborhood set N to be added to the cluster C is computed as follows:

$$h(N, T_{C \cup N}) = \frac{1}{\#N} \sum_i h(o_i, T_{C \cup N}) = \frac{1}{\#N} \sum_i \frac{1}{w+1} \sum_j h(o_i, T_j), \quad (1)$$

where $\#N$ is the cardinality of the neighborhood set N and $T_{C \cup N}$ is the cluster model of $C \cup N$ formed by both $\{T_1, \ldots, T_w\}$, i.e., the model of C and T_{w+1}, i.e., the model of N built as explained above. Since $T_j = H_{1j}, \ldots, H_{zj}$ ($z \geq 1$) with each H_{ij} a conjunctive formula in first-order formalism, we assume that:

$$h(o_i, T_j) = \frac{1}{z} \sum_i fm(o_i, H_{ij}), \tag{2}$$

where fm is a function returning the degree of matching of an object $o_i \in N$ against the conjunctive formula H_{ij}. In this way, the definition of homogeneity of a neighborhood set $N = \{o_1, \ldots, o_n\}$ with respect to some logical theory $T_{C \cup N}$ is closely related to the problem of comparing (matching) the conjunctive formula f_i representing an object $o_i \in N^1$ with a conjunctive formula H_{ij} forming the model T_j in order to discover likenesses or differences [19]. This is a directional similarity judgment involving a *referent* R, that is the description or prototype of a class (cluster model) and a *subject* S that is the description of an instance of a class (object to be clustered). In the classical matching paradigm, the matching of S against R corresponds to compare them just for equality. In particular, when both S and R are conjunctive formulas in first-order formalism, matching S against R corresponds to check the existence of a substitution θ for the variables in R such that $S = \theta(R)$. This last condition is generally weakened by requiring that $S \Rightarrow \theta(R)$, where $\Rightarrow$ is the logical implication. However, the requirement of equality, even in terms of logical implication, is restrictive in presence of noise or variability of the phenomenon described by the referent of matching. This makes necessary to rely on a flexible definition of matching that aims at comparing two descriptions and identifying their similarities rather than equalities. The result of such a flexible matching is a number in the interval $[0, 1]$ that is the probability of precisely matching S against R, provided that some change described by θ is possibly made in the description R.

The problem of computing flexible matching to compare structures is not novel. Esposito et al. [4] have formalized a computation schema for flexible matching on formulas in first-order formalism whose basic components (selectors) are the relational statements, that is, $f_i(t_1, \ldots, t_n) = v$, which are combined by applying different operators such as conjunction ($\wedge$) or disjunction ($\vee$) operator. In this work, we focus on the computation of flexible matching $fm(S, R)$ when both S and R are described by conjunctive formulas and $fm(S, R)$ looks for the substitution θ returning the best matching of S against R, as:

$$fm(S, R) = \max_\theta \prod_{i=1,\ldots,k} fm_\theta(S, r_i). \tag{3}$$

The optimal θ that maximizes the above conditional probability is here searched by adopting the branch and bound algorithm that expands the least cost partial path by performing quickly on average [4]. According to this formulation, fm_θ

---

[1] The conjunctive formula f_i is here intended as the description of $o_i \in N$ saturated according to the BK.

denotes the flexible matching with the tie of the substitution fixed by θ computed on each single selector $r_i \equiv f_{r_i}(t_{r_1}, \ldots, t_{r_n}) = v_{r_i}$ of the referent R where f_{r_i} is a function descriptor with either numerical (e.g. area or distance) or categorical (e.g. intersect) range. In the former case the function value v_{r_i} is an interval value ($v_{r_i} \equiv [a, b]$), while in the latter case v_{r_i} is a subset of values ($v_{r_i} \equiv \{v_1, \ldots, v_M\}$) from the range of f_{r_i}. This faces with a referent R that is obtained by generalizing a neighborhood of objects in O. Conversely for the subject S, that is, the description of a single object $o \in O$, the function value w_{s_j} assigned to each selector $s_j \equiv f_{s_j}(t_{s_1}, \ldots, t_{s_n}) = w_{s_j}$ is an exactly known single value from the range of f_{s_j}. In this context, the flexible matching $fm_\theta(S, r_i)$ evaluates the degree of similarity $fm(s_j, \theta(r_i))$ between $\theta(r_i)$ and the corresponding selector s_j in the subject S such that both r_i and s_j have the same function descriptor $f_r = f_s$ and for each pair of terms $\langle t_{r_i}, t_{s_i} \rangle$, $\theta(t_{r_i}) = t_{s_i}$. More precisely,

$$fm(s_j, \theta(r_i)) = fm(w_{s_j}, v_{r_i}) = \max_{v \in v_{r_i}} P(equal(w_{s_j}, v)). \tag{4}$$

The probability of the event $equal(w_{s_j}, v)$ is then defined as the probability that an observed w_{s_j} is a distortion of v, that is:

$$P(equal(w_{s_j}, v)) = P(\delta(X, v) \geq \delta(w_{s_j}, v)) \tag{5}$$

where X is a random variable assuming value in the domain D representing the range of f_r while $delta$ is a distance measure. The computation of $P(equal(w_{s_j}, v))$ clearly depends on the probability density function of X. For categorical descriptors, that is, D is a discrete set with cardinality $\#D$, it has be proved [4] that:

$$P(equal(w, v)) = \begin{cases} 1 \text{ if } w_{s_j} = v \\ \#D - 1/\#D \text{ otherwise} \end{cases} \tag{6}$$

when X is assumed to have a uniform probability distribution on D and $\delta(x, y) = 0$ if $x = y$, 1 otherwise. Although similar results have been reported for both linear non numerical and tree-structured domains, no result appears for numerical domains. Therefore, we have extended definitions reported in [4] to make flexible matching able to deal with numerical descriptors and we have proved that:

$$fm(c, [a, b]) = \begin{cases} 1 & \text{if } a \leq c \leq b \\ 1 - 2(a - c)/(\beta - \alpha) & \text{if } c < a \wedge 2a - c \leq \beta \\ (c - \alpha)/(\beta - \alpha) & \text{if } c < a \wedge 2a - c > \beta \\ (\beta - c)/(\beta - \alpha) & \text{if } c > b \wedge 2b - c < \alpha \\ 1 - 2(c - b)/(\beta - \alpha) & \text{if } c > b \wedge 2b - c \geq \alpha \end{cases} \tag{7}$$

by assuming that X has uniform distribution on D and $\delta(x, y) = |x - y|$. A proof of formula 7 is reported in the Appendix A of this paper.

3.3   Cluster Labeling

A cluster C can be naturally labeled with T_C that is the set of first-order clauses obtained from the generalization of neighborhoods merged in C. Each first-order clause is in the form $C \leftarrow s_1, \ldots, s_n$, where C represents the cluster label and each s_i denotes a selector in the form $f_i(t_{i_1}, \ldots, t_{i_l}) = v_i$. In this formalization, two selectors $s_1 : f_1(t_{1_1}, \ldots, t_{1_l}) = v_1$ and $s_2 : f_2(t_{2_1}, \ldots, t_{2_l}) = v_2$ are comparable according to some substitution θ when they involve the same descriptor $(f_1 = f_2 = f)$ and each pair of terms $\langle t_{1_i}, t_{2_i} \rangle$ is unifiable according to θ, i.e., $t_{1_i}\theta = t_{2_i}\theta = t_i$ $(\forall i = 1 \ldots l)$. In this case, the selector $s : f(t_1, \ldots, t_l) = \{v_1\} \cup \{v_2\}$ is intended as a generalization for both s_1 and s_2. In particular, the selectors s_1 and s_2 are equal when they are comparable and $v_1 = v_2 = v$ such that the generalization of s_1 and s_2 is built as $s : f(t_1, \ldots, t_l) = v$. Similarly, the selector s_1 (s_2) is contained in the selector s_2 (s_1) when they are comparable and $v_1 \subseteq v_2$ ($v_2 \subseteq v_1$), while the generalization s is $f(t_1, \ldots, t_l) = v_2$ ($f(t_1, \ldots, t_l) = v_1$). Note that equality of selectors implies containment, but not vice-versa. Similarly, the first-order clauses $H_1 : C \leftarrow s_{1_1}, \ldots, s_{1_n}$ and $H_2 : C \leftarrow s_{2_1}, \ldots, s_{2_n}$ are comparable according to some substitution θ when each pair of selectors $\langle s_{1_i}, s_{2_i} \rangle$ is comparable according to θ. Hence, H_1 is equal (contained) to H_2 when s_{1_i} is equal (contained) to s_{2_i} for each $i = 1, \ldots, n$. In both these cases (equality and containment condition), the pair of first-order clauses H_1, H_2 can be replaced without lost of information with the first-order clause H that is the generalization of H_1, H_2 built by substituting each pair of comparable selectors $\langle s_{1_i}, s_{2_i} \rangle \in \langle H_1, H_2 \rangle$ with the generalization obtained as stated above. This suggests the idea of merging a pair of comparable first-order clauses H_1, H_2 in a single clause H by preserving the equivalence of coverage, that is: (i) for each structured object o with $H_1, H_2, BK \models o$ then $H, BK \models o$ and vice-versa, (ii) for each structured object o with $H_1, H_2, BK \not\models o$ then $H, BK \not\models o$ and vice-versa, where BK is a set of first-order clauses. The equivalence of coverage between $\{H_1, H_2\}$ and H is obviously guaranteed when H_1 is either equal or contained in H_2 or vice-versa, but this equivalence cannot be guaranteed when H_1 and H_2 are comparable first-order clauses but neither equality condition nor containment condition are satisfied.

Example 1: Let us consider the pair of comparable first-order clauses:

$H_1 : cluster(X_1) = c \leftarrow distance(X_1, X_2) = [5..10], type(X_2) = street$
$H_2 : cluster(X_1) = c \leftarrow distance(X_1, X_2) = [3..7], type(X_2) = river$

where neither H_1 is equal to H_2 nor $H_1(H_2)$ is contained in $H_2(H_1)$. The first-order clause obtained by generalizing pairs of comparable selectors in both H_1 and H_2, is $H : cluster(X_1) = c \leftarrow distance(X_1, X_2) = [3..10], type(X_2) = \{street, river\}$, where $H \models o$ with $o : distance(X_1, X_2) = 3 \wedge type(X_2) = street$, but neither $H_1 \models o$ nor $H_2 \models o$.

The requirement of equality between H_1 and H_2 can be relaxed while preserving equivalence of coverage with respect to the generalization H. Indeed, when

$H_1 : C \leftarrow s_1(\_) = v_1, \ldots s_k(\_) = v_k, \ldots, s_n(\_) = v_n$
$H_2 : C \leftarrow s_1(\_) = v_1, \ldots s_k(\_) = w_k, \ldots, s_n(\_) = v_n$

are comparable first-order clauses differing only in the function value of a single selector (i.e. s_k), the first-order clause:

$$H : C \leftarrow s_1(\_) = v_1, \ldots s_k(\_) = \{v_k\} \cup \{w_k\}, \ldots, s_n(\_) = v_n$$

continues to preserve the equivalence of coverage with $\{H_1, H_2\}$.

Example 2: Let us consider the pair of comparable first-order clauses:

$$H_1 : cluster(X_1) = c \leftarrow distance(X_1, X_2) = [3..7], type(X_2) = street,$$
$$length(X_2) = [3, 5]$$
$$H_2 : cluster(X_1) = c \leftarrow distance(X_1, X_2) = [3..7], type(X_2) = street,$$
$$length(X_2) = [7, 10]$$

which differ only in the value of a single selector (length), the first-order clause obtained by generalizing the pairs of comparable selectors in both H_1 and H_2 is:

$$H : cluster(X_1) = c \leftarrow distance(X_1, X_2) = [3..7], type(X_2) = street,$$
$$length(X_2) = [3, 5] \cup [7, 10]$$

that is equivalent in coverage to the pair $\{H_1, H_2\}$.

Following this idea, it is possible to compactly describe the cluster theory T_C finally associated to a cluster C by iteratively replacing pairs of comparable first-order clauses H_1, H_2 with the generalization H, when H results equivalent in coverage to $\{H_1, H_2\}$ (see Algorithm 3.).

Algorithm 3. Build a compact theory to describe a cluster C

```
 1: function clusterLabel(T_C) → T'_C;
 2:   T'_C ← ∅
 3:   merge ← false;
 4:   while T_C is not empty do
 5:       H is a first-order clause in T_C;
 6:       T_C = T_C/H;
 7:       for each H' ∈ T_C do
 8:           if H and H' are generalizable without lost of information then
 9:               H = generalize(H,H'); T_C = T_C/H'; merge = true;
10:           end if
11:       end for
12:       T'_C = T'_C ∪ H;
13:   end while
14:   if merge is true then
15:       T'_C ←clusterLabel(T'_C);
16:   end if
17:   return T'_C;
```

Example 3: Let us consider T_C that is the set of first-order clauses including:

$$H_1 : cluster(X_1) = c \leftarrow distance(X_1, X_2) = [5..10], color(X_2) = red$$
$$H_2 : cluster(X_1) = c \leftarrow distance(X_1, X_2) = [5..6], color(X_2) = blue$$
$$H_3 : cluster(X_1) = c \leftarrow distance(X_1, X_2) = [5..10], color(X_2) = blue$$
$$H_4 : cluster(X_1) = c \leftarrow distance(X_1, X_2) = [6..10], area(X_2)in[30..40]$$

T_C can be transformed in the set of first-order clauses:

$$H'_1 : cluster(X_1) = c \leftarrow distance(X_1, X_2) = [5..10], color(X_2) = \{red, blue\}$$
$$H'_2 : cluster(X_1) = c \leftarrow distance(X_1, X_2) = [6..10], area(X_2)in[30..40]$$

where H_1' results by firstly merging H_1 and H_3, which are comparable and differ only in the function value of a selector $(color(X_2) = red$ vs $color(X_2) = blue)$, and obtaining $H_{13} : cluster(X_1) = c \leftarrow distance(X_1, X_2) = [5..10], color(X_2) = \{red, blue\}$ and then merging H_{13} and H_2 since H_2 is contained in H_{13}.

4   The Application: Two Case Studies

In this section, we describe the application of CORSO to two distinct real-world problems, namely topographic map interpretation and geo-referenced census data analysis. In the former problem, a topographic map is treated as a grid of square cells of same size, according to a hybrid tessellation-topological model such that adjacency among cells allows map-reading from a cell to one of its neighbors in the map. For each cell, geographical data is represented as humans perceive it in reality, that is, geometric (or physical) representation and thematic (or logical) representation. Geometric representation describes the geographical objects by means of the most appropriate physical entity (point, line or region), while thematic representation expresses the semantics of geographical objects (e.g., hydrography, vegetation, transportation network and so on), independently of their physical representation. Spatial clustering aims at identifying a mosaic of nearly homogeneous clusters (areas) including adjacent cells in the map such that geographical data inside each cluster properly models the spatial continuity of some morphological environment within the cluster region, while separate clusters model spatial variation over the entire space. In the second problem, the goal is to perform a joint analysis of both socio-economic factors represented in census data and geographical factors represented in topographic maps to support a good public policy. In this case, spatial objects are territorial units for which census data are collected as well as entities of geographical layers such as urban and wood areas. Spatial partitioning of CORSO is compared with the first-order clustering performed with logical decision trees [1], which are able to manage relational structure of spatial objects but ignore relations imposed with discrete spatial structure. The empirical comparison with GDBSCAN was not possible since the system is not publicly available. However, CORSO clearly improves GDBSAN clustering that is not able to manage complex structure of spatial data. In both applications, running time of CORSO refers to execution performed on a 2 Ghz IBM notebook with 256 Mb of RAM.

4.1   Topographic Map Interpretation

In this study we discuss two real-world applications of spatial clustering to characterize spatial continuity of some morphological elements over the topographic map of the Apulia region in Italy. The territory considered in this application covers 45 km^2 from the zone of Canosa in Apulia. The examined area is segmented into square areal units of 1 Km^2 each. Thus, the problem of recognizing spatial continuity of some morphological elements in the map is reformulated as the problem of grouping adjacent cells resulting in a morphologically homogeneous area, that is, a problem of clustering spatial objects according to the

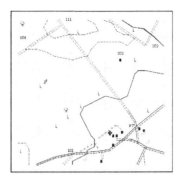

contain(c, f2) = true, ...,
contain(f, f70) = true,
type_of(c) = cell, ...,
type_of(f4) = vegetation,...,
subtype_of(f2) = grapewine,...,
subtype_of(f7) = cart_track_road,...,
part_of(f4, x4),
part_of(f7, x5), part_of(f7_x6),...,
extension(x7) = 111.018,...,
extension(x33) = 1104.74,
line_to_line(x7, x68) = almost_parallel, ...,
point_to_region(x4, x21) = inside,
point_to_region(x4, x18) = outside,...,
line_to_region(x8, x27) = adjacent, ...

Fig. 1. First-order description of a cell extracted from topographic chart of Apulia

discrete spatial structure imposed by the relation of "adjacency" among cells. Since several geographical objects, eventually belonging to different layers (e.g., almond tree, olive tree, font, street, etc) are collected within each cell, we apply algorithms derived from geometrical and topological reasoning [15] to obtain cell descriptions in first-order formalism (see Figure 1). For this task, we consider descriptions including spatial descriptors encompassing geometrical properties (*area, extension*) and topological relations (*regionToRegion, lineToLine, pointToRegion*) as well as non spatial descriptors (*typeOf, subtypeOf*). The descriptor *partOf* is used to define the physical structure of a logical object. An example is: $typeOf(f_1) = font \wedge partOf(f_1, x_1) = true$, where f_1 denotes a font which is physically represented by a point referred with the constant x_1. Each cell is here described by a conjunction of 946,866 ground selectors in average. To support some qualitative reasoning, a spatial background knowledge (BK) is expressed in form of clauses. An example of BK we use in this task is:

$fontToParcel(Font, Culture) = Relation \leftarrow typeOf(Font) = font,$

$\quad partOf(Font, Point) = true, typeOf(Parcel) = parcel,$

$\quad partOf(Parcel, Region) = true, pointToRegion(Point, Region) = Relation$

that allows to move from a physical to a logical level in describing the topological relation between the point that physically represents the font and the region that physically represents the culture and that are, respectively, referred to as the variables *Font* and *Culture*. The specific goal of this study is to model the spatial continuity of some morphological environment (e.g. cultivation setting) within adjacent cells over the map. This means that each cluster covers a contiguous area over the map where it is possible to observe some specific environment that does not occur in adjacent cells not yet assigned to any cluster. It is noteworthy that granularity of partitioning changes by varying homogeneity threshold (see Figure 2). In particular, when $h - threshold = 0.95$, CORSO clusters adjacent cells in five regions in 1821 secs. Each cluster is compactly labeled as follows:

$C_1 : cluster(X_1) = c_1 \leftarrow containAlmondTree(X_1, X_2) = \{true\},$

$\quad cultivationToCulture(X_2, X_3) = \{outside\},$

$\quad areaCulture(X_3) = [328..420112], fontToCulture(X_4, X_3) = \{outside\}.$

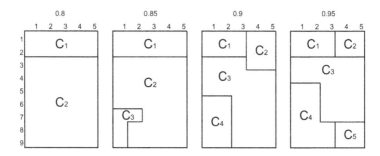

Fig. 2. Spatial clusters detected on map data from the zone of Canosa by varying $h - threshold$ value in $\{0.8, 0.85, 0.9, 0.95\}$

$C_2 : cluster(X_1) = c_2 \leftarrow containAlmondTree(X_1, X_2) = \{true\},$
$\quad cultivationToCulture(X_2, X_3) = \{inside\}, areaCulture(X_3) = [13550..$
$\quad 187525], areaCulture(X_3) = [13550..187525],$
$\quad cultivationToCulture(X_2, X_4) \in \{outside\}.$

$C_3 : cluster(X_1) = c_3 \leftarrow containGrapevine(X_1, X_2) = \{true\},$
$\quad cultivationToCulture(X_2, X_3) = \{inside\}, areaCulture(X_3) = [13550..$
$\quad 212675], cultivationToCulture(X_2, X_4) = \{outside\}.$
$\quad cluster(X_1) = c_3 \leftarrow containGrapevine(X_1, X_2) = \{true\},$
$\quad cultivationToCulture(X_2, X_3) = \{outside\}, areaCulture(X_3) = [150..$
$\quad 212675], cultivationToCulture(X_2, X_4) = \{outside, inside\}.$

$C_4 : cluster(X_1) = c_4 \leftarrow containStreet(X_1, X_2) = \{true\}$
$\quad streetToCulture(X_2, X_3) = \{adjacent\}, areaCulture(X_3) = [620..$
$\quad 230326], cultureToCulture(X_3, X_4) = \{outside, inside\}.$

$C_5 : cluster(X_1) = c_5 \leftarrow containOliveTree(X_1, X_2) = true,$
$\quad cultivationToCulture(X_2, X_3) \in \{outside\}, areaCulture(X_3) \in [620..$
$\quad 144787], oliviToParcel(X_2, X_4) = \{outside\}.$

Notice that each detected cluster effectively includes adjacent cells sharing a similar morphological environment, while separate clusters describe quite different environments. Conversely, the logical decision tree mined on the same data divides the territory under analysis in twenty different partitions where it is difficult to recognize the continuity of any morphology phenomenon.

4.2   Geo-referenced Census Data Analysis

In this application, we consider both census and digital map data concerning North West England (NWE) area that is decomposed into censual sections or wards for a total of 1011 wards. Census data is available at ward level and provides some measures of deprivation level in the ward according to index scores that combine information provided by 1998 Census. We consider Jarman Underprivileged Area Score that is designed to measure the need for primary care, the indices developed by Townsend and Carstairs that is used in health-related analysis, and the Department of the Environment's Index (DoE) that is used in targeting urban regeneration funds. The higher the index value the more deprived a ward is. Spatial analysis of deprivation distribution is enabled by the availability of vectorized boundaries of the 1010 census wards as well as by other Ordnance Survey digital maps of NWE, where several interesting layers are found, namely urban zones (including 384 large urban areas and 2232 small urban areas) and wood zones (including 859 woods). In particular, we focus attention on investigating continuity of socio-economic deprivation joined to geographical factors represented in linked topographic maps.

Both ward-referenced census data and map data are stored in an Object-Relational spatial database, i.e., Oracle Spatial 9i database, as a set of spatial tables, one for each layer. Each spatial table includes a geometry attribute that allows storing the geometrical representation (i.e. urban and wood zones are described by lines while wards are described by polygons) and the positioning of a spatial object with respect to some reference system. We adopt a topological algorithm based on the 9-intersection model [3] to detect both adjacency relation between NWE wards (i.e. wards which share some boundary) and overlapping relation between wards and urban areas (or woods). The former imposes a discrete spatial structure over NWE wards such that only adjacent wards may be grouped in the same cluster while the latter contributes to define the spatial structure embedded in each ward not only in terms of observed values of deprivation scores but also extension of urban areas and/or woods overlapping each ward. No BK is defined for this problem.

Granularity of partitioning changes when varying the value of $h-threshold$, that is, CORSO detects 79 clusters with $h-threshold = 0.80$, 89 clusters with $h-threshold = 0.85$, 122 clusters with $h-threshold = 0.90$ and 163 clusters with $h-threshold = 0.95$. In particular, when $h-threshold = 0.95$, CORSO clusters NWE area in 2160 secs and identifies adjacent regions modeling differently relational patterns involving deprivation and geographical environment. For instance, by analyzing these spatial clusters, we discover three adjacent areas, namely C_1, C_2 and C_3 compactly labeled as follows:

$C_1 : cluster(X_1) = c_1 \leftarrow townsend(X_1) = [-4.7.. - 0.6],$
$\quad doe(X_1) = [-12.4..2.7], carstairs(X_1) = [-4.5.. - 0.9],$
$\quad jarman(X_1) = [-32.7..7.5], overlapped\_by\_wood(X1, X2) = true.$
$\quad cluster(X_1) = c_1 \leftarrow townsend(X_1) = [-5.4.. - 2.3],$
$\quad doe(X_1) = [-10.9.. - 0.5], carstairs(X_1) = [-4.2.. - 1.6],$
$\quad jarman(X_1) = [-22.8..0.6], overlapped\_by\_wood(X1, X2) = true.$
$\quad cluster(X_1) = c_1 \leftarrow townsend(X_1) = [-5.4.. - 3.2],$
$\quad doe(X_1) = [-8.8.. - 2.1], carstairs(X_1) = [-4.4.. - 2.5],$
$\quad jarman(X_1) = [-22.8.. - 2.4], overlapped\_by\_wood(X1, X2) = true.$
$C_2 : cluster(X_1) = c_1 \leftarrow townsend(X_1) = [-2.0..0.6],$
$\quad doe(X_1) = [-4.2..1.6], carstairs(X_1) = [-2.6..2.1],$
$\quad jarman(X_1) = [-9.7..8.8], overlapped\_by\_largeUrbArea(X1, X2) = true.$
$\quad cluster(X_1) = c_1 \leftarrow townsend(X_1) = [-2.7..2.8],$
$\quad doe(X_1) = [-4.2..4.0], carstairs(X_1) = [-2.2..2.7],$
$\quad jarman(X_1) = [-8.8..21.3], overlapped\_by\_largeUrbArea(X1, X2) = true$

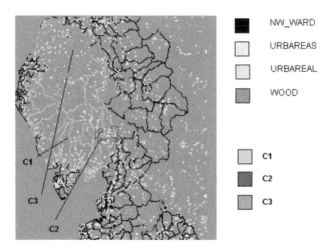

Fig. 3. Spatial clusters detected on NWE with $h-threshold = 0.95$

$C_3 : cluster(X_1) = c_1 \leftarrow townsend(X_1) = [-3.4..0.4],$
$\quad doe(X_1) = [-8.2.. - 0.2], carstairs(X_1) = [-3.7..0.6],$
$\quad jarman(X_1) = [-27.7.. - 1.5],$
$\quad overlapped\_by\_smallUrbArea(X1, X2) = true.$

C_1, C_2 and C_3 cover adjacent areas with quite similar range value for deprivation indexes but C_1 models the presence of woods while C_2 and C_3 model the presence of small urban areas and large urban areas, respectively. Discontinuity of geographical environments modeled by these clusters is confirmed by visualizing map data about the area (see Figure 3).

The logical decision tree mined on the same data discovers 58 different clusters. Clusters are built by minimizing the distance among relational descriptions of wards. However, the discrete structure imposed by the adjacency relation is ignored. Hence, wards which are not connected in the graph imposed by the adjacency relation are clustered together.

5   Conclusions

This paper presents a novel approach to discover clusters from structured spatial data taking into account relational constraints (e.g. spatial correlation) forming the discrete spatial structure. We represent this discrete spatial structure as a graph such that the concept of graph neighborhood is exploited to capture relational constraints embedded in the graph edges. Moreover, we resort to a relational approach to mine data scattered in multiple relations describing the structure that is naturally embedded in spatial data. As a consequence, only spatial units associated with (transitively) graph connected nodes can be clustered together according to judgment of similarity on relational descriptions representing their internal (spatial) structure. As future work, we intend to integrate

CORSO in a spatial data mining system that is able to extract both the spatial structure and the structure of spatial objects from a spatial database, cluster these spatial objects coherently with the extracted spatial structure and visualize discovered clusters. We also plan to employ CORSO for air pollution analysis.

Acknowledgment

The work presented in this paper is partial fulfillment of the research objective set by the ATENEO-2004 project on "Metodi di Data Mining Multi-relazionale per la scoperta di conoscenza in basi di dati".

References

1. L. De Raedt and H. Blockeel. Using logical decision trees for clustering. In S. Džeroski and N. Lavrač, editors, *Inductive Logic Programming, 7th International Workshop*, volume 1297, pages 133–140. Springer-Verlag, 1997.
2. S. Džeroski and N. Lavrač. *Relational Data Mining*. Springer-Verlag, 2001.
3. M. Egenhofer. Reasoning about binary topological relations. In *Symposium on Large Spatial Databases*, pages 143–160, 1991.
4. F. Esposito, D. Malerba, and G. Semeraro. Flexible matching for noisy structural descriptions. In *International Joint Conference on Artificial Intelligence*, pages 658–664, 1991.
5. M. Ester, H. P. Kriegel, and J. Sander. Algorithms and applications for spatial data mining. *Geographic Data Mining and Knowledge Discovery*, 5(6), 2001.
6. M. Ester, H.-P. Kriegel, J. Sander, and X. Xu. A density-based algorithm for discovering clusters in large spatial databases with noise. In *Knowledge Discovery in Databases*, pages 226–231, 1996.
7. V. Estivill-Castro and M. E. Houle. Robust distance-based clustering with applications to spatial data mining. *Algorithmica*, 30(2):216–242, 2001.
8. V. Estivill-Castro and I. Lee. Fast spatial clustering with different metrics and in the presence of obstacles. In *International Symposium on Advances in geographic information systems*, pages 142–147. ACM Press, 2001.
9. E. Hancock and M. Vento. *Graph Based Representations in Pattern Recognitions*. Springer-Verlag, 2003.
10. L. Holder and D. Cook. Graph-based relational learning: Current and future directions. *SIGKDD Explorations Special Issues on Multi-Relational Data Mining*, 5(1):90–93, 2003.
11. T. Horvath, S. Wrobel, and U. Bohnebeck. Relational instance-based learning with lists and terms. *Machine Learning*, 43(1/2):53–80, 2001.
12. L. Kaufmann and P. J. Rousseeuw. *Finding Groups in Data: An Introduction to Cluster Analysis*. John Wiley, 1990.
13. M. Kirsten and S. Wrobel. Relational distance-based clustering. In *Inductive Logic Programming, 8th International Conference*, volume 1446, pages 261–270. Springer-Verlag, 1998.
14. D. Malerba. Learning recursive theories in the normal ilp setting. *Fundamenta Informaticae*, 57(1):39–77, 2003.

15. D. Malerba, F. Esposito, A. Lanza, F. A. Lisi, and A. Appice. Empowering a gis with inductive learning capabilities: The case of ingens. *Journal of Computers, Environment and Urban Systems, Elsevier Science*, 27:265–281, 2003.

16. D. Mavroeidis and P. Flach. Improved distances for structured data. In T. Horváth and A. Yamamoto, editors, *Inductive Logic Programming, 13th International Conference*, volume 2835, pages 251–268. Springer-Verlag, 2003.

17. A. M. Neville, J. and J. D. Clustering relational data using attribute and link information. In *Text Mining and Link Analysis Workshop, 18th International Joint Conference on Artificial Intelligence*, 2003.

18. R. T. Ng and J. Han. Efficient and effective clustering methods for spatial data mining. In J. Bocca, M. Jarke, and C. Zaniolo, editors, *Very Large Data Bases, 20th International Conference*, pages 144–155. Morgan Kaufmann Publishers, 1994.

19. D. Patterson. *Introduction to Artificial Intelligence and expert systems*. Prentice-Hall, 1991.

20. L. D. Raedt and S. Dzeroski. First-order jk-clausal theories are pac-learnable. *Artificial Intelligence*, 70(1-2):375–392, 1994.

21. J. Sander, E. Martin, H.-P. Kriegel, and X. Xu. Density-based clustering in spatial databases: The algorithm gdbscan and its applications. *Data Mining and Knowledge Discovery*, 2(2):169–194, 1998.

22. W. Tobler. Cellular geography. In S. Gale and G.Olsson, editors, *Philosophy in Geography*, 1979.

23. G. Toussaint. Some unsolved problems on proximity graphs. In D. Dearholt and F. Harary, editors, *First Workshop on Proximity Graphs*, 1991.

24. M. Visvalingam. Operational definitions of area based social indicators. *Environment and Planning*, A(15):831–839, 1983.

A Appendix

Let us recall definitions (4) and (5) and apply them to numerical case. We have:

$$fm(c, [a, b]) = \max_{v \in [a,b]} P(equal(c, v)) = \max_{v \in [a,b]} P(\delta(X, v) \geq \delta(c, v))$$

By assuming that X has a uniform distribution on domain $D = [\alpha, \beta]$ with density function $f_D(x) = 1/(\beta - \alpha), \forall x \in D$ and fixing $\delta(x, y) = |x - y|$, $P(\delta(X, v) \geq \delta(c, v))$ can be rewritten as $P(|X - v| \geq |c - v|)$ that is maximized when minimizing $|c - v|$.

If $a \leq c \leq b$ then $\max_{v \in [a,b]} P(|X - v| \geq |c - v|) = P(|X - v| \geq |c - c|) = 1$.

If $c < a$ then $\max_{v \in [a,b]} P(|X - v| \geq |c - v|)$ is written as $\max_{v \in [a,b]} P(|X - v| \geq v - c)$.

Since the maximum of $P(|X - v| \geq v - c)$ is obtained for $v = a$, we have that $\max_{v \in [a,b]} P(|X - v| \geq v - c) = P(|X - a| \geq a - c) = P(X - a \geq a - c) + P(X - a \leq c - a) = P(X \geq 2a - c) + P(X \leq c)$ where:

1. $P(X \geq 2a - c) = \int_{\beta}^{2a-c} 1/(\beta - \alpha) dx = (\beta - 2a + c)/(\beta - \alpha)$ if $2a - c \leq \beta$, 0 otherwise;
2. $P(X \leq c) = (c - \alpha)/(\beta - \alpha)$.

Hence, we obtain that:

$$\max_{v\in[a,b]} P(|X-v| \geq v-c) = \begin{cases} 1 - 2(a-c)/(\beta-\alpha) & \text{if } c < a \wedge 2a - c \leq \beta \\ (c-\alpha)/(\beta-\alpha) & \text{if } c < a \wedge 2a - c > \beta \end{cases}$$

If $c > b$ then $\max_{v\in[a,b]} P(|X-v| \geq |c-v|)$ can be equivalently written as $\max_{v\in[a,b]} P(|X$ $-v| \geq c - v)$ that is obtained for $v = b$. Therefore, $\max_{v\in[a,b]} P(|X - v| \geq c - v) =$ $P(|X - b| \geq c - b) = P(X - b \geq c - b) + P(X - b \leq b - c) = P(X \geq c) + P(X \leq 2b - c)$. We have that:

$$\max_{v\in[a,b]} P(|X-v| \geq c-v) = \begin{cases} (\beta-c)/(\beta-\alpha) & \text{if } c > b \wedge 2b - c < \alpha \\ 1 - 2(c-b)/(\beta-\alpha) & \text{if } c > b \wedge 2b - c \geq \alpha \end{cases}$$

Generalization Behaviour
of Alkemic Decision Trees

K.S. Ng

Computer Sciences Laboratory,
Research School of Information Sciences and Engineering,
The Australian National University
kee@cslab.anu.edu.au

Abstract. This paper is concerned with generalization issues for a decision tree learner for structured data called ALKEMY. Motivated by error bounds established in statistical learning theory, we study the VC dimensions of some predicate classes defined on sets and multisets – two data-modelling constructs used intensively in the knowledge representation formalism of ALKEMY – and from that obtain insights into the (worst-case) generalization behaviour of the learner. The VC dimension results and the techniques used to derive them may be of wider independent interest.

1 Introduction

This paper is concerned with gaining some understanding of the generalization behaviour of ALKEMY, a logical decision-tree learner for structured data introduced under the higher-order logic learning framework of [17]. A brief (early) description of the learner appears in [6].

To get started on our goal, we turn to the rich body of literature on generalization issues. Inspection of error bounds established in statistical learning theory for general decision trees with arbitrary input domains and arbitrary node functions reveals that an important parameter governing the generalization behaviour of Alkemic decision trees is the VC dimension of node functions, and this is what we study in this paper. Specifically, we concentrate on some natural predicate classes defined on sets and multisets – two data-modelling constructs used intensively in the knowledge representation framework of [17] – and give bounds on their VC dimensions. The results turn out to have wider application beyond sets and multisets. Some indications of how they can be used to analyse common predicate classes defined on more complex data types like lists, trees, graphs, etc are given.

To the author's best knowledge, this is the first time that the VC dimensions of different predicate classes defined on sets and multisets have been analyzed *directly*. The only other relevant work I'm aware of is in [8], where the VC dimension of a class of predicates defined on sets is analyzed *indirectly* through a mapping to Blum's infinite attribute space model [5].

S. Kramer and B. Pfahringer (Eds.): ILP 2005, LNAI 3625, pp. 246–263, 2005.

The paper is organized as follows. Section 2 provides background information on ALKEMY. Error bounds suitable for use with it are stated in Section 3. Sections 4 and 5 present the new VC dimension results. A discussion of the main findings is given in Section 6. We conclude in Section 7.

2   Alkemy

We assume some familiarity with a functional programming language like Haskell [26] in the following.

Figure 1 gives a high-level view of the ALKEMY classification learning system. It accepts as inputs (1) a set of training examples and (2) a hypothesis space, and produces as output a logical decision tree. A variant of the standard TDIDT algorithm is used to construct the output tree.

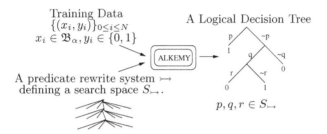

Fig. 1. A schematic diagram of Alkemy

Individuals (also known as instances) in the training set are represented using basic terms in the set $\mathfrak{B}_\alpha$ for some type α chosen appropriately according to the application. The formal basis for basic terms is provided in [17]; syntactically, they read like Haskell data constructs. A rich catalogue of data types is provided for data modelling via basic terms, and these include integers, floating-point numbers, characters, strings, booleans, data constructors, tuples, sets, multisets, lists, trees, graphs and composite types that can be built up from these.

Node functions are specified using predicate rewrite systems in ALKEMY. A detailed description of the mechanism is beyond the scope of this paper. Here we only provide sufficient detail in order to understand its use in Section 5.

Predicates are constructed incrementally by composing more basic functions called transformations. Composition is handled by the (reverse) composition function

$$\circ : (a \rightarrow b) \rightarrow (b \rightarrow c) \rightarrow (a \rightarrow c)$$

defined by $((f \circ g) \, x) = (g \, (f \, x))$.

Definition 1. *A* transformation *f is a function having a signature of the form*

$$f : (\varrho_1 \rightarrow \Omega) \rightarrow \cdots \rightarrow (\varrho_k \rightarrow \Omega) \rightarrow \mu \rightarrow \sigma,$$

where any type variables in $\varrho_1, \ldots, \varrho_k$ *and* σ *appear in* μ, *and* $k \geq 0$. *(Here* Ω *is the type of the booleans.) The type* μ *is called the* source *of the transformation, while the type* σ *is called the* target *of the transformation. The number* k *is called the* rank *of the transformation.*

The two constants 1 and 0 have type Ω. We now look at some examples of transformations.

Example 2. The transformation $\wedge_n : (a \rightarrow \Omega) \rightarrow \cdots \rightarrow (a \rightarrow \Omega) \rightarrow a \rightarrow \Omega$ defined by

$$\wedge_n \, p_1 \ldots p_n = \lambda x.((p_1 \; x) \wedge \cdots \wedge (p_n \; x)),$$

provides a conjunction of n predicates.

Example 3. Each projection $proj_i : a_1 \times \cdots \times a_n \rightarrow a_i$ defined by

$$proj_i \, (t_1, \ldots, t_n) = t_i,$$

for $i = 1, \ldots, n$, is a transformation of rank 0.

Example 4. There are two fundamental transformations $top : a \rightarrow \Omega$ and $bottom : a \rightarrow \Omega$ defined by $(top \; x) = 1$ and $(bottom \; x) = 0$, for each x. The transformation top is the weakest predicate on the type a and $bottom$, the strongest.

Example 5. Let μ be a type and suppose $A, B, C : \mu$ are constants of type μ. Then, corresponding to A, one can define a transformation $(= A) : \mu \rightarrow \Omega$ by

$$((= A) \, x) = x = A,$$

with analogous definitions for $(= B)$ and $(= C)$. Similarly, one can define the transformations $(\neq A), (\neq B)$ and $(\neq C)$.

Example 6. Consider a type such as *Nat* (the type of the natural numbers) which has various order relations defined on it. Then, for any natural number N, one can define the transformation $(< N) : Nat \rightarrow \Omega$ by

$$((< N) \, m) = m < N.$$

In a similar way, one can define the transformations $(> N)$, $(\geq N)$, and $(\leq N)$.

Example 7. Consider the transformation $domCard : (\mu \rightarrow \Omega) \rightarrow \{\mu\} \rightarrow Nat$ defined by

$$domCard \, b \, t = card \; \{x \mid (b \; x) \wedge x \in t\},$$

where *card* computes the cardinality of a set. Given a predicate b on type μ and a transformation on *Nat* such as (> 42), one can construct a predicate $(domCard \; b) \circ (> 42)$ on sets of type $\{\mu\}$ which selects the subset of elements that satisfy the predicate b and then checks that the cardinality of this subset is greater than 42.

One can similarly define *domMcard* for multisets.

Example 8. Consider the transformation $setExists_1 : (a \rightarrow \Omega) \rightarrow \{a\} \rightarrow \Omega$ defined by

$setExists_1\ b\ t = \exists x.((b\ x) \wedge (x \in t)).$

The predicate $(setExists_1\ b)$ checks whether a set has an element that satisfies b.

Transformations are used to define a particular class of predicates, called standard predicates.

Definition 9. *A* standard predicate *is a term of the form*

$$(f_1\ p_{1,1} \ldots p_{1,k_1}) \circ \cdots \circ (f_n\ p_{n,1} \ldots p_{n,k_n}),$$

where f_i is a transformation of rank k_i ($i = 1, \ldots, n$), the target of f_n is Ω, p_{i,j_i} is a standard predicate ($i = 1, \ldots, n$, $j_i = 1, \ldots, k_i$), $k_i \geq 0$ ($i = 1, \ldots, n$) and $n \geq 1$.

Example 10. If p, q, and r are standard predicates (having appropriate type) and $\neg : \Omega \to \Omega$ is negation, then $(\wedge_3\ p\ q\ r) \circ \neg$ is a standard predicate.

Now we can very informally define a predicate rewrite system. A *predicate rewrite* is an expression of the form

$$p \rightarrowtail q,$$

where p and q are standard predicates. The predicate p is called the *head* and q is the *body* of the rewrite. A *predicate rewrite system* is a finite set of predicate rewrites. One should think of a predicate rewrite system as a kind of grammar for generating a particular class of predicates. Roughly speaking, this works as follows. Starting from the weakest predicate *top*, all predicate rewrites that have *top* (of the appropriate type) in the head are selected to make up child predicates that consist of the bodies of these predicate rewrites. Then, for each child predicate and each redex in that predicate, all child predicates are generated by replacing each redex by the body of the predicate rewrite whose head is identical to the redex. This generation of predicates continues to produce the predicate class. The space of predicates defined this way using a predicate rewrite system $\rightarrowtail$ is denoted $S_{\rightarrowtail}$.

Example 11. Consider the predicate rewrite system $\rightarrowtail$ given for the Musk problem in §5.1. The following is a path in the predicate space defined by $\rightarrowtail$.

top

$setExists_1\ (\wedge_3\ top\ top\ top)$

$setExists_1\ (\wedge_3\ (proj_1 \circ (= -6))\ top\ top)$

$setExists_1\ (\wedge_3\ (proj_1 \circ (= -6))\ (proj_2 \circ (= 5))\ top)$

$setExists_1\ (\wedge_3\ (proj_1 \circ (= -6))\ (proj_2 \circ (= 5))\ (proj_{120} \circ (= 0)))$

3   Error Bounds

We now state a few error bounds for general decision trees. The purpose is to determine what are important parameters that one should look at in analysing the generalization behaviour of Alkemic decision trees.

We start with a reminder of some basic concepts. In what follows, log denotes logarithm to base 2, ln denotes the natural logarithm, and $\lceil \cdot \rceil$ and $\lfloor \cdot \rfloor$ denote, respectively, the ceiling and floor functions. The set of natural numbers $\{1, 2, 3, \ldots\}$ is denoted $\mathbb{N}$.

Let X be an arbitrary set and $\mathcal{F}$ a class of predicates over X. The growth function of $\mathcal{F}$, $\Pi_{\mathcal{F}} : \mathbb{N} \to \mathbb{N}$, is defined by $\Pi_{\mathcal{F}}(n) = \max\{|\mathcal{F}_{|x}| : x \in X^n\}$, where

$$\mathcal{F}_{|x} = \{(f(x_1), \ldots, f(x_n)) : f \in \mathcal{F}\}.$$

Given $x \in X^n$, if $|\mathcal{F}_{|x}| = 2^n$, then we say x is *shattered* by $\mathcal{F}$. (Equivalently, we say a subset Y of X is shattered by $\mathcal{F}$ if each subset Z of Y can be picked out by a predicate in $\mathcal{F}$, i.e., there exists $f \in \mathcal{F}$ such that $\forall z \in Z. \ f(z) = 1$ and $\forall z \in Y \setminus Z. \ f(z) = 0$.) The Vapnik-Chervonenkis (VC) dimension of $\mathcal{F}$ is defined by

$$VCD(\mathcal{F}) = \max\{n : \Pi_{\mathcal{F}}(n) = 2^n\}$$

or ∞ if no such maximum exists.

The following is a standard result we will need. More facts about VC dimension can be found in standard texts like [1].

Proposition 12. *Let $\mathcal{F}$ be a finite predicate class. Then $VCD(\mathcal{F}) \leq \lfloor \log |\mathcal{F}| \rfloor$.*

Proof. We need at least 2^d predicates to shatter a set of d elements.   □

Error bounds for decision trees obtained from classical VC theory suggest that the amount of training data needed for learning should grow at least linearly with the size of the tree and the VC dimension of the node functions. See, for example, [1], [12] and [13]. More recent results give data-dependent bounds that are qualitatively different from those earlier results. For example, in [14], the authors show how decision trees with node functions in $\mathcal{U}$ can be represented as thresholded convex combinations of functions in $\mathcal{U}$, and from that establish error bounds for decision trees using margin-based error bounds for two-layer neural networks (see [1] and [23]). We state the main theorem here. For more details, the reader is referred to [14] and [19].

Theorem 13 ([14]). *For a fixed $\delta > 0$, there is a constant c that satisfies the following. Let $\mathcal{D}$ be a distribution on $X \times \{0, 1\}$. Consider the class of decision trees of depth up to k, with node functions in $\mathcal{U}$. With probability at least $1 - \delta$ over the training set S of size m, every decision tree T satisfies*

$$\mathbf{P}_{(x,y)\sim\mathcal{D}}[T(x) \neq y] \leq \mathbf{P}_{(x,y)\sim S}[T(x) \neq y] + c\left(\frac{N_{\textit{eff}} \, VCD(\mathcal{U}) \log^2 m \log k}{m}\right)^{1/3}.$$

Here $N_{\textit{eff}}$ is a data-dependent quantity that measures the *effective* number of leave nodes in T, a number that can be significantly smaller than the actual number of leave nodes in T. See, for the exact definition, [14].

The classical theorems are suitable for use with small trees; Theorem 13 works better for large trees.

4   Tools for Calculating VC Dimensions

As shown in the last section, the VC dimension of node functions is an important parameter in the generalization behaviour of Alkemic decision trees. To understand the nature of learning with ALKEMY, we thus need to develop methods to calculate the VC dimensions of (more-or-less arbitrary) predicate classes definable using predicate rewrite systems. The problem seems difficult at first sight; in fact, it was listed as an open research question in [17, Exercise 6.6]. But recent progress has shown that solutions to some important aspects of the general problem are actually rather straightforward. These results are reported here.

We will first outline the development of some useful tools for analysing predicate classes defined on sets and multisets in this section. Armed with these, we will then proceed in Section 5 to calculate the VC dimensions of three illustrative predicate rewrite systems selected from [17]. We remark that the tools developed here have applications beyond ALKEMY, for example in the analysis of systems that learn from set-valued objects like [8].

In this section, for the most part, we will abstract away from predicate rewrite systems and just work on predicate classes defined on 'collections' of natural numbers. As we shall see, this is a useful simplification since there is a simple mapping between natural numbers and arbitrary finite sets that we can exploit.

4.1   Sets

We will start with the following basic observation.

Proposition 14. *Let $\mathcal{F}_\exists$ be the class of predicates $\mathcal{F}_\exists = \{f_{i,j} : i, j \in \mathbb{N}, j \geq i\}$ where each $f_{i,j} : 2^\mathbb{N} \to \{0, 1\}$ is defined by*

$$f_{i,j}(t) = \begin{cases} 1 & \text{if } \exists x \in t.\ i \leq x \leq j \\ 0 & \text{otherwise.} \end{cases}$$

Then $VCD(\mathcal{F}_\exists) = \infty$.

Proof. It suffices to show that the subset $\mathcal{F}'_\exists = \{f_{i,i} : i \in \mathbb{N}\}$ of $\mathcal{F}_\exists$ has infinite VC dimension. For each $n \in \mathbb{N}$, we can construct a set $\{X_1, X_2, \ldots, X_n\}$ that is shattered by $\mathcal{F}'_\exists$ as follows. Enumerate all the subsets of $N = \{1, 2, \ldots, n\}$, assigning them numbers from 1 to 2^n. For instance, when $n = 3$ we get

1	2	3	4	5	6	7	8	.
$\emptyset$	$\{1\}$	$\{2\}$	$\{3\}$	$\{1,2\}$	$\{1,3\}$	$\{2,3\}$	$\{1,2,3\}$	

Now define X_i to be the set of all numbers assigned to a subset of N having i as a member. Continuing with our example for $n = 3$, we obtain the set

$$\{X_1 = \{2, 5, 6, 8\},\ X_2 = \{3, 5, 7, 8\},\ X_3 = \{4, 6, 7, 8\}\}.$$

It is clear that $\{X_1, X_2, \ldots, X_n\}$ constructed this way is shattered by $\mathcal{F}'_\exists$. $\square$

We next give a useful generalization of Proposition 14. First, a definition.

Definition 15. *Let X be a set and $\mathcal{F}$ a class of predicates over X. We say a set $S \subseteq X$ is* disintegrated *by $\mathcal{F}$ if for every $x \in S$, there exists an $f \in \mathcal{F}$ such that $f(x) = 1$ and $f(y) = 0$ for all $y \in S \setminus \{x\}$.*

Lemma 16. *Let X be a set and suppose $\mathcal{F}$ is a class of predicates over X. Let $\mathcal{G} = \{g_f : f \in \mathcal{F}\}$ be the class of predicates where each $g_f : 2^X \to \{0,1\}$ is defined by*

$$g_f(t) = \begin{cases} 1 & \text{if } \exists x \in t.\ f(x) = 1 \\ 0 & \text{otherwise.} \end{cases}$$

If there exists a finite $S \subseteq X$ such that $|S| \geqslant 2$ and S is disintegrated by $\mathcal{F}$, then $VCD(\mathcal{G}) \geq \lfloor \log |S| \rfloor$.

Proof. Proceeding as in Proposition 14, we can assign a different element of S to each subset of $N = \{1, 2, \ldots, \lfloor \log |S| \rfloor\}$. Defining X_i to be the set of all elements assigned to a subset of N in which i occurs gives us a subset of 2^X that is shattered by $\mathcal{G}$. $\qquad\square$

As a simple application of Lemma 16, we give this next result for sets of tuples of constants.

Theorem 17. *Let N be a finite subset of $\mathbb{N}$ satisfying $|N| \geqslant 2$. Suppose $m \geq n > 0$ and let $\mathcal{G}_{m,n}$ be the class of predicates*

$$\mathcal{G}_{m,n} = \{g_{\{(i_l, j_l)\}_{1 \leq l \leq k}} : k \in \{1, \ldots, n\}, i_l \in \{1, \ldots, m\}, j_l \in N\}$$

where each $g_{\{(i_l, j_l)\}_{1 \leq l \leq k}} : 2^{N^m} \to \{0,1\}$ is defined by

$$g_{\{(i_l, j_l)\}_{1 \leq l \leq k}}(t) = \begin{cases} 1 & \text{if } \exists (x_1, \ldots, x_m) \in t.(x_{i_1} = j_1) \wedge \cdots \wedge (x_{i_k} = j_k) \\ 0 & \text{otherwise.} \end{cases}$$

Then

$$VCD(\mathcal{G}_{m,n}) \geq \begin{cases} \lfloor m \log |N| \rfloor & \text{if } n = m; \\ \lfloor \log(\sum_{k=1}^{n} \binom{m}{k}(|N| - 1)^k) \rfloor & \text{otherwise.} \end{cases}$$

Proof. Let

$$\mathcal{F}_{m,n} = \{f_{\{(i_l, j_l)\}_{1 \leq l \leq k}} : k \in \{1, \ldots, n\}, i_l \in \{1, \ldots, m\}, j_l \in N, i_1 < \cdots < i_k\}$$

where each $f_{\{(i_l, j_l)\}_{1 \leq l \leq k}} : N^m \to \{0,1\}$ is defined by

$$f_{\{(i_l, j_l)\}_{1 \leq l \leq k}}(x_1, \ldots, x_m) = \begin{cases} 1 & \text{if } (x_{i_1} = j_1) \wedge \cdots \wedge (x_{i_k} = j_k) \\ 0 & \text{otherwise.} \end{cases}$$

We use Lemma 16 to get the lower bounds here. When $n = m$, we can use for S the whole set N^m, which is clearly disintegrated by $\mathcal{F}_{m,m}$. When $n < m$, we construct S as follows. Pick an $x \in N$ at random and consider the following subset of $\mathcal{F}_{m,n}$:

$$\mathcal{F}_{m,n,x} = \{f_{\{i_l,j_l\}_{1 \leq l \leq k}} : k \in \{1,\ldots,n\},$$
$$i_l \in \{1,\ldots,m\}, j_l \in N \setminus \{x\}, i_1 < \cdots < i_k\}.$$

For each predicate $f_{\{(i_l,j_l)\}_{1 \leq l \leq k}} \in \mathcal{F}_{m,n,x}$ add to S the tuple that has value j_l at the i_l-th component, and x everywhere else. (For instance, when $m = 5, k = 2, N = \{1,2,3\}$ and $x = 3$, given $f_{\{(1,2),(3,1)\}}$, we add $(3,3,1,3,2)$ to S.) It is not hard to see that each element in S can be picked out by the predicate that generated it. Further,

$$|S| = |\mathcal{F}_{m,n,x}| = \sum_{k=1}^{n} \binom{m}{k} (|N| - 1)^k.$$

The condition $|N| \geqslant 2$ ensures that $|S| \geqslant 2$ in both cases.   □

It is perhaps of (independent) interest to note that the dual $\mathcal{F}_\forall$ (defined below) of $\mathcal{F}_\exists$ defined in Proposition 14 has finite VC dimension.

Proposition 18. *Let $\mathcal{F}_\forall$ be the class of predicates $\mathcal{F}_\forall = \{f_{i,j} : i, j \in \mathbb{N}, j \geq i\}$ where each $f_{i,j} : 2^\mathbb{N} \to \{0,1\}$ is defined by*

$$f_{i,j}(t) = \begin{cases} 1 & \text{if } \forall x \in t. \ i \leq x \leq j; \\ 0 & \text{otherwise.} \end{cases}$$

Then $VCD(\mathcal{F}_\forall) = 2$.

Proof. It is easy to show that $VCD(\mathcal{F}_\forall) \geqslant 2$. Assume there exists a set $S = \{X,Y,Z\}$ that is shattered by $\mathcal{F}_\forall$. Clearly, none of the elements in S can be the empty set, which evaluates to 1 for each $f \in \mathcal{F}_\forall$. Further, each element in S must be finite. (Shattering is impossible otherwise.) Denote by $\max(A)$ and $\min(A)$ the biggest and smallest numbers in a (finite) set A of numbers and define the range of A by $range(A) = \{\min(A),\ldots,\max(A)\}$. We have

$$\forall A, B \in S, \ A \neq B \Rightarrow range(A) \not\subseteq range(B)$$

since if $range(A) \subseteq range(B)$, there is no way to make B true without also making A true. Without loss of generality, assume $\min(X) < \min(Y) < \min(Z)$. This implies $\max(X) < \max(Y) < \max(Z)$. Now, there is no $f_{i,j} \in \mathcal{F}_\forall$ such that $f_{i,j}(X) = 1$, $f_{i,j}(Z) = 1$, and $f_{i,j}(Y) = 0$ since any (i,j)-interval that covers both $\min(X)$ and $\max(Z)$ must also cover every number in the range $\{\min(Y),\ldots,\max(Y)\} \supseteq Y$.   □

4.2   Multisets

We next look at multisets. The difference between a set and a multiset is that an element can occur multiple times in a multiset. Some of the results given for sets clearly carry over to multisets with little change. The multiplicity of elements allowed in multisets can sometimes be exploited, as done in our next result. First some notation.

Let A be a multiset of elements from some set X. In the following, we denote by $\#(A, x)$ the multiplicity of $x \in X$ in A. Further, we denote by $\mathbb{N}_0$ the set $\{0\} \cup \mathbb{N}$.

Definition 19. *Let A and B be multisets of elements from some set X. We define the pairwise maximum between A and B, denoted $A \sqcup B$, as follows: $A \sqcup B$ is the multiset that contains, for all $x \in X$, $\max\{\#(A, x), \#(B, x)\}$ occurrences of x. For example, $\{1, 1, 2, 2, 2\} \sqcup \{1, 2, 2, 2, 2, 3, 3, 3\} = \{1, 1, 2, 2, 2, 2, 3, 3, 3\}$.*

Theorem 20. *Suppose X and Y are non-empty finite subsets of $\mathbb{N}$. Let $\mathcal{F}$ be the class of predicates $\mathcal{F} = \{f_{i,j} : i \in X, j \in Y\}$ where each $f_{i,j} : \mathbb{N}_0{}^{\mathbb{N}} \to \{0, 1\}$ is defined by*

$$f_{i,j}(t) = \begin{cases} 1 & \text{if } \#(t, i) \geqslant j; \\ 0 & \text{otherwise.} \end{cases}$$

Let $d \in \mathbb{N}$. If $|Y| \geqslant d+1$ and $|X| \geqslant \binom{d}{i}$ for all $i \in \{1, \ldots, d\}$, then $VCD(\mathcal{F}) \geqslant d$.

Proof. The proof is in two stages. In the first stage, we show that given a function ψ from the powerset of $D = \{1, \ldots, d\}$ to $\mathbb{N}_0{}^{\mathbb{N}}$ satisfying a certain property, we can construct a set $Z = \{Z_1, \ldots, Z_d\}$ that is shattered by $\mathcal{F}$. In the second stage, we show that ψ exists and give a simple algorithm for constructing it.

Stage 1 We denote by (x, y) the multiset that contains y occurrences of x and nothing else. Assume ψ satisfies the following property: For all $S \subseteq D$, we have

1. $\psi(S) = (x, y)$ for some $x, y \in \mathbb{N}$, and
2. for all $A \subseteq D$ not equal to S, if $\psi(A) = (x, z)$ for some $z \in \mathbb{N}$ and $|A| \geq |S|$, then $S \subset A$ and $y > z$.

Given such a function ψ, define $Z_i = \bigsqcup \{\psi(S) : S \subseteq D, i \in S\}$ for each $i \in D$. (Example 23 below gives an example of a function ψ defined on the subsets of $D = \{1, 2, 3, 4\}$ that satisfy the property stated above. References there to the **Label** algorithm should be ignored for now. Each pair A (B, C) in the example should be interpreted as $\psi(A) = (B, C)$. For example, $\psi(\emptyset) = (1, 5)$. Note also the way each Z_i is defined using ψ.) We now argue that the set $Z = \{Z_1, \ldots, Z_d\}$ so-constructed is shattered by $\mathcal{F}$. Specifically, we show that for all $S \subseteq D$, $f_{x,y}(Z_i) = 1$ if $i \in S$ and $f_{x,y}(Z_i) = 0$ otherwise, given that $\psi(S) = (x, y)$.

Consider an arbitrary $S \subseteq D$ with $\psi(S) = (x, y)$. If $i \in S$, by construction, Z_i contains at least y occurrences of x and $f_{x,y}(Z_i) = 1$. Consider now the case when $i \notin S$. If $\#(Z_i, x) = 0$, then $f_{x,y}(Z_i) = 0$ as desired. If $\#(Z_i, x) > 0$, then there exists $A \subseteq D$ such that $i \in A$ and $\psi(A) = (x, z)$ for some $z \in \mathbb{N}$. We can assume without loss of generality that A is the set with the largest z. If $|A| \geq |S|$, then by the property of ψ, we have $y > z$ and $S \subset A$, which implies $f_{x,y}(Z_i) = 0$. If $|A| < |S|$, then by the property of ψ, we have $z > y$ and $A \subset S$. (Simply substitute the set A for the variable S and the set S for the variable A in the statement of the property of ψ.) This case can't arise since $A \subset S$ and $i \in A$ together imply $i \in S$, contradicting $i \notin S$.

Stage 2 It suffices to show that one such ψ exists. We will give a more general result that shows that not only does ψ exists, we can actually find many instances of it efficiently using well-studied algorithms in graph theory.

Given X and Y both non-empty finite subsets of $\mathbb{N}$, we first use the **Label** algorithm given below to label the subsets of D. For each $S \subseteq D$, we then define $\psi(S)$ to be the label assigned to S. To get some intuition, we first give a high-level description of the labelling algorithm. Conceptually, we first lay out in a sequence the subsets of D in groups, starting from the empty set (group 0), followed by the 1-subsets (group 1), the 2-subsets (group 2), $\ldots$, and finally finishing at D (group $|D|$). (A subset with k elements in it is called a k-subset here.) The algorithm starts by labelling the largest group and then iteratively label the next two largest unlabelled groups until every subset of D has a label.

We now give the algorithm. The variables l, u and m are integers. In the algorithm, we denote by $Y[i]$ and $X[i]$ the i-th largest elements in Y and X. The condition $|X| \geq \binom{d}{i}$ for all i comes about because of Step 2. The condition $|Y| \geq d + 1$ comes from the fact that there are $d + 1$ groups of subsets of D. Example 23 below gives a concrete example of the labelling. It is instructive to work through the example at this stage.

Alg. **Label**

1. $l \leftarrow 1$; $u \leftarrow 1$; $m \leftarrow \min\{i : \forall j.\ \binom{d}{j} \leqslant \binom{d}{i}\}$;
2. Label the m-subsets of D with $(X[i], Y[\lceil d/2 + 1 \rceil])$ in increasing order of i.
3. If $m - l < 0$, goto Step 6;
4. $C \leftarrow$ the $(m - l + 1)$-subsets of D;
5. For each $(m - l)$-subset S of D
   (a) Pick an $L \in C$ with label $(x, Y[m])$ such that $S \subset L$ and label S with $(x, Y[m + 1])$;
   (b) $C \leftarrow C \setminus L$;
6. If $m + u > d$, terminate;
7. $C \leftarrow$ the $(m + u - 1)$-subsets of D;
8. For each $(m + u)$-subset S of D
   (a) Pick an $L \in C$ with label $(x, Y[m])$ such that $L \subset S$ and label S with $(x, Y[m - 1])$;

(b) $C \leftarrow C \setminus L$;

9. $l \leftarrow l + 1$; $u \leftarrow u + 1$; Goto Step 3;

By design, the function ψ constructed from a labelling obtained by **Label**, assuming it terminates, satisfies the condition stated earlier. We now show that the **Label** algorithm always terminate successfully. For that, we need to show that Steps 5(a) and 8(a) can always be performed for each S. We will show this for Step 5(a); the argument for Step 8(a) is similar. What we are trying to do is in fact to find a matching in a bipartite graph. The vertices of the graph consists of the $(m - l)$ and $(m - l + 1)$-subsets of D, with the $(m - l)$-subsets forming the first partition, and the $(m - l + 1)$-subsets the second. There is an edge from an $(m - l)$-subset A to an $(m - l + 1)$-subset B iff $A \subset B$. By the choice of m, we have

$$\text{no. of } (m - l)\text{-subsets} = \binom{d}{m - l} \leqslant \binom{d}{m - l + 1} = \text{no. of } (m - l + 1)\text{-subsets.}$$

Thus we seek a matching of cardinality $\binom{d}{m-l}$.

To show that such a matching exists and can be found efficiently, we introduce a concept from graph theory.

Definition 21. *A vertex cover of a graph $G = (V, E)$ is a set $U \subseteq V$ such that every edge of G is incident with a vertex in U.*

We make use of the following known result. For a proof, see, for example, [9].

Theorem 22 (König 1931). *The maximum cardinality of a matching in a bipartite graph G is equal to the minimum cardinality of a vertex cover of G.*

The set of $(m - l)$-subsets with cardinality $\binom{d}{m-l}$ is clearly a vertex cover. A straightforward indirect argument shows that there is no smaller vertex cover. The existence of our desired matching then follows from Theorem 22. There are efficient network flow algorithms for finding (all) such matchings; see, for instance, [21, Chap. 10].

Finally, the labelling algorithm will always terminate at Step 6 by the choice of m in Step 1. ☐

Example 23. Suppose $X = \{1, \ldots, 6\}$ and $Y = \{1, \ldots, 5\}$. Let $\mathcal{F}$ be as defined in Theorem 20. To construct a set $Z = \{Z_1, Z_2, Z_3, Z_4\}$ that is shattered by $\mathcal{F}$, we first label the subsets of $D = \{1, 2, 3, 4\}$ according to the **Label** algorithm. One acceptable labelling is the following.

$$\emptyset \, (1, 5)$$
$$\{1\} \, (1, 4), \ \{2\} \, (4, 4), \ \{3\} \, (2, 4), \ \{4\} \, (3, 4)$$
$$\{1, 2\} \, (1, 3), \ \{1, 3\} \, (2, 3), \ \{1, 4\} \, (3, 3), \ \{2, 3\} \, (4, 3), \ \{2, 4\} \, (5, 3), \ \{3, 4\} \, (6, 3)$$
$$\{1, 2, 3\} \, (1, 2), \ \{1, 2, 4\} \, (5, 2), \ \{1, 3, 4\} \, (2, 2), \ \{2, 3, 4\} \, (6, 2)$$
$$\{1, 2, 3, 4\} \, (1, 1)$$

Based on the function ψ obtained from the labelling, we construct

$$Z = \{\, Z_1 = \{1,1,1,1,2,2,2,3,3,3,5,5\},$$
$$Z_2 = \{4,4,4,4,1,1,1,5,5,5,6,6\},$$
$$Z_3 = \{2,2,2,2,4,4,4,6,6,6,1,1\},$$
$$Z_4 = \{3,3,3,3,5,5,5,6,6,6,2,2,1\}\,\}.$$

It can be easily verified that Z is shattered by $\mathcal{F}$. ◄

Observation 24. *It is possible to weaken the condition on $|Y|$ in Theorem 20 using a more scrupulous grouping of the subsets, especially for large values of d. We note here a simple way to weaken that to $|Y| \geqslant d - 1$ by treating the empty set as part of the 1-subsets, and the whole set D as part of the $(d-1)$-subsets during labelling. Labelling is possible because the empty set, being a subset of every other set, is connected to all the 2-subsets; and the set D, being a superset of every other set, is connected to all the $(d-2)$-subsets.*

5 Some Illustrations

Building on results presented in the previous section, we now analyse three instructive examples of predicate rewrite systems taken from [17, Chap. 6]. For each illustration, we briefly introduce the problem and give details on (1) the way individuals are represented; and (2) the predicate rewrite system used. Readers can consult [17] for more information.

5.1 Musk

This first illustration is the Musk problem described in [10]. Briefly, the problem is to determine whether or not a molecule has a musk odour. Molecules generally have many different conformations and, presumably, only one conformation is responsible for the activity. Each conformation is a tuple of 166 floating-point numbers, where 162 of these represent the distance in angstroms from some origin in the conformation out along a radial line to the surface of the conformation and the other four numbers represent the position of a specific oxygen atom. For convenience, the floating-point numbers are discretized into 13 intervals, resulting in the following.

Representation of Individuals

$-6, -5, \ldots, 5, 6 : Distance$

$Conformation = Distance \times \cdots \times Distance$

$Molecule = \{\, Conformation \,\}$

Here the product type $Distance \times \cdots \times Distance$ contains 166 components. The function $musk$ to be learned has signature $musk : Molecule \to \Omega$.

Predicate Rewrite System

$$top \rightarrowtail setExists_1 \ (\wedge_3 \ top \ top \ top)$$
$$top \rightarrowtail proj_i \circ (= j) \ \text{ where } \ i \in \{1, 2, \dots, 166\}, j \in \{-6, -5, \dots, 6\}$$

Proposition 25. $VCD(S_\rightarrowtail) = 30.$

Proof. By Proposition 12, $VCD(S_\rightarrowtail) \leq \lfloor \log |S_\rightarrowtail| \rfloor = \lfloor \log 1,679,615,641 \rfloor = 30.$
We have the lower bound

$$VCD(S_\rightarrowtail) \geq \lfloor \log(\sum_{k=1}^{3} \binom{166}{k} (12)^k) \rfloor = \lfloor \log 1,295,658,552 \rfloor = 30$$

by Theorem 17. □

5.2 Climate

Consider next the problem of deciding whether a climate in some country is pleasant or not. The climate is modelled by a multiset. Each item in a multiset is a term characterizing the main features of the weather during a day and the multiplicity of the item is the number of times during a year a day with those particular weather features occurs.

Representation of Individuals

$$Sunny, Overcast, Rain : Outlook$$
$$Hot, Mild, Cool : Temp$$
$$High, Normal, Low : Humidity$$
$$Strong, Medium, Weak : Wind$$
$$Weather = Outlook \times Temp \times Humidity \times Wind$$

A climate is modelled as a multiset $Climate = Weather \rightarrow Nat$ and the function *pleasant* to be learned has signature $pleasant : Climate \rightarrow \Omega$.

Predicate Rewrite System

$$top \rightarrowtail (domMcard \ top) \circ (> 0);$$
$$top \rightarrowtail \wedge_4 \ (projOutlook \circ top) \ (projTemp \circ top)$$
$$(projHumidity \circ top) \ (projWind \circ top);$$
$$top \rightarrowtail (= Sunny); \ top \rightarrowtail (= Overcast); \ top \rightarrowtail (= Rain);$$
$$top \rightarrowtail (= Hot); \ top \rightarrowtail (= Mild); \ top \rightarrowtail (= Cool);$$
$$top \rightarrowtail (= High); \ top \rightarrowtail (= Low); \ top \rightarrowtail (= Normal);$$
$$top \rightarrowtail (= Strong); \ top \rightarrowtail (= Medium); \ top \rightarrowtail (= Weak);$$
$$(> i) \rightarrowtail (> i + 50) \ \text{ where } \ i \in \{0, 50, \dots, 300\}.$$

Proposition 26. $8 \leq VCD(S_\rightharpoonup) \leq 11$.

Proof. By Proposition 12, $VCD(S_\rightharpoonup) \leq \lfloor \log |S_\rightharpoonup| \rfloor = \lfloor \log 2057 \rfloor = 11$. We use Theorem 20 to establish the lower bound. All the tuples of type *Weather* can be numbered and form the set X, with $|X| = 81$. Each predicate in $S_\rightharpoonup$ of the form

$$(domMcard \ (\wedge_4 \ (projOutlook \circ (= A))$$
$$(projTemp \circ (= B)) \ (projHumidity \circ (= C)) \ (projWind \circ (= D)))) \circ (> j)$$

is equivalent to some $f_{i,j+1}$ as defined in Theorem 20, where i is the labelling number of (A, B, C, D). There are 81 ways to instantiate the variables A, B, C and D. The variable j can take on values in the set

$$Y = \{1, 51, 101, 151, 201, 251, 301, 351\}.$$

The largest d satisfying $|Y| \geq d - 1$ and $|X| \geq \binom{d}{i}$ for all i is $d = 8$.   □

5.3   Beyond Sets and Multisets

Results like Theorem 17 and Theorem 20 are actually more useful than they appear. A natural thing to do when learning from structured data is to check for existence of substructures common to individuals of the same class. For example, given a graph, it is common to pull out the set of all subgraphs of a certain size and check whether there exists one satisfying a certain property. Similarly for lists, trees and other complex data types. This means that transformations involving sets and multisets actually appear very often in predicate rewrite systems defined over a wide range of structured data, and these can be analysed using results presented in this paper. We remark that, in fact, *all* but one illustrations described in [17, Chap. 6], which cover many different data types in common use, can be analysed this way.

To illustrate the kind of reasoning involved, we give one final example, again taken from [17], involving lists. We consider the East-West challenge proposed by Michalski. Given trains and the directions they are traveling in, the task is to learn a rule that can differentiate between those heading east and those heading west.

The most natural type to model a train is a list. We first introduce the types *Direction*, *Shape*, *Length*, *Kind*, *Roof*, and *Object*.

East, West : *Direction*

Rectangular, DoubleRectangular, UShaped, BucketShaped,
Hexagonal, Ellipsoidal : *Shape*

Long, Short : *Length*

Closed, Open : *Kind*

Flat, Jagged, Peaked, Curved, None : *Roof*

Circle, Hexagon, Square, Rectangle, LongRectangle, Triangle,
InvertedTriangle, Diamond, Null : *Object*.

We also introduce the following type synonyms for convenience.

$NumWheels = Nat$

$NumObjects = Nat$

$Load = Object \times NumObjects$

$Car = Shape \times Length \times NumWheels \times Kind \times Roof \times Load$

$Train = List\ Car.$

The function *direction* to be learned has signature *direction* : $Train \to Direction$.

Before giving the predicate rewrite system, we first introduce a few transformations for lists. The transformation *listToSet* : $Train \to \{Car\}$ converts a list of carriages into a set of carriages. The transformation $(sublists\ N)$: $Train \to \{Train\}$ takes a list of carriages and returns the set of all sublists of size N. The transformation $(!!N)$: $Train \to Car$ takes a train and returns the N-th carriage in the train. The predicate rewrite system is as follows.

$top \rightarrowtail listToSet \circ (setExists_1\ (\wedge_2\ top\ top));$

$top \rightarrowtail (sublists\ 2) \circ (setExists_1\ (\wedge_2\ ((!!0) \circ top)\ ((!!1) \circ top)));$

$top \rightarrowtail projShape \circ top;\ top \rightarrowtail projLength \circ top;\ top \rightarrowtail projNumWheels \circ top;$

$top \rightarrowtail projKind \circ top;\ top \rightarrowtail projRoof \circ top;\ top \rightarrowtail projLoad \circ top$

$top \rightarrowtail projObject \circ top;\ top \rightarrowtail projNumObjects \circ top;$

$top \rightarrowtail (= A)$ where A a constant of type $Shape;$

$top \rightarrowtail (= B)$ where B a constant of type $Length;$

$top \rightarrowtail (= C)$ where C a constant of type $Kind;$

$top \rightarrowtail (= D)$ where D a constant of type $Roof;$

$top \rightarrowtail (= E)$ where E a constant of type $Object;$

$top \rightarrowtail (= 1);\ top \rightarrowtail (= 2);\ top \rightarrowtail (= 3).$

Proposition 27. $7 \leq VCD(S_{\rightarrowtail}) \leq 11.$

Proof. Given $|S_{\rightarrowtail}| = 2073$, we have $VCD(S_{\rightarrowtail}) \leq \lfloor \log |S_{\rightarrowtail}| \rfloor = 11$ by Proposition 12. The lower bound can be established by analysing the predicates generated by the first rewrite. The reasoning proceeds in a similar fashion as in Theorem 17, but taking into account the fact that the components of Car have different ranges. An element from each component is reserved as a default value, in the same way an $x \in N$ is used in Theorem 17. From that, we get a set X of Car objects that can be used to construct a shatterable set D of sets of Car objects, where $|D| = \lfloor \log |X| \rfloor$ by Lemma 16. Clearly, one can recover a $Train$ object from each element in D. A straightforward counting exercise yields $|X| = 230$, giving us the lower bound $\lfloor \log |X| \rfloor = 7$. $\qquad\square$

6   Discussion

In the three examples presented in the previous section, an upper bound on the VC dimension is established by counting the size of the predicate class. A lower bound is then given via an explicit construction of a set of individuals that is shattered by the predicate class, making use of the rich structures available. Interestingly, the upper and lower bounds are never too far apart, and this holds true for all the other illustrations in [17] we analysed. Now one would expect that it is possible to do a lot better than a naïve counting of the predicate class; apparently not. What are we to make of these results?

It was shown in [25] (see also [1, Chap. 5]) that for a predicate class with high VC dimension, there exist distributions that will force the learning algorithm to require a large number of examples to obtain good generalization. This, together with the results presented in this paper, implies that, in general, the true errors of hypotheses in the rich predicate classes used by ALKEMY cannot be easily estimated from empirical data, and that, *in the worst case*, the number of training examples needed grows rather quickly with the size and complexity of the hypothesis language used. The problem is that if we do not make any assumption about the underlying distribution, then we must be prepared to accept the possibility that everything can conspire against the learner – the more structures we introduce into the representation of individuals and the hypothesis language, the more structures there are to be exploited for producing bad cases.

7   Conclusion

We have looked at some generalization issues in relation to ALKEMY in this paper. In particular, we investigated the VC dimensions of some predicate classes defined on sets and multisets and studied their applications in the context of ALKEMY. The results provide valuable information on the nature of learning with sets and multisets, thus filling a gap in our understanding of the process of learning from structured data. On the practical side, the tools developed in this paper can be used to calculate the complexity of different predicate classes. In real applications, such calculations can be used to guide the selection and crafting of hypothesis languages.

Future Work. We have shown in this paper that some fairly natural predicate classes defined on sets and multisets have high VC dimension. This implies that these classes are hard to learn in the distribution-free setting. However, learning with predicate classes that have high VC dimensions is possible if the underlying distribution is benign, and this information can be obtained from the training data. For instance, [24] shows that the VC dimension of a predicate class on the training sample can be used as a measure of how helpful the distribution is in identifying the target concept, and gives error bounds in terms of that. More recently, [4] gives error bounds in terms of the Rademacher and Gaussian complexities of predicate classes, and these can be estimated easily from the training data. PAC-Bayes and PAC-MDL bounds, which are also data-dependent results, can also help us obtain tighter bounds. Some relevant work along this line of research include [18] and [22]. Investigation into such data-dependent analysis is our future work.

Related Work. A body of work in ILP has provided both upper and lower bounds on the number of examples required for learnability, mostly in the PAC setting. Upper bounds are usually obtained by analyzing concrete algorithms for learning restricted first-order classes; see, for example, [20], [11], [7] and [16]. Issues of computation and estimation, in the sense expounded in [1, §1.1], are usually tightly integrated in this kind of analyses, and this failure to separate concerns is slightly unsatisfactory.

Lower bounds, however, are usually obtained, independently of computation issues, using purely information-theoretic concepts like Vapnik-Chervonenkis dimensions. Examples of such work include [3], [15] and [2], and this paper is related to these. The fact that the same general conclusion was obtained from the analyses of two very different knowledge representation formalisms tells us something about the sample complexity of learning with rich expressive languages in general.

Acknowledgments

I'm grateful to John W. Lloyd and Evan Greensmith for valuable discussions.

References

1. Martin Anthony and Peter L. Bartlett. *Neural Network Learning: Theoretical Foundations.* Cambridge University Press, 1999.
2. Marta Arias and Roni Khardon. Complexity parameters of first order classes. In *Proceedings of the 13th International Conference on Inductive Logic Programming*, pages 22–37, 2003.
3. Hiroki Arimura. Learning acyclic first-order horn sentences from entailment. In *Proceedings of the International Conference on Algorithmic Learning Theory.* Springer-Verlag, 1997.
4. Peter L. Bartlett and Shahar Mendelson. Rademacher and Gaussian complexities: risk bounds and structural results. *Journal of Machine Learning Research*, 3:463–482, 2002.
5. Avrim Blum. Learning boolean functions in an infinite attribute space. *Machine Learning*, 9(4):373–386, 1992.
6. Antony F. Bowers, Christophe Giraud-Carrier, and John W. Lloyd. Classification of individuals with complex structure. In *Proceedings of the 17th International Conference on Machine Learning*, pages 81–88. Morgan Kaufmann, 2000.
7. William W. Cohen. PAC-learning recursive logic programs: Efficient algorithms. *Journal of Artificial Intelligence Research*, 2:501–539, 1995.
8. William W. Cohen. Learning trees and rules with set-valued features. In *Proceedings of the 13th National Conference on Artificial Intelligence*, pages 709–716, Menlo Park, CA, 1996. AAAI Press.
9. Reinhard Diestel. *Graph Theory.* Springer-Verlag, 2nd edition, 2000.
10. Thomas G. Dietterich, Richard H. Lathrop, and Tomás Lozano-Pérez. Solving the multiple instance problem with axis-parallel rectangles. *Artificial Intelligence*, 89:31–71, 1997.

11. Sašo Džeroski, Stephen Muggleton, and Stuart Russell. PAC-learnability of determinate logic programs. In *Proceedings of the Workshop on Computational Learning Theory*, 1992.
12. Andrzej Ehrenfeucht and David Haussler. Learning decision trees from random examples. *Information and Computation*, 82:231–246, 1989.
13. Usama Fayyad and Keki Irani. What should be minimized in a decision tree? In *Proc. the 8th National Conference on Artificial Intelligence*, pages 749–754, 1990.
14. Mostefa Golea, Peter L. Bartlett, Wee Sun Lee, and Llew Mason. Generalization in decision trees and DNF: Does size matter? In *Advances in Neural Information Processing Systems 10*, pages 259–265, 1998.
15. Roni Khardon. Learning function free horn expressions. *Machine Learning*, 37:241–275, 1999.
16. Jörg-Uwe Kietz and Sašo Džeroski. Inductive logic programming and learnability. *SIGART Bulletin*, 5(1):22–32, 1994.
17. John W. Lloyd. *Logic for Learning: Learning Comprehensible Theories from Structured Data*. Cognitive Technologies. Springer, 2003.
18. Yishay Mansour and David McAllester. Generalization bounds for decision trees. In *Proceedings of the 13th Annual Conference on Computational Learning Theory*, pages 69–80. Morgan Kaufmann, San Francisco, 2000.
19. Llew Mason. *Margins and Combined Classifiers*. PhD thesis, Research School of Information Sciences and Engineering, The Australian National University, 1999.
20. Stephen Muggleton and Cao Feng. Efficient induction of logic programs. In S. Muggleton, editor, *Inductive Logic Programming*, pages 281–298. Academic Press, 1992.
21. Christos H. Papadimitriou and Kenneth Steiglitz. *Combinatorial Optimization: Algorithms and Complexity*. Dover Publications, 1998.
22. Ulrich Rückert and Stefan Kramer. Towards tight bounds for rule learning. In *Proceedings of the 21st International Conference on Machine Learning*, 2004.
23. Robert E. Schapire, Yoav Freund, Peter Bartlett, and Wee Sun Lee. Boosting the margin: A new explanation for the effectiveness of voting methods. *The Annals of Statistics*, 26 (5):1651–1686, 1998.
24. John Shawe-Taylor, Peter L. Bartlett, Robert Williamson, and Martin Anthony. Structural risk minimization over data-dependent hierarchies. *IEEE Transactions on Information Theory*, 44(5):1926–1940, 1998.
25. Hans-Ulrich Simon. General bounds on the number of examples needed for learning probabilistic concepts. *J. of Computer and System Sciences*, 52:239–254, 1996.
26. Simon Thompson. *Haskell - The Craft of Functional Programming*. Addison-Wesley, 2nd edition, 1999.

Predicate Selection for Structural Decision Trees

K.S. Ng and J.W. Lloyd

Computer Sciences Laboratory,
Research School of Information Sciences and Engineering,
The Australian National University
{kee, jwl}@discus.rsise.anu.edu.au

Abstract. We study predicate selection functions (also known as split-ting rules) for structural decision trees and propose two improvements to existing schemes. The first is in classification learning, where we re-consider the use of accuracy as a predicate selection function and show that, on practical grounds, it is a better alternative to other commonly used functions. The second is in regression learning, where we consider the standard mean squared error measure and give a predicate pruning result for it.

1 Introduction

In this paper, we study predicate selection functions (also known as splitting rules in the literature) for structural decision trees and suggest two ways to improve existing schemes.

The first is in classification-tree learning, where we reconsider the use of accuracy as a predicate selection function and show that, on practical grounds, it is a better alternative to other commonly used functions in the context of structural trees, its primary advantage being the admission of a simple predicate pruning mechanism. With a small modification, we also show that two recognized problems associated with its use can be resolved easily. All these are discussed in Section 3.

The second, presented in Section 4, is in regression-tree learning. In that section, we consider the standard mean-squared error measure and give an effi-ciently computable predicate pruning result for it.

To avoid confusion, it's worth stressing that the two pruning mechanisms alluded to above happen *not* in the space of trees, but in the space of predicates we search to split a decision node. This form of pruning, called predicate pruning in this paper, is largely a search efficiency issue; in contrast, tree pruning deals with the more difficult problem of handling overfitting. This point should become clearer in Section 2.

We next give a high-level specification of a family of structural-tree induction systems. Every learner that fits the description can potentially benefit from the proposals of this paper.

S. Kramer and B. Pfahringer (Eds.): ILP 2005, LNAI 3625, pp. 264–278, 2005.

2   Induction of Structural Trees

We consider the family of decision-tree learners for *structured data* that uses (variants of) the top-down induction algorithm for learning. A high-level schema of such systems is shown in Figure 1.

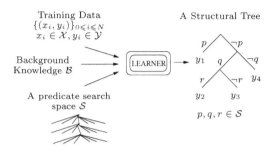

Fig. 1. Structural-tree learning systems

A learning algorithm of this kind takes three inputs:

1. a (finite) set of training examples $z \subseteq \mathcal{X} \times \mathcal{Y}$;
2. some background knowledge $\mathcal{B}$; and
3. a collection $\mathcal{S}$ of predicates over $\mathcal{X}$,

and produces as output a structural decision tree T with node functions in $\mathcal{S}$. The terminal nodes of T are labelled with elements from $\mathcal{Y}$. For classification, $\mathcal{Y}$ is a small finite set; for regression, $\mathcal{Y}$ is (usually a bounded interval of) $\mathbb{R}$. The input space $\mathcal{X}$ can be any arbitrary set. We assume $\mathcal{S}$ has the following structure:

1. $\mathcal{S}$ is a directed acyclic graph where each vertex is a predicate over $\mathcal{X}$ and there is an edge from a predicate p to a predicate q iff q can be obtained (in some way depending on the setting) from p.
2. Suppose p and q are both predicates in $\mathcal{S}$. If q is a descendant of p, then $\forall x \in \mathcal{X}, q(x) \implies p(x)$.

We permit the predicate search space to change from node to node in the decision tree.

The top-down induction algorithm makes binary splits at each node in the tree. If $\mathcal{E}$ is the set of examples at the current node, then a predicate $p \in \mathcal{S}$ induces a partition $\mathcal{P} = (\mathcal{E}_1, \mathcal{E}_2)$ of $\mathcal{E}$, where $\mathcal{E}_1 \subseteq \mathcal{E}$ is the set of examples that satisfy p and $\mathcal{E}_2 \subseteq \mathcal{E}$ is the set of examples that do not satisfy p. The quality of the partition $\mathcal{P}$ is determined by a real-valued predicate selection function $f(\mathcal{P})$. Given $\mathcal{S}$ and a set $\mathcal{E}$ of examples, we seek a predicate $p^* \in \mathcal{S}$ such that $f(\mathcal{P}^*)$, where $\mathcal{P}^*$ is the partition of $\mathcal{E}$ induced by p^*, is optimized.

The search space $\mathcal{S}$ can be huge, in which case some form of pruning is needed to explore the space efficiently. It is the form of the predicate selection function, together with the two properties of $\mathcal{S}$ stated earlier, that we will exploit in the design of our predicate pruning mechanisms.

Three learning systems that fit the description given here are Tilde [3], [2], S-CART [9], [10] and Alkemy [4], [11].

The underlying language for Tilde and S-CART is a subset of first-order logic. For both systems, $\mathcal{X}$ are Prolog programs, $\mathcal{B}$ is a Prolog program, and $\mathcal{S} = \{f_c \mid c \in \mathcal{C}\}$ where $\mathcal{C}$ is a set of program clauses. Given $x \in \mathcal{X}$, $f_c(x)$ evaluates to true iff the query $\leftarrow c$ succeeds in the program $x \wedge \mathcal{B}$. In trees induced by both Tilde and S-CART, variables are shared across decision nodes down true branches. For that reason, the predicate search space can be different from node to node.

For both systems, if we only consider the addition of a single literal at each node t in the process of growing a tree, the predicate search space $\mathcal{S}_t$ at t would be a one-level-deep tree that will not actually benefit from the proposals of this paper. In fact, existing predicate selection functions work rather well in this setting. However, if conjunctions of literals are considered, as can be done using the *lookahead* mechanism in Tilde and schemata declarations in S-CART (see, for details, [10, §6.4] and [2, §6.3]), then the pruning results presented here can exploit the richer structure of $\mathcal{S}_t$ to alleviate the usual computational problems associated with the use of such rich search spaces, thus solving an important, thorny problem for both learners.

The underlying language of Alkemy is a typed higher-order logic. In this case, $\mathcal{X}$ are basic terms of a certain type, $\mathcal{B}$ takes the form of transformations (and their definitions), and $\mathcal{S}$ consists of standard predicates over $\mathcal{X}$ defined using a predicate rewrite system. The predicate search space is the same for every node in the tree. See, for more details, [11].

We move on now to the discussion of a new accuracy-based predicate selection function for classification trees.

3   An Accuracy Heuristic for Classification-Tree Learning

The use of accuracy as a heuristic was called into question early on in classification-tree research. Two standard criticisms, stated in [6, §4.1], are as follows.

Criticism 1. *The use of accuracy can result in premature termination of tree growth. This is because tree nodes that are relatively pure, with examples coming from one predominant class, often cannot be split with a strict increase in accuracy.*

Criticism 2. *The accuracy heuristic does not take future growth into account in choosing the current best split. We use the example in [6, §4.1] to illustrate this point. Consider a set $\mathcal{E} = (400, 400)$ of 800 examples. (Here and in the following, $(n_1, \ldots, n_c)$ denotes a set of examples with n_i examples in the ith class.) Which of the following two is the better partition of $\mathcal{E}$?*

$\mathcal{P}_1 = ((300, 100), (100, 300));$ *or*
$\mathcal{P}_2 = ((200, 400), (200, 0)).$

$\mathcal{P}_2$ is intuitively the more appealing partition of the two, with potential to result in a smaller overall tree. But accuracy can't differentiate between them.

Criticisms 1 and 2 notwithstanding, in the context of structural decision trees, as pointed out in [4], the use of accuracy offers one important advantage that warrants reconsideration: its use admits a particularly simple predicate pruning mechanism. For completeness, we now review this result from [4].

Suppose there are c classes in all. Let $\mathcal{E}$ be a (non-empty) set of examples, N the number of examples in $\mathcal{E}$, n_i the number of examples in $\mathcal{E}$ in the ith class, and $p_i = n_i/N$, for $i = 1, \ldots, c$.

Definition 3. *The* majority class *of $\mathcal{E}$ is defined to be the class to which the greatest number of examples in $\mathcal{E}$ belong. (Ties are broken arbitrarily.)*

Definition 4. *The* accuracy, *$A_{\mathcal{E}}$, of a set $\mathcal{E}$ of examples is defined by*

$$A_{\mathcal{E}} = p_M,$$

where M is the index of the majority class of $\mathcal{E}$.

The accuracy is the fraction of examples which are correctly classified on the basis that the majority class gives the classification.

Definition 5. *Let $\mathcal{P} = (\mathcal{E}_1, \mathcal{E}_2)$ be a partition of a set $\mathcal{E}$ of examples. We define the accuracy, $A_{\mathcal{P}}$, of the partition $\mathcal{P}$ by*

$$A_{\mathcal{P}} = \frac{|\mathcal{E}_1|}{|\mathcal{E}|} A_{\mathcal{E}_1} + \frac{|\mathcal{E}_2|}{|\mathcal{E}|} A_{\mathcal{E}_2}.$$

In the predicate search space, if p' is a descendant of p, then p' implies p and the partition $(\mathcal{E}'_1, \mathcal{E}'_2)$ of $\mathcal{E}$ induced by p' has the property that $\mathcal{E}'_1 \subseteq \mathcal{E}_1$, where $(\mathcal{E}_1, \mathcal{E}_2)$ is the partition of $\mathcal{E}$ induced by p. These considerations lead to the following definition.

Definition 6. *Let $\mathcal{E}$ be a set of examples and $(\mathcal{E}_1, \mathcal{E}_2)$ a partition of $\mathcal{E}$. We say a partition $(\mathcal{E}'_1, \mathcal{E}'_2)$ of $\mathcal{E}$ is a* refinement *of $(\mathcal{E}_1, \mathcal{E}_2)$ if $\mathcal{E}'_1 \subseteq \mathcal{E}_1$.*

We now introduce the important measure of classification refinement bound.

Definition 7. *Let $\mathcal{P} = (\mathcal{E}_1, \mathcal{E}_2)$ be a partition of a set $\mathcal{E}$ of N examples, where n_i is the number of examples in $\mathcal{E}$ in the ith class and $n_{j,i}$ is the number of examples in $\mathcal{E}_j$ in the ith class, for $j = 1, 2$ and $i = 1, \ldots, c$. We define the classification refinement bound, $B_{\mathcal{P}}$, of the partition $\mathcal{P}$ by*

$$B_{\mathcal{P}} = \frac{1}{N} (\max_i \{n_i + \max_{k \neq i} n_{1,k}\}).$$

The intuitive idea behind the definition of $B_{\mathcal{P}}$ is that the refinement of $\mathcal{P}$ having the greatest accuracy can be obtained by moving all examples in one class from $\mathcal{E}_1$ across to $\mathcal{E}_2$. Here is an example to illustrate the concept of classification refinement bound.

Example 8. Let $\mathcal{E} = (6, 9, 3, 2)$ and suppose $\mathcal{P} = ((2, 1, 0, 2), (4, 8, 3, 0))$. Then $A_{\mathcal{P}} = 10/20$ and $B_{\mathcal{P}} = 11/20$. If $\mathcal{Q} = ((0, 9, 0, 0), (6, 0, 3, 2))$, then $A_{\mathcal{Q}} = B_{\mathcal{Q}} = 15/20$.   ◄

The next result shows that $B_{\mathcal{P}}$ is an upper bound for the accuracy of any refinement of a partition $\mathcal{P}$ of a set of examples.

Proposition 9 ([11]). *Let $\mathcal{E}$ be a set of examples and $\mathcal{P}$ a partition of $\mathcal{E}$. If $\mathcal{P}'$ is a refinement of $\mathcal{P}$, then $A_{\mathcal{P}'} \leq B_{\mathcal{P}}$. In particular, $A_{\mathcal{P}} \leq B_{\mathcal{P}}$.*

Proposition 9 can be used to prune the search space when searching for a predicate to split a node. During this search, we record the best partition $\mathcal{P}$ found so far and its associated accuracy $A_{\mathcal{P}}$. When investigating a new partition $\mathcal{Q}$, the quantity $B_{\mathcal{Q}}$ is calculated. According to the proposition, if $B_{\mathcal{Q}} < A_{\mathcal{P}}$, then the partition $\mathcal{Q}$ and all its refinements can be safely pruned. Here is an example to illustrate how this works.

Example 10. Let the set of examples be $(6, 9, 3, 2)$. Suppose the best partition found so far is $\mathcal{P} = ((6, 3, 0, 2), (0, 6, 3, 0))$, which has accuracy $12/20$. Suppose that later on in the search the partition $\mathcal{Q} = ((2, 4, 0, 1), (4, 5, 3, 1))$ is being investigated. Note that $B_{\mathcal{Q}} = 11/20$. Since $B_{\mathcal{Q}} < A_{\mathcal{P}}$, Proposition 9 shows that $\mathcal{Q}$ and its refinements can be pruned.

On the other hand, consider the partition $\mathcal{R} = ((6, 5, 3, 2), (0, 4, 0, 0))$, for which $B_{\mathcal{R}} = 15/20$. Thus $\mathcal{R}$ has refinements, which could be found by the system, whose accuracies exceed that of $\mathcal{P}$. Thus $\mathcal{R}$ should not be pruned.   ◄

The pruning mechanism just described has been shown to work well in many different applications. Table 1 gives an indication of its effectiveness. In it, we list six problems taken from [11, §6.2] and [5]. For each problem, we give (1) the size of the predicate search space $|\mathcal{S}|$ as defined in [11] and [5]; and (2) the number of predicates actually tested in a complete search of the predicate space aided by pruning. The percentage of the predicate space actually searched is also given. As shown, significant reduction in search can be achieved. It is worth pointing out that the effectiveness of the pruning mechanism is not a function of the size of the search space but a function of the structure of the search space and the way the training examples are actually labelled. In general, predicate search spaces that are formed by combining basic conditions in different ways, for example using conjunctions, stand to gain the most from the pruning mechanism. The predicate spaces defined for the last three datasets in Table 1 are of this kind.

It is not clear to the authors whether more commonly used functions like entropy admit similar (efficiently computable) pruning mechanisms. After several failed attempts to find such a result, it seems unlikely to us that there is one. Assuming there is no such result, then in the context of structural decision trees we can expect accuracy to be a better predicate selection function compared to other commonly used functions. To back up this claim, we examine two cases under the assumption that there is enough structure in the predicate space for predicate pruning to take effect. The first of these corresponds to the case when

Table 1. Efficiency of the predicate pruning mechanism

Dataset	$|\mathcal{S}|$	Searched
Int Trees	396	120 (30.30%)
Mutagenesis	535	108 (20.19%)
East West	2073	892 (43.03%)
Headline	2850	190 (6.66%)
Protein	9262	581 (6.27%)
Musk-1	1,679,615,641	2,914,727 (0.17%)

an exhaustive search of the predicate space is computationally feasible, and the second when it is not.

In the first case, *with the aid of pruning*, computing the most accurate predicate can be expected to be cheaper than computing the one with, say, the lowest entropy. Assuming accuracy and entropy both yield reasonably accurate decision trees and that their relative performances are not too far apart – we will come back to look at this shortly – then adopting accuracy as the predicate selection function is a good strategy, especially if time efficiency is an issue.

In the second case, we must resort to incomplete searches. Given the same amount of time, we can expect the predicate chosen using, say, entropy in the absence of a pruning mechanism to be, in all likelihood, worse than the predicate chosen using accuracy in the presence of pruning simply because a smaller percentage of the predicate space is actually searched.

To advocate the use of accuracy as a viable predicate selection function, we need to address the two criticisms stated in the beginning of this section. Both criticisms are valid arguments. Criticism 1 has a theoretical basis, as shown in [8]. Criticism 2, being an intuitive argument, is weaker but persuasive nonetheless. Interestingly, both problems can be addressed with an easy solution: one can adopt accuracy as the main predicate selection function and use a concave function like entropy to break ties between equally-accurate predicates. We will call this the Acc^* function.

This scheme addresses Criticism 1 because in the case where no predicate in the search space can achieve a strict increase in accuracy, splits can still be made in accordance with the tie-breaker function, which we know behaves well.

Criticism 2 can also be resolved this way. In the example given, Acc^* will pick $\mathcal{P}_2$ over $\mathcal{P}_1$, as desired.

One final question remains: Is a concave function like entropy, as a predicate selection function, always going to outperform Acc^*? We investigate this empirically. Two tree-growing algorithms are compared, the first uses Acc^*, and the second, entropy. Twelve datasets were used for this purpose. They consists of the first five datasets in Table 1 and seven other datasets chosen randomly from the UCI repository. (Musk-1 in Table 1 was excluded because an exhaustive search through the predicate space as required by the entropy-based algorithm is simply not feasible. It can, however, be handled using Acc^*.) The Alkemy learning system was used to perform the experiment. The results are shown in Tables 2 and 3. Table 2 gives the accuracies of the induced classifiers in the absence of tree

Table 2. Accuracy vs Entropy (w/o tree post-pruning)

Dataset	Acc^*	Accuracy			Time	
		Ent	$Ent > Acc^*$		Acc^*	Ent
Int Trees	0.400	0.400			0.26	0.82
Mutagenesis	0.820	0.840			186.370	232.63
East West	0.900	0.900			0.68	1.67
Headline	0.950	0.950			0.97	4.86
Protein	0.800	0.800			0.98	20.60
Audiology	0.735	0.765	✓		–	–
Lenses	0.833	0.833			–	–
Mushroom	1.000	1.000			–	–
Votes	0.947	0.942			–	–
Monks-1	0.894	0.886			–	–
Monks-2	0.692	0.692			–	–
Monks-3	0.884	0.876			–	–

Table 3. Accuracy vs Entropy (with tree post-pruning)

Dataset	Acc^*	Accuracy	
		Ent	$Ent > Acc^*$
Int Trees	0.700	0.700	
Mutagenesis	0.820	0.809	
East West	0.800	0.800	
Headline	0.900	0.900	
Protein	0.700	0.700	
Audiology	0.710	0.755	✓
Lenses	0.850	0.850	
Mushroom	0.999	0.999	
Votes	0.959	0.956	
Monks-1	0.920	0.887	×
Monks-2	0.634	0.638	
Monks-3	0.935	0.935	

post-pruning. The effects of post-pruning are shown in Table 3. In both tables, a ✓ is shown if the entropy-based algorithm is significantly more accurate; a × is shown if the Acc^*-based algorithm is better. Tree post-pruning is done using the cost-complexity pruning method of CART [6]. The accuracies reported are estimated using 10-fold cross validations.

It seems safe to conclude that the performance of Acc^* is comparable to most other predicate selection functions for the following reasons. The experiment above certainly suggests that Acc^* is comparable to entropy. We know from experience that entropy and the Gini index have similar behaviour. To top it off, it is shown in [12] and [7] that the Gini index is as good as any other known predicate selection function for the purpose of tree induction. In fact, the general agreement from [12] and [7] is that the exact predicate selection function used doesn't really matter all that much as long as the tree is allowed to grow sufficiently large, in which case tree post-pruning holds the key to the final performance. In that sense, the main problem with (plain) accuracy is that it results in premature termination of tree growth. With Acc^*, this is no longer an issue.

In a separate experiment, we also pitted Acc^* against (plain) accuracy on the twelve datasets. The experiment shows that Acc^* performs at least as well as, and usually better than, accuracy in all except one dataset (Audiology) after tree post-pruning.

Table 2 also records the time (measured in seconds) taken by the two algorithms on the first five datasets on a 1.2 GHz iBook. The results clearly show that non-trivial savings in learning time can be achieved. (The usual tests considered by C4.5 [14] are used for the UCI datasets. Such predicate spaces have no structure that can be exploited by the pruning mechanism, and naturally no reduction in computation time can be obtained – both algorithms need to evaluate every predicate in the search space.) When there is enough structure in the classification problem for predicate pruning to take effect, the only situation where the Acc^*-based algorithm would take longer time than the entropy-based algorithm is when a *significantly* larger tree is grown using the Acc^*-based algorithm. This scenario can probably occur, but it would be very rare.

In summary, we have proposed and shown the viability of a new accuracy-based predicate selection function for top-down induction of classification trees. In the context of structural decision trees, the pruning advantages it offers makes it, on practical grounds, the predicate selection function of choice. The pruning theorem was previously given in [4]; the contribution here is in the design of Acc^*, which overcomes some of the weaknesses of accuracy.

We end with a caveat. The working assumption throughout this section is that an efficiently computable pruning mechanism for some standard predicate selection function cannot be found. If one can be obtained, then the issues investigated here need to be revisited.

4   A Pruning Result for Regression-Tree Learning

We now present a predicate pruning result for structural regression-tree learning. We begin by stating the quadratic loss function commonly used in regression-tree learning. This is followed by the presentation of an efficient predicate pruning algorithm for this predicate selection function. The section ends with a discussion of some implementation issues.

Definition 11. *Given a set $\mathcal{E}$ of examples, we define the* mean squared error $E_{\mathcal{E}}$ *of $\mathcal{E}$ by*

$$E_{\mathcal{E}} = \min_{c} \sum_{(x,y) \in \mathcal{E}} (y - c)^2.$$

The unique minimizing c here is the empirical mean of the regression values in $\mathcal{E}$, and that is what we use to label the leaf nodes in a regression tree.

Definition 12. *Let $\mathcal{E}$ be a set of examples and $\mathcal{P} = (\mathcal{E}_1, \mathcal{E}_2)$ a partition of $\mathcal{E}$. We define the mean squared error, $Q_{\mathcal{P}}$, of $\mathcal{P}$ by*

$$Q_{\mathcal{P}} = E_{\mathcal{E}_1} + E_{\mathcal{E}_2}.$$

Given a predicate search space $\mathcal{S}$ and a set $\mathcal{E}$ of examples, the goal is thus to find a predicate in $\mathcal{S}$ that minimizes Q. As pointed in [1, §16.1], this formulation is well-founded since one can show that

$$\mathbb{E}(f(x) - y)^2 = \mathbb{E}(\mathbb{E}(y|x) - f(x))^2 + \mathbb{E}(\mathbb{E}(y|x) - y)^2,$$

which implies that choosing a function f to minimize Q is equivalent to finding the best approximation of the conditional expectation of y given x. See, for more details, [6, §8.3].

Proposition 13. *Let $\mathcal{E}_1$ and $\mathcal{E}_2$ be sets of examples. If $\mathcal{E}_1 \subseteq \mathcal{E}_2$, then $E_{\mathcal{E}_1} \leqslant E_{\mathcal{E}_2}$.*

Proof. Straightforward.   □

To search through the space of predicates efficiently by means of predicate pruning, we need a way to predict the smallest error that can be obtained from the descendants of a predicate. This motivates the next definition.

Definition 14. *Let $\mathcal{E}$ be a set of examples and $\mathcal{P} = (\mathcal{E}_1, \mathcal{E}_2)$ a partition of $\mathcal{E}$. We define the regression refinement bound of $\mathcal{P}$ by*

$$C_{\mathcal{P}} = \min_{\mathcal{P}'} Q_{\mathcal{P}'}$$

where $\mathcal{P}'$ is a refinement of $\mathcal{P}$. A refinement $\mathcal{P}^*$ of $\mathcal{P}$ that satisfies $Q_{\mathcal{P}^*} = C_{\mathcal{P}}$ is called a minimizing refinement of $\mathcal{P}$.

Proposition 15. *Let $\mathcal{E}$ be a set of examples and $\mathcal{P}$ a partition of $\mathcal{E}$. If $\mathcal{P}'$ is a refinement of $\mathcal{P}$, then $Q_{\mathcal{P}'} \geq C_{\mathcal{P}}$. In particular, $Q_{\mathcal{P}} \geq C_{\mathcal{P}}$.*

Proof. By the definition of $C_{\mathcal{P}}$.   □

The refinement bound $C_{\mathcal{P}}$ has the obvious definition, but can it be computed efficiently? Clearly, an exhaustive search through all possible refinements of $\mathcal{P}$ is impractical; a more efficient algorithm is needed. We next study this minimization problem.

A lower bound for $C_{\mathcal{P}}$ can be easily obtained.

Proposition 16. *Let $\mathcal{E}$ be a set of examples and $\mathcal{P} = (\mathcal{E}_1, \mathcal{E}_2)$ a partition of $\mathcal{E}$. Then $E_{\mathcal{E}_2} \leq C_{\mathcal{P}}$. In particular, when $\mathcal{E}_1 = \emptyset$, $E_{\mathcal{E}_2} = C_{\mathcal{P}}$.*

Proof. Let $\mathcal{P}^* = (\mathcal{E}_1^*, \mathcal{E}_2^*)$ be a minimizing refinement of $\mathcal{P}$. By Proposition 13, we have $E_{\mathcal{E}_2} \leq E_{\mathcal{E}_2^*}$ since $\mathcal{E}_2 \subseteq \mathcal{E}_2^*$. From that, we have

$$Q_{\mathcal{P}^*} = E_{\mathcal{E}_1^*} + E_{\mathcal{E}_2^*} \geq E_{\mathcal{E}_2^*} \geq E_{\mathcal{E}_2}.$$

Clearly, when $\mathcal{E}_1 = \emptyset$, $\mathcal{E}_1^* = \emptyset$ and $\mathcal{E}_2^* = \mathcal{E}_2$. □

It turns out that to compute $C_{\mathcal{P}}$ for a partition $\mathcal{P} = (\mathcal{E}_1, \mathcal{E}_2)$, we can restrict our attention to just those refinements that can be obtained by cutting a sorted version of $\mathcal{E}_1$ into two halves, and assigning one or the other to the new $\mathcal{E}_2$. Figure 2 gives an algorithm for computing $C_{\mathcal{P}}$. In the algorithm, $\mathcal{E}[i, j]$ denotes the subset of $\mathcal{E}$ formed from taking the i-th to j-th element(s). If $i > j$, we define $\mathcal{E}[i, j]$ to be $\emptyset$.

---

function *RegRefinementBound* $(\mathcal{P})$ **returns** $C_{\mathcal{P}}$;
input: $\mathcal{P} = (\mathcal{E}_1, \mathcal{E}_2)$, a partition;

if $\mathcal{E}_1 = \emptyset$ **return** $E_{\mathcal{E}_2}$;
sort$(\mathcal{E}_1)$;
minerr $:= Q_{\mathcal{P}}$;
for each i **from** 1 **to** $|\mathcal{E}_1|$ **do**

    $\mathcal{E}_{11} := \mathcal{E}_1[1, i]$;
    $\mathcal{E}_{12} := \mathcal{E}_1[i + 1, |\mathcal{E}_1|]$;
    $\mathcal{P}_1 := (\mathcal{E}_{11}, \mathcal{E}_{12} \cup \mathcal{E}_2)$;
    $\mathcal{P}_2 := (\mathcal{E}_{12}, \mathcal{E}_{11} \cup \mathcal{E}_2)$;
    minerr $:= \min\{$*minerr*$, Q_{\mathcal{P}_1}, Q_{\mathcal{P}_2}\}$

return *minerr*;

Fig. 2. Algorithm for calculating $C_{\mathcal{P}}$

The *sort* function in line 4 in Figure 2 is with respect to the following total order $\preccurlyeq$ on the examples. Examples are first ordered increasingly by their regression values. Examples with the same regression values are then ordered according to a lexicographic order on the individuals. We denote by $\max_{\preccurlyeq}(\mathcal{E})$ and $\min_{\preccurlyeq}(\mathcal{E})$ the largest and smallest examples in $\mathcal{E}$ as ordered by $\preccurlyeq$.

We now show the value returned by the algorithm *RegRefinementBound* on input $\mathcal{P}$ is $C_{\mathcal{P}}$. First, a technical lemma.

Proposition 17. *Let $\mathcal{E}$ be a set of examples and $\mathcal{P} = (\mathcal{E}_1, \mathcal{E}_2)$, $\mathcal{E}_1 \neq \emptyset$, a partition of $\mathcal{E}$. Suppose $\mathcal{P}_{min} = (\mathcal{E}_{11}, \mathcal{E}_{12} \cup \mathcal{E}_2)$ is a minimizing refinement of $\mathcal{P}$, where $\mathcal{E}_{11} \cup \mathcal{E}_{12} = \mathcal{E}_1$. Then $\mathcal{P}_{min}$ must satisfy the following property:*

1. $\forall (x_1, y_1) \in \mathcal{E}_{11}, \forall (x_2, y_2) \in \mathcal{E}_{12}, y_1 \leqslant y_2$; *or*
2. $\forall (x_1, y_1) \in \mathcal{E}_{12}, \forall (x_2, y_2) \in \mathcal{E}_{11}, y_1 \leqslant y_2$.

Proof. If either $\mathcal{E}_{11}$ or $\mathcal{E}_{12}$ is empty, then the property holds trivially. Now consider the case when both $\mathcal{E}_{11}$ and $\mathcal{E}_{12}$ are non-empty. Suppose the property does not hold. Then there exist (x_1, y_1) in $\mathcal{E}_{11}$ and (x_2, y_2) in $\mathcal{E}_{12}$ such that $y_1 > y_2$, and (x_3, y_3) in $\mathcal{E}_{12}$ and (x_4, y_4) in $\mathcal{E}_{11}$ such that $y_3 > y_4$. We have

$$\max_y(\mathcal{E}_{11}) \geqslant y_1 > y_2 \geqslant \min_y(\mathcal{E}_{12}); \quad \text{and} \tag{1}$$

$$\max_y(\mathcal{E}_{12}) \geqslant y_3 > y_4 \geqslant \min_y(\mathcal{E}_{11}). \tag{2}$$

We now show that we can always pick (x', e') from $\mathcal{E}_{11}$ and (x'', e'') from $\mathcal{E}_{12}$ and interchange them to produce another refinement of $\mathcal{P}$ with a lower error, thus contradicting the minimality of $\mathcal{P}_{min}$.

Let $\bar{y}_1$ and $\bar{y}_2$ denote, respectively, the empirical means of the regression values in $\mathcal{E}_{11}$ and $\mathcal{E}_{12} \cup \mathcal{E}_2$. There are two cases to consider, and we state the elements we choose in each case.

1. If $\bar{y}_1 \leqslant \bar{y}_2$, pick (x', e') to be $\max_{\preccurlyeq}(\mathcal{E}_{11})$, and (x'', e'') to be $\min_{\preccurlyeq}(\mathcal{E}_{12})$. We have $e' > e''$ from (1).

2. If $\bar{y}_1 > \bar{y}_2$, pick (x', e') to be $\min_{\preccurlyeq}(\mathcal{E}_{11})$, and (x'', e'') to be $\max_{\preccurlyeq}(\mathcal{E}_{12})$. We have $e'' > e'$ from (2).

Let $\mathcal{E}_1' = \mathcal{E}_{11} \cup \{e''\} \setminus \{e'\}$ and $\mathcal{E}_2' = \mathcal{E}_2 \cup \mathcal{E}_{12} \cup \{e'\} \setminus \{e''\}$. Clearly, $\mathcal{P}' = (\mathcal{E}_1', \mathcal{E}_2')$ is a refinement of $\mathcal{P}$. We have

$$Q_{\mathcal{P}_{min}} = \sum_{(x,y)\in\mathcal{E}_{11}} (y - \bar{y}_1)^2 + \sum_{(x,y)\in\mathcal{E}_2\cup\mathcal{E}_{12}} (y - \bar{y}_2)^2$$

$$= (e' - \bar{y}_1)^2 + \sum_{(x,y)\in\mathcal{E}_{11}\setminus\{e'\}} (y - \bar{y}_1)^2 + (e'' - \bar{y}_2)^2 + \sum_{(x,y)\in\mathcal{E}_2\cup\mathcal{E}_{12}\setminus\{e''\}} (y - \bar{y}_2)^2$$

$$\geqslant (e'' - \bar{y}_1)^2 + \sum_{(x,y)\in\mathcal{E}_{11}\setminus\{e'\}} (y - \bar{y}_1)^2 + (e' - \bar{y}_2)^2 + \sum_{(x,y)\in\mathcal{E}_2\cup\mathcal{E}_{12}\setminus\{e''\}} (y - \bar{y}_2)^2$$

$$> Q_{\mathcal{P}'}.$$

We can make the third step because

$$(e' - \bar{y}_1)^2 + (e'' - \bar{y}_2)^2 - [(e'' - \bar{y}_1)^2 + (e' - \bar{y}_2)^2] = 2(e'' - e')(\bar{y}_1 - \bar{y}_2) \geq 0$$

in both cases. The fourth step follows because $e' \neq e''$. (Recall Definition 11 and the remark following it.)   □

Proposition 18. *Given a partition $\mathcal{P}$, RegRefinementBound correctly finds $C_{\mathcal{P}}$.*

Proof. Let $\mathcal{P}$ be $(\mathcal{E}_1, \mathcal{E}_2)$. There are two cases. If $\mathcal{E}_1 = \emptyset$, the algorithm returns $E_{\mathcal{E}_2}$, which is equal to $C_{\mathcal{P}}$ by Proposition 16. If $\mathcal{E}_1$ is non-empty, then one of the minimizing refinements must satisfy the property stated in Proposition 17. The algorithm conducts an exhaustive search of all such partitions and must therefore find $C_{\mathcal{P}}$.   □

The *RegRefinementBound* algorithm, when implemented naïvely, has time complexity $O(|\mathcal{E}|^2)$, since there are $O(|\mathcal{E}|)$ iterations, and the computation of $Q_{\mathcal{P}_1}$ and $Q_{\mathcal{P}_2}$ in each iteration takes $O(|\mathcal{E}|)$ time. This can be significantly improved. We now give an implementation of *RegRefinementBound* that runs in time linear in the size of $\mathcal{E}$.

Proposition 19. *Given a set $\mathcal{E}$ of examples and a partition $\mathcal{P} = (\mathcal{E}_1, \mathcal{E}_2)$ of $\mathcal{E}$, assuming $\mathcal{E}_1$ is sorted according to $\preccurlyeq$, $C_{\mathcal{P}}$ can be computed in time $O(|\mathcal{E}|)$.*

Proof. Let $\bar{y}, \bar{y}_1, \bar{y}_2$ denote the empirical means of the regression values in $\mathcal{E}, \mathcal{E}_1$ and $\mathcal{E}_2$. We can rewrite the error function as follows.

$$
\begin{aligned}
Q_{\mathcal{P}} &= \sum_{(x,y)\in\mathcal{E}_1} (y - \bar{y}_1)^2 + \sum_{(x,y)\in\mathcal{E}_2} (y - \bar{y}_2)^2 \\
&= \sum_{(x,y)\in\mathcal{E}_1} [(y - \bar{y}) - (\bar{y}_1 - \bar{y})]^2 + \sum_{(x,y)\in\mathcal{E}_2} [(y - \bar{y}) - (\bar{y}_2 - \bar{y})]^2 \\
&= \sum_{(x,y)\in\mathcal{E}_1} [(y - \bar{y})^2 - (\bar{y}_1 - \bar{y})^2] + \sum_{(x,y)\in\mathcal{E}_2} [(y - \bar{y})^2 - (\bar{y}_2 - \bar{y})^2] \\
&= \sum_{(x,y)\in\mathcal{E}_1} (y - \bar{y})^2 - |\mathcal{E}_1|(\bar{y}_1 - \bar{y})^2 + \sum_{(x,y)\in\mathcal{E}_2} (y - \bar{y})^2 - |\mathcal{E}_2|(\bar{y}_2 - \bar{y})^2 \\
&= \sum_{(x,y)\in\mathcal{E}} (y - \bar{y})^2 - (|\mathcal{E}_1|\bar{y}_1^2 + |\mathcal{E}_1|\bar{y}^2 - |\mathcal{E}_1|2\bar{y}_1\bar{y} + |\mathcal{E}_2|\bar{y}_2^2 + |\mathcal{E}_2|\bar{y}^2 - |\mathcal{E}_2|2\bar{y}_2\bar{y}) \\
&= \sum_{(x,y)\in\mathcal{E}} (y - \bar{y})^2 - (|\mathcal{E}_1 + \mathcal{E}_2|\bar{y}^2 - 2\bar{y}(|\mathcal{E}_1|\bar{y}_1 + |\mathcal{E}_2|\bar{y}_2) + |\mathcal{E}_1|\bar{y}_1^2 + |\mathcal{E}_2|\bar{y}_2^2) \\
&= \sum_{(x,y)\in\mathcal{E}} (y - \bar{y})^2 + \bar{y}|\mathcal{E}|\bar{y} - (|\mathcal{E}_1|\bar{y}_1^2 + |\mathcal{E}_2|\bar{y}_2^2) \\
&= \sum_{(x,y)\in\mathcal{E}} (y-\bar{y})^2 + \frac{1}{|\mathcal{E}|}\Big(\sum_{(x,y)\in\mathcal{E}} y\Big)^2 - \left(\frac{1}{|\mathcal{E}_1|}\Big(\sum_{(x,y)\in\mathcal{E}_1} y\Big)^2 + \frac{1}{|\mathcal{E}_2|}\Big(\sum_{(x,y)\in\mathcal{E}_2} y\Big)^2\right).
\end{aligned}
$$
(3)

From that, we can reformulate the optimization problem as

$$
\begin{aligned}
C_{\mathcal{P}} &= \min_{\mathcal{P}'} Q_{\mathcal{P}'} \\
&= \sum_{(x,y)\in\mathcal{E}} (y-\bar{y})^2 + \frac{1}{|\mathcal{E}|}\Big(\sum_{\mathcal{E}} y\Big)^2 - \max_{\mathcal{P}'} \left(\frac{1}{|\mathcal{E}_1'|}\Big(\sum_{\mathcal{E}_1'} y\Big)^2 + \frac{1}{|\mathcal{E}_2'|}\Big(\sum_{\mathcal{E}_2'} y\Big)^2\right)
\end{aligned}
$$
(4)

where $\mathcal{P}' = (\mathcal{E}_1', \mathcal{E}_2')$ is a refinement of $\mathcal{P}$. Thus we are left with a maximization problem that can be computed in time linear in the size of $\mathcal{E}$. All that is required are a few preprocessing steps to compute the sum of all the regression values in $\mathcal{E}_2$ and the prefix sums ($S[i] = \sum_{1\leqslant j\leqslant i} \mathcal{E}_1[j]$) of each element in the sorted $\mathcal{E}_1$.

Here, $\mathcal{E}[j]$ denotes the regression value of the j-th element in $\mathcal{E}$. The details are given in Figure 3. In the algorithm, the function $div(x, y)$ is defined to be x/y if $y \neq 0$, and 0 otherwise. Note that the formula for $Q_{\mathcal{P}_1}$ and $Q_{\mathcal{P}_2}$ has the same general form as the last step in (3).

---

function $RegRefinementBound2(\mathcal{P})$ **returns** $C_\mathcal{P}$;
input: $\mathcal{P} = (\mathcal{E}_1, \mathcal{E}_2)$, a partition, $\mathcal{E}_1$ sorted;

if $\mathcal{E}_1 = \emptyset$ **return** $E_{\mathcal{E}_2}$;

$K := \sum_{(x,y)\in\mathcal{E}}(y - \bar{y})^2 + \frac{1}{|\mathcal{E}|}\left(\sum_{(x,y)\in\mathcal{E}} y\right)^2$;

$sum2 := \sum_{(x,y)\in\mathcal{E}_2} y$;

$S := prefixSum(\mathcal{E}_1)$;

$minerr := Q_\mathcal{P}$;

for each i **from** 1 **to** $|\mathcal{E}_1|$ **do**

$\qquad Q_{\mathcal{P}_1} := K - (\frac{1}{i}(S[i])^2 + div(1, |\mathcal{E}_2| + |\mathcal{E}_1| - i)(sum2 + S[|\mathcal{E}_1|] - S[i])^2)$;

$\qquad Q_{\mathcal{P}_2} := K - (div(1, |\mathcal{E}_1| - i)(S[|\mathcal{E}_1|] - S[i])^2 + \frac{1}{|\mathcal{E}_2| + i}(sum2 + S[i])^2)$;

$\qquad minerr := \min\{minerr, Q_{\mathcal{P}_1}, Q_{\mathcal{P}_2}\}$

return $minerr$;

Fig. 3. An implementation of $RegRefinementBound$

Each of the preprocessing steps can be done in $O(|\mathcal{E}|)$ time. There are $O(|\mathcal{E}|)$ iterations in the **for** loop, and each iteration takes $O(1)$ time. The overall complexity of the algorithm is thus $O(|\mathcal{E}|)$.   □

Can we avoid conducting an exhaustive search of the solution set? Given the form of the minimizing refinement, one might conjecture that given a partition $\mathcal{P} = (\mathcal{E}_1, \mathcal{E}_2)$, if $\bar{y}_1 < \bar{y}_2$, where $\bar{y}_1$ and $\bar{y}_2$ denote, respectively, the empirical means of the regression values in $\mathcal{E}_1$ and $\mathcal{E}_2$, then the minimizing refinement must be in the set

$$S1 = \{(\mathcal{E}_1', \mathcal{E}_2') : \mathcal{E}_1' = \mathcal{E}_1[1, i], \mathcal{E}_2' = \mathcal{E}_1[i + 1, |\mathcal{E}_1|] \cup \mathcal{E}_2, 1 \leqslant i \leqslant |\mathcal{E}_1|\}$$

where $\mathcal{E}_1$ here is assumed sorted. Similarly when $\bar{y}_1 > \bar{y}_2$. This is not true, as shown in the next example.

Example 20. Consider the partition

$$\mathcal{P} = (\{(x_1, 0.3), (x_2, 0.5), (x_3, 0.98)\}, \{(x_4, 0.41), (x_5, 0.53), (x_6, 0.77), (x_7, 0.9)\})$$

with $\bar{y}_1 = 0.59$ and $\bar{y}_2 = 0.65$. The best refinement in the set $S1$, with error 0.255, is

$$(\{(x_1, 0.3), (x_2, 0.5)\}, \{(x_3, 0.98), (x_4, 0.41), (x_5, 0.53), (x_6, 0.77), (x_7, 0.9)\}).$$

Table 4. Efficiency of the predicate pruning mechanism for regression

Dataset	$|\mathcal{S}|$	Searched
Int Trees	396	120 (30.30%)
Mutagenesis	535	124 (23.18%)
East West	2073	633 (30.54%)
Headline	2850	148 (5.19%)
Protein	9262	581 (6.27%)
Musk-1	1,679,615,641	3,814,746 (0.23%)

The actual minimizing refinement is

$$(\{(x_3, 0.98)\}, \{(x_1, 0.3), (x_2, 0.5), (x_4, 0.41), (x_5, 0.53), (x_6, 0.77), (x_7, 0.9)\})$$

with error 0.254. ◄

Another conjecture is that the errors obtained by increasing the index i in both $S1$ and $S2$ (defined similarly to $S1$, see below) traces a quadratic curve with a single (local) minimum. This also turns out to be false, as shown in the next example.

Example 21. Consider the partition

$$\mathcal{P} = (\{(x_1, 0.29), (x_2, 0.36), (x_3, 0.81), (x_4, 0.92)\}, \{(x_5, 0.95)\}).$$

The refinements in the set

$$S2 = \{(\mathcal{E}'_1, \mathcal{E}'_2) \, : \, \mathcal{E}'_1 = \mathcal{E}_1[i+1, |\mathcal{E}_1|], \, \mathcal{E}'_2 = \mathcal{E}_1[1, i] \cup \mathcal{E}_2, 0 \leqslant i \leqslant |\mathcal{E}_1|\}$$

where $\mathcal{E}_1$ is assumed sorted produces the following sequence of errors with increasing values of i: $[0.3001, 0.3938, 0.2689, 0.3202, 0.4009]$. ◄

To get an indication of the effectiveness of the pruning mechanism, we conducted a small experiment using the same six datasets given in Table 1. Each of these was converted into a regression problem by appropriate relabellings of the individuals, with individuals coming from the same class relabelled with random numbers chosen from the same subinterval of the real line. A complete search through the predicate space was then performed for each. The results are shown in Table 4. It is clear from the table that significant reduction in computation time can be achieved in practice.

5   Related Work and Conclusion

The idea of predicate pruning is, of course, not new in ILP. For example, both Progol and Aleph have such mechanisms for some standard rule-evaluation functions; see [13, §7.4.7] and [15, §3.2.3]. This paper extends such techniques to top-down induction of structural trees, in both the classification and regression settings. The pruning theorem for classification has been established in [4] before; the contribution here is in the design of Acc^*. The pruning theorem for regression is new and it is the main contribution of this paper.

Acknowledgements

We would like to thank Evan Greensmith and Mathi Nagarajan for helpful discussions on the subject matter of this paper. Thanks are also due to the anonymous reviewers whose comments helped improve the presentation of the paper.

References

1. Martin Anthony and Peter L. Bartlett. *Neural Network Learning: Theoretical Foundations.* Cambridge University Press, 1999.
2. Hendrik Blockeel. *Top-Down Induction of First Order Logical Decision Trees.* PhD thesis, Departement Computerwetenschappen, Katholieke Universiteit Leuven, 1998.
3. Hendrik Blockeel and Luc De Raedt. Top-down induction of first-order logical decision trees. *Artificial Intelligence*, 101(1-2):285–297, 1998.
4. Antony F. Bowers, Christophe Giraud-Carrier, and John W. Lloyd. Classification of individuals with complex structure. In P. Langley, editor, *Proceedings of the 17th International Conference on Machine Learning*, pages 81–88. Morgan Kaufmann, 2000.
5. Antony F. Bowers, Christophe Giraud-Carrier, and John W. Lloyd. A knowledge representation framework for inductive learning. Available at http://rsise.anu.edu.au/~jwl/, 2001.
6. Leo Breiman, Jerome Friedman, Richard Olshen, and Charles Stone. *Classification and Regression Trees.* Chapman & Hall, New York, 1984.
7. Wray Buntine and Tim Niblett. A further comparison of splitting rules for decision-tree induction. *Machine Learning*, 8:75–85, 1992.
8. Michael Kearns and Yishay Mansour. On the boosting ability of top-down decision tree learning algorithms. In *Proceedings of the 28th Annual ACM Symposium on the Theory of Computing*, pages 459–468. ACM Press, 1996.
9. Stefan Kramer. Structural regression trees. In *Proceedings of the 13th National Conference on Artificial Intelligence*, pages 812–819. AAAI Press, 1996.
10. Stefan Kramer and Gerhard Widmer. Inducing classification and regression trees in first order logic. In Sašo Džeroski and Nada Lavrač, editors, *Relational Data Mining*, chapter 6. Springer, 2001.
11. John W. Lloyd. *Logic for Learning: Learning Comprehensible Theories from Structured Data.* Cognitive Technologies. Springer, 2003.
12. John Mingers. An empirical comparison of selection measures for decision-tree induction. *Machine Learning*, 3:319–342, 1989.
13. Stephen Muggleton and John Firth. Relational rule learning with CPROGOL4.4: A tutorial introduction. In Sašo Džeroski and Nada Lavrač, editors, *Relational Data Mining*, chapter 7. Springer, 2001.
14. John Ross Quinlan. *C4.5: Programs for Machine Learning.* Morgan Kaufmann, 1993.
15. Ashwin Srinivasan. The Aleph Manual. Technical report, Computing Laboratory, Oxford University, 2000.

Induction of the Indirect Effects of Actions by Monotonic Methods

Ramon P. Otero

Department of Computer Science,
University of Corunna,
Corunna 15071, Galicia, Spain
otero@udc.es

Abstract. In [1] a method for inducing the effects of actions was introduced which provides a solution to the frame problem in induction. The method relied on well-known monotonic methods of ILP making it as efficient as induction of Horn Logic Programs. That proposal is not intended for the induction of the ramifications of the effects of actions (indirect effects) thus providing domain descriptions with the so-called ramification problem. In this work we introduce the induction of such ramification rules describing effects directly from other effects without mentioning the action. A framework based on causality in action formalisms is used to induce causal ramification rules. The method is shown sound and complete while efficient as the induction of action rules.

1 Introduction

Action descriptions of dynamic systems can be represented in Logic Programming (LP). The set of actions and fluents of the domain are represented by predicates with a situation argument $a(s)$, $f(s)$ denoting the time point the action a is performed and the time point the property f holds in the domain. In action descriptions the rules that model the dynamics of the domain are restricted to have a particular form. The behavior of the dynamic system is described with *action laws* and, sometimes, with *ramification laws*. Action laws are rules in the form

$$e(S) \leftarrow a(S), prev(S, P), e'_1(P), \ldots, e'_n(P).$$

where $e(S)$, $e'_i(P)$ are fluent predicates, $a(S)$ is an action predicate, and $prev(S, P)$ is the successor predicate predefined to hold on consecutive situations. Note that the rule mentions just two consecutive situations, P and S, and that the rule holds for every such situations S, P. Action rules describe the model of the dynamic domain by describing the effect the execution of actions have on the properties —fluents— under some condition on other fluents, $e'_1(P), \ldots, e'_n(P)$, at the previous situation. A logic program with a collection of action rules for the different effects in the domain can then be used to predict the effects of a sequence of actions from a given initial situation, called the *temporal prediction problem*. But the same description can be also used, e.g., for *planning*

S. Kramer and B. Pfahringer (Eds.): ILP 2005, LNAI 3625, pp. 279–294, 2005.

problems, namely, given an initial state of the domain and a goal state —both described as a collection of ground fluent instances at two given situations— infer the sequences of actions that lead from one state to the other. Planning problems can be solved when these actions descriptions are executed on suitable Logic Programming frameworks, for instance in Answer Set Programming (ASP) [2] [3].

Sometimes *ramification laws* are also allowed in the description. Ramification laws are rules in the form

$$e(S) \leftarrow e'_1(S), \ldots, e'_n(S).$$

where $e(S)$, $e'_i(S)$ are fluent predicates. This rule mentions just one situation S, and the rule holds at any situation. Ramification rules describe the effect on some fluent $e(S)$ as an *indirect* effect of other effects in the domain at the same situation. Some effects are better described by ramification rules instead of using action rules for them.

Consider the following motivating example (Lin's suitcase scenario [4]). There is a suitcase with two locks and a spring-loaded mechanism such that when the two locks are open the suitcase opens. In a description of this domain we have an action to toggle each one of the two locks, $t1$ and $t2$, and fluents stating whether each lock is open, $l1$ and $l2$, and whether the suitcase is open, o. An example narrative in this domain is the following: initially $l2$ is open ($l2$ true), $l1$ is not open and the suitcase is not open, then action $t1$ toggles lock $l1$ and as (indirect effect) the suitcase opens, o.

time	*action*	*fluents*
0		$l2(0)$
1	$t1(1)$	$l1(1)$, $l2(1)$, $o(1)$

With induction of the (direct) effects of actions we would arrive to a description of the domain like the following

$$l1(S) \leftarrow t1(S),\ prev(S,P),\ nl1(P).$$

where S,P are situation variables representing time points, and $nl1$ is the complementary fluent to $l1$ (we do not want negation as failure for representing fluents in Logic Programming, see later.) This rule is an action law with action $t1$ as condition in the body and some other condition literals on fluents in the previous situation P. A similar rule would be induced for $l2$. For the case of fluent o the rule induced could be the following

$$o(S) \leftarrow t1(S),\ prev(S,P),\ nl1(P),\ l2(P).$$

which can be read as the suitcase opens, $o(S)$, when we toggle lock1, $t1(S)$, and it was not open before, $nl1(P)$, while lock2 was open, $l2(P)$. Another rule is needed for the symmetrical case of toggling lock2 when lock1 was open (or its generalization with variables for locks.) Nevertheless there is a simpler description of fluent $o(S)$

$$o(S) \leftarrow l1(S),\ l2(S).$$

which together with the action rules for the direct effects $l1$ and $l2$ would complete the description. This rule does not mention actions in its body, but just other fluents, it is a ramification rule describing that some effects ($l1$, $l2$ in this case) have other effects as consequence (o).

When an action description does not allow for ramification rules every fluent of the domain is represented as a direct effect of the actions with an action rule. Representing everything with action rules makes the description longer, action rules are longer than ramification rules and more rules are needed. (Consider two different actions that lead to the same (direct) effect under some conditions, then the effect has in its turn other (indirect) effects, a different action rule is needed for each action on the indirect effect, while just a single ramification from the direct effect would be enough.) Furthermore ramification rules is an extension on the language which provides for descriptions which are easier to understand.

In this work we introduce the induction of ramification rules with a method that is sound and complete while efficient. The task could seem as simple as allowing these rules for induction in the language bias, but induction of action descriptions is not induction in Horn logic programs. In action descriptions, fluents persist from a situation to the next situation when there is no consequence on the contrary, even when none of the action rules, which have it as a consequence, is applicable. Representing this persistence without a suitable non-monotonic mechanism like negation as failure in Logic Programming, leads to the frame problem. Finding a suitable representation of persistence when ramification rules are allowed is solving the ramification problem. Utilizing Logic Programming solutions of these problems, e.g., as stated in Answer Set Programming [2] [3] (Logic Programming with stable models semantics), persistence can be represented with an inertia rule, like the following for fluent o,

$$o(S) \leftarrow prev(S, P), \ o(P), \ not \ no(S).$$

where S, P are situation variables representing consecutive time points, and no is the complementary fluent to o. Doing induction with such inertia rules in the background would provide for a solution of the ramification problem in induction. We will show an alternative method, following that of [1], which identifies a Horn induction problem. The solutions of the Horn problem correspond to solutions of the original problem, thus allowing for the application of efficient induction methods.

2   The Problem of Inducing Ramifications

We will follow the definition of induction in action given in [1], so e.g., the current results will provide enhanced descriptions of the domains with ramification rules from the same evidence.

2.1   Narratives as Evidence

Evidence on the behavior of the dynamic domain is assumed in the form of narratives representing facts true in the domain at different time points. Given fluents

$\mathcal{F}$ and actions $\mathcal{A}$, a *narrative* is a pair of two sets, one for action instances and another for effect instances, both given as ground unit clauses of corresponding predicates, and verifying consistency, e.g.

$$F \subseteq \{f(s_i), \neg f(s_i) \mid f \in \mathcal{F}, \, 0 \leq s_i \leq n\}$$

$$A \subseteq \{a(s_i) \mid a \in \mathcal{A}, \, 1 \leq s_i \leq n\}$$

where $f(s_i)$ and $\neg f(s_i)$ are literals on fluent f, complementary to each other. The natural number s_i is the situation constant and 0 names the initial situation.

Using the example in Section 1 the narrative would be

$$(F, A) = (\{l2(0), \, nl1(0), \, no(0), \, l1(1), \, l2(1), \, o(1)\}, \, \{t1(1)\})$$

Evidence will usually contain a collection of different narratives for different sequences of actions and for different initial states of the domain (fluents at time 0).

2.2   Examples and Background

A single narrative (or a collection of them) is enough for the induction of the different effects involved in the domain. For each problem of inducing one of the effects the narrative would be split in two sets, the predicates corresponding to the target effect are extracted to form the positive and negative examples for induction, while the remaining fluent instances and the action instances would be background knowledge for induction. Given a narrative (F, A) and some effect literal e of a fluent in $\mathcal{F}$, the sets of *positive examples* E^+ and *negative examples* E^- on e are

$$E^+ = \{e(s_i) \mid e(s_i) \in F, \, 1 \leq s_i\}$$

$$E^- = \{e(s_i) \mid \overline{e(s_i)} \in F, \, 1 \leq s_i\}$$

where $\overline{e(s_i)}$ is the literal complementary to $e(s_i)$. With the notation we are following, $\overline{e(s_i)}$ is $ne(s_i)$ when learning $e(s_i)$, but $\overline{e(s_i)}$ is $e(s_i)$ when learning $ne(s_i)$. Note that the negation of a fluent is explicitly represented with another predicate in Logic Programming to reserve negation as failure for the representation of inertia. So we will get rules for the fluent and rules for its complementary, we are calling both, effects. Indeed a constraint $\leftarrow e(S), ne(S)$. is needed in the description to avoid inconsistent models.

Background knowledge for induction would be, given a narrative (F, A) and the sets of examples E^+ and E^- for target effect e the set

$$B = F' \cup A = (F \setminus E^+) \cup A$$

Note that negative examples in the form of instances on the complementary effect belong to B, and that target instances at time 0, part of the initial state, are not considered examples but background. Action descriptions usually do not contain rules for the initial state, e.g. note that action rules by their form do not apply to the initial state. Sometimes the possible initial states of the domain are described with rules for time point 0, these rules can be induced with basic methods as they are static rules and inertia does not apply at the initial state. (Ramifications—at least some types of them, as we will see later—can be made applicable at initial state too).

2.3   Non-monotonic Background for Persistence

If induction is made without further background knowledge, we will get the frame problem in induction. Consider the example in Section 1, for target $l2$ we have $l2(0)$ and $l2(1)$, it is likely that the following rule would be induced, $l2(S) \leftarrow t1(S), prev(S, P), l2(P)$. As more actions are defined in the domain, as it would be the case for not so simple domains, we will induce one such rule for $l2$ on any other action that, like $t1$, does not affect fluent $l2$. This way of describing the persistence of the effects present in dynamic domains has several drawbacks, mainly the length of the description and the difficulty on elaborating on it (introduce more features in the description). To solve the frame problem, the usual persistence of the effects in dynamic domains is represented with a non-monotonic mechanism. In Logic Programming, negation as failure can be used, thus for every fluent an inertia rule is added to the program. An *inertia* rule on an effect e is a clause I

$$e(S) \leftarrow prev(S, P), e(P), not\ \overline{e(S)}$$

where S, P are situation variables (universally quantified), $\overline{e(S)}$ is the literal complementary to $e(S)$. Intuitively the inertia rule says that $e(S)$ will be true at a situation S if it was previously true and the complementary fluent cannot be proved true at the same situation S. Just one of these rules is needed for each effect vs. one frame rule for each effect and action combination. And as far as induction, this rule is known in advance and will cover target instances when the effect persists, thus no need to induce rules for these cases. Then background knowledge will include inertia rules for the fluents. In brief, to induce descriptions free from the frame problem we need background knowledge which includes negation as failure in recursive rules on the target predicate.

2.4   Hypotheses Language for Ramifications

To complete the definition of the induction problem, we define the hypotheses language. Action descriptions in Logic Programming already establish the allowed form of action rules and ramification rules, thus defining the hypotheses language. On introducing ramification rules in induction we have two choices for each target effect, either inducing an action rule for it or a ramification rule. In this work we assume the target effect is described by a ramification rule, see [1] for the action rule case. Although note that domains cannot usually be described by only ramification rules for all the effects, while action rules for all the effects are able to describe it. On the other hand, once ramification rules are allowed, most of the effects are usually better described by them.

Definition 1. *(Hypotheses) A ramification rule on an effect e (target effect) is a clause H*

$$e(S) \leftarrow e'_1(S), \ldots, e'_n(S)$$

where $e(S)$ is $f(S)$ or $\neg f(S)$ for some fluent $f \in \mathcal{F}$; S is a situation variable (universally quantified); $e'_1(S), \ldots, e'_n(S)$ may be missing and each $e'_i(S)$ is an effect literal $f'(S)$ or $\neg f'(S)$, with $f' \in \mathcal{F}$.

Ramification rules describe an effect from other effects at the same situation without mentioning the action.

2.5 Types of Ramification Rules

On describing effects from other effects several types of dependence can be identified that are relevant for learning. We will consider three types of dependence present in domains, called definitions, regular and causal. We present these three types of dependencies in the order of their inductive computational complexity. Domains with causal dependencies are the more complex and also the most general case.

1) *(Definitions)* Fluents that do not need inertia. Some (indirect) effects when represented with ramifications do not need inertia, the case arises when the rules (completely) define the effect and its complementary. So given the fluents the effect depend on, and their persistence, it is always the case that at least one of the rules on the indirect effect is applicable.

   In the example of Section 1 consider that the suitcase is open when (and only when) the two locks are open, the rules $o(S) \leftarrow l1(S)$, $l2(S)$ and for the complementary "not_open" effect $no(S) \leftarrow nl1(S).$, and $no(S) \leftarrow nl2(S).$, completely define the fluent. Thanks to the persistence of $l1$ and $l2$, either o or no will be deduced at any situation, thus its persistence does not need to be represented. Nevertheless, if an inertia rule is present for fluent o, though useless in this case, it does not prevent the mentioned behavior.

   Note that these fluents when represented with action rules do need inertia, otherwise when the action is no longer present at the next situation, the fluent cannot be proved.

2) *(Regular)* Fluents that do need inertia. The ramification rules do not define the fluent at any possible situation. Thus persistence (as usual) is assumed from the previous situation. This is the general case of regular ramifications. In the example we are following, consider a different behavior for the suitcase, it opens when the two locks are open (because of the spring mechanism), but we can later close the locks while the suitcase is open, without actually closing it (assume an additional action c is needed to close the suitcase.) The ramification rule will be $o(S) \leftarrow l1(S)$, $l2(S)$, but there are situations at which one lock is not true while the suitcase is open, as it was previously.

3) *(Causal)* The (indirect) effect not only depends on conditions on the truth of other effects, but also on the fact of other effects *becoming* true.

Let start with an example, consider the suitcase opens only when their locks are opened in some order, assume the order open $l2$ then $l1$ does not work, but the other do work. The regular ramification $o(S) \leftarrow l1(S), l2(S)$ is not valid, as would make open true when the order is not correct. The key observation is that the rule needs something more than the truth of fluents in its condition. Note that in action representations, an effect $e(S)$ may be true at a situation because it has been made true by the current action or because of persistence. Simply considering its truth does not tell us in which of these two cases the effect is. In the example, assume we have a predicate $pl2(S)$ for effect $l2(S)$ that is true only when $l2(S)$ is an effect of the current action. Then the rule $o(S) \leftarrow l1(S), pl2(S)$ would be valid for the mentioned behavior of the domain.

For including causal ramifications under Logic Programming representations of actions, we define the following,

i) For each effect $e(S)$ (intended to be used on causal rules) we define a causal predicate $pe(S)$.

ii) Action or ramification rules with head $e(S)$ are changed to head $pe(S)$. Inertia rule remains on head $e(S)$.

iii) A small rule $e(S) \leftarrow pe(S)$ is added to the description for every effect.

Note that no inertia rule is defined for $pe(S)$, it will not persist. Predicate $pe(S)$ will tell us whether the effect $e(S)$ is caused at the situation S. (Intuitively you may consider "caused" as "directly or indirectly affected by the current action".)

We are following the kind of causality in action from [5], see e.g. [4] for another alternative. To follow more accurately that proposal a further requirement is needed for causal ramifications, namely,

iv) Every ramification rule with head $pe(S)$ must include at least one condition literal on some $pe'(S)$ causal predicate.

The evidence narratives on a domain available for induction implicitly contain the type of the ramification rules needed for the domain. If induction is restricted to ramifications in the form of definitions, i.e., inertia of the (indirect) effects is not considered during learning, then domains which demand other types of ramifications —as the example in 2) above— may not have solution in the form of definitions. Similarly, if induction is restricted to regular ramifications, domains which demand causal ramifications will not have solution.

2.6 The Problem of Inducing Causal Ramifications

Causal ramifications extend the framework we are using, so we review the definitions made for the general problem of inducing ramifications.

Initially there is no evidence in the narratives about the causal predicates $pe(S)$ introduced for causality.

In the example we are using if we want to induce a causal ramification for effect o there are no instances on causal predicates at all in the evidence.

Given a narrative (F, A) its extension for causality (F_C, A) is as follows, i) $F \subset F_C$; and ii) for each effect e a causality predicate pe is defined such that for each instance $e(s_i) \in F$ the instance $pe(s_i) \in F_C$ iff $e(s_i) \in F$ and $\overline{e(s_{i-1})} \in F$.

We can define as many causal predicates as we like up to one for each effect in the domain.

The remaining update on the definition of the induction problem to include causality is on the hypotheses language. The condition of the ramification rules will allow literals on causal predicates $pe(S)$, at the same situation, just like any other regular effect predicate.

2.7   Solutions to Induction of Ramifications

Solutions to the induction of ramification rules for the indirect effects of action, without the frame problem can be defined as follows.

Definition 2. *(Induction of the indirect effects of actions) Given some evidence (F, A) on a narrative of a domain and a target effect literal e on a fluent in $\mathcal{F}$, a solution to induction of the indirect effect e is a set of ramification rules H_I on it, verifying*

$$(I \cup F' \cup A \cup H_I) \models e^+(s_i) \quad \text{for every } e^+(s_i) \in E^+$$

$$(I \cup F' \cup A \cup H_I) \not\models e^-(s_i) \quad \text{for every } e^-(s_i) \in E^-$$

$$(I \cup F' \cup A \cup H_I) \not\models \bot$$

where $F' = (F \setminus E^+)$, E^+ and E^- are the set of positive and negative examples on e, and I is the inertia rule on e.

This induction problem is a case of (explanatory) induction in ILP, with background $B = (I \cup F' \cup A)$. However, B is a normal logic program using negation as failure, the *not* operator, in the inertia rule. Unfortunately, it is not known how to efficiently solve an induction problem under normal background knowledge. But see [6] for a characterization of induction in normal logic programs. As an indication of the nonmonotonic behavior note that it will usually be the case that $B \models e^-(s_i)$ for some $e^-(s_i) \in E^-$, while this will not imply that there is no solution. For this reason this condition was omitted from this definition, even though it is a usual and common condition in standard ILP.

3   Efficient Method for Inducing Ramifications

The background knowledge needed to induce ramifications is a normal logic program which compromises efficiency as the induction methods of ILP for Horn logic programs cannot be applied.

In [1] a method has been presented to circumvent a related difficulty for the case of inducing action rules. In this work we will show a similar approach for inducing ramifications that extends that result providing a method to induce action descriptions with both action and ramification rules.

The method is based on identifying a Horn induction problem whose solutions correspond one-to-one to those of the original problem (Def. 2.) The identification of the corresponding problem begins by considering a subset of the positive examples of Def. 2. As in [1] we will present the method in two steps, first for a restricted case requiring no missing instances of the target fluent in the narratives, then for the general case. A narrative (F, A) is complete on fluent f iff for every situation s_i, $0 \leq s_i \leq n$ there is either $f(s_i) \in F$ or $\neg f(s_i) \in F$, where $(n + 1)$ is the length of the narrative.

Given a narrative (F, A) and some target effect e, the set of *positive examples on change* to e is

$$PE^+ = \{e(s_i) \mid e(s_i) \in F \text{ and } \overline{e(s_{i-1})} \in F\}$$

where $\overline{e(s_i)}$ is the literal complementary to $e(s_i)$.

Definition 3. *(Monotonic induction of the indirect effects of actions) Given some evidence (F, A) on a narrative of a domain and a target effect literal e on a fluent in $\mathcal{F}$, a solution to monotonic induction of the indirect effect e is a set of ramification rules H_M on it, verifying*

$$(F' \cup A \cup H_M) \models e^+(s_i) \quad \text{for every} \quad e^+(s_i) \in PE^+$$

$$(F' \cup A \cup H_M) \not\models e^-(s_i) \quad \text{for every} \quad e^-(s_i) \in E^-$$

$$(F' \cup A \cup H_M) \not\models \bot$$

where $F' = (F \setminus E^+)$, PE^+ is the set of positive examples on change to e, E^+ and E^- are the sets of positive and negative examples on e.

The background knowledge in Def. 3. does not contain inertia rules, furthermore B, H_M, PE^+, and E^- are sets of Horn clauses, thus most efficient methods of ILP can be applied to this problem.

3.1   Correspondence Between the Two Induction Problems

Proposition 1. *(Correspondence) From evidence on narratives complete on the target fluent, H_I is a solution of nonmonotonic induction with inertia (Definition 2) if and only if it is a solution of monotonic induction (Definition 3).*

Proof. Consider the proof of [1] Prop. 2. (correspondence), though that proof was devised for the induction of action rules, we will work on it showing its applicability to the current case, instead of repeating the proof that is relatively long.

The form of H solutions that is the main difference wrt ramification rules is not directly mentioned in the proof though indirectly used. But actually most of the proof is valid as presented there for H different from action rules. The proof *strongly relies on the form of the inertia rule used (parts 1.a. (persistent instances case), 1.b, 1.c, and 2.a), we use here the same representation of inertia —that is the standard one for Logic Programming representations of action formalisms, in particular in Answer Set Programming— thus these parts of the proof are valid to show that H in the form of ramification rules obtained with the monotonic method on change makes it sound and complete wrt the nonmonotonic induction with inertia.*

The form of H is used in the proof (indirectly) only in parts 1.a (change instances), 2.b, and 2.c. The fact used is that H together with the background (but without inertia rules) is a Horn program. The ramification rules we use here are positive rules thus, these parts of the proof are applicable to our case, when H in the form of ramification rules is considered instead of action rules.

Finally when narratives extended for causality are considered, the proof is also valid as the fluents available for condition literals in H are not used in the proof. ∎

3.2 General Efficient Method for Inducing Ramifications: Missing Target Instances

The general method for inducing ramifications works on any narrative including those with missing target instances (the restriction previously made). In this case, circumventing the nonmonotonic nature of induction in action is more difficult. But as in the case for the induction of action rules in [1], a corresponding Horn induction problem can be identified.

For the general case the subset of the positive examples considered in Def. 3 is not complete for the problem. Note that the selection of the examples on change relied on target instances at two consecutive situations; in general, the change in the effect may show on two non-consecutive complementary targets, because of some missing instances in-between.

We start by defining a new predicate $me(s', s)$ on situations. The predicate $me(s', s)$ will characterize the missing segments on the narrative for the target predicate. A (new) name is given to each segment (first argument, s') and the situation instances s that fall inside the segment are described in the second argument.

Given a narrative (F, A) and some target effect e, the set of instances of *missing segments* ME is

$$ME = \{me(s'_i, s_j) \mid e(s_i) \in F,\ e(s_{i-1}) \notin F,\ \overline{e(s_{i-1})} \notin F \text{ and}$$
$$\overline{e(s_{i-k})} \in F \text{ such for all } s_l,\ s_{i-k} < s_l < s_i,\ e(s_l) \notin F \text{ and } \overline{e(s_l)} \notin F$$
$$\text{and } s_{i-k} < s_j \leq s_i,\ s'_i \text{ new } \}$$

where $\overline{e(s_i)}$ is the literal complementary to $e(s_i)$ and corresponding to each $e(s_i)$ instance in the condition, the constant s'_i is a new situation constant not present elsewhere in the description.

There is an instance $me(s'_i, s_j)$ whenever there is at least one missing target instance—thus instance at s_{i-1} is missing in F— between two complementary instances of target ($e(s_i)$ and $\overline{e(s_{i-k})}$); then the extension of predicate $me(s'_i, s_j)$ would be given as one new constant s'_i for this missing segment and one instance for each situation s_j from situation s_i back to s_{i-k+1} (one after the situation of the complementary). For example, consider

$$F = \{ne(0), ne(1), ne(2), e(5), e(6), ne(8), ne(9), e(11), ne(12), e(13)\}$$

recall notation, ne and e are complementary effects; then

$$ME = \{me(m25, 3), me(m25, 4), me(m25, 5), me(m911, 10), me(m911, 11)\}$$

for target e, and $ME = \{me(m68, 7), me(m68, 8)\}$ for target ne. We used the edge situation numbers to build the new constant naming each missing segment.

Then the general definition of positive examples is a follows. Given a narrative (F, A) and some target effect e, the set of *positive examples on change* to e is

$$PME^+ = \{e(s_i) \mid e(s_i) \in F \text{ and } \overline{e(s_{i-1})} \in F\} \cup$$
$$\{e(s'_i) \mid me(s'_i, s_j) \in ME\}$$

where $\overline{e(s_i)}$ is the literal complementary to $e(s_i)$ and ME is the set of missing segments in F for target e.

In the previous example, $PME^+ = \{e(m25), e(m911), e(13)\}$ for target e, and $PME^+ = \{ne(m68), ne(12)\}$ for target ne.

As the reader may have realized, the general method we propose demands the use of the multiple instance framework for induction. Intuitively, a missing segment from s_i back to s_{i-k} has a collection of k target instances $e(s_i), \dots, e(s_{i-k+1})$ for which one of them is a positive example but it is not known which one. The multiple instance framework needs a redefinition of the hypotheses language for the problem.

Definition 4. *(Multiple instance hypotheses) A multiple instance ramification rule on an effect e (target effect) is a clause H_{MI}*

$$e(S') \leftarrow me(S', S), e'_1(S), \dots, e'_n(S)$$

where $e(S')$ is $f(S')$ or $\neg f(S')$ for some fluent $f \in \mathcal{F}$; S, S' are situation variables (universally quantified); $e'_1(S), \dots, e'_n(S)$ may be missing and each $e'_i(S)$ is an effect literal $f'(S)$ or $\neg f'(S)$, with $f' \in \mathcal{F}$; $me(S', S)$ is a literal of the predicate for missing segments, it may be missing in which case $e(S')$ is $e(S)$.

When $me(S', S)$ is missing, we are in the basic definition of hypotheses given before. Note that only one literal $me(S', S)$ is allowed at most in H_{MI}.

Definition 5. *(General monotonic induction of the indirect effects of actions) Given some evidence (F, A) on a narrative of a domain and a target effect literal e on a fluent in $\mathcal{F}$, a solution to monotonic induction of the indirect effect e is a set of multiple instance ramification rules H_{MI} on it, verifying*

$$(F' \cup A \cup ME \cup H_{MI}) \models e^+(s_i) \quad \text{for every } e^+(s_i) \in PME^+$$

$$(F' \cup A \cup ME \cup H_{MI}) \not\models e^-(s_i) \quad \text{for every } e^-(s_i) \in E^-$$

$$(F' \cup A \cup ME \cup H_{MI}) \not\models \bot$$

where $F' = (F \backslash E^+)$, PME^+ is the set of positive examples on change to e, ME is the set of missing segments, E^+ and E^- are the sets of positive and negative examples on e.

The background knowledge in Def. 5. does not contain inertia rules, F', A, ME, H_{MI}, PME^+, and E^- are sets of Horn clauses, thus efficient methods of ILP can be applied to this problem.

With respect to [1], that also solves in general the induction problem including missing instances, the multiple instance method there for action rules is not applicable for ramification rules. The reason is that the multiple instance representation for action rules takes advantage of the use of action predicates in the action rules, there is always one such predicate in the condition.

The proposal made here is more general and applies to ramification rules, but can be used also for action rules (or in general for other kind of hypotheses in dynamic domains), being [1] a particular case.

3.3   Correspondence Between the Two Induction Problems

The multiple instance hypotheses are syntactically different to the regular ramifications intended as solution to the problem. A transformation can be defined to regular ramification rules.

Given a multiple instance ramification rule on an effect e, $H_{MI} = e(S') \leftarrow me(S', S), e'_1(S), \ldots, e'_n(S)$ its transformation to regular ramification is $H^T_{MI} = e(S) \leftarrow e'_1(S), \ldots, e'_n(S)$. The missing segments literal is deleted and the situation variable of the head effect is moved to S. Note that an hypothesis that does not mention the predicate me transforms to itself, and that the inverse transformation is defined.

Proposition 2. *(Correspondence general) From evidence on narratives, H_I is a solution of nonmonotonic induction with inertia (Definition 2) if and only if H_{MI} is a solution of general monotonic induction (Definition 5) and H_{MI} transforms to H_I.*

Proof. We only show the part of the proof that differs from the restricted case in Prop. 1, mainly related to the different positive examples PME^+ instead of PE^+.

1. ($H_I \Leftarrow H_{MI}$) Consider a monotonic solution H_{MI}, transformed to the regular form H^T_{MI}, is not a solution of the nonmonotonic induction problem with inertia.

The relevant case (different from Prop. 1) occurs when there is some $e(s_i) \in E^+$ such that $(I \cup F' \cup A \cup H^T_{MI}) \not\models e(s_i)$ and, in particular, $e(s_i)$ belongs to a missing segment. Then the segment is from s_i back to s_{i-k}, by definition of general monotonic induction, there is some $e(s'_i) \in PME^+$ such that $(F' \cup A \cup ME \cup H_{MI}) \models e(s'_i)$. The instance at $e(s'_i)$ of H_{MI}, $e(s'_i) \leftarrow me(s'_i, s_j), e'_1(s_j), \ldots, e'_n(s_j)$ verifies that there is some s_j, $s_{i-k} < s_j \le s_i$ such that $e'_1(s_j), \ldots, e'_n(s_j)$

is true under the background $(F' \cup A \cup ME)$ thus also under background $(F' \cup A)$. Then in its transformed form $H_{MI}^T = e(S) \leftarrow e_1'(S), \ldots, e_n'(S)$, the instance at that s_j would entail $e(s_j)$, namely, $(F' \cup A \cup H_{MI}^T) \models e(s_j)$.

If it is the case $s_j = s_i$ then we proved $(I \cup F' \cup A \cup H_{MI}^T) \models e(s_i)$ (because $e(s_i)$ is monotonically entailed without inertia) which contradicts the assumption. In any other case $s_j < s_i$ and $\overline{e(s_l)} \notin F'$ for $s_j \leq s_l < s_i$ because there is a missing segment at those situations. Thus inertia rule $e(s_{j+1}) \leftarrow prev(s_{j+1}, s_j), e(s_j), not \ \overline{e(s_{j+1})}$ applies as its condition is true, this happens "starting" from the entailed instance $e(s_j)$ up to $e(s_i)$. Thus $(I \cup F' \cup A \cup H_{MI}^T) \models e(s_i)$ which contradicts the assumption.

2. $(H_I \Rightarrow H_M)$ Consider a nonmonotonic solution H_I is not a solution of the monotonic induction problem.

The interesting case (different from Prop. 1) occurs when there is some $e(s_i') \in PME^+$ such that $(F' \cup A \cup ME \cup H_{MI}) \not\models e(s_i')$ where $H_{MI}^T = H_I$ and, in particular, $e(s_i')$ corresponds to a missing segment. Consider the missing segment named s_i' extends from s_i back to s_{i-k}, thus $e(s_i) \in E^+$ and $\overline{e(s_{i-k})} \in F'$. Then $(I \cup F' \cup A \cup H_I) \models e(s_i)$ and $(I \cup F' \cup A \cup H_I) \not\models e(s_{i-k})$ as it is solution. As the complementary effect holds at the start of the missing segment, and the effect holds at the end, it must be some situation in between, say s_j at which $(I \cup F' \cup A \cup H_I) \models e(s_j)$ and $(I \cup F' \cup A \cup H_I) \not\models e(s_{j-1})$. At that situation s_j the inertia rule is not applicable as previously the effect is not entailed, thus $(F' \cup A \cup H_I) \models e(s_j)$. Now extend the rule H_I to H_{MI} form such that $H_{MI}^T = H_I$, its instance $e(s_i') \leftarrow me(s_i', s_j), e_1'(s_j), \ldots, e_n'(s_j)$ makes $(F' \cup A \cup ME \cup H_{MI}) \models e(s_i')$, which contradicts the assumption. ∎

3.4   Monotonic Induction of Causal Ramification Rules

Recall from Sections 2.5, 2.6, that the behavior of some dynamic domains have to be described with causal ramification rules, in order to cover the observed evidence. The causal ramification problem introduces a new causal predicate $pe(S)$ for each effect $e(S)$ that is made available at the narrative F for induction. Thus the hypotheses can use those predicates as condition literals.

The method described here includes the induction of causal ramifications, as the results do not depend on the kind of condition literals available in the background for the hypotheses.

3.5   Efficiency of the Method

From the point of view of efficiency of the method, Prop. 2 and Prop. 1 reduce the effort of learning ramifications rules, including causal ramifications, to that of the Horn induction problem of Def. 5 (resp. Def. 3.)

In Figure 1 an algorithm is outlined to induce action descriptions including ramification and action rules. A suitable Horn induction solver is used; the definitions stated in this work were intentionally made simple, wrt the background knowledge, to avoid unnecessary complication for the presentation of

Induction of actions (N, H_P)
input collection of narratives $N = \{(F, A)\}$
output action description in Logic Programming H_P

> $H_P = $ empty set
>   >   (**if** some narrative F is inconsistent **then exit**)
>   define causal predicates for each $e \in F$
>   >   and add them to F.
>   **for** each effect $e \in F$ **do**
>   >   select e as target predicate
>   >   extract the positive and negative examples E^+, E^- for e from F
>   >   extract the positive examples on change PE^+, for e from F
>   >   identify the missing segments ME for e on F
>   >   extract the positive missing examples on change PME^+, for e from F
>   >   decide whether to induce H action rule or ramification rule form
>   >   **call** Horn induction method with
>   >   >   background $B = (F \setminus E^+) \cup A \cup ME$ and
>   >   >   positive examples PME^+, negative examples E^- and
>   >   > H bias, (multiple instance) ramification or action rule on target e
>   >   **endcall**
>   >   transform H output from multiple instance form to regular.
>   >   add H effect instances e to F
>   >   >   or H itself to next B
>   >   add H to H_P
>   **end for**
>   **output** H_P

Fig. 1. Algorithm for monotonic induction of action descriptions, outlined

the method, but also to allow a wide range of available Horn induction systems of ILP suitable to the method. Note e.g. that background knowledge and examples are sets of ground facts, and the hypotheses are function-free positive rules. Under these conditions most of the solvers are able to work, and what is more important some are sound and complete, i.e. if there is a solution to induction they find it and it is correct. Thus the monotonic method provides a sound and complete induction of the effects of actions without the frame problem from the most basic evidence on its narratives.

Indeed, the efficiency of the Horn induction method applied determines the efficiency of our method. For example, the *ij-determinacy* of hypotheses [7], guarantees that the Horn problem is tractable. The restricted method without missing target instances verifies this condition. Unfortunately, the general method, as a multiple instance induction requires the induction of *nondeterminate* clauses — the missing segments literal is nondeterminate with respect to the background and examples. This compromises efficiency, as induction of 12-nondeterminate clauses is not PAC-learnable [8].

Finally note that other issues have to be considered for the whole problem, for instance, the algorithm of Figure 1 describes the induction of rules for all the effects which involves a multiple predicate learning problem that is not considered there. Also, e.g., the for loop and the call to Horn induction solver has to be repeated for alternative solutions to the input problem. An implementation based on an extension of that algorithm will be available soon.

4   Discussion

The main contribution of this work is a method to induce action descriptions in Logic Programming —also valid for Answer Set Programming [2] [3]— from evidence in the simplest form of narratives observed in the dynamic domain.

The method generalizes a previous result in [1] that is applicable to action rules, inducing also ramification rules, including causal ramifications. This completes the induction of action descriptions providing a sound and complete method that makes it as efficient as basic induction in Horn logic programs. Recall that a direct induction of action requires normal programs as background for the representation of persistence present in any dynamic domain, without having the frame problem. As there are no efficient methods for induction under normal programs, the result of this work is a bit surprising and indeed suggests investigating other cases of induction in normal programs which might also be solvable efficiently.

For induction in dynamic domains in general, the results of this work solve one of the main problems, discovering the knowledge model of the dynamic domain. The problem is solved in its general form, without restrictions —the complete narrative restriction is usually found in other works—, or without prior knowledge on the domain, etc. Induction in dynamic domains has other general problems the method is not directly intended, e.g. induction of alternative models of the domain, for instance, reactive models. In this case hypotheses have action literals on its head, which is never the case in action description rules. This kind of model provides for efficient inference of plans (sequences of actions) to achieve goals (sets of fluent instances). But the descriptions induced in this work can be also used for that task, this is the case of planning with action formalisms. Just to mention another important area of learning in dynamic domains, relational reinforcement learning (RRL) framework is able to work on evidence on the domain that is a subset of the evidence used here for action induction, namely, the set of relevant fluent instances of the domain does not need to be known/observed. Unfortunately the induced descriptions from this method does not have as good symbolic features as action descriptions.

Finally this work opens a wide set of tasks to be done on induction of dynamics domains with action descriptions. It can be viewed as a foundational initial step on which extensions can rely. To mention one, being able to work with reduced evidence as in RRL.

Acknowledgements. I would like to thank the anonymous reviewers for helpful comments. This research is partially supported by the European Union, grant

IST-2001-37004 WASP, Working Group on Answer Set Programming and by the Government of Spain, National Commission of Science and Tecnology grant TIC-2001-0393 and by the Government of Galicia, Spain, Secretary of R&D grant PGIDIT-02-PXIC-10502PN.

References

1. Otero, R.: Induction of the effects of actions by monotonic methods. In: Proc. of the 13th Int. Conference on Inductive Logic Programming, ILP 03, LNAI 2835. (2003) 299–310
2. Gelfond, M., Lifschitz, V.: The stable model semantics for logic programming. In Kowalski, R., Bowen, K., eds.: Logic Programming: Proc. of the Fifth Int'l Conf. and Symp. (1988) 1070–1080
3. Lifschitz, V.: Action languages, answers sets and planning. Artificial Intelligence **13** (1995) 245–286
4. Lin, F.: Embracing causality in specifying the indirect effects of actions. In: Proc. of the 14th International Joint Conference on Artificial Intelligence, IJCAI'95. (1995) 1985–1991
5. Otero, R.P.: Pertinence logic for reasoning about actions and change. Technical Report TR-AI-97-03, AILab, University of Corunna, Galicia, Spain (1997)
6. Otero, R.: Induction of stable models. In: Proc. of the 11th Int. Conference on Inductive Logic Programming, ILP 01, LNAI 2157. (2001) 193–205
7. Muggleton, S., Feng, C.: Efficient induction of logic programs. Inductive Logic Programming (1992)
8. Kietz, J.: Some lower bounds on the computational complexity of inductive logic programming. In: Proc. of the 6th European Conference on Machine Learning, ECML 93, LNAI 667. (1993) 115–123

Probabilistic First-Order Theory Revision from Examples

Aline Paes[1], Kate Revoredo[1], Gerson Zaverucha[1], and Vitor Santos Costa[1,2]

[1] Department of Systems Engineering and Computer Science - COPPE,
Federal University of Rio de Janeiro (UFRJ),
PO Box 68511, 21945-970, Rio de Janeiro, RJ, Brasil
{ampaes, kate, gerson, vitor}@cos.ufrj.br
[2] Department of Biostatistics and Medical Informatics,
University of Wisconsin-Madison,
1210 West Dayton Street, Madison, WI 53706, USA

Abstract. Recently, there has been significant work in the integration of probabilistic reasoning with first order logic representations. Learning algorithms for these models have been developed and they all considered modifications in the entire structure. In a previous work we argued that when the theory is approximately correct the use of techniques from theory revision to just modify the structure in places that failed in classification can be a more adequate choice. To score these modifications and choose the best one the log likelihood was used. However, this function was shown not to be well-suited in the propositional Bayesian classification task and instead the conditional log likelihood should be used. In the present paper, we extend this revision system showing the necessity of using specialization operators even when there are no negative examples. Moreover, the results of a theory modified only in places that are responsible for the misclassification of some examples are compared with the one that was modified in the entire structure using three databases and considering four probabilistic score functions, including conditional log likelihood.

1 Introduction

The ability of representation of individuals, their properties and their relationships, makes first-order logic (FOL) a very expressive knowledge representation system. On the other hand FOL is limited by its inability to represent uncertainty. Recently, there has been a great interest in integrating FOL based formalism with mechanisms for probabilistic reasoning, thus defining first-order probabilistic theories. Examples include: *Probabilistic Relational Models (PRM)* [Koller, 1999] [Friedman et al., 1999], *Independent Choice Logic (ICL)* [Poole, 1993], *Bayesian Logic Programs (BLP)* [Kersting and De Raedt, 2001], *Constraint Logic Programming (CLP(BN))* [Costa et al., 2003] and *Stochastic Logic Program (SLP)* [Muggleton, 2002], among others.

Consider that one is supplied with a probabilistic first-order theory. The theory is known to be approximately correct, i.e., only some points of its structure

S. Kramer and B. Pfahringer (Eds.): ILP 2005, LNAI 3625, pp. 295–311, 2005.

prevent it from reflecting the database correctly. It is much more efficient to identify these points through using the database and then propose modifications only to these points than to use an algorithm that considers modifications over the entire structure. Therefore [Revoredo and Zaverucha, 2002] proposed a Bayesian Logic Programs Revision system (RBLP), which receives an initial BLP and through the examples discovers points that fail in covering some of them. RBLP then considers modifications only for those points choosing the best one through a probabilistic evaluation function. The returned BLP will be consistent with the database.

RBLPs introduce new questions over first-order theory revision. When learning or revising probabilistic first-order theories negative examples are incorporated into the set of positive examples, since the distributions of probabilities will reflect this difference in accordance with the domain of the predicates. At first, this would suggest only using generalization operators to revise the theory. The question arises of whether using specialization operators can improve the result of the probabilistic evaluation function.

A second question considers how to evaluate the proposed modifications. Previous RBLP work used the log likelihood function [Revoredo and Zaverucha, 2002]. However, [Grossman and Domingos, 2004] showed that this function was not well-suited on domains such as the propositional Bayesian classification task; instead, the conditional log likelihood should be used.

In the present paper, we extend RBLP by showing the necessity of using specialization operators even when there are no negative examples. Moreover, we compare the results of a theory modified only in places that are responsible for the misclassification of some examples versus modifying the entire structure. Our evaluation uses three datasets and considers four probabilistic scoring functions: conditional log likelihood, log likelihood, Minimum Description Length (MDL) and Akaike's Information Criterion (AIC).

This paper is organized as follows: in section 2 we review some background knowledge; in section 3 the extended probabilistic first-order theory revision system is presented; the probabilistic evaluation functions used are described in section 4; the experimental results are described in section 5; and finally some conclusions and future works are presented in section 6.

2   Background Knowledge

In this section, first-order theory refinement, revision points, revision operators and BLP are briefly reviewed.

2.1   Theory Refinement

The acquisition of knowledge is a difficult task, time consuming and with the possibility of error. The process of improving automatically an knowledge base using learning methods can be achieved through theory refinement systems [Wrobel, 1996].

Theory refinements can be divided into two classes: theory revision and theory restructuring. Both aim at improving the quality of the theory. The revision task involves changing the answer set of the given theory, i.e., improving its inferential capabilities by adding previously missing answers (generalization) or by removing incorrect answers (specialization). On the other hand, the task of restructuring does not change the answer set of the given theory; its objective is to improve performance and/or user understandability of the theory. The focus of this paper is on theory revision.

A theory revision system starts from an initial theory which will be minimally modified to become consistent with the set of examples. This initial theory can be divided in two parts: background knowledge, which is assumed to be correct, and another that can be modified by the revision. Learning in Inductive Logic Programming (ILP), can be seen as a theory revision where the initial theory consists of the background knowledge. Revision occurs only through the addition of new clauses.

The theory revision problem can be defined in the following way, [Wrobel, 1996]:

Definition 1. *Given:*

- *a initial theory T*
- *a set of positive (C^+) and negative (C^-) examples.*

  Find:

- *a revised theory T′*
- *that logically implies all the positive examples (completeness), $T′ \vDash C^+$*
- *and none of the negative examples (consistency), $\forall c^- \in C^- : T′ \nvDash c^-$*
- *and satisfies a minimality criteria.*

Several authors have shown that both propositional [Towell and Shavlik, 1994], [Garcez and Zaverucha, 1999], [Buntine, 1991], [Ramachandran and Mooney, 1998] and first-order theory revision systems [Wogulis and Pazzani, 1993], [Wrobel, 1996], [Richards and Mooney, 1995] can learn more precisely theories with less data than purely inductive systems.

2.2   Revision Points

When the theory to be revised has only one predicate the selected example, positive or negative, determines the type of operator that must be used, a generalization or a specialization operator.

In the case of a theory with multiple-predicate definitions many clauses can be involved in the proof of a negative example or in no proof of a positive example. Therefore, the indication of which type of operator that must be used is not immediate. It thus becomes necessary to find the theory′s points that need to be correct. Depending on the type of example that is being considered we can define two types of revision points:

- *Generalization* - if the literal in a clause is responsible for the failure of proving positive examples (failure point) and other antecedents (contributing points) that may have contributed to this failure;
- *Specialization* - clauses used in successful proofs of negative examples.

The specification of the revision point determines the type of revision operator that will be applied to make the theory consistent with the dataset.

2.3   Revision Operators

Theory revision relies on operators that propose modifications at each revision point. Any operator used in machine learning (first-order) can be used in a theory revision system. Below we describe the main operators, originally defined in [Richards and Mooney, 1995].

The operators for specialization are:

- *delete-rule* - there are two restrictions for this operator. It cannot delete a clause that is neither the only base case of a recursive predicate nor the only clause for a top-level concept. In the latter replace the clause to be deleted with the rule: *concept :- fail.*
- *add-antecedent* - add antecedents to a clause in an attempt to make all negative examples unprovable. If adding these antecedents also makes some positive examples unprovable, this specialized clause is added to the theory and the specialization begins again with the original clause, looking for alternative specializations that retain the proofs of the other positive examples while still eliminating the negatives. There are two algorithms to add antecedents to a clause: the first one is hill-climbing antecedent addition: it adds one antecedent at a time to find which one increases the accuracy of the theory. Sometimes none of the antecedents decreases accuracy, but in order to actually increase it, several antecedents must be added at once. To do so one can use relational pathfinding, which tries to find the related antecedents [Richards and Mooney, 1995]). Alternatively, one can use the literals from the bottom clause [Muggleton, 1995].

The operators for generalization are:

- *delete-antecedent* - we have two methods: a) the first one is hill-climbing antecedent deletion. This method tries to delete each antecedent in the specified clause at a time, and deletes the one increasing the accuracy while not allowing any negatives to be proven. This process is repeated until the theory's accuracy cannot be improved. The method b) is to delete multiple antecedents - sometimes the provability of an example is just affected by deleting many antecedents at once. First, it collects all antecedents whose deletion does not allow any negative examples to be proven, and then it generates combinations of these antecedents, looking for the one whose deletion allows proofs of one or more positives but no negatives. It does not stop when positives have became provable, it delete as many antecedents as

possible. This algorithm is computationally expensive; therefore, it is only
called when hill-climbing does not improve any revision.

- *add-rule* - it is a clause-based revision. It leaves the original clause in the theory and generates new ones based on the original. The process is made in two
  ways. First it copies the original clause and, using hill-climbing antecedent
  deletion, deletes antecedents without allowing any negatives to be proven,
  and also those that allows one or more previously unprovable positives to be
  proven (even if doing so allows proofs of negatives). Then it creates one or
  more specializations of this core rule using the add-antecedents operator, to
  allow proofs of the desired positives while eliminating the negatives.
- *identification* - it constructs a new clause to generalize the definition of
  an antecedent that failed in the proof of a positive example. Rather than
  developing the clause from scratch, it performs an inverse resolution step
  [Muggleton, 1992] using two existing rules in the domain theory.
- *absorption* - it looks for an existing clause c whose antecedents subsume
  the failing antecedent (and possibly other antecedents in the clause), and
  which has alternate clauses that will allow the failing positive examples to
  be proven; then it replaces the failure antecedents by c's head.

2.4   Bayesian Logic Program

In a BLP [Kersting and De Raedt, 2001] each ground atom represents a random
variable. Each random variable can take on various possible values from the
(finite) domain D_q of the corresponding Bayesian predicate q. In any state of
the world a random variable takes exactly one value. Thus, the main difference
between Bayesian and classical clauses is that Bayesian atoms represent classes
of similar random variables.

A Bayesian definite clause is of the form: $A|A_1, ..., A_n$ where A is a Bayesian
atom and $A_1, ..., A_n$ are Bayesian and logic atoms and all variables are implicitly
universally quantified (similarly to Prolog). As an example:

1. class(A) | obj(A,B),in(A,B,C),obj(A,C).
2. obj(A,B) | dom(A,B).

where the domain (D) of all the predicates is binary ($D_{dom} = D_{obj} = \{triangle,$
$circle\}, D_{in} = \{true, false\}, D_{class} = \{positive, negative\}$). Roughly speak-
ing a Bayesian definite clause $A|A_1, ..., A_n$ specifies that for each substitution
β [Lloyd, 1989] that grounds the clause, the random variable $A\beta$ depends on
$A_1\beta, ..., A_n\beta$.

Similarly to Bayesian networks, for each Bayesian definite clause there is a
CPD associated with it (see table 1).

Since a Bayesian predicate is defined by a set of definite Bayesian clauses, so-
called *combining rules* (as noisy-or) are used to obtain the combining probability
distribution of those clauses from the CPDs of each one (they are decomposable).

Table 1. CPDs of the clauses

P(dom(A,B))
< 0.40, 0.60 >

P(in(A,B,C))
< 0.20, 0.80 >

dom(A,B)	**P**(obj(A,B))
triangle	0.99
circle	0.01

obj(A,B)	in(A,B,C)	obj(A,C)	**P**(class(A))
triangle	false	triangle	0.70
circle	false	triangle	0.70
triangle	true	triangle	0.005
circle	true	triangle	0.001
triangle	false	circle	0.06
circle	false	circle	0.8
triangle	true	circle	0.999
circle	true	circle	0.001

3   Probabilistic First-Order Theory Revision

The Probabilistic First-Order Theory (PFOT) revision problem can be defined as follows:

Definition 2. *Given:*

- *an initial probabilistic first-order theory T.*
- *a set of examples C.*
- *a probabilistic evaluation function F*

  Find:

- *a revised probabilistic first-order theory T'*
- *that logically implies all the examples* $T' \models C^+$
- *maximizes the probabilistic evaluation function*
- *and satisfies a minimality criteria*

  The (PFOT) considered in the present paper is a BLP.

  When we use PFOT the examples which were considered as negatives in the logical approach (see definition 1) will become positive examples, since the probability distribution will reflect this difference according to the predicate's domain.

  The dataset **C** is a set of ground atoms. For each proven ground atom a Bayesian network is constructed using the notion of Knowledge-based Model Construction (KBMC)[Haddawy, 1999]. Each node of these Bayesian Networks is a random variable where its domain is from its corresponding predicate's domain. At the end, a new dataset **B** is formed, composed of the resultant Bayesian networks. This dataset will be used for learning the parameters and to apply the probabilistic evaluation function. Any Bayesian network inference algorithm can be applied in order to find the example's probability.

Therefore, the revision can be divided in two parts: the PFOT´s logical revision (structure revision) and the PFOT´s probabilistic revision (parameters revision).

When revising the PFOT´s parameters the current structure is retained and the probability distributions, which maximize a given probabilistic evaluation function, are searched. The algorithms considered in the literature, such as EM [Kersting and De Raedt, 2002] [Koller and Pfeffer, 1997] and the gradient ascent [Kersting and De Raedt, 2002], can be used for learning the parameters.

```
Let C be the dataset;
Let H' be the initial PFOT;
Best_revision := H';
if there are examples not covered by H' then
    repeat
        initialize S_MR;
        for each logical revision point do
            generate revisions (H);
            for each H" ∈ H do
                if H" logically improves the PFOT then
                    S_{H"} := score(H");
                    if S_{H"} > S_MR then
                        Best_revision := H";
                        S_MR := S_{H"};
                    end if
                end if
            end
        end
    until there is no revision that logically improves the PFOT
end if
if there are examples covered by Best_revision, but misclassified then
    repeat
        for each probabilistic revision point
            generate revisions (H);
            for each H" ∈ H do
                S_{H"} := score(H");
                if S_{H"} > S_MR then
                    Best_revision := H";
                    S_MR := S_{H"};
                end if
            end
        end
    until there is no revision that probabilistically improves the PFOT
end if
returns Best_revision;
```

Fig. 1. Algorithm for PFOT revision

3.1   Structure Revision

Similarly to first-order theory revision, in PFOT revision it is also necessary to identify the revision points. The points that failed in covering (proof) some example are considered as *logical revision points* and the points that covered the examples, but did not classify them correctly i.e. the value with the highest probability was not the same value given by the example, are considered as *probabilistic revision points*. Generalization and specialization operators are respectively applied.

One might argue that since there are no negative examples, specialization operators would not be necessary. However, they still must be applied, because we may want to improve the value of the probabilistic evaluation function. These operators are as described in the section 2.1, except for the add-antecedents operator, which is modified to specialize the rules while improving the probabilistic evaluation function. Example covering must be kept for both the specialization operators.

Generalization operators are also the same described in section 2.1, except for the add-rule operator, since it uses the add-antecedent operator, which was modified as aforementioned.

When an operator is applied to a revision point the probabilistic parameters are learned and the revision is evaluated by the probabilistic evaluation function (*score*). We define the function *score*(PFOT) as being responsible for the construction of the Bayesian networks (B), the CPDs learning and the determination of the probabilistic evaluation function value. The algorithm is shown in figure 1.

4   Probabilistic Evaluation Functions

As it was previously mentioned, four probabilistic evaluation functions are considered:

1. Likelihood - the Likelihood function is defined as:

$$L(H : \mathbf{B}) = \mathbf{P}(\mathbf{B}|H, \mathbf{\Theta}) \tag{1}$$

where $\mathbf{H}$ is the current PFOT, $\mathbf{B}$ is the dataset and $\mathbf{\Theta}$ are the conditional probability distributions. Considering that the examples are independent, we have:

$$P(\mathbf{B}|\mathbf{\Theta}, H) = \prod_{i=1}^{m} P(B_i|\mathbf{\Theta}, H) \tag{2}$$

where m is the number of examples in the dataset. Since the logarithm is monotone and easier to manipulate then $\log L(H : \mathbf{B})$ (LL) can be used.

$$LL(H : \mathbf{B}) = \sum_{i=1}^{m} \log P(B_i|\mathbf{\Theta}, H) \tag{3}$$

The negative log-likelihood (NLL) is a standard measure of training error and is defined as $NLL(H|B) = -LL(H|B)$.

2. Conditional likelihood - in a classification task, the ideal would be to find a theory with the smallest classification error. In [Friedman et al., 1997] it was shown that maximizing the conditional likelihood (see formula 4) of the class is equivalent to minimizing classification error. This occurs because for classification purposes only the conditional log likelihood of the class given the attributes is relevant. Therefore this function is preferable over the likelihood in classification problems.

$$CLL(H|B) = \sum_{i=1}^{m} \log P(y_i|x_{i,1}, ..., x_{i,v-1}) \qquad (4)$$

where $B_i = \{y_i, x_{i,1}, ..., x_{i,v-1}\}$ and y_i represents the class in the example i. Similarly the negative conditional log-likelihood can be defined as $NCLL(H|B) = -CLL(H|B)$.

3. Minimum Description Length (MDL) - both the likelihood and the conditional likelihood are monotonic functions when an antecedent is added in a rule and therefore will favour more complex theories. To resolve this problem, a complexity penalty can be added to the likelihood (or to the conditional likelihood), as MDL [Lam and Bacchus, 1994]:

$$MDL\_LL(H|B) = \frac{1}{2}n \log m + NLL(H|B) \qquad (5)$$

where n is the number of probabilistic parameters. If so desired one can change the log-likelihood to conditional log-likelihood.

$$MDL\_CLL(H|B) = \frac{1}{2}n \log m + NCLL(H|B) \qquad (6)$$

4. Akaike Information Criterion (AIC) - the probabilistic evaluation function AIC [Stone, 1977] adds a smaller complexity penalty to the likelihood than the MDL, in an attempt to prevent underfitting problems that can appear with the later.

$$AIC\_LL(H|B) = n \log e + NLL(H|B) \qquad (7)$$

Similarly to MDL, conditional log-likelihood can be used instead of log-likelihood.

$$AIC\_CLL(H|B) = n \log e + NCLL(H|B) \qquad (8)$$

5   Experimental Results

We apply four probabilistic evaluation functions to the extended revision system and compare the results experimentally in three domains. The first one is the Bongard domain [1]. The dataset is composed of 60 examples where the concept we try

---

[1] The Bongard problems, due to the Russian scientist M. Bongard, are well-known within inductive logic programming.

to learn is the one mentioned in [Kersting and De Raedt, 2002]: "there is a triangle in a circle". We consider that 30% of the random variables are hidden. The others domains considered are the Family domain [Quinlan, 1990] and the School domain [Costa et al., 2003]. Both datasets are completely observed and have 353 and 554 examples, respectively. Table 2 shows the original theories (PFOT1). For the Bongard domain this PFOT1 was the one used to generate the examples.

Table 2. Original PFOT

Domain	PFOT1
bongard	class(A)|obj(A,B),in(A,B,C),obj(A,C)
	obj(A,B)|dom(A,B)
Family	wife(A, B) | gender(A), married(A,B).
	husband(A,B) | gender(A), married(A, B).
	mother(A, B) | gender(A),parent(A, B).
	father(A, B) | gender(A), parent(A, B).
	daughter(A, B) | gender(A), parent(B, A).
	son(A, B) | gender(A), parent(B, A).
	sister(A, B) | gender(A), sibling(A,B).
	brother(A, B) | gender(A), sibling(A, B).
	sibling(A,B) | parent(C, A), parent(C, B), A \ = B.
School	student_ranking(S) | registration_grade(R), registration(R, C, S).
	course_rating(C) | registration_satisfaction(R), registration(R, C, S).
	registration_satisfaction(R) | registration_grade(R),professor_ability(P),
	course(C, P), registration(R, C, S).
	registration_grade(R) | course_difficulty(C),student_intelligence(S),
	registration(R, C, S).
	professor_popularity(P) | professor_ability(P).

Table 3. PFOT provided to the Revision System

Domain	PFOT2
bongard	obj(A,B)|dom(A,B)
Family	wife(A, B) | married(A,B).
	husband(A, B) | gender(A), married(A, B).
	father(A, B) | gender(A), parent(A,B).
	daughter(A, B) | gender(A), parent(A, B).
	son(A, B)| gender(A), parent(B, A), sibling(C,A).
	sister(A, B) | gender(A), sibling(A, B).
	brother(A, B) | gender(A),sibling(A, B).
	sibling(A, B) | parent(C, A), parent(C, B), A= B.
School	professor_popularity(A)| course_difficulty(A), course(B,A).
	registration_grade(A)|course_difficulty(B),student_intelligence(C),
	registration(A,B,C).
	registration_satisfaction(A)| professor_ability(A), course(B,C).
	course_rating(A)|registration_satisfaction(B), registration(B,A,C).

We introduced some errors in the PFOT1s such as delete rule, delete antecedent, add antecedent, change antecedent and change variable. The corrupted PFOTs (PFOT2) are exhibited in table 3.

As in [Baião et al., 2003], to overcome the overfitting problem during training, we applied k-fold cross validation approach to split the input data into disjoint training and test sets and, within that, a t-fold cross-validation approach to split training data into disjoint training and tuning sets [Kohavi, 1995, Mitchell, 1997]. We considered k=4 and t=3. In each k-fold the best PFOT (in accordance with the probabilistic evaluation function) is kept and applied to the test set.

The revised PFOTs (PFOT3) for each domain are shown in tables 4, 5 and 7. For each PFOT3 we exhibit in tables 6, 8 and 9 the probabilistic evaluation function's value (PEFV), the logic accuracy (LA) (percentage of covering examples)

Table 4. PFOT revised for the Family domain

Function	PFOT3	
NLL	mother(A,B)|parent(A,B). son(A,B)|parent(A,B). daughter(A,B)|parent(B,A). wife(A,B)|married(A,B). husband(A,B)|gender(A),married(A,B).	sibling(A,B)|A\ =B,gender(A). sister(A,B)|gender(A),sibling(A,B). brother(A,B)|gender(A),sibling(A,B). father(A,B)|gender(A),parent(A,B).
NCLL	son(A,B)|parent(A,B). daughter(A,B)|parent(B,A). wife(A,B)|married(A,B). father(A,B)|gender(A),parent(A,B). husband(A,B)|gender(A),married(A,B). sibling(A,B)|parent(C,A),parent(C,B), A\ =B.	mother(A,B)|parent(A,B),gender(A). brother(A,B)|gender(A),sibling(A,B). sister(A,B)|gender(A),sibling(A,B).
MDL_LL	mother(A,B)|parent(A,B). son(A,B)|parent(A,B). daughter(A,B)|parent(B,A). wife(A,B)|married(A,B). husband(A,B)|gender(A),married(A,B).	sibling(A,B)|A\ =B,gender(A). sister(A,B)|gender(A),sibling(A,B). brother(A,B)|gender(A),sibling(A,B). father(A,B)|gender(A),parent(A,B).
MDL_CLL	son(A,B)|parent(A,B). daughter(A,B)|parent(B,A). wife(A,B)|married(A,B). father(A,B)|gender(A),parent(A,B). husband(A,B)|gender(A),married(A,B). sibling(A,B)|parent(C,A),parent(C,B), A\ =B.	mother(A,B)|parent(A,B),gender(A). brother(A,B)|gender(A),sibling(A,B). sister(A,B)|gender(A),sibling(A,B).
AIC_LL	mother(A,B)|parent(A,B). son(A,B)|parent(A,B). daughter(A,B)|parent(B,A). wife(A,B)|married(A,B). husband(A,B)|gender(A),married(A,B).	sibling(A,B)|A\ =B,gender(A). sister(A,B)|gender(A),sibling(A,B). brother(A,B)|gender(A),sibling(A,B). father(A,B)|gender(A),parent(A,B).
AIC_CLL	son(A,B)|parent(A,B). daughter(A,B)|parent(B,A). wife(A,B)|married(A,B). father(A,B)|gender(A),parent(A,B). husband(A,B)|gender(A),married(A,B). sibling(A,B)|parent(C,A),parent(C,B), A\ =B.	mother(A,B)|parent(A,B),gender(A). brother(A,B)|gender(A),sibling(A,B). sister(A,B)|gender(A),sibling(A,B).

Table 5. PFOT revised for the Bongard domain

Function	PFOT3
NLL	class(A)|in(A,B,C) obj(A,B)|dom(A,B)
NCLL	class(A)|obj(A,B),in(A,B,C),obj(A,C) obj(A,B)|dom(A,B)
MDL_LL	class(A)|in(A,B,C) obj(A,B)|dom(A,B)
MDL_CLL	class(A)|obj(A,B),in(A,B,C),dom(A,C) obj(A,B)|dom(A,B)
AIC_LL	class(A)|in(A,B,C) obj(A,B)|dom(A,B)
AIC_CLL	class(A)|obj(A,B),in(A,B,C),dom(A,C) obj(A,B)|fdt:dom(A,B)

Table 6. Experimental Results for the Family domain, where PEFV is the probabilistic evaluation function's value, LA the logic accuracy and PA the probabilistic accuracy

Function	Theory	PEFV	LA(%)	PA(%)
NLL	PFOT2	3.55	38	18
	PFOT3	2.47	100	71
NCLL	PFOT2	3.17	36	16
	PFOT3	1.32	100	73
MDL_LL	PFOT2	5.64	38	16
	PFOT3	3.27	100	72
MDL_CLL	PFOT2	5.24	39	19
	PFOT3	2.59	100	76
AIC_LL	PFOT2	4.38	35	16
	PFOT3	2.49	100	73
AIC_CLL	PFOT2	4.20	36	15
	PFOT3	2.02	100	76

and the probabilistic accuracy (PA) (percentage of correctly classified examples) found by the revision system.

When the probabilistic evaluation function used was the log likelihood or the conditional log likelihood we limited the number of antecedents in three for Bongard and Family domains and in four for School domain similar to [Grossman and Domingos, 2004].

Since we are considering the negative (conditional) log-likelihood, the best PFOT is the one that minimizes the probabilistic evaluation function.

The logical accuracy for all PFOT3 is 100% showing that the revised theories are consistent with the datasets. Moreover, the probabilistic accuracy is improved and the probabilistic evaluation is minimized in most of the PFOTs, which is a good result since the main task is classification.

Table 7. PFOT revised for the School domain

Function	PFOT3

NLL	s_ranking(A)| s_intelligence(A)
	p_popularity(A)| p_ability(A)
	registration_grade(A)|course_difficulty(B),s_intelligence(C),
	    registration(A,B,C)
	registration_satisfaction(A)|registration(A,B,C),course(B,D),p_ability(D)
	course_rating(A)|registration_satisfaction(B),registration(B,A,C),
	    course(A,D), p_ability(D)

NCLL	s_ranking(A)| s_intelligence(A)
	p_popularity(A)| p_ability(A)
	registration_grade(A)|course_difficulty(B),s_intelligence(C),
	    registration(A,B,C)
	registration_satisfaction(A)|registration_grade(A),registration(A,B,C),
	    course(B,D), p_ability(D)
	course_rating(A)|registration_satisfaction(B),registration(B,A,C),
	    course(A,D), p_ability(D)

MDL_LL	s_ranking(A)| s_intelligence(A) p_popularity(A)| course(B,A), registration(C,B,D),s_intelligence(D) registration_grade(A)|course_difficulty(B),s_intelligence(C), registration(A,B,C) registration_satisfaction(A)|registration(A,B,C),course(B,D),p_ability(D) course_rating(A)|registration_satisfaction(B),registration(B,A,C)

MDL_CLL	s_ranking(A)| registration(B,C,A), course(C,D),s_intelligence(A),
	    registration_grade(B), p_ability(D), course_difficulty(C)
	p_popularity(A)|course(B,A),registration(C,B,D),p_ability(A),
	    s_intelligence(D)
	registration_grade(A)|course_difficulty(B),s_intelligence(C),
	    registration(A,B,C)
	registration_satisfaction(A)|registration_grade(A),registration(A,B,C),
	    course(B,D), p_ability(D),s_intelligence(C), course_difficulty(B)
	course_rating(A)|registration_satisfaction(B),registration(B,A,C)

AIC_LL	s_ranking(A)| s_intelligence(A) p_popularity(A)| p_ability(A) registration_grade(A)|course_difficulty(B),s_intelligence(C), registration(A,B,C) registration_satisfaction(A)|registration(A,B,C),course(B,D),p_ability(D) course_rating(A)|registration_satisfaction(B),registration(B,A,C)

AIC_CLL	s_ranking(A)|registration(B,C,A),course(C,D),registration_grade(B),
	    s_intelligence(A), p_ability(D), registration_satisfaction(B)
	p_popularity(A)| p_ability(A)
	registration_grade(A)|course_difficulty(B),s_intelligence(C),
	    registration(A,B,C)
	registration_satisfaction(A)|registration_grade(A),registration(A,B,C),
	    course(B,D), p_ability(D), s_intelligence(C), course_difficulty(B)
	course_rating(A)|registration_satisfaction(B),registration(B,A,C)

Table 8. Experimental Results for the Bongard domain, where PEFV is the probabilistic evaluation function's value, LA the logic accuracy and PA the probabilistic accuracy

Function	Theory	PEFV	LA(%)	PA(%)
NLL	PFOT2	0	0	0
	PFOT3	1.18	100	60
NCLL	PFOT2	0	0	0
	PFOT3	0.27	100	87
MDL_LL	PFOT2	0	0	0
	PFOT3	1.81	100	63
MDL_CLL	PFOT2	0	0	0
	PFOT3	4.8	100	67
AIC_LL	PFOT2	0	0	0
	PFOT3	5.26	100	73
AIC_CLL	PFOT2	0	0	0
	PFOT3	1.12	100	79

Table 9. Experimental Results for the School domain, where PEFV is the probabilistic evaluation function's value, LA the logic accuracy and PA the probabilistic accuracy

Function	Theory	PEFV	LA(%)	PA(%)
NLL	PFOT1	3.81	37	10
	PFOT2	2.41	100	53
NCLL	PFOT1	1.98	36	10
	PFOT2	1.40	100	70
MDL_LL	PFOT1	6.65	37	10
	PFOT2	3.33	100	53
MDL_CLL	PFOT1	4.65	39	10
	PFOT2	12.99	100	68
AIC_LL	PFOT1	4.32	40	10
	PFOT2	2.25	100	53
AIC_CLL	PFOT1	2.73	39	10
	PFOT2	6.86	100	67

As the result shows, the probabilistic evaluation functions that use the conditional log likelihood return the best probabilistic accuracy; additionally, the NCLL was the best choice in Bongard and School domains. These results confirm that in a classification task the use of conditional log-likelihood is a more appropriate choice, even in a first-order approach.

For comparison purpose, we consider a maximization procedure that looks for a PFOT with higher probabilistic evaluation in the entire search space (restrict to PFOTs consistent with the dataset) [Revoredo and Zaverucha, 2002]. The resultant PFOT was the same, showing that the revision system could find the best PFOT.

6   Conclusion

In this paper, we extended the probabilistic first-order theory revision system proposed in [Revoredo and Zaverucha, 2002] showing the necessity of using specialization operators, even when there are no negative examples. We compared experimentally a theory revised only in points responsible for the misclassification, with the one that was modified in the entire structure. The resultant probabilistic theory was the same, showing that the use of theory revision can be a more adequate choice.

In [Grossman and Domingos, 2004] has shown that the log likelihood function was not adequate for the propositional Bayesian classification task and that conditional log likelihood should be used instead. In this work, we compared experimentally the results when using different probabilistic evaluation functions, including conditional log likelihood, in a probabilistic first order theory revision. Our results also point to an improvement in probabilistic accuracy when using the conditional log likelihood function.

As future work, we intend to extend these results for other datasets, in particular [Baião et al., 2003].

Acknowledgements

The first author is partially financially supported by CAPES and the others by the Brazilian Research Council, CNPq.

References

[Baião et al., 2003] Baião, F., Mattoso, M., Shavlik, J., and Zaverucha, G. (2003). Applying theory revision to the design of distributed databases. In *Proceedings of the the 13th Int. Conference on Inductive Logic Programming,LNAI 2835, Springer Verlag*, pages 57–74.

[Buntine, 1991] Buntine, W. (1991). Theory refinement on Bayesian networks. In *Proceedings 17th Conference Uncertainty in Artificial Intelligence*, pages 52–60, San Mateo, CA.

[Costa et al., 2003] Costa, V., Page, D., Qazi, M., and Cussens., J. (2003). CLP(BN): Constraint logic programming for probabilistic knowledge. In *Proceedings of the 19th Annual Conference on Uncertainty in Artificial Intelligence (UAI-03)*, pages 517–524.

[Friedman et al., 1997] Friedman, N., Geiger, D., and Goldszmidt, M. (1997). Bayesian network classifiers. *Machine Learning*, 29:131–163.

[Friedman et al., 1999] Friedman, N., Getoor, L., Koller, D., and Pfeffer, A. (1999). Learning probabilistic relational models. In *Proceedings of the 16th International Joint Conference on Artificial Intelligence*, pages 1300–1309, Stockholm, Sweeden.

[Garcez and Zaverucha, 1999] Garcez, A. and Zaverucha, G. (1999). The connectionist inductive learning and logic programming system. *Applied Intelligence*, 11:59–77.

[Grossman and Domingos, 2004] Grossman, D. and Domingos, P. (2004). Learning bayesian network classifiers by maximizing conditional likelihood. In *Proceedings of the 21th International Conference on Machine Learning (ICML-04)*, pages 361–368.

[Haddawy, 1999] Haddawy, P. (1999). An overview of some recent developments on bayesian problem solving techniques. *AI Magazine - Special issue on Uncertainty in AI*, 20(2):11–29.

[Kersting and De Raedt, 2001] Kersting, K. and De Raedt, L. (2001). Towards combining inductive logic programming with Bayesian networks. In *Proceedings of the 12th Int. Conference on Inductive Logic Programming, LNAI 2157 Springer Verlag*, pages 118–131, Strasbourg, France.

[Kersting and De Raedt, 2002] Kersting, K. and De Raedt, L. (2002). Basic principles of learning bayesian logic programs. Technical Report 174, University of Freiburg, Institute for Computer Science, Freiburg, German.

[Kohavi, 1995] Kohavi, R. (1995). A study of cross-validation and bootstrap for accuracy estimation and model selection. In *Proceedings of the International Joint Conference on Artificial Intelligence(IJCAI)*, pages 1137–1145.

[Koller, 1999] Koller, D. (1999). Probabilistic relational models. In *Proceedings of the 9th Int. Conference on Inductive Logic Programming, LNAI 1634, Springer Verlag*, pages 3–13.

[Koller and Pfeffer, 1997] Koller, D. and Pfeffer, A. (1997). Learning probabilities for noisy first-order rules. In *Proceedings of the 15th International Joint Conference on Artficial Intelligence (IJCAI-97)*, pages 1316–1323.

[Lam and Bacchus, 1994] Lam, W. and Bacchus, F. (1994). Learning Bayesian belief networks: an approach based on the MDL principle. *Computational Intelligence*, 10(4):269–293.

[Lloyd, 1989] Lloyd, J. (1989). *Foundations of Logic Programming*. Springer Verlag, 2 edition.

[Mitchell, 1997] Mitchell, T. (1997). *Machine Learning*. McGraw-Hill, New York.

[Muggleton, 1992] Muggleton, S. (1992). *Inductive logic programming*. Academic Press, New York.

[Muggleton, 1995] Muggleton, S. (1995). Inverse entailment and progol. *New Generation Computing Journal*, 13:245–286.

[Muggleton, 2002] Muggleton, S. (2002). Learning structure and parameters of stochastic logic programs. In *Proceedings of the 12th Int. Conference on Inductive Logic Prgramming,LNAI 2583, Springer Verlag*, pages 198–206.

[Poole, 1993] Poole, D. (1993). Probabilistic Horn abduction and Bayesian networks. *Artificial Intelligence*, 64(1):81–129.

[Quinlan, 1990] Quinlan, J. (1990). Learning logical definitions from relations. *Machine Learning*, 5:239–266.

[Ramachandran and Mooney, 1998] Ramachandran, S. and Mooney, R. (1998). Theory refinement of bayesian networks with hidden variables. In *Proceedings of the 15th International Conference on Machine Learning (ICML)*, pages 454–462.

[Revoredo and Zaverucha, 2002] Revoredo, K. and Zaverucha, G. (2002). Revision of first-order Bayesian classifiers. In *Proceedings of the 12th Int. Conference on Inductive Logic Programming, LNAI 2583,Springer Verlag*, pages 223–237.

[Richards and Mooney, 1995] Richards, B. L. and Mooney, R. J. (1995). Automated refinement of first-order Horn-clause domain theories. *Machine Learning*, 19:95–131.

[Stone, 1977] Stone, M. (1977). An asymptotic equivalence of choice of model by cross-validation and akaike´s criterion. *Journal of the Royal Statistical Society series B*, 39:44–47.

[Towell and Shavlik, 1994] Towell, G. and Shavlik, J. (1994). Knowledge-based artificial neural networks. *Artificial Intelligence*, 70(1–2):119–165.

[Wogulis and Pazzani, 1993] Wogulis, J. and Pazzani, M. (1993). A methodology for evaluationg theory revision systems: results with Audrey II. In *Proceedings of the 13th International Join Conference on Artificial Intelligence*, pages 1128–1134, Chambery, France.

[Wrobel, 1996] Wrobel, S. (1996). First-order theory refinement. In Raedt, L. D., editor, *Advances in Inductive Logic Programming*, pages 14–33. IOS Press.

Inductive Equivalence of Logic Programs

Chiaki Sakama[1] and Katsumi Inoue[2]

[1] Department of Computer and Communication Sciences,
Wakayama University, Sakaedani, Wakayama 640-8510, Japan
sakama@sys.wakayama-u.ac.jp
[2] National Institute of Informatics,
2-1-2 Hitotsubashi, Chiyoda-ku, Tokyo 101-8430, Japan
ki@nii.ac.jp

Abstract. This paper studies equivalence issues in inductive logic programming. A background theory B_1 is *inductively equivalent* to another background theory B_2 if B_1 and B_2 induce the same hypotheses for any given set of examples. Inductive equivalence is useful to compare inductive capabilities among agents having different background theories. Moreover, it provides conditions for optimizing background theories through appropriate program transformations. In this paper, we consider three different classes of background theories: clausal theories, Horn logic programs, and nonmonotonic extended logic programs. We show that logical equivalence is the necessary and sufficient condition for inductive equivalence in clausal theories and Horn logic programs. In nonmonotonic extended logic programs, on the other hand, *strong equivalence* is necessary and sufficient for inductive equivalence in general. Interestingly, however, we observe that several existing induction algorithms require weaker conditions of equivalence under restricted problem settings. We also discuss connection to equivalence in abductive logic and conclude that the notion of strong equivalence is useful to characterize equivalence of non-deductive reasoning.

1 Introduction

The issue of equivalence between logic programs is receiving increasing attention. In knowledge representation, a logic program is used for representing knowledge of a problem domain. The same problem may be encoded in different manners by different experts. Equivalence of two programs is then useful to identify different knowledge bases. In program development, one program may give a declarative specification of some problem and another program may give an efficient coding of it. In this case, equivalence of two programs guarantees a correct implementation of the given specification. Various criteria for program equivalence are proposed in the literature [5,10,13,14,15,25]. Of these, *weak equivalence* and *strong equivalence* of two programs are widely studied. Two logic programs P_1 and P_2 are *weakly equivalent* if they have the same declarative meaning. On the other hand, P_1 and P_2 are *strongly equivalent* if for any logic program R, $P_1 \cup R$ and $P_2 \cup R$ have the same declarative meaning. By the definition, strong equivalence implies weak equivalence.

S. Kramer and B. Pfahringer (Eds.): ILP 2005, LNAI 3625, pp. 312–329, 2005.

Equivalence relations presented above are intended to compare capabilities of deductive reasoning between programs. When we consider realizing intelligent agents that can perform commonsense reasoning, however, comparing capabilities of *non-deductive* reasoning between programs is also necessary and important. Recently, Inoue and Sakama argue equivalence in *abductive logic* [11]. They introduce two different types of abductive equivalence: *explainable equivalence* and *explanatory equivalence*. The former considers whether two theories have the same explainability for any observation, while the latter considers whether two theories have the same explanations for any observation. These two notions compare capabilities of abductive reasoning among agents, and [11] provides necessary and sufficient conditions for abductive equivalence in first-order logic and *abductive logic programming* [4]. *Induction* is also known as non-deductive reasoning, which is often distinguished from abduction [6]. In computational logic, induction is realized by *inductive logic programming* (ILP) [19,21]. A typical ILP problem is to induce new rules which explain given examples together with a background theory. There are several parameters which should be considered in defining equivalence notions in ILP. Several questions then arise, for instance: When can we say that induction with a background theory is equivalent to induction with another background theory? When can we say that induction from a set of examples is equivalent to induction from another set of examples? When can we say that induced hypotheses are equivalent to another induced hypotheses? Do conditions for these equivalence depend on underlying logics? These equivalence issues are important and meaningful for comparing different induction tasks, but no study answers these questions as far as the authors know.

This paper focuses on the first question presented above. A background theory B_1 is said *inductively equivalent* to another background theory B_2 if B_1 and B_2 induce the same hypothesis H (under the same hypothesis language) in face of an arbitrary set E of examples. Intuitively, if an agent has a background theory B_1 that is inductively equivalent to another background theory B_2 of another agent, then these two agents are considered equivalent with respect to inductive capability. In this case, we can identify those two agents as far as induction is concerned. On the other hand, if a theory B_1 is transformed to another syntactically different B_2, inductive equivalence of two theories guarantees identification of results of induction from each theory. This provides guidelines for optimizing background theories in ILP. The problem of interest is syntactic/semantic conditions for inductive equivalence in ILP. Conditions for inductive equivalence are arguable in different logics of background theories. In this paper, we consider three different classes of background theories – clausal theories, Horn logic programs, and nonmonotonic extended logic programs. We show that logical equivalence is the necessary and sufficient condition for inductive equivalence in clausal theories and Horn logic programs. In nonmonotonic extended logic programs, on the other hand, strong equivalence is necessary and sufficient for inductive equivalence in general. Interestingly, however, we observe that several induction algorithms require weaker conditions of equivalence between programs under restricted problem settings. We also discuss connection to equivalence in abductive logic, and conclude that the notion of strong equivalence is useful to characterize equivalence of non-deductive reasoning.

The rest of this paper is organized as follows. Section 2 introduces the notion of inductive equivalence. Section 3 and Section 4 present inductive equivalence in clausal theories and Horn logic programs, respectively. Section 5 provides results in nonmonotonic extended logic programs. Section 6 discusses related issues and Section 7 summarizes the paper.

2 Inductive Equivalence

In this paper, we consider logical theories whose domain is given as the *Herbrand universe* and interpretations/models are defined as subsets of the *Herbrand base* HB. Given a logical theory B, let $Mod(B)$ be the set of all (Herbrand) models of B, and $SEM(B)$ the set of all *canonical* models of B. Canonical models are models that are selected from $Mod(B)$ based on some preference criterion, and the relation $SEM(B) \subseteq Mod(B)$ holds. Let L be a logic of a theory B whose semantics is given by $SEM(B)$. Then, a theory B *entails* a formula F under L (written as $B \models_L F$) if F is true in any $I \in SEM(B)$. B entails a set G of formulas under L (written as $B \models_L G$) if B entails every formula in G under L.

Remark: The meaning of the entailment relation $\models_L$ depends on underlying logic L. In this paper, different entailment relations are considered based on different logic L. As a special case, we use the reserved symbol $\models$ for logical entailment in first-order logic.

The induction problem considered in this paper is described as follows:[1]

Given: a *background theory* B, and a set E of *examples*;

Find: a *hypothesis* H such that $B \cup H$ is consistent and

$$B \cup H \models_L E. \tag{1}$$

When H satisfies the relation (1), we say that a hypothesis H *explains* E with respect to B (under L). Throughout the paper, a background theory B is assumed to be consistent. The examples E are *positive* examples and we do not consider negative examples in this paper.

When two different theories B_1 and B_2 are compared, they are assumed to have the common underlying (hypothesis) language. In logic programming, there are different notions of equivalence between theories. In this paper, we consider three different types of equivalence relations. Two theories B_1 and B_2 are:

- *logically equivalent* (written as $B_1 \equiv B_2$) if $Mod(B_1) = Mod(B_2)$.
- *weakly equivalent* (written as $B_1 \equiv_w B_2$) if $SEM(B_1) = SEM(B_2)$.

---

[1] This type of induction is called *explanatory induction*. An alternative type is considered in Section 3.2.

– *strongly equivalent* (written as $B_1 \equiv_s B_2$) if $B_1 \cup Q \equiv_w B_2 \cup Q$ for any theory Q under the same language.

By the definition, $B_1 \equiv_s B_2$ implies $B_1 \equiv_w B_2$. In particular, when $SEM(B) = Mod(B)$ holds in first-order logic, three equivalence relations coincide [5]. As canonical models, *minimal models* are often considered. The set of all minimal models of B (denoted by $MM(B)$) is defined as $MM(B) = \{ M \in Mod(B) \mid \neg \exists N \in Mod(B) \text{ s.t. } N \subset M \}$. We first show that logical equivalence coincides with strong equivalence when $SEM(B) = MM(B)$ in first-order logic. In what follows, $M^* = M \cup \{ \neg A \mid A \in HB \setminus M \}$. Then, any $M(\subseteq HB)$ is a model of B if $B \cup M^*$ is satisfiable.

Proposition 2.1. *For any first-order theories B_1 and B_2, $B_1 \equiv B_2$ iff $MM(B_1 \cup Q) = MM(B_2 \cup Q)$ for any first-order theory Q.*

Proof. The only-if part is obvious. Let $MM(B_1 \cup Q) = MM(B_2 \cup Q)$ for any Q. If $B_1 \not\equiv B_2$, there is $M \in Mod(B_1) \setminus Mod(B_2)$. Since M is not a model of B_2, $B_2 \cup M^*$ is unsatisfiable. Thus, $MM(B_2 \cup M^*) = \emptyset$. On the other hand, $M \in Mod(B_1 \cup M^*)$, so $MM(B_1 \cup M^*) \neq \emptyset$. This contradicts the assumption. Hence, $B_1 \equiv B_2$. □

By contrast, logical equivalence does not coincide with weak equivalence when $SEM(B) = MM(B)$.

Example 2.1. Consider two propositional theories:

$$B_1 : \quad a \vee b, \quad c \vee \neg a, \quad c \vee \neg b,$$
$$B_2 : \quad a \vee b, \quad c.$$

If we set $SEM(B_i) = Mod(B_i)$ for $i = 1, 2$, then $Mod(B_1) = Mod(B_2) = \{\{a, c\}, \{b, c\}, \{a, b, c\}\}$. Hence, $B_1 \equiv B_2$ and $B_1 \equiv_s B_2$. On the other hand, consider

$$B_3 : \quad a \vee b, \quad \neg a \vee \neg b, \quad c.$$

Then, $B_1 \not\equiv B_3$ and $B_2 \not\equiv B_3$. If we set $SEM(B_i) = MM(B_i)$ for $i = 1, 2, 3$, then $MM(B_1) = MM(B_3)$ and $MM(B_2) = MM(B_3)$. Hence, $B_1 \equiv_w B_3$ and $B_2 \equiv_w B_3$. By contrast, $B_1 \not\equiv_s B_3$ nor $B_2 \not\equiv_s B_3$ because the addition of $Q = \{a, b\}$ makes B_3 inconsistent.

The next definition provides a general framework of inductive equivalence between two theories.

Definition 2.1. Two theories B_1 and B_2 are *inductively equivalent* under a logic L if it holds that $B_1 \cup H \models_L E$ iff $B_2 \cup H \models_L E$ for any set E of examples and for any hypothesis H such that $B_1 \cup H$ and $B_2 \cup H$ are consistent.

By the definition, inductive equivalence presents that two background theories have the same explanation power for any example. Background theories can be represented by different logics, so that conditions of inductive equivalence are argued in respective logic L. In the following sections, we provide general conditions for inductive equivalence in different logics, and argue the issue in specific ILP algorithms.

3   Clausal Theories

We start with clausal theories in general. A *clausal theory* B is a set of clauses of the form:

$$A_1 \vee \cdots \vee A_m \vee \neg A_{m+1} \vee \cdots \vee \neg A_n$$

where A_i $(1 \leq i \leq n)$ are atoms. In the context of logic programming, it is also written as

$$A_1 \vee \cdots \vee A_m \leftarrow A_{m+1}, \ldots, A_n . \tag{2}$$

If $m \leq 1$ for every clause (2) in B, B is a *Horn logic program*. A Horn logic program B is *definite* if $m = 1$ for every clause (2) in B. Horn logic programs are handled in detail in Section 4. A theory, a clause or an atom is *ground* if it contains no variable. A theory or a clause with variables stands for the set of its ground instances. A *propositional* theory is a finite set of ground clauses.

Given a background theory B as a clausal theory and a set E of clauses as examples, induction produces a set H of clauses as hypothesis. As usual, a set of clauses is identified with the conjunction of clauses included in the set. We first set $SEM(B) = Mod(B)$. In this case, logical equivalence of background programs is necessary and sufficient.[2]

Theorem 3.1. *Two clausal theories B_1 and B_2 are inductively equivalent under clausal logic iff $B_1 \equiv B_2$.*

Proof. B_1 and B_2 are inductively equivalent under clausal logic
iff $B_1 \cup H \models E \Leftrightarrow B_2 \cup H \models E$ for any set E of clauses and for any set H of clauses such that $B_1 \cup H$ and $B_2 \cup H$ are consistent
iff $B_1 \models H \rightarrow E \Leftrightarrow B_2 \models H \rightarrow E$ for any H and E such that $B_1 \cup H$ and $B_2 \cup H$ are consistent
iff $B_1 \equiv B_2$.   □

Since logical equivalence coincides with strong/weak equivalence under the setting $SEM(B) = Mod(B)$ in clausal logic, the above result implies that strong/weak equivalence of two theories is also necessary and sufficient.

Next, we set $SEM(B) = MM(B)$ for the semantics of a clausal theory B. Such a setting is considered as the *minimal model semantics* of disjunctive logic programs [17] or *circumscription* [16]. Then, we write $B \models_{MM} C$ if a clause C is satisfied in any $I \in MM(B)$. For any set D of clauses, we write $B \models_{MM} D$ if $B \models_{MM} C$ for every clause C in D. Under the setting, the notion of inductive equivalence *under the minimal model semantics* is defined in the same manner as Definition 2.1 with the only difference that the entailment relation $\models_L$ is replaced by $\models_{MM}$. In this case, we have the next result.

Theorem 3.2. *Two clausal theories B_1 and B_2 are inductively equivalent under the minimal model semantics iff $B_1 \equiv B_2$.*

---

[2] This result is also obtained as a special case of explanatory equivalence of abductive frameworks by allowing any clause as a candidate hypothesis in [11, Theorem 3.6].

Proof. Suppose that B_1 and B_2 are inductively equivalent under the minimal model semantics. Then, $B_1 \cup H \models_{MM} E$ iff $B_2 \cup H \models_{MM} E$ for any set H and for any set E of clauses such that $B_1 \cup H$ and $B_2 \cup H$ are consistent. By putting $E = B_1 \cup H$, it holds that $B_1 \cup H \models_{MM} B_1 \cup H$ iff $B_2 \cup H \models_{MM} B_1 \cup H$. By putting $E = B_2 \cup H$, it holds that $B_1 \cup H \models_{MM} B_2 \cup H$ iff $B_2 \cup H \models_{MM} B_2 \cup H$. As $B_1 \cup H \models_{MM} B_1 \cup H$ and $B_2 \cup H \models_{MM} B_2 \cup H$ always hold, $B_1 \cup H \models_{MM} B_2 \cup H$ and $B_2 \cup H \models_{MM} B_1 \cup H$ also hold. By $B_1 \cup H \models_{MM} B_2 \cup H$, any minimal model M of $B_1 \cup H$ satisfies every clause in $B_2 \cup H$. If $M \notin MM(B_2 \cup H)$, there is a minimal model $N \in MM(B_2 \cup H)$ such that $N \subset M$ and N satisfies $B_2 \cup H$. By $B_2 \cup H \models_{MM} B_1 \cup H$, N satisfies every clause in $B_1 \cup H$. But this is impossible because M is a minimal model of $B_1 \cup H$. Hence, $M \in MM(B_2 \cup H)$. Likewise, $M \in MM(B_2 \cup H)$ implies $M \in MM(B_1 \cup H)$. Therefore, $MM(B_1 \cup H) = MM(B_2 \cup H)$, so that $B_1 \equiv B_2$ by Proposition 2.1.

Conversely, if $B_1 \equiv B_2$, $MM(B_1 \cup H) = MM(B_2 \cup H)$ holds for any set H of clauses (Proposition 2.1). Then, $B_1 \cup H \models_{MM} E$ iff $B_2 \cup H \models_{MM} E$ for any set E of clauses and $B_1 \cup H$ is consistent iff $B_2 \cup H$ is consistent. Hence, B_1 and B_2 are inductively equivalent. $\qquad\square$

Theorem 3.2 and Proposition 2.1 imply that strong equivalence of two theories is also necessary and sufficient for inductive equivalence under the minimal model semantics. Note that weak equivalence of two theories is not sufficient for inductive equivalence.

Example 3.1. Two theories $B_1 = \{\, p(x) \vee \neg q(x), \quad r(a)\,\}$ and $B_2 = \{\, r(a)\,\}$ have the same minimal model $\{r(a)\}$, thereby weakly equivalent. However, they are not inductively equivalent. In fact, for the example $E = \{p(a)\}$, the clause $H = (q(x) \vee \neg r(x))$ explains $p(a)$ in B_1, but not in B_2.

Theorems 3.1 and 3.2 imply that in full clausal theories the notion of inductive equivalence under $SEM(B) = Mod(B)$ and the one under $SEM(B) = MM(B)$ coincide.

Corollary 3.3. *Two clausal theories are inductively equivalent under clausal logic iff they are inductively equivalent under the minimal model semantics.*

Given two propositional clausal theories B_1 and B_2, the problem of testing $B_1 \equiv B_2$ is equivalent to the problem of testing unsatisfiability of $B_1 \wedge \neg B_2$, which is coNP-complete. Then, the next result follows by Theorems 3.1 and 3.2.

Corollary 3.4. *Deciding inductive equivalence of two propositional clausal theories is coNP-complete.*

In what follows, we pick up two induction methods for full clausal theories and investigate conditions for inductive equivalence.

3.1   CF-Induction

Inoue [9] provides a method for induction from full clausal theories. It is based on the technique of *consequence finding* (CF). Given a background theory B as a clausal theory and a set E of examples as clauses, *CF-induction* computes a hypothesis H as follows: First, the condition $B \cup H \models E$ of (1) is converted to

$$B \cup \{\neg E\} \models \neg H$$

where $\neg E$ is a formula in a disjunctive normal form. The above relation is interpreted as $B \cup \{\neg E\} \models CC(B, E)$ and $CC(B, E) \models \neg H$ with some clausal theory $CC(B, E)$. The relation $CC(B, E) \models \neg H$ is then rewritten as

$$H \models \neg CC(B, E).$$

Then, a hypothesis H is constructed as a clausal theory which entails $\neg CC(B, E)$.[3] $CC(B, E)$ is a set of clauses that are computed by the *characteristic clauses* of $B \cup \{\neg E\}$. The characteristic clauses of a set Σ of clauses are defined as follows. A clause C *subsumes* a clause D if $C\theta \subseteq D$ for some substitution θ. C *properly subsumes* D if C subsumes D but D does not subsume C. Then,

$$Carc(\Sigma) = \{\, C \in Th(\Sigma) \mid \neg \exists\, D \in Th(\Sigma) \text{ s.t. } D \text{ properly subsumes } C \,\}.$$

That is, each characteristic clause is a theorem of Σ that is not properly subsumed by any clause in the set of theorems. Then, it holds that

$$Carc(B \cup \{\neg E\}) \models CC(B, E).$$

Inductive equivalence under CF-induction is then defined as follows.

Definition 3.1. Let B_1 and B_2 are two clausal theories. Then, B_1 and B_2 are *inductively equivalent under CF-induction* if $Carc(B_1 \cup \{\neg E\}) = Carc(B_2 \cup \{\neg E\})$ for any set E of clauses.

Then, we have the next result.

Theorem 3.5. *Let B_1 and B_2 be two clausal theories. Then, B_1 and B_2 are inductively equivalent under CF-induction iff $B_1 \equiv B_2$.*

Proof. If $Carc(B_1 \cup \{\neg E\}) = Carc(B_2 \cup \{\neg E\})$ for any set E of clauses, $Carc(B_1) = Carc(B_2)$ by putting $E = \emptyset$. This implies $B_1 \equiv B_2$. The converse is straightforward. $\square$

The above result, together with Theorem 3.1, implies that B_1 and B_2 are inductively equivalent under clausal logic iff they are inductively equivalent under CF-induction.

3.2   Confirmatory Induction

Confirmatory induction (or *descriptive induction*) is an alternative framework of induction [2]. In this framework, a hypothesis H explains an example E with respect to a background theory B iff H is satisfied by every $I \in SEM(B \cup E)$.

---

[3] This extends Muggleton's *inverse entailment* in Horn theories. Muggleton's method is explained in Section 4.2.

The system CLAUDIEN [3] realizes this type of induction under the minimal model semantics $SEM = MM$.

The notion of inductive equivalence in this context is distinguished as *confirmatorily inductive equivalence* (*c-inductive equivalence*, for short). The notion of c-inductive equivalence is defined as follows.

Definition 3.2. Two theories B_1 and B_2 are *c-inductively equivalent* under a logic L if it holds that $B_1 \cup E \models_L H$ iff $B_2 \cup E \models_L H$ for any set E of examples and for any hypothesis H such that $B_1 \cup H$ and $B_2 \cup H$ are consistent.

When a background theory is given as a clausal theory, c-inductive equivalence under the minimal model semantics is characterized as follows.

Theorem 3.6. *Two clausal theories B_1 and B_2 are c-inductively equivalent under the minimal model semantics iff $B_1 \equiv B_2$.*

Proof. Suppose that B_1 and B_2 are c-inductively equivalent under the minimal model semantics. Then, $B_1 \cup E \models_{MM} H$ iff $B_2 \cup E \models_{MM} H$ for any set E and for any set H of clauses such that $B_1 \cup H$ and $B_2 \cup H$ are consistent. Then, $B_1 \equiv B_2$ holds by Theorem 3.2. The converse is shown in a straightforward manner.   □

The above theorem presents that in clausal theories two notions of inductive equivalence coincide (under the minimal model semantics). That is, B_1 and B_2 are inductively equivalent in explanatory induction iff they are inductively equivalent in confirmatory induction.

4   Induction in Horn Logic Programs

Next we consider the case where a background theory, examples, and hypotheses are all Horn logic programs. A lot of ILP systems handle Horn logic programs and some algorithms are known for Horn ILP. So we discuss here inductive equivalence in Horn logic programs apart from Section 3.

The declarative semantics of a Horn logic program is given by the unique minimal model, called the *least model*. Thus, for any Horn logic program B, $SEM(B) = MM(B)$ and we write $MM(B)$ as $LM(B)$. We write $B \models_{LM} C$ if a Horn clause C is satisfied in $LM(B)$. For a set D of Horn clauses, we write $B \models_{LM} D$ if $B \models_{LM} C$ for every Horn clause C in D. Notice that $\models_{LM}$ does not coincide with $\models$. For instance, given $B = \{p \leftarrow q\}$, $B \models_{LM} \neg p$ but $B \not\models \neg p$. Thus, $\models_{LM}$ has the effect of the *closed world assumption*.

Definition 4.1. Two Horn logic programs B_1 and B_2 are *inductively equivalent (under the least model semantics)* if it holds that $B_1 \cup H \models_{LM} E$ iff $B_2 \cup H \models_{LM} E$ for any set E of examples and for any hypothesis H such that $B_1 \cup H$ and $B_2 \cup H$ are consistent.

For inductive equivalence in Horn logic programs, the next result follows by Theorem 3.2.

Theorem 4.1. *Let B_1 and B_2 be two Horn logic programs. Then, B_1 and B_2 are inductively equivalent iff $B_1 \equiv B_2$.*

Logical equivalence of two propositional Horn logic programs is tested in polynomial-time, so that:

Proposition 4.2. *Deciding inductive equivalence of two propositional Horn logic programs is done in polynomial-time.*

Several algorithms are known for induction in Horn logic programs. We investigate conditions for inductive equivalence in two popular algorithms.

4.1   Relative Least General Generalization

Plotkin's *relative least general generalization* [24] is a well-known algorithm for induction, which is used in the Horn ILP system GOLEM [18]. We first remind terms and basic results. A clause C_1 *subsumes* another clause C_2 *relative to* a program B, denoted by $C_1 \succeq_B C_2$, if there is a substitution θ such that $B \models C_1\theta \rightarrow C_2$. A clause D is a *relative least general generalization* (RLGG) of C_1 and C_2 with respect to B if D is the least upper bound of C_1 and C_2 under the ordering $\succeq_B$ over the clausal language. The RLGG does not always exist but exists when B is a ground program.

Inductive equivalence under RLGG is defined as follows. Given a ground Horn logic program B and a set E of ground Horn clauses, let $RLGG(B, E)$ be the set of clauses which are the RLGG of clauses in E with respect to B.

Definition 4.2. *Let B_1 and B_2 be two ground Horn logic programs. Then, B_1 and B_2 are inductively equivalent under RLGG if $RLGG(B_1, E) = RLGG(B_2, E)$ for any set E of ground Horn clauses.*

Given a ground Horn logic program B and examples E as a set of ground Horn clauses, GOLEM constructs inductive hypothesis H as follows:

$$B \cup H \models E$$
$$\Leftrightarrow \quad H \models B \rightarrow E$$
$$\Leftrightarrow \quad \models H \rightarrow (\neg B \vee E).$$

At this point, GOLEM replaces B with the conjunction of ground atoms included in a finite subset of $LM(B)$. Here we suppose that the $LM(B)$ is finite. Then, we replace B with $LM(B)$ as GOLEM does. Let $E = \{C_1, \ldots, C_k\}$. Then, the RLGG of E with respect to B is computed as the least general generalization (LGG) of clauses $(C_1 \vee \neg LM(B)), \ldots, (C_k \vee \neg LM(B))$, where $\neg LM(B) = \bigvee_{A_i \in LM(B)} \neg A_i$, which becomes a solution H. Then, we have the following result.[4]

Theorem 4.3. *Let B_1 and B_2 be two ground Horn logic programs. Then, B_1 and B_2 are inductively equivalent under RLGG iff $B_1 \equiv_w B_2$.*

---

[4] We assume the result in the context of GOLEM.

Proof. Suppose that B_1 and B_2 are inductively equivalent under RLGG. Then, for any set $E = \{C_1, \ldots, C_k\}$ of ground clauses, $RLGG(B_1, E) = RLGG(B_2, E)$ implies $LGG(C_1 \vee \neg LM(B_1), \ldots, C_k \vee \neg LM(B_1)) = LGG(C_1 \vee \neg LM(B_2), \ldots, C_k \vee \neg LM(B_2))$. Put $E = \{A\}$ for any ground atom A. Then, $LGG(A \vee \neg LM(B_1)) = A \vee \neg LM(B_1)$ and $LGG(A \vee \neg LM(B_2)) = A \vee \neg LM(B_2)$, so $LGG(A \vee \neg LM(B_1)) = LGG(A \vee \neg LM(B_2))$ implies $LM(B_1) = LM(B_2)$. Hence, $B_1 \equiv_w B_2$.

Conversely, if $B_1 \equiv_w B_2$, $LM(B_1) = LM(B_2)$. Then, for any set $E = \{C_1, \ldots, C_k\}$ of ground clauses, $LGG(C_1 \vee \neg LM(B_1), \ldots, C_k \vee \neg LM(B_1)) = LGG(C_1 \vee \neg LM(B_2), \ldots, C_k \vee \neg LM(B_2))$, so $RLGG(B_1, E) = RLGG(B_2, E)$. Hence, the result holds. □

Example 4.1. Consider two programs:

$$B_1 : \quad has\_wings(joe) \leftarrow bird(joe),$$
$$bird(tweety) \leftarrow,$$
$$bird(polly) \leftarrow .$$
$$B_2 : \quad bird(tweety) \leftarrow,$$
$$bird(polly) \leftarrow .$$

Given the example $E = \{flies(tweety), flies(polly)\}$, both the RLGG of E wrt B_1 and the RLGG of E wrt B_2 become

$$flies(x) \leftarrow bird(x).$$

This means that the first clause in B_1 is of no use for induction under $RLGG$. Note that B_1 and B_2 are not strongly equivalent.

4.2   Inverse Entailment

Next, we consider Muggleton's *inverse entailment* (IE) algorithm which is used in the Horn ILP system PROGOL [20]. Given a Horn logic program B and a ground Horn clause E as an example, suppose a Horn clause H satisfying

$$B \cup \{H\} \models E.$$

By inverting the entailment relation it becomes

$$B \cup \{\neg E\} \models \neg H.$$

Put $\neg Bot(B, E)$ as the conjunction of ground literals which are true in every model of $B \cup \{\neg E\}$. Then, a clause H is induced by *inverse entailment* (IE) if $H \models Bot(B, E)$.

Remark: The process of inverting entailment is similar to CF-induction in clausal theories [9], but IE supposes a Horn logic program B, and a single Horn clause H and E. Another difference is that CF-induction is sound and complete for finding hypotheses, but IE is sound but not complete in general [27].

Given a Horn logic program B and a ground Horn clause E, let $IE(B, E)$ be the set of clauses which is induced by IE from E with respect to B. Then, inductive equivalence under IE is defined as follows.

Definition 4.3. Two Horn logic programs B_1 and B_2 are *inductively equivalent under IE* if $IE(B_1, E) = IE(B_2, E)$ for any ground Horn clause E.

Then, we have the following result.

Theorem 4.4. *Two Horn logic programs B_1 and B_2 are inductively equivalent under IE iff $B_1 \equiv B_2$.*

Proof. B_1 and B_2 are inductively equivalent under IE iff $Bot(B_1, E) = Bot$ (B_2, E) for any E. Then, $B_1 \cup \{\neg E\} \models L$ iff $B_2 \cup \{\neg E\} \models L$ for any ground Horn clause E and for any literal L. Put $E = A_0 \leftarrow A_1, \ldots, A_n$. Then, $B_1 \cup \{\neg A_0, A_1, \ldots, A_n\} \models L$ iff $B_2 \cup \{\neg A_0, A_1, \ldots, A_n\} \models L$ for any $\{\neg A_0, A_1, \ldots, A_n\}$. Thus, for any set F of ground atoms $B_1 \cup F$ and $B_2 \cup F$ have the same least model. Hence, $B_1 \equiv_s B_2$, thereby $B_1 \equiv B_2$ (by Proposition 2.1). The converse is straightforward.   □

The results of Sections 4.1 and 4.2 show that inductive equivalence under RLGG requires a weaker condition of equivalence than IE.

5   Induction in Nonmonotonic Logic Programs

Nonmonotonic logic programs are logic programs with *negation as failure* [1]. We consider the class of *extended logic programs* [8] in this paper. An extended logic program (ELP) is a set of *rules* of the form:

$$L_0 \leftarrow L_1, \ldots, L_m, not\, L_{m+1}, \ldots, not\, L_n \quad (n \geq m) \tag{3}$$

where each L_i is a literal and *not* represents *negation as failure* (NAF). The literal L_0 is the *head* and the conjunction $L_1, \ldots, L_m, not\, L_{m+1}, \ldots, not\, L_n$ is the *body*. A rule with the empty head of the form:

$$\leftarrow L_1, \ldots, L_m, not\, L_{m+1}, \ldots, not\, L_n \quad (n \geq 1) \tag{4}$$

is an *integrity constraint*. A rule with the empty body $L \leftarrow$ is a *fact* and identified with the literal L. An ELP is called a *normal logic program* (NLP) if every literal appearing in the program is an atom. Let Lit be the set of all ground literals in the language of a program. Any element in $Lit^+ = Lit \cup \{ not\, L \mid L \in Lit \}$ is called an *LP-literal* and an LP-literal $not\, L$ is called an *NAF-literal*. A rule is *NAF-free* if it contains no NAF-literal. A program is NAF-free if it consists of NAF-free rules. A program, a rule or an LP-literal is *ground* if it contains no variable. A program or a rule with variables stands for the set of its ground instances. A *propositional* program is a finite set of ground rules.

Remark: A primary difference between nonmonotonic logic programs and clausal theories is that a rule (3) is *not* a clause even if it is NAF-free. For instance, a rule $L_1 \leftarrow L_2$ has meaning different from $\neg L_2 \leftarrow \neg L_1$ or $L_1 \vee \neg L_2$.

A set $S(\subset Lit)$ *satisfies* a ground rule R of the form (3) if $\{L_1, \ldots, L_m\} \subseteq S$ and $\{L_{m+1}, \ldots, L_n\} \cap S = \emptyset$ imply $L_0 \in S$. In particular, S satisfies a ground integrity constraint of the form (4) if $\{L_1, \ldots, L_m\} \not\subseteq S$ or $\{L_{m+1}, \ldots, L_n\} \cap S \neq \emptyset$. When a rule R contains variables, S satisfies R if S satisfies every ground instance of R. The semantics of ELPs is given by the *answer set semantics* [8]. First, let B be an NAF-free program and $S \subset Lit$. Then, S is an *answer set* of B if (i) S is a minimal set which satisfies every ground rule in the ground instantiation of B, and (ii) S does not contain both L and $\neg L$ for any $L \in Lit$. Next, let B be any ELP and $S \subset Lit$. Then, define the NAF-free program B^S as follows: a rule $L_0 \leftarrow L_1, \ldots, L_m$ is in B^S iff there is a ground rule $L_0 \leftarrow L_1, \ldots, L_m, not\, L_{m+1}, \ldots, not\, L_n$ in the ground instantiation of B such that $\{L_{m+1}, \ldots, L_n\} \cap S = \emptyset$. Here, L_0 is possibly empty. Then, S is an *answer set* of B if S is an answer set of B^S. In NLPs, answer sets coincide with *stable models* [7]. An ELP may have none, one, or multiple answer sets. The set of all answer sets of B is denoted by $AS(B)$. An ELP B is *consistent* if it has an answer set; otherwise B is *inconsistent*. An ELP B is called *categorical* if it has the unique answer set [1]. If a ground rule R is satisfied in every answer set of B, it is written as $B \models_{AS} R$. In particular, $B \models_{AS} L$ if a ground literal L is included in every answer set of B. For a set E of ground rules/literals, we write $B \models_{AS} E$ if $B \models_{AS} R$ for any $R \in E$.

An induction problem considered in this section is stated as follows. Given a consistent ELP B as a background theory and a set E of rules as examples, find a set H of rules such that $B \cup H$ is consistent and

$$B \cup H \models_{AS} E. \tag{5}$$

We put $SEM(B) = AS(B)$ in this section.

Definition 5.1. Two ELPs B_1 and B_2 are *inductively equivalent (under the answer set semantics)* if it holds that $B_1 \cup H \models_{AS} E$ iff $B_2 \cup H \models_{AS} E$ for any set E of examples and for any hypothesis H such that $B_1 \cup H$ and $B_2 \cup H$ are consistent.

We proceed to build conditions for inductive equivalence in ELPs. In what follows, we assume the underlying language of programs is function-free and Lit is finite. In this setting, every answer set is a finite set of ground literals.

Theorem 5.1. *Let B_1 and B_2 be two ELPs. Then, B_1 and B_2 are inductively equivalent iff $B_1 \equiv_s B_2$.*

Proof. When B_1 and B_2 are inductively equivalent, it holds that $B_1 \cup H \models_{AS} E$ iff $B_2 \cup H \models_{AS} E$ for any set E of rules and any set H of rules such that $B_1 \cup H$ and $B_2 \cup H$ are consistent. Suppose that there is a set S such that $S \in AS(B_1 \cup H) \setminus AS(B_2 \cup H)$ for some H. Let $S = \{L_1, \ldots, L_m\}$ and $Lit \setminus S = \{L_{m+1}, \ldots, L_n\}$. Put $E = \{\leftarrow L_1, \ldots, L_m, not\, L_{m+1}, \ldots, not\, L_n\}$. Then, every answer set of $B_2 \cup H$ satisfies E, but S does not satisfy E. This contradicts the assumption. Thus, no such S exists for any H and $AS(B_1 \cup H) = AS(B_2 \cup H)$. Hence, $B_1 \equiv_s B_2$. The converse is proved in a straightforward manner. □

The complexity of testing strong equivalence of two propositional ELPs is coNP-complete [14]. This implies the next result.

Proposition 5.2. *Deciding inductive equivalence of two propositional ELPs is coNP-complete.*

5.1   Induction from Answer Sets

Sakama [26] introduces an algorithm called *induction from answer sets (IAS)*. He provides procedures for handling positive/negative examples, and we review the procedure for positive examples here.

Some notions are defined. For any LP-literal L, $pred(L)$ denotes the predicate of L and $const(L)$ denotes the set of constants appearing in L. A rule (3) is *negative-cycle-free* if $pred(L_0) \neq pred(L_i)$ for any $i = m + 1, \ldots, n$. Let L be a ground LP-literal and S a set of ground LP-literals. Then, L_1 in S is *relevant* to L if either (i) $pred(L_1) = pred(L)$ and $const(L_1) = const(L)$, or (ii) for some LP-literal L_2 in S, $const(L_1) \cap const(L_2) \neq \emptyset$ and L_2 is relevant to L. A ground NAF-literal *not L* is *involved* in B if L appears in the ground instance of B. For simplicity reasons, the following conditions are assumed; a function-free and categorical ELP B as a background program; and a positive example as a ground literal L such that $B \not\models_{AS} L$ and $pred(L)$ appears nowhere in B.

Suppose that B has the answer set S. Then, construct a rule $L \leftarrow \Gamma$ where $\Gamma \subseteq S \cup \{not\ L \mid L \in Lit \setminus S\}$ and every element in Γ is relevant to L and is involved in B. Next, the rule $L \leftarrow \Gamma$ is generalized to R as $R\theta = (L \leftarrow \Gamma)$ with some substitution θ.

Example 5.1. ([26]) Suppose the background program B

$$B : \ bird(x) \leftarrow penguin(x),$$
$$bird(tweety) \leftarrow,$$
$$penguin(polly) \leftarrow .$$
$$E : \ flies(tweety),$$

which has the answer set

$$S = \{\, bird(tweety),\ bird(polly),\ penguin(polly)\}.$$

Given the example $L = flies(tweety)$, the rule $L \leftarrow \Gamma$ becomes

$$flies(tweety) \leftarrow bird(tweety),\ not\ penguin(tweety)\,.$$

Replacing *tweety* by a variable x, the rule

$$R : \ flies(x) \leftarrow bird(x),\ not\ penguin(x)$$

becomes a solution.

It is shown in [26] that the rule $H = \{R\}$ satisfies the condition (5) for $E = \{L\}$ if R is negative-cycle-free.

Let $IAS(B, L)$ be the set of rules which is computed by the above procedure using B and L. Then, inductive equivalence under IAS is defined as follows.

Definition 5.2. Two function-free categorical ELPs B_1 and B_2 are *inductively equivalent under IAS* if $IAS(B_1, L) = IAS(B_2, L)$ for any ground literal L.

The necessary and sufficient condition for inductive equivalence under IAS is as follows.

Theorem 5.3. *Two function-free categorical ELPs B_1 and B_2 are inductively equivalent under IAS iff $B_1 \equiv_w B_2$.*

Proof. Since the rule R is constructed by the answer set of a program, the result immediately follows.   □

5.2   Induction of Stable Models

Otero [22] characterizes induction problems in normal logic programs (NLPs) under the stable model semantics. He introduces different types of induction for positive/negative examples, but here we consider the so-called *induction from non-complete sets* which is the usual ILP setting for positive examples.

Suppose a background program B as an NLP, and a set E of ground atoms as positive examples such that $B \not\models_{AS} E$.[5] The goal is to find a set H of rules satisfying the relation (5). An interpretation M is a *monotonic model* of an NLP if M satisfies every rule in B. Given a set E of examples, an interpretation M (of $B \cup E$) is an *extension* of E iff $E \subseteq M$. He then captures H satisfying (5) as an extension M of E that becomes a stable model of $B \cup M$. Note that in this definition a hypothesis H is given as a set of ground atoms.

Let $ISM(B, E)$ be the collection of H defined as above. Then, inductive equivalence under ISM is defined as follows.

Definition 5.3. Two NLPs B_1 and B_2 are *inductively equivalent under ISM* if $ISM(B_1, E) = ISM(B_2, E)$ for any set E of ground atoms.

Lemma 5.4. *[22] Given an NLP B, M is a monotonic model of B iff M is a stable model of $B \cup M$.*

Let $MonMod(B)$ be the set of monotonic models of B. Then, we have the following result.

Theorem 5.5. *Two NLPs B_1 and B_2 are inductively equivalent under ISM iff $MonMod(B_1) = MonMod(B_2)$.*

Proof. Suppose that B_1 and B_2 are inductively equivalent under ISM. For any $M \in ISM(B_1, E)$, M is a stable model of $B_1 \cup M$ and a monotonic model of B_1 (Lemma 5.4). Then, $ISM(B_1, E) = ISM(B_2, E)$ implies $MonMod(B_1) = MonMod(B_2)$. The converse is proved in a similar manner.   □

---

[5] Recall that answer sets coincide with stable models in NLPs.

Example 5.2. Let $B_1 = \{ p \leftarrow not\,q \}$ and $B_2 = \{ q \leftarrow not\,p \}$. For $E = \{p\}$, put its extension as $M = \{p\}$. Then, $H = \{ p \leftarrow \}$ becomes a solution in both B_1 and B_2. Note that $B_1 \not\equiv_w B_2$ but $MonMod(B_1) = MonMod(B_2)$.

6   Discussion

Equivalence of logic programs has been studied in various aspects, but to our best knowledge, equivalence issue in inductive logic programming has never been discussed. Recently, Inoue and Sakama study equivalence of abductive frameworks [11]. They introduce two different types of abductive equivalence: *explainable equivalence* and *explanatory equivalence*. Given a background theory B and a set H of candidate hypotheses (called *abducibles*), an abductive framework is defined as a tuple $\langle B, H \rangle$. Two abductive frameworks $\langle B_1, H_1 \rangle$ and $\langle B_2, H_2 \rangle$ are called *explainable equivalent* if, for any observation O, there is an explanation of O in $\langle B_1, H_1 \rangle$ iff there is an explanation of O in $\langle B_2, H_2 \rangle$. On the other hand, two programs are called *explanatorily equivalent* if, for any observation O, E is an explanation of O in $\langle B_1, H_1 \rangle$ iff E is an explanation of O in $\langle B_2, H_2 \rangle$. Explanatory equivalence is stronger than explainable equivalence, and the former implies the latter.

Comparing [11] with our present work, some interesting connections are observed. When underlying logic is first-order logic, logical equivalence of two theories is a necessary and sufficient condition for explanatory equivalence. When a background theory is represented by a (nonmonotonic) logic program, on the other hand, $\langle B_1, H \rangle$ and $\langle B_2, H \rangle$ are explanatorily equivalent iff B_1 and B_2 are strongly equivalent. Those results have connection to the results of Theorems 3.1, 3.2, 4.1 and 5.1 of this paper. In particular, in clausal logic the notion of inductive equivalence coincides with the notion of explanatory equivalence if one permits arbitrary clauses as abducibles. However, there is an important difference between explanatory equivalence in abductive frameworks and inductive equivalence in this paper, which stems from the difference between abduction and induction. In an abductive framework, a hypothesis space is prespecified as H and possible explanations for a given observation are constructed as a subset of abducibles. The existence of H in abductive logic programs results in characterization by *relative* strong equivalence, i.e., B_1 and B_2 are explanatory equivalent iff they are strongly equivalent *with respect to H*. Moreover, in abductive logic programming, abducibles and observations are usually restricted to (ground) literals. In ILP, on the other hand, hypotheses and examples are general rules rather than facts. Besides these differences, both abduction and induction require strong equivalence of two (nonmonotonic) logic programs to identify the results of abductive/inductive inference. The essence of this lies in the fact that abduction and induction are both *ampliative* reasoning and extend theories. Strong equivalence takes the influence of addition of a rule set to each program into account, so that it succeeds in characterizing the effect of abduction/induction that are not captured by weak equivalence of programs. In [13], it is argued that strong equivalence is useful to simplify a part of a program without looking at the other parts. On the other hand, the study [11] and the result of this paper reveal that strong equivalence has another important applications for testing equivalence in abductive and inductive logic programming.

From the computational viewpoint, testing strong equivalence of propositional nonmonotonic logic programs is converted to the problem of propositional entailment in classical logic [14]. The problem of testing strong equivalence is then solved using existing SAT solvers. For predicate programs without function symbols, strong equivalence testing is also possible by instantiating a program into a finite propositional one. There is a system for testing strong equivalence of function-free nonmonotonic logic programs, e.g., [12]. Existence of no procedure for testing strong equivalence of logic programs with functions would restrict practical application of inductive equivalence in ILP. Nevertheless, inductive equivalence is useful when background knowledge is given as a function-free Datalog or a database that is a collection of propositional sentences.

Apart from the general ILP setting, we have shown that several existing ILP algorithms require weaker conditions of equivalence between programs. Each algorithm is designed to work in some restricted problem setting for theoretical/practical reasons, and such restriction has the effect of relaxing conditions of inductive equivalence. Note that it may happen that some algorithm may produce different hypotheses from two background theories due to its incompleteness. Thus, if two strongly equivalent programs produce different hypotheses in face of some common examples, it indicates that the algorithm is incomplete or incorrect. Thus, inductive equivalence would be used for testing correctness/completeness of an algorithm. In this respect, inverse entailment in Horn logic programs is incomplete, but Theorem 4.4 guarantees that under the restricted problem setting the algorithm correctly judges inductive equivalence of two Horn logic programs. For another application, inductive equivalence would be used for comparing different induction algorithms under the common problem setting. Let $\alpha(B, E)$ be the set of hypotheses induced by an algorithm α using a background theory B and examples E. For two different algorithms α_1 and α_2 in the common problem setting, suppose that $\alpha_1(B_1, E) = \alpha_1(B_2, E)$ implies $\alpha_2(B_1, E) = \alpha_2(B_2, E)$, but not vice versa. In this case, α_1 is considered inductively more sensitive than α_2 in the sense that α_1 may distinguish different background theories that are not distinguished by α_2. For instance, suppose any ground Horn logic program B and any ground Horn clause E. In this problem setting, we can say that IE is inductively more sensitive than $RLGG$ by the result of Section 4. Thus, the notion of inductive equivalence is also useful to compare capabilities of different induction algorithms.

From the viewpoint of program development, it is known that some basic transformations including *unfolding/folding* do not preserve strong equivalence of logic programs [23]. This fact, together with the result of this paper, implies that such basic program transformations are *not* applicable to optimize background theories in ILP. If applied, the result of induction may change in general. Those transformations are still effective as far as one uses induction algorithms that require the condition of weak equivalence.

7 Conclusion

This paper has studied equivalence issues in inductive logic programming. We introduced the notion of inductive equivalence which compares inductive capabilities between different background theories. Three different logics are considered – clausal theories, Horn logic programs, and nonmonotonic extended logic programs. Logical equivalence is necessary and sufficient for inductive equivalence in clausal theories and Horn logic programs, while strong equivalence is necessary and sufficient in nonmonotonic extended logic programs. Under restricted problem settings, on the other hand, we also observed that several existing ILP algorithms require weaker conditions of equivalence. The results of this paper, together with those of [11], reveal that the notion of strong equivalence is useful to characterize equivalence in non-deductive reasoning.

In the introduction, we posed several questions on equivalence issues which may arise in ILP. This paper has answered one question regarding equivalence of background theories. Answering other questions is left for future study.

References

1. C. Baral and M. Gelfond. Logic programming and knowledge representation. *Journal of Logic Programming*, 19/20:73–148, 1994.
2. L. De Raedt. Logical settings for concept-learning. *Artificial Intelligence*, 95:187–201, 1997.
3. L. De Raedt and L. Dehaspe. Clausal discovery. *Machine Learning*, 26:99–146, 1997.
4. M. Denecker and A. Kakas. Abductive logic programming. In: A. C. Kakas and F. Sadri (eds.), *Computational Logic: Logic Programming and Beyond—Essays in Honour of Robert A. Kowalski, Part I*, Lecture Notes in Artificial Intelligence, vol. 2407, pp. 402–436, Springer-Verlag, 2002.
5. T. Eiter and M. Fink. Uniform equivalence of logic programs under the stable model semantics. In: *Proceedings of the 19th International Conference on Logic Programming*, Lecture Notes in Computer Sciences, vol. 2916, pp. 224–238, Springer-Verlag, 2003.
6. P. A. Flach and A. C. Kakas (eds.). *Abduction and Induction — Essays on their Relation and Integration*. Kluwer Academic, 2000.
7. M. Gelfond and V. Lifschitz. The stable model semantics for logic programming. In: *Proceedings of the 5th International Conference and Symposium on Logic Programming*, pp. 1070–1080, MIT Press, 1988.
8. M. Gelfond and V. Lifschitz. Logic programs with classical negation. In: *Proceedings of the 7th International Conference on Logic Programming*, pp. 579–597, MIT Press, 1990.
9. K. Inoue. Induction as consequent finding. *Machine Learning*, 55:109–135, 2004.
10. K. Inoue and C. Sakama. Equivalence of logic programs under updates. In: *Proceedings of the 9th European Conference on Logics in Artificial Intelligence*, Lecture Notes in Artificial Intelligence, vol. 3229, pp. 174–186, Springer-Verlag, 2004.
11. K. Inoue and C. Sakama. Equivalence in abductive logic. In: *Proceedings of the 19th International Joint Conference on Artificial Intelligence*, to appear, 2005.

12. T. Janhunen and E. Oikarinen. LPEQ and DLPEQ – translators for automated equivalence testing of logic programs. In: *Proceedings of the 7th International Conference of Logic Programming and Nonmonotonic Reasoning*, Lecture Notes in Artificial Intelligence, vol. 2923, pp. 336–340, Springer-Verlag, 2004.

13. V. Lifschitz, D. Pearce and A. Valverde. Strongly equivalent logic programs. *ACM Transactions on Computational Logic*, 2:526–541, 2001.

14. F. Lin. Reducing strong equivalence of logic programs to entailment in classical propositional logic. In: *Proceedings of the 8th International Conference on Principles of Knowledge Representation and Reasoning*, pp. 170–176, Morgan Kaufmann, 2002.

15. M. J. Maher. Equivalence of logic programs. In: J. Minker (ed.), *Foundations of Deductive Databases and Logic Programming*, pp. 627–658, Morgan Kaufmann, 1988.

16. J. McCarthy. Circumscription – a form of nonmonotonic reasoning. *Artificial Intelligence*, 13(1&2):27–39, 1980.

17. J. Minker. On indefinite data bases and the closed world assumption. In: *Proceedings of the 6th International Conference on Automated Deduction*, Lecture Notes in Computer Science, vol. 138, pp. 292–308, Springer-Verlag, 1982.

18. S. Muggleton and C. Feng. Efficient induction algorithm. In: [19], pp. 281–298, 1992.

19. S. Muggleton (ed.). *Inductive Logic Programming*, Academic Press, 1992.

20. S. Muggleton. Inverse entailment and Progol. *New Generation Computing*, 13:245–286, 1995.

21. S.-H. Nienhuys-Cheng and R. De Wolf. *Foundations of inductive logic programming*. Lecture Notes in Artificial Intelligence, vol. 1228, Springer-Verlag, 1997.

22. R. P. Otero. Induction of stable models. In: *Proceedings of the 11th International Conference on Inductive Logic Programming*, Lecture Notes in Artificial Intelligence, vol. 2157, pp. 193–205, Springer-Verlag, 2001.

23. M. Osorio, J. A. Navarro, and J. Arrazola. Equivalence in answer set programming. In: *Proceedings of the 11th International Workshop on Logic Based Program Synthesis and Transformation*, Lecture Notes in Computer Science, vol. 2372, pp. 57–75, Springer-Verlag, 2001.

24. G. D. Plotkin. A further note on inductive generalization. In: B. Meltzer and D. Michie (eds.), *Machine Intelligence*, vol. 6, pp. 101–124, Edinburgh University Press, 1971.

25. Y. Sagiv. Optimizing Datalog programs. In: J. Minker (ed.), *Foundations of Deductive Databases and Logic Programming*, pp. 659–668, Morgan Kaufmann, 1988.

26. C. Sakama. Induction from answer sets in nonmonotonic logic programs. *ACM Transactions on Computational Logic*, 6(2):203–231, 2005. Preliminary version: Learning by answer sets. In: *Proceedings of the AAAI Spring Symposium on Answer Set Programming*, pp. 181–187, AAAI Press, 2001.

27. A. Yamamoto. Which hypotheses can be found with inverse entailment? In: *Proceedings of the 7th International Workshop on Inductive Logic Programming*, Lecture Notes in Artificial Intelligence, vol. 1297, pp. 296–308, Springer-Verlag, 1997.

Deriving a Stationary Dynamic Bayesian Network from a Logic Program with Recursive Loops

Yi-Dong Shen[1] and Qiang Yang[2]

[1] Laboratory of Computer Science, Institute of Software,
Chinese Academy of Sciences, Beijing 100080, China
ydshen@cqu.edu.cn
[2] Department of Computing Science,
Hong Kong University of Science and Technology, Hong Kong, China
qyang@cs.ust.hk

Abstract. Recursive loops in a logic program present a challenging problem to the PLP framework. On the one hand, they loop forever so that the PLP backward-chaining inferences would never stop. On the other hand, they generate cyclic influences, which are disallowed in Bayesian networks. Therefore, in existing PLP approaches logic programs with recursive loops are considered to be problematic and thus are excluded. In this paper, we propose an approach that makes use of recursive loops to build a stationary dynamic Bayesian network. Our work stems from an observation that recursive loops in a logic program imply a time sequence and thus can be used to model a stationary dynamic Bayesian network without using explicit time parameters. We introduce a Bayesian knowledge base with logic clauses of the form $A \leftarrow A_1, ..., A_l, true, Context, Types$, which naturally represents the knowledge that the A_is have direct influences on A in the context $Context$ under the type constraints $Types$. We then use the well-founded model of a logic program to define the direct influence relation and apply SLG-resolution to compute the space of random variables together with their parental connections. We introduce a novel notion of influence clauses, based on which a declarative semantics for a Bayesian knowledge base is established and algorithms for building a two-slice dynamic Bayesian network from a logic program are developed.

Keywords: Probabilistic logic programming (PLP), the well-founded semantics, SLG-resolution, stationary dynamic Bayesian networks.

1 Introduction

Probabilistic logic programming (PLP) is a framework that extends the expressive power of Bayesian networks with first-order logic [18,21]. The core of the PLP framework is a backward-chaining procedure, which generates a Bayesian

S. Kramer and B. Pfahringer (Eds.): ILP 2005, LNAI 3625, pp. 330–347, 2005.

network graphic structure from a logic program in a way quite like query evaluation in logic programming. Therefore, existing PLP methods use a slightly adapted *SLD-* or *SLDNF-resolution* [16] as the backward-chaining procedure.

Recursive loops in a logic program is of the form

$$A_1 \leftarrow \ldots A_2 \leftarrow \ldots A_3 \leftarrow \ldots A_4 \leftarrow \ldots \tag{1}$$

where for any $i \geq 1$, A_i is the same as A_{i+1} up to variable renaming. Such loops present a challenging problem to the PLP framework. On the one hand, they loop forever so that the PLP backward-chaining inferences would never stop. On the other hand, they generate cyclic influences, which are disallowed in Bayesian networks. Two representative approaches have been proposed to avoid recursive loops. The first one is by Ngo and Haddawy [18] and Kersting and De Raedt [15], who restrict to considering only acyclic logic programs [1]. The second approach, proposed by Glesner and Koller [11], uses explicit time parameters to avoid occurrence of recursive loops. It enforces acyclicity using time parameters in the way that every predicate has a time argument such that the time argument in the rule head is at least one time step later than the time arguments of the predicates in the rule body. In this way, each predicate $p(X)$ is changed to $p(X, T)$ and each clause like $p(X) \leftarrow q(X)$ is rewritten into $p(X, T1) \leftarrow q(X, T2), T2 = T1 - 1$, where T, $T1$ and $T2$ are time parameters.

In this paper, we propose a solution to the problem of recursive loops under the PLP framework. Our method is not restricted to acyclic programs, nor does it rely on explicit time parameters. Instead, it makes use of recursive loops to derive a stationary dynamic Bayesian network. We will make two novel contributions. First, we introduce the *well-founded* semantics [29] of logic programs to the PLP framework; in particular, we use the well-founded model of a logic program to define the direct influence relation and apply *SLG-resolution* [4] (or *SLTNF-resolution* [25]) to make the backward-chaining inferences. As a result, termination of the PLP backward-chaining process is guaranteed. Second, we observe that under the PLP framework recursive loops (cyclic influences) define feedbacks, thus implying a time sequence. For instance, the following two clauses

$$aids(X) \leftarrow aids(X),$$
$$aids(X) \leftarrow aids(Y), contact(X, Y)$$

model that the direct influences on $aids(X)$ (in the current time slice t) come from whether X was already infected with aids earlier (in the last time slice $t-1$) or whether X had contact with someone Y who was infected (in time slice $t-1$). As a result, recursive loops of form (1) imply a time sequence

$$A_1 \underset{t}{\leftarrow} \ldots A_2 \underset{t-1}{\leftarrow} \ldots A_3 \underset{t-2}{\leftarrow} \ldots A_4 \leftarrow \ldots \tag{2}$$

It is this observation that leads us to viewing a logic program with recursive loops as a special temporal model. Such a temporal model corresponds to a stationary dynamic Bayesian network and thus can be compactly represented as a two-slice dynamic Bayesian network.

1.1   Preliminaries and Notation

We assume the reader is familiar with basic ideas of Bayesian networks [19] and logic programming [16]. In particular, we assume the reader is familiar with the well-founded semantics [29] as well as SLG-resolution [4]. Here we review some basic concepts concerning dynamic Bayesian networks (DBNs). DBNs are introduced to model the evolution of the state of the environment over time [14]. Briefly, a DBN is a Bayesian network whose random variables are subscripted with time slices (or intervals). For instance, $Weather_{t-1}$, $Weather_t$ and $Weather_{t+1}$ are random variables representing the weather situations in time slices $t-1$, t and $t+1$, respectively. We can then use a DBN to depict how $Weather_{t-1}$ influences $Weather_t$.

A DBN is represented by describing the intra-probabilistic relations between random variables in each individual time slice t and the inter-probabilistic relations between the random variables of each two consecutive time slices $t-1$ and t. If both the intra- and inter-probabilistic relations are the same for all time slices (in this case, the DBN is a repetition of a Bayesian network over time; see Figure 1), the DBN is called a *stationary* DBN [22]; otherwise it is called a *flexible* DBN [11]. As far as we know, most existing DBN systems reported in the literature are stationary DBNs.

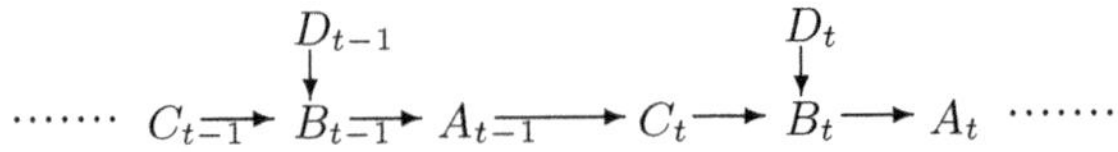

$$\cdots\cdots \quad C_{t-1} \rightarrow B_{t-1} \rightarrow A_{t-1} \rightarrow C_t \rightarrow B_t \rightarrow A_t \quad \cdots\cdots$$

with D_{t-1} above B_{t-1} and D_t above B_t.

Fig. 1. A stationary DBN structure

In a stationary DBN as shown in Figure 1, the state evolution is determined by random variables like C, B and A, as they appear periodically and influence one another over time. Such variables are called *state variables*. Note that D is not a state variable. Due to the characteristic of stationarity, a stationary DBN is often compactly represented as a two-slice DBN.

Definition 1. A *two-slice* DBN for a stationary DBN consists of two consecutive time slices, $t-1$ and t, which describes (1) the intra-probabilistic relations between the random variables in slice t and (2) the inter-probabilistic relations between the random variables in slice $t-1$ and the random variables in slice t.

A two-slice DBN models a feedback system. For convenience, we depict feedback connections with dashed edges. Moreover, we refer to nodes coming from slice $t-1$ as *state input nodes*.

Example 1. The stationary DBN of Figure 1 can be represented by a two-slice DBN as shown in Figure 2. It can also be represented by a two-slice DBN starting from a different state input node (C_{t-1} or B_{t-1}). These two-slice DBN structures are equivalent in the sense that they can be unrolled into the same stationary DBN (Figure 1).

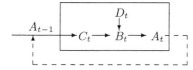

Fig. 2. A two-slice DBN structure (a feedback system)

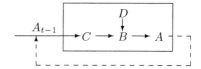

Fig. 3. A simplified two-slice DBN structure

Observe that in a two-slice DBN, all random variables except state input nodes have the same subscript t. In the sequel, the subscript t is omitted for simplification of the structure. For instance, the two-slice DBN of Figure 2 is simplified to Figure 3.

In the rest of this section, we introduce some necessary notation for logic programs. We use $p(.)$ to refer to any atom/predicate whose predicate symbol is p and use $p(\vec{X})$ to refer to $p(X_1, ..., X_n)$ where all X_is are variables. There is one special atom, *true*, which is always logically true. A predicate $p(\vec{X})$ is *typed* if its arguments $\vec{X}$ are typed so that each argument takes on values in a well-defined finite domain. A (general) logic program P is a finite set of clauses of the form

$$A \leftarrow B_1, ..., B_m, \neg C_1, ..., \neg C_n \qquad (3)$$

where A, the B_is and C_js are atoms. We use $HU(P)$ and $HB(P)$ to denote the Herbrand universe and Herbrand base of P, respectively, and use $WF(P) = <I_t, I_f>$ to denote the well-founded model of P, where $I_t, I_f \subseteq HB(P)$, and every A in I_t is true and every A in I_f is false in $WF(P)$. By a *(Herbrand) ground instance* of a clause C we refer to a ground instance of C that is obtained by replacing all variables in C with some terms in $HU(P)$.

A logic program P is a *positive logic program* if no negative literal occurs in the body of any clause. P is a *Datalog program* if no clause in P contains function symbols. P is an *acyclic logic program* if there is a mapping *map* from the set of ground instances of atoms in P into the set of natural numbers such that for any ground instance $A \leftarrow B_1, ..., B_k, \neg B_{k+1}, ..., \neg B_n$ of any clause in P, $map(A) > map(B_i)$ $(1 \leq i \leq n)$ [1]. P is said to have the *bounded-term-size property* w.r.t. a set of predicates $\{p_1(.), ..., p_t(.)\}$ if there is a function $f(n)$ such that for any $1 \leq i \leq t$ whenever a top goal $G_0 =\leftarrow p_i(.)$ has no argument whose term size exceeds n, no atoms in any backward derivations for G_0 have an argument whose term size exceeds $f(n)$ [28].

2   Bayesian Knowledge Bases

Definition 2. A *Bayesian knowledge base* is a triple $<PB \cup CB, T_x, CR>$, where

- $PB \cup CB$ is a logic program, each clause in PB being of the form

$$p(.) \leftarrow \underbrace{p_1(.), ..., p_l(.)}_{direct\ influences}, true, \underbrace{B_1, ..., B_m, \neg C_1, ..., \neg C_n}_{context},$$

$$\underbrace{member(X_1, DOM_1), ..., member(X_s, DOM_s)}_{type\ constraints} \qquad (4)$$

where (i) the predicate symbols $p, p_1, ..., p_l$ only occur in PB and (ii) $p(.)$ is typed so that for each variable X_i in it with a finite domain DOM_i (a list of constants) there is an atom $member(X_i, DOM_i)$ in the clause body.

- T_x is a set of conditional probability tables (CPTs) of the form $\mathbf{P}(p(.)|p_1(.),$ ..., $p_l(.))$, each being attached to a clause (4) in PB.
- CR is a combination rule such as *noisy-or, min* or *max* [15,18,22].

A Bayesian knowledge base contains a logic program that can be divided into two parts, PB and CB. PB defines a direct influence relation, each clause (4) saying that the atoms $p_1(.), ..., p_l(.)$ have direct influences on $p(.)$ in the context that $B_1, ..., B_m, \neg C_1, ..., \neg C_n, member(X_1, DOM_1), ..., member(X_s, DOM_s)$ is true in $PB \cup CB$ under the well-founded semantics. Note that the special literal *true* is used in clause (4) to mark the beginning of the context; it is always true in the well-founded model $WF(PB \cup CB)$. For each variable X_i in the head $p(.)$, $member(X_i, DOM_i)$ is used to enforce the type constraint on X_i, i.e. the value of X_i comes from its domain DOM_i. CB assists PB in defining the direct influence relation by introducing some auxiliary predicates (such as $member(.)$) to describe contexts. Clauses in CB do not describe direct influences. Note that recursive loops are allowed in PB and CB.

In this paper, we focus on Datalog programs, although the proposed approach applies to logic programs with the bounded-term-size property (w.r.t. the set of predicates appearing in the heads of PB) as well. Datalog programs are widely used in database and knowledge base systems [27] and have a polynomial time complexity in computing their well-founded models [29]. In the sequel, we assume that except for the predicate $member(.)$, $PB \cup CB$ is a Datalog program.

For each clause (4) in PB, there is a unique CPT, $\mathbf{P}(p(.)|p_1(.), ..., p_l(.))$, in T_x specifying the degree of the direct influences. Such a CPT is shared by all instances of clause (4).

A Bayesian knowledge base has the following important property.

Theorem 1. *(1) All unit clauses in PB are ground. (2) Let $G_0 = \leftarrow p(.)$ be a goal with p being a predicate symbol occurring in the head of a clause in PB. Then all answers of G_0 derived from $PB \cup CB \cup \{G_0\}$ by applying SLG-resolution are ground.*

For simplicity of presentation, in the sequel for each clause (4) in PB, we omit all of its type constraints $member(X_i, DOM_i)$ $(1 \leq i \leq s)$. Therefore, when we say that the context $B_1, ..., B_m, \neg C_1, ..., \neg C_n$ is true, we assume that the related type constraints are true as well.

3   Declarative Semantics

In this section, we formally describe the space of random variables and the direct influence relation defined by a Bayesian knowledge base KB. We then derive formulas for computing probability distributions induced by KB.

3.1   Space of Random Variables and Influence Clauses

A Bayesian knowledge base KB defines a direct influence relation over a subset of $HB(PB)$. Recall that any random variable in a Bayesian network is either an input node or a node on which some other nodes (i.e. its parent nodes) in the network have direct influences. Since an input node can be viewed as a node whose direct influences come from an empty set of parent nodes, we can define a space of random variables from a Bayesian knowledge base KB by taking all unit clauses in PB as input nodes and deriving the other nodes iteratively based on the direct influence relation defined by PB. Formally, we have

Definition 3. The *space of random variables* of KB, denoted $\mathcal{S}(KB)$, is recursively defined as follows:

1. All unit clauses in PB are random variables in $\mathcal{S}(KB)$.
2. Let $A \leftarrow A_1, ..., A_l, true, B_1, ..., B_m, \neg C_1, ..., \neg C_n$ be a ground instance of a clause in PB. If the context $B_1, ..., B_m, \neg C_1, ..., \neg C_n$ is true in the well-founded model $WF(PB \cup CB)$ and $\{A_1, ..., A_l\} \subseteq \mathcal{S}(KB)$, then A is a random variable in $\mathcal{S}(KB)$. In this case, each A_i is said to have a *direct influence* on A.
3. $\mathcal{S}(KB)$ contains only those ground atoms satisfying the above two conditions.

Definition 4. For any random variables A, B in $\mathcal{S}(KB)$, we say A is *influenced by* B if B has a direct influence on A, or for some C in $\mathcal{S}(KB)$ A is influenced by C and C is influenced by B. A *cyclic influence* occurs if A is influenced by itself.

Let $WF(PB \cup CB) = <I_t, I_f>$ be the well-founded model of $PB \cup CB$ and let $I_{PB} = \{p(.) \in I_t | p$ occurs in the head of some clause in $PB\}$. The following result shows that the space of random variables is uniquely determined by the well-founded model.

Theorem 2. $\mathcal{S}(KB) = I_{PB}$.

Theorem 2 suggests that the space of random variables can be computed by applying an existing procedure for the well-founded model such as SLG-resolution or SLTNF-resolution. Since SLG-resolution has been implemented as the well-known XSB system [23], in this paper we apply it for the PLP backward-chaining inferences. Let $\{p_1, ..., p_t\}$ be the set of predicate symbols occurring in the heads of clauses in PB, and let $G_0 = \leftarrow p_1(\overrightarrow{X_1}), ..., p_t(\overrightarrow{X_t})$ be a top goal where $\overrightarrow{X_i}$ and $\overrightarrow{X_j}$ are disjoint for any $i \neq j$. During the process of evaluating G_0, SLG-resolution stores answers of each $p_i(\overrightarrow{X_i})$ in a space called *table*, denoted $\mathcal{T}_{p_i(\overrightarrow{X_i})}$.

Algorithm 1: Computing random variables.

1. Compute all answers of G_0 by applying SLG-resolution to $PB \cup CB \cup \{G_0\}$.
2. Return $\mathcal{S}'(KB) = \bigcup_{i=1}^{t} \mathcal{T}_{p_i(\overrightarrow{X_i})}$.

Theorem 3. *Algorithm 1 terminates, yielding a finite set $\mathcal{S}'(KB) = \mathcal{S}(KB)$.*

When evaluating G_0, SLG-resolution will construct a proof tree, rooted at $\leftarrow p_i(\overrightarrow{X_i})$, for each subgoal $p_i(\overrightarrow{X_i})$ $(1 \leq i \leq t)$ [4]. For each answer A' of $p_i(\overrightarrow{X_i})$ in $\mathcal{S}'(KB)$ there must be a success branch (i.e. a branch starting at the root node and ending at a node marked with *success*) in the tree that generates the answer. Let

$$p_i(.) \leftarrow A_1, ..., A_l, true, B_1, ..., B_m, \neg C_1, ..., \neg C_n$$

be the k-th clause in PB that was applied to expand the root goal $\leftarrow p_i(\overrightarrow{X_i})$ in the success branch and let θ be the composition of all the mgus (most general unifiers) along the branch. Then $A' = p_i(.)\theta$ and $(A_1, ..., A_l, true, B_1, ..., B_m, \neg C_1, ..., \neg C_n)\theta$ is true in $WF(PB \cup CB)$. In this case, we refer to

$$k. \quad p_i(.)\theta \leftarrow A_1\theta, ..., A_l\theta \tag{5}$$

as an *influence clause* (the prefix "k." would be omitted sometimes for simplicity of presentation). Obviously, every success branch in the proof tree for $\leftarrow p_i(\overrightarrow{X_i})$ produces an influence clause. All influence clauses from the proof trees for $\leftarrow p_i(\overrightarrow{X_i})$ $(1 \leq i \leq t)$ constitute the *set of influence clauses* of KB, denoted $\mathcal{I}_{clause}(KB)$.

Let $G_0 = \leftarrow p_1(\overrightarrow{X_1}), ..., p_t(\overrightarrow{X_t})$ be a top goal as in Algorithm 1. The above process of generating influence clauses can be described more formally as follows.

Algorithm 2: Computing influence clauses.

1. Compute all answers of G_0 by applying SLG-resolution to $PB \cup CB \cup \{G_0\}$, while for each success branch starting at a root goal $\leftarrow p_i(\overrightarrow{X_i})$ $(1 \leq i \leq t)$, we collect an influence clause from the branch into $\mathcal{I}_{clause}(KB)$.
2. Return $\mathcal{I}_{clause}(KB)$.

Influence clauses have two principal properties.

Theorem 4. *Let $A \leftarrow A_1, ..., A_l$ be an influence clause. Then A and all the A_is are ground atoms.*

Theorem 5. *For any $A, A_i \in HB(PB)$, A_i has a direct influence on A, which is derived from the k-th clause in PB, if and only if there is an influence clause in $\mathcal{I}_{clause}(KB)$ of the form $k. \ A \leftarrow A_1, ..., A_i, ..., A_l$.*

Corollary 1. *For any $A \in HB(PB)$, A is in $\mathcal{S}(KB)$ if and only if there is an influence clause in $\mathcal{I}_{clause}(KB)$ whose head is A.*

Example 2. Let us consider the AIDS program, adapted from [11]. Let KB_1 be a Bayesian knowledge base with $CB_1 = \emptyset$ and PB_1 containing the following eleven clauses:

1-3. $aids(pi)$. $(i = 1, 2, 3)$
   4. $aids(X) \leftarrow aids(X)$.
   5. $aids(X) \leftarrow aids(Y), contact(X, Y)$.
6-11. $contact(pi, pj)$. $(i, j = 1, 2, 3$ and $i \neq j)$

Let $G_0 = \leftarrow aids(X), contact(Y, Z)$. Algorithm 2 will generate two proof trees rooted at $\leftarrow aids(X)$ and $\leftarrow contact(Y, Z)$, respectively, and produce the set $\mathcal{I}_{clause}(KB_1)$ with the following eighteen influence clauses:

1-3. $aids(pi)$. $(i = 1, 2, 3)$
   4. $aids(pi) \leftarrow aids(pi)$. $(i = 1, 2, 3)$
   5. $aids(pi) \leftarrow aids(pj), contact(pi, pj)$. $(i, j = 1, 2, 3$ and $i \neq j)$
6-11. $contact(pi, pj)$. $(i, j = 1, 2, 3$ and $i \neq j)$

For example, the third line above represents six influence clauses that are derived by applying the 5-th clause in PB_1 to the root goal $\leftarrow aids(X)$.

3.2   Probability Distributions Induced by KB

For any random variable A in $\mathcal{S}(KB)$, we use $pa(A)$ to denote the set of random variables that have direct influences on A; namely $pa(A)$ consists of random variables in the body of all influence clauses whose head is A. Assume that the probability distribution $\mathbf{P}(A|pa(A))$ is available (see Section 4.2). Furthermore, we make the following independence assumption.

Assumption 1. For any random variable A in $\mathcal{S}(KB)$, we assume that given $pa(A)$, A is probabilistically independent of all random variables in $\mathcal{S}(KB)$ that are not influenced by A.

Theorem 6. *When no cyclic influence occurs, the probability distribution induced by KB is $\mathbf{P}(\mathcal{S}(KB)) = \prod_{A_i \in \mathcal{S}(KB)} \mathbf{P}(A_i|pa(A_i))$ under the independence assumption.*

When there are cyclic influences, we cannot have a partial order on $\mathcal{S}(KB)$. By Definition 4 and Theorem 5, any cyclic influence, say "A_1 is influenced by itself," must be resulted from a set of influence clauses in $\mathcal{I}_{clause}(KB)$ of the form

$$
\begin{aligned}
A_1 &\leftarrow ..., A_2, ... \\
A_2 &\leftarrow ..., A_3, ... \\
&...... \\
A_n &\leftarrow ..., A_1, ...
\end{aligned}
\tag{6}
$$

Observe that these clauses generate a chain of direct influences

$$A_1 \leftarrow A_2 \leftarrow A_3 \leftarrow ... \leftarrow A_n \leftarrow A_1$$

which defines a feedback connection. Since a feedback system can be modeled by a two-slice DBN (see Section 1.1), the above clauses represent the same knowledge as the following ones

$$A_1 \leftarrow ..., A_2, ...$$
$$A_2 \leftarrow ..., A_3, ...$$
$$...... \tag{7}$$
$$A_n \leftarrow ..., A_{1_{t-1}}, ...$$

Here the A_is are state variables and $A_{1_{t-1}}$ is a state input variable. That is, A_1 being influenced by itself becomes A_1 being influenced by $A_{1_{t-1}}$. By applying this transformation (from clauses (6) to (7)), we can get rid of all cyclic influences and obtain a *generalized set* $\mathcal{I}_{clause}(KB)_g$ of influence clauses from $\mathcal{I}_{clause}(KB)$.[1]

Let $\mathcal{V}_{input}(KB)$ be the set of state input variables introduced in $\mathcal{I}_{clause}(KB)_g$ and let $\mathcal{S}(KB)_g = \mathcal{S}(KB) \cup \mathcal{V}_{input}(KB)$. By extending the independence assumption from $\mathcal{S}(KB)$ to $\mathcal{S}(KB)_g$ and defining $pa(A_i)$ over $\mathcal{I}_{clause}(KB)_g$, we obtain the following result.

Theorem 7. *When $\mathcal{I}_{clause}(KB)$ produces cyclic influences, the probability distribution induced by KB is $\mathbf{P}(\mathcal{S}(KB)_g) = \prod_{A_i \in \mathcal{S}(KB)_g} \mathbf{P}(A_i|pa(A_i))$ under the independence assumption.*

4 Building a Bayesian Network from a Bayesian Knowledge Base

4.1 Building a Two-Slice DBN Structure

From a Bayesian knowledge base KB, we can derive a set of influence clauses $\mathcal{I}_{clause}(KB)$, which defines the same direct influence relation over the same space $\mathcal{S}(KB)$ of random variables as $PB \cup CB$ does (see Theorem 5). For any influence clause $A \leftarrow A_1, ..., A_l$, its head A and the body atoms A_js are all ground and true in the well-founded model. Therefore, given a probabilistic query together with some evidences, we can depict a network structure from $\mathcal{I}_{clause}(KB)$, which covers the random variables in the query and evidences, by backward-chaining the related random variables via the direct influence relation.

Let Q be a probabilistic query and E a set of evidences, where all random variables (with time subscripts removed, if any) come from $\mathcal{S}(KB)$ (i.e., they

---

[1] Depending on starting from which influence clause to generate an influence cycle, a different generalized set containing different state input variables would be obtained. All of them are equivalent in the sense that they define the same feedback connections and can be unrolled into the same stationary DBN.

are heads of some influence clauses in $\mathcal{I}_{clause}(KB)$). Let TOP consist of these random variables. An *influence network* of Q and E, denoted $\mathcal{I}_{net}(KB)_{Q,E}$, is constructed from $\mathcal{I}_{clause}(KB)$ using the following algorithm.

Algorithm 3: Building an influence network.

1. Initially, $\mathcal{I}_{net}(KB)_{Q,E}$ has all random variables in TOP as nodes.
2. Remove the first random variable A from TOP. For each influence clause in $\mathcal{I}_{clause}(KB)$ of the form $k.\ B \leftarrow ...,A,...$, if B is not in $\mathcal{I}_{net}(KB)_{Q,E}$ then add B to $\mathcal{I}_{net}(KB)_{Q,E}$ as a new node and to the end of TOP. For each influence clause in $\mathcal{I}_{clause}(KB)$ of the form $k.\ A \leftarrow A_1,...,A_l$, if $l = 0$ then add to $\mathcal{I}_{net}(KB)_{Q,E}$ an edge $A \xleftarrow{k}$. Otherwise, for each A_i in the body:
   (a) If A_i is not in $\mathcal{I}_{net}(KB)_{Q,E}$ then add A_i to $\mathcal{I}_{net}(KB)_{Q,E}$ as a new node and to the end of TOP.
   (b) Add to $\mathcal{I}_{net}(KB)_{Q,E}$ an edge $A \xleftarrow{k} A_i$.
3. Repeat step 2 until TOP becomes empty.

$\mathcal{I}_{net}(KB)_{Q,E}$ covers all random variables in TOP. Moreover, for any node A in $\mathcal{I}_{net}(KB)_{Q,E}$, its parent nodes come from the body atoms of all influence clauses of the form $k.\ A \leftarrow A_1,...,A_l$. Each parent node A_i is connected to A via an edge $A \xleftarrow{k} A_i$, indicating that the parental relationship comes from applying an influence clause that is derived from the k-th clause in PB. We see that an influence network is a Bayesian network structure unless it contains loops (cyclic influences).

Let $\mathcal{I}_{net}(KB)_{\mathcal{S}(KB)}$ denote an influence network that covers all random variables in $\mathcal{S}(KB)$. It is easy to show the following. First, for any node A_i in $\mathcal{I}_{net}(KB)_{\mathcal{S}(KB)}$, the set $parents(A_i)$ of its parent nodes is $pa(A_i)$, as defined in Theorem 6. Second, A_i is a descendant node of A_j if and only if A_i is influenced by A_j. This means that the independence assumption (Assumption 1) applies to $\mathcal{I}_{net}(KB)_{\mathcal{S}(KB)}$ as well, and that $\mathcal{I}_{clause}(KB)$ produces a cycle of direct influences if and only if $\mathcal{I}_{net}(KB)_{\mathcal{S}(KB)}$ contains the same loop. Combining these facts leads to the following immediate result.

Theorem 8. *When no cyclic influence occurs, the probability distribution induced by KB can be computed over $\mathcal{I}_{net}(KB)_{\mathcal{S}(KB)}$. That is,* $\mathbf{P}(\mathcal{S}(KB)) = \prod_{A_i \in \mathcal{S}(KB)} \mathbf{P}(A_i|pa(A_i)) = \prod_{A_i \in \mathcal{S}(KB)} \mathbf{P}(A_i|parents(A_i))$ *under the independence assumption.*

Let us consider influence networks with loops. Loops in an influence network are generated from recursive influence clauses of form (6). They establish feedback connections like that in Figure 3, which can be unrolled into a stationary DBN as in Figure 1. This means that an influence network with loops can be converted into a two-slice DBN, simply by converting each loop of the form

$$A_1 \xleftarrow{k_1} A_2 \xleftarrow{k_2} ...... \xleftarrow{k_{n-1}} A_n \overset{k_n}{\frown}$$

into a two-slice DBN path

$$A_1 \overset{k_1}{\leftarrow} A_2 \overset{k_2}{\leftarrow} ... \overset{k_{n-1}}{\leftarrow} A_n \overset{k_n}{\leftarrow} \mathbf{A_{1_{t-1}}}$$

by introducing a state input node $A_{1_{t-1}}$.

As illustrated in Section 1.1, a two-slice DBN is a snapshot of a stationary DBN across any two time slices, which can be obtained by traversing the stationary DBN from a set of state variables backward to the same set of state variables (i.e., state input nodes). This process corresponds to generating an influence network $\mathcal{I}_{net}(KB)_{Q,E}$ from $\mathcal{I}_{clause}(KB)$ incrementally (adding nodes and edges one by one) while wrapping up loop nodes with state input nodes (like A_{t-1}). This leads to the following algorithm for building a two-slice DBN structure, $2\mathcal{S}_{net}(KB)_{Q,E}$, directly from $\mathcal{I}_{clause}(KB)$, where Q, E and TOP are as defined in Algorithm 3.

Algorithm 4: Building a two-slice DBN structure.

1. Initially, $2\mathcal{S}_{net}(KB)_{Q,E}$ has all random variables in TOP as nodes.
2. Remove the first random variable A from TOP. For each influence clause in $\mathcal{I}_{clause}(KB)$ of the form k. $B \leftarrow ..., A, ...$, if B is not in $\mathcal{I}_{net}(KB)_{Q,E}$ then add B to $\mathcal{I}_{net}(KB)_{Q,E}$ as a new node and to the end of TOP. For each influence clause in $\mathcal{I}_{clause}(KB)$ of the form k. $A \leftarrow A_1, ..., A_l$, if $l = 0$ then add to $2\mathcal{S}_{net}(KB)_{Q,E}$ an edge $A \overset{k}{\leftarrow}$. Otherwise, for each A_i in the body:
   (a) If A_i is not in $2\mathcal{S}_{net}(KB)_{Q,E}$ then add A_i to $2\mathcal{S}_{net}(KB)_{Q,E}$ as a new node and to the end of TOP.
   (b) If adding $A \overset{k}{\leftarrow} A_i$ to $2\mathcal{S}_{net}(KB)_{Q,E}$ produces a loop, then add to $2\mathcal{S}_{net}(KB)_{Q,E}$ a node $A_{i_{t-1}}$ and an edge $A \overset{k}{\leftarrow} A_{i_{t-1}}$, else add an edge $A \overset{k}{\leftarrow} A_i$ to $2\mathcal{S}_{net}(KB)_{Q,E}$.
3. Repeat step 2 until TOP becomes empty.

Algorithm 4 is Algorithm 3 enhanced with a mechanism for cutting loops (item 2b), i.e. when adding the current edge $A \overset{k}{\leftarrow} A_i$ to the network forms a loop, we replace it with an edge $A \overset{k}{\leftarrow} A_{i_{t-1}}$, where $A_{i_{t-1}}$ is a state input node. This is a process of transforming influence clauses (6) to (7). Therefore, $2\mathcal{S}_{net}(KB)_{Q,E}$ is essentially built from a generalized set $\mathcal{I}_{clause}(KB)_g$ of influence clauses.

Let $\mathcal{S}(KB)_g$ be the set of random variables in $\mathcal{I}_{clause}(KB)_g$, as defined in Theorem 7. Let $2\mathcal{S}_{net}(KB)_{\mathcal{S}(KB)}$ denote a two-slice DBN structure (produced by applying Algorithm 4) that covers all random variables in $\mathcal{S}(KB)_g$. We have the following result.

Theorem 9. *When $\mathcal{I}_{clause}(KB)$ produces cyclic influences, the probability distribution induced by KB can be computed over $2\mathcal{S}_{net}(KB)_{\mathcal{S}(KB)}$. That is,*
$$\mathbf{P}(\mathcal{S}(KB)_g) = \prod_{A_i \in \mathcal{S}(KB)_g} \mathbf{P}(A_i|pa(A_i)) = \prod_{A_i \in \mathcal{S}(KB)_g} \mathbf{P}(A_i|parents(A_i)) \text{ under the independence assumption.}$$

Remark 1. Note that Algorithm 4 does not use any time parameters. It only requires the user to specify, via the query and evidences, what random variables are necessarily included in the network. Algorithm 4 builds a two-slice DBN structure for any given query and evidences whose random variables are heads of some influence clauses in $\mathcal{I}_{clause}(KB)$. When no query and evidences are provided, we may apply Algorithm 4 to build a *complete* two-slice DBN structure, $2\mathcal{S}_{net}(KB)_{\mathcal{S}(KB)}$, which covers the space $\mathcal{S}(KB)$ of random variables, by letting TOP consist of all heads of influence clauses in $\mathcal{I}_{clause}(KB)$. This is a very useful feature, as in many situations the user may not be able to present the right queries unless a Bayesian network structure is shown.

Example 3 (Example 2 continued). Suppose that we want to build a Bayesian network from KB_1 that covers $aids(p1)$, $aids(p2)$ and $aids(p3)$. We may present a query ? $- \mathbf{P}(aids(p1))$ along with the evidences $aids(p2) = yes$ and $aids(p3) = no$. Thus $TOP = \{aids(p1), aids(p2), aids(p3)\}$. Algorithm 4 builds from $\mathcal{I}_{clause}$ (KB_1) a two-slice DBN structure $2\mathcal{S}_{net}(KB_1)_{Q,E}$ as shown in Figure 4 where for simplicity, edges of the form $A \xleftarrow{k}$ are omitted. Note that loops are cut by introducing three state input nodes $aids(p1)_{t-1}$, $aids(p2)_{t-1}$ and $aids(p3)_{t-1}$. We see that the two-slice DBN structure $2\mathcal{S}_{net}(KB_1)_{Q,E}$ concisely depicts a feedback system where the feedback connections are as shown in Figure 5.

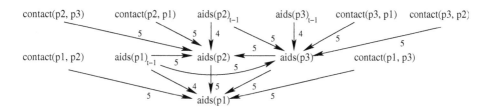

Fig. 4. A two-slice DBN structure built from the AIDS program KB_1

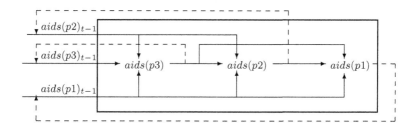

Fig. 5. The feedback connections created by the AIDS program KB_1

4.2   Building CPTs

After a Bayesian network structure $2\mathcal{S}_{net}(KB)_{Q,E}$ has been constructed from a Bayesian knowledge base KB, we associate each (non-state-input) node A in the network with a CPT. There are three cases. (1) If A only has unit clauses in

$\mathcal{I}_{clause}(KB)$, we build from the unit clauses a *prior* CPT for A as its prior probability distribution. (2) If A only has non-unit clauses in $\mathcal{I}_{clause}(KB)$, we build from the clauses a *posterior* CPT for A as its posterior probability distribution. (3) Otherwise, we prepare for A both a prior CPT (from the unit clauses) and a posterior CPT (from the non-unit clauses). In this case, A is attached with the posterior CPT; the prior CPT for A would be used, if A is a state variable, as the probability distribution of A in time slice 0 (only in the case that a two-slice DBN is unrolled into a stationary DBN starting with time slice 0; see Section 1.1).

Assume that the parent nodes of A are derived from n ($n \geq 1$) different influence clauses in $\mathcal{I}_{clause}(KB)$. Suppose these clauses share the following CPTs in T_x: $\mathbf{P}(A_1 | B_1^1, ..., B_{m_1}^1)$, ..., and $\mathbf{P}(A_n | B_1^n, ..., B_{m_n}^n)$. (Recall that an influence clause prefixed with a number k shares the CPT attached to the k-th clause in PB.) Then the CPT of A is computed by combining the n CPTs in terms of the combination rule CR.

5   Related Work

A recent overview of existing representational frameworks that combine probabilistic reasoning with logic (i.e. logic-based approaches) or relational representations (i.e. non-logic-based approaches) is given by De Raedt and Kersting [6]. Typical non-logic-based approaches include probabilistic relational models (PRM), which are based on the entity-relationship (or object-oriented) model [10,13,20], and relational Markov networks, which combine Markov networks and SQL-like queries [26]. Representative logic-based approaches include frameworks based on the KBMC (Knowledge-Based Model Construction)idea [2,3,8,11,12,15,18,21], stochastic logic programs (SLP) based on stochastic context-free grammers [5,17], parameterized logic programs based on distribution semantics (PRISM) [24], and more. Most recently, a unifying framework, called *Markov logic*, has been proposed by Domingos and Richardson [7]. Markov logic subsumes first-order logic and Markov networks. Since our work follows the KBMC idea focusing on how to build a Bayesian network directly from a logic program, it is closely related to three representative existing PLP approaches: the context-sensitive PLP developed by Haddawy and Ngo [18], Bayesian logic programming proposed by Kersting and Raedt [15], and the time parameterbased approach presented by Glesner and Koller [11].

5.1   Comparison with the Context-Sensitive PLP Approach

The core of the context-sensitive PLP is a probabilistic knowledge base (PKB). In order to see the main differences from our Bayesian knowledge base (BKB), we reformulate its definition here.

Definition 5. A *probabilistic knowledge base* is a four tuple $<PD, PB, CB, CR>$, where

- PD defines a set of probabilistic predicates (*p-predicates*) of the form $p(T_1, ..., T_m, V)$ where all arguments T_is are typed with a finite domain and the last argument V takes on values from a probabilistic domain DOM_p.
- PB consists of *probabilistic rules* of the form

$$P(A_0|A_1, ..., A_l) = \alpha \leftarrow B_1, ..., B_m, \neg C_1, ..., \neg C_n \qquad (8)$$

where $0 \leq \alpha \leq 1$, the A_is are p-predicates, and the B_js and C_ks are context predicates (*c-predicates*) defined in CB.
- CB is a logic program, and both PB and CB are acyclic.
- CR is a combination rule.

In a probabilistic rule (8), each p-predicate A_i is of the form $q(t_1, ..., t_m, v)$, which simulates an equation $q(t_1, ..., t_m) = v$ with v being a value from the probabilistic domain of $q(t_1, ..., t_m)$. For instance, let $DOM_{nbrhd} = \{average, good, bad\}$ be the probabilistic domain of $nbrhd(X)$, then the p-predicate $nbrhd(X, good)$ simulates $nbrhd(X) = good$, meaning that the neighborhood of X is *good*. The left-hand side $P(A_0|A_1, ..., A_l) = \alpha$ expresses that the probability of A_0 conditioned on $A_1, ..., A_l$ is α. The right-hand side $B_1, ..., B_m, \neg C_1, ..., \neg C_n$ is the *context* of the rule where the B_js and C_ks are c-predicates. Note that the sets of p-predicate and c-predicate symbols are disjoint. A separate logic program CB is used to evaluate the context of a probabilistic rule. As a whole, the above probabilistic rule states that for each of its (Herbrand) ground instances

$$P(A_0'|A_1', ..., A_l') = \alpha \leftarrow B_1', ..., B_m', \neg C_1', ..., \neg C_n'$$

if the context $B_1', ..., B_m', \neg C_1', ..., \neg C_n'$ is true in CB under the program completion semantics, the probability of A_0' conditioned on $A_1', ..., A_l'$ is α.

PKB and BKB have the following important differences.

First, probabilistic rules of form (8) in PKB contain both logic representation (right-hand side) and probabilistic representation (left-hand side) and thus are not logic clauses. The logic part and the probabilistic part of a rule are separately computed against CB and PB, respectively. In contrast, our BKB uses logic clauses of form (4), which naturally integrate the direct influence information, the context and the type constraints. These logic clauses are evaluated against a single logic program $PB \cup CB$, while the probabilistic information is collected separately in T_x.

Second, logic reasoning in PKB relies on the program completion semantics and is carried out by applying SLDNF-resolution. But in BKB, logic inferences are based on the well-founded semantics and are performed by applying SLG-resolution. The well-founded semantics resolves the problem of inconsistency with the program completion semantics, while SLG-resolution eliminates the problem of infinite loops with SLDNF-resolution. Note that the key significance of BKB using the well-founded semantics lies in the fact that a unique set of influence clauses can be derived, which lays a basis on which both the declarative and procedural semantics for BKB are developed.

Third, most importantly PKB has no mechanism for handling cyclic influences. In PKB, cyclic influences are defined to be *inconsistent* (see Definition

9 of the paper [18]) and thus are excluded (PKB excludes cyclic influences by requiring its programs be acyclic). In BKB, however, cyclic influences are interpreted as feedbacks, thus implying a time sequence. This allows us to derive a stationary DBN from a logic program with recursive loops.

Recently, Fierens, Blockeel, Ramon and Bruynooghe [9] introduced *logical Bayesian networks* (LBN). LBN is similar to PKB except that it separates logical and probabilistic information. That is, LBN converts rules of form (8) into the form

$$A_0|A_1, ..., A_l \leftarrow B_1, ..., B_m, \neg C_1, ..., \neg C_n$$

where the A_is are p-predicates with the last argument V removed, and the B_js and C_ks are c-predicates defined in CB. This is not a standard clause of form (3) as defined in logic programming [16]. Like PKB, LBN differs from BKB in the following: (1) it has no mechanism for handling cyclic influences (see Section 3.2 of the paper [9]), and (2) although the well-founded semantics is also used for the logic contexts, neither declarative nor procedural semantics for LBN has been formally developed.

5.2   Comparison with Bayesian Logic Programming

Building on Ngo and Haddawy's work, Kersting and De Raedt [15] introduce the framework of Bayesian logic programs. A *Bayesian logic program* (BLP) is a triple $<P, T_x, CR>$ where P is a well-defined logic program, T_x consists of CPTs associated with each clause in P, and CR is a combination rule. According to [15], we understand that a *well-defined* logic program is an acyclic positive logic program satisfying the range restriction.[2] For instance, a logic program containing clauses like $r(X) \leftarrow r(X)$ (cyclic) or $r(X) \leftarrow s(Y)$ (not range-restricted) is not well-defined. BLP relies on the least Herbrand model semantics and applies SLD-resolution to make backward-chaining inferences.

BLP has two important differences from our BKB framework. First, it applies only to positive logic programs. Due to this, it cannot handle contexts with negated atoms. (In fact, no contexts are considered in BLP.) Second, it does not allow cyclic influences. BKB can be viewed as an extension of BLP with mechanisms for handling contexts and cyclic influences in terms of the well-founded semantics. Such extension is clearly non-trivial.

5.3   Comparison with the Time Parameter-Based Approach

The time parameter-based framework proposed by Glesner and Koller [11] is also a triple $<P, T_x, CR>$, where CR is a combination rule, T_x is a set of CPTs that are represented as decision trees, and P is a logic program with the property that each predicate contains a time parameter and that in each clause the time argument in the head is at least one time step (unit) later than the time arguments in

---

[2] A logic program is said to be *range-restricted* if all variables appearing in the head of a clause appear in the body of the clause.

the body. This framework is implemented in Prolog, i.e. clauses are represented as Prolog rules and goals are evaluated applying SLDNF-resolution. Glesner and Koller [11] state: "... In principle, this free variable Y can be instantiated with every domain element. (This is the approach taken in our implementation.)" By this we understand that they consider typed logic programs with finite domains.

An obvious difference is that our BKB framework is devoted to modeling stationary DBNs, whereas the time parameter-based framework targets flexible DBNs. One may say that stationary DBNs can also be modeled with the time parameter-based framework, as they are special cases of flexible DBNs. This appears not the case. We observe two major limitations of the time parameter-based framework. First, it uses time steps as time slices, thus for any A and B such that A is influenced by B, A and B will not be allowed to occur in the same time slice. Due to this, we are unable to use the time parameter-based framework to model intra-probabilistic relations between the random variables within a time slice t (like those in Figure 1). Second, introducing time parameters to enforce acyclicity may lose answers to some queries. Let P be a logic program and P_t be P with additional time parameters. It is easy to prove that P_t is acyclic. Let $p(.)$ be a query and $p(., N)$ be $p(.)$ with a ground time argument N added. Then evaluating $p(., N)$ over P_t (applying SLDNF-resolution) achieves the same effect as evaluating $p(.)$ over P with some depth-bound M (i.e. derivations are cut at depth M). Since the loop problem in logic programming is undecidable in general, it is impossible to determine an appropriate depth-bound (rep. a ground time argument) for an arbitrary query without losing answers.

6   Conclusions and Discussion

We have developed an approach to deriving a stationary DBN from a logic program with recursive loops. We observed that recursive loops in a logic program imply a time sequence and thus can be used to model a stationary DBN without using explicit time parameters. We introduced a Bayesian knowledge base with logic clauses of form (4). These logic clauses naturally integrate the direct influence information, the context and the type constraints, and are evaluated against a single logic program $PB \cup CB$ under the well-founded semantics. We established a declarative semantics for a Bayesian knowledge base and developed algorithms that build a two-slice DBN from a Bayesian knowledge base.

We emphasize the following two points. First, recursive loops (cyclic influences) and recursion through negation are unavoidable in modeling real-world domains, thus the well-founded semantics together with its top-down inference procedures is well suitable for the PLP application. Second, recursive loops define feedbacks, thus implying a time sequence. This allows us to derive a two-slice DBN from a logic program containing no time parameters. We point out, however, that the user is never required to provide any time parameters during the process of constructing such a two-slice DBN. A Bayesian knowledge base defines a unique space of random variables and a unique set of influence clauses, whether it contains recursive loops or not. From the viewpoint of logic, these random variables are ground atoms in the Herbrand base; their truth values are determined by the well-founded model and will never change over time.[3] Therefore, a Bayesian network is built over these random variables, independently of any time factors (if any). Once a two-slice DBN has been built, the time intervals over it would become clearly specified, thus the user can present queries and evidences over the DBN using time parameters at his/her convenience.

Acknowledgements

We thank the anonymous referees for their constructive comments, which have greatly improved the presentation. Yi-Dong Shen is supported in part by Chinese National Natural Science Foundation (grant # 60373052 and 60421001) and Trans-Century Training Program Foundation for the Talents by the Chinese Ministry of Education. Qiang Yang is supported in part by HKUST/6187/04E.

References

1. K. R. Apt and M. Bezem, Acyclic programs, *New Generation Computing* 29(3):335-363 (1991).
2. F. Bacchus, Using first-order probability logic for the construction of Bayesian networks, in: *Proc. of the Ninth Conference on Uncertainty in Artificial Intelligence*, 1994, pp. 219-226.
3. J. S. Breese, Construction of belief and decision networks, *Computational Intelligence* 8(4):624-647 (1992).
4. W. D. Chen, T. Swift and D. S. Warren, Efficient top-down computation of queries under the well-founded semantics, *Journal of Logic Programming* 24(3):161-199 (1995).
5. J. Cussens, Stochastic logic programs: sampling, inference and applications, in: *Proc. of The Sixteenth Annual Conference on Uncertainty in Artificail Intelligence*, 2000, pp. 115-122.
6. L. De Raedt and K. Kersting, Probabilistic logic learning, *SIGKDD Explorations* 5(1):31-48 (2003).
7. P. Domingos and M. Richardson, Markov logic: a unifying framework for statistical relational learning, in: *Proc. of the ICML-2004 Workshop on Statistical Relational Learning and its Connections to Other Fields* , Banff, Canada, 2004, pp. 49-54.
8. I. Fabian and D. A. Lambert, First-order Bayesian reasoning. In: *Proc. of the 11th Australian Joint Conference on Articial Intelligence*, number 1502 in LNAI. Springer, 1998, pp. 131-142.
9. D. Fierens, H. Blockeel, J. Ramon and M. Bruynooghe, Logical Bayesian networks, in: *3rd Workshop on Multi-Relational Data Mining*, Seattle, USA, 2005
10. L. Getoor, *Learning Statistical Models from Relational Data*, Ph.D. thesis, Stanford University, 2001.
11. S. Glesner and D. Koller, Constructing flexible dynamic belief networks from first-order probabilistic knowledge bases, in: C. Froidevaux and J. Kohlas, eds., *Proceedings of the European Conference on Symbolic and Quantitative Approaches to Reasoning under Uncertainty*, Fribourg, Switzerland, July 1995, pages 217-226.

---

[3] However, from the viewpoint of Bayesian networks the probabilistic values of these random variables (i.e. values from their probabilistic domains) may change over time.

12. R. Goldman and E. Charniak, A language for construction of belief networks, *IEEE Transactions on Pattern Analysis and Machine Intelligence* 15(3):196-208 (1993).
13. M. Jaeger, Relational Bayesian networks, in: *Proc. of The Thirteenth Annual Conference on Uncertainty in Artificail Intelligence*, 1997, pp. 266-273.
14. K. Kanazawa, D. Koller and S. Russell, Stochastic simulation algorithms for dynamic probabilistic networks, in: *Proc. of the Eleventh Annual Conference on Uncertainty in Artificail Intelligence*, 1995.
15. K. Kersting and L. De Raedt, Bayesian logic programs, in: J. Cussens and A. Frisch, eds, *Work-in-Progress Reports of the Tenth International Conference on Inductive Logic Programming*, London,U.K., 2000. (A full version: Technical Report 151, University of Freiburg Institute for Computer Science.)
16. J. W. Lloyd, *Foundations of Logic Programming*, 2nd ed., Springer-Verlag, Berlin, 1987.
17. S. Muggleton, Stochastic logic programs, in: *Advances in Inductive Logic Programming*, IOS Press, 1996.
18. L. Ngo and P. Haddawy, Answering queries from context-sensitive probabilistic knowledge bases, *Theoretical Computer Science*, 171:147-177 (1997).
19. J. Pearl, *Probabilistic Resoning in Intelligent Systems: Networks of Plausible inference*, Morgan Kaufmann, 1988.
20. A. Pfeffer and D. Koller, Semantics and inference for recursive probability models, in: *Proc. of the Seventeenth National Conference on Artificial Intelligence*, AAAI Press, 2000, pp.538-544.
21. D. Poole, Probabilistic Horn abduction and Bayesian networks, *Artificial Intelligence* 64(1):81-129 (1993).
22. S. Russell and P. Norvig, *Artificial Intelligence: A Modern Approach*, Prentice-Hall, 1995.
23. K. Sagonas, T. Swift, D.S. Warren, J. Freire and P. Rao, *The XSB Programmer's Manual (Version 1.8)*. Department of Computer Science, SUNY at Stony Brook. Available from http://www.cs.sunysb.edu/ sbprolog/xsb-page.html.
24. T. Sato and Y. Kameya, Parameter learning of logic programs for symbolic-statistical modeling, *Journal of Artificial Intelligence Research* 15:391-454 (2001).
25. Y. D. Shen, J. H. You and L. Y. Yuan, Enhancing global SLS-resolution with loop cutting and tabling mechanisms, *Theoretical Computer Science* 328(3):271-287(2004).
26. B. Taskar, P. Abeel and D. Koller, Discriminative probabilistic models for relational data, in: *Proc. of the Eighteenth Conf. on Uncertainty in Artificial Intelligence*, Edmonton, Canada, 2002, pp.485-492.
27. J. D. Ullman, *Database and Knowledge-Base Systems*, vols. I and II, Computer Science Press, 1988.
28. A. Van Gelder, Negation as failure using tight derivations for general logic programs, *Journal of Logic Programming* 6(1&2):109-133 (1989).
29. A. Van Gelder, K. Ross, J. Schlipf, The well-founded semantics for general logic programs, *J. ACM* 38(3):620-650 (1991).

A Study of Applying Dimensionality Reduction to Restrict the Size of a Hypothesis Space

Ashwin Srinivasan and Ravi Kothari

IBM India Research Laboratory,
Block 1, Indian Institute of Technology,
New Delhi 110 016, India
{ashwin.srinivasan, rkothari}@in.ibm.com

Abstract. Given sample data and background knowledge encoded in the form of logic programs, a predictive Inductive Logic Programming (ILP) system attempts to find a set of rules (or clauses) for predicting classification labels in the data. Most present-day systems for this purpose rely on some variant of a generate-and-test procedure that repeatedly examines a set of potential candidates (termed here as the "hypothesis space"). On each iteration a search procedure is employed to find the "best" clause. The worst-case time-complexity of such systems depends critically on: (1) the size of the hypothesis spaces examined; and (2) the cost of estimating the goodness of a clause. To date, attempts to improve the efficiency of such ILP systems have concentrated either on examining fewer clauses within a given hypothesis space, or on efficient means of estimating the goodness of clauses. The principal means of restricting the size of the hypothesis space itself has been through the use of language and search constraints. Given such constraints, this paper is concerned with investigating the use of a dimensionality reduction method to reduce further the size of the hypothesis space. Specifically, for a particular kind of ILP system, clauses in the search space are represented as points in a high-dimension space. Using a sample of points from this geometric space, feature selection is used to discard dimensions of little or no (statistical) relevance. The resulting lower dimensional space translates directly, in the worst-case, to a smaller hypothesis space. We evaluate this approach on one controlled domain (graphs) and two real-life datasets concerning problems from biochemistry (mutagenesis and carcinogenesis). In each case, we obtain unbiased estimates of the size of the hypothesis space before and after feature selection; and compare the the results obtained using a complete search of the two spaces.

1 Introduction

Given sample data and background knowledge encoded in the form of logic programs, a category of Inductive Logic Programming (ILP) systems attempt to find a set of rules (or clauses) for predicting classification labels in new data. Many present-day systems for this purpose rely on some variant of a generate-and-test procedure that repeatedly examines a set of potential candidates (termed here

S. Kramer and B. Pfahringer (Eds.): ILP 2005, LNAI 3625, pp. 348–365, 2005.

as the "hypothesis space", or sometimes, the search space). On each iteration a search procedure is employed to find the "best" clause. A straightforward analysis (see Section 2) shows that under fairly general considerations, the worst-case time-complexity depends on: (1) the size of the hypothesis spaces examined; and (2) the cost of estimating the goodness of a clause. To date, attempts to improve the efficiency of such ILP systems have concentrated either on examining fewer clauses within a given hypothesis space (for example, using a greedy search [20,17], restricting the number of clauses examined in a branch-and-bound search [16], or employing randomized restarted methods [29,30]); or on efficient means of estimating the goodness of clauses (for example, using stochastic matching [24], sampling [25], clause optimization techniques [3], neural-network models for clause utility [4]).

Practical problems and the flexibility of using first-order logic as a representation language can often engender intractably large hypothesis spaces. Under such conditions, it is clearly infeasible to perform any kind of exhaustive search. Indeed, there appears to be some evidence that even if feasible, such an extended search may be undesirable. Experiments with feature-based rule learning [21] suggests that as the number of candidates examined increases, so does the probability of obtaining a "fluke" – a clause that scores well on the sample data simply due to chance effects. This can be seen as a procedural analogue of overfitting and Fig. 1 shows a manifestation of this phenomenon in two prominent problems addressed by ILP. Related theoretical developments in the field of computational learning theory have also shown the need to restrict the hypothesis space in order to arrive at learnability results [2].

The principal means of restricting the size of the hypothesis space has been through the use of language and search constraints (mode declarations, restrictions on the maximum length of clauses, "prune" statements and so on). These are provided by the user, usually with some knowledge of the problem being studied. In this paper, we investigate whether it is possible to restrict the size a hypothesis space further by using the sample data provided to the ILP system and statistical techniques for dimensionality reduction (or feature selection, as they are sometimes called in the literature). Specifically, the investigation is an empirical study in which clauses in the hypothesis space examined by an ILP system are represented as points in a high-dimension (Boolean) space. Using a sample of points from this geometric space, feature selection is used to discard dimensions of little or no statistical (as opposed to logical) relevance. The resulting lower dimensional space translates directly, in the worst-case, to a smaller hypothesis space. We evaluate this approach on one controlled domain (graphs) and two real-life datasets concerning problems from biochemistry (mutagenesis and carcinogenesis). In each case, we obtain unbiased estimates of the size of the hypothesis space before and after feature selection; and compare the results obtained using a complete search of the two spaces.

This paper is organized as follows. Section 2 summarizes the features of an ILP algorithm to the extent that is relevant to the paper. Section 3 describes the

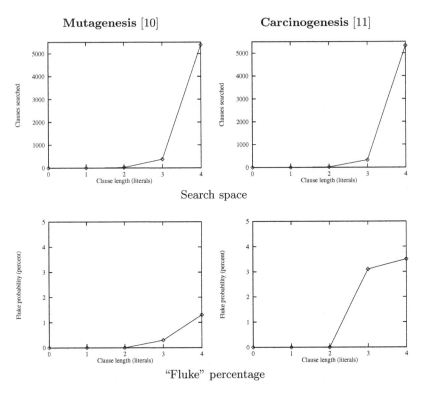

Fig. 1. Search space size and "fluke" percentages for two applications of ILP. The top row of graphs shows the size of the space searched for each clause-length (up to a maximum of 5000 clauses at any length). Our interest here is in flukes – clauses that appear "good" when evaluated on the sample ("training") data provided, but are revealed to be "bad" when evaluated on new ("test") data. For the illustration here, a clause is classified "good" on either data set if it is in the top 5 percent of the clause-ranking obtained by scores on that data set. A fluke is thus in the top 5 percent when evaluated on training data, but outside it when evaluated on the test data. The fluke percentage is then simply the ratio of flukes to the total number of clauses examined. The lower row of graphs shows this percentage when using the evaluation function described in [16].

use of dimensionality reduction for restricting the size of the hypothesis space. An empirical evaluation is in Section 4. Section 5 concludes the paper.

2   "Predictive" ILP

The term "predictive ILP" has been used to describe the function of a class of programs that construct theories for discriminating accurately amongst two sets of examples ("positive" and "negative"). The partial specifications provided by [15] have been adopted as the basis for deriving programs in this class. With some minor changes to the formulation in [15], an ILP algorithm for constructing predictive theories is taken to be one that conforms to at least the following:

Given:
> B: background knowledge consisting of a set of definite clauses.
> I: a set of constraints.
> $\mathcal{L}$: a language describing acceptable hypotheses.
> E: a finite set of examples $= E^+ \cup E^-$ where:
>> $E^+ = \{e_1, e_2, \ldots\}$ is a set of definite clauses (these are "positive examples");
>> $E^- = \{\overline{f_1}, \overline{f_2} \ldots\}$ is an optional set of Horn clauses (these are "negative examples"); and
>> $B \not\models E^+$

Find: $H \in \mathcal{L}$, $H = \{D_1, D_2, \ldots\}$, such that the following conditions are met:
>   *Weak Sufficiency (WS).* $\forall D_i \in H \; \exists e \in E^+$ s.t. $B \cup \{D_i\} \models e$
>   *Strong Sufficiency (SS).* $B \cup H \models E^+$;
>   *Weak Consistency (WC).* $B \cup H \not\models \Box$;
>   *Strong Consistency 1 (SC1).* $B \cup H \cup E^- \not\models \Box$; and
>   *Strong Consistency 2 (SC2).* $B \cup H$ is consistent with the I

The first requirement under Strong Consistency ensures that H does not contain any "over-general" clauses. Often, implementations do not require clauses to meet this requirement, as some members of E^- are taken to be "noisy". This specification is then refined to allow theories to be inconsistent with some negative examples. We have deliberately left SC2 imprecise to allow a flexible interpretation of the I; and will use the phrase "H explains E" to denote that at least WS, SS, WC, and SC2 are met.

The reader would have noted that this specification does not state how the D_i are to be constructed. This is an implementation-dependent detail and some variant of the greedy cover set procedure in Fig. 2 is the most popular (reproduced, with minor changes, from [25]).

At the heart of each iteration i is a search through a set of candidate clauses in $\mathcal{L}$. This set is called the "hypothesis space" for iteration i and denoted $\mathcal{H}_i$. For each iteration i we will assume:

A1. $\mathcal{H}_i$ will only contain definite clauses composed of at most $c+1$ literals drawn without replacement from a "most specific" definite clause $\perp_i \in \mathcal{L}$. The value of c is pre-specified.[1]

---

[1] The notion of a most specific clause is described in [16] and ensures clauses in the hypothesis space satisfy the requirement of Weak Sufficiency. For our purpose, $\perp_i$ will be a definite clause. Typically this would consist of 10s-100s of literals. Each clause that consists of literals drawn from $\perp_i$ θ-subsumes it as defined in [18] and in some sense, can be taken to be "more general" than it. The reader should be aware that such clauses are only a subset of all clauses that θ-subsume $\perp_i$. We have assumed that the ordering of literals in the clause can affect its coverage – this is the case with the computation rule used by standard Prolog. For simplicity, we do not include any tests in the search for equivalences arising from literal re-orderings.

$generalise(B, I, \mathcal{L}, E)$: Given background knowledge B, hypothesis constraints I, a finite training set $E = E^+ \cup E^-$, returns a hypothesis H in $\mathcal{L}$ such that H explains the E.

1. $i = 0$
2. $E_i^+ = E^+$, $H_i = \emptyset$
3. if $E_i^+ = \emptyset$ return H_i otherwise continue
4. increment i
5. $Train_i = E_{i-1}^+ \cup E^-$
6. $D_i = search(B, H_{i-1}, I, \mathcal{L}, Train_i)$
7. $H_i = H_{i-1} \cup \{D_i\}$
8. $E_p = \{e_p : e_p \in E_{i-1}^+ \ s.t. \ B \cup H_i \models \{e_p\}\}$.
9. $E_i^+ = E_{i-1}^+ \backslash E_p$
10. Go to Step 3

Fig. 2. An ILP implmentation. The function $search(\ldots)$ in Step 6 is some search procedure that returns the "best" clause from all candidates in $\mathcal{L}$ (using some estimate of clause utility). The requirement SC1 that D_i be consistent with all the negative examples may be weakened by allowing the D_i to be inconsistent with some number of negative examples. This number would then have to be provided as an additional parameter to the search procedure.

A2. The evaluation function induces a partial ordering on the set of clauses in $\mathcal{H}_i$.

Remark 1. **Time complexity.** $\mathcal{H}_i$ consists of definite clauses that are obtained by selecting literals from $\bot_i$. Since $\bot_i$ is definite, there is only 1 definite clause with a single literal. On the other hand, there can be at most $1 \times (|\bot_i| - 1)$ two-literal definite clauses, $1 \times (|\bot_i| - 1) \times (|\bot_i| - 2)$ three-literal definite clauses and so on. $|\mathcal{H}_i|$ is therefore at most $1 + (|\bot_i| - 1) + \ldots + (|\bot_i| - 1) \times \ldots (|\bot_i| - c)$ $\leq 1 + |\bot_i| + \ldots + |\bot_i|^c = \frac{|\bot_i|^{(c+1)} - 1}{|\bot_i| - 1}$. If $|\bot|$ is an upper bound on the size of the most specific clause then the number of clauses in the hypothesis space on any iteration is $O(|\bot|^c)$. As a first approximation, for a given B, we take the cost of estimating the utility of any clause as being some monotonically increasing function of $Train_i$, say $f(|Train_i|)$. The time complexity of the search on any one iteration of Fig. 2 is then $O(f(|E|) \times |\bot|^c)$ (since $|E|$ is an upper bound on $Train_i$). It is evident that the procedure in Fig. 2 iterates no more than $|E^+|$ times. The time complexity of the entire procedure in Fig. 2 is therefore $O(f(|E|) \times |\bot|^c \times |E|)$.

We can therefore envisage a naive (exhaustive) search that does the following on each iteration i: (1) Obtain the set of all clauses $\{C_{i,1}, C_{i,2}, \ldots, C_{i,N_i}\}$ in $\mathcal{H}_i$. From the remark above, $N_i \leq |\bot|^c$; (2) Obtain a total order on the $C_{i,j}$ based on the evaluation function used. This follows from A2 above and the fact that there is a consistent enumeration for any partially ordered set; and (3) Return the clause that has the highest utility in this order (the "best" clause). A complete, but not necessarily exhaustive, search can be achieved by a branch-and-bound technique [19], but the worst-case time-complexity of the procedure would remain remains unaltered.

From Remark 1, it is clear that the size of the hypothesis space on any given iteration i of the procedure in Fig. 2 is at most $|\perp_i|^c$. We now examine obtaining an unbiased estimate for the true size of the hypothesis space.

Remark 2. **Unbiased estimation of** $|\mathcal{H}_i|$ Let the number of definite clauses in $\mathcal{L}$ obtained by selecting exactly l literals from $\perp_i$ be n_l, the total number of definite clauses obtained by selecting exactly l literals from $\perp_i$ be N_l and $p_l = n_l/N_l$. Then $|\mathcal{H}_i| = n_1 + n_2 + \cdots + n_{c+1} = p_1 N_1 + p_2 N_2 + \cdots + p_{c+1} N_{c+1}$. Let $\hat{p}_1, \hat{p}_2, \ldots, \hat{p}_{c+1}$ be sample proportion estimates of $p_1, p_2, \ldots, p_{c+1}$ respectively. It is known that these estimates are unbiased [28] (that is, with some abuse of notation, $E(\hat{p}_i) = p_i$). An unbiased estimate of $|\mathcal{H}_i|$ is then $\hat{p}_1 N_1 + \hat{p}_2 N_2 + \cdots + \hat{p}_{c+1} N_{c+1}$.

Fig. 3 shows the steps for obtaining this estimate using a modified version of the procedure described in [26].

$hsize(\perp, \mathcal{L}, n, s)$: Given a definite clause $\perp$ and a natural number $n > 0$, returns an estimate, using a sample of size s, of the number of definite clauses in $\mathcal{L}$ with at most n literals drawn from $\perp_i$.
  1. $\hat{H}_1 = 1$
  2. $l = 2$
  3. while $l \leq n$ do
      (a) Sample s clauses of length l from $\perp$. Each such clause consists of the positive ("head") literal in $\perp$ and a random selection, without replacement, of $l - 1$ literals from the negative ("body") literals in $\perp$.
      (b) Let $\hat{p}_l$ be the proportion of the s clauses that are in $\mathcal{L}$.
      (c) $\hat{n}_l = \hat{p}_l \times (|\perp| - 1) \times \ldots \times (|\perp| - l + 1)$
      (d) $\hat{H}_l = \hat{H}_{l-1} + \hat{n}_l$
  4. return $\hat{H}_n$

Fig. 3. A procedure for estimating the number of "legal" clauses of length at most n drawn from $\perp$. The number is computed using estimates of the proportion of legal clauses p_l for $l = 1 \ldots n$. These estimates are proportions of legal clauses in samples of size s. Randomly sampling clauses of a particular length is done using a procedure described in [26]. The size of s needs to be specified in advance: one option is to be guided by statistical estimation theory. This states that if values of the p_l are not too close to 0 or 1, then we can be at least $100 \times (1 - \alpha)\%$ confident that the error will be less than a specified amount e when $s = z_{\alpha/2}^2/(4e^2)$ [28]. Here z represents the standard normal variable as usual.

Remark 3. **Vector representation of a clause.** Any clause $C_{i,j} \in \mathcal{H}_i$ is composed of literals drawn without replacement from $\perp_i$. Let $n = |\perp_i|$, and assume a total ordering over literals in $\perp_i$. $C_{i,j}$ can be seen as a point in $\{0,1\}^n$, represented by the vector $\boldsymbol{C_{i,j}} = (x_1, x_2, \ldots, x_n)$ where $x_k = 1$ iff the kth literal from $\perp_i$ is in $C_{i,j}$. Actually, since we are only concerned with definite clauses, we can represent $C_{i,j}$ as a point in $\{0,1\}^{n-1}$ (instead of $\{0,1\}^n$) since the positive literal in $\perp_i$ will always be in $C_{i,j}$.)

Figure 4 shows an example of representing clauses in this manner. The example is from the "trains" problem, originally proposed in [14]. As a result of the language restrictions in $\mathcal{L}$, not all vectors may represent legal clauses in the hypothesis space (see Fig. 4(c) and associated text).

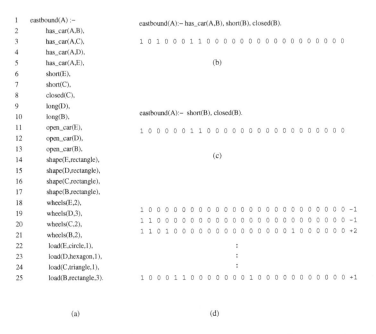

Fig. 4. The trains problem. (a) The most specific clause within some $\mathcal{L}$ for an "eastbound" train (with an ordering on its literals); (b) A clause and its vector representation; (c) A vector representing a clause outside an $\mathcal{L}$ that stipulates that "short" literals require to be preceded by "has_car" literals. Such a clause would not be in the hypothesis space; and (d) A sample of clauses from the hypothesis space, along with their utility values.

3   Dimensionality Reduction

Our goal in using dimensionality reduction is this: clauses represented by n-dimensional vectors are to be represented instead by m-dimensional ones, where $m < n$. Further, we will seek to achieve this by discarding those dimensions that appear to contain little or no information. It is evident that removing dimensions in this manner corresponds directly to removing literals from the most specific clause used to construct the clauses. From Remark 1, the upper bound on the size of the hypothesis space is, in turn, lowered.[2]

---

[2] It does not, of course, follow that the actual size is also smaller. This is the subject of the empirical investigation in Section 4.

Given a set of vectors of the form shown in Fig 4(d): $\{(\boldsymbol{x}^{(i)}, t^{(i)})\}_{i=1}^{N}$, where $\boldsymbol{x}^{(i)}$ is some n-dimensional vector and $t^{(i)}$ is the target value (this is not always needed), the goal of dimensionality reduction is to represent the $\boldsymbol{x}^{(i)}$ in some m-dimensional space ($m < n$), by discarding those dimensions that are found to be statistically irrelevant or redundant (usually obtained using some correlation measure). To achieve this, techniques for dimensionality reduction either require that a target value be supplied with each vector (the resulting techniques are called "supervised" methods) or they do not (resulting in "unsupervised" methods). With this broad distinction, a large number of methods have been proposed: the reader is referred to [7] for a good introduction to the area and to [8,9] for some additional approaches. In this paper, we are simply concerned with their application to reducing the number of dimensions in the vector representation of clauses.

3.1 Using Dimensionality Reduction to Restrict the Hypothesis Space

We return here to the $search(\ldots)$ procedure in Fig. 2. Recall that it was assumed there that this procedure would return the "best" clause in a set containing definite clauses constructed from a most specific clause. The main conceptual steps are shown in Fig. 5.

$search(B, H, I, \mathcal{L}, E)$: Given background knowledge B, hypothesised clauses H, hypothesis constraints I, a finite training set $E = E^+ \cup E^-$, returns a clause D in $\mathcal{L}$ such that $B \cup H \cup D \models E_p$, where: $E_p \subseteq E^+, E_p \neq \emptyset$; and $B \cup H \cup D$ is consistent with the I.
  1. If $E^+ = \emptyset$ then return $\emptyset$
  2. Let e be a randomly selected example in E^+
  3. Construct $\perp$ s.t. $\perp \models \overline{B \cup H \cup \{\overline{e}\}}$
  4. Let $S = \{C : \square \succeq [C] \succeq [\perp]$ and $C \in \mathcal{L}\}$
  5. Let D be the best clause in S consistent with B, H, I.
  6. return D

Fig. 5. The conceptual steps of the search procedure in Fig. 2. Here $\succeq$ denotes a generality ordering (like $\theta-$subsumption) and $[\cdot]$ denotes an equivalence class. In practice, the set S would not actually be constructed in Step 4.

We intend to modify the steps in Fig. 5 along the lines shown in Fig. 6. A complication arises in Step 7: some literals may necessarily have to be included to ensure a "high ranking" literal is retained in $\perp'$. For example, in Fig. 4, literal 7 may be ranked highest, but $\mathcal{L}$ may require that it can appear in $\perp'$ only if literal 3 is present. This means that $\perp'$ may not necessarily contain all the top p-percentile of literals. Some may have to be left out to ensure other necessary literals are included.

$rsearch(B, H, I, \mathcal{L}, E, s, p)$: Given background knowledge B, hypothesised clauses H,
   hypothesis constraints I, a finite training set $E = E^+ \cup E^-$, numbers s and p
   $(0 < s, p \leq 100)$, returns a clause D in $\mathcal{L}$ such that $B \cup H \cup D \models E_p$, where:
   $E_p \subseteq E^+$, $E_p \neq \emptyset$; and $B \cup H \cup D$ is consistent with the I.
   1. If $E^+ = \emptyset$ then return $\emptyset$
   2. Let e be a randomly selected example in E^+
   3. Construct $\perp$ s.t. $\perp \models \overline{B \cup H \cup \{\overline{e}\}}$
   4. Let $S = \{C : \square \succeq [C] \succeq [\perp]$ and $C \in \mathcal{L}\}$
   5. Randomly draw $\frac{s}{100}|S|$ clauses from S and construct a table T of feature
      vectors representing the clauses
   6. Use a dimensionality reduction method on T to rank the binary features in
      decreasing order of relevance
   7. Use the ranking to retain at most $\frac{p}{100}|\perp|$ literals. Let the resulting clause be
      called $\perp'$.
   8. Let $S' = \{C : \square \succeq [C] \succeq [\perp']$ and $C \in \mathcal{L}\}$
   9. Let D be the best clause in S' consistent with B, H, I.
   10. return D

Fig. 6. The conceptual steps of the search procedure which uses dimensionality reduction to remove literals from $\perp$. As before, in practice, neither S or S' would actually
be constructed. If $|\perp| = n$ then the table T will consist either of n columns or $n + 1$
columns (depending on whether the dimensionality reduction method is unsupervised
or supervised).

4   Empirical Evaluation

In this section we evaluate empirically the use of dimensionality reduction to restrict the size of a hypothesis space. Using well-known statistical methods on some
standard ILP datasets, we attempt to find answers to the following questions:

1. Does the use of dimensionality reduction actually reduce the size of the
   hypothesis space? and
2. Does the resulting search space after dimensionality reduction still contain
   as good a clause as the original space?

4.1   Materials

Problem Domains. We examine the use of dimensionality reduction on three
ILP tasks considered in the literature. These are: a synthetic problem concerned
with finding clauses in randomly constructed directed graphs [30]; and the standard problems of mutagenesis (the subset containing 188 examples: see [10]) and
carcinogenesis [11]. Of these, the last two problems have been well studied and
we refer the reader to the literature cited for specific details. The graphs problem
is less well known. The data here consist of 5,000 directed graphs (containing in
total 16,000 edges). Every node in a graph is coloured to red or black. In [30],
examples were generated using a target clause consisting of 11 literals. Here we
consider two problems: an "easy" one in which there is a clause that precisely

separates the positive examples from the negatives, given the language restrictions[3]; and a "hard" one in which no such clause exists[4]. Clearly, if no good clause exists, then the answer to the second question above is trivially "yes". The answer to the first question remains to be determined. Figure 7 tabulates the data characteristics of the different problems considered here (all datasets can be obtained from the first author).

Property	Easy Graphs	Hard Graphs	Mutagenesis	Carcinogenesis
Origin	Artificially generated	Artificially generated	Biochemical literature	Biochemical literature
Noise	No	No	Yes	Yes
'Target' theory	1 short clause	No	No	No
# pos/neg examples	2480/2420	20/20	125/63	182/148

Fig. 7. Data characteristics of the problem domains

Algorithms and Machines. All experiments use the ILP program Aleph (Version 5). Aleph is available at: `http://www.comlab.ox.ac.uk/oucl/research/areas/machlearn/Aleph/aleph.pl`. We consider two dimensionality reduction methods: Principal Component Analysis (PCA, which is unsupervised); and RReliefF, a supervised feature selection method proposed in [22] as an extension to Relief [12] enabling it to problems in which the response variable is numerical (more correctly, RReliefF is an extension to ReliefF [13]). PCA by itself does not produce a ranking over the original set of features. We extract this ordering from the eigenvectors. More specifically, we start by choosing the dominant eigenvector (the one with the largest eigenvalue) and choose the variable with the largest absolute value of the coefficient. This variable is the most relevant. We then move to the next eigenvector and repeat the process leaving out the variables previously chosen to obtain the second most relevant variable. In this way we obtain an ordering of all the variables [23]. We use Matlab for performing PCA (the program is available from the authors), and the implementation within the WEKA program of RReliefF (WEKA is available at: `http://www.cs.waikato.ac.nz/ ml/weka/`). All experiments were conducted on a machine equipped with an two Intel Pentium IV 1.2GHz processors and 512 megabytes of random access memory.

4.2 Method

We are primarily concerned with assessing the utility of using $rsearch(\ldots)$ as a search procedure instead of $search(\ldots)$ (see Figs. 5,6). The principal parame-

---

[3] We have elected to restrict clauses to at most 4 literals. This is in line with the original published work on mutagenesis and carcinogenesis.

[4] That is, no 4-literal clause exists that can discriminate amongst the examples provided (the target theory is a 10-literal clause).

ters of interest are s (the percentage of the hypothesis space to be provided as "training" data for dimensionality reduction); and p (the percentage of the most specific clause to be retained). We adopt the following method in investigating the use of $rsearch(\ldots)$:

> For each task (Graphs, Mutagenesis and Carcinogenesis) and dimensionality reduction method (PCA and RReliefF):
> - For $s \in \{s_1, s_2, \ldots\}$ and $p \in \{p_1, p_2, \ldots\}$
>   - Repeat R times
>   1. Randomly select an example and construct a most specific clause $\perp$
>   2. Let $\hat{H}$ be the estimated size of the hypothesis space with $\perp$ (obtained using the procedure in Fig. 3)
>   3. Let F be the utility of the best clause found by conducting a complete search over $\hat{H}$ nodes (using $\perp$ as the most specific clause).
>   4. Generate a sample T of $\frac{s}{100}\hat{H}$ clauses and represent them in the vector form appropriate for the dimensionality reduction method.
>   5. Obtain a ranking over the literals in $\perp$ using T and the dimensionality reduction method and use this ranking to construct a new clause $\perp'$ that retains at most $\frac{p}{100}|\perp|$ literals from $\perp$
>   6. Let $\hat{H}'$ be the estimated size of the hypothesis space with $\perp'$.
>   7. Let F' be the utility of the best clause found by conducting a complete search over $\hat{H}'$ nodes (using $\perp'$ as the most specific clause).
>   8. Record $\hat{H}, \hat{H}', F, F'$
>   - Compute the average values $\hat{H}_{av}, \hat{H}'_{av}, F_{av}, F'_{av}$ over the R trials.
>   - Compare the differences between $\hat{H}_{av}, \hat{H}'_{av}$; and F_{av}, F'_{av}.

The following details are relevant: (1) For the purposes of this study, we will consider s values of 5% and 10%, and p values of 25%, 50% and 75%; (2) We will average over $R = 3$ trials. This is lower than what we would have liked, but was forced by the relatively long time to conduct complete searches in the biochemical problems. It is not the dimensionality reduction step that takes up the time here, but the complete search of the hypothesis space both before and after selecting literals (we use a branch-and-bound algorithm for the complete search); (3) Estimating the sizes $\hat{H}$ and $\hat{H}'$ require drawing samples from the hypothesis space. We use samples of size 400 to estimate the proportions required by the procedure in Fig. 3; (4) We compute clause utilities F and F' by the difference in the positive and negative coverage of the clause. This is consistent with the original applications; (5) The use of RReliefF requires the user to provide values of two parameters: m (the number of instances sampled) and k (the number of neighbors examined). We have used a m value of 250 and a k value of 10. The m value is as recommended in the original RReliefF paper. The value for k is less evident: a value of 10 is common in the literature for problems with discrete response variables. Problems with numeric response variables usually employ a

k value of 100. Although our response variable (clause utility) is numeric, we have elected to use the lower value since typically, only a few different values for the response variable appear in the data (a lot of clauses have the same positive and negative coverages); (6) We present the comparisons of $\hat{H}_{av}$, $\hat{H}'_{av}$; and F_{av}, F'_{av} after normalizing against $\hat{H}_{av}$ and F_{av} respectively. For example, if $\hat{H}_{av}$ is 100,000 and $\hat{H}'_{av}$ is 6,000, then these numbers will be presented as 100 percent and 6 percent respectively. This is done for two reasons: the actual values of the quantities are of less interest here than the ratio of their values; and the quantities are on different scales.

4.3   Results and Discussion

Figures 8 and 9 tabulate the normalized values of the sizes of the hypothesis spaces before and after dimensionality reduction; and normalized values of the best clause in the different hypothesis spaces. If dimensionality reduction plays a useful role, we would expect to see the size of the hypothesis space to be reduced (that is, $\hat{H}'_{av}$ should be substantially lower than 100 percent) without much change in the clause utility (that is, F'_{av} should be fairly close to 100 percent).

The results tabulated clearly show that for the problems considered, there is no compelling evidence for the usefulness of unsupervised dimensionality reduction (at least in the form of Principal Components Analysis). Although the size of the hypothesis space is reduced, the best clause in the resulting space is always substantially worse. This is not surprising, since there is no *a priori* reason to expect that the relevance of features obtained from the eigenvectors should be correlated with clause utility. In general, we would also expect that as s is increased—a larger data sample is provided to the dimensionality reduction technique—the ranking of features produced would improve. This is not observed with PCA (using F'_{av} values as a guide, in many cases it gets worse), suggesting that it is not being able to extract a reliable ranking from the data.

The PCA based method we have used for ranking the variables usually identifies very good subsets. Further, if there are groups of correlated variables, then it selects just one variable from the group since there is exactly one high variance principal component associated with each group. However, the method occasionally also identifies bad or moderate subsets. In part, this is a drawback of unsupervised dimensionality reduction methods in general. By not using the class information, the most appropriate subspace (where a certain optimality criteria is maximized) cannot be identified and one has to resort to using an optimality criteria that does not necessarily align with the task at hand. In the case of PCA, the optimality criteria is the preservation of the variance *i.e.*, the subspace should retain as much of the variance in the data as possible. This is not usually related to notions such as separability of the classes.

In contrast, supervised dimensionality reduction appears to hold more promise. Setting aside the "Easy Graphs" problem for the moment, it is possible to restrict the hypothesis space to nearly half its original size, without loss on the utility front. Performance is also as expected when s is increased (the few cases where F'_{av} values are lower are artifacts, either of sampling or small numbers).

p	s 5%				10%			
	$\hat{H}_{av}$	$\hat{H}'_{av}$	F_{av}	F'_{av}	$\hat{H}_{av}$	$\hat{H}'_{av}$	F_{av}	F'_{av}
25%	100	1	100	0	100	1	100	0
50%	100	10	100	39	100	10	100	28
75%	100	39	100	64	100	38	100	28

(a) Easy Graphs

p	s 5%				10%			
	$\hat{H}_{av}$	$\hat{H}'_{av}$	F_{av}	F'_{av}	$\hat{H}_{av}$	$\hat{H}'_{av}$	F_{av}	F'_{av}
25%	100	8	100	100	100	8	100	100
50%	100	11	100	100	100	10	100	100
75%	100	39	100	100	100	37	100	100

(b) Hard Graphs

p	s 5%				10%			
	$\hat{H}_{av}$	$\hat{H}'_{av}$	F_{av}	F'_{av}	$\hat{H}_{av}$	$\hat{H}'_{av}$	F_{av}	F'_{av}
25%	100	3	100	30	100	6	100	23
50%	100	28	100	63	100	22	100	58
75%	100	44	100	79	100	44	100	71

(c) Mutagenesis

p	s 5%				10%			
	$\hat{H}_{av}$	$\hat{H}'_{av}$	F_{av}	F'_{av}	$\hat{H}_{av}$	$\hat{H}'_{av}$	F_{av}	F'_{av}
25%	100	3	100	4	100	4	100	20
50%	100	28	100	30	100	37	100	14
75%	100	77	100	54	100	75	100	60

(d) Carcinogenesis

Fig. 8. Results of using PCA. s represents the percentage of the hypothesis space provided as a sample to PCA and p represents the percentage of the most specific clause retained using the ranking of literals produced by dimensionality reduction. $\hat{H}_{av}$ and F_{av} are the size of the hypothesis space and the utility of the best clause before dimensionality reduction. $\hat{H}'_{av}$ and F'_{av} are the corresponding values after dimensionality reduction. All entries are normalized against $\hat{H}_{av}$ and F_{av} values and the result expressed as a percentage. As a matter of interest, the actual $\hat{H}_{av}$ values are in the tens of thousands (Graphs) or hundreds of thousands (Mutagenesis and Carcinogenesis). The actual F_{av} values are 2480 (Simple Graphs), 1 (Hard Graphs), between 7 and 60 (Mutagenesis), and between 1 and 6 (Carcinogenesis). The absence of any good clause within the search space in "Hard Graphs" results in F'_{av} being always equal to F_{av}.

p	s 5%				10%			
	$\hat{H}_{av}$	$\hat{H}'_{av}$	F_{av}	F'_{av}	$\hat{H}_{av}$	$\hat{H}'_{av}$	F_{av}	F'_{av}
25%	100	1	100	56	100	1	100	31
50%	100	9	100	61	100	10	100	59
75%	100	38	100	100	100	38	100	67

(a) Easy Graphs

p	s 5%				10%			
	$\hat{H}_{av}$	$\hat{H}'_{av}$	F_{av}	F'_{av}	$\hat{H}_{av}$	$\hat{H}'_{av}$	F_{av}	F'_{av}
25%	100	1	100	100	100	1	100	100
50%	100	10	100	100	100	10	100	100
75%	100	40	100	100	100	37	100	100

(b) Hard Graphs

p	s 5%				10%			
	$\hat{H}_{av}$	$\hat{H}'_{av}$	F_{av}	F'_{av}	$\hat{H}_{av}$	$\hat{H}'_{av}$	F_{av}	F'_{av}
25%	100	7	100	44	100	9	100	48
50%	100	25	100	99	100	37	100	98
75%	100	28	100	96	100	47	100	100

(c) Mutagenesis

p	s 5%				10%			
	$\hat{H}_{av}$	$\hat{H}'_{av}$	F_{av}	F'_{av}	$\hat{H}_{av}$	$\hat{H}'_{av}$	F_{av}	F'_{av}
25%	100	8	100	40	100	17	100	50
50%	100	41	100	67	100	49	100	100
75%	100	53	100	100	100	63	100	83

(d) Carcinogenesis

Fig. 9. Results of using RReliefF. s, k, $\hat{H}_{av}$, F_{av} $\hat{H}'_{av}$ and F'_{av} are as in Fig. 8. As before, the entries are normalised against $\hat{H}_{av}$ and F_{av} values and the result expressed as a percentage.

The results also suggest that an s value of 10 percent and a p value of 50 percent yield the best results. For reference, Fig. 10, shows the values obtained by using the same method, but with a random assignment of relevance to features in the Mutagenesis and Carcinogenesis domains.

Problem	Method							
	RReliefF				Random			
	$\hat{H}_{av}$	$\hat{H}'_{av}$	F_{av}	F'_{av}	$\hat{H}_{av}$	$\hat{H}'_{av}$	F_{av}	F'_{av}
Mutagenesis	100	37	100	98	100	30	100	41
Carcinogenesis	100	49	100	100	100	28	100	67

Fig. 10. Comparison of supervised dimensionality reduction against a method that randomly assigns relevance to features. We have shown values for $s = 10\%$ and $p = 50\%$ only.

Turning now to the performance on "Easy Graphs": it is evident that the performance of supervised dimensionality reduction is not as stable. A conservative approach seems to suggest that for problems with relatively easy target concepts (here, a single short clause that can perfectly discriminate amongst the examples), it is best not to perform any form of statistical dimensionality reduction. It is a moot point whether we could know in advance that such a target concept exists. To some extent the issue is not of immediate relevance: we expect the methods here to be used when we know that easy target concepts do *not* exist.

Of course, the use of a supervised method has the additional overhead of having to obtain clause utility values for s percent of the hypothesis space; making the whole procedure only worthwhile for problems that require substantial search to find the best clause.

5   Concluding Remarks

This paper has been a study of using general-purpose statistical dimensionality reduction methods to restrict the size of a hypothesis space. The test-beds used in experiments here have involved search spaces of the order of 10s–100s of thousands of clauses. By combinatorial standards, these are of very modest size. Nevertheless they have been sufficient to investigate the use of both unsupervised and supervised methods for dimensionality reduction. Our results suggest that when "easy" target concepts do not exist, supervised dimensionality reduction schemes may be able to play an important role in restricting the size of a hypothesis space. Specifically, we have been able to show that an ILP program, equipped with a supervised dimensionality reduction scheme, can detect and discard substantial portions of the hypothesis space that is not relevant to identifying good clauses.

The study can be seen as part of an on-going effort to improve the efficiency of ILP systems by concentrating on ways to improve search performance. So far, this effort has concentrated on either changing the time-complexity of clause evaluation, or simply exploring fewer clauses within a given hypothesis space. The task of circumscribing the space itself has been left to the user, using tools of language and search restrictions. The approach here can be seen as augmenting this by attempting to discover statistical relevancies in the search space using sample data. In a sense, this is related to, but not the same as the work in [4], where sample data about clause properties are used to learn an efficient approximation to the clause utility function. The point that statistical techniques for dimensionality reduction could be useful in ILP was noted some time ago [6], and the techniques themselves have been used in an indirect manner more recently in [1] (by transforming the relational problem to an approximate attribute-value one). Here we have demonstrated how feature selection methods could be used directly by an ILP system that constructs rules using most-specific clauses. A different approach to restricting the size of the hypothesis space by dynamic construction of the most-specific clause during the search has been investigated in [27]. This is not based on detecting statistical redundancies in the manner we suggest.

The paper itself has a number of limitations: (1) Results from three domains, however realistic, clearly can only be suggestive. The variance in estimates of gains that we have obtained is also high, given the small number of trials we have been able to perform; (2) The dimensionality reduction methods we have used are standard, but by no means the best available. For example, an extensive series of experiments in [5] show that a form of classifiability-based feature selection may perform much better (although it would have to be altered to account for numeric response variables); (3) The techniques described here are for rule-learning using a most-specific clause as described in [16]. This is by no means the only kind of ILP system possible; (4) The use of the earlier work on improving clause evaluation and reduced search are outside the scope here.

These issues suggest several directions for future work, namely: (1) Further testing: on new domains, and using better statistical methods; (2) A study of the role for statistical relevance discovery in other ILP settings: it is conceivable, for example, that unsupervised dimensionality reduction may be better suited to the "explanatory" ILP setting which only seeks descriptive patterns; (3) The development and application of ILP engines that contain techniques that combine all three techniques of improving search performance (efficient clause evaluation, hypothesis space reduction and reduced search).

Acknowledgements

The study in this paper was suggested by a conversation with Stepen Muggleton during the course of ILP 2004. Thanks are also due to Mark Hall and Eibe Frank for their help with the feature selection programs within WEKA and to the Oxford University Computing Laboratory for continuing to host the Aleph program.

References

1. E. Alphonse and S. Matwin. Filtering Multi-Instance Problems to Reduce Dimensionality in Multi-Relational Learning. *Journal of Intelligent Information Systems*, 22(1):23–40, 2004.

2. W. Cohen and C.D. Page. Polynomial learnability and inductive logic programming: Methods and results. *New Generation Computing*, 13(3,4):369–409, 1995.
3. V. S. Costa, A. Srinivasan, R. C. Camacho, H. Blockeel, B.Demoen, G. Janssens, J. Struyf, H. Vandecasteele, and W. Van Laer. Query Transformations for Improving the Efficiency of ILP Systems. *Journal of Machine Learning Research*, 4(Aug):465–491, 2003.
4. F. DiMaio and J. Shavlik. Learning an Approximation to Inductive Logic Programming Clause Evaluation. In *Proceedings of the Fourteenth International Conference on Inductive Logic Programming (ILP2004)*, LNAI 3194, pages 80–97, Berlin, 2004. Springer.
5. M. Dong and R. Kothari. Feature subset selection using a new definition of classifiability. *Pattern Recognition Letters*, 24(9–10):1215–1225, 2003.
6. J. Furnkranz. Dimensionality Reduction in ILP: A Call to Arms. In *Proceedings of the IJCAI-97 Workshop on Inductive Logic Programming*, pages 81–86, 1997.
7. I. Guyon and A. Elisseeff. An Introduction to Variable and Feature Selection. *Journal of Machine Learning Research*, 3:1157–1182, 2003.
8. R. Lotlikar and R. Kothari. Bayes-Optimality Motivated Linear and Multi-Layered Perceptron Based Dimensionality Reduction. *IEEE Transactions on Neural Networks*, 11:452–463, 2000.
9. R. Lotlikar and R. Kothari. Fractional-Step Dimensionality Reduction. *IEEE Transactions on Pattern Analysis and Machine Intelligence*, 22:623–627, 2000.
10. R.D. King, S.H. Muggleton, A. Srinivasan, and M.J.E. Sternberg. Structure-activity relationships derived by machine learning: The use of atoms and their bond connectivities to predict mutagenicity by inductive logic programming. *Proc. of the National Academy of Sciences*, 93:438–442, 1996.
11. R.D. King and A. Srinivasan. Prediction of rodent carcinogenicity bioassays from molecular structure using inductive logic programming. *Environmental Health Perspectives*, 104(5):1031–1040, 1996.
12. K. Kira and L.A. Rendell. The feature selection problem: traditional methods and a new algorithm. In *Proceedings of the Tenth National Conference on AI*, pages 129–134, Menlo Park, CA, 1992. AAAI Press.
13. I. Kononenko. Estimating attributes: analysis and extensions of Relief. In *Proceedings of the Seventh European Conference on Machine Learning*, pages 171–182, Berlin, 1994. Springer.
14. R.S. Michalski. A theory and methodology of inductive learning. In R. Michalski, J. Carbonnel, and T. Mitchell, editors, *Machine Learning: An Artificial Intelligence Approach*, pages 83–134. Tioga, Palo Alto, CA, 1983.
15. S. Muggleton. Inductive Logic Programming: derivations, successes and shortcomings. *SIGART Bulletin*, 5(1):5–11, 1994.
16. S. Muggleton. Inverse Entailment and Progol. *New Gen. Comput.*, 13:245–286, 1995.
17. S.H. Muggleton and C. Feng. Efficient induction of logic programs. In *Proceedings of the First Conference on Algorithmic Learning Theory*, Tokyo, 1990. Ohmsha.
18. S. Nienhuys-Cheng and R. de Wolf. *Foundations of Inductive Logic Programming*. Springer, Berlin, 1997.
19. C.H. Papadimitriou and K. Steiglitz. *Combinatorial Optimisation*. Prentice-Hall, Edgewood-Cliffs, NJ, 1982.
20. J.R. Quinlan. Learning logical definitions from relations. *Machine Learning*, 5:239–266, 1990.

21. J.R. Quinlan and R.M. Cameron-Jones. Oversearching and Layered Search in Empirical Learning. In *Proceedings of the Fourteenth International Joint Conference on Artificial Intelligence (IJCAI'95)*, Los Angeles, CA, 1995. Morgan Kaufmann.
22. M. Robnik-Sikonja and I. Kononenko. An adaption of Relief for Attribute Estimation in Regression. In *Proceedings of the Fourteenth International Conference on Machine Learning*, pages 296–304. Morgan Kaufmann, 1997.
23. I.T. Jolliffe. Principal Component Analysis. Springer-Verlag, 1986.
24. M. Sebag and C. Rouveirol. Tractable Induction and Classification in First-Order Logic via Stochastic Matching. In *Proceedings of the Fifteenth International Conference on Artificial Intelligence (IJCAI-97)*. Morgan Kaufmann, Los Angeles, CA, 1997.
25. A. Srinivasan. A study of two sampling methods for analysing large datasets with ILP. *Data Mining and Knowledge Discovery*, 3(1):95–123, 1999.
26. A. Srinivasan. A study of two probabilistic methods for searching large spaces with ILP. Technical Report PRG-TR-16-00, Oxford University Computing Laboratory, Oxford, 2000.
27. L.R. Tang, R.J. Mooney and P. Melville. Scaling Up ILP to Large Examples: Results on Link Discovery for Counter Terrorism. In *Proceedings of the KDD 2003 Workshop on Multi-Relational Data Mining (MRDM-2003)*, 107–121, 2003.
28. R.E. Walpole and R.H. Myers. *Probability and Statistics for Engineers and Scientists*. Collier Macmillan, New York, 1978. 2nd Edition.
29. F. Zelezny, A. Srinivasan, and C.D. Page. Lattice-Search Runtime Distributions May Be Heavy-Tailed. In *Proceedings of the Twelfth International Conference on Inductive Logic Programming (ILP2002)*, LNAI, Berlin, 2002. Springer.
30. F. Zelezny, A. Srinivasan, and C.D. Page. A Monte-Carlo Study of Randomised Restarted Search in ILP. In *Proceedings of the Fourteenth International Conference on Inductive Logic Programming (ILP2004)*, LNAI 3194, pages 341–358, Berlin, 2004. Springer.

Polynomial Time Inductive Inference of TTSP Graph Languages from Positive Data

Ryoji Takami[1], Yusuke Suzuki[2], Tomoyuki Uchida[2],
Takayoshi Shoudai[3], and Yasuaki Nakamura[2]

[1] Department of Computer and Media Technologies,
Hiroshima City University, Hiroshima 731-3194, Japan
r_takami@toc.cs.hiroshima-cu.ac.jp
[2] Faculty of Information Sciences, Hiroshima City University,
Hiroshima 731-3194, Japan
{y-suzuki, uchida, nakamura}@cs.hiroshima-cu.ac.jp
[3] Department of Informatics, Kyushu University, Kasuga 816-8580, Japan
shoudai@i.kyushu-u.ac.jp

Abstract. Two-Terminal Series Parallel (TTSP, for short) graphs are used as data models in applications for electric networks and scheduling problems. We propose a TTSP term graph which is a TTSP graph having structured variables, that is, a graph pattern over a TTSP graph. Let $\mathcal{TG}_{TTSP}$ be the set of all TTSP term graphs whose variable labels are mutually distinct. For a TTSP term graph g, the TTSP graph language of g, denoted by $L(g)$, is the set of all TTSP graphs obtained from g by substituting arbitrary TTSP graphs for all variables in g.

Firstly, when a TTSP graph G and a TTSP term graph g are given as inputs, we present a polynomial time matching algorithm which decides whether or not $L(g)$ contains G. The minimal language problem for the class $\mathcal{L}_{TTSP} = \{L(g) \mid g \in \mathcal{TG}_{TTSP}\}$ is, given a set S of TTSP graphs, to find a TTSP term graph g in $\mathcal{TG}_{TTSP}$ such that $L(g)$ is minimal among all TTSP graph languages which contain all TTSP graphs in S. Secondly, we give a polynomial time algorithm for solving the minimal language problem for $\mathcal{L}_{TTSP}$. Finally, we show that $\mathcal{L}_{TTSP}$ is polynomial time inductively inferable from positive data.

1 Introduction

We consider the learnability of Two-Terminal Series Parallel (TTSP, for short) graph languages from positive data. A TTSP graph is a graph constructed by recursively applying "series" and "parallel" operations. A TTSP graph is a planar graph and used as a data model in applications for problems on electrical networks and scheduling problems. The purpose of this paper is to show that the class of languages on TTSP graphs is polynomial time inductively inferable from positive data.

Uchida et al. [11] proposed the concepts of a graph pattern having graph structures and structured variables, called a *term graph*, and a graph pattern language, called a *graph language*. Based on the concept of a term graph and a

S. Kramer and B. Pfahringer (Eds.): ILP 2005, LNAI 3625, pp. 366–383, 2005.
© Springer-Verlag Berlin Heidelberg 2005

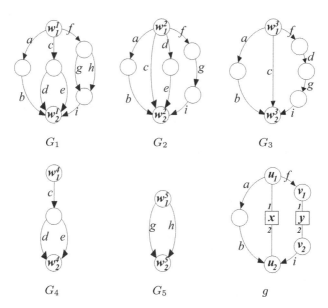

Fig. 1. TTSP graphs G_1, G_2, G_3, G_4, G_5 and a TTSP term graph g. A variable is drawn by a box with lines to its elements. The numbers at these lines indicates the order of the vertices which a variable consists of. The symbol inside a box shows the label of the variable.

graph language given in [11], we define a *TTSP term graph* as a graph pattern having a TTSP graph structure and structured variables. A variable in a TTSP term graph is a pair of its distinct vertices. For a TTSP term graph g, we also define a *TTSP graph language* of g as the set of all TTSP graphs obtained from g by substituting arbitrary TTSP graphs for all variables in g. $\mathcal{TTSP}$ denotes the set of all TTSP graphs. $\mathcal{TG}_{TTSP}$ denotes the set of all TTSP term graphs whose variable labels are mutually distinct. For a TTSP term graph $g \in \mathcal{TG}_{TTSP}$, the TTSP graph language of g is denoted by $L(g)$. In Fig. 1, we give TTSP graphs G_1, G_2, G_3, G_4, G_5 in $\mathcal{TTSP}$ and a TTSP term graph g in $\mathcal{TG}_{TTSP}$ as examples. And the TTSP graph G_1 in Fig. 1 is obtained from the TTSP term graph g by replacing variables having label x and y with TTSP graphs G_4 and G_5 so that u_1, u_2, v_1, v_2 of g are identified with w_1^4, w_2^4, w_1^5, w_2^5 of TTSP graphs G_4 and G_5, respectively.

Angluin [2] and Shinohara [7] gave the framework of inductive inference from positive data and showed that if a class $\mathcal{C}$ has finite thickness, and the membership problem and the minimal language (MINL) problem for $\mathcal{C}$ are computable in polynomial time then $\mathcal{C}$ is polynomial time inductively inferable from positive data. Based on this framework, in this paper, we consider the polynomial time learnability of $\mathcal{L}_{TTSP} = \{L(g) \mid g \in \mathcal{TG}_{TTSP}\}$ from positive data.

Firstly, we show that, for any nonempty set S of TTSP graphs, the cardinality of the set $\{L \in \mathcal{L}_{TTSP} \mid S \subseteq L\}$ is finite, that is, $\mathcal{L}_{TTSP}$ is finite thickness. Secondly, we consider the membership problem for $\mathcal{L}_{TTSP}$ which is,

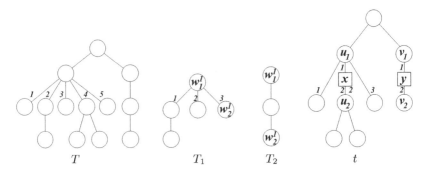

Fig. 2. Trees T, T_1, T_2 and a term tree t

given a TTSP term graph $g \in \mathcal{TG}_{TTSP}$ and a TTSP graph $G \in \mathcal{TTSP}$, to decide whether or not $L(g)$ contains G. In [6,8,9], we presented a term tree all of whose internal vertices are ordered, called an *ordered term tree*, and a term tree all of whose internal vertices are unordered, called an *unordered term tree*. In order to show that the membership problem for $\mathcal{L}_{TTSP}$ is solvable in polynomial time, we present a polynomial time matching algorithm for solving the membership problem for the set of languages of term trees each of whose internal vertices has ordered or unordered children, by modifying polynomial time matching algorithms for ordered term trees and unordered term trees in [6,9]. In Fig. 2, we give a term tree t as an example. A tree T in Fig. 2 is obtained from t by replacing two variables having labels x and y with trees T_1 and T_2 in Fig. 2, respectively. Thirdly, we consider the minimal language problem, MINL problem for short, for $\mathcal{L}_{TTSP}$ which is, given a set S of TTSP graphs, to find a TTSP term graph $g \in \mathcal{TG}_{TTSP}$ such that $S \subseteq L(g)$ and there exists no TTSP term graph $g' \in \mathcal{TG}_{TTSP}$ with $S \subseteq L(g') \subsetneq L(g)$, that is, $L(g)$ is minimal in the set $\{L \in \mathcal{L}_{TTSP} \mid S \subseteq L\}$. g is called a *minimally generalized TTSP term graph* explaining S. For example, the TTSP graph g in Fig. 1 is a minimally generalized TTSP term graph such that $\{G_1, G_2, G_3\} \subseteq L(g)$, where G_1, G_2, G_3 are TTSP graphs in Fig. 1. Finally, we show that the class $\mathcal{L}_{TTSP}$ is polynomial time inductively inferable from positive data.

There are many studies [10,12,13] for many graph theoretical problems on TTSP graphs such as *Recognition, Decomposition, Maximum independent set, Minimum dominating set, Maximum matching*. We considered the polynomial time learnabilities of ordered term tree languages and unordered term tree languages from positive data in [6,8,9]. In other learning models such as query learning, the learnability of the class of finite unions of ordered term tree languages was considered in [4,5].

2   Preliminaries

In this section, we introduce a two-terminal series parallel (TTSP, for short) graph and present a TTSP term graph having structured variables and its TTSP graph language by restricting the notion of a term graph given in [11]. Then, we formally define a membership problem and a minimal language problem for TTSP graph languages. For a set S, $|S|$ denotes the cardinality of S, that is the number of elements of S.

A *multidag* is a directed connected graph which allows multiple edges and does not contain any cycle. Let g be a multidag. For a vertex v in g, the number of edges entering v, called the *indegree* of v, is denoted by $indeg(v)$, and the number of edges leaving v, called the *outdegree* of v, is denoted by $outdeg(v)$. A vertex v with $indeg(v) = 0$ (resp., $outdeg(v) = 0$) is called a *source* (resp., a *sink*) of g. A multidag is said to be *two-terminal* if it has exactly one source and one sink. Let Λ be a finite alphabet.

Definition 1 (TTSP graphs). A TTSP graph is a two-terminal multidag defined as follows.

(1) A directed connected graph consisting of two vertices u and v, and a single edge from u to v labeled with an element in Λ is a TTSP graph. The vertices u and v are its source and its sink, respectively.
(2) For $i = 1, 2$, let G_i be a TTSP graph which has u_i as its source and v_i as its sink. Then the graph obtained by either of the following two operations is a TTSP graph.
   (a) *Parallel operation*: Identify u_1 with u_2, and identify v_1 with v_2. The resulting graph, denoted by $G_1//G_2$, has $u_1(= u_2)$ as its source and $v_1(= v_2)$ as its sink.
   (b) *Series operation*: Identify u_2 with v_1. The source and the sink of the resulting graph, denoted by $G_1 * G_2$, are u_1 and v_2, respectively.

The set of all TTSP graphs is denoted by $\mathcal{TTSP}$.

For example, for each i ($1 \leq i \leq 5$), G_i given in Fig. 1 is a TTSP graph having w_1^i as the source and w_2^i as the sink, respectively. For two TTSP graphs G_4 and G_5 given in Fig. 1, we give an example of a TTSP graph $G_4//G_5$ (resp., $G_4 * G_5$) in Fig. 3 which is obtained by applying the Parallel operation (resp., the Series operation) to G_4 and G_5.

Let $\mathcal{X}$ be an infinite alphabet such that $\Lambda \cap \mathcal{X} = \emptyset$.

Definition 2 (TTSP Term Graphs). Let $G = (V_G, E_G)$ be a TTSP graph, where V_G and E_G are sets of vertices and edges, respectively. Let E_g and H_g be a partition of E_G, i.e., $E_g \cup H_g = E_G$ and $E_g \cap H_g = \emptyset$. And let $V_g = V_G$. Then, a triplet $g = (V_g, E_g, H_g)$ is called a *TTSP term graph*. We call an element in V_g, E_g and H_g a *vertex*, an *edge* and a *variable*, respectively. A variable has an element in $\mathcal{X}$ as a label. If $H_g = \emptyset$, a TTSP term graph $g = (V_g, E_g, H_g)$ is said to be *ground* and is identified with the TTSP graph $G = (V_g, E_g)$.

From the definitions of a TTSP graph and a TTSP term graph, we note that every edge and every variable of a TTSP term graph have elements in Λ and $\mathcal{X}$ as labels, respectively, but every vertex has no label. Labels of an edge and a variable are called an *edge label* and a *variable label*, respectively. Let $g =$

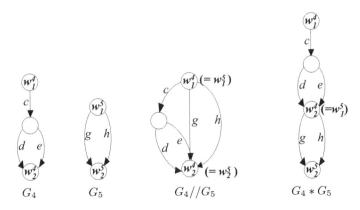

Fig. 3. TTSP graphs $G_4//G_5$ and $G_4 * G_5$, where G_4 and G_5 are given in Fig. 1

(V_g, E_g, H_g) be a TTSP term graph. An edge in E_g from a vertex u to v with a label a in Λ is denoted by a triplet (u, a, v). For an edge $(u, a, v) \in E_g$, u is said to be the *parent* of v and v is a *child* of u. In the same way, a variable in H_g, which consists of two vertices u and v and has an element x in $\mathcal{X}$ as a variable label, is denoted by a triplet $[u, x, v]$. For a variable $[u, x, v] \in H_g$, we call u the *parent port* of $[u, x, v]$ and v the *child port* of $[u, x, v]$. We call a sequence $v_1, v_2, \ldots, v_i$ of distinct vertices of g a *path* from v_1 to v_i if for any j with $1 \leq j < i$, there exists an edge or a variable which consists of v_j and v_{j+1}. In the same way as a TTSP graph, for a vertex v in a TTSP term graph g, $indeg(v)$ denotes the sum of all edges entering v and all variables whose child port is v, and $outdeg(v)$ denotes the sum of all edges leaving v and all variables whose parent port is v. A vertex v with $indeg(v) = 0$ (resp., $outdeg(v) = 0$) is called a *source* (resp., a *sink*) of g. It is easy to see that that a TTSP term graph has exactly one source and one sink. For example, g in Fig. 1 is a TTSP term graph having two variables $[u_1, x, u_2]$ and $[v_1, y, v_2]$, the source u_1 and the sink u_2.

Definition 3 (Linear TTSP term graph). A TTSP term graph g is *linear* if all variables in g have mutually distinct variable labels in $\mathcal{X}$.

The set of all linear TTSP term graphs is denoted by $\mathcal{TG}_{TTSP}$. Since a ground TTSP term graph is regarded as a TTSP graph, the set of all ground TTSP term graphs is equal to $\mathcal{TTSP}$, that is, $\mathcal{TTSP} \subset \mathcal{TG}_{TTSP}$. In this paper, we deal with linear TTSP term graphs only. Hence, unless otherwise indicated, we call a linear TTSP term graph a TTSP term graph simply.

Definition 4. For two TTSP term graphs $g = (V_g, E_g, H_g)$ and $f = (V_f, E_f, H_f)$, g and f are *isomorphic*, denoted by $g \equiv f$, if there exists a bijection $\pi : V_g \to V_f$ satisfying the following conditions.

(1) The vertices u and v are the source and the sink of g, respectively, if and only if the vertices $\pi(u)$ and $\pi(v)$ are the source and the sink of f, respectively.

(2) $(u, a, v) \in E_g$ if and only if $(\pi(u), a, \pi(v)) \in E_f$.
(3) $[u, x, v] \in H_g$ if and only if $[\pi(u), y, \pi(v)] \in H_f$ for some x and y in $\mathcal{X}$.

Definition 5 (Bindings and substitutions). Let g be a TTSP term graph with at least two vertices and x a variable label in $\mathcal{X}$. Let $\sigma = [u, u']$ be a list of two vertices in g where u is the source of g and u' is the sink of g. The form $x := [g, \sigma]$ is called a *binding* for x. A *substitution* is a finite collection of bindings $\{x_1 := [g_1, \sigma_1], \cdots, x_n := [g_n, \sigma_n]\}$, where x_i's are mutually distinct variable labels in $\mathcal{X}$ and g_i's are ground TTSP term graphs.

Let $f = (V_f, E_f, H_f)$ and $g = (V_g, E_g, H_g)$ be two TTSP term graphs. A new TTSP term graph $f\{x := [g, [u, u']]\}$ is obtained by applying the binding $x := [g, [u, u']]$ to f in the following way. Let $e = [v, x, v']$ be a variable in f. Let g' be one copy of g and w, w' the vertices of g' corresponding to u, u' of g, respectively. For the variable $e = [v, x, v']$, we attach g' to f by removing the variable e from H_f and by identifying the vertices v, v' with the vertices w, w' of g', respectively. Let $\theta = \{x_1 := [g_1, \sigma_1], \cdots, x_n := [g_n, \sigma_n]\}$ be a substitution. The TTSP term graph $f\theta$, called the *instance* of f by θ, is obtained by applying all the bindings $x_i := [g_i, \sigma_i]$ to f simultaneously. We remark that the source and the sink of f are the source and the sink of $f\theta$, respectively. For example, let g be a TTSP term graph in Fig. 1 and $\theta = \{x := [G_4, [w_1^4, w_2^4]], y := [G_5, [w_1^5, w_2^5]]\}$ a substitution, where G_4 and G_5 are TTSP graphs in Fig. 1. Then the instance $g\theta$ of the term tree g by θ is the TTSP graph G_1 in Fig. 1.

Definition 6 (TTSP graph languages). For a TTSP term graph $g \in \mathcal{TG}_{TTSP}$, the *TTSP graph language* of g, denoted by $L(g)$, is defined as $\{G \in \mathcal{TTSP} \mid G \equiv g\theta \text{ for a substitution } \theta\}$.

For a class $\mathcal{C}$, Angluin [1] and Shinohara [7] showed that if $\mathcal{C}$ has finite thickness, and the membership problem and the minimal language problem for $\mathcal{C}$ are solvable in polynomial time then $\mathcal{C}$ is polynomial time inductively inferable from positive data. In this paper, we consider the class $\mathcal{L}_{TTSP} = \{L(g) \mid g \in \mathcal{TG}_{TTSP}\}$ as a target of inductive inference.

It is easy to see that the following lemma holds, that is, for any nonempty finite set $S \subseteq \mathcal{TTSP}$, the cardinality of the set $\{L \in \mathcal{L}_{TTSP} \mid S \subseteq L\}$ is finite.

Lemma 1. *The class $\mathcal{L}_{TTSP}$ has finite thickness.*

Proof. (Sketch) Let S be a nonempty finite subset of $\mathcal{TTSP}$ and $G = (V_G, E_G)$ a TTSP graph in S. If $g = (V_g, E_g, H_g)$ is a TTSP term graph in $\mathcal{TG}_{TTSP}$ such that $L(g)$ includes G, then $|V_g| \leq |V_G|$ and $|E_g| + |H_g| \leq |E_G|$. Moreover, the number of all edge labels in G is finite. Therefore $\mathcal{L}_{TTSP}$ has finite thickness. $\square$

Next, the membership problem for $\mathcal{L}_{TTSP}$ is defined as follows.

Membership Problem for $\mathcal{L}_{TTSP}$.
Instance: A TTSP term graph $g \in \mathcal{TG}_{TTSP}$ and a TTSP graph $G \in \mathcal{TTSP}$.
Question: Does $L(g)$ contain G?

In Section 3, by presenting a polynomial time matching algorithm for solving the membership problem for the set of languages of term trees each of whose internal vertices has ordered or unordered children, we show that the membership problem for $\mathcal{L}_{TTSP}$ is solvable in polynomial time. A *minimally generalized TTSP term graph* explaining a given set of TTSP graphs $S \subseteq TTSP$ is a TTSP term graph g such that $S \subseteq L(g)$ and there is no TTSP term graph g' satisfying that $S \subseteq L(g') \subsetneq L(g)$. Then, The Minimal Language Problem (MINL Problem, for short) for $\mathcal{L}_{TTSP}$ is defined as follows.

> **Minimal Language (MINL) Problem for $\mathcal{L}_{TTSP}$.**
> **Instance**: A nonempty set of TTSP graphs $S \subseteq TTSP$.
> **Question**: Find a minimally generalized TTSP term graph $g \in T\mathcal{G}_{TTSP}$ explaining S.

In Section 4, by presenting a polynomial time algorithm for the MINL problem for $\mathcal{L}_{TTSP}$, we show that the MINL problem for $\mathcal{L}_{TTSP}$ is solvable in polynomial time. Therefore, we show the following main result.

Theorem 1. *The class $\mathcal{L}_{TTSP}$ is polynomial time inductively inferable from positive data.*

3   An Efficient Matching Algorithm for TTSP Term Graphs

In this section, we give a polynomial time matching algorithm for the membership problem for $\mathcal{L}_{TTSP}$ by presenting a matching algorithm for the membership problem for the set of languages of term trees each of whose internal vertices has ordered or unordered children. Firstly, based on notions of an ordered term tree and unordered term tree presented in [6,9], we formally define a term tree each of whose internal vertices has ordered or unordered children and call such a term tree a *partially-ordered term tree*. Moreover, we define a membership problem for the set of the languages of partially-ordered term trees. Next, we give a polynomial time matching algorithm for the membership problem for the set of the languages of partially-ordered term trees. Finally, we give a polynomial time algorithm for the membership problem for $\mathcal{L}_{TTSP}$ by reducing this problem to the membership problem for the set of the languages of a special kind of partially-ordered term trees.

3.1   Partially-Ordered Term Trees and Partially-Ordered Term Tree Languages

In this paper, unless otherwise indicated, we call a rooted tree each of whose internal vertices has ordered or unordered children a *tree* simply. We call an internal vertex having ordered children (resp., unordered children) an *o-vertex* (resp., a *u-vertex*) simply.

Definition 7 (Linear partially-ordered term trees). Let $T = (V_T, E_T)$ be a tree where V_T and E_T are sets of vertices and edges, respectively. Let E_t and H_t be a partition of E_T, i.e., $E_t \cup H_t = E_T$ and $E_t \cap H_t = \emptyset$. And let $V_t = V_T$. A triplet $t = (V_t, E_t, H_t)$ is called a *partially-ordered term tree*. A partially-ordered term tree $t = (V_t, E_t, H_t)$ is *linear* if all variables in H_t have mutually distinct variable labels in $\mathcal{X}$.

In this paper, we deal with only linear partially-ordered term trees. Hence, unless otherwise indicated, we call a linear partially-ordered term tree a *term tree* simply. $\mathcal{TT}$ denotes the set of all term trees. A term tree with no variable is called a *ground term tree*, which is a tree. $\mathcal{T}$ denotes the set of all ground term trees. In the same way as a TTSP term graph, we assume that every edge and every variable have elements in Λ and $\mathcal{X}$ as labels, respectively, but every vertex has no label. Hence, we use the same notations of an edge and a variable as those of a TTSP term graph. For a term tree t and two vertices u, v of t, u is an ancestor of v and v is a descendant of u if there exists a path from u to v. For a tree or a term tree T, we call the *height* of T the maximum length of paths from the root of T to leaves.

For a term tree t and every internal vertex u in t having ordered children, all children of u have a total ordering on all children of u. The ordering on the children of u is denoted by $<_u^t$. Let $s = (V_s, E_s, H_s)$ and $t = (V_t, E_t, H_t)$ be two term trees. We say that s and t are *isomorphic*, denoted by $s \equiv t$, if there is a bijection φ from V_s to V_t such that

(1) the root of s is mapped to the root of t by φ,
(2) u is an o-vertex of s if and only if $\varphi(u)$ is an o-vertex in t,
(3) $(u, a, v) \in E_s$ if and only if $(\varphi(u), a, \varphi(v)) \in E_t$,
(4) $[u, x, v] \in H_s$ if and only if $[\varphi(u), y, \varphi(v)] \in H_t$, for some x and y in $\mathcal{X}$, and
(5) for any o-vertex u in s which has more than one child, and for any two children u' and u'' of u, $u' <_u^s u''$ if and only if $\varphi(u') <_{\varphi(u)}^t \varphi(u'')$.

Definition 8 (Bindings and Substitutions of term trees). Let t be a term tree with at least two vertices and x a variable label in $\mathcal{X}$. Let $\sigma = [u, u']$ be a list of two vertices in t where u is the root of t and u' is a leaf of t. The form $x := [t, \sigma]$ is called a *binding* for x. A *substitution* is a finite collection of bindings $\{x_1 := [t_1, \sigma_1], \cdots, x_n := [t_n, \sigma_n]\}$, where x_i's are mutually distinct variable labels in $\mathcal{X}$ and t_i's are ground term trees.

In the same way as a TTSP term graph, for a term tree t and a substitution θ, we define an *instance* of t by θ, denoted by $t\theta$, as a term tree obtained from t by applying θ to t. We define the root of the instance $t\theta$ of t by θ as the root of t. Further we have to give a new total ordering $<_v^{f\theta}$ on every vertex v of $f\theta$. These orderings are defined in a natural way.

Definition 9 (Child orderings on an instance of a term tree). Let $s = (V_s, E_s, H_s)$ be a term tree and $\theta = \{x_1 := [t_1, \sigma_1], \cdots, x_n := [t_n, \sigma_n]\}$ a substitution. Suppose that v is an o-vertex in $s\theta$ which has more than one child and let u' and u'' be two children of v of $s\theta$. If v is the parent port of variables $[v, x_1, v_1], \ldots, [v, x_k, v_k]$ of s with $v_1 <_v^s \cdots <_v^s v_k$, we have the following four cases. Let t_i be a term tree which is substituted for $[v, x_i, v_i]$ for $i = 1, \ldots, k$. *Case 1*: If $u', u'' \in V_s$ and $u' <_v^s u''$, then $u' <_v^{s\theta} u''$. *Case 2*: If u', u'' are vertices of t_i and $u' <_v^{t_i} u''$ for some i, then $u' <_v^{s\theta} u''$. *Case 3*: If u' is a vertex of V_{t_i}, u'' is a vertex of s, and $v_i <_v^s u''$ (resp. $u'' <_v^s v_i$), then $u' <_v^{s\theta} u''$ (resp. $u'' <_v^{s\theta} u'$). *Case 4*: If u' is a vertex of t_i, u'' is a vertex of t_j ($i \neq j$), and $v_i <_v^s v_j$, then $u' <_v^{s\theta} u''$. If v is not the parent port of any variable, then u', u'' are vertices of s, therefore we have $u' <_v^{s\theta} u''$ if $u' <_v^s u''$.

For example, let t be a term tree in Fig. 2 and $\theta = \{x := [T_1, [w_1^1, w_2^1]], y := [T_2, [w_1^2, w_2^2]]\}$ a substitution, where T_1 and T_2 are trees in Fig. 2. Then the instance $t\theta$ of the term tree t by θ is the tree T in Fig. 2.

Definition 10 (Term tree languages). For a term tree $t \in \mathcal{TT}$, the *term tree language* of t, denoted by $L(t)$, is defined as $\{s \in \mathcal{T} \mid s \equiv t\theta$ for a substitution $\theta\}$.

3.2   A Polynomial Time Algorithm for Solving the Membership Problem for Term Trees

In this section, by extending the polynomial time matching algorithm in [6,9], we give a polynomial time matching algorithm for solving the membership problem for the class $\mathcal{L}_{\mathcal{TT}} = \{L(t) \subseteq \mathcal{T} \mid t \in \mathcal{TT}\}$ defined as follows.

Membership Problem for $\mathcal{L}_{\mathcal{TT}}$.
Instance: A term tree $t \in \mathcal{TT}$ and a tree in $T \in \mathcal{T}$.
Question: Does $L(t)$ contain T ?

For a tree or a term tree t and its vertex v, $t[v]$ denotes the subtree consisting of v and all descendants of v in t. We note that v is the root of $t[v]$. Let $t = (V_t, E_t, H_t)$ be a term tree and T a tree. We assume that all vertices of a term tree t are associated with mutually distinct numbers, called *vertex identifiers*. We denote by $I(u)$ the vertex identifier of $u \in V_t$. A *correspondence set*, C-set for short, is a set of vertex identifiers which are with or without parentheses.

We employ a dynamic programming method. Our matching algorithm proceeds by constructing C-sets for each vertex of a given tree T in the bottom-up manner, that is, from the leaves to the root of T. Let u be a vertex of t and $c_1, \cdots, c_m$ all ordered (or unordered) children of u. The *C-set-attaching rule* of u is of the form $I(u) \leftarrow \xi(c_1), \ldots, \xi(c_m)$, where $\xi(c_i) = (I(c_i))$ if c_i is the child port of a variable, $\xi(c_i) = I(c_i)$ otherwise. The C-set-attaching rule of t, denoted by $Rule(t)$, is defined as follows.

$$Rule(t) = \bigcup_{u \in V_t} (\{I(u) \xleftarrow{o} \xi(c_1), \ldots, \xi(c_m) \mid u \text{ is an o-vertex of } t\}$$
$$\cup \{I(u) \xleftarrow{u} \xi(c_1), \ldots, \xi(c_m) \mid u \text{ is a u-vertex of } t\}$$
$$\cup \{(I(u)) \longleftarrow (I(u)) \mid u \text{ is the child port of a variable}\}).$$

For example, for a TTSP term tree t given in Fig. 4, we give the C-set-attaching rule $Rule(t)$ of t in Fig. 4.

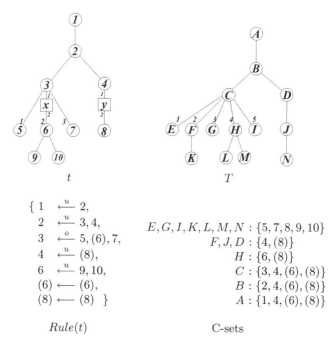

$$\{\ 1 \xleftarrow{u} 2,$$
$$2 \xleftarrow{u} 3, 4,$$
$$3 \xleftarrow{o} 5, (6), 7,$$
$$4 \xleftarrow{u} (8),$$
$$6 \xleftarrow{u} 9, 10,$$
$$(6) \longleftarrow (6),$$
$$(8) \longleftarrow (8)\ \}$$

$$E, G, I, K, L, M, N : \{5, 7, 8, 9, 10\}$$
$$F, J, D : \{4, (8)\}$$
$$H : \{6, (8)\}$$
$$C : \{3, 4, (6), (8)\}$$
$$B : \{2, 4, (6), (8)\}$$
$$A : \{1, 4, (6), (8)\}$$

$Rule(t)$ C-sets

Fig. 4. A term tree t, the C-set-attaching rule $Rule(t)$ of t, a tree T and C-sets which are attached for vertices in T

In Fig.5, we present an efficient algorithm TT-MATCHING for solving the membership problem for $\mathcal{L}_{TT}$. In TT-MATCHING, by using CS-ATTACHING given in Fig.5, we repeatedly attach a C-set to each vertex of a given tree T in the bottom-up manner, that is, from the leaves to the root of T. When we can not apply this procedure to any more vertex, if the C-set of the root of T has the vertex identifier of the root of t, then we conclude that $L(t)$ contains T. For example, given a term tree t and a tree T in Fig. 4, TT-MATCHING constructs the C-set-attaching rule $Rule(t)$ of t in Fig. 4 and attaches the C-set in Fig. 4 to each vertex of T. In this example, TT-MATCHING returns "*yes*", because the C-set of the root A of T includes the vertex identifier 1 of the root of t.

Theorem 2. *The membership problem for $\mathcal{L}_{TT}$ is solvable in polynomial time.*

Proof. (Sketch) First of all, it is easy to see that TT-MATCHING certainly terminates. Because the number of vertices not attached C-sets always decreases after executing the procedure CS-ATTACHING.

Secondly, we can prove that for a tree T and a term tree t, $L(t)$ contains T if and only if TT-MATCHING returns "yes", by showing the following claims.

(1) For a vertex u of T and a vertex v of t, $L(t[v])$ contains $T[u]$ if and only if $I(v) \in CS(u)$.
(2) Let u' be a descendant of u in T and v' the child port of a variable of t. $L(t[v'])$ contains $T[u']$ if and only if $(I(v')) \in CS(u)$.

Algorithm TT-MATCHING(T, t);
input T: a tree, t: a term tree;
        /* Let r_T and r_t be the roots of T and t, respectively; */
output "*yes*" or "*no*";
begin
    Construct the C-set-attaching rule $Rule(t)$ of t;
    For each leaf v of T, attach $CS(v) = \{I(\ell) \mid \ell$ is a leaf of $t\}$ to v;
    while there exists a vertex v of T which is not attached any C-set but all of
            whose children are attached C-sets, respectively
    do CS-ATTACHING$(v,\ Rule(t))$;
    if $CS(r_T)$ contains $I(r_t)$ **then output** "*yes*" **else output** "*no*"
end.

Procedure CS-ATTACHING$(v, Rule(t))$;
begin
1. $CS := \emptyset$;
2. Let $CS(c_1), \cdots, CS(c_m)$ be C-Sets of all children $c_1, \ldots, c_m$ of v in T, respectively;
3. **if** v is an o-vertex **then**
4.   **foreach** $I(u') \overset{o}{\longleftarrow} \xi(c_1'), \cdots, \xi(c_{m'}')$ in $Rule(t)$ **do begin**
5.   **if** for the list $\rho = [1, 2, \ldots, m]$, there is a partition $[\ell_1, \ldots, \ell_2 - 1], \ldots,$
                $[\ell_{m'}, \ldots, \ell_{m'+1} - 1]$ of ρ satisfying the following condition, where $1 = \ell_1 \leq$
                $\ell_2 \leq \cdots \leq \ell_{m'} \leq \ell_{m'+1} - 1 = m$:
            For each i $(1 \leq i \leq m')$,
                1. if $\xi(c_i') = I(c_i')$ then $\ell_i = \ell_{i+1} - 1$ and $I(c_i') \in CS(c_{\ell_i})$,
                2. if $\xi(c_i') = (I(c_i'))$ then $CS(c_{k_i})$ has $I(c_i')$ or $(I(c_i'))$
                    for some $k(i)$ $(\ell_i \leq k(i) \leq \ell_{i+1} - 1)$.
6.   **then** $CS := CS \cup \{(I(u')\}$
7.   **end**;
8. **if** v is a u-vertex **then**
9.   **foreach** $I(u') \overset{u}{\longleftarrow} \xi(c_1'), \cdots, \xi(c_{m'}')$ in $Rule(t)$ **do begin**
10.   Construct a bipartite graph $G = (\{I(c_1'), \ldots, I(c_{m'}')\}, \{CS(c_1), \ldots, CS(c_m)\}, E)$
                where E is the set $\{\{I(c_i'), CS(c_j)\} \mid 1 \leq i \leq m', 1 \leq j \leq m, I(c_i') \in CS(c_j)\}$
                $\cup \{\{I(c_i'), CS(c_j)\} \mid 1 \leq i \leq m', 1 \leq j \leq m, (I(c_i')) \in CS(c_j)$ and $\xi(c_i') = (I(c_i'))\}$;
11.   **if** for any i $(1 \leq i \leq m')$, $\xi(c_i') = I(c_i')$ **then**
12.   **if** there exists a perfect matching on G **then** $CS := CS \cup \{I(u')\}$;
13.   **else if** there exists a matching of size m' **then** $CS := CS \cup \{I(u')\}$
14.   **end**;
15. **foreach** $(I(u')) \longleftarrow (I(u'))$ in $Rule(t)$ **do**
16.   **if** there is a set in $CS(c_1), \cdots, CS(c_m)$ which has $I(u')$ or $(I(u'))$ **then**
17. $CS := CS \cup \{(I(u')\}$;
18. Attach CS to v
end;

Fig. 5. Algorithm TT-MATCHING and Procedure CS-ATTACHING

We can prove the above two claims by using an induction on the height of $T[u]$. Due to the lack of space, we omit proofs of the above claims.

Finally, we show that TT-MATCHING can solve the membership problem for $\mathcal{L}_{TT}$ in polynomial time as follows. Given a tree T and a term tree t, we consider the time complexity of TT-MATCHING. Let N and n be the numbers of vertices of T and t, respectively. We can show that the time complexity of TT-MATCHING is $O(\sum_{v \in Q_T} \Phi(v, Rule(t)))$, where Q_T is the set of internal vertices in T and $\Phi(v, Rule(t))$ is the time complexity of the procedure CS-ATTACHING for v and $Rule(t)$.

In [3], Hopcroft and Karp presented an $O(\sqrt{|V|}|E|)$ time algorithm for finding a maximum cardinality matching for a given bipartite graph $G = (V, E)$. By using the algorithm RULE_MATCHING given in [9] and Hopcroft and Karp's algorithm for the line 5 and lines 11-13 of CS-ATTACHING, respectively, the time complexity $\Phi(v, Rule(t))$ of CS-ATTACHING is $\sum_{r \in Rule(t)}(\sqrt{D_v + d_r} \times D_v \times d_r)$, where D_v is the number of children of v and d_r is the number of elements in the righthand side of the rule r. Since $d_r < D_v$, $\sum_{r \in Rule(t)} d_r = n - 1$, $\sum_{v \in Q_T} D_v = N - 1$ and for each $v \in Q_T$, $D_v \leq D_{max}$,

$$O\left(\sum_{v \in Q_T} \sum_{r \in Rule(t)} (\sqrt{D_v + d_r} \times D_v \times d_r) \right) = O(\sqrt{D_{max}} \times N \times n),$$

where $D_{max} = \max_{v \in Q_T} D_v$. Hence, this theorem holds. $\square$

3.3   A Polynomial Time Algorithm for Solving the Membership Problem for $\mathcal{L}_{TTSP}$

In this section, we present a polynomial time algorithm for solving the membership problem for $\mathcal{L}_{TTSP}$ by reducing this problem to the membership problem for $\mathcal{L}_{TT}$. A tree whose vertices have labels is called by a *colored-tree*.

Definition 11. A *decomposition tree* of a TTSP term graph is recursively defined as follows.

(1) A colored-tree consisting of only one vertex having a label a in Λ is a decomposition tree of a TTSP term graph consisting of two vertices u, v and an edge (u, a, v).
(2) A colored-tree consisting of only one vertex having a label x in $\mathcal{X}$ is a decomposition tree of a TTSP term graph consisting of two vertices u, v and an variable $[u, x, v]$.
(3) Let $T_1 = (V_1, E_1)$ and $T_2 = (V_2, E_2)$ be decomposition trees of TTSP term graphs g_1 and g_2, respectively, and r_1 and r_2 roots of T_1 and T_2, respectively. Let a be a label in Λ. Then, the following two colored-trees are decomposition trees.
    (a) A colored-tree $T = (V_T, E_T)$ having a u-vertex r_u as the root and having T_1 and T_2 as children of r is a decomposition tree of the TTSP term graph $g_1//g_2$. Namely, $V_T = V_1 \cup V_2 \cup \{r_u\}$, and $E_T = E_1 \cup E_2 \cup \{(r_u, a, r_1), (r_u, a, r_2)\}$.

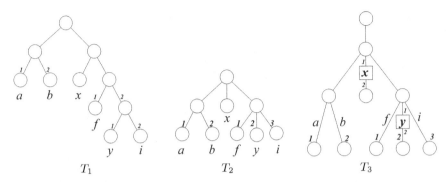

Fig. 6. A decomposition tree T_1 of the TTSP term graph g given in Fig. 1, the contraction tree T_2 of T_1 and the parse tree T_3 of g in Fig. 1

(b) A colored-tree $T = (V_T, E_T)$ having an o-vertex r_o as the root and having T_1 and T_2 as children of r with $r_1 <_r^T r_2$ is a decomposition tree of the TTSP term graph $g_1 * g_2$. Namely, $V_T = V_1 \cup V_2 \cup \{r_o\}$ and $E_T = E_1 \cup E_2 \cup \{(r_o, a, r_1), (r_o, a, r_2)\}$.

We remark that a decomposition tree is a tree whose internal vertices are o-vertices or u-vertices, all of whose leaves have labels in $\Lambda \cup \mathcal{X}$ and all of whose edges have the label a.

Let T be a decomposition tree having at least two vertices. We call an edge whose both endpoints are o-vertices (resp., u-vertices) an *o-edge* (resp., a *u-edge*). Let $e = (u, a, v)$ be an o-edge or a u-edge of T. A *contraction* of e is an operation of removing e from T, identifying u with v and, if u and v are o-vertices, updating a total ordering $<_u^{T'}$ on the o-vertex $u(= v)$ of the result tree T' as follows.

(1) For w and w' are children of u if $w <_u^T w'$ then $w <_u^{T'} w'$.
(2) For w and w' are children of v if $w <_v^T w'$ then $w <_u^{T'} w'$.
(3) For w and w' are children of u and v, respectively, if $w <_u^T v$ then $w <_u^{T'} w'$.
(4) For w and w' are children of u and v, respectively, if $v <_u^T w$ then $w' <_u^{T'} w$.

Let g be a TTSP term graph and T_g a decomposition tree of g. A *contraction tree* of T_g is the tree obtained from T_g by recursively applying contractions of o-edges and u-edges until there exists neither o-edges nor u-edges. For the TTSP term graph g in Fig. 1, for example, T_1 shown in Fig. 6 is a decomposition tree of g and T_2 shown in Fig. 6 is the contraction tree of T_1.

Let g be a TTSP term graph. And let $T = (V_T, E_T)$ be the contraction tree of a decomposition tree of g and r the root of T. A *parse tree* of g is the term tree $t_g = (V_t, E_t, H_t)$ such that $V_t = V_T \cup \{v_0\}$, $E_t = \{(v_0, a, r)\} \cup \{(u, a, v) \mid (u, a, v) \in E_T, v$ is an internal vertex of $T\} \cup \{(u, b, v) \mid (u, b, v) \in E_T, v$ is a leaf labeled with $b \in \Lambda \}$ and $H_t = \{[u, x, v] \mid (u, x, v) \in E_T, v$ is a leaf labeled with $x \in \mathcal{X}\}$. For example, for a TTSP term graph g in Fig. 1, T_3 presented in Fig. 6 is the parse tree of g.

Algorithm TTSPTG-MATCHING(G, g);
input G: a TTSP graph, g: a TTSP term graph;
output *"yes"* or *"no"*;
begin
1. $T := $ PARSE(G);   // Construct the parse tree T of G
2. $t := $ PARSE(g);   // Construct the parse tree t of g
3. **output** TT-MATCHING(T, t)
end.

Procedure PARSE(G);
input G: a TTSP term graph;
output T_G: the parse tree of G;
begin
    Construct a decomposition tree T of G;
    Construct the contraction tree T' of T;
    Construct the parse tree T_G of G from T';
    return T_G
end;

Fig. 7. Algorithm TTSPTG-MATCHING

Lemma 2. *Let g_1 and g_2 be TTSP term graphs. Let t_1 and t_2 be the parse trees of g_1 and g_2, respectively. Then, $g_1 \equiv g_2$ if and only if $t_1 \equiv t_2$.*

Proof. (Sketch) Let T_1 and T_2 be the contraction trees of g_1 and g_2, respectively. Then, from the definition of a parse tree, by showing that $g_1 \equiv g_2$ if and only if $T_1 \equiv T_2$, we can prove Lemma 2. We can show that if $g_1 \equiv g_2$ then $T_1 \equiv T_2$ by using an induction on $|E_1 \cup H_1|$, where $g_1 = (V_1, E_1, H_1)$. Moreover, we can prove that if $T_1 \equiv T_2$ then $g_1 \equiv g_2$ by using an induction on the height of a subtree of T_1.   □

Lemma 3. *Let g be a TTSP term graph and G a TTSP graph. Let T_g and T_G be the parse trees of g and G, respectively. Then, $G \in L(g)$ if and only if $T_G \in L(T_g)$.*

In Fig. 7, we give a polynomial time algorithm TTSPTG-MATCHING which solves the membership problem for $\mathcal{L}_{TTSP}$.

Theorem 3. *The membership problem for $\mathcal{L}_{TTSP}$ is solvable in polynomial time.*

Proof. It is easy to see that TTSPTG-MATCHING certainly terminates. From Lemma 3, given a TTSP graph $G = (V_G, E_G)$ and a TTSP term graph $g = (V_g, E_g, H_g)$, TTSPTG-MATCHING correctly decides whether or not $L(g)$ contains G. By using a linear time algorithm presented by Valdes et al. [12], we can construct the parse trees of G and g in time proportional to $|V_G| + |E_G|$. Moreover, by using TT-MATCHING given in Fig. 5, Line 3 can be executed in

$O(|E_G|^{1.5} \times |E_g \cup H_g|)$. Hence, for a given TTSP graph G and a given TTSP term graph g, the algorithm TTSPTG-MATCHING decides whether or not $L(g)$ contains G in $O(|E_G|^{1.5} \times |E_g \cup H_g|)$ time.   □

4   An Algorithm for Finding a Minimally Generalized TTSP Term Graph

Let Λ be a set of edge labels. In this section, we assume that $|\Lambda| = \infty$. Let g and f be TTSP term graphs. We denote $g \preceq f$ if there exists a substitution θ such that $g \equiv f\theta$. For any TTSP term graph g, we denote by $s(g)$ the TTSP term graph obtained from g by replacing each of all edges of g with a variable, i.e., for $g = (V_g, E_g, H_g)$, $s(g) = (V_g, \emptyset, H_g')$ where $H_g' = H_g \cup \{[u, x_e, v] \mid e = (u, a, v) \in E_g$ and x_e is a new variable label only for $e\}$. For any two TTSP term graphs g and f, we write $g \approx f$ if $s(g) \equiv s(f)$. It is easy to see the following lemma since $|\Lambda| = \infty$.

Lemma 4. *Let g and f be two TTSP term graphs in $\mathcal{TG}_{TTSP}$. If $g \approx f$ and $L(g) \subseteq L(f)$ then $g \preceq f$.*

The algorithm MINL-$\mathcal{TTSP}$ (Fig. 8) solves the MINL problem for $\mathcal{L}_{TTSP}$. The procedure VARIABLE-EXTENSION (Fig. 8) extends a TTSP term graph g by adding variables as much as possible while $S \subseteq L(g)$ holds. EDGE-REPLACING (Fig. 8) tries to replace each variable in g with a labeled edge if possible. We use the following three substitutions in the algorithm. These substitutions are called *refinement operators.*

$Par(h)$: Replace $h = [u, x, v] \in H_g$ with $h' = [u, x', v]$ and $h'' = [u, x'', v]$,
        where x' and x'' are new variable labels in $\mathcal{X}$.
$Ser(h)$: Replace $h = [u, x, v] \in H_g$ with $h' = [u, x', w]$ and $h'' = [w, x'', v]$,
        where w is a new vertex and x' and x'' are new variable labels in $\mathcal{X}$.
$Lab(h)_\lambda$: Replace $h = [u, x, v] \in H_g$ with (u, λ, v) where $\lambda \in \Lambda$.

Lemma 5. *Let $g \in \mathcal{TG}_{TTSP}$ be the TTSP term graph just after the procedure VARIABLE-EXTENSION for an input S finishes. Let g' be another TTSP term graph. If $S \subseteq L(g') \subseteq L(g)$ then $g' \approx g$.*

Proof. (Sketch) Let $T(g')$ and $T(g)$ be the contraction trees of decomposition trees of g' and g, respectively. In the procedure VARIABLE-EXTENSION (Fig. 8), for one variable popped up from a queue of variables, a refinement operator Par is executed first as much as possible (line 5–9), and then for each variable which is newly added by those Par operators, Ser is executed as much as possible (line 15–19). From this algorithm, we can show that $T(g)$ must be equivalent to $T(g')$ if the labels of leaves are not considered. The statement follows from this fact.   □

Lemma 6. *Let $g \in \mathcal{TG}_{TTSP}$ be the output of the algorithm MINL-$\mathcal{TTSP}$ for an input S. Let g' be a TTSP term graph such that $S \subseteq L(g') \subseteq L(g)$ holds. Then $g' \equiv g$.*

Algorithm MINL-$\mathcal{TTSP}(S)$;
input: a set of TTSP graphs $S \subseteq \mathcal{TTSP}$;
output a minimally generalized TTSP term graph g in $\mathcal{TG}_{\mathcal{TTSP}}$ for S;
begin

    $g := (\{u, v\}, \emptyset, \{[u, x, v]\})$, where u and w are new vertices and x is in $\mathcal{X}$;
    Let q be a queue $[[u, x, v]]$, which stores variables of g as elements;
    VARIABLE-EXTENSION(g, S, q); EDGE-REPLACING(g, S);
    output g
end.

Procedure VARIABLE-EXTENSION(g, S, q);
begin

 1: **while** q is not empty **do begin**
 2:     // *Parallel Extensions*
 3:     Let q' be an empty queue;
 4:     $h_{target} := pop(q)$;
 5:     $g' := g\,Par(h_{target})$;
 6:     **while** $S \subseteq L(g')$ **do begin**
 7:       $g := g'$; Let h' and h'' be two variables newly added by $Par(h_{target})$;
 8:       $h_{target} := h'$; $q' := q'\&[h'']$; $g' := g\,Par(h_{target})$.
 9:     **end**;
10:     $q' := q'\&[h_{target}]$;
11:     // *Series Extensions*
12:     **while** q' is not empty **do begin**
13:       Let q'' be an empty queue;
14:       $h_{target} := pop(q')$;
15:       $g' := g\,Ser(h_{target})$;
16:       **while** $S \subseteq L(g')$ **do begin**
17:         $g := g'$; Let h' and h'' be two variables newly added by $Ser(h_{target})$;
18:         $h_{target} := h'$; $q'' := q''\&[h'']$; $g' := g\,Ser(h_{target})$
19:       **end**;
20:       **if** q'' is not empty **then** $q := q\&q''\&[h_{target}]$
21:     **end**
22: **end**
end;

Procedure EDGE-REPLACING(g, S);
begin

    Let Λ_S be the set of edge labels which appear in S;
    foreach variable h in g **do**
      foreach edge label $\lambda \in \Lambda_S$ **do begin**
        $g' := g\,Lab(h)_\lambda$; **if** $S \subseteq L(g')$ **then begin** $g := g'$; **break end**
      end
end;

Fig. 8. Algorithm MINL-$\mathcal{TTSP}$: For a queue q, $pop(q)$ represents an operation which removes the first element from q and returns it. A notation $q\&q'$ represents a concatenation of two queues q and q'.

Proof. (Sketch) From Lemmas 4 and 5, we have $g' \preceq g$. The procedure EDGE-REPLACING (Fig. 8) replaces all possible variables with labeled edges. Therefore from $S \subseteq L(g')$, $g' \equiv g$ holds.   □

Theorem 4. *The algorithm* MINL-$\mathcal{TTSP}$ *finds a minimally generalized TTSP term graph in* $\mathcal{TG}_{\mathcal{TTSP}}$ *for a given set of TTSP graphs in* $\mathcal{TTSP}$ *in polynomial time.*

Proof. The correctness follows from Lemma 6. Let $S = \{G_1, \ldots, G_m\}$ be an input set of TTSP graphs, where $G_i = (V_i, E_i)$ $(1 \leq i \leq m)$. Let $N_{\min} = \min_{1 \leq i \leq m} |E_i|$ and $N_{\max} = \max_{1 \leq i \leq m} |E_i|$. Let $g = (V_g, E_g, H_g)$ be the TTSP term graph generated by the algorithm MINL-$\mathcal{TTSP}$ for S. It is easy to see that $|E_g \cup H_g| \leq N_{\min}$. Therefore $O(N_{\min})$ refinement operators are totally executed at lines 5–9 and 15–19 in VARIABLE-EXTENSION. From Theorem 3, one inclusion test at lines 6 or 16 needs $\sum_{1 \leq i \leq m} O(|E_i|^{1.5} \times |E_g \cup H_g|) = O(mN_{\max}^{1.5} N_{\min})$ time. Since one inclusion test is executed every refinement operation, the procedure VARIABLE-EXTENSION needs $O(mN_{\max}^{1.5} N_{\min}^2)$ time. Let Λ_S be the set of edge labels which appear in S. Since EDGE-REPLACING tries to replace variables with labeled edges at most $|\Lambda_S|N_{\min}$ times, the procedure needs totally $|\Lambda_S|N_{\min} \times O(mN_{\max}^{1.5} N_{\min})$ time. Hence the total time for all executions in the algorithm MINL-$\mathcal{TTSP}$ is $O(|\Lambda_S|mN_{\max}^{1.5} N_{\min}^2)$, which is polynomial w.r.t. S.   □

5   Conclusion

We have shown the polynomial time learnabilities of TTSP graph languages from positive data by giving a reduction to that of a special kind of term tree languages. Firstly, we have introduced a TTSP term graph as a graph pattern consisting of a TTSP graph structure and structured variables. Moreover, for a TTSP term graph g, we have defined a TTSP graph language $L(g)$ as the set of all TTSP term graphs obtained from g by substituting arbitrary TTSP graphs for all variables in g. Secondly, we have given a set $\mathcal{TT}$ of term trees such that there exists a bijection from the set $\mathcal{TG}_{\mathcal{TTSP}}$ of all TTSP term graphs to $\mathcal{TT}$, and have presented a polynomial time matching algorithm for solving the membership problem for $\mathcal{L}_{\mathcal{TTSP}} = \{L(g) \mid g \in \mathcal{TG}_{\mathcal{TTSP}}\}$ by giving a polynomial time matching algorithm for solving the membership problem for $\mathcal{L}_{\mathcal{TT}} = \{L(t) \mid t \in \mathcal{TT}\}$. Finally, we have presented a polynomial time algorithm for solving the minimal language problem for $\mathcal{L}_{\mathcal{TTSP}}$. By using the above polynomial time algorithms for $\mathcal{L}_{\mathcal{TTSP}}$, we have shown the polynomial time learnability of $\mathcal{L}_{\mathcal{TTSP}}$ from positive data.

Our results given in this paper lead us to study the learnability of languages over other classes of graphs such as series parallel graphs, outerplanar graphs, graphs of bounded treewidth (see [13]). As future works, we consider the learnability of languages on other classes of graph patterns. We also consider the learnability of $\mathcal{L}_{\mathcal{TTSP}}$ in other learning models (e.g., query learning model) and the learnability of the class of finite unions of TTSP graph languages from positive data. Moreover, we consider applications our results in this paper to other fields such as data mining from graph structured data.

References

1. D. Angluin. Finding patterns common to a set of strings. *Journal of Computer and System Science*, 21:46–62, 1980.
2. D. Angluin. Inductive inference of formal languages from positive data. *Information and Control*, 45:117–135, 1980.
3. J. Hopcroft and R. Karp. An $n^{5/2}$ algorithm for maximum matching in bipartite graphs. *SIAM J. Comput.*, 2:225–231, 1973.
4. S. Matsumoto, T. Shoudai, T. Miyahara, and T. Uchida. Learning of finite unions of tree patterns with internal structured variables from queries. *Proc. ALT-2002, Springer-Verlag, LNAI 2557*, pages 523–534, 2002.
5. Y. Matsumoto, S. Suzuki, T. Shoudai, T. Miyahara, and T. Uchida. Learning of finite unions of tree patterns with repeated internal structured variables from queries. *Proc. ALT-2003, Springer-Verlag, LNAI 2842*, pages 144–158, 2003.
6. T. Miyahara, T. Shoudai, T. Uchida, T. Kuboyama, K. Takahashi, and H. Ueda. Discovering new knowledge from graph data using inductive logic programming. *Proc. ILP-99, Springer-Verlag, LNAI 1634*, pages 222–233, 1999.
7. T. Shinohara. Polynomial time inference of extended regular pattern languages. In *Springer-Verlag, LNCS 147*, pages 115–127, 1982.
8. T. Shoudai, T. Uchida, and T. Miyahara. Polynomial time algorithms for finding unordered tree patterns with internal variables. *Proc. FCT-2001, Springer-Verlag, LNCS 2138*, pages 335–346, 2001.
9. Y. Suzuki, R. Akanuma, T. Shoudai, T. Miyahara, and T. Uchida. Polynomial time inductive inference of ordered tree patterns with internal structured variables from positive data. *Proc. COLT-2002, Springer-Verlag, LNAI 2375*, pages 169–184, 2002.
10. K. Takamizawa, T. Nishizeki, and N. Saito. Linear-time computability of combinatorial problems on series-parallel graphs. *Journal of the Association for Computing Machinery*, 29(3):623–641, 1982.
11. T. Uchida, T. Shoudai, and S. Miyano. Parallel algorithm for refutation tree problem on formal graph systems. *IEICE Trans. Inf. Syst.*, E78-D(2):99–112, 1995.
12. J. Valdes, R.E. Tarjan, and E.L. Lawler. The recognition of series parallel digraphs. *SIAM J. Comput.*, 11:298–313, 1982.
13. Jan van Leeuwen, editor. *Handbook of theoretical computer science (vol. A): algorithms and complexity*. Elsevier and MIT Press, 1990.

Classifying Relational Data
with Neural Networks

Werner Uwents and Hendrik Blockeel

Katholieke Universiteit Leuven,
Department of Computer Science,
Celestijnenlaan 200A, B-3001 Leuven
{werner.uwents, hendrik.blockeel}@cs.kuleuven.be

Abstract. We introduce a novel method for relational learning with neural networks. The contributions of this paper are threefold. First, we introduce the concept of relational neural networks: feedforward networks with some recurrent components, the structure of which is determined by the relational database schema. For classifying a single tuple, they take as inputs the attribute values of not only the tuple itself, but also of sets of related tuples. We discuss several possible architectures for such networks. Second, we relate the expressiveness of these networks to the 'aggregation vs. selection' dichotomy in current relational learners, and argue that relational neural networks can learn non-trivial combinations of aggregation and selection, a task beyond the capabilities of most current relational learners. Third, we present and motivate different possible training strategies for such networks. We present experimental results on synthetic and benchmark data sets that support our claims and yield insight in the behaviour of the proposed training strategies.

1   Introduction

Neural networks are a very popular learning method. However, their use is still mainly limited to propositional data. A number of approaches exist to extend them to structured domains, such as logical terms, trees and graphs [9, 18, 8]. However, none of them is specifically oriented to relational databases. Other research focuses on the combination of neural networks and first-order logic [3, 1], but the relational problem should be simpler to solve. In this paper, we will discuss a possible extension of propositional neural networks to relational databases.

In general, learning concepts over relational data can be considered as learning a combination of aggregation and selection. The distinction between aggregation and selection is basically a distinction between two different ways of handling sets. The difficulties for current relational learners to make combinations of both are an important motivation for our relational neural networks (RNNs).

This problem of combining aggregation and selection will be elaborated in section 2. In the context of neural networks, these combinations can be learned

S. Kramer and B. Pfahringer (Eds.): ILP 2005, LNAI 3625, pp. 384–396, 2005.

using a neural network consisting of feedforward and recurrent parts. The precise structure of relational neural networks will be explained in section 3. The training method for the networks is based on the well-known backpropagation algorithm. Some specific issues for training relational neural networks are discussed in section 4. To test our approach, four experiments were conducted and the results are presented in section 5. Finally, some conclusions will be formulated in section 6.

2   Aggregation Versus Selection

In propositional learning, an example is described by a single tuple of a fixed type (i.e., each example is described by the same attributes). In relational learning, an example is essentially described by a set of tuples that are somehow related to each other. The tuples may be of different types and the size of such a set is in general not constrained. Because of the latter property, the set cannot be reduced to a single tuple without loss of information. Thus, we can say that the essential difference between propositional and relational learning is that relational learners need to be able to handle sets in some way. They need to be able to construct tests on sets rather than on scalar attributes.

Some relational learners use what is called a propositionalisation approach: they transform the data into a propositional format using a number of predefined features, and let the propositional learner choose those features that are most relevant. Other relational learners integrate the construction of such features in the learning process.

Independent of the question whether feature construction happens before or during learning, we can also look at the type of features that are constructed. In relational algebra terminology, we can say that such features are of the form $\mathcal{F}(\sigma_C(S))$ where $\mathcal{F}$ is some aggregate function, σ_C maps the set S into its subset of elements that fulfill condition C, and S is the natural join of all the tuples linked by foreign keys to the tuple to be classified [2].

We can classify symbolic relational learners according to what kind of aggregate functions and selection conditions they consider. It then turns out that many propositionalisation approaches choose $\mathcal{F}$ from a predefined set of functions (typically count, sum, average, max, min; note that except for count, one has to specify an attribute in combination with the function, which means the actual number of features to be considered is linear in the number of attributes), and use for C a trivial or very simple condition.

Many propositionalisation approaches consider C to be true. The number of possible features then derived is still $O(fa)$ with f the number of aggregate functions and a the number of attributes. For instance, the RELAGGS approach [12, 13] considers several aggregate functions, and atomic conditions of the form $A\theta v$ with A an attribute, v a value, and θ a comparison operator. This makes the number of possible features $O(fa^2)$. Building a more complex C, for instance, one involving multiple conjuncts, is difficult because the number of possible conjunctions grows exponentially in the number of conjuncts.

Inductive logic programming systems can be considered as constituting the other side of the spectrum: they build complex conditions C but a trivial aggregate function $\mathcal{F}$ that returns true if $\sigma_C(S)$ is non-empty. Indeed, a clause such as

```
pos(X) :- page(X), hub(X), linked(X,Y), hub(Y).
```

can be seen as constructing a boolean feature that expresses whether the page is linked to by a hub. (In other words, the set of pages linking to this page that are hubs, is non-empty.) An ILP system could add further conditions on Y to the clause, possibly introducing more variables somehow linked to Y, thus making the C condition arbitrarily complex.

As ILP systems focus on the construction of the selection condition, we call them selection-oriented. Systems that include aggregate functions with only very simple selection conditions, can be called aggregation-oriented. The question then arises whether systems could be built that look for patterns involving both aggregation and non-trivial selection conditions.

It turns out that this is difficult because of several reasons. First, clearly, the feature space that has to be searched becomes much larger. Second, it is more difficult to navigate this space in an efficient and structured way. One approach towards combining aggregation and selection is the work by Knobbe et al. [11]. They propose a method to search this more complex feature space for aggregations over complex selections. In order to keep the search well-behaved, however, they have to restrict the aggregate functions to monotone ones. Vens et al. [20] propose an approach where any aggregate functions can be combined with complex selections; their random forests [4] based approach involves a random sampling of the feature space, which makes the search feasible.

Perlich and Provost [16] provide an alternative characterization of relational learners in terms of probability distributions; what we call an aggregate over a complex conjunction, in their terminology boils down to summarizing statistics of a joint distribution over multiple variables. They essentially arrive at the same conclusion with respect to the position of ILP and aggregation-oriented relational learning approaches: both are at different sides of a spectrum that is very sparsely populated (if at all) in between.

The relational learning approach that we propose here, is a non-symbolic approach, and as such does not make a distinction between searching for aggregate functions and searching for complex conditions. It does both in parallel, and yields models that may be closer to selection-oriented models, or closer to aggregation-oriented ones, depending on what seems most fit for the dataset under consideration. In addition, they are not constrained to using only predefined aggregation functions, or to using a specific kind of conditions. Our approach is unique in this respect and makes it possible to learn patterns that none of the current relational learners can model.

3   The Structure of Relational Neural Networks

The structure of a relational neural network (RNN) is based on the schema of the relational database. More specifically, it is influenced by the different types of tuples in the data set, the number of attributes for each tuple type and the relationships that are allowed. It is important that every attribute should be a real value, because these are the only values a neural network can process. Other types of attributes require a transformation to a fixed number of real values. Standard transformations for this are known.

A good starting point to address the relational learning task, is the typical setting for solving propositional learning tasks. The usual method to construct a neural network for a propositional data set is illustrated in figure 1(a). In a propositional data set, only one type of tuple is present, in this case account tuples. All tuples of this kind are characterized by three attributes, X_1, X_2 and X_T, as is shown on the left side of the figure. On the right side, a corresponding neural network is depicted. More specifically, a standard feedforward neural network with two layers is used. X_1 and X_2 are used as inputs to this network. X_T is a special attribute, because it is the target attribute, which must be predicted. This value is used to train the neural network at the output.

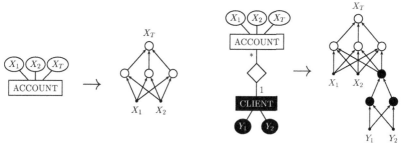

(a) Propositional case.

(b) One-to-one or many-to-one relationship, complete participation.

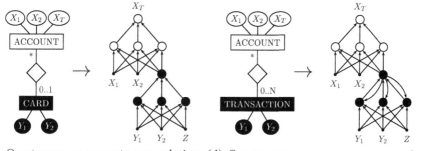

(c) One-to-one or many-to-one relationship, partial participation.

(d) One-to-many or many-to-many relationship.

Fig. 1.

Starting from this propositional case, an extension can now be proposed to solve relational tasks. This extension is developed in three steps. The first step is to handle one-to-one relationships with complete participation. Figure 1(b) shows how a new type of tuple, client, is added to the original data set. This new type of tuple has a one-to-one relationship with account tuples. It means that each account is related to exactly one client. This case could easily be transformed into a propositional case by adding some extra inputs for the related client tuple to the original network.

However, we will follow a different approach here, that is more similar to the use of combinations of aggregation and selection. When using such a combination, the related tuples are actually summarized and the result is used in predicting the target. Similarly, we can use a neural network, representing a combination of aggregation and selection, to summarize related tuples. The outputs of this network are then used as extra inputs into the original network so that it can predict the target.

In the case of a one-to-one relationship, this summarizing is performed by a feedforward network. On the right side of figure 1(b), the original propositional network, indicated by the white neurons, can still be distinguished. However, a new neural network, indicated by the black neurons, has been added. The attributes Y_1 and Y_2 of the client tuples are used as inputs to this network and the outputs are used as extra inputs to the original propositional network.

More generally, we are assuming that we have a data set with a target relation R_T and some other relations $R_1, \ldots, R_M$. The attribute set of R_i is denoted by U_i. $S_1(R)$ can now be defined as the set of all relations R_i with which R has a one-to-one or many-to-one relationship with complete participation. For all R_i in $S_1(R_T)$, where R_T is the target relation, a feedforward neural network N_i is created. The inputs I_i of N_i are equal to U_i in this case. The outputs O_i of N_i are used as inputs for N_T, so $I_T = U_T \cup (\cup_{i:R_i \in S_1(R_T)} O_i)$.

The second step is very similar to the first one. Instead of a one-to-one or many-to-one relationship with complete participation, a one-to-one or many-to-one relationship with only partial participation is considered here. This could be a relationship between account and card tuples for example, as shown in figure 1(c). Compared to the neural network for the first relational extension, only a new input Z is added. As there is only a partial participation between account and card, not every account has a card tuple related to it. The variable Z is therefore used to indicate whether there is a card tuple related to the account tuple or not. This variable has two possible values, for instance zero and one.

Again, this result can be described more formally for a target relation R_T and a number of other relations $R_1, \ldots, R_M$. Now we define $S_{01}(R)$ as the set of all relations R_i with which R has a one-to-one or many-to-one relationship with partial participation. For all R_i in $S_{01}(R_T)$ we define a feedforward network N_i, with inputs $I_i = U_i \cup \{Z\}$. The domain of Z is $\{0, 1\}$. The outputs O_i of N_i are used again as inputs for N_T, so $I_T = U_T \cup (\cup_{i:R_i \in S_1(R_T) \cup S_{01}(R_T)} O_i)$ so far.

A third step is required to facilitate handling sets, which involves recurrent neural networks. Instead of a one-to-one relationship, a one-to-many relationship is now added to the data set in the form of a relationship between account and transaction tuples. An account can not only have one or zero transactions, as with cards, but also multiple transactions. An extra variable Z is used to indicate whether or not there is at least one transaction present. To be able to process multiple transactions, the added network is now a recurrent network. It contains recurrent connections which feed signals from the second layer back into the first layer. This enables the processing of a sequence of input vectors, so the set of transaction tuples is fed in the recurrent network as a sequence.

Formally, we define the set $S_M(R)$ of all relations R_i with a one-to-many or many-to-many relationship from R to R_i. This time a recurrent network N_i is constructed for each R_i in $S_M(R_T)$. The inputs for N_i are $I_i = U_i \cup \{Z\}$, where $Z \in \{0, 1\}$. The outputs O_i of N_i are added again to the inputs of N_T, resulting in $I_T = U_T \cup (\cup_{i:R_i \in S_1(R_T) \cup S_{01}(R_T) \cup S_M(R_T)} O_i)$.

The described method of constructing a new neural network and using its outputs as extra inputs to the original network, can also be applied to further relationships. If transaction tuples have a relationship with a bank, for instance, a new network to process this bank tuple can be added and the outputs used as extra inputs to the recurrent network for transaction tuples. This results in a tree structure, where every node is a network that processes tuples of some type and its children process tuples involved in some relationship with the parent tuple. The signals are propagated from bottom to top.

The most expressive recurrent networks are fully connected networks in which each neuron is connected to all other neurons. However, this makes the number of connections increase quadratically with respect to the number of neurons and therefore we prefer the Jordan recurrent network [10]. In the latter type of recurrent network, each neuron in the second layer is connected to all neurons in the first layer. This is the same as using the outputs of the neurons in the second layer as extra inputs for the network in the next update step. The number of recurrent connections is then $n_1 \times n_2$, with n_1 and n_2 the number of neurons in the first and second layer respectively. This results in a good trade-off between expressiveness and the number of neurons and connections in the network.

4   Training

The described relational neural network consists of feedforward as well as recurrent parts. Both are trained using the backpropagation algorithm. For the feedforward parts, standard backpropagation is used and the recurrent parts are trained with backpropagation through time. The latter is an adapted version of standard backpropagation for recurrent networks [21]. The key idea to backpropagation through time is to unfold the recurrent network into a feedforward network. As many folds or copies of the original network are created as there are instances in the input sequence. All recurrent connections are converted into feedforward connections between successive folds. The resulting feedforward network is trained using standard backpropagation, except for the fact that all weight updates are added to the original weights.

As explained above, the recurrent networks are used to process sets of tuples. This means that all tuples in the set are fed in the recurrent network as a sequence. The particular order of these sequences is arbitrary, as there is no real order in the set of tuples. To avoid imposing an artificial order on the data, it is possible to reshuffle or reorder these sequences randomly to train the network. Thus, the variation in the data presented to the network is increased, which should improve learnability. Reshuffling can also be done for testing where each sample is tested in different orders and the results are averaged, which should improve prediction.

There are two ways of reshuffling for training. In a first setting, simply reshuffle the training set after every iteration. This method presents a maximum of variation to the network, at least in the long term. Another possibility is to expand the original training set with a number of reshuffled copies. The latter method will increase the size of the training set initially, but during the training process the training samples remain the same. At first sight, reshuffling after every iteration would seem to give the best result as it produces maximal variation in the data presented to the network. However, it also changes the gradient from one iteration to the next, which can make it difficult for the training algorithm to converge.

5   Experiments

The described approach was tested on four different data sets. Experiments were conducted using ten-fold cross-validation and the results are averages over five different runs. Three different settings were used for training: without reshuffling, using continuous reshuffling and using ten reshuffled copies. When reshuffling is used for training, the accuracy on the test set is measured over twenty reshuffled tests for each sample. At least two questions should be answered by conducting these experiments. First, we want to know how the results obtained with relational neural networks compare to results for other systems, such as first-order random forests (FORFs) [20]. This should indicate whether our RNNs are indeed able to learn relational concepts. Second, the effect of reshuffling on learning such concepts should become clear.

5.1   Musk

Musk is actually a multi-instance data set, but multi-instance learning can be seen as a special, simple case of relational learning [5]. The data set consists of two parts, each containing a number of molecules and a bag of conformations for each molecule [14]. A conformation is described by 166 numerical attributes. Each molecule has to be classified as musk or not. There are 92 molecules in the first data set and 102 in the second one. A further difference between the two data sets is the average number of conformations per molecule. For the first data set there are 5 conformations per molecule on average, for the second data set the average is 65.

Table 1. Accuracies for relational neural networks on all tested data sets. Average accuracy and standard deviation over five runs are given for ten-fold cross-validation.

	no reshuffling	continuous reshuffling	10 reshuffled copies
musk 1	80±3%	82±3%	84±3%
musk 2	78±2%	79±2%	80±2%
trains 1	76±4%	91±3%	93±3%
trains 2	74±4%	86±3%	87±3%
trains 3	86±3%	94±3%	96±3%
trains 4	83±4%	85±3%	89±3%
mutagenesis	86±3%	88±3%	86±4%
diterpenes	81±2%	78±2%	79±2%

Table 2. Accuracies on musk data set compared to other methods. Results were obtained from [6] and [17].

	method	musk 1	musk 2
1	iterated-discrim APR	92.4%	89.2%
2	GFS elim-kde APR	91.3%	80.4%
3	GFS elim-count APR	90.2%	75.5%
4	GFS all-positive APR	83.7%	66.7%
5	all-positive APR	80.4%	72.6%
6	simple backpropagation	75.0%	67.7%
7	multi-instance neural networks	88.0%	82.0%
8	C4.5	68.5%	58.8%
9	1-nearest neighbor (euclidean distance)	/	75%
10	neural network (standard poses)	/	75%
11	1-nearest neighbor (tangent distance)	/	79%
12	neural network (dynamic reposing)	/	91%
13	relational neural networks	84%	80%

Table 1 shows the results obtained with relational neural networks for different settings. These results illustrate that reshuffling gives an improvement of the final accuracy and that copy reshuffling works better than continuous reshuffling in this case. Table 2 compares the best results for relational neural networks with the results for other methods. These other results come from [6], except for the results for multi-instance neural networks [17]. It should be noted that methods 11 and 12 require computation of the molecular surface, which cannot be done using the feature vectors in the data set.

Comparing the different neural network approaches, we see that RNNs do not perform as well as multi-instance neural networks, but substantially better than simple backpropagation. This method ignores the multi-instance character of the musk data set and treats all of the positive instances as positive examples. This is actually some kind of propositional approach. As RNNs perform clearly better than this method, it seems that they are able to learn a real multi-instance concept, which is also a relational concept.

5.2 Trains

The trains data set is an artificially created data set containing a number of trains. Every train consists of a number of cars, carrying some load. Some of the trains are eastbound, the others are westbound. This target concept is based on the properties of the cars of a train and their loads. A data generator for this train problem was used to create the data set [15]. A simple (trains 1 and 2) and a more complicated concept (trains 3 and 4) were defined to generate the data sets. The simple concept defines trains that are eastbound as trains with at least two circle loads, the other trains are westbound. The more complicated concept defines westbound trains as trains that have more than seven wheels in total but not more than one open car with a rectangle load, or trains that have more than one circle load; the other trains are eastbound. There is also a distinction between data sets without noise (trains 1 and 3) and those with 5% noise added (trains 2 and 4).

Training was done with learning rate 0.1 and during 5000 iterations. Results for the different settings can be found in table 1 and a comparison with first-order random forests (FORFs) [20] in table 5. Apparently, the first two data sets, containing 100 samples, are too small to train the network sufficiently. Therefore, better performance for these data sets is obtained with FORF. For data set 3 and 4, the results are very similar to those obtained with FORF. Using reshuffling clearly outperforms no reshuffling for this experiment. This indicates that reshuffling does indeed help to learn relational concepts.

5.3 Mutagenesis

Mutagenesis is a well-known ILP data set [19]. It consists of 230 molecules which have to be classified as mutagenic or not. A structural description of each molecule is given, stating all atoms of the molecule and the bonds between them. In this case, best results were achieved when using 20% of the training set as validation set to do early stopping. This means that after every training iteration the performance on this validation set and on the test set is computed and after training the iteration with the lowest validation error is used to select the test accuracy.

The network was trained for 20000 iterations with a learning rate of 0.5. The large number of training iterations was needed because convergence seems to be quite slow for this experiment. Results for different settings are shown in table 1. Best results are obtained using continuous reshuffling. The reason that this works better than copy reshuffling, could be the large number of training iterations. A comparison with FORF can be found in table 4. For this data set, RNNs achieve substantially better results than FORFs.

5.4 Diterpenes

For the last experiment, the diterpenes data set is used [7]. This data set contains information about 1503 diterpene structures. For each of the 20 carbon atoms

Table 3. Accuracy results for the diterpenes data set compared to other systems. Results for FOIL, RIBL and ICL come from [7], the result for FORF is obtained from [20].

RNN	FORF	FOIL	RIBL	ICL
81%	93%	78%	91%	86%

Table 4. Accuracy results for the mutagenesis data set compared to those for FORF [20]

RNN	FORF
88%	79%

Table 5. Results for trains data sets compared with FORF

	concepts	samples	noise	RNN	FORF
trains 1	simple	100	none	93%	100%
trains 2	simple	100	5%	87%	93%
trains 3	complex	800	none	96%	96%
trains 4	complex	800	5%	89%	90%

in the diterpene structure, multiplicity and frequency are given. The results are shown in table 1. Again, training was done over 20000 iterations and with 0.5 learning rate. A comparison with other results can be found in table 3. For this data set, relational neural networks do not perform very well and reshuffling gives worse results than using no reshuffling at all. It is not very clear why this is so.

5.5   Experimental Conclusions

One must be careful to draw straightforward conclusions from the four experiments as a whole. It seems to be partially problem dependent which training setting gives the best results. Copy reshuffling improves accuracy for musk and trains for instance, but for mutagenesis continuous reshuffling is better and best results for diterpenes are obtained without any reshuffling. Moreover, some results are rather sensitive to changes in the training setting. Even small changes for parameters can produce quite different results. This is also the reason why the training methodology is not uniform in the conducted experiments. There is not one setting that produces acceptable results for all experiments.

Another problem is that convergence tends to be slow. Probably, this is partially due to the use of recurrent neural networks. It is known that these networks are harder to train than feedforward networks. The fact that we increased the number of layers, decreases learnability further. These problems are related to the use of backpropagation as training method, which has problems to backpropagate an error signal over too long distances.

However, some conclusions can be made. For instance, the improvement of the accuracy when using reshuffling for the trains data set is remarkable. Because this data set is artificially created, we are sure that the concept to be learned is a combination of aggregation and selection. As the results improve so much, this is a strong indication that reshuffling is indeed helping to learn this kind of concepts. If we look at the overall accuracies achieved for the different data sets and compare them to other approaches, we can also conclude that RNNs seem to be able to express relational concepts quite well.

6   Conclusions

In this paper, we presented a novel neural network approach to relational learning. The fact that current relational learners are very limited in making combinations of aggregation and selection is an important motivation for this work. By using neural networks, such combinations can be made in an implicit way and we should be able to avoid a bias to either aggregation or selection.

The structure of a RNN is based on the relational database schema. It is a combination of feedforward and recurrent networks to process a tuple together with its related tuples. The fact that sets of tuples are fed in the recurrent networks as sequences, is also used to improve training and testing. By reordering these sequences, the variation in the data can be increased, which should increase learnability.

Experiments on four different data sets give some insight in the capacities of RNNs. They seem to be able to learn relational concepts reasonably well. The beneficial effect of reshuffling in training and testing could also be demonstrated. But issues as verifying what concepts are actually learned and a training algorithm that is better suited to train this kind of neural networks, are worth further investigation. Understandability is an important issue in ILP, but it is a known problem for neural networks. A lot of work has been done in rule extraction from neural networks, but relational neural networks present some complications. With regard to the training method, a genetic algorithm could be a better method than backpropagation.

Acknowledgements

Hendrik Blockeel is a postdoctoral fellow of the Fund for Scientific Research of Flanders (FWO-Vlaanderen). Werner Uwents is supported by IDO/03/006 'Development of meaningful predictive models for critical disease'.

References

[1] R. Basilio, G. Zaverucha, and V. C. Barbosa. Learning logic programs with neural networks. In *Proceedings of the Eleventh International Conference on Inductive Logic Programming*, Lecture Notes in Artificial Intelligence. Springer-Verlag, 2001.
[2] H. Blockeel and M. Bruynooghe. Aggregation versus selection bias, and relational neural networks. In *IJCAI-2003 Workshop on Learning Statistical Models from Relational Data, SRL-2003, Acapulco, Mexico, August 11, 2003*, 2003.

[3] M. Botta, A. Giordana, and R. Piola. Fonn: Combining first order logic with connectionist learning. In *Proceedings of the 14th International Conference on Machine Learning*, pages 46–56. Morgan Kaufmann, 1997.

[4] L. Breiman. Random forests. *Machine Learning*, 45(1):5–32, 2001.

[5] L. De Raedt. Attribute-value learning versus inductive logic programming: the missing links (extended abstract). In D. Page, editor, *Proceedings of the Eighth International Conference on Inductive Logic Programming*, volume 1446 of *Lecture Notes in Artificial Intelligence*, pages 1–8. Springer-Verlag, 1998.

[6] T. G. Dietterich, R. H. Lathrop, and T. Lozano-Pérez. Solving the multiple-instance problem with axis-parallel rectangles. *Artificial Intelligence*, 89(1-2):31–71, 1997.

[7] S. Džeroski, S. Schulze-Kremer, K. R. Heidtke, K. Siems, D. Wettschereck, and H. Blockeel. Diterpene structure elucidation from ^{13}C NMR spectra with inductive logic programming. *Applied Artificial Intelligence*, 12(5):363–384, July-August 1998.

[8] P. Frasconi, M. Gori, and A. Sperduti. A general framework for adaptive processing of data structures. *IEEE-NN*, 9(5):768–786, September 1998.

[9] C. Goller and A. Küchler. Learning task-dependent distributed representations by backpropagation through structure. In *Proceedings of the IEEE International Conference on Neural Networks (ICNN-96)*, pages 347–352, 1996.

[10] M. I. Jordan. Attractor dynamics and parallelism in a connectionist sequential machine. In *Proceedings of the Eighth Annual Conference on Cognitive Science*, pages 531–546, 1986.

[11] A. Knobbe, A. Siebes, and B. Marseille. Involving aggregate functions in multi-relational search. In *Principles of Data Mining and Knowledge Discovery, Proceedings of the 6th European Conference*, pages 287–298. Springer-Verlag, August 2002.

[12] M.-A. Krogel and S. Wrobel. Transformation-based learning using multi-relational aggregation. In *Proceedings of the Eleventh International Conference on Inductive Logic Programming*, pages 142–155, 2001.

[13] M.-A. Krogel and S. Wrobel. Facets of aggregation approaches to propositionalization. In T. Horváth and A. Yamamoto, editors, *Proceedings of the Work-in-Progress Track at the 13th International Conference on Inductive Logic Programming*, pages 30–39, 2003.

[14] C. Merz and P. Murphy. UCI repository of machine learning databases [http://www.ics.uci.edu/~mlearn/mlrepository.html], 1996. Irvine, CA: University of California, Department of Information and Computer Science.

[15] D. Michie, S. Muggleton, D. Page, and A. Srinivasan. To the international computing community: A new east-west challenge. Technical report, Oxford University Computing Laboratory, Oxford, UK, 1994. Available at ftp.comlab.ox.ac.uk.

[16] C. Perlich and F. Provost. Aggregation-based feature invention and relational concept classes. In *Proceedings of the ninth ACM SIGKDD international conference on Knowledge discovery and data mining*, pages 167–176. ACM Press, 2003.

[17] J. Ramon and L. De Raedt. Multi instance neural networks. In *Proceedings of the ICML-Workshop on Attribute-Value and Relational Learning*, 2000.

[18] A. Sperduti and A. Starita. Supervised neural networks for the classification of structures. *IEEE Transactions on Neural Networks*, 8(3):714–735, May 1997.

[19] A. Srinivasan, R. King, and D. Bristol. An assessment of ILP-assisted models for toxicology and the PTE-3 experiment. In *Proceedings of the Ninth International Workshop on Inductive Logic Programming*, volume 1634 of *Lecture Notes in Artificial Intelligence*, pages 291–302. Springer-Verlag, 1999.

[20] C. Vens, A. Van Assche, H. Blockeel, and S. Džeroski. First order random forests with complex aggregates. In R. Camacho, R. King, and A. Srinivasan, editors, *Proceedings of the 14th International Conference on Inductive Logic Programming*, pages 323–340. Springer, 2004.

[21] P. J. Werbos. Back propagation through time: What it does and how to do it. In *Proceedings of the IEEE*, volume 78, pages 1550–1560, 1990.

Efficient Sampling in Relational Feature Spaces

Filip Železný

Czech Technical University in Prague,
Technická 6, 166 27, Prague 6, Czech Republic
zelezny@fel.cvut.cz

Abstract. State-of-the-art algorithms implementing the 'extended transformation approach' to propositionalization use backtrack depth first search for the construction of relational features (first order atom conjunctions) complying to user's mode/type declarations and a few basic syntactic conditions. As such they incur a complexity factor exponential in the maximum allowed feature size. Here I present an alternative based on an efficient reduction of the feature construction problem on the propositional satisfiability (SAT) problem, such that the latter involves only Horn clauses and is therefore tractable: a model to a propositional Horn theory can be found without backtracking in time linear in the number of literals contained. This reduction allows to either efficiently enumerate the complete set of correct features (if their total number is polynomial in the maximum feature size), or otherwise efficiently obtain a random sample from the uniform distribution on the feature space. The proposed sampling method can also efficiently provide an unbiased estimate of the total number of correct features entailed by the user language declaration.

1 Introduction

A major stream of approaches to propositionalization [6] is based on constructing relational features in the form of Datalog queries, such as the one below

$$\texttt{car(C)} \land \texttt{load(C,L)} \land \texttt{small(L)} \land \texttt{triangle(L)}$$

from the well-known Michalski's east-west trains domain, querying whether there is car carrying a small, triangle shaped load (in a train). In this paper I constrain myself to expressions that are conjunctions of non-negated atoms without constants (thus avoiding atoms such as `numOfWheels(Car, 2)` and rather considering an atom `has2Wheels(Car)`). Much like traditional ILP systems suffer from two sources of computational complexity–the size of the hypothesis space and the complexity of proving examples from a hypothesis–the burden of this propositionalization approach is also twofold, represented by these factors:

1. the complexity of constructing a syntactically well-formed feature definition
2. the complexity of finding the extension of a feature, ie. the subset of data instances for which the feature holds true.

S. Kramer and B. Pfahringer (Eds.): ILP 2005, LNAI 3625, pp. 397–413, 2005.

A lot of research has been conducted to make subsumption check based proving (ie. the problem underlying Item 2) more efficient. This includes both enhancements preserving completeness and correctness [2] as well as those representing tractable approximations to the subsumption check [11]. In contrast, Item 1 is in state-of-the-art propositionalization systems approached through an exhaustive, usually depth-first search, which of course becomes quickly intractable once language bounds (eg. the maximum number of atoms in a feature) are softened.

Note the complexity trade-off between Items 1 and 2. The finer conditions are stipulated on the acceptable syntactical form of a feature, the fewer correct features exist in the search space, decreasing the effort needed to exert in Item 2, but the more difficult it may be to find a correct feature if one resorts to a naive backtrack search.

Correct Feature. In this paper, I constrain the notion of a well-formed feature[1] in a natural way, by combining two popular language-bias specification techniques. First, as in many successful ILP systems (such as Progol [8]), I assume the user to pre-specify the set of predicates which can be employed in a feature, as well as *types* and *modes* of each argument place therein. In a correct feature, no variable appears at two, differently typed arguments. For each argument, the mode is either '+', or '−' and a variable occurrence at that argument is called an input, or output, respectively. Furthermore, the maximum *branching factor* (maximum number of occurrences of a given predicate in a feature with the same input variables[2]), and the maximum *size* of a feature (maximum number of atoms contained), are pre-set. Second, I impose the provisos suggested in the Extended Transformation Approach propositionalization framework [7], namely that (i) each variable in a feature is used exactly once as an output and at least once as an input, (ii) no correct feature is an atom-wise union of two or more correct features.

Conditions (i) and (ii) actually distinguish the feature construction process from the clause-enumeration procedures at the heart of most ILP systems. While (i) is motivated primarily by the ease of human interpretation of a relational feature, (ii) prevents the assembly of features by simply conjoining simpler ones– an excess expressivity given that propositional algorithms, to which the resulting features are subjected, are themselves able to construct conjunctions.

Assume the user declaration is specified, including n, β representing the bounds on the feature size and branching-factor, respectively. Here I mainly show that if the declaration obeys certain easily acceptable restrictions, one can either efficiently (in time polynomial in n and β) enumerate the complete set of correct features (if the number N of actually existing correct features is polynomial in n), or efficiently obtain a polynomial-size random sample of correct features (if N is exponential in n) from a uniform probability distribution on the set of all correct features. Although it is not known beforehand, whether or not N is polynomial in n given a declaration and varying n, running the two respective

---

[1] I will use interchangeably the terms 'feature', 'correct feature' and 'well-formed feature'.

[2] This parameter is called *recall* in Progol.

algorithms in parallel would of course result in obtaining one of the two results efficiently. The fundamental technique I exploit is a polynomial-time reduction of the feature-construction problem onto an instance of HORN-SAT, ie. finding a model of a propositional Horn theory. It is interesting to note that HORN-SAT is the only non-trivial tractable subclass of the generally NP-complete SAT problem [10]. A model to a propositional Horn theory can be found without backtracking, in time linear in the number of literals in the theory [5].

Let me now present three specific reasons why the method here presented is an important contribution to both propositionalization and state-of-the-art relational learning in general.

1. The first reason is practical. Even if a user requires to obtain the complete set of correct features rather than a sample, and thus resorts to an exhaustive enumerative method, there is presently no way of efficiently determining how large a set of correct features is entailed by the current language declaration. Thus the typical propositionalization modus operandi consists of repeated executions of the feature construction process stopped after a long run time and an unacceptable number of features generated, followed by iterative re-tuning of the declaration.[3] A consequence of my sampling method is that the total number of correct features can be efficiently and accurately estimated prior to enumerating all features.

2. Recent research [14,4,1] indicates the possibility that rather than using an exhaustive set of features enumerated from a small space of simple expressions, it may be beneficial to uniformly sample (eg. the same number of) features from a larger space (for which an exhaustive method is intractable), allowing for more descriptive complexity as well as variability between the features. My method provides the necessary bits for this sake.

3. A recent, very interesting paper [13] shows the advantages of constructing random-forest classifiers based on relational features. A random sample of features provided by the method presented here can be used as an input to construct a randomized decision tree, as a component of a random forest.[4] Experimental evaluation of this idea is however out of the scope of this paper.

2   Correct Features as HORN-SAT Solutions

Before exposing details, here is a brief outline of my strategy. Recall the definition of a *correct feature* from the introduction. Let me call a finite set of constant-free Datalog atoms[5] an expression and, given a mode/type declaration, let every expression be called *proper* if all its variables have exactly one output and at least one input occurrence, and *connected* if it all its atoms are pairwise connected.

---

[3] This argument of course follows solely from my subjective experience.

[4] My method only generates one of two types of features considered in the mentioned paper, there called *selective* features.

[5] For simplicity I work with sets, although examples of such expressions will be shown as conjunctions of the elements.

Two atoms a and b in an expression are connected if they share a variable or both a and b are connected with another atom c in the expression. Clearly, any correct feature is connected (remind the requirement of the undecomposability of a feature into two or more features). In this section, the adjective *polynomial (exponential)* will stand for *polynomial (exponential) in n* (the maximum feature size). By definition of the branching factor β, it must hold $\beta \leq n$, so for simplicity of analysis, I will use the upper-bound $\beta := n$ and then make sure that the time complexity of the algorithm is polynomial in n implying it is also polynomial in β.

I first construct a 'bottom feature' $\perp$ – a proper expression complying to the type/mode declaration, which is an atom-wise superset (up to variable renaming) of all correct features. Slight restrictions on the user declaration will guarantee that $\perp$ exists, has a polynomial number of atoms, and can be constructed in polynomial time. As $\perp$ complies to typing and moding constraints, so do all its subsets. What remains to do then is to find all proper, connected subexpressions of $\perp$ of size $\leq n$, A straightforward verification of all subexpression of size $\leq n$ would obviously require exponential time, however, I show that this problem may be efficiently reduced onto a polynomial-size HORN-SAT instance, for which an efficient solving algorithm exists.

2.1   Bottom Feature Construction

I now regard the first step, ie. constructing the bottom feature $\perp$ given a type/ mode declaration and n, the maximum feature size. To encode a declaration, I employ a simple form used with slight variations in numerous ILP systems. Here, available predicates are listed with mode and type indicators plugged into the argument places. An example declaration follows

car(-c), hasRoof(+c), load(+c,-l), triangle(+l), box(+l)

The modes -/+ denote outputs/inputs, respectively, and c, l represent the respective car and load argument types. I now impose two natural, yet important restrictions on declarations. First, a declaration has a finite size and each declared predicate has a finite arity. Second, there exists a partial irreflexive order $\prec$ on types, such that for any two types t_1, t_2 it holds $t_1 \prec t_2$ whenever t_1 occurs at an input position of a declared predicate and t_2 appears at an output position in the same predicate. This assumption is trivially met by the example declaration above (here $c \prec l$). The declaration would remain valid if eg. tows(+c,+c) was added to it, but not if tows(+c,-c) was added. Finally, for clarity of explanation I will only consider predicates with at most one output argument, although the further presented principles do not require that condition.

To demonstrate the construction of $\perp$, I will distinguish two cases: (SI) any declared predicate has at most one input, (MI) some have two or more inputs. I will first exemplify the former case, using the sample declaration above. Due to the $\prec$ existence and the assumption (SI), every correct feature can be represented as a tree, where vertices correspond to atoms and edges connect pairs of atoms where one contains a variable as an output and the other contains the same

$$\beta \leq n \begin{cases} \texttt{car(C)} -\texttt{hasRoof(C)} \\ \qquad\quad -\texttt{load(C, L1)} -\texttt{box(L1)} \\ \qquad\qquad\qquad\qquad -\texttt{triangle(L1)} \\ \qquad\quad -\texttt{load(C, L2)} -\texttt{box(L2)} \\ \qquad\qquad\qquad\qquad -\texttt{triangle(L2)} \\ \qquad\qquad \vdots \qquad\qquad \vdots \\ \qquad\quad -\texttt{load(C, Ln)} \ \vdots \end{cases}$$

$$\underbrace{\phantom{-\texttt{load(C, Ln)} \qquad\qquad\qquad\qquad\qquad\qquad}}_{\Delta \leq \Delta_{max}}$$

Fig. 1. A tree graph representing the bottom feature $\perp$ whose size is a polynomial function of n. Vertices correspond to atoms in $\perp$. β denotes the branching factor, Δ stands for the tree depth, bounded by some constant Δ_{max}.

variable as an input. Similarly, $\perp$ also corresponds to a tree, which must contain all correct features as root-sharing subtrees. The tree form of $\perp$, whose size depends on n, is sketched in Fig. 1.

Due to the feature connectivity requirement and assumption (SI), no correct feature may regard two or more cars: such an expression would necessarily be disconnected.[6] Therefore, only one `car/1` atom is present in $\perp$, as the root. Due to the assumed partial ordering of types $\prec$ and the finiteness of the declaration, the depth of the tree is bounded by some constant Δ_{max}. Also its branching factor can be upper-bounded by n (eg. no feature of size at most n can address more loads than n; this upper bound may of course be quite easily improved). The number of nodes, ie. the size of the bottom set is thus of order $n^{\Delta_{max}}$, ie. polynomial.

Consider now the more general (MI) case where a declaration contains a predicate with multiple inputs. This is a natural case in domains where a feature may relate two substructures of the individual. An example declaration follows capturing a simplified version of the Mutagenesis problem [12].

$$\texttt{atm(-a), crb(+a), nit(+a), oxy(+a), hyd(+a),}$$
$$\texttt{bond(+a,+a,-b), single(+b), double(+b)}$$

With respect to the graph representation I introduced in the previous paragraph, due to the presence of the `bond/3` predicate with 2 inputs, correct features no longer form a tree and neither does $\perp$.[7] The proof of $\perp$ still having a polynomial size now relies on the fact that $\perp$'s atoms can still be organized in 'layers' (corresponding to the columns in Fig. 2 on Page 404), using the assumed partial type order $\prec$. Up to n atoms are in the first layer, so the first layer generates $O(n)$ output variables. The cardinality of the second layer is thus $O(n^I)$, where

---

[6] I ignore the case when the declaration has more than one predicate with only output variables (such as `car/1`), while assuming (SI): again due to the connectivity requirement, this case can be treated as two separate feature construction problems.

[7] Also, the `atm/1` predicate will need to be placed n times in $\perp$ with distinct output variables, unlike the `car/1` predicate in the (SI) case.

I is the maximum number of input arguments in an atom, among atoms in the declaration. The third layer may use $O(n^I)$ variables, so its cardinality is at most $O(n^{I \times I})$. Thus in general, $O(|\bot|)$ may be upper bounded by $n^{I^{\Delta_{max}}}$. Since the exponential factor is a constant, I accept this as a polynomial bound as I intended to achieve in this section.[8]

2.2   Avoiding Improperness

Having constructed $\bot$, I now proceed to the problem of how to efficiently extract $\bot$'s proper subexpressions of size $\leq n$. The basic idea is to assign a propositional variable to each atom of $\bot$ and use the variables to construct a clause set, encoding the properness requirements, so that every solution of the clause set corresponds to a proper expression. Interestingly, encoding the constraints turns out to require only Horn clauses. Again, I will illustrate the procedure by way of example in the East-West train domain, continuing with its previous predicate declaration. Let $n = 3$. Then $\bot =$

$$\underset{P_1}{\texttt{car(C)}} \wedge \underset{P_2}{\texttt{hasRoof(C)}} \wedge \underset{P_3}{\texttt{load(C,L)}} \wedge \underset{P_4}{\texttt{triangle(L)}} \wedge \underset{P_5}{\texttt{box(L)}}$$

is a correct bottom feature. Note that using the branching-factor upper-bound $\beta := n$ used above for bounding $|\bot|$, I would include three $\texttt{load/2}$ atoms into $\bot$ (refer to the corresponding branches in Fig. 1), however, in this case all correct features of length up to 3 atoms are clearly subsets (up to variable renaming) of this shorter $\bot$. As the lower line indicates, I assign one propositional variable (P_1 to P_5) to each atom. A truth assignment to these variables will represent a $\bot$'s subexpression as follows: if and only if a variable has the *false* value, the corresponding atom *belongs* to the subexpression.[9] As the reader will easily verify, the following set of clauses is satisfied if and only if each variable present in the subexpression has at least one input occurrence (the first clause relating to C, the second to L).

$$\neg P_2 \vee \neg P_3 \vee P_1 \tag{1}$$
$$\neg P_4 \vee \neg P_5 \vee P_3 \tag{2}$$

In each clause, I introduced a negative literal corresponding to each atom containing the respective variable as an input, and the positive literal in each clause corresponds to the atom with an output appearance of the respective variable. Since I assume each variable to have exactly one output occurrence, I necessarily obtain Horn clauses. It of course remains to make sure that the mentioned

---

[8] This, in general rapid polynomial growth of $|\bot|$ may be reduced by imposing a small branching factor bound β.

[9] With this choise the dual propositional problem will acquire a HORNSAT form. I may equally have assigned the *true* value to denote the membership thus arriving instead at a NON-HORNSAT problem, ie. one with at most one negative literal in each clause.

assumption is indeed satisfied. Note first that by construction of $\perp$ (refer to Fig. 1), each output argument is assigned a distinct variable and therefore each variable in any subexpression of $\perp$ appears as an output *at most* once. I now need to make sure that it appears as an output *at least* once. Evidently, this is the case if and only if the following four clauses, which I add to the constructed clause set, are satisfied (the upper two for C, the lower two for L).

$$\neg P_1 \vee P_2 \qquad \neg P_1 \vee P_3 \qquad\qquad (3)$$
$$\neg P_3 \vee P_4 \qquad \neg P_3 \vee P_5 \qquad\qquad (4)$$

Here the negative (positive) literals correspond to input (output) occurrences of the respective variables in $\perp$. Since, as the reader has already seen, there is at most one output occurrence of each variable, also these clauses are necessarily Horn. Let me now determine the total number of Horn clauses obtained in general by the procedure so far. A simple insight yields that I get one clause per every output argument in $\perp$ (such as the two clauses 1 - 2) and one clause per every input in $\perp$ (such as the four clauses 3 - 4). Due to assigning a single propositional variable to every atom in $\perp$, the number of literals in each clause is at most $|\perp|$. As I have constructed a polynomial size $\perp$, the resulting HORN-SAT instance (consisting of all clauses 1 - 4) has a polynomial number of clauses with a polynomial number of literals in each. A trivial solution simply makes true all involved propositional variables (note the omnipresence of a positive literal). To avoid this useless solution–corresponding to the empty feature–I append one more Horn clause

$$\neg P_1 \vee \neg P_2 \vee \ldots \vee \neg P_5 \qquad\qquad (5)$$

2.3 Avoiding Disconnected Features

At this stage, whenever a solution satisfying all clauses constructed so far makes false n or fewer of the propositional variables, it corresponds to a correct feature. Although I constructed no dedicated clauses guaranteeing connectedness of extracted expressions, due to the (SI) character of the particular example at hand, this property is satisfied automatically: from Fig. 1 it is easy to see that any disconnected subgraph of the tree would represent an expression with an input variable with no output occurrence. Such a non-proper expression would be eliminated by the so-far constructed clauses. However, the (MI) setting allows for proper yet disconnected expressions such as

$$\mathtt{atm(A)} \wedge \mathtt{crb(A)} \wedge \mathtt{atm(B)} \wedge \mathtt{oxy(B)}$$

–an example taken from the Mutagenesis domain. The method to avoid obtaining disconnected expressions such as the above, is based on a polynomial extension of the generated Horn set. Let a *primary predicate (atom)* be a declared predicate (atom based thereon) with no input argument (ie. one relating directly to the individual, such as $\mathtt{atm/1}$ or $\mathtt{car/1}$). I will distinguish two (MI) subcases: (MI-S) only one primary predicate is declared, and (MI-M) more than one primary predicates are declared.

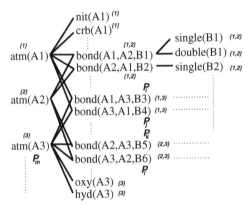

Fig. 2. A fraction of the ⊥ graph representation in a (MI) setting. Chemical bonds are not oriented so half of the shown **bond/3** atoms are semantically superfluous, however, I am not concerned here with feature semantics.

I first regard (MI-S). In the layer-wise construction of ⊥ (enabled again by assuming the ≺ order, refer to Fig. 2), I assign a distinct integer singleton label to each (necessarily primary) atom in the first layer. Then the label of every vertex in layer l ($l \geq 2$) is the union of the labels of its parents in layer $l-1$. Now I am able to identify atoms ('joints'), which are simultaneously descendants of more than one primary atoms. The idea now is to allow the inclusion of a second or further primary atom in a feature, only if there is a joint for it with another primary atom in the feature. For example, for the primary atom **atm(A3)**, I can facilitate that by adding the following Horn clause into the HORN-SAT instance (refer to the $P_m \ldots P_l$ variables assigned to vertices in the figure)

$$P_m \vee \neg P_i \vee \neg P_j \vee \neg P_k \vee \neg P_l \qquad (6)$$

In general, assume that $P_1 \ldots P_{|\perp|}$ are variables assigned to atoms in ⊥, and let $L(P_s)$ ($1 \leq s \leq |\perp|$) be a function yielding the label of the vertex corresponding to the to variable P_s. For each primary atom, corresponding to variable P_r and having the label $\{\lambda\} = L(P_r)$, the following Horn clause will be added to the HORN-SAT instance:

$$P_r \bigvee_{1 \leq s \leq |\perp|,\ \{\lambda\} \subset L(P_s),\ \forall \rho \in L(P_s):\ \rho \leq \lambda} \neg P_s \qquad (7)$$

This extension has a polynomial size since it generates at most $|\perp|$ additional clauses each with at most $|\perp|$ literals. The $\rho \leq \lambda$ inequality in the selector line exploits the order imposed on primary atoms by the vertex labelling (I reflect here the order also in output-variable naming). It prevents the construction of disconnected expressions such as

atm(A1)∧atm(A2)∧bond(A1,A2,B1)∧single(B1)
∧atm(A3)∧atm(A4)∧bond(A3,A4,B2)∧single(B2)

This expression is disqualified since atm(A3) has no joint with with atm(A1) or atm(A2) (although it has one with atm(A4)). At first sight it seems incorrect that this technique thus also disqualifies connected expressions such as

$$\texttt{atm(A1)} \wedge \texttt{atm(A2)} \wedge \texttt{atm(A3)} \wedge \texttt{bond(A1,A3,B1)}$$
$$\wedge \texttt{bond(A2,A3,B2)} \wedge \texttt{single(B1)} \wedge \texttt{single(B2)}$$

since atm(A2) has no joint with atm(A1). This expression, however, is equivalent to the non-discarded counterpart where A1 and A3 are mutually exchanged. In can be shown also generally that no connected proper feature will be discarded by this technique, as long as one adheres to the (MI-S) assumption, that is, only one primary predicate is declared.

Unfortunately, I cannot provide any efficient feature connectivity verification technique for the remaining, most general (MI-M) case (multiple input arity + multiple primary predicates). I do not believe that one can be implemented without solving the general intractable graph connectivity testing problem. The (MI-M) case would correspond to a problem where individuals would be structured by two or more different manners, and it would be required to mutually relate such multiple kinds of substructures. This fortunately does not seem to be a typical case in applied propositionalization.

2.4   Avoiding Multiple Equivalent Features

The reader has certainly noticed an evident deficiency of the feature set corresponding to the set of all solutions to the dual HORN-SAT problem. The set may contain classes of equivalent features, only differing in variable naming. Indeed, if $\perp$ contains eg. multiple occurrences of the load/2 predicate, as necessary for large enough n (refer to Fig. 1), two distinct solutions to the corresponding HORN-SAT instance will represent for instance the following, equivalent features:

$$\texttt{car(C)} \wedge \texttt{load(C,L1)} \wedge \texttt{triangle(L1)}$$
$$\texttt{car(C)} \wedge \texttt{load(C,L2)} \wedge \texttt{triangle(L2)}$$

Such cases may however be remedied by an extension of the generated HORN-SAT instance in the following way. Let $P_{b_1}, P_{b_2}, \ldots P_{b_n}$ be the propositional variables corresponding the (up to) n roots of the branches stemming from an atom in $\perp$ (again, refer to Fig. 1 for quicker insight). I add the following polynomial number (again due to the bounded branching factor and depth) of Horn clauses

$$\neg P_{b_1} \vee P_{b_2} \ , \ \neg P_{b_2} \vee P_{b_3} \ , \ldots \neg P_{b_{n-1}} \vee P_{b_n} \tag{8}$$

In the continuing example, $P_{b_1}, P_{b_2}, \ldots P_{b_n}$ correspond to the multiple hasLoad/2 atoms contained and the clauses above will guarantee that load(C,L$_{i+1}$) ($i \geq 1$) will appear in a feature only if it also includes load(C,L$_i$). To see that this technique does not eliminate features that are not redundant, realize that in the $\perp$ graph representation all children vertices of a given parent vertex have the same (up to variable naming) descendant subgraph, so any feature containing load(C,L_{i+1}) and not load(C,L_i) has its equivalent containing load(C,L_i) and not load(C,L_{i+1}).

Still, the technique just explained does guarantee syntactic uniqueness of every feature in the resulting set. A thorough discussion of redundancy elimination is out of the scope of this paper; I just note here that the residual redundancy, exemplified by the following two equivalent features

$$\text{car(C)} \wedge \text{load(C,L1)} \wedge \text{load(C,L2)} \wedge \text{triangle(L1)} \wedge \text{box(L2)}$$
$$\text{car(C)} \wedge \text{load(C,L1)} \wedge \text{load(C,L2)} \wedge \text{triangle(L2)} \wedge \text{box(L1)}$$

manifests itself as well in the standard backtrack-search based feature construction systems and in neither framework there seems to be an apparent syntactic redundancy removal method not resorting to the NP-complete subsumption check.

2.5 Extracting Correct Features from the Bottom Feature

I am now in the position to extract correct features from $\perp$ by finding a satisfying assignment to a polynomial-size set of propositional Horn clauses. Horn satisfiability was identified as a tractable problem as early as in the 1970's [10] and later, efficient algorithms have been designed [5] able to find a *maximal (minimal)* solution, that is, one that assigns the *true* value to the greatest (smallest) possible number of variables, or determine that no solution exists. In this paper's context, a maximal solution corresponds to the smallest connected proper subexpression of $\perp$ (remind that a $\perp$'s atom belongs to the extracted subexpression if its corresponding propositional variable is false). Consequently, if the efficiently found maximal solution makes false n or fewer variables, I have found a correct feature. Otherwise, I can conclude that the declaration allows for no correct feature. In the continuing example, a maximal solution to the clauses constructed above makes true P_3, P_4 and P_5 (the reader will check that all seven clauses 1 – 5 are indeed satisfied), thus P_1 and P_2 are false. This corresponds to the correct feature car(C)$\wedge$hasRoof(C).

So far I have merely shown how to efficiently decide the *feature existence* problem by finding a correct feature if one exists. In practice though, one will need to enumerate the entire set of correct features. For this purpose, fortunately, one can accommodate the algorithm proposed in [3] able to produce the set of all HORN-SAT instance solutions by iterative executions of the core procedure for finding a single solution. The input clause set is at each call modified in a way guaranteeing that the successive solutions form the entire (lexicographically ordered) set of solutions to the original HORN-SAT instance. A favorable property of the algorithm is that the total number of calls to the core procedure is polynomial in (i) the total number of literals in the original clause set, (ii) the number of existing solutions, that is, the algorithm does not introduce an exponential complexity factor when upgrading a single solution finding onto finding of all solutions. I refer the reader to [3] for further details. By employing this algorithm (in the way described in Fig. 3) to find all solutions to the HORN-SAT instance

EnumerationOfFeatures($\mathcal{D}, n$) : Given a correct user predicate declaration $\mathcal{D}$ and a number $n \geq 0$, produces the set of all proper connected features of size $\leq n$, satisfying $\mathcal{D}$.

1. Construct bottom feature $\bot = \bot(\mathcal{D}, n)$.
2. Construct HORN-SAT instance $\mathcal{H}$ from $\bot$.
3. $\mathcal{S} := AllModels(\mathcal{H})$.
4. For all $s \in \mathcal{S}$ with at most n false assignments, convert s into the corresponding feature f and output f.

Fig. 3. Enumeration of all correct features through the HORN-SAT reduction strategy. Steps 1 and 2 are detailed in Section 2. Step 3, ie. procedure *AllModels* implements [3]: it terminates in polynomial time if the number of all models is polynomial. A correct declaration $\mathcal{D}$ complies to assumptions described in Section 2 (finiteness, $\prec$ order on types) and one of the (SI) or (MI-S) assumptions.

corresponding to the feature construction problem instance, I do not conduct significant 'excess computation' (corresponding to exploring exponentially large search subspaces containing no solution in the case of standard backtrack feature construction approaches), and specifically, if the actual number of correct features is polynomial, they are all enumerated in polynomial time.

3   Sampling the Feature Space

For the case when the total number of correct features allowed by the user declaration is exponential in n (maximal feature size) and complete feature enumeration is intractable, I offer two algorithms for feature sampling. Both of them approach the task by sampling in the space of models for the dual HORN-SAT problem.

The first algorithm described in Fig. 4 simply generates random truth assignments with at most n false-valued variables (corresponding to the maximal feature size n) to the dual HORN-SAT instance and checks (through a linear time algorithm) if they are models. To obtain a uniform sample of features, care must be taken to generate the truth assignments equiprobably, given the maximal feature length (n) constraint. The corresponding technique is explained in the Figure. Due to the uniformity, this algorithm is also able to produce an unbiased estimate of the total number of existing features. The number of iterations (truth assignments made) in the algorithm is linear in s (the required sample size) and $1/p$, where p is the actual proportion of the number of all models to the number of all possible truth assignments, which grows exponentially in n. Therefore, if the number of all correct features, ie. the number of all models of the dual problem is also exponential in n, the number of iterations is at most polynomial.

The second, locally deterministic algorithm shown in Fig. 6 can be viewed as a middle-ground between complete enumerative search and sampling. At each iteration it generates a random partition of the search space by assigning the true value to at least $|\mathcal{V}| - n$ randomly chosen variables in the dual HORN-SAT instance with $|\mathcal{V}|$ variables, thereby guaranteeing that any found model will convert to a feature of at most n atoms. The completion to a total truth

$SampleFeatures(\mathcal{D}, n, s)$: Given a correct user predicate declaration $\mathcal{D}$ and a number $n \geq 0$, produces a set $\mathcal{F}$ of s random features of size $\leq n$, satisfying $\mathcal{D}$ and an estimate e of the total number of such features.

1. Construct bottom feature $\bot = \bot(\mathcal{D}, n)$.
2. $\mathcal{H} = ConvertToHornSAT(\bot, n)$; $\mathcal{V} :=$ the set of propositional variables in $\mathcal{H}$.
3. $t := 0$; $f := 0$; $\mathcal{F} := \{\}$
4. $\mathcal{T} := RandomTruthAssignment(\mathcal{V}, n)$; $t := t + 1$
5. if $ModelCheck(\mathcal{H}, \mathcal{T})$ then $\mathcal{F} := \mathcal{F} \cup \{ConvertToFeature(\bot, \mathcal{T})\}$; $f := f + 1$
6. if $f = s$ then return $\mathcal{F}$ and $e = f/t * \sum_{i=0}^{n} \binom{|\mathcal{V}|}{i}$, else go to 4

Fig. 4. Sampling features by generating random truth assignments to the dual HORN-SAT problem and checking whether they are models thereof. Procedures $ConvertToHornSAT$ and $ConvertToFeature$ implement reduction principles described in Section 2. Procedure $ModelCheck$ implements a linear time HORN-SAT model checking algorithm. Proc. $RandomTruthAssignment$ is described in Fig. 5.

$RandomTruthAssignment(\mathcal{V}, n)$: Given a set of propositional variables $\mathcal{V}$ and a number $n \leq |\mathcal{V}|$, produces a random truth assignment to $\mathcal{V}$ with at most n false assignments, with equal probability among all such assignments.

1. Choose a random number $0 \leq r \leq n$ with probability

$$P(r) = \frac{\binom{|\mathcal{V}|}{r}}{\sum_{i=0}^{n} \binom{|\mathcal{V}|}{i}} \tag{9}$$

2. Choose a random combination C^r of r variables from $\mathcal{V}$ with equal probability among all such combinations.
3. Output the assignment $\{false \leftarrow v_i | v_i \in C^r\} \cup \{v_j \leftarrow true | v_j \notin C^r\}$.

Fig. 5. Procedure $RandomTruthAssignment$ ensures equiprobability by first selecting the number $r \leq n$ of false valued variables in the selected assignment with probability proportional to the number of all assignments with r false valued variables, and then drawing a random combination of r variables to be falsified

assignment is then done by formally adding the instantiated variables as positive singletons to the Horn clause set and then using a simple linear time-algorithm [5] for finding a minimal HORN-SAT model (instantiating the rest of the variables). Unlike the previous sampling algorithm, this locally deterministic algorithm does not guarantee that resulting features form a sample from a uniform distribution on all correct features, and thus it cannot provide an unbiased estimate of the total number of correct clauses. The non-uniformity is a consequence of both the bias toward the minimal model in each search space partition as well as the possible overlaps between individual partitions.

Although I formally use the name $ModelCheck$ in Fig. 4 and $HornModel$ in Fig. 6, I implemented the two procedures naturally by a single binary Prolog predicate, where the model carrying argument may or may not be instantiated

LocalSearchOfFeatures$(\mathcal{D}, n, s)$: Given a correct user predicate declaration $\mathcal{D}$ and a number $n \geq 0$, produces a set $\mathcal{F}$ of s random features of size $\leq n$, satisfying $\mathcal{D}$.

1. Construct bottom feature $\bot = \bot(\mathcal{D}, n)$.
2. $\mathcal{H} = ConvertToHornSAT(\bot, n)$; $\mathcal{V} :=$ the set of propositional variables in $\mathcal{H}$.
3. $f := 0$; $\mathcal{F} := \{\}$
4. Choose a random number $|\mathcal{V}| - n \leq r \leq |\mathcal{V}|$ with probability

$$P(r) = \frac{\binom{|\mathcal{V}|}{r}}{\sum_{i=|\mathcal{V}|-n}^{|\mathcal{V}|} \binom{|\mathcal{V}|}{i}} \tag{10}$$

5. Choose a random combination C^r of r variables from $\mathcal{V}$ with equal probability among all such combinations.
6. $\mathcal{H}^{ext} := \mathcal{H} \cup \{v_i \leftarrow true | v_i \in C^r\}$
7. if $\mathcal{T} := HornModel(\mathcal{H}^{ext})$ succeeds then
   $\mathcal{F} := \mathcal{F} \cup \{ConvertToFeature(\bot, \mathcal{T})\}$; $f := f + 1$
8. if $f = s$ then return $\mathcal{F}$, else go to 4

Fig. 6. Sampling features by generating a random, partial truth assignment to variables in the dual HORN-SAT theory, and then verifying if the assignment can be completed to a model of the theory. Procedure *HornModel* terminates in linear time [5].

when calling the predicate. The total number of calls to this predicate will represent a parameter used in comparing the two methods.

4   Implementation and Experiments

The algorithms presented in this paper have been implemented in SWI Prolog. The implementation is available for download from `http://labe.felk.cvut.cz/~zelezny/feature_sampling.pl` .

Let me now consider the following mode/type declaration

`car(-c)`, `connected(+c, +c)`, `load(+c,-l)`, `big(+l)`, `small(+l)`

and set the maximum branching factor $\beta = 2$ and maximum feature size $n = 10$. The bottom feature for this declaration has 18 atoms, and consequently there exist $\sum_{i=0}^{10} \binom{18}{i} = 199140$ possible truth assignments in the dual HORN-SAT instance (out of which 567 are models to the corresponding Horn theory).

I have two goals in this exercise. First, I want to verify that the estimate e of the total number of correct features provided by the algorithm *SampleFeatures* in Fig. 4 converges sufficiently rapidly to the correct value with growing sample size, in comparison to an estimate based on enumerating subsets of the bottom feature in systematic manners, either top-down or bottom-up. Second, I want to compare the efficiency of algorithms *SampleFeatures* in Fig. 4 and *LocalSearchOfFeatures* in Fig. 6 to see whether abandoning the distributional uniformity in *LocalSearchOfFeatures* trades off for a significant speedup of the feature sample construction, with respect to *SampleFeatures*.

Figure 7 answers the first question by demonstrating that the uniform sampling method (unlike the systematic top-down or bottom-up procedures) pro-

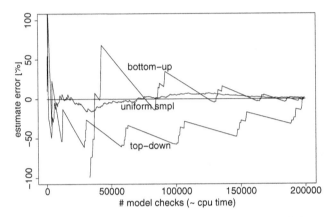

Fig. 7. The diagram plots the per cent error of the estimate e of the total number of correct features provided by the uniform sample in the *SampleFeatures* algorithm and by measuring the proportion of models of the dual HORN-SAT theory among possible truth assignments in a systematic enumeration of assignments starting either with n false valued variables (so that largest features are found first, denoted as bottom-up in the figure), or with 0 false valued variables (so that smallest features are found first, denoted as top-down in the figure). The error value is plotted against the growing number of verified truth assignments to the dual HORN-SAT problem.

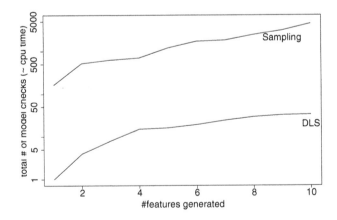

Fig. 8. The diagram plots the total number of calls to the *ModelCheck* (*HornModel*, respectively) procedure made in a pure sampling approach by the Algorithms *SampleFeature* (denoted as Sampling) and in a deterministic local search (denoted as DLS) by the *LocalSearch* algorithm. The value corresponds to the cpu time spent and is plotted on a logarithmic scale, against the growing number of features generated.

vides a stable estimate, which remains in a 15% error margin once about 5,000 truth assignments (about 2.5% of the search space) are sampled.

The second question is addressed in Fig. 8, showing that the rate at which the algorithm runtime increases with the growing number of feature sampled is reduced by $LocalSearchOfFeatures$ to about 1/100 of that invested by $SampleFeatures$.

5   Related Work

Similarly to the work of Pfahringer and Holmes [9], my approach aims at generating randomized features, viewable as extracting some constrained random subgraphs of some graph G. While in my approach, G (the bottom feature) is derived from a user's syntactic declaration, in [9], G is a structural representation of a chosen example of a class for which the features are generated. This difference has two fundamental consequences. First, unlike [9], my approach is class-blind and as such it is not apriori biased towards constructing features with discriminative power, which needs to be assessed (and possibly used for posterior feature selection) after the feature syntax has been generated. Second, Pfahringer's and Holmes' features are, to my best understanding, less expressive than my features. Assuming ground descriptions of examples, their feature graphs correspond to ground logic formulas, so unlike in my approach, they eg. cannot express the feature 'there are two carbon atoms c_1, c_2 both connected to some other atom A.

My method includes a number of ingredients, whose application in relational machine learning is not original. Namely, the concept of a bottom feature derived on the basis of user moding and typing declarations deliberately adopts the ideas of the mode directed inverse entailment [8] technique popular in ILP, where a *bottom clause* is constructed to constrain the search space. To my best knowledge though, there is no previous approach exploiting the 'bottom' concept for feature construction. The crucial point where I diverge from the traditional approach is in the utilization of the bottom feature: rather than using it as a constraint for a backtrack search, I translate it into a propositional Horn theory whose models represent correct features.

Furthermore, the basic idea of estimating the number of features by sampling in the feature space was inspired by an analogous technique implemented by Ashwin Srinivasan in the ILP system Aleph for estimating the number of existing legal clauses (see eg. [14]). Again, the principal difference of my materialization of that idea from the one in Aleph stems from the conversion of feature construction onto a propositional satisfiability problem enabling to carry out the sampling in the 'easily conquerable' space of propositional truth assignments.

6   Conclusion, Future Work

I have presented an approach to relational feature construction based on its poly-time reduction to the tractable HORN-SAT problem. Under acceptable restrictions on user language declarations, I am able to either efficiently enumerate the complete set of proper, connected, declaration compliant relational features (if their total number is polynomial in the maximum feature size), or otherwise efficiently obtain their random sample from the uniform distribution on the feature space.

The assumptions I imposed on the user declarations to achieve the results were its finite size, existing partial irreflexive order on types, which 'agrees' with the input-output order of types in any declared predicate (see Section 2 for details), and the 'non (MI-M)' condition which stipulates that either no two different declared predicates are primary (without input arguments), or no declared predicate has more than one input. Dropping the 'non (MI-M)' condition has the consequence that solutions arising from the dual HORN-SAT problem may correspond to disconnected features, which may be decomposed into two or more correct features and therefore are redundant.

Intuition suggests that the efficient technique used for solving the dual, satisfiability problem in linear time without backtracking, should have its 'mirror' procedure applicable directly on the primary problem of correct feature search. I have not yet been able to exactly determine what form such search procedure would acquire and this is a goal of my future work.

The approach admittedly needs more experimental evaluation. Also, the presented method for estimating the number of correct features (or, equivalently, their relative frequency $0 \leq p \leq 1$ in the search space) calls for a statistical analysis to determine the required size of the sample which, with a given probability, leads to an estimate $\hat{p}$ of p in a given error bound. Altough simple statistical techniques are available for calculating the error bound, they assume p not too close to 0 or 1. Unfortunately, p is typically very close to zero in the expression spaces in question. An alternative way, suggested by a reviewer, is to approach the estimate-reliability analysis empirically, eg. by repeated sampling.

Acknowledgement. Thanks go to the ILP 2005 reviewers for their informative suggestions and particularly for pointing out the relevant paper [9]. I am supported by the Czech Ministry of Education through the project 1ET101210513 "Relational Machine Learning for Biomedical Data Analysis" in the "Information Society" programme.

References

1. J. Blatak and L. Popelinsky. Distributed mining maximal first-order patterns. In *Work in Progress track of Inductive Logic Programming, 14th Inf. Conf*, 2004.
2. V. S. Costa, A. Srinivasan, R. Camacho, H. Blockeel, B.Demoen, G. Janssens, J. Struyf, H. Vandecasteele, and W.V. Laer. Query transformations for improving the efficiency of ilp systems. *J. Mach. Learn. Res.*, 4:465–491, 2003.
3. R. Dechter and A. Itai. Finding all solutions if you can find one. In *AAAI-92 Workshop on Tractable Reasoning*, 1992.
4. P. Domingos. Process-oriented estimation of generalization error. In *IJCAI97*, pages 714–721, 1999.

5. W. F. Dowling and J. H. Gallier. Linear time algorithms for testing the satisfiability of propositional horn formula. *Journal of Logic Programming*, 3:267–284, 1994.
6. M-A. Krogel, S. Rawles, F. Železný, S. Wrobel, P. Flach, and N. Lavrac. Comparative evaluation of approaches to propositionalization. In *Proceedings of the 13th International Conference on Inductive Logic Programming*. Springer-Verlag, 2003.
7. N. Lavrač and P. A. Flach. An extended transformation approach to inductive logic programming. *ACM Transactions on Computational Logic*, 2(4):458–494, October 2001.
8. S. Muggleton. Inverse entailment and Progol. *New Generation Computing, Special issue on Inductive Logic Programming*, 13(3-4):245–286, 1995.
9. B. Pfahringer and G. Holmes. Propositionalization through stochastic discrimination. In *Work in Progress Track at Inductive Logic Programming, 13th Inf. Conf*, 2003.
10. T. J. Schaefer. The complexity of satisfiability problems. In *Tenth Annual Symposium on Theory of Computing*, pages 216–226, 1978.
11. M. Sebag and C. Rouveirol. Tractable induction and classification in first-order logic via stochastic matching. pages 888–893, 1997.
12. A. Srinivasan, S. H. Muggleton, M. J. E. Sternberg, and R. D. King. Theories for mutagenicity: a study in first-order and feature-based induction. *Artif. Intell.*, 85(1-2):277–299, 1996.
13. C. Vens, A.Van Assche, H. Blockeel, and Saso Dzeroski. First order random forests with complex aggregates. In *ILP*, pages 323–340, 2004.
14. F. Železný, A. Srinivasan, and D. Page. Lattice-search runtime distributions may be heavy-tailed. volume 2583, pages 333–345, 2003.

Why Computers Need to Learn About Music

Gerhard Widmer[1,2]

[1] Department of Computational Perception,
Johannes Kepler University (JKU) Linz,
A-4040 Linz, Austria
[2] Austrian Research Institute for Artificial Intelligence,
Vienna, Austria
gerhard.widmer@jku.at

The goal of this presentation is to convince the research community that music is much more than an interesting and "nice", but ultimately esoteric toy domain for machine learning experiments. I will try to show that right now is the time for machine learning to really make an impact in both the arts, the (music) sciences, and, not least, the music market. In order to demonstrate that, some impressions will be given of what computers can currently do with music.

In the domain of classical music, I will show how machine learning can give us new insights into complex artistic behaviours such as expressive music performance, with examples ranging from the automatic discovery of characteristic stylistic patterns to automatic artist identification and even computers that learn to play music with "expression".

In the (commercially more relevant) domain of popular music, the currently ongoing rapid shift of the music market towards digital music distribution opens myriads of application possibilities for machine learning, from intelligent music recommendation services to content-based music search engines to adaptive radio stations. Again, some ongoing work in this area will be briefly demonstrated.

A number of challenges for machine learning research will be identified throughout the presentation, and my hope is that after the conferences, a large part of the ICML and ILP attendants will go back to their labs and get involved in machine learning and music right away.

S. Kramer and B. Pfahringer (Eds.): ILP 2005, LNAI 3625, p. 414, 2005.

Tutorial on Statistical Relational Learning

Lise Getoor

Computer Science Department,
University of Maryland,
College Park, MD 20742, USA
getoor@cs.umd.edu

Statistical machine learning is in the midst of a "relational revolution". After many decades of focusing on independent and identically-distributed (iid) examples, many researchers are now studying problems in which the examples are linked together into complex networks. These networks ca be a simple as sequences and 2-D meshes (such as those arising in part-of-speech tagging and remote sensing) or as complex as citation graphs, the world wide web, and relational data bases.

Statistical relational learning raises many new challenges and opportunities. Because the statistical model depends on the domain's relational structure, parameters in the model are often tied. This has advantages for making parameter estimation feasible, but complicates the model search. Because the "features" involve relationships among multiple objects, there is often a need to intelligently construct aggregates and other relational features. Problems that arise from linkage and autocorrelation among objects must be taken into account. Because instances are linked together, classification typically involves complex inference to arrive at "collective classification" in which the labels predicted for the test instances are determined jointly rather than individually. Unlike iid problems, where the result of learning is a single classifier, relational learning often involves instances that are heterogeneous, where the result of learning is a set of multiple components (classifiers, probability distributions, etc.) that predict labels of objects and logical relationships between objects.

In this tutorial, we will survey several of the major branches of this newly emerging field : rule-based approaches, frame-based approaches and stochastic/ functional programming approaches. We will describe representational issues, learning and inference. Many of the approaches are based in some way on graphical models, and we will describe approaches which are based on both directed and undirected graphical models. We will describe several useful inference tasks such as link prediction, group detection and entity resolution and applications areas including citation graphs, the world wide web and social networks.

S. Kramer and B. Pfahringer (Eds.): ILP 2005, LNAI 3625, p. 415, 2005.
© Springer-Verlag Berlin Heidelberg 2005

Machine Learning for Systems Biology

S.H. Muggleton

Department of Computing, Imperial College London

Abstract. In this paper we survey work being conducted at Imperial College on the use of machine learning to build Systems Biology models of the effects of toxins on biochemical pathways. Several distinct, and complementary modelling techniques are being explored. Firstly, work is being conducted on applying Support-Vector ILP (SVILP) as an accurate means of screening high-toxicity molecules. Secondly, Bayes' networks have been machine-learned to provide causal maps of the effects of toxins on the network of metabolic reactions within cells. The data were derived from a study on the effects of hydrazine toxicity in rats. Although the resultant network can be partly explained in terms of existing KEGG (Kyoto Encyclopedia of Genes and Genomes) pathway descriptions, several of the strong dependencies in the Bayes' network involve metabolite pairs with high separation in KEGG. Thirdly, in a complementary study KEGG pathways are being used as background knowledge for explaining the same data using a model constructed using Abductive ILP, a logic-based machine learning technique. With a binary prediction model (up/down regulation) cross validation results show that even with a restricted number of observed metabolites high predictive accuracy (80-90%) is achieved on unseen metabolite concentrations. Further increases in accuracy are achieved by allowing discovery of general rules from additional literature data on hydrazine inhibition. Ongoing work is aimed at formulating probabilistic logic models which combine the learned Bayes' network and ILP models.

1 Introduction

In the past experimental analysis of any single biological component, such as a gene or its protein product, was extremely time consuming. Consequently a single biology laboratory could study only a handful of such components at any one time. The recent revolution in high-throughput technologies offers an exciting opportunity to study such complex biological systems as an integrated whole. This new integrated approach to modelling of biological entities is known as Systems Biology. Systems Biologists use graph-based descriptions of bio-molecular interactions which describe cellular activities such as gene regulation, metabolism and transcription. Biologists build and maintain these network models based on the results of experiments in wild and mutated organisms. This paper will provide an overview of recent research in this area involving a consortium of computer scientists and biologists at Imperial College London. Some of the intrinsic interest in the area from a logic-based machine learning perspective include:

1. the availability of large-scale background knowledge on existing known biochemical networks from publicly available resources such as KEGG [2] (used in data sets such as those in [1,11,5]);

S. Kramer and B. Pfahringer (Eds.): ILP 2005, LNAI 3625, pp. 416–423, 2005.

	MSE	R-squared
CHEM	1.04	0.48
PLS	1.03	0.47
TOPKAT	2.2	0.26
SVILP	**0.8**	**0.57**

Fig. 1. MSE and R-squared for CHEM, PLS, TOPKAT and SVILP

2. an abundance of training and test data from a variety of sources including microarray experiments (see for instance [3]) and metabolomic data [10] from NMR and mass spectroscopy experiments;
3. the inherent importance of the problem (see [6,7]) owing to its application in biology and medicine;
4. the inherent relational structure in the form of spatial and temporal interactions of the molecules involved;

From a logical perspective the objects within this area include genes, proteins, metabolites, inhibitors and cofactors. The relations include biochemical reactions in which one set of metabolites is transformed to another in a biochemical reaction catalysed by an enzyme. One of the representational challenges is that within various databases the same object can be referred to in several ways.

A large part of the incentive for using machine learning techniques in this area comes from the incompleteness of detailed knowledge concerning the effects of inhibitors on known biochemical reactions. The requirement to infer such objects and relations indirectly from observational data necessitates the use of a mixture of abduction and induction within the ILP approaches to modelling in this problem.

Such models have wide potential application. For instance, in the new area of personalised medicines techniques which allow the construction of models of the toxic reactions of individuals to drug treatment would be of great benefit. Non-invasive testing, such as the NMR analysis of urine used in these studies, would be an appropriate basis for such modelling.

The paper is arranged as follows. Section 2 describes a novel approach to combining Support Vector Machines and ILP for directly predicting the effects of toxins on the basis of molecular features of the inhibitors. Section 3 describes the use of Bayes' network technology to estimate the structure and parameters of the causal network of interactions between metabolites whose up and down regulation patterns are observable within the NMR data. An ILP model built on the same data is described in Section 4. The model provides more detailed and testable predictions of the inhibited enzymes. Finally we conclude the paper in Section 5.

2   SVILP Prediction of Toxins

In [9] an accurate means of screening high-toxicity molecules is described. This approach uses a general method for constructing kernels for Support Vector Inductive Logic Programming (SVILP). The kernel not only captures the semantic and syntactic relational information contained in the data but also provides the flexibility of using

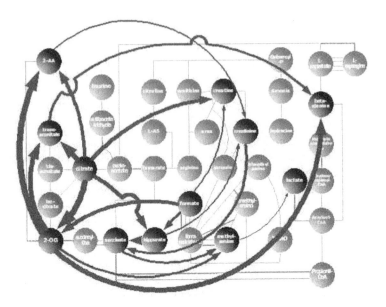

Fig. 2. Metabolic network showing the effects of hydrazine on rat metabolism. The thickness of arcs indicates the strength of dependencies between observable metabolites.

arbitrary forms of structured and non-structured data coded in a relational way. While specialised kernels have been developed for strings, trees and graphs the approach uses declarative background knowledge to provide the learning bias. The use of explicitly encoded background knowledge distinguishes SVILP from existing relational kernels which in ILP-terms work purely at the atomic generalisation level.

The SVILP approach is a form of generalisation relative to background knowledge, though the final combining function for the ILP-learned clauses is an SVM rather than a logical conjunction. SVILP was evaluated empirically against related approaches, including an industry-standard toxin predictor called TOPKAT. Evaluation was conducted on a broad-ranging toxicity dataset DSSTox [12]. Figure 1 shows the cross-validated error of SVILP compared to a number of alternative predictors on the DSSTox dataset. The results demonstrate that the approach significantly outperforms other state-of-the-art approaches on the wide-ranging set of toxins represented.

Such toxin-substructure based techniques, much like the ILP approach to predicting mutagenesis in [4,13], are appropriate for large-scale screening of potential toxic side-effects of drugs. By contrast, techniques for detailed analysis of the causes of toxic reaction are addressed in the next two sections.

3   Bayes' Network Model for Metabolic Pathways

Metabolism comprises the network of chemical reactions involved in the biological processes of cells. These reactions are typically catalysed by enzymes and are highly interconnected.

In [15] a modular approach for representing metabolic pathways using Bayes' networks is described. The authors examined different models for a single reaction metabolism and introduced a Bayes' network model for this purpose. The performance of the model was compared to a Stochastic Logic Program representation for learning the aromatic amino acid pathway of yeast.

In subsequent work the authors have used this approach to model the effects of the toxin hydrazine administered to rats. The data were derived from Nuclear Magnetic Resonance (NMR) studies conducted by the Consortium for Metabonomic Toxicology (COMET) [10]. The derived Bayes' network is shown in Figure 2. Although the resultant network can be partly explained in terms of existing KEGG pathway descriptions, several of the strong dependencies in the Bayes' network involve metabolite pairs which are distant in the KEGG network.

4   Abductive ILP Models of Toxicity

In [14] the hydrazine NMR toxicity data studied previously using Bayes' nets was re-analysed within an ILP framework using Progol5.0 [8]. Figure 3 shows the approach adopted. KEGG pathway descriptions were used as background knowledge. Only a limited subset (less than 10%) of the up/down regulation levels of metabolites in the KEGG model were directly observable within the NMR data. Progol5.0 was given this data as examples together with background knowledge consisting of the KEGG model and some general background rules concerning the transitive behaviour of the inhibitory effects of the toxin on various enzymes. From this it generated a set of ground hypotheses to explain the data in terms of inhibition of various enzymes. These ground hypotheses were then further generalised inductively together with known facts concerning the inhibition of various enzymes by hydrazine.

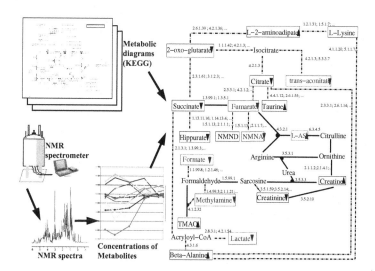

Fig. 3. Abductive ILP modelling of hydrazine toxicity

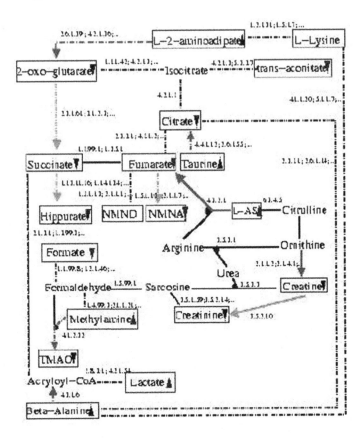

Fig. 4. Predicted inhibitions within the network. Modes represent metabolites with up and down regulation indicated by arrows when observable. Solid arcs represent single reactions, labelled by the catalysing enzyme's classification number. Dotted lines indicate a reaction sequence, with the list of associated enzymes. Red/green arrows indicate an inhibited/uninhibited (respectively) reaction (or reaction sequence). The arrow head shows the direction of inhibition.

The resulting set of predicted inhibitions are shown in Figure 4. Owing to the spareseness of the known and documented inhibitory effects of hydrazine, all but one of the predicted inhibitory effects is novel. With the help of biological experts the model has been compared in detail with the Bayes' net model shown in Figure 2. In general the ILP model gives more detailed suggestions for the location of the inhibitory effects of the toxin. This level of detail allows for the possibility of laboratory testing of the inhibitory effects suggested by the ILP model.

The model was tested by randomly leaving out subsets of the examples and testing the predictions on the remaining observations. The resulting learning curves for abduction on its own versus the combination of abduction and subsequent induction are shown in Figure 5.

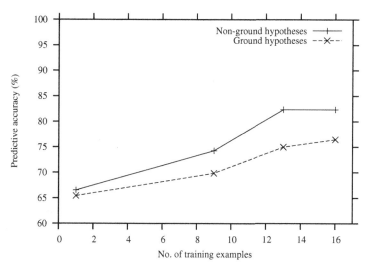

Fig. 5. Learning curves for abduction on its own versus abduction and subsequent induction. The X-axis indicates the number of examples in the training test after removal of a randomly chosen test set of varying sizes. The Y-axis gives predictive accuracy on the test set for results averaged over multiple trials.

5   Conclusions and Further Work

In this paper we have described three distinct machine learning approaches to modelling the toxic effects of molecules. These three approaches should not be considered as being in competition, but rather as complementary approaches to the problem which can be used in a series of analytical phases. During drug development it is usual to consider a large set of potential candidates in the early stages of development. The SVILP toxicity predictor described in Section 2 has been proved to be at least as good as alternative state-of-the-art toxicity predictors in such a setting.

Having selected a particular candidate for further investigation it would be advantageous to apply more detailed analysis to the compound in question to understand its toxic effects better. NMR analyses of urine could then be conducted. Such an analysis incurs experimental costs, but could potentially be applied non-invasively in both animal and human testing. The results could then be modelled in a broad-brush fashion using the Bayes' network technology described in Section 3. An advantage of this approach is that no additional background knowledge of metabolism need be considered.

A more detailed analysis of inhibitory effects of the compound could be produced using the ILP modelling approach. It makes sense to apply ILP modelling last, since both the development of appropriate background knowledge and the computational costs of running ILP models incur more costs than the other two modelling approaches.

Many open questions are still to be addressed in this work. In particular, the treatment of time in both the Bayes' network and ILP models is presently inadequate. The NMR data are available as a time series measured at intervals of several hours over a 72 hour period. Within the Bayes net setting it may seem attractive to build dynamic

Bayes' nets to deal with this temporal data. However, such models do not adequately account for the underlying causality of the domain. Metabolic reactions and fluxes take place within a period of under 1 millisecond, while the intervals between readings are at least 8 hours. Persistence of inhibitory effects are due to the toxin remaining in the blood stream over an extended period of time. While it is possible to model such persistence axiomatically within a logical model, it is unclear how this could be achieved in the case of the Bayes' model.

Work is presently progressing on including aspects of both the Bayes' and ILP models within a Probabilistic Logic Programming model. Such integration holds the promise of allowing uncertainty to be expressed explicitly within ILP-generated models.

Finally, modelling within Systems Biology is a key application area for Machine Learning in general. The studies described in this paper indicate that ILP has the potential to be a key technology in an area which is now drawing major scientific interest internationally.

Acknowledgements

Many thanks are due to my wife, Thirza and daughter Clare for the support and happiness they give me. This work was supported by the DTI Beacon project "Metalog - Integrated Machine Learning of Metabolic Networks Applied to Predictive Toxicology", Grant Reference QCBB/C/012/00003, the ESPRIT IST project "Application of Probabilistic Inductive Logic Programming II (APRIL II)", Grant Reference FP-508861 and BBSRC Bio-informatics and E-Science Programme, "Studying Biochemical networks using probabilistic knowledge discovery", Grant Reference 28/BEP17011.

References

1. C.H. Bryant, S.H. Muggleton, S.G. Oliver, D.B. Kell, P. Reiser, and R.D. King. Combining inductive logic programming, active learning and robotics to discover the function of genes. *Electronic Transactions in Artificial Intelligence*, 5-B1(012):1–36, November 2001.
2. S. Goto, Y. Okuno, M. Hattori, T. Nishioka, , and M. Kanehisa. Ligand: database of chemical compounds and reactions in biological pathways. *Nucleic Acids Research*, 30:402–404, 2002.
3. T.R. Hughes, M.J. Marton, A.R. Jones, C.J. Roberts, R. Stoughton, C.D. Armour, H.A.Bennett, E. Coffey, H. Dai, Y.D. He, M.J. Kidd, A.M. King, M.R. Meyer, D. Slade, P.Y. Lum, S.B. Stepaniants, D.D. Shoemaker, D. Gachotte, K. Chakraburtty, J. Simon, M. Bard, and S.H. Friend. Functional discovery via a compendium of expression profiles. *Cell*, 102(1):109–126, 2000.
4. R.D. King, S.H. Muggleton, A. Srinivasan, and M. Sternberg. Structure-activity relationships derived by machine learning: the use of atoms and their bond connectives to predict mutagenicity by inductive logic programming. *Proceedings of the National Academy of Sciences*, 93:438–442, 1996.
5. R.D. King, K.E. Whelan, F.M. Jones, P.K.G. Reiser, C.H. Bryant, S.H. Muggleton, D.B. Kell, and S.G. Oliver. Functional genomic hypothesis generation and experimentation by a robot scientist. *Nature*, 427:247–252, 2004.

6. H. Kitano. Computational systems biology. *Nature*, 420:206–210, 2002.

7. H. Kitano. Systems biology: a brief overview. *Science*, 295:1662–1664, 2002.

8. S.H. Muggleton and C.H. Bryant. Theory completion using inverse entailment. In *Proc. of the 10th International Workshop on Inductive Logic Programming (ILP-00)*, pages 130–146, Berlin, 2000. Springer-Verlag.

9. S.H. Muggleton, H. Lodhi, A. Amini, and M.J.E. Sternberg. Support Vector Inductive Logic Programming. In D. Holmes and L.C. Jain, editors, *Recent Advances in Machine Learning*. Springer-Verlag, 2005. To appear.

10. J.K. Nicholson, J. Connelly, J.C. Lindon, and E. Holmes. Metabonomics: a platform for studying drug toxicity and gene function. *Nature Drug Discovery*, 1:153–161, 2002.

11. P.G.K. Reiser, R.D. King, D.B. Kell, S.H. Muggleton, C.H. Bryant, and S.G. Oliver. Developing a logical model of yeast metabolism. *Electronic Transactions in Artificial Intelligence*, 5-B2(024):223–244, November 2001.

12. A.M. Richard and C.R. Williams. Distributed structure-searchable toxicity (DSSTox) public database network: A proposal. *Mutation Research*, 499:27–52, 2000.

13. A. Srinivasan, S.H. Muggleton, R. King, and M. Sternberg. Theories for mutagenicity: a study of first-order and feature based induction. *Artificial Intelligence*, 85(1,2):277–299, 1996.

14. A. Tamaddoni-Nezhad, A. Kakas, S.H. Muggleton, and F. Pazos. Modelling inhibition in metabolic pathways through abduction and induction. In *Proceedings of the 14th International Conference on Inductive Logic Programming*. Springer-Verlag, 2004.

15. A. Tamaddoni-Nezhad, S. Muggleton, and J. Bang. A Bayesian model for metabolic pathways. In *International Joint Conference on Artificial Intelligence (IJCAI03) Workshop on Learning Statistical Models from Relational Data*, pages 50–57. IJCAI, 2003.

Five Problems in Five Areas for Five Years

Ashwin Srinivasan

IBM India Research Laboratory,
Block 1, Indian Institute of Technology,
Hauz Khas, New Delhi 110 016, India
ashwin.srinivasan@in.ibm.com

I have chosen the title of this talk in the same spirit as the early Buddhists, who often resorted to enumeration as a mnemonic device. (*cf.* the Three Jewels, the Four Noble Truths, the Eight-Fold Path containing the Five Elementary Precepts, the Six Virtues, the 84,000 Teachings and so on). Specifically, it is my intention to remind you of an invited talk at ILP 2000 by David Page, in which five areas were proposed as pressing issues for Inductive Logic Programming to address. For those who came in late, these were[1]:

1. Incorporating probabilities.
2. Novel search methods.
3. Techniques for parallel ILP.
4. Using special-purpose reasoners.
5. Enhancing human-computer interaction.

Five years is a reasonable length of time to take stock and ask: has progress been made on each of these fronts? We know different approaches have been proposed for incorporating probabilities, some unusual search methods have been developed and a few techniques for concurrent processing have been investigated. But can we do things now that we could not five years ago (or at least, could do so only with great difficulty then)? The principal hindrances to a direct answer are that there are no yardsticks established for measuring progress, nor has the same ILP system been used in all cases. As a result, we can do little more that list out who has done what and how over the past five years.

It is my belief—unsurprising, given my own training and inclination—that we need a well-defined engineering R&D project to implement and apply conceptual advances being made in these five areas. Consider what this means. It means a band of engineers working together to design and develop an ILP system that is routinely updated to incorporate advances made in each of the five areas. As with any well-engineered tool, demonstrations of robustness and efficiency using standard tests will be necessary. It is also common for such projects to be driven by a performance wish-list. For this I propose that we agree on five problems—one for each area above—that are beyond the capabilities of current

---

[1] A description can be found in C.D. Page and A. Srinivasan (2003), "ILP: A Short Look back and a Longer Look Forward", *Journal of Machine Learning Research*, 4:415–430.

S. Kramer and B. Pfahringer (Eds.): ILP 2005, LNAI 3625, pp. 424–425, 2005.

ILP systems, but ones that we would want to solve routinely in say, five years or so.

Having spent the last decade or so in developing and maintaining the ILP system Aleph, I have some good reasons to advocate such a project. First, it has been my experience and those of many others that there is some significant value in having a tool that incorporates many ILP advances within a single system. Second, I am acutely aware that the Aleph approach cannot scale-up. It is limited by the interests, understanding, received wisdom, skills and availability of one person (and friends). This works as a hobby, but cannot scale to even being a cottage industry. Instead, what I have in mind is more along the lines of collaborative projects like Wikipedia, Linux, or even like WEKA. Third, all too often ILP has been described as "an interesting approach, but still not robust or efficient enough for tackling industrial problems." Any response to this will necessarily require a well-engineered tool. Finally, nothing spurs development more than research problems that are hard nuts to crack: much of the early development of Progol was fuelled by simply trying to get it do something useful with the "mutagenesis" problem. Similar problems will be needed to motivate the development of ILP systems for the next decade.

I am concious that the project that I propose has the smell of oil and grease. But if ILP is to truly fulfil its potential and boldly go where other machine learning methods have not, then it will need its share of Montgomery Scotts.

Author Index

Lecture Notes in Artificial Intelligence (LNAI)

Vol. 3396: R.M. van Eijk, M.-P. Huget, F. Dignum (Eds.), Agent Communication. X, 261 pages. 2005.

Vol. 3394: D. Kudenko, D. Kazakov, E. Alonso (Eds.), Adaptive Agents and Multi-Agent Systems II. VIII, 313 pages. 2005.

Vol. 3392: D. Seipel, M. Hanus, U. Geske, O. Bartenstein (Eds.), Applications of Declarative Programming and Knowledge Management. X, 309 pages. 2005.

Vol. 3374: D. Weyns, H. V.D. Parunak, F. Michel (Eds.), Environments for Multi-Agent Systems. X, 279 pages. 2005.

Vol. 3371: M.W. Barley, N. Kasabov (Eds.), Intelligent Agents and Multi-Agent Systems. X, 329 pages. 2005.

Vol. 3369: V. R. Benjamins, P. Casanovas, J. Breuker, A. Gangemi (Eds.), Law and the Semantic Web. XII, 249 pages. 2005.

Vol. 3366: I. Rahwan, P. Moraitis, C. Reed (Eds.), Argumentation in Multi-Agent Systems. XII, 263 pages. 2005.

Vol. 3359: G. Grieser, Y. Tanaka (Eds.), Intuitive Human Interfaces for Organizing and Accessing Intellectual Assets. XIV, 257 pages. 2005.

Vol. 3346: R.H. Bordini, M. Dastani, J. Dix, A.E.F. Seghrouchni (Eds.), Programming Multi-Agent Systems. XIV, 249 pages. 2005.

Vol. 3345: Y. Cai (Ed.), Ambient Intelligence for Scientific Discovery. XII, 311 pages. 2005.

Vol. 3343: C. Freksa, M. Knauff, B. Krieg-Brückner, B. Nebel, T. Barkowsky (Eds.), Spatial Cognition IV. XIII, 519 pages. 2005.

Vol. 3339: G.I. Webb, X. Yu (Eds.), AI 2004: Advances in Artificial Intelligence. XXII, 1272 pages. 2004.

Vol. 3336: D. Karagiannis, U. Reimer (Eds.), Practical Aspects of Knowledge Management. X, 523 pages. 2004.

Vol. 3327: Y. Shi, W. Xu, Z. Chen (Eds.), Data Mining and Knowledge Management. XIII, 263 pages. 2005.

Vol. 3315: C. Lemaître, C.A. Reyes, J.A. González (Eds.), Advances in Artificial Intelligence – IBERAMIA 2004. XX, 987 pages. 2004.

Vol. 3303: J.A. López, E. Benfenati, W. Dubitzky (Eds.), Knowledge Exploration in Life Science Informatics. X, 249 pages. 2004.

Vol. 3301: G. Kern-Isberner, W. Rödder, F. Kulmann (Eds.), Conditionals, Information, and Inference. XII, 219 pages. 2005.

Vol. 3276: D. Nardi, M. Riedmiller, C. Sammut, J. Santos-Victor (Eds.), RoboCup 2004: Robot Soccer World Cup VIII. XVIII, 678 pages. 2005.

Vol. 3275: P. Perner (Ed.), Advances in Data Mining. VIII, 173 pages. 2004.

Vol. 3265: R.E. Frederking, K.B. Taylor (Eds.), Machine Translation: From Real Users to Research. XI, 392 pages. 2004.

Vol. 3264: G. Paliouras, Y. Sakakibara (Eds.), Grammatical Inference: Algorithms and Applications. XI, 291 pages. 2004.

Vol. 3259: J. Dix, J. Leite (Eds.), Computational Logic in Multi-Agent Systems. XII, 251 pages. 2004.

Vol. 3257: E. Motta, N.R. Shadbolt, A. Stutt, N. Gibbins (Eds.), Engineering Knowledge in the Age of the Semantic Web. XVII, 517 pages. 2004.

Vol. 3249: B. Buchberger, J.A. Campbell (Eds.), Artificial Intelligence and Symbolic Computation. X, 285 pages. 2004.

Vol. 3248: K.-Y. Su, J. Tsujii, J.-H. Lee, O.Y. Kwong (Eds.), Natural Language Processing – IJCNLP 2004. XVIII, 817 pages. 2005.

Vol. 3245: E. Suzuki, S. Arikawa (Eds.), Discovery Science. XIV, 430 pages. 2004.

Vol. 3244: S. Ben-David, J. Case, A. Maruoka (Eds.), Algorithmic Learning Theory. XIV, 505 pages. 2004.

Vol. 3238: S. Biundo, T. Frühwirth, G. Palm (Eds.), KI 2004: Advances in Artificial Intelligence. XI, 467 pages. 2004.

Vol. 3230: J.L. Vicedo, P. Martínez-Barco, R. Muñoz, M. Saiz Noeda (Eds.), Advances in Natural Language Processing. XII, 488 pages. 2004.

Vol. 3229: J.J. Alferes, J. Leite (Eds.), Logics in Artificial Intelligence. XIV, 744 pages. 2004.

Vol. 3228: M.G. Hinchey, J.L. Rash, W.F. Truszkowski, C.A. Rouff (Eds.), Formal Approaches to Agent-Based Systems. VIII, 290 pages. 2004.

Vol. 3215: M.G.. Negoita, R.J. Howlett, L.C. Jain (Eds.), Knowledge-Based Intelligent Information and Engineering Systems, Part III. LVII, 906 pages. 2004.

Vol. 3214: M.G.. Negoita, R.J. Howlett, L.C. Jain (Eds.), Knowledge-Based Intelligent Information and Engineering Systems, Part II. LVIII, 1302 pages. 2004.

Vol. 3213: M.G.. Negoita, R.J. Howlett, L.C. Jain (Eds.), Knowledge-Based Intelligent Information and Engineering Systems, Part I. LVIII, 1280 pages. 2004.

Vol. 3209: B. Berendt, A. Hotho, D. Mladenic, M. van Someren, M. Spiliopoulou, G. Stumme (Eds.), Web Mining: From Web to Semantic Web. IX, 201 pages. 2004.

Vol. 3206: P. Sojka, I. Kopecek, K. Pala (Eds.), Text, Speech and Dialogue. XIII, 667 pages. 2004.

Vol. 3202: J.-F. Boulicaut, F. Esposito, F. Giannotti, D. Pedreschi (Eds.), Knowledge Discovery in Databases: PKDD 2004. XIX, 560 pages. 2004.

Vol. 3201: J.-F. Boulicaut, F. Esposito, F. Giannotti, D. Pedreschi (Eds.), Machine Learning: ECML 2004. XVIII, 580 pages. 2004.

Vol. 3194: R. Camacho, R. King, A. Srinivasan (Eds.), Inductive Logic Programming. XI, 361 pages. 2004.

Vol. 3192: C. Bussler, D. Fensel (Eds.), Artificial Intelligence: Methodology, Systems, and Applications. XIII, 522 pages. 2004.

Vol. 3191: M. Klusch, S. Ossowski, V. Kashyap, R. Unland (Eds.), Cooperative Information Agents VIII. XI, 303 pages. 2004.

Vol. 3187: G. Lindemann, J. Denzinger, I.J. Timm, R. Unland (Eds.), Multiagent System Technologies. XIII, 341 pages. 2004.

Vol. 3176: O. Bousquet, U. von Luxburg, G. Rätsch (Eds.), Advanced Lectures on Machine Learning. IX, 241 pages. 2004.